ROUTLEDGE HANDBOOK OF COMPARATIVE POLICY ANALYSIS

This Handbook presents the first comprehensive study of policy analytical practices from a comparative perspective.

It explores emerging developments and innovations in the field and advances knowledge of the nature and quality of policy analysis across different countries and at different levels of government by all relevant actors, both inside and outside government, who contribute to the diagnosis of problems and the search for policy solutions.

The chapters of the Handbook examine all aspects of the science, art and craft of policy analysis. They do so both at the often studied national level, and also at the less well-known level of sub-national and local governments. In addition to studying governments, the Handbook also examines for the first time the practices and policy work of a range of non-governmental actors, including think tanks, interest groups, business actors, labour groups, media, political parties and non-profit organizations.

Bringing together a rich collection of cases and a renowned group of scholars, the Handbook constitutes a landmark study in the field.

Marleen Brans is Professor at the KU Leuven Public Governance Institute, and visiting Professor at Université catholique de Louvain, Belgium.

Iris Geva-May is Professor Emerita at Simon Fraser University, Burnaby, British Columbia, Canada, and Visiting Professor, Baruch College School of Public Affairs, CUNY. She is Founding Editor-in-Chief of Routledge's *Journal of Comparative Policy Analysis: Research and Practice*, and Founding President of the International Comparative Policy Analysis Forum.

Michael Howlett is Burnaby Mountain Chair in the Department of Political Science at Simon Fraser University, Canada, and Yong Pung How Chair Professor in the Lee Kuan Yew School of Public Policy at the National University of Singapore. He specializes in public policy analysis, Canadian political economy, and Canadian resource and environmental policy.

ROUTLEDGE HANDBOOK OF COMPARATIVE POLICY ANALYSIS

Edited by Marleen Brans, Iris Geva-May and Michael Howlett

Routledge
Taylor & Francis Group

NEW YORK AND LONDON

First published 2017
by Routledge
711 Third Avenue, New York, NY 10017

and by Routledge
2 Park Square, Milton Park, Abingdon, Oxon, OX14 4RN

Routledge is an imprint of the Taylor & Francis Group, an informa business

© 2017 Taylor & Francis

The right of Marleen Brans, Iris Geva-May, Michael Howlett to be
identified as the authors of the editorial material, and of the authors
for their individual chapters, has been asserted in accordance with
sections 77 and 78 of the Copyright, Designs and Patents Act 1988.

All rights reserved. No part of this book may be reprinted or reproduced
or utilised in any form or by any electronic, mechanical, or other means,
now known or hereafter invented, including photocopying and recording,
or in any information storage or retrieval system, without permission in
writing from the publishers.

Trademark notice: Product or corporate names may be trademarks or
registered trademarks, and are used only for identification and
explanation without intent to infringe.

Library of Congress Cataloging in Publication Data
Names: Brans, M. (Marleen), editor. | Geva-May, Iris, editor. | Howlett, Michael, 1955– editor.
Title: Routledge handbook of comparative policy analysis / edited by Marleen Brans,
    Iris Geva-May, and Michael Howlett.
Description: New York, NY : Routledge, 2017. | Includes bibliographical references and index.
Identifiers: LCCN 2016045292 | ISBN 978113895977
Subjects: LCSH: Policy sciences. | Comparative government.
Classification: LCC H97 .R677 2017 | DDC 320.6—dc23LC record available at
    https://lccn.loc.gov/2016045292

ISBN: 978-1-138-95977-4 (hbk)
ISBN: 978-1-315-66056-1 (ebk)

Typeset in Bembo
by RefineCatch Limited, Bungay, Suffolk

CONTENTS

List of Figures	*viii*
List of Tables	*ix*
Notes on Contributors	*x*

1 Policy Analysis in Comparative Perspective: An Introduction   1
Marleen Brans, Iris Geva-May and Michael Howlett

PART I
The Styles and Methods of Public Policy Analysis   **25**

2 The Policy Analysis Profession   27
Yukio Adachi

3 The Choice of Formal Policy Analysis Methods   43
Claudia Scott

4 From Policy Analytical Styles to Policymaking Styles   56
Patrick Hassenteufel and Philippe Zittoun

5 Policy Analysis and Bureaucratic Capacity   70
Jose-Luis Mendez and Mauricio I. Dussauge-Laguna

6 Reflections on a Half Century of Policy Analysis   85
Beryl A. Radin

Contents

PART II
Policy Analysis by Governments   **101**

7 Policy Analysis in the Central Government   103
Arnošt Veselý

8 Policy Analysis in Sub-National Governments   118
Joshua Newman

9 Policy Analysis at the Local Level   131
Martin Lundin and PerOla Öberg

10 Evidence-Based Budgetary Policy: Speaking Truth to Power?   143
Frans K. M. van Nispen and Maarten de Jong

PART III
**Committees, Public Inquiries, Research Institutes, Consultants and
Public Opinion**   **167**

11 Public Inquiries   169
Patrik Marier

12 Expert Advisory Bodies in the Policy System   181
Kate Crowley and Brian W. Head

13 Policy Analysis in the Legislative Branch   199
Wouter Wolfs and Lieven De Winter

14 Management Consultancy and the Varieties of Capitalism   213
Denis Saint-Martin

15 Public Opinion and Policy Analysis   229
Christine Rothmayr Allison

PART IV
Parties and Interest-Group-Based Policy Analysis   **243**

16 Who are The Political Parties' Ideas Factories? On Policy Analysis by
Political Party Think Tanks   245
Valérie Pattyn, Gilles Pittoors and Steven Van Hecke

17 Business Associations and the Public Policy Process: When Do They
Do Policy Analysis?   261
Aidan R. Vining and Anthony E. Boardman

Contents

18 Policy Analysis by the Labour Movement: A Comparative Analysis
of Labour Market Policy in Germany, Denmark and the United States   276
Michaela Schulze and Wolfgang Schroeder

19 Policy Analysis and the Voluntary Sector   291
Bryan Evans, Juniper Glass and Adam Wellstead

PART V
Advocacy-Based and Academic Policy Analysis   **307**

20 Media and Policy Analysis   309
Yu-Ying Kuo and Ming Huei Cheng

21 Policy Analysis and Think Tanks in Comparative Perspective   324
Diane Stone and Stella Ladi

22 Academic Policy Analysis and Research Utilization in Policymaking   341
Sonja Blum and Marleen Brans

23 Public Policy Studies in North America and Europe   360
Johanu Botha, Iris Geva-May and Allan M. Maslove

Index   *380*

FIGURES

10.1	Schematic presentation of the PPB System	144
10.2	Breakdown of 27 programs rated ineffective by PART for FY2008	146
10.3	Performance budgeting index (PBI) for a selected number of OECD countries	148
10.4	The frequency of performance utilization during budget negotiations per category in OECD countries	149
10.5	The utilization of performance information in OECD countries	149
10.6	Diversified approach of performance budgeting depending on policy characteristics	152
10.7	Modes of policy analysis and evaluation	155
10.8	The utilization of program evaluation in the budget negotiations in OECD countries	156
10.9	A classification of budget reviews	157
10.10	Overview of the main actor in charge of spending reviews per category of activity in OECD countries	158
10.11	The utilization of spending reviews in the budget negotiations in OECD countries	158
16.1	Think tank functions	257
17.1	The role of business associations in the policy process	266
19.1	Relationship among various types of 'advocacy' activities	297
22.1	Actors and arenas in the policy advisory system	348

TABLES

4.1	The French policymaking style	66
4.2	The German policymaking style	66
4.3	The US policymaking style	67
5.1	A supply-demand matrix of governmental policy analysis	74
7.1	Policy analysis in central government	112
12.1	Policy advisory system actors classified by policy types	183
12.2	The 'externalization' of advisory councils	187
12.3	Comparative approaches to studying advisory bodies/systems	189
12.4	Policy advisory systems—ILPA single country comparisons	192
12.5	Key findings on cross-national variation in advisory bodies/systems	194
14.1	European consulting market, 2010	218
16.1	Level of autonomy	247
16.2	Political party think tank function	252
17.1	Business associations that have the most contact with Canadian federal officials	262
17.2	Canadian business associations: scope and production of policy analyses	271
19.1	Role within organization	302
19.2	At what stage of the government process is your organization invited to participate?	303
20.1	i-Voting on performance of Taipei City Government Departments	311
20.2	2013 participants in internet use in Japan	312
20.3	Internet users in Japan, 2012-2016	313
20.4	Respondents of survey on child abuse	314
20.5	Areas covered by the OPEN system	317
20.6	The top 10 provincial microblogs in China	318
20.7	The top 10 government microblogs in Beijing	318
20.8	Message content in Beijing announcements	319
22.1	Ladder of research utilization	345

CONTRIBUTORS

Yukio Adachi is Professor of Public Policy and Political Philosophy at Kyoto Sangyo University, Faculty of Law (Professor Emeritus, Kyoto University).

Sonja Blum is Senior Researcher at the Austrian Institute for Family Studies at the University of Vienna. She is currently Visiting Professor of Research at the KU Leuven Public Governance Institute.

Anthony Boardman is the Van Dusen Professor of Business Administration in the Strategy and Business Economics Division at the University of British Columbia.

Johanu Botha is a PhD Candidate at the Carleton University, Ottawa's School of Public Policy and Administration (SPPA). He holds one of the Social Sciences and Humanities Research Council of Canada's prestigious Joseph-Armand Bombardier Awards for doctoral research.

Marleen Brans is Professor at the KU Leuven Public Governance Institute and visiting Professor at Université catholique de Louvain, Belgium.

Ming Huei Cheng is Associate Professor in the School of Public Economics at Nanjing Audit University, China.

Kate Crowley is Associate Professor of Public and Environmental Policy at the University of Tasmania.

Maarten de Jong, PhD is senior budget specialist at the Dutch Ministry of Finance in The Hague, and has been contracted as a researcher/lecturer by the World Bank, the OECD and the European Commission.

Lieven De Winter is Professor at the Université catholique de Louvain, Belgium.

Mauricio I. Dussauge-Laguna is Professor-Researcher at the Public Administration Department, Centro de Investigación y Docencia Económicas (CIDE), Mexico City. He

Contributors

obtained his MPA from the Maxwell School of Syracuse University and his PhD in Political Science from the London School of Economics and Political Science.

Bryan Evans is Professor in the Department of Politics and Public Administration at Ryerson University.

Iris Geva-May is Professor Emerita at Simon Fraser University and Visiting Professor, Baruch College School of Public Affairs, CUNY. She is Founding Editor-in-chief of Routledge's *Journal of Comparative Policy Analysis: Research and Practice* and Founding President of the International Comparative Policy Analysis Forum Scholarly Society.

Juniper Glass is a specialist in philanthropic and nonprofit strategy. She holds a Master of Philanthropy & Nonprofit Leadership from Carleton University, Ottawa.

Patrick Hassenteufel is Professor of Political Science at the Université de Versailles-Paris-Saclay and member of the Printemps (CNRS) research centre.

Brian W. Head is Professor of Public Policy in the School of Political Science, University of Queensland, Australia.

Michael P. Howlett is Burnaby Mountain Chair in the Department of Political Science at Simon Fraser University and Yong Pung How Chair Professor in the Lee Kuan Yew School of Public Policy at the National University of Singapore.

Yu-Ying Kuo is Professor in the Department of Public Policy and Management and Dean of Academic Affairs at Shih Hsin University, Taiwan.

Stella Ladi is Senior Lecturer in Public Management in the School of Business and Management at Queen Mary University of London and Assistant Professor in European Policies and Public Policy at Panteion University, Athens.

Martin Lundin is Associate Professor at the Institute for Evaluation of Labour Market and Education Policy. He is also affiliated with the Department of Government at Uppsala University.

Patrik Marier is Professor, Political Science at Concordia University and Concordia University Research Chair in Aging and Public Policy.

Allan M. Maslove is Distinguished Research Professor Emeritus at Carleton University, Ottawa. His research primarily focuses on financing of health care in Canada, with a focus on the federal-provincial fiscal arrangements, and public budgeting.

Jose-Luis Mendez is a research professor at El Colegio de México in Mexico City. His research focuses on public policy, civil service, state reform and political leadership.

Joshua Newman is a Lecturer in the School of Social and Policy Studies at Flinders University, in Adelaide, South Australia.

PerOla Öberg is Professor in Political Science at the Department of Government, Uppsala University, Sweden.

Contributors

Valérie Pattyn is Assistant Professor in Public Administration and Public Policy at the Institute of Public Administration at Leiden University.

Gilles Pittoors is a PhD candidate and junior assistant at the department of Political Science of Ghent University. He holds an MA in European Studies (2010) and an MSc in European Politics and Policies (2011), both obtained at KU Leuven.

Beryl A. Radin is a member of the faculty at the McCourt School of Public Policy of Georgetown University in Washington, DC. She has written extensively about the development of the policy analysis field and currently is the Editor of the Georgetown University Press book series, Public Management and Change.

Christine Rothmayr Allison is Professor in the Department of Political Science at the University of Montreal. Her two main fields of interest are: comparative public policy, focusing on the fields of biotechnology, biomedicine and higher education; and courts and politics, in particular, the impact of court decisions on public policy making in North America and Europe.

Denis Saint-Martin is Professor at the Université de Montréal Department of Political Science. His research examines the institutions of collective action and the dilemmas that arise when the rational pursuit of individual interests leads to irrational results for public policy.

Wolfgang Schroeder, Prof. Dr, is Professor of Political Science at the University of Kassel, Germany.

Michaela Schulze, Dr, is Lecturer of Political Science at the University of Kassel, Germany.

Claudia Scott is Professor of Public Policy at the School of Government at Victoria University of Wellington. She was Professor of Public Policy at the Australia and New Zealand School of Government (ANZSOG) from 2002–2014, and was appointed as an ANZSOG Fellow in 2015.

Diane Stone is Centenary Professor of Governance at the Institute of Governance and Policy Analysis, University of Canberra, and Professor in Politics and International Studies, University of Warwick.

Steven Van Hecke is Assistant Professor at the Public Governance Institute of the Faculty of Social Sciences, KU Leuven.

Frans van Nispen is Affiliated Professor of Public Administration at the Erasmus University of Rotterdam, the Netherlands and Visiting Fellow at the Department of Political and Social Sciences of the European University Institute in San Domenico di Fiesole, Italy.

Arnošt Veselý is Professor of Public and Social Policy and Head of the Department of Public and Social Policy, Faculty of Social Sciences, Charles University in Prague, Czech Republic. His research interests include empirical analysis of policy work in public administration, policy advisory systems and problem structuring in public policy, focusing on educational policy.

Contributors

Aidan R. Vining is the Centre for North American Business Studies (CNABS) Professor of Business and Government Relations in the Beedie School of Business, Simon Fraser University, in Vancouver.

Adam Wellstead is Associate Professor of Environmental and Energy Policy at Michigan Technological University.

Wouter Wolfs is a researcher at the Public Governance Institute of KU Leuven.

Philippe Zittoun is Research Professor of political science, LAET-ENTPE, University of Lyon, France and General Secretary of the International Public Policy Association.

1

POLICY ANALYSIS IN COMPARATIVE PERSPECTIVE: AN INTRODUCTION

Marleen Brans, Iris Geva-May and Michael Howlett

Part A: Conceptual Foundations and Contribution

The Handbook of Comparative Policy Analysis provides the first comprehensive examination of policy analysis in a comparative perspective. It covers an international meta study of the state of the art knowledge about the science, art and craft of policy analysis in different countries, at different levels of government and by all relevant actors in and outside government who contribute to the analysis of problems and the search for policy solutions.

This book's ambition is to advance the comparative knowledge of policy analysis, and it does so by a unique configuration of internationally diverse authors and internationally based evidence. It is comparative in both the international scope of the cases presented and in the overarching theoretical conclusions that are generalizable enough to be applicable for understanding the field.

The book brings together invited experts who, as editors of/or contributors to country studies on policy analysis, are experienced in collating theories and empirical evidence from a wide range of countries. Many of the contributors are at the forefront of studying comparative policy analysis and policy advice, and several are leading scholars advancing policy analysis internationally. They are active in promoting policy analysis studies in various international research networks, such as the International Comparative Policy Analysis Forum and the *Journal of Comparative Policy Analysis* (ICPA/JCPA), the International Political Science Association (IPSA), the European Group of Public Administration (EGPA), the Midwest Political Science Association (MPSA) and the International Public Policy Association (IPPA). Some contributors to this volume were specifically invited to close particular theoretical and empirical gaps that have until now never been systematically approached from a policy analytical angle.

In terms of the perspective of policy analysis as a subject for comparative research and in terms of its structure, the Handbook follows the International Library for Policy Analysis book series (Geva-May & Howlett, 2013–2018) sponsored by the ICPA Forum and the *Journal of Comparative Policy Analysis*, and is informed by a common template and content orientation derived from Dobuzinskis, Howlett and Laycock's *Policy Analysis in Canada* (2007).

The definition of policy analysis is seen by the editors of this volume as applied social and scientific research as well as more implicit forms of practical knowledge. Compliant with

Lasswell's (1971) distinction between 'analysis for policy' and 'analysis of policy', this book studies practices of analysis *for* policy in order to inform the analysis *of* policy. Referring to the first aspect, 'for policy', one is reminded that analysis for policy refers to applied policy analysis, and includes both formal and informal professional practices that organizations and actors entertain to define a problem marked for government action, as well as to prescribe the measures to solve that problem by policy action or change. In this meaning, policy analysis relies upon policy work by actors, and encompasses the garnering of information about the problem situation and its context, the demarcation of problem definitions, the design and comparison of policy instruments, and the assessment of policy alternatives reached and capable of feasibly mitigating the problem situation. The outcome of policy analysis is eventually policy advice, which in this book is understood as a recommendation or opinion for future courses of government action or inaction.

By an explanatory observation of applied policy analysis by different policy actors, in different social or policymaking units, the Handbook also aims to make a significant contribution to the meta study of policy, or what Lasswell (1971) calls the analysis 'of policy'. Analysis of policy refers to the more theoretical and/or generalizable investigation of the ways in which policies are made and the roles policy actors play in the policy cycle. It investigates the ways in which their policy analytical work sets the agenda, informs the search for solutions, supports decision making, impacts upon implementation, and eventually helps to evaluate policies.

This Handbook's anchoring points for studying the bearing of policy analytical activities on policymaking, however, do not necessarily follow the distinct stages of the policy analysis process (DeLeon, 1999; Dunn, 1994; Patton & Sawicki, 1993; Dye, 1995; Geva-May with Wildavsky, 2011; Geva-May, 2017; Bardach, 2015) or those of the policymaking process (Patton, 1997; Howlett, Ramesh & Perl, 2009). Rather, given the actor and client orientation of the policy analysis process in policymaking (Wildavsky, 1979; Weimer & Vining, 2010; Radin, 2013, 2016; May, 2005) the book offers a useful heuristic tool to map actors and their influence over policy choices, and reviews the nature of their policy analytical activities and the difference they make in the policy process (Howlett, Ramesh & Perl, 2009). Some of the studied actors may put their policy analysis to use for agenda setting but not for policy evaluation, while others may a have a more encompassing impact across different stages. With this conceptual orientation in mind, the organizing principles for the majority of the chapters are related to the locus and focus of public policy analysis by policy-relevant actors in and outside of government.

To be sure, it is not the first time that these actors and their roles in the policy process have been analysed. Several actors and their roles have featured in theories of the policymaking process, from neo-corporatist and pluralist studies to policy networks or subsystems approaches (Polsby, 1960; Schmitter & Lehmbruch, 1979; Schmitter & Streeck, 1999; Rhodes, 1997; Richardson, 2000), in public choice (Dunleavy, 1991), actor-centred institutionalism (Scharpf, 1997), as well as in approaches such as the policy streams theory (Kingdon, 1984), the advocacy coalition framework (Sabatier & Jenkins-Smith, 1993), resource theory on lobbying and advocacy (Bouwen, 2002), and finally in work on policy advisors and the configuration of policy advisory systems (Halligan, 1995, 1998; Craft & Howlett, 2012, 2013).

But this is the first time the policy-relevant actors are comprehensively approached with a focus on their policy analytical activities. As policy analytical work has long been recognized as a core function of modern bureaucracies (Lasswell, 1971; Meltsner, 1976, Geva-May, 2017; Page & Jenkins, 2005), bureaucrats' policy analysis can count on a longer-standing research tradition than that of actors outside executive government. But even then, attention has mostly focused on policy analysis in central government, and has left policy analysis in subnational and local governments largely unexplored. There are also some actors outside government who have attracted research attention for a while, such as academic researchers (Weiss, 1979) and think tanks (Stone, 1996). But for other actors, such as voluntary organizations or management consultancies, academic interest in the nature of their policy analytical work is relatively recent, for some even absent up till now. Political parties and parliaments are cases in point.

While the policy analysis tenet of transparency, effectiveness, efficiency and accountability through systematic and evidence-based analysis started in the US in the 1960s, it only began to spread internationally in the late 1990s as the global village became increasingly smaller through technology, transportation and commerce, and more economically, environmentally and politically interdependent. In seeking to better understand the local adoption of policy analysis by different loci, and their respective interpretations, as well as the effect on international interactions—whether explicit or implicit—the Handbook promises to substantively advance the comparative knowledge about policy analysis across the globe.

The Handbook's content relies on contributions that connect the broader literature, existing comparative research and supplementary secondary analysis with the evidence garnered in a collection of single case studies that were published in Policy Press's International Library of Policy Analysis (ILPA) book series (Geva-May & Howlett, 2013–2018) and the comparative policy analytical tenets pioneered and enhanced by the *Journal of Comparative Policy Analysis*. Throughout the three volumes per year of the ILPA, each focusing on policy analysis in a different country, the country cases build consensus on the definition of policy analysis, answer the same set of central research questions, and consider the same range of actors that configure the policy advisory systems in different jurisdictions. Together these country studies have provided the ground material with which the chapters of this volume proceed, as well as the contextual description necessary for the higher comparative aims of classification, typology building and explanation. They also significantly enlarged the geographical scope of current policy analysis literature. This Handbook brings together evidence from countries other than the usual Anglo-Saxon countries that have much dominated the literature to date. From continental Europe, the chapters feature policy analytical practices in France, Germany, the Netherlands, Belgium, Sweden and Denmark. From Asia, evidence is brought in from Japan, China and Taiwan. South American cases include Brazil and Mexico.

First, apart from addressing a larger than usual geographical scope in their investigations, the contributors to this volume substantively advance the state of comparative policy analysis. They do this by departing from *operational definitions* that are devoid of national bias so that they are encompassing enough to capture similarities and differences of policy analysis across the globe. The definitions and concepts entertained are necessarily broad enough to capture functional equivalents of the same phenomenon across a variety of jurisdictions and languages. This is the case for the definitions of 'policy analysis as a profession' (Geva-May, 2005); 'formal policy analytical methods'; or 'policy analytical activities' (Weimer & Vining, 2010; Bardach, 2015; Geva-May with Wildavsky, 2011); 'policy analysis' and 'policy research' as academic subjects (JPA, NASPAA publications), as well as for defining such policy-relevant actors as 'committees of inquiry', 'expert advisory bodies', 'non-profits', 'think tanks' (Radin, 2000, 2002, 2016; Fischer & Forester, 1993; Stone, 1996).

Second, the authors of this collection move their analysis up the ladder of comparison, and provide heuristic tools and frameworks for further studies. Several of the chapters apply, for instance, a policy analysis *supply-and-demand framework*. The chapter on the relationship between policy analysis and policy capacity offers a way to map different jurisdictions along different combinations of strong or weak demand and supply of policy analysis. An additional chapter on professional policy analysis uses a supply-and-demand logic. The chapter on policy analysis in central governments presents a consistent set of material research subjects, such as the context of policy analysis, the *institutionalization of policy analysis* in central government vis-à-vis other institutions, the people that perform policy analysis, and the challenges they face. *Legislative policy analysis*, in turn, is approached with a comprehensive set of units of analysis, ranging from the people and units that perform parliamentary policy analysis to the instruments that legislators have at their disposal to garner knowledge and expertise. One of the more comprehensive heuristic matrices in this book considers policymaking styles. It provides legitimacy and guidance for future studies of the way in which different policy analytical styles are produced and circulated in a country's *policymaking system*.

Third, the role of the policy-relevant actors vis-à-vis the nature of policy analysis shows divergence across the cases featuring in this book. Several chapters have succeeded to reduce the 'world of complexity' of policy analysis actors and activities with the use of classifications and by constructing typologies that reveal the features that cases share or do not share. *Formal policy analytical methods* are classified alongside *participatory and consensus-oriented approaches*. *Policy analytical styles* include policy predictive analysis, problem causal analysis, trial/error policy analysis, policy process analysis and normative policy analysis. The repertoire of resources for *parliamentary policy analysis* includes Members of Parliament's (MPs) personal assistants and group assistants, and parliamentary support services to the MPs. The *roles of particular policy actors* are also classified. *Committees of inquiry* (COIs) play a variety of roles, from facilitating learning, to adjudication and political roles. *Expert advisory bodies* are traditional professionalized advisory bodies, or modernized interactive responsive bodies. *Management consultancy firms* feature as rational planners, cost-cutters, or partners in the new governance. *Think tanks* also come in many guises, each exposing different modes of policy analysis: 'ideological tanks' or 'advocacy tanks', 'academic, non-partisan think tanks', 'specialist' think tanks, 'generalist' think tanks, and 'think and do' tanks. The more-specific *party political think tanks* appear in four types, depending on the temporal and ideational focus of their advice: 'ideological guardians', 'policy experts', 'policy advisors' and 'policy assistants'. As to *types of policy analysis instruction*, finally, the country profiles reviewed in this Handbook are either mixed-policy analysis-policy research, mixed-policy-research heavy, or mixed-policy-analysis heavy.

Fourth, next to offering descriptions, classifications and typologies, the Handbook chapters also venture into explaining the observed similarities and differences across different jurisdictions. The explanatory candidates originate from variations in *institutions, political and epistemological cultures and economies*. The Anglo-Saxon family of nations share a great number of similarities. Compared to other jurisdictions, they share a stronger acknowledgement of policy analysis as a profession, a stronger institutionalization of formal rational policy analysis, a longer tradition of policy analytical instruction in academia, the expert composition of advisory bodies, and a relatively greater receptiveness to management consultancy firms and think tank advocacy. While some continental European countries such as the Netherlands share some of these features, policy analysis is relatively less recognized as a profession outside the Anglo-Saxon world. Formal rational policy analysis is variably present in some policy sectors but not in others. Overall, rational policy analysis is blended with more political and participatory policy analytical activities. In academia, policy analysis is younger as a discipline. Advisory bodies have mixed memberships with representation from civil society organizations.

Management consultancy firms play a smaller role in advising government, and think tanks are but an emerging discursive force.

The tentative explanations of patterns of divergence rest on the enduring influence of institutions, cultures and market characteristics. These include differences between majority and consensual systems; between elitist, pluralist or neo-corporatist forms of interest intermediation; between rational versus political epistemological cultures; and between liberal or coordinated markets. There are also within-group differences. To explain these one needs to take into account different historical paths and transitions, classic divisions between presidential and parliamentary systems, differences in political cultures of social units, and differences in politico-administrative relations and parliamentary cultures.

To sum up, the chapters included in this Handbook describe, categorize and offer explanations for the nature of policy analysis and its actors in different countries. At the same time, they point at trends and issues that confront policy analysis across the cases. These include a number of global developments that create sources of convergence.

Conducive to the quality of policy analysis is the evidence-based movement that has gained momentum since the start of the millennium. The move to knowledge-intensive policies and public services has required that governments across the globe make a commitment to *evidence-based policymaking* along the lines of the basic definition of policy analysis as the 'use of reason and evidence to choose the best policy among a number of alternatives' (MacRae & Wilde, 1979, p. 14; Dror, 1972, 1983; Weimer & Vining, 2010; Geva-May with Wildavsky, 2011; Geva-May, 2017; Sanderson, 2011; Nutley, Morton, Jung & Boaz, 2010; Straßheim & Kettunen, 2014). In some countries with relatively weak government policy analytical capacity, this movement did much to strengthen the policy analytical base in policy formulation practices. In other countries, the evidence-based policy movement had to compete with a move to the externalization of policy advice, or the 'diversification of supply from the traditionally dominant public service to a plurality of suppliers' (Craft & Halligan, 2015, p. 3).

Externalization has taken many forms. In some cases, it involved the marketization of policy advice to agencies at arm's length from government or to management consultancy firms. Another manifestation of this movement is what could be called the *societalization* of policy analysis. Democratic governments need expertise to tackle complex problems, but also want to garner support for their decisions, and to (appear to) be following the wishes of the people and/or at least acting with their interests in mind. Policy decisions down this path involve direct consultation and interaction with target groups, bringing citizens directly into the policymaking process with the assumption that their support will mean that the policy solutions are not only in the public's interest but are also sustainable. This type of externalization has led to the blending of expert policy analysis with public consultation and participation in the policymaking process. It has broadened the sources of advice and made advice more competitive and contested.

In the last decade, the value of the technical and scientific base of policy analysis is contested against the value of those with so-called experience-based expertise, or lay expertise, and even the 'wisdom of crowds' (Surowiecki, 2004; Radin, 2013). Expert domain expertise is bouncing back on the policy analysis pendulum of the field's methodology, even among recent Association for Public Policy Analysis and Management (APPAM) and *Journal of Policy Analysis and Management* (*JPAM*) scholarship and evidence of practice. *Politicization* is another competing trend, and refers to the many faces of attempts by elected politicians to restore the primacy of political judgement in the policymaking process, at the expense of technical or scientific evidence. The majority of chapters in this book deal with the translation of these challenges in a variety of national contexts, but the question to what extent they mediate national heterogeneity merits further research.

This Handbook's contribution to the advancement of the comparative study of policy analysis is anchored on (a) the basis that it extends for middle-range theory development on the production and consumption of policy analysis, and on (b) the models of configurations of policy advisory systems that it offers comparatively. Further, some individual chapters point at the need for avenues for improving future comparative research on policy analysis as a domain of study and of practice. There are still a great number of case types that remain under described and ill understood. In particular, an expansion to policy analysis on the African continent certainly deserves attention.

Several contributors have also pointed at the need to further improve operational definitions of policy analysis activities and policy-relevant actors, to further capture functional equivalents of the application of different kinds of applied knowledge in the policy process and to better study the actors who perform it. They also call for enhanced sophistication of research tools such as surveys, interviews and longitudinal time series research.

Recent developments in the international arena, and in particular the 'Brexit' referendum results, seem to indicate more than ever that this comparative policy analysis research agenda for structured scientific comparative research is worth pursuing. The domestic and global policy problems that governments face in the second decade of the new millennium are formidable. In our view, the capacity of governments to deal with these problems is aided by strong policy analytical capacity in government as well as in society and academia. This is reminiscent of the argument that policy problems are satisfactorily dealt with in societies where there is both a strong state and a strong civil society.

True to the credo of the founding fathers of modern-day policy analysis, we believe that policy analysis has a role to play in contributing to create a better world. Comparisons and a meta understanding of the role of policy analysis can facilitate a more informed dialogue among countries, as well as among decision makers and their respective constituencies.

Part B: On the Content of the Routledge Handbook of Comparative Policy Analysis

The book consists of five parts. Part I first discusses how policy analysis as a profession is understood, and how policy analytical methods vary. It then constructs policy analytical styles and investigates the relationship between policy analysis and bureaucratic capacity. It ends with a critical reflection on 30 years of policy analysis development.

Part II deals with policy analysis in central, subnational and local governments, and zooms in on the much-debated relationship between policy analysis and the budgetary process.

In Part III, the discussions move away from executive government departments and agencies to explore the nature of policy analysis in parliaments and semi-autonomous bodies such as COIs and expert advisory bodies. Also included is an analysis of management consultancy and public opinion research.

Part IV extends the analysis outside the public sector to include chapters on the nature and influence of policy analysis by independent non-governmental actors such as political parties, business associations, labour unions and the voluntary sector.

After considering the ascent of social media, Part V concludes the book with an investigation of policy analysis by advocates and academics, and with an overview of how policy analysis is nurtured in academic teaching.

Part I: The Styles and Methods of Public Policy Analysis

In chapter 2, Adachi attempts to portray policy analysis as a profession and views it as a sophisticated tool in the policymaking process. He considers what a profession means, and what is the primary mission of policy analysis in the political process of a democracy. He critically examines the different perspectives on policy analysis, but reserves the denotation of policy analysis as a profession to mean knowledge work that meets a number of conditions. He details: the application of a set of sophisticated skills based on deep and wide theoretical knowledge and a certain amount of experience; a considerable demand for the work or service that is provided by members of the profession; the orientation of policy analysts to the public good; and a minimum level of occupational ethics shared among the practitioners of policy analysis.

Adachi finds that the extent to which policy analysis as a profession is established as an occupation with a considerable demand for the work or service that is provided by its members, varies from nation to nation. Applying a demand focus, he finds variation in the demand for policy analysis. In the US, demand for policy analysis is high both inside and outside government. In Canada, he notes an active demand for policy advice, with government seeking ways to tap into expertise within and across government, as well as from outside sources. He also finds a growing demand for quality policy analysis in Australia and New Zealand as well as in international organizations. In other cases, policy analysis is absent as a profession, or emerging, with only recent moves to academic policy analysis education, and a weak demand for policy analysis by government and civil society actors. Japan belongs to this latter group.

According to Adachi's definition of the policy analytical profession, sophisticated skills are what policy analysis professionals should master. Such skills include the aptitude to use formal policy analytical methods—also the focus of Scott's analysis in chapter 3.

Scott's chapter (3) considers variations in the use of formal methods. She recounts that the sophistication and use of formal methods of policy analysis were at the heart of the development of policy analysis in the US in the 1960s. Formal methods were recognized as fruitful by governments, and several schools of public policy activity contributed to the growth of academic literature, supporting the development of policy analysis as a distinct field, and advising as a profession. While the origin of policy analysis goes back to the US, many governments in both developed and developing countries have introduced formal methods to enhance the policy analytical capability of policy advisors, often following a policy cycle model in which policy analytical tools help to define policy problems, compare solutions, and evaluate the results against specific goals and objectives.

Scott notes, however, that the spread of formal methods has not been equal across the globe, and these have been mainly welcomed in Westminster-style governments, which place comparatively more reliance upon a cadre of public policy advisors who serve ministers as clients. However, more recently, there seems to be some convergence due to transformations of policy analysis in the government. In countries with a weak tradition of formal policy analysis, formal methods have been introduced in part, for distinct policy analytical tasks, in distinct policy sectors, or in support of new accountability procedures. Countries with a strong tradition of rationalist formal policy analysis have come to embrace participatory consensus-oriented methods of problem definition and solution analysis, responding to such trends as co-design with civil society or to a greater consideration of balancing rational analysis with political judgement. This also means that there is now a great variation in the selection and use of policy analysis methods, models and techniques, with analytical practices becoming less mechanistic, and calling upon a greater diversity of hard and soft skills of policy analysis.

Following up on the variation that the authors of chapters 2 and 3 found in the nature of policy analytical methods in different professional traditions, and on the comparative manifestation of rationalists and participatory practices in different countries, Hassenteufel and Zittoun move on to consider policymaking styles in chapter 4. They develop these as a heuristic tool for comparing the use of different policy analytical methods in relation to systems of policy advice, policy formulation and public debate, thus encompassing the whole policymaking system. In order to analyse variations in style, the definition of policy analysis they entertain is necessarily broad: it is understood as an activity that produces different kinds of knowledge on and for public policies. Policy analysis is seen as applied knowledge activities producing problem-solving statements, proposals, arguments, frames and evidence for the policymaking process. Thus defined, policy analysis is not the 'playground' for policy analyst bureaucrats and policy analyst academics alone, but also of policy analyst advocates and policy analyst politicians, who all aspire to influence policy decisions by producing usable knowledge in support of problem-solving statements.

To understand further where and which kind of problem-solving statements are produced and disseminated, the policy style heuristic builds upon four types of policy systems, differentiated on the basis of rules a problem-solving statement must follow: the policy academic system (comprising academics and researchers), the policy advisory system (comprising policy advisors in and outside government), the policy formulation system (comprising specialized bureaucratic agents), and the public debate system (comprising all actors engaged in public confrontations).

They also identify five policy analytical styles: policy predictive analysis, problem causal analysis, trial/error policy analysis, policy process analysis, and normative policy analysis. Further dimensions for analysis are the degree of compartmentalization between each system, the level of conflict and cooperation in each policy system, the level of substantive controversies in each system, and finally the relative openness of the systems. The constructed types and dimensions are then combined by the authors in a policymaking styles matrix.

In a first test of this heuristic matrix based on the empirical material in the ILPA book series, Hassenteufel and Zittoun promisingly identify three distinct national types of policymaking styles. The French style is characterized by high levels of compartmentalization and a dominant role of public experts using predictive and causal analytical styles. Academics locked in their policy academic system, which mainly seeks to demonstrate causal and process-oriented styles, shy away from the policy formulation system, hence supporting high levels of conflict in the public debate system. The German policymaking style, on the other hand, is characterized by the importance of collaboration between different levels of government, and between government and civil society actors. The German policy systems are more porous, even if the policy analytical styles are rather similar to those practised in France. Finally, the US policymaking style is characterized by strong exchange between the different policy systems, by a high level of conflict in the policy formulation system, and by a greater reliance upon predictive and trial-and-error policy analysis.

While chapter 4's heuristic for understanding policy analytical styles and policymaking styles considers a range of policy systems, chapter 5 zooms in on the policy formulation system itself. Mendez and Dussauge-Laguna theoretically and empirically revisit the relationship of policy analysis with bureaucratic capacity, and argue, as others have before them, that higher levels of policy analytical capacity are expected to better equip public organizations for solving problems, whether in the short term or in the long term. To understand what the authors call the level of policy analysis and policy analytical capacity, they develop a demand-and-supply matrix of governmental policy analysis.

The authors hypothesize in chapter 5 that policy analytical capacity in governments is higher where there are high levels of both demand and supply for policy analysis, while countries with low demand and low supply will demonstrate lower policy analytical capacity. One would find country cases with high levels of demand and supply, the authors assert, in consolidated democracies such as most Western European states, the US and Canada, as well as Australia, New Zealand and some East Asian countries. On the other extreme, low demand and low supply would be represented by authoritarian regimes as well as by clientelist bureaucracies in Africa. Intermediate levels would be found in cases where the demand is low but the supply of policy analysis high. In the governments of Mexico and several South American nations, policy analysis is at an intermediate level because, even if not highly demanded by the state, good-quality analysis can eventually be subcontracted from national think tanks or universities. Conversely, the governments of several Central American countries and the Caribbean are hypothesized to have to turn to analyses provided by international organizations such as the UN and the World Bank, in the absence of domestic policy analytical supply. In this latter case the demand for analysis is high but the supply is low.

Taking the country studies of Australia, Canada, Germany, Brazil and Mexico in the ILPA book series (Geva-May & Howlett, 2013–2018) as foci cases, Mendez and Dussauge-Laguna place these countries on their supply-and-demand matrix. Australia, Canada and Germany broadly fit the high demand–high supply type, albeit with some variations between these cases as to where and how governments seek and source policy analysis. While Brazil is shown to have a somewhat longer tradition in building policy analytical capacities in the bureaucracy than Mexico, both countries tend to find a place in the low demand–high supply quadrant. The authors' review of the five cases points at differences between the countries' level of policy analytical capacity. Yet, their analysis also shows that there are common trends which all cases face, and which have also been evidenced in country cases beyond the ILPA series. Of note is the common agenda to build or re-build policy analytical capacity, either springing from limited initial capacity, or from the re-articulation of policy analytical structures after periods of managerial reform or the externalization of policy analysis.

In chapter 6, Radin observes common issues and concerns that are confronted by academics and practitioners across the unique configurations of different cultures, structures and experiences. These spring from technological changes and changes in the structure and processes of governments both internally and globally, as well as from new expectations about accountability and transparency. Radin considers these and other changes by revisiting the seminal works that since the 1960s laid out the expectations of what policy analysis is, and how it is, or should be, practised.

She describes how the expansion of the field of policy analysis across the Atlantic and Pacific oceans modified the view of American policy analysis scholars. Compliant with differences between the Westminster and presidential systems, UK policy analysts are traditionally career civil servants and generalists, whose mission it is to advise individuals as clients. The advising process in which they are involved has traditionally not focused on separate organization structures that collectively present advice. By contrast, in the US, policy analysts were highly trained professionals drawn in from universities or think tanks and employed in organizational units with significant autonomy in their operations. However, this image of the policy analyst as a quasi-academic staffer no longer describes policy analysts in the US. While some may still fit the original model, for many the stylized approach to analysis has been replaced by interactions in which the analyst is one of a number of participants in policy discussions. The boundaries between managers and policy analysts, and between government and non–government-located analysis, have become blurred. Together with the increased speed and scope of information, these blurred boundaries have moved policy analysis beyond a positivist orientation, closer to one found in Westminster systems, where the consideration of interests and ideology are equally valid concerns in advising ministerial clients as providing reliable information.

Part II: Policy Analysis by Governments

In chapter 7, on policy analysis in central governments, Veselý engages in a tentative comparison of policy analysis in the central governments of Australia, Canada, the Netherlands and Germany. He specifically and systematically analyses the context of policy analysis, the institutionalization of policy analysis vis-à-vis other institutions, the type of people doing policy analysis, and the core issues or challenges identified. Although all four cases project a comparatively strong tradition of policy analysis, the author finds substantial differences between them, but also the common manifestation of two trends: externalization and politicization.

As to the institutionalization of policy analysis, Australia and the Netherlands are identified as two cases where building policy analytical capacity inside the government has not been a priority. Australia has a strong tradition of reliance upon policy analysis by royal commissions and COIs, whereas the Netherlands strongly depends upon policy analysis in advisory bodies and planning bureaus. Canada and Germany share a traditional focus on building in-house capacity. But also here there are some comparative differences. Canada has originally focused on rational policy analysis and has gradually shifted to include more participatory approaches. In Germany, policy analysts, although one would rarely find them under this specific title, are expected to master political and coordination skills. The observed differences in the institutionalization of policy analysis are tentatively explained by the governance context, the traditions of policy analytical training and the recruitment of civil service personnel.

While the core issues identified in the four cases are not the same, it does seem that all four countries face increased politicization and externalization. Politicization comes under different forms, one of which is the rise of political advisors. Externalization shows a relocation of advisory activities previously performed inside government. Veselý makes two important observations. First, to the extent that externalization differs across sectors, national aggregates can be misleading. Second, the discourse on externalization should be approached with caution as evaluations of in-house policy capacity are fraught with normative considerations on what the level of in-house policy analysis in central government should be.

Newman's chapter (8) on policy analysis makes a strong case for studying policy analysis at the subnational level and discusses particular methodological challenges typical for such units of analysis. Policy analysis at the subnational level deserves more attention than it has so far received, first because it is relevant in an ever-increasing number of countries around the globe. Well-known federations, formerly unitary states, and increasingly also developing countries, have been devolving policy responsibilities to subnational jurisdictions. Second, subnational policy issues are unique. States and regions deliver hands-on public services, and often regulate the most tangible aspects of people's lives, while central governments often have their policies confined to money transfers in domains such as social insurance or taxation. Third, subnational governments allow for ethnic, cultural and religious variation of policies, thus allowing subnational governments to act as policy experimentation labs and active agents in policy transfer and lesson drawing. Fourth, subnational policymaking is beautifully complex given the malalignment of central and subnational parties in government and the number of intergovernmental strings that can be attached, as in the case of financial dependencies or rules imposed by central government.

Because of the variation in job titles such as policy advisors, policy officers and policy analysts, it is notoriously difficult to identify who the actual policy advisors are and what they do, and thus studying them at the subnational level poses challenges. This may become ever-more complicated where subnational units utilize different languages in their operations. In researching who policy advisors are and what they do, further methodological complications arise from the application of the dominant research methods such as surveys and interviews. These pose serious limitations because of administrations' (un)willingness to disclose details about their workforce, and thus research encounters the technical difficulty of determining the exact target population. Surveys are necessarily based on purposive sampling and the statistically weaker method of asking human resource departments or managers to distribute surveys or requests for interviews. At the present state of research, Newman finds that it is difficult to discern general international trends or patterns since the research instruments used in cross-country studies are not identical. In addition, a lack of longitudinal data has so far made it challenging to establish whether and how such international trends as New Public Management (NPM) or the alleged decline of in-house policy capacity have affected subnational policy analysis.

What holds for the subnational government's role in delivering tangible services also holds for local government. Many of the services with which citizens are most acquainted in their daily lives are decided and administered by local governments. But local governments' engagement in policy analysis will vary significantly depending on their power, size and autonomy. To the extent that policy decisions are made locally, and in view of the established relation between trust and local government performance, local governments' capacity to provide decision makers with accurate and enough information may matter a great deal.

In chapter 9, Lundin and Öberg consider the role of local civil servants, who play a key role in collecting information and writing memos for the use of the local politicians they advise. In Canada, for instance, the local knowledge producers are mainly local civil servants, but in other countries, for instance in Brazil, local governments are found to use knowledge produced by experts and academics. In Sweden, research has shown that local administrations primarily generate information themselves, but will also use reports and documents from national authorities, from local government associations, or from other local authorities. Geographical proximity seems moreover to foster the engagement of local authorities in networks where they maintain relationships with business actors and interest groups, as well as with other actors in the local community. But exactly how these complex governance structures affect local policy analysis is still under evidenced. In addition, the questions of how information flows in interlocal learning hubs and how the popular tool of benchmarking impacts on local policy analysis call for further research.

Lundin and Öberg find indications that policy analysis at the local level is more problematic than it is at the national level. Policy analytical capacity is often low within local authorities and the resources to perform advanced analyses are missing. Overall, local governments depend very much on the quality of information by national authorities and on peer learning with other local governments. In addition, local politicians are often not of the same calibre as politicians at the national level, and may be quite variably inclined to disregard available information or to fail to crank up local policy analysis. The available evidence from the countries reviewed by the authors reveals that local capacities for policy analysis are rather weak. The same holds true for the comparative study of local policy analysis as a theme of inquiry. Current empirical evidence is restricted to a rather limited geographical scope, and based mainly on studies in the US, the UK and the Scandinavian countries. Cross-country comparisons are rare and are complicated by a great variation in the size, status and power of local governments in an intergovernmental perspective. Yet, despite the sorry state of comparative local policy analysis, Lundin and Öberg succeed in identifying a number of international trends, an example of which is the introduction of NPM. NPM elements such as performance management have been introduced in many local governments, but their implementation faces sceptical local politicians and managers. Another trend is the increased experimentation with various democratic innovations for engaging citizens in local problem definition and solution finding.

In chapter 10, van Nispen and de Jong focus on an area of policy analysis in central governments that has great historical relevance for both the discipline and practice of policy analysis. The relationship between policy analysis and public budgeting has been a hot point of debate since the rise and demise of the Planning-Programming-Budgeting-System (PPBS) in the 1960s and 1970s, and again with the NPM move to performance budgeting. Looking back at 50 years of budgetary reform, the authors assess the progress that has been made towards a more evidence-based budgetary policy. They succinctly narrate the story of the life and death of the PPBS system in the US, and its French, Dutch and UK variants, as well as the same fate of later efforts such as the US's Zero-Based Budgeting (ZBB). They attribute the failure of these systems to a variety of factors, ranging from a lack of leadership, bureaucratic politics, and the fundamentally anti-analytic nature of conventional budgetary routines. Performance budgeting was revived under the NPM movement that spread from New Zealand to the rest of the Anglo-Saxon world and beyond, much aided by the policy diffusion role of the OECD. The latest offsprings were the Program Assessment Rating Tool (PART) in the US and the Korean Self-Assessment of Budgetary Programs (SABP).

Building upon data from the OECD, van Nispen and de Jong survey the availability and utilization of performance information for a selected number of OECD countries across the globe. They demonstrate great variation between the South Korean government, on the one side of the continuum, and Portugal on the other. The evidence further shows that, while in many cases performance information is available across a wide range of countries, about one-third do not use non-financial information in their budgetary process. With the sovereign debt crisis in the EU, the authors expect a strengthening of government priorities for performance measurement and budgeting, although, as they point out, the attention to budgeting has not been matched by the use of non-financial information. They find evidence of a massive return to incremental budgeting based on inputs rather than outputs, even in countries such as New Zealand, which had been one of the original drivers of performance budgeting.

Even with the demise of performance budgeting, however, the demand for non-financial information has not disappeared. Programme evaluation and, in times of austerity, spending reviews increasingly generate non-financial information. As to performance budgeting itself, 50 years of experience show that the chances for incremental budgeting being substituted by performance budgeting are not high. The authors conclude that it stands to reason to scale down the high expectations on the use of performance information in the budget cycle. Performance information is just one piece of information competing with other sources of information. The added value of performance budgeting does not lie in its utility for the allocation of services, and the pursuit of efficiency and effectiveness, but rather in increased government transparency.

Comparative Policy Analysis: An Introduction

Part III: Committees, Public Inquiries, Research Institutes, Consultants and Public Opinion

While the chapters in Part II describe and compare in-house policy analysis in central, subnational and local governments, Part III moves the analysis away from the inner circles of executive government. The contributors to this part of the Handbook investigate comparative differences and similarities of policy analysis in COIs, expert advisory councils, legislatures and management consultancy work, as well as explore the use of public opinion research in policy analysis.

In chapter 11 Marier reviews the literature and comparative research on COIs, which in some countries like the UK and Sweden have a century-long tradition. In view of facilitating cross-national comparison, Marier promotes a broad definition of COI as 'any working group created and mandated by a government to study a particular policy and/or program'. COIs are distinguished from other public organizations in that they are temporary and consist of experts external to the government.

Classifications of COIs can be made on the basis of the roles they perform, accepting that a COI can play more than one role. A first such role is the facilitation of learning by helping to better understand a problem, which is the main role played by COIs in Sweden. Adjudication is a second role, with a long-standing presence in Westminster systems. This role is also projected by such COIs as the Truth and Reconciliation Commission in South Africa, where the outcome of adjudication is not the attribution of blame but the fostering of forgiveness. Political roles constitute a third type to consider when analysing COIs. Political roles are observed with executives calling in to life COIs to facilitate the implementation of intended policy programmes or, conversely, to stall progress in the policymaking process. This role pertains at all times and all places. Another object of comparative research on COIs is their changing nature in terms of composition and independence, with indications of the UK Royal Commissions making way for alternative arrangements, or of the Swedish COIs' allowances for a more prominent role of politicians at the expense of the usual social actors. One other fruitful domain of research lies in the study of the influence COIs exert on policy change or agenda setting. According to Marier, there are five kinds of policy influence that COIs have (in some cases simultaneously): alarm raising, reinforcing the status quo, incremental policy change, idea shaking, and policy engineering. Among five key variables to determine this influence are governmental responses ranging from counteraction to full endorsement.

Chapter 12 reviews the comparative roles and changing functions of semi-permanent institutions that provide recommendations on government policy. Crowley and Head explain the origin and development of expert advisory councils against the background of five developments: (1) the post-war indispensability of science and technology and the need for expert advice to support this growth; (2) the diffusion since the 1980s of efficiency and effectiveness concerns to public sector policies and programs; (3) the growing complexity of policy challenges owing to globalization; (4) the increased politicization of decision making; (5) the externalization of policy advice beyond the civil service. At present, expert advisory bodies are best understood as entities established by government to provide advice on matters requiring scientific and technical analysis, and whose membership consists largely of experts drawn from non-governmental organizations and research groups. The accepted function of expert advisory councils is to consolidate scientific and technical knowledge for recommendations in policy areas where lay expertise or stakeholder input is not sufficient. However, the authors also point out that this function is shifting, and that science and technological knowledge are no longer the main sources of advice.

There are currently two perspectives on the roles of expert advisory councils: either they are traditional professionalized advisory bodies, or they are modernized interactive responsive bodies. In several European countries advisory bodies are described as no longer traditional sources of expert policy advice for government, but as being part of the contemporary complex policy environment in which they operate as boundary organizations between multiple players. Building upon and synthesizing available comparative studies in continental Europe, the Anglo-Saxon world, and on a number of single case studies (including Japan, the Czech Republic, and Taiwan of the ILPA book series 2013–2018), and using different criteria such as configuration, administration and composition, the authors find remarkable similarities but also enduring differences. In the US, the pluralist nature of the advisory system puts advisory bodies at a fair distance from government. In Europe, advisory bodies are more neo-corporatist, in Japan they are elitist/neo-corporatist, and they are highly controlled in the post-communist world, such as in the Czech Republic. Despite noted differences there are also signs of convergence. Advisory bodies develop similar strategies to maximize their relevance and legitimacy in policy advisory systems characterized by growing competition for advice. Advisory councils must also gain and sustain access to the policymaking process, and hence deal with the risk of politicization.

Legislative studies need a policy turn, as Wolfs and De Winter assert in chapter 13. To date, the rich domain of legislative research has contributed little to understanding parliamentary policy analysis. This is surprising, given the crucial role that parliamentary policy analysis could play in reducing the widely acknowledged information asymmetry between legislatures and executive governments. The authors make important headway in providing a general framework for advancing the knowledge on parliamentary policy analysis and support. Building upon empirical data from the countries covered in the ILPA volumes, as well as from the European Parliament, they explore similarities and differences in the contribution of different actors engaged in providing parliamentary policy analysis: the personal assistants of MPs, the advisors of political groups, and the support services of parliamentary administrations. They also examine variations in the political structures and instruments that legislators use to extract information from the executive and expertise from external actors: committees, hearings, and also less conventional methods of consultation, such as research and study visits.

Overall, the analysis provided by Wolfs and De Winter demonstrates a wide variation in parliamentary policy analysis. They tentatively account for these differences by referring to constitutional differences (Westminster versus presidential), parliamentary cultures (transformative or debating parliaments), and majority–opposition politics. Marked differences exist between the numbers of MPs' supporting staff (1-60), the organization of staffing (staff-based or allowance-based) and the type of roles that staff play (administrative, policy analysis, constituency service). In most parliaments with limited staff numbers, assistants combine several roles, while a high degree of specialization is afforded in more generous systems such as the US Congress. Advisors to the political groups, in turn, are found to follow three types of logic. In a logic of centralization, such as found in Brazil and the US, a significant portion of advisors is allocated to party leaders. In a logic of decentralization, like in Germany, staff are dispersed among the different parliamentary committees. A logic of secondment is observed when advisors are posted at party headquarters, as is the case in 'partitocratic' systems. The in-house policy analytical capacity also differs, both in size and in the kind of policy work that is performed by parliament staffers and research units.

In the studied cases, the number of staffers varies between five and 30. In most parliaments, staffers provide support on request and their work mainly consists of data collection, and to a lesser extent of data analysis and research utilization. Next to being supported by three kinds of parliamentary staff, MPs can actively use a number of informational strategies. The best-known instruments are parliamentary committees. The informational role of committees and the extent to which committees engage in policy work vary between what are called 'transformative' or 'working' parliaments, and 'debating parliaments'. A working parliament, as identified for Germany, puts emphasis on legislative and policy work in the committees, while a debating parliament such as in the UK is focused on plenary discussions and law-making, and policy work is less important. A common instrument for bringing in external experts is through parliamentary COIs which investigate a certain policy problem or failure. Hearings, as meetings with stakeholders and experts, have become increasingly popular across the world. Yet, the authors contend that the exact nature of the policy analytical support that these instruments provide to legislators presents a venue for further comparative research.

In chapter 14, Saint-Martin deals with the comparative origin and rise of global management consultancies. As agents of isomorphism, consultancies are active in defining the norms and in disseminating models of appropriate action in the management of large organizations, including in the public sector. Increasingly they have also established themselves as legitimate actors in public debates on policy problems and solutions, a development that has been coined by the author as the *think tank-ization* of consultancy. Saint-Martin's comparative analysis shows how management consultancies have developed earlier and more successfully in countries with liberal market economies (LMEs) than in countries with coordinated market economies (CMEs) as per Peter A. Hall and David Soskice (2001).

Management consultancy emerged in the early 20th century under the impetus of 'scientific management' (Taylor, 1911), but started booming in the 1960s when major accounting firms in the US capitalized on their privileged access to clients. With the exception of the UK, Europe originally proved a less fertile ground for home-grown consultancies to develop, not only because government regulation restricted accountants from providing consultancy services to the same clients, but also because of the relatively smaller size of European companies. Yet with the growing presence of big US firms and the Marshall Plan-aided spread of American management ideas and models, the big American consultancies succeeded in enlarging their action terrain to Europe. The success with which they permeated the European public sector, however, is largely explained by the nature of market economies. In the UK, like in the US, the public sector has been a more important client of consultancies than in the coordinated market economy of Germany, for instance. Liberal market economies have also been keener to adopt the NPM ideas that were developed and disseminated by consultancy firms. The UK, together with New Zealand, the US, Canada and Australia were so-called first-mover countries, all characterized by majoritarian political traditions and an individualist pro-market culture, both of which have traditionally not featured in most continental European countries.

In addition to the origin of management consultancy work and its access to the public sector, Saint-Martin reviews the actual roles and content of management consultancy work. He identifies interesting historical and comparative paths: from rational planners in the 1960s, to cost-cutters in the 1980s, and finally to partners in new governance in the 21st century. In the rational planning era of the 1960s, government efforts to rationalize state interventions opened up the civil service to draw lessons from the private sector, hence also opening up to management consultants, for instance by secondment programmes between Whitehall and consultancy firms. Also influential was the effect of PPBS in fuelling openness to the booming business of systems theory. In the 1980s a new push came along, particularly in LMEs, with

NPM as a vehicle for importing management consultants' ideas in the public sector. From the mid-1990s, with a greater emphasis on policymaking rather than on management alone, major consulting firms repositioned themselves as partners in governance.

In conclusion, Saint-Martin identifies a range of strategies that consultancy firms deploy to keep and expand their market share: they establish formal associations to lobby governments, they offer free consultants on secondment, they create hubs for networking and they serve as revolving doors for high-ranking civil servants and politicians.

While chapter 14 highlights the discursive power that global management consultancies exercise in public debates on the definition of policy problems and solutions, chapter 15 turns to another source of discursive power: public opinion. Rothmayr approaches public opinion research, constructed through a collection of census and other data by various tools of research, as an important but relatively under-studied tool for generating data for policy analysis. She offers three perspectives to advance the understanding of the relationship between public opinion and policymaking. At the macro level, she addresses the question of public responsiveness of policies. At the meso level, she opens the black box of the relationship between policy choices and public opinion. At the micro level, she focuses on how various actors utilize public opinion data in the crafting of public policies, which is to date the least empirically developed theme of public opinion research. In her review of the state of literature and of current research, the author contends that public opinion matters and provides some evidence on important mitigating factors such as electoral cycles and issue salience. Whereas there appears to be general agreement that public opinion influences policymaking, there is disagreement on whether public opinion is an independent factor or a social construct of political and media elites.

Several policy process theories have tried to open up the black box of the role of public opinion for policy choice and policy change. While there is substantive variation between these theories, they also share a number of commonalities: the ways in which public opinion as a resource is put to use in policymaking depends on the strategies of the actors involved; the relationship between public opinion and public policy is bidirectional in that public opinion can in itself be influenced by framing processes; public opinion is neither a sufficient nor a necessary condition to explain policy change.

As to micro-level perspective, how politicians and policymakers actually use public opinion, the available evidence is limited. In parliaments, public opinion is used either in a partisan fashion or in support of intended policy proposals. Political actors refer not only to mediated polls but also to polling specifically conducted by interest groups for their respective use in various representational arenas.

It also appears that the nature of political systems matters with reference to public opinion data utilization. In parliamentary systems, electoral results are more important than public opinion expressed through organized interests or mass opinion in parliamentary systems; the opposite holds true in presidential systems. The available evidence shows, however, that the influence of public opinion over policy choices should not be overestimated. Media and government polls do play a signalling role in agenda setting, and help to direct instrument choices and evaluations in policy formulation and implementation respectively. Yet, according to evidence from the US, Canada and Switzerland, the most useful role of public opinion polls seems to be their fit with the communicative and persuasion strategies of policy actors.

Part IV: Parties and Interest-Group-Based Policy Analysis

Part IV delves particularly into the political and corporatist dimensions of policy analysis, with a focus on political parties, business associations, labour unions, and the voluntary sector.

Chapter 16 presents a comparative analysis of political party think tanks. Comprehensively exploring cases in North and South America, Europe, and Asia-Pacific, Pattyn, Pittoors and Van Hecke build two heuristic typologies to classify different types and functions of party think tanks worldwide. Party think tanks with high autonomy are typically found in the US and Canada. In these countries, political parties have little in-house capacity, and intellectual support for party ideas and policies relies on the external expertise of research centres, political consultant firms and think tanks. In these cases, parties turn for research input and policy ideas to party-affiliated bodies, such as the well-known German foundations. Medium autonomy is characteristic of political foundations and party-affiliated research institutes, such as found in Germany, the Netherlands, Wallonia and the European Union. Low autonomy is typical of Brazilian, Japanese and Flemish in-house party study services or departments.

As to the actual policy analytical functions of political party think tanks, the authors' classification rests on two dimensions of the nature of the advice that party think tanks provide to their political patrons or mother parties. These dimensions relate to whether they produce short-term or long-term ('hot' or 'cold') advice (Craft & Howlett, 2012), whether they focus on applied technical policy issues, or on more-fundamental ideological questions. On the basis of these dimensions, the authors identify four types of political party think tanks. 'Ideological guardians' combine long-term advice with an ideological focus and are typical of the political foundations in Germany, the Netherlands and the European Union generally. 'Political advisors' such as Brazilian and Japanese think tanks analyse fundamental questions with a short-term purpose. 'Policy assistant' think tanks, such as found in Flanders, assist MPs with short-term, applied advice. 'Policy experts' perform research on applied longer-term issues. This is the case for the North American private think tanks. To explain the variation in the autonomy and functions of party think tanks, Pattyn, Pittoors and Van Hecke tentatively point at the role of party leadership, but also at the influence of enduring traditions of pluralism in North America and political pillarization in a number of continental European countries.

In chapter 17, Vining and Boardman examine the role of business associations in the policy process and particularly in performing policy analysis. The geographical scope of their analysis is North America, the UK and Australia, where business associations are voluntary organizations whose members consist of individual firms. Still, the composition of business associations varies substantively along industrial activities, size and shared interests. Generally, business associations can be classified into industry-based associations, professional organizations, and chambers of commerce. In Vining and Boardman's issue-based policymaking model, business associations will only consider conducting policy analysis and proposing solutions that are consistent with their own interests, that will maximize benefits to their members, or at a minimum, will not reduce the profitability of their members. The authors identify important restraints on the incentives of business associations to engage in policy analysis. Policy analysis is costly in money and effort, and has to face divergent interests among association members. In addition, the profit-making logic of member firms might clash with the public interest or the social-values logics of public policy debates, which renders the legitimate usage of profit-making arguments difficult. Alternative strategies, such as direct or indirect lobbying, are seen as potentially more cost-effective.

In their empirical analysis of Canadian business associations, the authors indeed find that there are only a few business associations that conduct and publish policy analysis with wide and transparent appeal. For most business associations, it is cumbersome to ignore profit and downplay equity demands in favour of scientific argument and analysis. The only exception to this rule may be the professional associations of lawyers, doctors or accountants, whose expertise carries more legitimacy in the public domain than the claims of businesses.

Similar to business associations, unions defend the interests of their members. In chapter 18, Schulze and Schroeder show how the unions' preoccupation with the defence of members' interests is one factor in explaining the limited knowledge transfer from labour-union research institutes to labour-market policy agenda setting and formulation. Against the background of global welfare state retrenchment and declining union membership, the authors investigate the utilization of union research institutions in developing the unions' claims in the policy process. Their study is a comparative case analysis across three countries with different welfare state profiles, two stages of the policy cycles (agenda setting and formulation), and one policy (labour–market activation).

Germany is a conservative regime and labour unions are well connected to Parliament and committees. Denmark is a social democratic regime with strong representation of unions in the political arena. The US in turn represents a liberal regime, where unions are weak and only indirectly active in the political arena. In these countries the authors examine the policy analysis and role of one of two research institutes of the German Hans Böckler Foundation, the Danish Economic Council of the Labour Movement, and the relatively younger US Economic Policy Institute. These institutes publish different studies and reports on employment and provide input to the policy positions of labour unions. Schulze and Schroeder's analysis shows that the knowledge transfer of these studies to agenda setting and policy change has been modest. At least in the domain of labour-market studies and active labour-market policies, the unions' receptiveness to scientific analysis is hampered by the particular dilemmas that labour unions face: opposing or partaking in reforms, and trade-offs between the defence of high social protection or shaping a policy in the making.

In the new public governance, where policymaking has allegedly pluralized, non-state actors are potential contributors to generating and advocating policy ideas. In chapter 19, Evans, Glass and Wellstead theorize on the role of non-profits in the policy process and explore what are the types of policy advocacy activities of non-profits, the extent of organizational investments in such work, and the tools and instruments put to use. Their analysis excludes business associations of the type discussed in chapter 17, but includes non-profits that have a mission to contribute to the public good in domains such as healthcare, culture, recreation, housing, volunteerism promotion and international activities. The role of non-profits in policymaking is variably restricted or facilitated by government regulation and oversight, with pluralist countries showing more liberal regulation compared to restrictive regulation by the autocratic governments in many developing countries. There remain important methodological problems of operational definition, measurement and causality in analysing the variation of non-profits' advocacy activities. Even so, the authors have managed to identify the key factors for understanding these variations as the strength of commitment to specific causes and venue selection.

In addition, the chapter points at various exogenous and endogenous factors that constrain or facilitate policy engagements and advocacy mobilization. Although the empirical evidence across North American and European studies is not conclusive, the (exogenous) nature of funding relations between government and non-government actors in a chain of service delivery constrains non-profits' latitude in engagement in policy advocacy. Among the endogenous factors, the limited resource capacity of non-profits reduces their opportunities to effectively mobilize knowledge. Insufficient capacity of non-profits to be effective participants in co-construction of policies ultimately questions the optimist perspective of the new public governance model.

Part V: Advocacy-Based and Academic Policy Analysis

Part V focuses on advocacy-based and academic policy analysis in think tanks, academic research and university teaching.

Chapter 20 deals with social media and policy analysis. Kuo and Cheng explore social media policies and policy analysis in four capital cities in Asia with a focus on the application of social media for citizen participation. Social media differ from traditional media. The latter are a one-way transmission platform lacking participation, feedback and communication with stakeholders. Social media promise to be more participatory, interactive and transparent. The author finds that government agencies in Taipei, Seoul, Tokyo and Beijing use social media to improve the quality of government services and improve citizen engagement. In Taipei, the city government uses a platform called i-Voting to encourage citizens to express their opinions and vote on issues. Tokyo metropolitan government uses internet surveys to garner citizens' opinions on important policy issues. In Seoul, the 'OPEN' system discloses administrative procedures through the internet. Beijing, finally, has developed micro-blogs and diffuses these to other government agencies at all levels. Beijing's 'Announcement' is an example of a microblog used extensively by local government for information transmission, public communication and the development of mobilization. Whether these blogs are used as an input for policymaking or as an instrument of propaganda is an interesting question meriting further research.

In chapter 21, Stone and Ladi entertain a broad definition of think tanks with which they cover a wider global comparative analysis of their many faces and functions. They note that think tanks 'engage in research, analysis and communication for policy development within local communities, national governments and international institutions in both public and private domains'. There is substantial variation in the legal constitution of think tanks, ranging from non-governmental organizations in North America, to semi-governmental units in Asia and Europe, and to the party-affiliated foundations in the European Union. The authors trace the history of think tanks and the type of analysis they perform, identify a number of types, and explore their respective influence.

Stone and Ladi identify three past historical stages and an emerging new phase. In the early 20th century, think tanks developed in the Anglo-Saxon world, mainly the US, in response to state intervention and the 'progressive era'. The character of policy analysis was strongly rationalist. In the ever-stronger state expansion of the post-war era, think tank development got a second push, this time also in European liberal and social democracies. Policy analysis in this era became more sophisticated and professional in carrying out its role in providing rational knowledge inputs to policymaking. From the 1980s, a worldwide boom of think tanks saw Anglo-American think tanks mature and diversify their policy analytical activities in the direction of advocacy and publicity. Countries in Europe, Asia, Africa and the former Soviet Union all witnessed an increase in think tanks, albeit under different legal forms and with varying sizes, scopes, and policy analytical activities. In the current internet era, the authors find some, albeit modest, evidence of the emergence of transnational think tanks.

As to policy analytical modes, Stone and Ladi relate these variations to different types of think tanks. 'Ideological tanks' or 'advocacy tanks' typically choose their research topics in light of their ideological identity. 'Academic, non-partisan think tanks' provide high-quality analysis, often with the application of quantitative data analysis and formal models. There are also 'specialist' think tanks, for instance in the domain of foreign policy, which are prone to use mixed methods of research. The 'generalist' think tanks also display the use of a variety of research tools. Another type is the 'think and do tanks', undertaking applied research targeted at direct policy results.

Think tanks perform policy analysis but also spend considerable efforts to disseminate their results. According to Stone and Ladi, these include acting as information interlocutors, policy entrepreneurs, and network entrepreneurs. Whether these efforts are successful in influencing policy development is a question the authors can only tentatively answer. Beyond the very number of think tanks being indicators of their functionality, there is no accepted evidence of think tanks' direct influence in policymaking. On a positive note, think tanks are well positioned to provide rational input into policy development, and help to contribute to a more participatory and educated populace. More sceptically, think tanks are instruments used to maintain hegemonic class interests. Or, instead of providing rational policy analysis, they function as agenda setters and provide attractive narratives for the definition of problems and for framing the terms of a debate. Their ultimate influence is eventually mediated by national institutional arrangements and the interplay of political and economic interests.

What are academics doing? Which kind of policy analysis? Where, how, with what purpose in mind, and with what effect on the real world of policymaking? These are the questions that Blum and Brans attempt to answer in Chapter 22 in a comparative investigation of policy analysis by academics. The authors' distinction between policy studies and policy analysis is similar to the distinction made in the last chapter and labelled policy research and policy analysis.

From the available literature and country evidence, Blum and Brans posit that the nature of policy analysis by academics is influenced by the institutional habitat of academics and their position in the policy advisory system. In principle, academics have greater independence than policy analysts in the government or in the political party organizations and interest groups. But the extent to which the academic branch in a country does independent policy research or engages in more practice-oriented policy analysis depends on a country's specific epistemological tradition, and on self-understandings of the discipline. Some countries, like France, keep their academic policy research at a distance from authorities, and researchers assume roles of mainstream academics or policy critics. Another tradition, such as found in the US, shows a more pragmatic orientation, where policy researchers engage in applied policy analysis, evaluation and technical advice or advice on policy options. The most common type of self-understanding of the discipline in Europe appears to be mixed, and combines both mainstream and critical policy studies with applied policy analysis, yet with what seems to be a dominance of the former.

In this context, different kinds of policy researchers undertake different kinds of analysis, and portray a variety of roles and engagements vis-à-vis policymaking. But what are the results of these engagements in the real world of policymaking? In this chapter, Blum and Brans hypothesize that policy-research utilization is aided by at least three features: a mature academic policy analysis at universities; strongly institutionalized policy analysis as a practice in government and governance; and an epistemological culture of instrumental rationality or technocratic orientations in policymaking. Yet, next to cross-sectoral characteristics, the authors also find that the influence of national features of policy-research utilization is mediated by international trends.

In the last two decades, at least three movements influenced the interaction between policy research and policymaking: the evidence-based policy movement; the trend towards interactive policymaking (or, to use the more fashionable terms, towards co-creation and co-design of policies), and pressures for the restoration of primacy of politics over evidence in policy choices. Against the background of these trends of scientification, societalization and politicization, more research is needed on the extent to which there is convergence in policy-research utilization or whether national heterogeneities prevail.

The kind of policy analysis conducted by policy professionals depends to a large extent on the nature of policy analytical education at universities. In the last chapter of this book, Botha, Geva-May and Maslove compare the policy analytical content of academic degree programmes across three regions: the US, Canada and Europe. Their study is based on a statistical analysis of curriculum components and website information. To understand the content of programmes, the authors distinguish between policy analysis and policy research (also coined 'policy studies', as in chapter 22). Policy analysis trains graduates to understand and master skills meant to inform the actions and decisions of specific clients in the public sector. Policy research deepens graduates' understanding 'about' the policymaking process as a social, economic and political phenomenon worthy of study in its own right.

In the US, programmes are mixed but policy-analysis heavy. In Canada, degree programmes are typically policy-research heavy, and have embraced policy analysis more recently than in the US. In Western Europe, programmes promote policy analysis alongside policy research. In Central and Eastern Europe, finally, capacity building in post-communist administrations has brought along a policy-analysis-heavy profile. Variable historical paths account for these differences. In the US, pragmatism and the revolving door between academics and policy professionals have supported a client orientation that is typical for policy analysis. In Canada, concerns about academic independence are key in understanding the prioritization of policy research. In Western Europe, mixed profiles hide many national variations and are best understood as the results of American policy analytical influence on different academic traditions. Consistent with legal, public governance, and corporate traditions in teaching public sector approaches, there are indeed many academic homes to teaching public policy in Europe: law, political science and public administration departments, and business schools. In Central and Eastern Europe, there are within-region differences behind the apparently keen adoption of policy analysis in post-communist curricula.

Variations in the prominence of policy analytical components in public policy degree programmes are also visible in variations in the extent to which the latter require their students to take up practical internships in policy analysis and policymaking. Internships feature prominently in US curricula, less so in Canadian programmes, and to a varying degree in European programmes. What is more, the pattern of accreditation seems to fit the observed regional differences. Standardized accreditation is well developed in the US with the Network of Schools of Public Policy, Affairs, and Administration (NASPAA), while it is resisted in Canada. In Europe, given the diversity of national contexts, the mission-based accreditation of the European Association for Public Administration Accreditation (EAPAA) makes allowances for different identities and approaches of programmes and for the constraints of different educational systems.

The pendulum of policy analysis as a profession and as an academic field of study has swung in the last decade from the initial 'speaking truth to power' and rigorous policy analysis methodology originated in the US, to a more diffuse position in the policymaking process. In lieu of 'speaking truth to power', we note a myriad of policy analytical loci—not only in the government but also in agencies, parliaments, consultancy firms, interest groups and various other civil society organizations. The exposure to communication, technology and domain-specific niches requires teams of analysts widely involving experts as policy analysts. As a result, the policy analysis domain has moved to a more advisory rather than a definitive policy solution orientation. In this book, through comparison and generalization achieved through the myriad of international cases and variety of foci in which policy analysis is involved, we sought to draw universal conclusions about the state of the art today.

References

Bardach, E. (1996). *A practical guide for policy analysis: The eightfold path to more effective problem solving (1st edition)*. Berkeley, CA: Berkeley Academic Press.

Bardach, E. (2005, 2008, 2011, 2015). *A practical guide for policy analysis: The eightfold path to more effective problem solving (2nd, 3rd, 4th & 5th editions)*. Washington, DC: CQ Press.

Bouwen, P. (2002). Corporate lobbying in the European Union: The logic of access. *Journal of European Public Policy 9*(3): 365–390.

Craft, J. & Halligan, J. (2015). Looking back and thinking ahead: 30 years of policy advisory system scholarship. Paper prepared for the Second International Conference on Public Policy, Milan 2015.

Craft, J. & Howlett, M. (2012). Policy formulation, governance shifts and policy influence: Location and content in policy advisory systems. *Journal of Public Policy 32*(2): 79–98.

Craft, J. & Howlett, M. (2013). The dual dynamics of policy advisory systems: The impact of externalization and politicization on policy advice. *Policy and Society 32*(3): 187–197.

DeLeon, P. (1999). The stages approach to the policy process: What has it done? Where is it going. *Theories of the Policy Process 1*: 19–32.

Dobuzinskis, L., Howlett, M. & Laycock, D. (2007). *Policy analysis in Canada: The state of the art.* Toronto: University of Toronto Press.

Dror, Y. (1972). The challenge of policy sciences. *Policy Studies Journal 1*(1): 4–5.

Dror, Y. (1983). *Public policy making reexamined.* New Brunswick, NJ: Transaction.

Dunleavy, P. (1991). *Democracy, bureaucracy and public choice.* London: Pearson Education.

Dunn, W. N. (1994). *Public policy analysis: An introduction.* Englewood Cliffs, NJ: Prentice Hall.

Dye, T. R. (1995). *Understanding public policy (8th edition)*. Englewood Cliffs, NJ: Prentice Hall.

Fischer, F. & Forester, J. (Eds) (1993). *The argumentative turn in policy analysis and planning.* Durham, NC: Duke University Press.

Geva-May, I. (Ed.) (2005). *Thinking like a policy analyst: Policy analysis as a clinical profession.* New York: Palgrave Macmillan.

Geva-May, I. (2017). *A methodology for policy analysis.* New York: Routledge.

Geva-May, I. & Howlett, M. (Eds) (2013–2018). International Library of Policy Analysis (Vols. 1–21), Bristol, UK: Policy Press.

Geva-May, I. with Wildavksy, A. (1997, 2011). *An operational approach to policy analysis: The craft—Prescriptions for better analysis.* Boston: Kluwer Academic Publishers.

Hall, P. A. & Soskice, D. (2001). An introduction to varieties of capitalism, in P. A Hall & D. Soskice (Eds), *Varieties of capitalism: The institutional foundations of comparative advantage.* Oxford: Oxford University Press.

Halligan, J. (1995). Policy advice and the public sector. In B. G Peters & D. J Savoie (Eds), *Governance in a changing environment.* Montreal: McGill-Queen's University Press: 138–172.

Halligan, J. (1998). Policy Advice. In *International Encyclopedia of Public Policy and Administration*, 3 (1): 686–688. Boulder, CO: Westview.

Howlett, M., Ramesh, M. & Perl, A. (2009). *Studying public policy: Policy cycles and policy subsystems (3rd edition)*. Toronto: Oxford University Press.

Kingdon, J. W. (1984). *Agendas, alternatives and public policies.* Boston: Little, Brown.

Knott, J. & Wildavsky, A. (1980). If dissemination is the solution, what is the problem? *Knowledge: Creation, Diffusion, Utilization 1*(4): 537–578.

Lasswell, H. (1971). *A pre-view of the policy sciences.* New York: American Elsevier.

Meltsner, A. J. (1976). *Policy analysts in the bureaucracy.* Berkeley, CA: University of California Press.

MacRae, D. & Wilde, J. A. (1979). *Policy analysis for public decisions.* Lanham, MD: University Press of America.

May, J. P. (2005). Policy maps and political feasibility. In I. Geva-May (Ed.), *Thinking like a policy analyst: Policy analysis as a clinical profession.* New York: Palgrave Macmillan.

Nutley, S. M., Morton, S., Jung, T. & Boaz, A. (2010). Evidence and policy in six European countries: Diverse approaches and common challenges. *Evidence & Policy 6*(2): 131–144.

Page, E. C. & Jenkins, B. (2005). *Policy bureaucracy: Government with a cast of thousands.* Oxford: Oxford University Press.

Patton, C. V. & Sawicki, D. S. (1993). *Basic methods of policy analysis and planning.* Englewood Cliffs, NJ: Prentice Hall.

Polsby, N. W. (1960). How to study community power: The pluralist alternative. *The Journal of Politics* 22(3): 474–484.

Radin, B. A. (2000). *Beyond Machiavelli: Policy analysis comes of age.* Washington, DC: Georgetown University Press.

Radin, B. A. (2002). *The accountable juggler: The art of leadership in a federal agency.* Washington, DC: Congressional Quarterly Press.

Radin, B. A. (2013). Policy analyses reaches midlife. *Central European Journal of Public Policy* 7(1): 8–27.

Radin, B. A. (2016). Policy analysis and advising decisionmakers; Don't forget the decisionmaker/client. *Journal of Comparative Policy Analysis* 18(3): 290–301.

Rhodes, R. A. W. (1997). *Understanding governance: Policy networks, governance, reflexivity and accountability.* Buckingham: Open University Press.

Richardson, J. J. (2000). Government, interest groups and policy change. *Political Studies* 48(5): 1006–1025.

Sabatier, P. A. & Jenkins-Smith, H. (1993). *Policy change and learning: An advocacy coalition approach.* Boulder, CO: Westview Press.

Sabatier, P. A. & Weible, C. M. (Eds) (2014). *Theories of the policy process* (3rd edition). Boulder, CO & Oxford, UK: Westview Press.

Sanderson, Ian (2011). Evidence-based policy or policy-based evidence? Reflections on Scottish experience. *Evidence & Policy: A Journal of Research, Debate and Practice* 7(1): 59–76

Scharpf, F. W. (1997). *Games real actors play: Actor-centered institutionalism in policy research.* Boulder, CO: Westview Press.

Schmitter, P. C. & Lehmbruch, G. (1979). *Trends toward corporatist intermediation.* Beverley Hills, CA & London: Sage.

Schmitter, P. C. & Streeck, W. (1999). *The organisation of business interests: Studying the associative action of business in advanced industrial societies.* Köln: Max-Planck-Institut für Gesellschaftsforschung.

Stone, Diane. (1996). *Capturing the political imagination: Think tanks and the policy process.* London: Frank Cass.

Straßheim, H. & Kettunen, P. (2014). When does evidence-based policy turn into policy-based evidence? Configurations, contexts and mechanisms. *Evidence & Policy* 10(2): 259–277.

Surowiecki, J. (2004). *The wisdom of crowds.* New York: Doubleday.

Taylor, F. W. (1911). *The principles of scientific management.* New York & London: Harper & Brothers.

Weimer, D. L. & Vining, A. R. (1988, 1991, 1999, 2005). *Policy analysis: Concepts and practice (1st, 2nd, 3rd, 4th editions).* Upper Saddle River, NJ: Prentice Hall.

Weimer, D. L. & Vining, A. R. (2010). *Policy analysis: Concepts and practice* (5th edition). Boston: Longman.

Weiss, C. H. (1979). The many meanings of research utilization. *Public Administration Review* 39(5): 426–431.

Wildavsky, A. (1979). *Speaking truth to power: The art and craft of policy analysis.* Boston: Little, Brown.

PART I

The Styles and Methods of Public Policy Analysis

2

THE POLICY ANALYSIS PROFESSION

Yukio Adachi

Introduction

This chapter portrays the discipline of policy analysis as a sophisticated tool for effectively tackling serious, complicated, value-laden public problems, and to consider whether policy analysis may appropriately be recognized as a 'profession', in the classic sense of the term. The first of four sections below critically examines the conception of the elevated level of vocational occupations referred to as 'professions' that was formulated by British sociologist G. Millerson more than half a century ago. While Millerson's conception is still most often referred to by sociologists of professionalism as the standard definition of the term, this chapter argues that the increase in new types of post-industrial and knowledge-based occupations requires us to revisit the traditional conception.

The second section focuses on the identification of the primary mission of policy analysis in the political process of democracy, followed by a critical examination of the formal/rationalist, positivist/empiricist, and post-positivist frameworks (models) of policy analysis. The third section turns to the design-oriented approach to policy analysis, recognizing the significance of its requirement that analysts be knowledgeable about as many versions of each of the existing analytical frameworks as possible, and apply the most appropriate one for the context and the design of workable policy prescriptions in that context. The final section considers how to reformulate the conception of 'profession' so that newly developed knowledge fields, including policy analysis, can be legitimately recognized as 'professions', emphasizing that whether policy analysis will be so recognized can vary from nation to nation.

The Concept of 'Professionalism'

The word 'profession' has a long history in all Latin-based European languages, and was primarily used to refer to the university-educated occupations of medicine, law and the clergy throughout the medieval period.[1] In the sixteenth century, however, another usage of the term developed, referring to the whole range of occupations by which people were identified and made their living. This extension of the scope of the term inevitably caused its devaluation, with the relegation of the original, prestigious connotation to the background.[2] Such a devaluation is mirrored, for example, in the pejorative sense of contrast between *professional* and *amateur*, by which prestige is associated with the amateur who engages in an activity simply for pleasure rather than for financial benefit, while professionals make a trade of anything that is properly pursued with higher motives, such as a 'professional politician'. Another contrast reverses such an evaluation and measures the quality of activity that one may expect of each: something characterized as the work of an 'amateur' implies poor or untrained work, while a 'professional' job implies good, reliable work of skill and quality.

The development of capitalist industrialism in nineteenth-century Europe and the United States gave rise to a number of new types of occupational frameworks. In contrast with continental Europe, where a demand for the designation of 'professional' was not as great,[3] professional status was zealously sought by certain occupational echelons in Britain, and then later in the United States, to distinguish them from the 'lowly' trades. Gaining recognition as a profession was vital in Anglo-American occupational culture not only because it was associated with traditional gentry status, but also because the traditional connotations of dedication and learning provided political legitimation in the competitive labour market (Freidson, 1986, p. 33). Furthermore, the descriptive term 'professional' was adopted as part of the official occupational classification scheme in both countries. Occupations such as surveying, medicine, actuarial science, law, dentistry, civil engineering, logistics, architecture, accounting, pharmacy, veterinary medicine, psychology, nursing, teaching, librarianship, optometry and social work had allegedly gained 'professional' status by 1900. Of particular importance in understanding the fundamental difference between continental European and Anglo-American occupational cultures is the broad perspective of the more egalitarian Anglo-American societies in which one's distinction and position in the market place depended less on the prestige of the institutions in which one was educated than on the substance of education and training one received, and one's identity as a credentialed member of a highly regarded professional association.[4]

With the development and rapid spread of 'professionalization' in the Weberian sense,[5] the demand for professionals has dramatically spiked, not only in the public sector, but also in the market and civic sectors. As a result, what was originally an Anglo-American occupational culture, valuing training and credentials over education at prestigious institutions for professional standing, has been introduced in, and often successfully transplanted into, a surprisingly large number of industrialized nations on almost every continent, including continental Europe, and recently by some of the developing countries still in the process of modernization and industrialization. It may not be too much to say, then, that this sense of 'professionalism' is now well established at the centre of public life both as a mode of organization and as a discursive episteme, almost all over the world (Butler, Chillas & Muhr, 2012, p. 260).

But what are the vital characteristics that qualify a vocation as a 'profession'? British sociologist G. Millerson published a book in 1964 entitled *The Qualifying Associations: A Study in Professionalization*, in which he presented a still widely endorsed concept of the term *profession*. Millerson compared 21 proposed definitions, identified 14 traits referred to in all of them, and focused on the following six as the critical requirements characterizing a 'profession' (1964, p. 10):

- The use of skills based on theoretical knowledge;
- Formal education and training in those skills;
- Competence to practise accredited by formal examination;
- A standard of integrity maintained by adherence to a code of professional conduct;

- Commitment to the public good;
- Organization into a professional association with the power to limit to its credentialed members the right to deliver a service.

An occupational group that finds little or no difficulty in identifying a body of knowledge that can be systematized to a high level of abstraction is, in general, in a more advantageous position to organize a closed professional association with the power to effectively control its members' practice. From this position, the group can successfully achieve social recognition as an occupation that provides a quality professional service for the public. Law, medicine and accountancy are typical cases of such occupations. In fact, these occupational groups are not allowed to practise their work unless they have demonstrated a certain amount of professional knowledge and acquired formal certification, which involves going through a lengthy period of training and passing exams (Butler et al., 2012, p. 262).

In stark contrast are those occupational groups that find it more difficult to carve out a formal body of knowledge, standardized programmes of education and training, qualifying exams, or codes of conduct to be strictly observed by their members. In fact, it is often the case with recently developed occupations, such as management consultancy, personal coaching, project management, research and development management, fund management, programming and system engineering, that it is neither illegal nor uncommon to engage in professional practice without a relevant degree or equivalent qualification. Occupations of this kind have increased in number with the development of the post-industrial or knowledge-based society.

However, occupational groups do not need to satisfy all of Millerson's requirements to serve the public. Therefore, there is good reason to doubt whether it is, in fact, appropriate to apply this prestigious designation of 'profession' only to that limited number of occupational groups that can easily satisfy the requirements.

Historical Overview of Policy Analysis as an Academic and Practical Enterprise

In contemporary advanced democracies, citizens are encouraged to actively participate in the political process through various political associations. As they do so, the politicians who are endowed with the formal authority to make policy will come under increasing scrutiny and behave accordingly, hoping to avoid accusations of serving special interests. Inevitably, politicians will try to strike compromises to meet the demands of conflicting parties.

The easiest way for politicians to accomplish this balance is to secure the maximum returns for their client groups—on whom they rely for financial backing and votes. They will give the leftovers to non-client groups, while charming as many voters as possible with excessive promises. The vast majority of politicians will resort to exploiting this tactic on a regular basis, whenever they deem it feasible, which necessarily causes a gross inflation of public expenditures.

The harm of such behaviour is not so desperately overwhelming, as long as the principle of a balanced budget is basically adhered to with very limited exceptions. When this principle is reduced to the status of a false pledge, however, democracy lapses into a 'bargaining democracy' (Hayek, 1960), resulting in myopic tendencies that may lead society down a path to self-destruction. Hence, for the very survival of democracy itself, there is a vital need to monitor and correct any myopic tendencies (Adachi, 2014, pp. 142–143). What should be done to decrease the possibility of such policies that conflict both with the long-term interest of society as a whole and with the ethics of inter-generational justice being adopted and implemented through 'legitimate' democratic channels?

The first, seemingly paradoxical, thing to be done is to fully explore the possibility of making the democracy more substantive and engaging. Specifically, attempts must be made to remove, to the greatest extent possible, factors that may inhibit the proper functioning of the mechanisms of 'partisan mutual adjustment' (Lindblom, 1965). In addition, the number of opportunities for citizen participation in the political process must be expanded. What is further required, lest the democracy degenerate into the sheer tyranny of the myopic majority, is a set of self-restraint mechanisms built into the democracy itself. The most important of these are constitutional restraints on the behaviour of law-makers and governments, independent courts, independent career civil servants and a parliamentary system in which a high-quality second chamber with significant but secondary powers to make occasional checks on, and recommend reconsideration of, public policies formulated by the first chamber[6] (Adachi, 2014; Hayek, 1960). Yehezkel Dror of the Hebrew University of Jerusalem went even further in advocating that 'consultative councils enjoying constitutional status, and composed of outstanding individuals, should therefore be set up to engage in policy deliberation on long-term critical issues, presenting evaluations, analysis, options and recommendations, to governance and the public at large' (Dror, 2001, p. 166).

To this end, policy analysis as an occupation undoubtedly has much to contribute. Policy analysis as an academic and practical activity can reasonably expect to function as an effective and powerful measure for decreasing the possibilities of myopic policies being adopted and implemented. Nevertheless, it never follows from this that policy analysis should be a substitute for democracy. As Deborah Stone reminds us, a large number of citizens in advanced democracies still harbour the 'view'—or, more correctly, 'feeling'—that politics should be replaced with rational decision making, inspired by a vague sense that reason is clean and politics is dirty (Stone, 1997, p. 373). Distrust of, or even hostility towards, politics in the wicked sense of 'majoritarianism', which has its intellectual roots in Plato and was later refined by the French utopian socialists Henri de Saint-Simon and Auguste Comte, could be easily detected in the advocates and practitioners of both planning and policy analysis in the early days of their development (Adachi, 2014, p. 140). This is no longer the case, however. It is now widely acknowledged, at least by policy researchers and practitioners, not to mention citizens in general, that the raison d'être of policy analysis is not to be a substitute for democracy, but to complement it, by providing major policy actors with evidence-based information vital for formulating informed policy options, thereby increasing the possibility that quality solutions—effective, efficient, feasible, and morally justifiable public policies—will be adopted and implemented through the political process of democracy (Adachi, 2015a).

What, then, are the activities that should be conducted in the name of policy analysis? What are the processes or phases that constitute policy analysis? What is a body of knowledge that can be systematized to a high level of abstraction for professional policy analysts? Can policy analysis as an occupation identify such a body of knowledge? If so, there is a fair chance for policy analysis as an academic and practical activity to be socially acknowledged as a 'profession'. Questions concerning the substance of policy analysis can be broadly divided into the following.

- Is the task of formulating and proposing solutions, which consists of two successive processes (examination and selection of policy objectives, and conceptualization and selection of specific prescriptions), an integral part of policy analysis?
- What are the guidelines or criteria for policy analysts to skilfully perform a series of activities that constitute policy analysis?

The Policy Analysis Profession

On one hand is the rationalist approach to policy analysis, which expects policy analysts to learn and apply a range of qualitative and quantitative techniques in specific circumstances, providing advice to decision makers about optimal strategies and outcomes to pursue in the resolution of public problems (Dobuzinskis, Howlett & Laycock, 2007, p. 7). On the other hand is the post-positivist approach, which views as naïve, or worse, dangerous the idea that expert policy analysts are society's problem solvers. From the post-positivist analytical framework, 'the job of the analysts is better conceived as a task of interpretation and facilitation: understanding the different perspectives that create the conflict of values and judging them on their own terms. "What should we do?" is a question best answered by reflective deliberation and discourse among these various perspectives, not by a causal theory or a regression coefficient' (Smith & Larimer, 2009, p. 102).

Precautions must be taken against this dichotomy, however. Undoubtedly, in thus rigidly dividing the field of policy analysis into two camps, rationalist and post-positivist, there is a risk of inculcating beginners to the field with an over-simplified conception of policy analysis. There are in fact numerous degrees of each of these positions. The orientation of policy analysis is more accurately described as a continuum rather than as two competing camps (Smith & Larimer, 2009, p. 102). Furthermore, not all of the existing approaches are placed somewhere on the continuum between the two camps. For example, Lejano detects not only divergence but also commonalities between the two camps. Both are, in his terminology, 'constructionist', in the sense that policy, even reality, is whatever is constructed by the analyst's will, from which he differentiates his analytical framework, post-constructionism (Lejano, 2006, p. 12).

Seen as an intellectual movement in government, policy analysis represents the efforts of actors inside and outside the formal political decision-making processes to improve policy outcomes by applying systematic evaluative rationality.[7] Policy analysis, in this sense, is a relatively recent phenomenon, dating back to the 1960s with the U.S. experience with formalized large-scale planning processes and statistical analyses in areas such as defence, urban development and budgeting (Wildavsky, 1979; MacRae & Wilde, 1979; Heineman, Bluhm, Peterson & Kearny, 2001; Howlett & Lindquist, 2007). Particularly important at this time was the movement of Robert MacNamara and his 'whiz kids' into leadership positions in the U.S. Defense Department. Impressed by the contribution of formal/rationalist analytical methods such as cost-benefit analysis, operations research, systems analysis, linear programming and the PPBS (Planning, Programming, and Budgeting System) to better decision making in the military, these officials passionately introduced them into the analysis of management and policy issues in almost all policy fields (Heineman et al., 2001, p. 16). In the early days of the development of policy analysis, the formal/rationalist approach, which focused on providing advice to decision makers about optimal strategies and outcomes to pursue in the resolution of public problems, was by far the dominant analytical style (Dobuzinskis et al., 2007, p. 7).

From the 1970s, the research interests of policy professionals rapidly shifted to policy implementations and evaluations. Policy analysts increasingly refrained from the value-laden task of conceptualizing and formulating specific prescriptions and began to identify their role in the policy process with the purely instrumental/technocratic task. As Linder and Peters lamented, the emphasis on fashioning solutions that once characterized the planning profession (with its emphasis on social reform) gave way to a limited focus on evaluating the short- and long-term consequences of alternative policies. A great majority of policy analysts, trained primarily in the social sciences,[8] came to de-emphasize the design of solutions, preferring instead to concentrate on the comparison and evaluation of given alternatives. Professional policy analysts who are committed to such an ascetic, rigidly positivist/empiricist approach to policy analysis typically accept the sets of alternatives as given, and see their primary role not as remaking the alternatives, but as predicting their impact and evaluating their prospects for enactment and trouble-free implementation (Linder & Peters, 1984, p. 252).

Post-positivists, however, have mounted a fierce attack both on the fact–value dichotomy, characterizing the positivist/empiricist analytical framework, and on the formal/rationalist planning-oriented analytical framework. Advocates and supporters of the post-positivist approach to policy analysis have steadily increased in number since the beginning of the 1990s. Policy intellectuals lumped together as post-positivists are far from monolithic; they diverge in philosophical (ethical) foundations and analytical styles, as evident from such leading figures as Forester, Dryzeck, Fischer and DeLeon, to mention just a few. All agree, however, that the role of a policy analyst is neither that of a scientist nor a privileged advisor expected to be 'speaking truth to power' (Wildavsky, 1979), but that of a mediator, making processes and forums available to stakeholders, listening to them as they make sense of their own situations, and facilitating the joint construction of meaning. Post-positivists could undoubtedly make no small contribution to policy design, though they are generally not that interested in advocating specific policy options in the policymaking process.[9] Closer attention to the processes of meaning construction and the way in which these processes are affected by power differentials would undoubtedly lead to ideas for reforming institutions for public deliberation, and a better-designed deliberative process might actually help the group of stakeholders come to some common understanding of the situation (Lejano, 2006, p. 112).

By way of comparison, since the turn of the century, a series of books and articles discussing policy design have been published, and a policy-design perspective has arguably gained the status of an alternative to the three analytical frameworks discussed above (formal/rationalist, positivist/empiricist, and post-positivist). A policy designer's primary mission lies in searching for and conceptualizing a policy, or more commonly, a policy package, that is coherent with the given context of the characteristics of the very problems to be tackled by policies and the various types of constraints limiting the range of feasible (workable) policy options. To successfully carry out this mission, policy designers should have a good command of as many analytical approaches as possible, since a specific approach is expected to provide an analytical tool-kit that enables them to reach a penetrating insight into what Lejano (2006) calls a 'thick description' of a specific aspect or a set of aspects of the given context, and/or a set of relevant and usable criteria for comparing and ranking the alternatives for tackling the problems at hand. A policy-design perspective for policy analysis is, then, not only an alternative to, but also an integrative analytical framework that incorporates, the above-mentioned three analytical frameworks. The following section identifies a set of core knowledge, skills and ethics required of design-oriented professional policy analysts.

The Policy-Design Approach to Policy Analysis[10]

To design things, whatever they may be, entails a number of common elements. The first element is obtaining a penetrating insight into the context in which the design activity is being conducted. Designers are not normally given carte blanche to create whatever they like. In fact, their freedom is often restricted to a surprising degree. For example, architectural designers are greatly constrained by the preferences and budget of their clients, the natural and physical conditions of the building site, construction law, and various types of regulations such as ancillary restraints, administrative guidance, local ordinances and community agreements. Designers must have the ability to clearly differentiate between those things that must be accepted as given preconditions or constraints on the design activity and those that could be changed by their own talent and efforts. The arrogant attitude of not taking one or more of the critical constraints seriously—that is, being insensitive to the design context—and enforcing their own preferences and sense of values on their clients exists at the opposite end of the spectrum from a design-oriented mode of thinking.

Another common element of design is achieving target values. Value judgements are an integral part of design activity, regardless of what is being designed. Taking automobile design as an example, a glance at an automobile catalogue shows that there is a highly diverse range of concepts represented by cars on the market today. Differences in concept boil down to how much importance is placed on which values—safety, fuel efficiency, eco-friendliness, roominess, amenities, accelerating performance, appearance, price, etc.—that consumers may seek in a car. An integral part of design activity is fixing the concept of a product to be designed, either by choosing from among existing concepts or newly creating an original one.

A third common element in design activity is the process of fleshing out the concept, or 'fashioning an instrument that will work in a desired manner' (Linder & Peters, 1984, p. 253). Fleshing out the concept does not happen automatically once the objective has been established. Rather, it is a creative process relying heavily on a high degree of tacit and experiential knowledge.

While these three elements are common to design activity in general, be it architectural, industrial or any other type, public policy design entails an additional element unique to the field. Even when the direct or immediate client for policy analysis is a specific politician, governmental bureau, political party, interest group, non-profit or non-governmental organization, the ultimate client for policy analysts[11] is, and should be, every member of society, or all those members of society who fulfil a given condition. Architectural designers have only to focus on designing and completing the best possible structure that maximizes the client's satisfaction under various constraints. Likewise, industrial designers usually only need to consider whether the products they design will be accepted by a particular consumer segment. If they are designing an economy car, for example, they do not have to consider the preferences of sports car or luxury car buyers at all. This is not the case with public policy analysts. The design object for them is a public policy intended to tackle a specific public problem, and a public problem is completely different in nature either from a purely private matter, or from a collective issue shared only by members of a specific group or organization in the society. Its impacts more or less extend over every member of society, or all those members of society who fulfil a given condition (or conditions). That is why the cogency or 'goodness' of a public policy is, and should be, ultimately evaluated from the public point of view—that is, in terms of the interests of society as a whole. Public policy analysts must always keep this in mind when carrying out their tasks.

This characteristic is further complicated by the 'wicked' nature of the problems that public policies address,[12] the high degree of uncertainty inherent both in the policy environment and the expected costs and benefits of the policy, and issues of feasibility that unavoidably limit the application of purely scientific/rationalist methods. As a result, it is particularly difficult to accomplish the above-mentioned three tasks—obtaining a penetrating insight into the context in which the design activity is carried out, achieving target values, and fleshing out the concept.

A clinical physician, through patient interview, palpation, and various tests, obtains an accurate understanding of a patient's symptoms, identifies the illness causing these symptoms, decides what to describe and embarks upon a certain course of treatment. A symptom or a set of symptoms can be caused by numerous factors, and the same illness can cause different symptoms in different patients. Furthermore, medication can act differently depending on the individual, and the degree of effects and the seriousness of side effects can vary greatly from patient to patient. Therefore, in order to reach an accurate diagnosis and determine an effective treatment plan, a physician must have a solid store of expert knowledge pertaining to pathology, pharmacology and other branches of medicine, as well as being a thoroughly experienced clinician.

Identifying the cause of disease and determining a course of treatment is like solving a riddle—ruling out the possibilities of other diseases one by one through a systematic trial-and-error approach to diagnosis and treatment. Causal reasoning plays a central role in this process, where a set of signs or phenomena are reviewed to arrive at an estimation of the factor underlying or causing the symptoms.

The work of a policy analyst is similar to that of a physician, in that both try to discover the causes of a problem or symptoms and search for an effective treatment to solve the problem. Both are required to have not only sophisticated theoretical knowledge of relevant disciplines, but also tacit/practical knowledge and skill (art and craft) gained only through wide and rich clinical experience to make an accurate diagnosis and develop an effective prescription. However, there are a number of significant differences between the two that overwhelm all similarities, the most important of which by far is that physicians, unlike policy analysts, rarely face the serious conflict of values.[13]

Phases of Policy Analysis as Policy Design[14]

In contemporary democracies characterized by the somewhat clichéd phrase 'from government to governance', policy analysis is no longer the sole province of governments, though the ultimate responsibility of implementing and managing policies approved by legislators still resides in them. Today, political parties, think tanks, industrial organizations, labour organizations, citizen groups, non-profit organizations, non-governmental organizations, journalists, policy researchers and diverse other policy actors are also expected to serve as policy advocates. It has become more and more important for policy actors to be able to engage in policy analysis, or at least be able to distinguish a quality analysis from a perfunctory one. Acquiring this ability is now the *sine qua non* for every policy actor in democracies, including the citizenry in general. Of special importance in this respect is to understand the three 'phases' of policy analysis: identification of the problems that policies are designed to address, examination and selection of policy objectives, and design of specific prescriptions.

Policy analysis starts with the recognition of a problem that needs to be addressed through a policy package. This phase is not an objective process independent of the subjectivity of the observer or analyst, but a highly subjective or inter-subjective process where a discrepancy between the *status quo* and any desirable future state of affairs can create problems. How the existing condition is perceived and the nature of what a successful policy outcome would look like may differ, depending on the observer or analyst. There are no objective, universally applicable criteria or standards. Most problems subject to public policy are given life only upon their recognition by an observer or analyst as problems, and may not pre-exist as an objective reality.

In view of the foregoing, it can be said that the core aspect of identifying a problem is to strongly impress upon the public that the existing condition is intolerable, and that any desirable future condition a policy is designed to bring about is not only worth pursuing but is actually realizable if the necessary efforts are made.

The Policy Analysis Profession

The next task for a policy analyst is to investigate the causes of the problem identified, although these are rarely easy to pinpoint, and only in rare cases is a problem caused by a single factor. How much in resources, including time, should be allocated to this task? If careful research into the history and background of the problem is not made and action is taken in haste, it is very easy to overlook key contributory factors and, as a result, the situation is unlikely to improve and may even be aggravated, making it more difficult to solve the problem. That said, if too much time is given to the task, and nothing is decided or carried out until a fail-safe solution has been found, a prime opportunity to improve the situation may be lost; eventually, the problem itself may worsen or change. When to stop looking for causes must be determined separately for each individual case.

Of special importance in this process of problem identification is the examination into what government action or inaction has contributed to or been involved in creating, intensifying or prolonging problems, and to what degree. This task is a process of critical importance, one that enables analysts to provide a foundation for change and improvement.

Effective policy analysis requires, in addition to cause-and-effect reasoning, the ability to imagine a sophisticated conceptual road map for change, as well as the ability to persuasively communicate the benefits that will accrue from a new policy direction. Once the problem has been identified and reviewed and a direction has been established for new government policy, the remaining task is to flesh out the specific character of the new policy. This process consists of two consecutive phases: establishing the policy objective and the desired changes that it will support, and designing the specific means by which the policy objective will be achieved.

In essence, the core task of establishing the policy objective is to define what kind of public value is to be achieved, to what degree, and by when. However, such a definition is no easy task, primarily because there are multiple public values that are in conflict with each other.[15] Therefore, the public desirability or justifiability of a policy aimed at contributing to the attainment of a given public value (or a set of values) can only be guaranteed *ceteris paribus*— that is, other things being equal.

In general, conflict with other public values increases as the level of the public value targeted by a policy rises, or the strength of commitment towards achieving or enhancing a given value increases. For example, once the level of public safety and security passes a threshold value—if surveillance cameras are placed all over town as in London these days, or if people are encouraged or required to report to the authorities whenever they notice any suspicious characters as in Nazi Germany or Japan immediately before and during World War II—it may be possible to reduce 'crime' and realize the maximum level of public safety and security. However, such actions come with a high price in the form of privacy invasion and a weakening of basic trust within a community; serious infringement of privacy can result (Adachi, 2011b, p. 68). The higher the targeted level of safety and security, the greater the negative effects on privacy. Conversely, if privacy is considered inviolable under any circumstance, the options for protecting public safety and security are very limited.

The same can be said about timeframe. A shorter timeframe for achieving the policy objective can make it more difficult to satisfy the demands for other public values. Conversely, a longer timeframe tends to make it easier to achieve adjustment and coordination among values.

There are no universal guidelines for determining how high to set a policy objective or what timeframe to establish for achieving that objective. Judgements must be made on a case-by-case basis in line with conditions specific to the situation, and responsibility for the consequences must be accepted. There may be times when analysts are forced to set the policy objective at a much lower level than theoretically or technically possible, or establish a long timeframe, owing to an overriding need to achieve social integration and gain consensus. On the other hand, there may be times when immediate efforts to realize the highest possible level of a given public value are allowed or demanded.

The exploration of means (prescriptions) cannot be performed without some idea of the objective to work towards; in general, it is neither possible nor desirable to establish a policy objective at the early stages of policy analysis. In reality, the analyst follows a zigzagging process consisting of an initial cycle of problem analysis, identification of policy objective and exploration of specific measures, followed by additional cycles of problem re-analysis, adjustment of policy objective and adjustment of specific measures. Finally, at the end of all these repeated cycles, the analyst is able to simultaneously determine the policy objective and the means for achieving that objective.

The activity of designing a specific prescription, therefore, is not a linear, instrumentally rational process of exploring and finding the most effective means for achieving a clearly defined policy objective. Rather, it is a process consisting of conceptualizing as many objectives–means combinations as possible, predicting what social consequences are likely to arise and to what degree of probability, and selecting the one that is expected to produce the most preferable consequences for the society as a whole. Choosing the lesser of two evils is often the only option available for policy analysts.

Problems that may be addressed by public policies are enormously diverse, and no two problems are entirely the same in real life. Because of this, the task of designing a specific prescription that is the means to tackle a specific problem is essentially a unique, one-time endeavour, one that requires flexible thinking adapted to the situation at hand, as well as the capacity to make sound judgements.

This does not mean, however, that there is no tool-kit to assist this difficult task. Of special importance in this respect is the idea of generic policies or stock strategies persuasively put forward in Weimer and Vining (1989). Generic policies are the categories of policies or strategies that have been proven, through past successes and failures in policy implementation, to have a certain level of effectiveness as prescriptions against similar problems occurring under similar conditions.[16] When conceptualizing a prescription, it is worth considering whether one of the generic policies that vary greatly in the degree and form of government involvement can be used, or whether it is possible to increase effectiveness by combining some of them. Of course, there may be times when none of the generic policies appears useful and therefore original thinking is called for. It is also important to avoid the trap of relying excessively on generic policies to the extent of losing the ability to make necessary changes or adjustments.

Once the basic form has been determined, the remaining task is to decide the specifics. This task could be successfully performed by comparing widely shared criteria and ranking the multitude of similar prescriptions that are available, resulting in an extremely challenging process that compares cost-effectiveness, feasibility, preparedness for uncertainties and complexities and the ethical justifiability of different prescriptions.

Capacity for Systemic Thinking

Given that public policies in various policy fields are linked together to be incorporated into a single overall system or network, policy analysts, when designing a policy to tackle a specific problem in a specific policy field, must take seriously the impact of its adoption and implementation not only on other policies in the same field, but also on various other policies in other fields, in a systemic fashion. However, what does it mean to analyse a problem from a systemic point of view? How is it possible for an analyst to design a policy option from the perspective of the overall public policy system?

To gain possession of something of value, one must usually sacrifice other things that are no less important, be they time, money, opportunity or any other valued asset. Policy is no exception. By implementing a certain policy we gain a great number of things, but a great number of things are also lost in the process. The enjoyment of a benefit always bears a cost. Every policy actor, especially policymakers, should be always aware of the cost to the same extent, if not to a greater extent, that they are of the benefit. This is the first requirement of systemic policy thinking.

A great majority of politicians and policy advocates, however, have a tendency to overestimate benefits while underestimating, occasionally even ignoring, costs. Policy analysts are in a position to check such wishful thinking on the part of politicians and policy advocates. They must expend the maximum effort to ensure that the largest favourable impact on society will be achieved with the smallest cost, consisting of implementation cost—that is, the opportunity cost of resources actually consumed or sacrificed in the implementation process—and the negative side effects. Having a good command of micro-economics in general and sophisticated techniques of cost–benefit or cost-effectiveness analysis in particular, is vital for policy analysts.

These skills are needed because the public sector should, and generally does operate under extremely severe resource limitations,[17] and must ration the limited resources available for the public sector among a great number of policies in a great number of fields vying with each other for resource use. Rationing would not be that troublesome if the public sector could set a clear precedence among a variety of policies in a variety of fields, but the public sector is normally reluctant to do so, except in an emergency (Adachi, 2011a, pp. 40–41).

The second element of systemic thinking is a prudential or pragmatic attitude towards public values, which makes a good contrast with the utopian or ideological commitment to a specific value or a specific *Weltanschauung* (a comprehensive/systematized social philosophy). There is of course nothing wrong in struggling to formulate a constellation of public values deemed justifiable, to be attained in an ideal future society. It is, on the contrary, one of the most critical virtues required of policymakers and analysts living in an age of 'after virtue' (MacIntyre, 1984). However, as already implied herein, there is a serious problem with committing too much to one's *Weltanschauung* and looking upon public policies simply as a means for materializing one's conception of a good society (Burke, 1987; Oakeshott, 1962; Popper, 1971; Crick, 1993; Braybrook & Lindblom, 1963; Jonsen & Toulmin, 1988; Lejano, 2006; Bluhm & Heineman, 2007).

Conclusion: Policy Analysis as a Profession

Policy analysis as an academic and practical enterprise has yet to succeed, in any nation including the United States, in organizing a closed professional association with the power to limit practice to those credentialed members that have demonstrated a certain amount of professional knowledge and acquired formal certification, and requiring a lengthy period of training and passing exams. Neither has it been successful in developing a code of conduct that should be strictly observed by its practitioners. Given these facts, Radin is quite right in arguing that, despite the growth of the field over the past several decades, policy analysis has not gained a place in the world of professions equal to that of law, medicine or engineering (Radin, 2000, p. 1). In a similar vein, Geva-May, who has long endeavoured to establish policy analysis as a profession, also admits that there is no professional association for policy analysts equivalent to that for lawyers, doctors and other professional groups—one that sets out a code of professional ethics and standards, specifying duties and rights (Geva-May, 2005, p. 41).

As implied in the first section, when uncritically following the traditional but still influential definition of 'profession' formulated by Millerson, thereby allowing this prestigious occupational designation only to those limited number of occupational groups that can successfully satisfy all of his defined requirements, a great number of newly developed knowledge works deemed eligible enough to claim this title are prevented from doing so, and are thereby deprived of the chance to be socially acknowledged as a 'profession'. However, the development of a post-industrial, knowledge-based society, accompanied by a drastic change in the occupational structure and culture, makes it imperative to revisit and reformulate the conception of the term 'profession'. This chapter suggests that there is neither inconvenience nor injustice in permitting this prestigious occupational designation for every knowledge work that successfully satisfies the following four conditions.

- It is widely acknowledged as a professional occupation that requires of its practitioners a set of sophisticated skills based on deep and wide theoretical knowledge and a certain amount of experience;
- There is a considerable demand for the work or service that is provided by its members;
- It commits to the public good;
- A minimum level of occupational/professional ethics is widely shared among its practitioners.

As discussed in the previous section, policy analysis is undoubtedly a professional enterprise requiring of its practitioners the following: first, a specific mode of thinking that consists of the capacity for systemic thinking, an ability to be engaged in a special type of thought-experiment by asking what policy they would choose if they were in a position to formally make a final decision (Adachi, 2011a, pp. 42–44), and design orientation; second, a body of knowledge that can be systematized to a high level of abstraction—that is, theoretical/methodological knowledge—in addition to practical/local knowledge in a specific policy field; and third, an analytical tool-kit, or 'tricks of the trade' (Geva-May, 2005). A great majority of contemporary practising policy analysts identify themselves as agents for the public good, their ultimate client being the public at large, even when they do not work for the public sector but for a specific organization in the market or civic sector. They should, then, be able to justify their policy claims from the public point of view. It is also widely acknowledged among them that 'an assumption that should form the basis for any legitimate conception of policy analysis as a profession is that the analyst is a person of professional integrity' (Heineman et al., 2001, p. 25). According to Meltsner, 'those who are dishonest, distort their work, and deliberately lie should have no place in the analytic fraternity' (1976, p. 282). Similarly, Tong argues that the analyst should demonstrate the attributes of honesty, candour, competence, diligence, loyalty and discretion as components of trustworthiness (1986, p. 92).

Whether and to what extent policy analysis is established as an occupation with a considerable demand for the work or service that is provided by its members, however, varies from nation to nation. In the United States, 'the demand for policy analysis is considerable, and it comes both from inside and outside of governments' (Mintrom, 2007, p. 151). In Canada, 'the national government has more actively demanded policy advice, which has led to departments seeking creative ways to tap into expertise within and across governments, and with analysts and researchers in consulting firms, universities, think tanks, and associations'

(Howlett & Lindquist, 2007, p. 104). Demand for quality policy analysis (and analysts) has also steadily increased in Australia, New Zealand and a growing number of major European Union countries. At the global level, key coordinating organizations, such as the World Bank, IMF, WTO and OECD, 'have made extensive use of the skills of policy analysts to monitor various transnational developments and national-level activities of particular relevance and interest' (Mintrom, 2007, p. 151). There still remain, however, a great many nations where this is not the case, including Japan.

It has been a long time since the social significance of policy research in general, and policy analysis in particular, was first recognized in Japan. In the mid-1990s academia began to realize the urgent need of fostering highly knowledgeable and skilled policy professionals, and major universities and graduate schools soon started to introduce new public policy programmes that feature policy analysis as part of their core courses. After all these years, however, most public policy programmes are still struggling to attract intellectual and public-minded candidates, while surprisingly few graduates trained in policy analysis manage to find a job in a relevant field (Adachi, 2015a; Watanabe, 2015). Very few independent think tanks that are prosperous enough to employ professional policy analysts, have been established. Even governments, of various levels, have not attached much weight to the knowledge and skill in policy analysis either in hiring or in promoting their employees. The application or use of policy analysis has also been quite limited. Only a few members in the public, market and civic sectors realize the vital need of consulting policy analysts when selecting and adopting a general stance on policy issues. Politicians and political parties are no exception.

Consequently, there will be no hope for policy analysis to gain the prestigious occupational designation 'profession' in any nation, including Japan, unless and until the potential contributions that professional policy analysts can make for improved policymaking and policy implementation come to be widely acknowledged, with policy analysis being established as an occupation (Adachi, 2015b, p. 289).

Notes

1 In addition to these three occupations, this title was often used to refer to the gentlemanly occupation of the military.

2 This is not to imply, however, that the original gentlemanly, prestigious connotation of profession had simply been replaced. Rather, it is more correct to say that 'as early as the sixteenth century the word profession could be used to mean either a very exclusive set of occupations or the exact opposite—any occupation at all' (Freidson, 1986, p. 22).

3 The main reason why the 'professional' orientation was so weak in nineteenth-century continental Europe lies in the historical fact that what assured ambitious youngsters elite positions not only in public but also in market and civic sectors was their attendance at state-controlled elite institutions of higher education: being a graduate of a *gymnasium* in Russia and Poland (Gella, 1976); an *Akademiker* (a university graduate) in Germany (Reuschemeyer, 1973); or a graduate of one of the *grandes écoles* in France (Suleiman, 1978). A great majority of state-controlled elite institutions of higher education in continental Europe, which found their primary mission in cultivating talented human resources—future elites working in the public, market and civic sectors—required students to acquire a high-level of *Bildung* (self-cultivation or self-instruction, linking philosophy and education) through a wide and intensive study of disciplines in liberal arts and sciences, and encouraged them to build as many personal connections (social network) as possible, deemed advantageous for their future career; a 'professional' or an 'expert' in a narrow specific field of discipline or practice was long destined, at least in continental Europe, to be occupying an inferior position in the occupational/organizational hierarchy vis-à-vis a 'generalist'.

4 This does not necessarily apply now, for instance, to the information industry, where what matters most is one's 'post-modern' talent such as creativity, imagination, resilience, systemic thinking or

even eccentricity. Being a credentialed member of a profession is no longer a necessary or sufficient condition to gain a reputation as a talented professional or expert.

5 Max Weber defined *professionalization* roughly as a process of acquiring authority based on recognized expert credentials that may include formal training, degrees, certifications, and particular types of experience (Brooks, 2007, p. 23).

6 This applies only to nations with parliamentary systems. In the Japanese context, the 'first' chamber refers to the House of Representatives, while the 'second' chamber refers to the 'House of Councillors'. The House of Councillors is ideally expected to play such a role, though the reality is far from this ideal.

7 Mintrom terms this intellectual movement in government the 'policy analysis movement' (2007, p. 145).

8 Apart from economists, social scientists have tended to resist the conceptualization and selection of specific prescriptions for tackling pressing public issues, which is a normative enterprise in essence requiring them to formulate a set of criteria for ranking alternative prescriptions. For the social scientists determined to engage only in purely positivist/empiricist analyses of social phenomena, to commit themselves to such a value-laden 'analysis' is the last thing they would be willing to accept. This group normally views with suspicion any effort to combine judgements about values with empirical propositions.

9 In fact, proponents of participatory policy analysis (PPA) such as DeLeon and Fischer urge the policy analyst to be an active advocate of a policy proposal they deem most desirable as well as to work as an interpreter, meditator, and a facilitator for the citizenry, assisting them to effectively express themselves in the political process of deliberative democracy (Fischer, 2003; DeLeon, 1988).

10 This section is partly based on Adachi (2011b).

11 In the policy design approach to policy analysis, the terms 'policy analysis' and 'policy design' are used interchangeably. The word 'policy analyst' refers, then, to a policy analyst engaged in policy design activity.

12 Rittel and Weber characterized 'wicked' problems as follows:

> There is no definite formulation of a wicked problem; wicked problems have no stopping rule; solutions to wicked problems are not true or false, but good or bad; there is no immediate and ultimate test of a solution to a wicked problem; every solution to a wicked problem is a 'one-shot' operation; wicked problems do not have an enumerable (or an exhaustively describable) set of potential solutions, nor is there a well-described set of permissible operations that may be incorporated into the plan; every wicked problem is essentially unique; every wicked problem can be considered to be a symptom of another problem; the existence of discrepancy representing a wicked problem can be explained in numerous ways; the planner has no right to be wrong. (abbreviated from Rittel & Webber, 1973, pp. 161–167)

> In contrast with the scientific community, which does not blame its members for postulating hypotheses that are later refuted so long as the author abides by the rules of the game, in the world of planning and wicked problems, no such immunity is tolerated. Planners are liable for the consequences of the actions they generate.

13 Whether or not to assist an induced abortion, surrogate motherhood, and death with dignity are among a few exceptions in which a physician is forced to make a difficult value judgement.

14 For more detail on this topic, see Adachi (2015a, pp. 4-10); Bardach (2005); MacRae & Wilde (1979); Weimer & Vining (1989).

15 Efficiency, equity, citizenship, participation, equality, welfare, public safety and security, privacy, economic development and environmental preservation are among the most important public values.

16 Weimer and Vining classify generic policies into the following five categories:

- freeing, facilitating and stimulating markets;
- using subsidies and taxes to alter incentives;
- establishing rules;
- supplying goods through non-market mechanisms;
- providing insurance and cushions (economic protection).

17 The public sector operates under severe resource limitations because it is in a competitive relationship with the private sector, and almost always falls far short of the private sector in the effective use of

these resources; excessive consumption of resources by the public sector leads to fear of an economic recession.

References

Adachi, Y. (2011a) 'What Are the Core Knowledge and Skills for Policy Professionals?: Public Policy Studies in Japan', *Seisaku-Souzou-Kenkyu* 4.

Adachi, Y. (2011b) 'The Process of Policy Design', *Seisaku-Souzou-Kenkyu* 5.

Adachi, Y. (2014) 'Democracy in Transition Management for Sustainable Development', in Ueta, K. and Adachi, Y. eds., *Transition Management for Sustainable Development*, Tokyo: United Nations University Press.

Adachi, Y. (2015a) 'Introduction: Policy Analysis in Japan: The State of the Art', in Adachi, Y., Hosono, S., Iio, J. eds., *Policy Analysis in Japan*, Bristol, UK: Policy Press.

Adachi, Y. (2015b) 'Conclusion: Future Directions of the Theory and Practice of Public Policy Analysis in Japan', in Adachi et al. *Policy Analysis in Japan*.

Bardach, E. (2005) *A Practical Guide for Policy Analysis: The Eightfold Path to More Effective Problem Solving*, Washington, DC: CQ Press.

Bluhm, W.T. and Heineman, R.A. (2007) *Ethics of Public Policy: Method and Cases*, Englewood Cliffs, NJ: Prentice Hall.

Braybrook, D. and Lindblom, C.E. (1963) *A Strategy of Decision*, New York, NY: Free Press.

Brooks, S. (2007) 'The Policy Analysis Profession in Canada', in Dobuzinskis, L., Howlett, M., Laycock, D. eds., *Policy Analysis in Canada: The State of the Art*, University of Toronto Press.

Burke, E. (1987 [1790]) *Reflections on the Revolution in France*, Indianapolis, IN: Hackett Publishing.

Butler, N., Chillas, S., Muhr, S.L. (2012) 'Professions at the Margins', *Ephemera: Theory & Politics in Organization* 12–13.

Crick, B. (1993) *In Defence of Politics*, 4th edition, Chicago, IL: The University of Chicago Press.

DeLeon, P. (1988) *Advice and Consent: The Development of Policy Sciences*, New York, NY: Russell Sage Foundation.

Dobuzinskis, L., Howlett, M., Laycock, D. (2007) 'Policy Analysis in Canada: The State of the Art' in Dobuzinskis et al. *Policy Analysis in Canada: The State of the Art*.

Dror, Y. (2001) *The Capacity to Govern: A Report to the Club of Rome*, London: Frank Cass.

Fischer, F. (2003) *Reframing Public Policy: Discursive Politics and Deliberative Practices*, Oxford University Press.

Freidson, E. (1986) *Professional Powers: A Study of the Institutionalization of Formal Knowledge*, The University of Chicago Press.

Gella, A. (1976) 'An Introduction to the Sociology of the Intelligentsia', in Gella, A. ed. *The Intelligentsia and the Intellectuals*, Beverly Hills, CA: Sage Publications.

Geva-May, I. (2005) *Thinking Like a Policy Analyst: Policy Analysis as a Clinical Profession*, New York, NY: Palgrave Macmillan.

Hayek, F.A. (1960) *The Constitution of Liberty*, University of Chicago Press.

Heineman, R.A., Bluhm, W.T., Peterson, S.A., Kearny, E.N. (2001) *The World of the Policy Analyst*, New York, NY: Chatham House Publishers.

Howlett, M. and Lindquist, E. (2007) 'Beyond Formal Policy Analysis: Governance Context, Analytical Styles, and the Policy Analysis Movement in Canada' in Dobuzinskis et al. *Policy Analysis in Canada: The State of the Art*.

Jonsen, A.L. and Toulmin, S. (1988) *The Abuse of Casuistry: A History of Moral Reasoning*, Berkeley, CA: University of California Press.

Lejano, R.P. (2006) *Frameworks for Policy Analysis: Merging Text and Context*, New York, NY: Routledge.

Lindblom, C.E. (1965) *The Intelligence of Democracy: Decision Making Through Mutual Adjustment*, New York, NY: The Free Press.

Linder, S.H. and Peters, B.G. (1984) 'From Social Theory to Policy Design', *Journal of Public Policy* 4–3.

MacIntyre, A. (1984) *After Virtue: A Study in Moral Philosophy*, 2nd edition, Notre Dame, IN: University of Notre Dame Press.

MacRae, D. and Wilde, J. (1979) *Policy Analysis for Public Decision*, Pacific Grove, CA: Duxbury Press.

Meltsner, A.J. (1976) *Policy Analysis in the Bureaucracy*, Berkeley, CA: University of California Press.

Millerson, G. (1964) *The Qualifying Associations*, London: Routledge & Kegan Paul.

Mintrom, M. (2007) 'The Policy Analysis Movement' in Dobuzinskis et al., *Policy Analysis in Canada: The State of the Art*.

Oakeshott, M. (1962) *Rationalism in Politics and Other Essays*, London: Methuen.

Popper, K. (1971) *The Open Society and Its Enemies*, Princeton University Press.

Radin. B.A. (2000) *Beyond Machiavelli: Policy Analysis Comes of Age*, Washington DC: Georgetown University Press.

Reuschemeyer, D. (1973) *Lawyers and their Society*, Cambridge, MA: Harvard University Press.

Rittel, H. and Webber, M. (1973) 'Dilemmas in a General Theory of Planning', *Policy Sciences* 4–1.

Smith, K.B. and Larimer, C.W. (2009) *The Public Policy Theory Primer*, Boulder, CO: Westview Press.

Stone, D.A. (1997) *Policy Paradox: The Art of Political Decision Making*, New York, NY: W.W. Norton.

Suleiman, E.N. (1978) *Elites in French Society*, Princeton University Press.

Tong, R. (1986) *Ethics in Public Policy*, Englewood Cliffs, NJ: Prentice Hall.

Watanabe, S.P. (2015) 'Job Market for Public Policy Programmes Graduates in Japan' in Adachi et al. *Policy Analysis in Japan*.

Weimer, D.L. and Vining, A.R. (1989) *Policy Analysis: Concepts and Practice*, Englewood Cliffs, NJ: Prentice Hall.

Wildavsky, A. (1979) *Speaking Truth to Power: The Art and Craft of Policy Analysis*, New York, NY: Little, Brown.

3

THE CHOICE OF FORMAL POLICY ANALYSIS METHODS

Claudia Scott

Introduction

In the 1960s, formal policy analysis methods were adopted by US federal government agencies on a large scale. Academic expertise was recruited into government agencies, and academics were tasked with conducting formal analyses to underpin public policy decisions, bringing elements from many disciplines.

The adoption of formal policy analysis approaches helped analysts and advisers to interpret the information and evidence base, design alternative policy solutions, and introduce more transparent and rigorous processes for making informed judgements by evaluating alternative courses of action. The adoption of these methods equipped governments and their advisers with a more professional set of processes and practices, resembling those in the private sector.

The term formal methods cannot be defined precisely—covering a range of quantitative methods and analytical techniques borrowed from economics, operations research and other social sciences. These methods were also called rational methods or techniques. Economists contributed cost-benefit analysis to help measure the efficiency and effectiveness of government projects and programmes. Multi-criteria analysis broadened the focus to take in the values and consequences of concern to decision makers. Carley's book, *Rational Techniques in Policy Analysis*, published in 1980, included cost utility, impact assessment, forecasting and futures research, and social indicator research.

Academics from many disciplines contributed to a new multi-disciplinary field of 'policy sciences', which cast a rational lens on real-world problems to seek solutions consistent with the norms and beliefs of the era (see DeLeon & Vogenbeck, 2007). Discussion among academics and practitioners led to extensive debate about the strengths and weaknesses of specific formal policy analysis methods and the relative emphasis to be given to analytical, political and other dimensions of decision making by governments on policies and programmes.

Some methods were recognized as particularly useful to practitioners, and some governments mandated the use of specific techniques. Over several decades, schools of public policy were founded and the academic and practitioner literatures grew, contributing to the development of policy analysis as a distinct field and advising as a distinct profession. Policy analysis during this time relied heavily on 'formal' or 'rational' policy analysis methods and techniques.

This chapter explores the selection and choice of formal policy analysis methods from several vantage points. It begins by looking at the influence of formal methods on the development of policy analysis as a distinct field and on the profession of policy analysis and advising. The precise role of formal methods depends on practices that vary from place to place and over time. There is also some potential for confusion arising from the lack of consistency in the way that policy terms such as formal methods, models, frameworks, tools and techniques are used by academics and practitioners.

A brief discussion of cost-benefit and multi-criteria analysis highlights the strengths and weaknesses of these widely used formal methods, and describes their contribution to policy advisory work. The changing nature of policy analysis practices is considered, including, implications for the use of formal and other methods, models, frameworks and other tools and techniques in the policy adviser's repertoire, drawing on experiences from New Zealand by way of illustration.

While the trend of formal methods emerged in the US, similar approaches were adopted in other countries. Many governments in both developed and developing countries have introduced formal methods in an effort to enhance the policy analysis capability of advisers. While formal methods and other policy analysis practices have been adopted in many countries, the patterns in their use and popularity are rarely smooth and consistent between or within countries, for many different reasons.

The Influence of Formal Methods on the Development of Policy Analysis

Many factors can shape trends in the use and choice of formal methods, including changes in the institutional, political and governance arrangements that determine the role of policy advisers in and outside of government; and the changing roles of citizens, stakeholder groups, research institutions and actors and institutions in the private and community sectors.

The formalization of public policy analysis produced various models and heuristics for the methods and practices used for certain steps and stages in preparing policy analysis and advice for a client or decision maker. In some countries, the prevailing model assumes the government is the client of policy advice; in others, the client may be an individual, group, organization, or institution from the public, private or community sector. Definitions of policy analysis are often linked to providing advice, with attention to values and the evaluation of policy options to enhance the quality of advice. However the process is conceptualized or formalized, advisers and policy practitioners must wrestle with issues and look for ways to design policy processes and practices to support and inform public decisions and decision makers.

Models of policy analysis and advising were an early introduction into the field of policy analysis. They reflect the institutional and governance arrangements in the particular countries in which they were developed and applied.

Policy-process models specify a series of steps or stages of applied decision making, such as identifying the problem, gathering information and evidence, designing policy options, evaluating options against criteria, choosing an option to implement the policy, and evaluating policy outcomes in relation to specific policy goals and objectives. These tasks reflect problem-solving methods and techniques utilized in many disciplines and fields of enquiry. The models and heuristics developed to guide policy practitioners in designing processes and selecting specific methods, tools and techniques remain widely applied and discussed to this day. A multi-step policy-cycle model brought some order to the tasks of addressing simple and more complex problems. Policy practitioners linked specific formal methods, tools and techniques to particular steps and stages in the policy process.

Formal Policy Analysis Methods

Alongside and sometimes competing with policy-cycle models, there arose a range of 'network-participatory' models, which in effect challenged the assumption that formal methods are sufficient and universally applicable. Rather than process, they focus on the various actors and institutions—at state, society and international levels—in policy issues (see Howlett & Ramesh, 2003). Such models challenged the objective reality of more rational and more formal approaches to policy analysis, and acknowledged a wider policy system; they proposed values reflecting more collective and participatory approaches to policy work, and the democratization of efforts to address public policy problems. Some authors acknowledged both rational client- and state-centric models of policy development as well as network-participatory models, suggesting that the two can co-exist (see Colebatch 2002, 2006).

Literature on the selection and use of formal methods has been primarily concerned with their specific and various suitability for addressing real-world public policy problems and challenges. Commentary by Vining and Boardman (2007) and Howlett and Lindquist (2007) on the merits and limitations of formal policy methods on policy practices in Canada reflect an on-going tension between the analytical and political dimensions of policy analysis and advisory practices.

Support for formal quantitative methods came from those seeking analytical rigour. Qualitative methods were regarded as inherently inferior, and there was scepticism about methods that imported information on values and criteria from sources outside of government. Such evidence was regarded as lacking scientific and objective rigour, and as introducing bias into the analysis.

As the field evolved, more experimentation and discussion of formal methods surfaced in the academic and practitioner literatures. Models of the policy process, nevertheless, were an early and lasting contribution to policy analysis as a field. Many of the models and heuristics developed to guide policy analysis, understood as a multi-step approach to problem solving, remain widely used to this day.

Policy-process models can be useful for guiding policy practice when there is a clearly identified client seeking professional policy advice (see Bardach & Patashnik, 2015; Althaus, Bridgman & Davis, 2013). Policy-process approaches are popular when governments and their advisers have prominent roles in designing and evaluating policies and implementing policy through legislation and regulation, as is common in some Westminster-style governments. Guidance documents issued by government agencies sometimes link policy models to project management techniques, which has been shown to improve the efficiency of policy advisory work.

The approach of Mayer, van Daalen, and Bots (2004) shifted attention from policy processes to the roles and tasks that policy advisers undertake, and the suitability of different policy methods, tools and techniques for performing specific tasks. This model was developed by academics who examined actual policy practices, drawing on written advice provided to governments on policy issues and the analytic practices used to prepare the advice. Their model described how policy advisers undertook their work and the processes, methods and tools they used. The model has several analytical roles in common with other models, but also some distinctive interactive and participatory roles involving stakeholders or the public.

A model based on tasks accommodated rational analytical and strategic tasks as well as those involving participation, engagement and collaboration with citizens and stakeholders. This suggested that a dedicated policy process should emerge from consideration of the particular instance. Quality was now associated with analysis that was specifically designed for the particular purpose; steps in the process were to be selected and sequenced to suit the specific policy issue and context. This approach drew attention to policy advisers' need for design and crafting skills.

Scott and Baehler (2010) adopted a 'systems approach' to policy work, which involved cultivating awareness of the interactions between the state and non-state actors and institutions influencing the policy space. This approach sought to encourage public servants to be aware of options other than government interventions and initiatives; it called for more extensive regard for the private and community sectors in policy and programmes, and encouraged public–private partnerships.

In Australia and New Zealand, this approach to policy analysis and advising was shown to lead to more creativity and innovation in designing policy options. The approach encouraged less attention to process and no longer assumed that there was a single client for policy advice. Public servants became skilled in designing and choosing specific methods, frameworks and tools to suit the specific contexts, issues and tasks (see Scott, 2013).

Discussion of the benefits and limitations of various formal policy approaches often focuses on the role of policy analysts and advisers and their responsibility and accountability in governmental advisory systems. A Washington-style policy system typically has different relationships between elected members and advisers from those in a Westminster-style parliamentary system (see Patapan, 2005). The career of policy advisers or analysts in the US may include working for the public, private or community sectors, and policy practice experience at local, regional, national and international levels.

A Westminster-style government, on the other hand, may have a career public service tradition where apolitical public servants provide 'free and frank' advice to current and future governments. There is provision in Australia for ministers to have political advisers, alongside the professional advice offered by public servants. In some Australian jurisdictions the number of political advisers can be large, but there are clear protocols distinguishing the roles and accountabilities of the two groups. In New Zealand, changes in the electoral system have produced a series of coalition governments; a government must now bargain with minor parties to secure sufficient support in Parliament to pass legislation, which can also require a government to support and adopt policy proposals and priorities that are supported by minor parties. Coalition deals can lead to policy settings that have had no scrutiny from public sector advisers. Some Westminster executive governments rely on their policy advisers to lead policy innovation and change; alternatively, new ideas may be developed outside of government, leaving the public service with the role of overseeing policy processes and implementation, rather than more fundamental policy design.

Beryl Radin (2000; 2013) has authored two volumes describing changing policy advisory practices in the US and observing some differences between Washington- and Westminster-style advisory systems. *Beyond Machiavelli: Policy Analysis Comes of Age* (Radin, 2000) describes policy analysis practices in the US government as involving at their peak 'duelling swords', meaning the pressures of balancing the analytical and political inputs into policy work. Her second volume, *Policy Reaches Midlife* (Radin, 2013) observes a decline in analytical skills and a growing emphasis on political dimensions in the Washington advisory system. Radin also observes trends in parliamentary systems: less dominance by central agencies in some countries; movement of analysts outside of government; greater use of whole-of-government approaches; and new influences on practice coming out of the academic study of policy analysis in various countries.

The fact that many policy issues affect future as well as current populations is an incentive for governments to consider the long-term implications of policy options. Countries vary in the degree to which advisers working within government can think independently and serve the interests of both current and future governments. In New Zealand, the State Sector Act 1988 was modified in 2013 to require chief executives of government departments to demonstrate 'stewardship' and ensure sufficient policy capability to provide the advice required by current and future governments.

The selection and use of one or more formal policy methods remains one of many important choices to be made in a complex policy project. However, the earlier tendency to mandate specific formal methods for certain policy tasks and stages of the policy cycle is no longer routine. The increasing complexity of some policy challenges has encouraged the use of other methods, frameworks, tools and techniques that may be more appropriate.

The choice of formal methods must suit the context of policy advising and the scope of the policy, and be able to deal with complex issues in a world where policy settings are influenced by international trends, multiple actors and institutions, and a policy agenda seeking challenging economic, social, and environmental outcomes. Two formal methods frequently used and sometimes mandated by governments are cost-benefit analysis (CBA) and, to a lesser extent, multi-criteria analysis (MCA).

Cost-benefit analysis (see Goldbach & Leleur, 2004; New Zealand Treasury, 2015) is a highly developed technique that performs well for assessing alternative options on the basis of efficiency. It is less successful in incorporating difficult-to-measure efficiency impacts on third parties, and the approach is of limited use in dealing with trade-offs involving social, environmental and cultural outcomes, or policy issues where there are multiple values and impacts of concern. Multi-criteria analysis takes account of multiple criteria and the various values and impacts related to particular options. MCA also provides ways of weighting criteria to give them selective emphasis to reflect priorities.

Vining and Boardman (2006, 2007) provide useful guidance on meta-choices between cost-benefit and multi-criteria analyses. Cost-benefit analysis is suited to assessing efficiency, as are related approaches such as cost-effectiveness and cost-utility analyses. Cost-effectiveness analysis and cost-utility analysis are close relations to cost-benefit analysis, and can be used where projects have to be ranked within a fixed budget and the benefits can be quantified but not expressed in monetary units. CBA is useful for ranking alternatives when costs and benefits can be measured in the same units.

MCA techniques are diverse in themselves and in the kind of problems they address. CBA and MCA are sometimes mandated to ensure that specific criteria such as efficiency, equity and cost to government are included in the analysis. The benefits of analytical rigour must sometimes be sacrificed to incorporate multiple criteria and accommodate technical problems, such as measuring externalities, establishing important costs and benefits, and fixing the discount rate (see Gamper & Turcanu, 2007).

Cost-benefit and multi-criteria analysis are both useful techniques for the evaluation of options, though multi-criteria analysis can incorporate a much wider range of values and impacts. More refined comparisons give welcome attention to the specific strengths of each approach, and some commentators and guidance documents now portray the two approaches as complements rather than substitutes. This is reflected in recent guidance provided by the New Zealand Treasury (2015), which suggests that MCA is not to be used as a substitute for CBA, but should be used as a complement when dealing with policies that have economic, social and environmental impacts.

The balance needed between analytical skills and skills relating to political and institutional contexts varies from one government to another. Responsibilities, accountability and relationships between decision-makers and advisers differ between and within countries, and shift over time as they are adapted to address different policy issues. Devolution and decentralization of governance and service delivery in some countries, coupled with an increase in partnerships involving government and the private and community sectors, has made the clients and users of policy advice more numerous and diverse. This is especially so in the US, where the government is less involved than in welfare states.

The choice of formal method in policy practice must be suited to the country context and the nature of the issue under investigation. Policy settings change over time and the policy environment shifts. Public policy as a field of study is now addressing more complex issues than ever, and the focus of decision making is no longer on 'government' as the primary client of policy advice. The changing role of government in many countries requires advisers to consider multiple clients and customers of policy advice as they work to address complex issues.

The choice of method cannot be made arbitrarily: it will ultimately affect many stakeholders, and the methods must be suitable for evaluating alternative policy proposals with diverse potential impacts on the state, the economy and society. The choice of methods and frameworks is an integral part of the policy analysis design, depending on the level of analysis called for, the complexity of the issue, and the nature of the particular problem or opportunity.

Changing Policy Practices

Over the years, far more attention has been given to the theory and practice of policy analysis as process than the selection and application of a specific formal policy analysis method. The use of formal methods in policy analysis has made a lasting contribution towards effective and efficient policy decisions. These approaches bring some practical benefits to the empirical and normative tasks of policy analysis, and their benefits and shortcomings encourage the development of new theory and practices to address public policy challenges. The selection and application of formal methods remains an important topic for academics and practitioners in the field.

The history of policy analysis practice in many countries has been influenced by the US and other early entrants to the field, but there remains a wide spectrum of practice and emphasis. Global trends and governments' diminishing influence on policy relative to other sectors have put pressure on governments to adopt policy settings conducive to investment, trade and reputation. Westminster-style systems place more reliance on a cadre of public policy advisers who serve ministers as clients. However, fiscal constraints and closer relationships with the private and community sectors in some countries have expanded the quantum of actors and institutions involved in policy matters, and led to competing sources of policy analysis and advice.

In several countries, policy practices have undergone substantial and rapid change regarding the role of public-sector advisers relative to stakeholders and organizations outside the public sector. This has happened in countries including Australia, the Netherlands, New Zealand, South Korea, Sweden and the United Kingdom. Some countries have maintained earlier changes while others have reverted to earlier practices. Policy analysis in the Netherlands has shifted from a rationalist scientific approach to a participatory and consensus-oriented approach (van Nispen & Scholten, 2015). In other countries, formal methods have often been adopted in part, for specific policy analysis tasks, but not on a larger scale.

There are many different reasons for these varying responses to adopted formal policy analysis methods. In Japan, for example, the use of formal policy analysis methods was restricted to certain economic, political and historical approaches. It is now suggested that there are unexploited opportunities to adopt a wider range of formal methods to build policy capability (Adachi, Hosono & Iio, 2016).

Over time, public policy analysis developed its own body of theory, drawing on its inheritance from other disciplines. This has led to sophisticated and diverse policy practices, and consequently more choice between specific models, tools and methods for policy analysis and advice. More variety has emerged in the selection and use of policy analysis methods, models and techniques. Practice as a result has become less mechanistic and more diverse, calling upon multiple skills. Policy work is now recognized to be an art and a craft as well as a science.

Official guidance documents provide advice on various practices, including processes, choices of methods, frameworks, tools and techniques. In New Zealand, policy guides are one of a number of initiatives undertaken by central or line agencies to build policy capability at the individual, organizational, sectoral and system levels.

Policy guidance documents are now common in many countries. In New Zealand and Australia the guidance may be provided at the national, regional and local levels and for specific government departments and ministries. For example, the New Zealand Ministry for the Environment developed a Policy Guide to professionalize policy advising, which was then followed by a Natural Resources Framework that involved collaboration with many departments and agencies concerned with environmental policy issues (see New Zealand Ministry for the Environment, 2011, 2013). Other ministries in New Zealand have drawn up detailed specifications of the knowledge, skills, competencies and behaviours they expect their analysts and advisers to demonstrate as a prerequisite for holding policy positions at different levels in the organization.

More emphasis is now placed on commissioning policy projects with the awareness that policy issues are often under review. A broader 'systems' approach to policy development has challenged the process view, particularly when the problem is complex and governments lack the mandate and ability to solve problems if they pursue solutions in isolation without contributions from other participants.

Policy analysts now possess a wide range of knowledge, skills, competencies and behaviours, and an array of policy frameworks, tools, instruments and methods. They must demonstrate the ability to apply different frameworks to the analysis of diverse policy issues. Specific policy tools and methods include, for example, consultation, intervention logic, stakeholder analysis and data analysis. It is recognized now that these means can be applied at various points and sometimes multiple stages in a policy process. The challenges of designing policies for more complex issues include the selection of appropriate methods and policy tools, and also the appropriate sequencing of multiple policy tasks for the issue at hand.

Policy advisers must judge the likely value and limitations of particular models and methods, and develop the skills to select and apply a wide range of tools and methods, tailoring them to the specific context and policy problem or opportunity. The economic and governance context must also be taken into account, along with the quality of the information and evidence available to support the analysis.

A key choice for policy practitioners is finding the appropriate balance between formal methods and analytical approaches to problem solving, on the one hand, and approaches that are more sensitive to context on the other. Alternative approaches can incorporate the values and political influences that motivate governments to take action, and are thus an integral part of public policy choices.

In New Zealand, various public sector agencies have invested in developing their own policy models and have created agency-specific frameworks to guide policy practice. Some of the frameworks that have been developed to guide policy development involve the British Crown and indigenous Maori in the context of the Treaty of Waitangi, and other legislation involves the New Zealand Government and Maori as treaty partners. An opportunity-oriented Maori Potential Framework has also been developed. A Policy Framework for Pacific People has been designed to take account of cultural and other dimensions to policy development. A gender analysis framework and corresponding training was developed by the Ministry for Women's Affairs.

A recent addition is a 'Living Standards Framework' (Karacaoglu, 2015) which establishes a set of common goals and objectives, measures the impact of policies on the four capitals (financial and physical, natural, social and human capitals) and provides useful measures of trade-offs among these policy goals. The 'Living Standards Framework' is being applied to arrive at a more consistent ranking of specific policy proposals against a set of common criteria for measuring well-being. Concern about the environment and sustainability has also encouraged the development of methods and techniques that incorporate related goals and objectives, and the expansion of analytical tools such as CBA to incorporate social, environmental and cultural well-being.

The creation of explicit frameworks has brought more formality into analysis. Examples of widely used frameworks are market and government failure, human rights, gender analysis, and frameworks tailored to specific issues and population groups. Policy analysis has borrowed and also inspired the design of new frameworks for addressing specific policy issues, in turn advancing the design of policy options and instruments. Such newer frameworks for analysis have addressed market and government failure and the expression of values and impacts as criteria, and the development of performance measures for help in ranking options.

The use of specific policy frameworks has led to new tools, techniques and methods to deal more comprehensively with specific policy developments. Frameworks regarding market and government failure are very useful when designing options assigning different roles to government and others. Weimer and Vining (2015) are particularly strong on identifying different types of market and government failure and linking them to specific kinds of policy interventions. The market and government failure frameworks continue to be used, and have been expanded to include other frameworks to address failures relating to human rights and gender issues. More attention is now given to the selection and choice of policy instruments, and various taxonomies have been developed to classify policy instruments in relation to specific policy frameworks.

Policymakers now have more regard for policy goals and more awareness of criteria such as sustainability and the impact of policies on future generations. There is now greater awareness that options analysis should project outcomes, and policy alternatives are often valued because of their influence on specific economic, social, environmental and cultural outcomes. Specific analytical frameworks have also become embedded in criteria for assessing the quality of policy analysis and advice.

In both Australia and New Zealand, an independent Productivity Commission has been established and funded by governments to address important policy and regulatory topics. Governments can also engage on policy issues by establishing dedicated working groups, task forces and policy advisory groups which are serviced by public servants and sometimes bring together a wider range of expertise and opinions on policy issues. Such groups are more independent and can encourage discussion of a much wider range of issues and options than is likely to be put forward by public sector advisers.

More attention is now given to the selection and choice of policy instruments, and various taxonomies have been developed to classify policy instruments in relation to specific policies.

New tools and approaches to consultation, participation and engagement (such as www.iap2.org) contribute to policy developments. A single tool, such as intervention (programme) logic, is now selected to assist with many tasks and stages when developing policy issues such as problem definition, designing options and dealing with risk management in policy design (see Baehler, 2002). Analysis is becoming more sophisticated, with new approaches to selecting and designing values and criteria to assess options and project outcomes. MCA analyses will sometimes weight criteria, and computer software can now assist the analyst by identifying when weights will take on values that will alter the ranking of the alternatives. Contingent recommendations provide opportunities to associate specific options with particular values and impacts to create if/then statements, allowing decision makers to decide which options perform well against the criteria they prioritize (see Congressional Budget Office, 2013); computer software shows the impact of the weights on the choice of options, and contingent (if/then) recommendations create linkages between particular policy goals and criteria and preferred options.

Policy practices continue to reflect institutional and governance arrangements and can change suddenly in response to a new government, to changes in world events and crises, and to changing expectations regarding the role of governments and other actors in contributing to policy processes and resulting policy decisions. The association of specific tools and techniques with a particular stage of the policy process has given way to policy practices that have expanded the use of tools and techniques such as intervention/programme logic and system and causal mapping. The association of specific tools and techniques with particular steps and stages is less common. Co-production can be used at any stage in the policy process and is useful when there is limited consensus across stakeholders though such processes can be expensive and carry a significant risk of failure. Co-production has been used to develop scenarios and strategies for the future, and to design services in many country contexts. Co-production and co-design are being used for strategic and operational policies and provide direct input for the clients and users of services (Dunrose & Richardson, 2015).

The New Zealand Prime Minister's chief science adviser has produced various reports on the role of evidence in policy formation and implementation (Gluckman, 2013), suggesting that scientific advice can improve public policy outcomes and in no way weakens the authority of the political process. He supports the wider use of randomized control trials (RCT) and other formal methods for gathering evidence on public policy issues and asserts that greater reliance on scientific advice will strengthen rather than weaken the authority of the political process.

Discussions surrounding the use of information and evidence have led to an expansion of the information and evidence base, including the use of big data to support policy analysis and advisory work. Policy practitioners are more aware of the need for good information to inform policy design and implementation and the importance of research results to inform policy work. At the same time, the call for evidence-based policy requires considerable care and attention. Evidence-based policy is sometimes associated with the use and application of large data sets to inform policy work. It is still common for policy advisers to lack the kind of information that is needed to address the complex issues on current policy agendas. The focus on introducing greater rigour to the analysis of information and evidence is reflected in greater investments in data analysis and policy research.

The construction and use of evidence hierarchies provides the basis for advisers to balance and weigh up the rigour of methods with the relevance of the research to the specific policy issues under consideration. Greater attention to the role of evidence in supporting policy has sometimes promoted approaches that are rigorous but not always relevant. Evidence hierarchies are important and useful when policies are being considered which draw on knowledge and experiences from different country contexts.

In New Zealand and Australia, independent productivity commissions have been established and funded by governments to conduct enquiries on important public policy and regulatory topics. Another way for governments to engage on policy issues is to establish dedicated working groups, task forces and policy advisory groups that are serviced by public servants and which bring together a wide range of expertise and opinions on policy issues. Such groups are more independent and can encourage discussion of a much wider range of issues and options than is likely to be put forward by public sector advisers.

Changes in the nature of public policy theory and practice have broadened the bodies of knowledge, skills and competencies of policy analysts and advisers. The focus on the choice of formal methods, while relevant, is now part of a much larger range of choices as analysts select and also create new approaches involving various methods, models, tools and frameworks in analysing complex issues in diverse governance settings.

Greater complexity in dealing with policy issues has diminished mechanistic and technical approaches to policy work. It has alerted practitioners to the need to develop 'design' skills so they can create analysis and advice which suits the specific issue, context and environment. There is now a demand for 'crafting skills' that require knowledge and experience built up over time. Globalization puts pressure on countries to consider the selection of methods that have been used successfully in other countries and in some cases set a good-practice approach.

There is a need to balance analytical and political elements of public decision making to find policy solutions that are workable and sustainable, both analytically and politically. Policy analysis is increasingly done by groups and teams rather than individuals. Theories surrounding policy analysis have given considerable attention to models of policy processes rather than to the relationships between various methods, tools and specific tasks. Sometimes countries have excessively focused on the role of institutions and processes, and paid less attention to external influences and policy transfer from other countries. In a connected world, more attention must be placed on settings and practices in other countries and contexts.

Today's policy practitioners draw from a wide range of formal and informal methods, models, frameworks, and various tools and techniques when conducting policy analysis to address a real-world problem. Evidence suggests that the skills of policy advisers grow primarily by experience working on a wide range of different policy issues. This allows advisers and analysts to experiment with and share experiences regarding the selection and choice of approaches to be used. Through experience and reflection and learning from others, they can hone their knowledge, skills and competencies and become more proficient at understanding what works well and why. The word 'craft' also recognizes a repertoire of knowledge and skills and the ability to apply them to meet the requirements of a specific issue or client (Scott & Baehler, 2010; Bardach & Patashnik, 2015; Parsons, 2004; Weimer & Vining, 2015; Weimer, 1998).

These trends can be seen in the changing curriculum of some policy schools, which are now more strongly linking public policy and public management and bringing in expertise in human resources management, organizational behaviour and leadership. Expertise in formal methods has been and remains an important contribution to policy analysis as a field— as do knowledge, skills and competencies across a wide range of different theories, frameworks, methods, tools and techniques that contribute to the analysis of a specific policy issue or problem.

The priority given to different frameworks, methods and techniques for conducting policy analysis can be observed in various standards for assessing quality policy analysis and advice.

Individual agencies often purchase independent reviews of their written policy advice from a private sector organization. Many agencies specify the knowledge, skills, competencies and behaviours that are required to be appointed to junior and senior policy analyst and advisory positions.

While policy analysis and advising is not regulated and formalized compared with other professions such as law and economics, various initiatives have been undertaken to enhance the capability of policy advisers and analysts and to 'professionalize' the public service advisory system. They include establishing programmes to build skills and capability in partnership with universities. Some countries have formed explicit partnerships between the government and specific universities to credential public policy and public management qualifications. Such offerings are far less common than in-house civil service training programmes and university-based academic programmes.

As policy analysis developed as a profession, issues were raised regarding the degree to which quality policy analysis and advice should be assessed by standards and criteria of best practice, drawing on the expertise of professionals working in the field and/or the client(s) for policy advisory services. There is growing interest within governments to establish objective measures and criteria to evaluate the quality of analytical, written and oral advice.

Approaches to assessing the quality of analysis and advice within government are associated with measures of the quality of inputs and policy processes, and also the selection and application of rigorous analytical methods. The selection and choice of formal policy analysis methods, frameworks, tools and techniques are important aspects of policy analysis design and implementation. One measure that has been considered and used from time to time is a measure of the proportion of advice that is accepted by decision makers, though this approach has limitations and has the potential to discourage advisers from offering 'free and frank' advice as is the norm in some Westminster advisory systems.

There is now more focus on 'good practice' (for a specific context), rather than 'best practice', which can result in a one-size-fits-all approach. Current practices are more successful in bringing together the art, science and craft elements of policy analysis, including new frameworks, tools and techniques and methods to respond to changing policy priorities, county contexts and governance arrangements (New Zealand Department of Prime Minister and Cabinet, 2015; New Zealand Treasury, 2010; UK Civil Service Board, 2013).

Conclusions

The concept of formal policy methods has been promoted and also challenged by academics and practitioners working on policy issues. The growing multi-disciplinary and applied nature of policy analysis theory and practice has led to less clarity as regards the concept of 'formal methods' and there is now greater integration and linkages across methods, frameworks, tools and techniques. This mirrors what has happened with CBA and MCA, which were previously viewed as competing methods.

With the increase and wider use of more transparent analysis, both academics and practitioners in the field have recognized the need to balance the political and analytical dimensions of policy analysis and advisory work. There are numerous actors and institutions who form part of the wider policy system and provide a set of influences on policy option design, evaluation and choice, and who have a major impact on specific goals, objectives and outcomes.

Doing policy analysis involves bringing together elements relating to the arts and social sciences and crafting skills in order to design a policy process that reflects the complexity of the issue and context, builds analysis on a strong information and evidence base, and draws lessons from international experiences and evidence while also acknowledging local knowledge and experience.

Formal methods can play an important role in deriving valuable information, alongside a good information base and evidence to support and shape policy analysis. However, the choice of single method will rarely comprise a standalone approach to the analysis of a policy issue. Context and values are integral to addressing policy issues in a more global, complex and changing world.

Rather than seeking to discern 'best practices' that may be associated with the use of more sophisticated analytical methods, quality analysis should focus on policy analysis designs that are fit for purpose. More attention should be given to developing crafting skills and using a variety of methods, tools and techniques for a specific task with a focus on what works well and what does not.

References

Adachi, Yukio, Hosono, Sukehiro and Iio, Jun (eds) (2016) *Policy Analysis in Japan*, International Library of Policy Analysis, Bristol, UK: Policy Press.

Althaus, Catherine, Bridgman, Peter and Davis, Glyn (2013) *The Australian Policy Handbook*, Sydney, Australia: Allen & Unwin.

Baehler, K. (2002) 'Intervention Logic: A User's Guide', *Public Sector, 25*(3), 13–19.

Bardach, Eugene and Patashnik, Erik (2015) *A Practical Guide for Policy Analysis*, Washington, DC: CQ Press.

Carley, Michael (1980) *Rational Techniques in Policy Analysis*, London: Heinemann Education.

Colebatch, Hal (2002) *Policy*, Buckingham, UK: Open University Press.

Colebatch, Hal (2006) *Beyond the Policy Cycle: The Policy Process in Australia*, Sydney: Allen & Unwin.

Congressional Budget Office (2013) *The Army's Ground Combat Vehicle Program and Alternatives*, Washington, DC.

DeLeon, Peter and Vogenbeck, Danielle (2007) 'The Policy Sciences at the Crossroads' in F. Fischer, G. Miller and M. Sidney (eds), *Handbook of Public Policy Analysis*, New York: CRC Press.

Dunrose, Catherine and Richardson, Liz (2015), *Designing Policy for Co-production*, Bristol, UK: Policy Press.

Fischer, Frank (2003) *Reframing Public Policy: Discursive Politics and Deliberative Practices*, Sydney, Australia: Pearson Longman.

Gamper, Catherine and Turcanu, Catrinel (2007) 'Multi-Criteria Analysis: A Tool for Going Beyond Monetization?' in A. Jordan and J. Turnpenny (eds), *Tools of Policy Formulation: Actors, Capacities, Venues and Effects*, Cheltenham, UK: Edward Elgar.

Gluckman, Peter (2013) 'The Role of Evidence in Policy Formation and Implementation', *Report of the Prime Minister's Chief Science Adviser*, Wellington, New Zealand.

Goldbach, Stine and Leleur, Steen (2004) *Cost-Benefit Analysis (CBA) and Alternative Approaches from the Centre for Logistics and Goods (CLG) Study of Valuation Techniques.* Available from www.systemicplanning.dk.

Howlett, Michael and Lindquist, Evert (2007) 'Beyond Formal Policy Analysis: Governance Context, Analytical Styles and the Policy Movement in Canada', in L. Dobuzinskis, M. Howlett and D. Laycock (eds), *Policy Analysis in Canada: The State of the Art*, University of Toronto Press.

Howlett, Michael and Ramesh M. (2003) *Studying Public Policy: Policy Cycles and Policy Subsystems*, Toronto, ON: Oxford University Press.

Karacaoglu, G. (2015) *The New Zealand Treasury's Living Standards Framework: Exploring a Stylised Model*, Wellington: New Zealand Treasury.

Mayer, Igor, van Daalen, Els and Bots, Pieter (2004) 'Perspectives on Policy Analysis: A Framework for Understanding and Design', *International Journal of Technology, Policy and Management, 4*(2), 169–191.

New Zealand Department of Prime Minister and Cabinet (2015) *The Policy Project: Narrative and Direction of Travel*, Wellington, NZ: New Zealand Government, www.dpmc.govt.nz/policyproject.

New Zealand Ministry for the Environment (2011) *The Cobra Guide*, Wellington, NZ: New Zealand Government, www.mfe-cobra.

New Zealand Ministry for the Environment (2013) *Natural Resources Framework: Guidance for Users.* Wellington: Ministry for the Environment, http://nrs.mfe.govt.nz/content/natural-resources-framework.

New Zealand Treasury (2010) *Review of Expenditure on Policy Advice*, Wellington, NZ: New Zealand Government, www.treasury.govt.nz/statesector/policyexpenditurereview.

New Zealand Treasury (2015) *Guide to Social Cost Benefit Analysis*, Wellington, NZ: New Zealand Government, www.treasury.govt.nz/publications/guidance/planning/costbenefitanalysis/guide/cba-guide-jul15.pdf.

Pal, Lesley (2013) *Beyond Policy Analysis: Public Issue Management in Turbulent Times*, 5th edition, Canada: Nelson College Indigenous.

Parsons, Wayne (2004) 'Not Just Steering but Weaving: Relevant Knowledge and the Craft of Building Policy Capability and Coherence', *Australian Journal of Public Administration*, *63*(1), 43–57

Patapan, Haig (ed.) (2005) *Westminster Legacies: Democracy and Responsible Government in Asia and the Pacific*. Sydney, Australia: University of New South Wales Press.

Radin, Beryl (2000) *Beyond Machiavelli: Policy Analysis Comes of Age*, Washington, DC: Georgetown University Press.

Radin, Beryl (2013) *Beyond Machiavelli: Policy Reaches Midlife*, Washington, DC: Georgetown University Press.

Scott, Claudia (2013) 'Teaching Policy Analysis in Cross-National Settings: A System Approach', *Journal of Public Education Affairs*, *19*(3), 433–443.

Scott, Claudia and Baehler, Karen (2010) *Adding Value to Policy Analysis and Advice*, Sydney, Australia: NSW Press.

UK Civil Service Board (2013) *Twelve Actions to Professionalise Policy Work*. London.

van Nispen, Frans and Scholten Peter (eds) (2015) *Policy Analysis in the Netherlands*, International Library of Policy Analysis, Bristol, UK: Policy Press.

Vining, Aidan and Boardman Anthony (2006) 'Metachoice in Policy Analysis', *Journal of Comparative Policy Analysis: Research and Practice, 8*(1), 77–87.

Vining, Aidan and Boardman, Anthony (2007) 'The Choice of Formal Policy Analysis Methods in Canada', in L. Dobuzinskis, M. Howlett, and D. Laycock (eds), *Policy Analysis in Canada: The State of the Art*, University of Toronto Press.

Weimer, David (1998). 'Policy Analysis and Evidence: A Craft Perspective', *Policy Studies Journal, 26*(1), 114–129.

Weimer, David and Vining, Aidan. (2015) *Policy Analysis Concepts and Practice* 5th Edition, Upper Saddle River, NJ: Prentice Hall.

Wolf, Amanda (1997) Building Advice: The Craft of the Policy Professional, Working Paper No. 7, State Services Commission, Wellington, New Zealand.

4

FROM POLICY ANALYTICAL STYLES TO POLICYMAKING STYLES

Patrick Hassenteufel and Philippe Zittoun

Inspired by Lowi's works that proposed a typology of public policies (1964, 1972) and thus by a wide range of comparative studies since the 1970s (Smith, 1975; Heidenheimer, Adams & Heclo, 1975; Hayward & Watson, 1975; Feldman et al., 1978), the heuristic concept of 'style' aims to transform an incomparable and singular policy or policy process into a comparable one through the identification of a relevant characterization (policy domain, time period, policy tools, etc.). By allowing the commensurability of policy, this concept also contributes to identify the divergence or convergence between 'different systems of the decision-making process, different procedures of making societal decisions' (Richardson, Gustafsson & Jordan, 1982, p. 2).

One of the best-known usages of the concept of 'policy style' is Richardson et al.'s (1982) comparison of national policy styles across two dimensions: the kind of relationship between government and interest groups (conflict or negotiation) and the dominant time horizon of public policies (short-term reactive policies or long-term anticipatory policies). Based on this analytical framework, Richardson et al. identified a 'British style', corresponding to 'broad characterizations of the British (and possibly European) policy processes, particularly in terms of the relationship between government and interest groups' (Jordan & Richardson, 1982). They argued that, irrespective of the policy field, Britain's policymaking characteristics were slightly different from those of other countries. They characterized the British policy style as a kind of 'bureaucratic accommodation' producing reactive policies. In contrast, in France— where the state imposed anticipatory policies—the relationship between government and interest groups was more conflict-oriented.

The notion of policy style took a new turn in the early 2000s following the reflections of Igor Mayer, C. Els van Daalen and Pieter Bots. Mayer et al. (2004) proposed to use the notion to distinguish and characterize different kinds of policy analysis rather than policy processes, as previous studies had done. They perceived the concept of 'style' not only as useful for qualifying different kinds of policy analysis, but also as capable of replacing the concept of paradigm and facilitating comparability of policy approaches. While the paradigm concept implies opposition, i.e. stronger differentiation, they presented the different kinds of policy analysis as complementary. They identified six policy analytical styles (rational, argumentative, client advice, participatory, process and interactive) and transformed a long tradition of incompatible paradigms into a typology of complementary analytical methods.

The concept of 'style' can be considered as a heuristic method of building a typology and transforming incomparable objects or processes into comparable ones. How, then, might we use it for the study of policy analysis? This question is particularly complex if we consider that the concept of 'policy analysis' is itself used in multiple ways; it has been used to identify an applied scientific field, to identify knowledge production by practitioners, and even to speak about a broad field with applied and non-applied dimensions (Wildavsky, 1987; Bardach & Patashnik, 2015; Peters & Pierre, 2006; Majone, 1989).

The main purpose of this chapter is to underpin the notion that, while the concept of style might not be able to take the place of the paradigm concept in the academic field, it can prove quite useful in comparing the use of different policy analytical methods in relation to the systems of policy advice, policy formulation and public debate across various countries. Following the perspective proposed by Craft and Howlett (2012), we propose that the concept of policy analytical style might provide a heuristic channel to reconsider the whole policymaking process, from policy analysis to policy formulation and policy debate.

Policy Analysis: A Scientific Discipline or Field of Expertise?

To develop the concept of policy analytical style, Mayer, van Daalen and Bots proposed to bridge the gap between the various, incompatible 'policy analysis' paradigms by combining them into knowledge activities (Mayer et al., 2004). By defining what constitutes an academic 'discipline' ('if we are unable to construct cohesion and unity behind this great diversity, we cannot speak of a discipline', p. 170), and proposing to build a unique model transforming policy analysis into different 'styles', they paved the way for relevant debate on the status of policy analysis and the possibility of defining 'styles'.

Mayer et al.'s definition of academic discipline does not consider that most academic disciplines, especially in the social sciences, are largely structured around different non-compatible paradigms. As Popper suggests, the epistemological distinction of different approaches is very constitutive of academic knowledge production (Popper, 1959). In policy studies, for example, the argumentative approach considers that all policy analyses are argumentative activities, even the rational ones. From this perspective, it is not possible to combine the argumentative paradigm with the rational paradigm; these different 'styles' are based on different conceptions of what a public policy is and with what methods it should be analysed.

Contrary to Mayer et al., Dobuzinskis, Howlett and Laycock (2007) consider epistemologically policy analysis as 'applied social and scientific research—but also involving more implicit forms of practical knowledge—pursued by government officials and non-governmental organizations usually directed at designing, implementing, and evaluating existing policies, programs and other courses of action adopted or contemplated by states' (p. 1). They distinguish policy analysis from policy study, which 'is conducted mainly by academics and relates to "meta-policy" or the overall nature of the activities of the state. It is generally concerned with understanding the development, logic and implications of overall state policy processes and the models used by investigators to analyze those processes' (p. 1).

The debate on the epistemological status of policy analysis and its ambiguity is not new. Aaron Wildavsky evoked rather late the issue of definition of policy analysis[1] and explained that policy analysis is not a science but, rather, an art and a craft: 'Without art, analysis is doomed to repetition; without craft, analysis is unpersuasive' (Wildavsky, 1987, p. 389). However, he merely challenged the epistemological status of policy analysis as a scientific discipline. When Charles Lindblom developed the paradoxical concept of the 'science of muddling through', he criticized 'theorists' who developed non-scientific and non-rigorous policy analyses because they forgot that 'no one can practice the rational–comprehensive method for really complex problems' (Lindblom, 1958b, p. 84). Lindblom considered their theory 'of extremely limited helpfulness in policy-making' (p. 87). Eugene Bardach also suggested that 'policy analysis is more art than science [which] draws on intuition as much as on method' (Bardach, 2008, p. xvi), thus reinforcing the idea that policy analysis as an activity is not scientific. This is in opposition to the policy science perspective (Lerner & Lasswell, 1951) that was dominant at that time.

Following Dobuzinskis et al. (2007)[2] and these different authors, we make a clear distinction between the academic field of policy studies, which seeks to understand the policy process, and the non-academic field of policy analysis, which is a specific knowledge field bringing together the different kinds of knowledge produced on and for public policies. Policy analysis is not based on shared scientific methods, nor is there an academic community responsible for organizing formal procedures to differentiate 'genuine' problem-solving statements from those that are not genuine. Rather, it is an applied knowledge activity that produces problem-solving statements, proposals, arguments, ways of thinking and evidence for the policymaking process. As Wildavsky suggested, the main objective of policy analysis is to persuade decision makers of a policy's efficiency rather than to publish scientific articles and obtain academic acclaim. This kind of knowledge does not seek validation through the persuasion of peers involving a formal process of scientific evaluation: rather, it seeks to transform a proposal statement into a decision by policymakers (Zittoun, 2014). It is interesting to note that in countries such as France (Halpern, Hassenteufel & Zittoun, 2017) or Germany (Blum & Schubert, 2013), where there is a clear distinction between the academic community and the policy process, policy analysis is underdeveloped and policy studies are focused on the policy process as a means through which to grasp governmental activities.

Taking this assumption into account and based on the epistemological status of knowledge, it becomes impossible to clearly distinguish between a policy analyst academic, a policy analyst expert, a policy analyst bureaucrat or even a policy analyst politician, all of whom produce proposals supported by knowledge and arguments. By considering policy analysis as applied knowledge rather than as scientific knowledge, the academic community is prevented from occupying a specific position with regard to these activities, while the other actors—experts, bureaucrats and politicians—aspire to influence the policy process by proposing problem-solving statements.

Lindblom contrasted 'theorists' who produce policy analysis knowledge with practitioners who produce 'profane' knowledge, which is generally just as useful and rigorous as policy analysis knowledge (Lindblom, 1958b, 1958a). Policy analysis may also be considered as knowledge activities and separated from the question of who produces and uses this knowledge, based on empirical observations.

Policy analysis must therefore be considered not as an academic field, but rather as a set of knowledge activities that practitioners, policymakers, academics, politicians and experts produce. The concept of 'style' thus becomes relevant to tackle two questions. First, is it possible to identify sufficient specific characteristics to establish a typology of policy analysis independently of who uses it and who produces it? Second, is there a link between this typology and the configuration of the producers and users of this knowledge?

A Typology of Policy Analytical Styles

To build a typology of policy analysis as a knowledge-producing activity, we must begin by defining policy analysis. Although this task is particularly complex, we examine the cognitive operations that make it possible to produce 'usable' knowledge in order to influence the policy process (Lindblom & Cohen, 1979). Indeed, it would be too complex to take all kinds of knowledge into account to organize a typology. We thus focus here on all 'usable' knowledge that seeks to support and justify a problem-solving statement.

A problem-solving statement is a statement that proposes to associate the definition of a problem with the policy instruments aimed at solving it. Following Wittgenstein, we do not focus on the content of these linking operations, but rather examine the statement as a "language game" associating two concepts—public problems and policy instruments—and translating this into a 'causal link' that transforms the choice of an instrument into a way of solving a given problem (Wittgenstein, 2005). To avoid making assumptions about what comes first between a problem and a solution—presuming either that the solution is always the result of the resolution of a problem, or that the solution arises first and is only later associated with a problem—we suggest going beyond this opposition by considering problems and solutions independently. From this perspective, the linking operation that Kingdon referred to as 'coupling' (1995) stands apart from the policy analysis process which produces knowledge (arguments, evidence and proofs) to justify the couplage and to reorder it.

In his practical guide to policy analysis, Eugene Bardach (2008) considers 'policy analysis' as a problem-solving process that can be deconstructed into eight parts: defining the problem, assembling evidence, constructing alternatives, selecting criteria, projecting the outcomes, confronting the trade-offs, deciding, and telling the story. In his classical style of analysis, the process begins with the identification of the different components of policy analysis (problem, evidence, alternatives, criteria, etc.), followed by their transformation into specific operations for each problem (defining policy, selecting criteria, etc.), which is also some form of analysis, making it possible to solve the problem in a complex way. Like Russian dolls, policy analysis contains different kinds of analysis. Wshile it is difficult to identify all the operations required by policy analysis in the problem-solving process they are all linked to the most important component—the problem-solving statement. Inspired by Bardach (2008), we propose a typology structured around five types of analysis. The typology is not exhaustive, but attempts to understand a large number of policy analysis methods, focusing on the production of usable knowledge to support problem-solving statements. The analyses are not mutually exclusive and they are generally combined.

Policy Predictive Analysis

The link between a proposal and its consequences is one of the least known and most problematic links. A typical case is that of the US prohibition policy in the early 20th century, which had more unexpected consequences than expected ones. Taking into account the fragile link between a proposal and its consequences, many policy analyses have mobilized different methods and strategies to predict the impact of a proposal. The approach typically depicts an image of the future which is actually a reproduction of the present modified by the expected consequences.

One of the best-known predictive analyses employs rational choice theory and cost-benefit analysis to predict what may happen in the future should a specific policy instrument be chosen (Peters, 2015). By proposing to objectivize human behaviour through its constant preferences and its calculation of scales of interest, rational choice theory allows for the simulation of future human behaviour, among other things. Cost-benefit analysis largely develops predictive cost evolution. It aims to establish indicators, principles of evolution and general laws that make it possible to predict different components, discipline human behaviour and build fictions. A good example is the 'consumer's surplus' proposed by Mishan and Quah (2007), which identifies some laws to simulate and predict behaviour. In this case, the fiction is essentially the present modified by the consequence of the policy measure. For example, to justify the construction of a tramway as a solution to pollution, a policy analyst might develop a form of behaviour modelling that makes it possible to build a fiction and simulate the number of people who might take the tramway after its construction (Zittoun, 2014). The model is essentially built on behaviour laws and preferences that human beings follow in both the present and the future. In this example, the assumption is that most people would prefer to take the fastest transport and the most-direct path. Based on this, the analyst could establish the number of people who would take the new tramway and compare different layouts. By simulating the future and comparing it to the present, the analyst justifies the policy.

In addition to rational choice, comparative policy analysis can also be used as a method to predict the consequence of a policy proposal. It is of primary importance in establishing a link between a public policy implemented in one country and its effects, then transforming this link into a predictive link able to sustain a proposal. The relationship between the flexibility of the labour market and the unemployment rate is a good example of this kind of reasoning.

Problem Causal Analysis

In this analytical style, the goal is to attach a causal factor to a problem by proposing correlations between some specific phenomena and the problem to be solved. Unlike predictive analysis, which focuses on policy consequences in the future, causal analysis focuses on the past and the present in order to identify the cause of the problem to be addressed. Like medicine, which tries to identify and eliminate the cause of an illness, this analytical style essentially seeks to transform the cause into a new problem to solve. For example, in the case of housing policy, problem causal analysis could point out that the main problem is an insufficient amount of new housing; hence a solution to the problem should include instruments that contribute to new housing construction (Zittoun, 2001).

Problem causal analysis aims to develop knowledge to transform correlation into causality between two phenomena. While the context of the phenomenon is specific, the primary objective of the analysis is to find evidence to transform the problem into a cause. This supposes that every time the first phenomenon appears, it provokes the apparition of the second. Comparative analysis is one of the main classical styles of analysis and is based on the idea that one can find the same correlation in the past or in a different country. The main difficulty encountered by this kind of analysis is that, to enable comparability, the specificity of every situation must be transformed. Popper (1960) suggests that, irrespective of the number of cases, confirmation alone is not sufficient to constitute scientific proof.

Trial/Error Policy Analysis

This associates an experimental approach with evaluative analysis. Inspired by Popper and developed by Dahl and Lindblom (1953), this analytical style considers that it is epistemologically impossible to have a rigorous predictive or causal analysis. Because every policy always provokes unexpected consequences, one must study policy, observe it and analyse its consequences. The trial-and-error approach is based on the repetition and multiplication of experiments, often on a small scale with the purpose of generalization. It can also be introduced directly on a bigger scale with the purpose of adjustment. The trial-and-error approach to policy analysis can be incremental, as it seeks to test policy proposals similar to an existing policy. This method, which has been inspired by the experimental method in natural science (Popper, 1935), has primarily been developed in public policy with tests carried out at the micro level. The analysis essentially seeks to build and/or use experimentation as the primary evidence to support a problem-solving statement. It has been widely developed in the last fifteen years by economists under the label of 'evidence-based policy'.

Policy Process Analysis Producing Knowledge on the Process

This approach is based on the idea that understanding the process is the most relevant way to define an efficient strategy. Since the beginning of policy analysis, social scientists have developed knowledge of the process itself and have attempted to grasp the complexity of the various actors and the constraints generated by the different stages of the process. Knowledge about the policy process was one of the most important fields nurtured by social scientists in the initial studies on the decision-making process undertaken in the 1950s and 1960s (Lasswell, 1956; Simon, 1944; Bachrach & Baratz, 1963; Lindblom, 1972), on policy implementation (Pressman & Wildavsky, 1973), and on the policy process as a whole in the 1970s (Jones, 1970; Anderson, 1975; Lasswell, 1971).

Normative Policy Analysis

This last type of analytical style produces knowledge that makes it possible to legitimize the link between a proposal and the norms, values and references that give meaning to the proposal. For example, a policy analysis may use data and arguments to justify the notion that a particular instrument contributes to 'sustainable development', 'freedom' or 'equality'. The relationship between a norm and a proposal can be justified through a complex chain of links.

Although Lindblom distinguished knowledge *for* the policy process from knowledge *on* the policy process (Lindblom & Woodhouse, 1993), he undoubtedly underestimated the fact that the knowledge on the policy process is often used to grasp and designate a cartography of actors, networks and policy paths, i.e. to justify a problem-solving statement. For instance, all measures proposed to simplify administration, organize citizen participation or reach a compromise between multiple interests can be supported by an analysis of the policy process that underlines its restrictions and its limits.

The Different Policy Systems in the Policymaking Process

If policy analysis is 'usable' knowledge that supports problem-solving statements, we must also examine how this analysis is used in the policy process and by whom. This will make it possible to differentiate policy analytical styles on the basis of both their content and the manner in which they are used by policy actors in different governance contexts and at three levels in particular: national traditions, policy sectors and departments (Howlett & Lindquist, 2007).

The first and easiest approach to tackle these issues is to use the 'location-based model' (Craft & Howlett, 2012; Wilson, 2006), which seeks to identify the loci where policy analysis (in the form of reports, publications or data) is produced. These locations might be universities, academic research units, think tanks, interest groups or governmental offices dedicated to the production of data. Craft and Howlett clearly distinguish between locations that produce knowledge and those that make decisions, and between political and technical content. There are a number of limitations to the location-based model, however. The inclusion of a new category of analysis gives rise to new challenges such as the differentiation between the short term and the long term, based on location. A second limitation is related to the fact that some policy analysts might engage in activities other than knowledge production; for instance, they may defend their problem-solving statements within government and try to directly persuade decision makers. Third, different kinds of activities might be carried out in the same institution, meaning that activities do not always define the specificity of an institution. For example, in a governmental office one may find civil servants who produce knowledge and others who use this knowledge to advise and persuade others. These limitations make it difficult to elaborate a completely convincing typology. The idea of a location-based model is interesting but needs to be enlarged to embrace the entire policymaking process, from the formulation of policy proposals to the finalization of policy decisions.

A second model is function-based, which separates the knowledge function into different individual components: the function of knowledge production, the function of using knowledge, and the function of discussing knowledge. When Wildavsky distinguishes art and craft activities (1987), he separates the production of knowledge and its use. However, he focuses mainly on one kind of use, i.e. the manner in which decision makers can be persuaded to choose between different proposals. This distinction suggests that the knowledge used as evidence to support a problem-solving statement needs to be transformed into arguments to persuade decision makers. To understand the distinction between policy analysis as evidence to support problem-solving statements and policy analysis as an argument to persuade decision makers, we must return to Lindblom, one of the first scholars trying to understand the role of policy analysis in policymaking. He asked: 'How far do analysis and reasoning discussion go in policy making?' (Lindblom & Woodhouse, 1993, p. 13), and compared 'reaching policy choices by informed analysis and thoughtful discussion versus setting policy by bargaining, trading of favors, voting or otherwise exerting power' (p. 7). Lindblom considered, however, that 'analysis and politics always intertwine' (p. 7): 'Why, given the obvious merits, do governments not make even more use of analysis? Why is there not less decision making on the basis of power and more on the basis of reasoned inquiry?' (p. 15).

The main challenge of this approach is how to epistemologically separate knowledge making from knowledge use. As Perelman has suggested, all knowledge, except in mathematics, is generally developed as an argument to persuade others of the likelihood of the purpose (Perelman & Olbrechts-Tyteca, 1950). When knowledge is developed in the academic world, researchers have to persuade other researchers using specific rules and methods. It is clear that the use of knowledge in the political arena always involves some transformation and simplification. More generally, separating knowledge production from knowledge use might lead one to overlook the fact that while knowledge is used, there is no additional testing during the argumentative exchange.

The third approach combines elements of the first two in the policy system-based model (Jobert, 1994; Easton, 1965; Edelman, 1988; Bourdieu & Christin, 1990; Sabatier & Jenkins-Smith, 1993; Marsh & Rhodes 1992). This model identifies the different policy systems in which a policy statement is formulated, analysed, negotiated, discussed and tested, based on autonomous rules and using specific actors or, more precisely, specific social roles and strategies, a specific distribution of acknowledgement and power, specific institutions and resources, some institutionalized likelihood statements, truth, and some dominant types of critiques. The same actor or the same institution might be involved in multiple policy systems, and in each one may play a different role and have different resources, a different position and different authority, and develop different kinds of arguments. Each policy system is like an autonomous game with its own rules, strategies and roles.

Defining different policy systems in this way offers a heuristic for understanding the dynamics of policy proposal statements within each specific system and better grasping the circulation between them. Each system can be differentiated based on the rules a policy proposal statement must follow to succeed. Subsequently, one must also take into account the kind of public one needs to persuade and the system of critiques the proposal must evade or resist. The first task therefore is to identify the different policy systems.

The Policy Academic System

This system, largely studied by the sociology of sciences (Latour, 1988), has specific rules that revolve around the production and the testing of academic knowledge. This system mainly includes researchers and academics whose careers and legitimacy are built upon their publications and citations within the academic system. This system is fragmented as it is composed of different disciplines, each with its own sub-system—though all disciplines share a relatively similar process. The key to recognition and academic career progression is largely based on publishing. While public policy is generally not an autonomous field, it is important to identify the dominant disciplines in the academic study of public policies.

The Policy Advisory System

This brings together all producers of 'usable' knowledge to support problem-solving statements. 'Expertise' is the main social role; it can be organized within bureaucracies, think tanks, interest groups and, less systematically, within political parties and non-profit organizations. It has become increasingly difficult to determine where expertise begins and ends. The main rules of this system are the publication of reports, notes, books and communications addressed to different kinds of publics (mostly specialized but also to the larger public via the media) in order to persuade, but also to resist the multiple critiques they reinforce. Generally, the system of expertise is organized into a policy community with its own rules of acknowledgement and its own language. Another key dimension is the degree of differentiation between public expertise (in governmental departments and agencies) and private expertise (in think tanks, interest groups and non-government organizations, which frequently overlap).

The Policy Formulation System

This generally revolves around a specific policy domain and is related to a specialized bureaucracy, formalized decision mechanisms, different official interlocutors, and a multitude of roles, discourses and practices. In this system, the main rules are direct persuasion through discursive interaction and the production of official texts, laws, decrees, budgets, instruments and other policy measures, as well as negotiations and conflicts. For instance, a country's national housing policy system associates the housing policy with a large number of laws, policy instruments, the Department of Housing, the Minister and the Ministry of Housing, the national spokesmen of owners and renters, the spokesman of building companies and of banks, and other dominant discourses and statements about housing.

The Public Debate System

This last system refers to the complex public confrontations between different actors (political actors, the media, interest groups, experts, etc.). This is the most visible part of the policymaking process, during which different actors argue and discuss problem-solving statements. This arena revolves around convictions, conflicts and critiques. While politicians play an important role in this system, they are not the only actors: journalists, experts, interest-group spokesmen, academics and—less frequently—bureaucrats participate in public debates. One of the main characteristics of this system is that policy proposals and their critiques seek to persuade a large public. This is in contrast to other systems where the audience to be persuaded is more restricted and specialized.

The Structure of Policy Systems and Their Interaction

These four different policy systems can be identified everywhere. Differences across countries can be grasped by analysing the structure and the relationships between them, based on the identification of the actors who compose the different systems, the circulation (or absence of circulation) between the systems and the type of interactions they share (i.e. the level of conflict between policy actors).

The first step in this comparative analysis is to identify the different categories of actors. Key criteria include the actor's professional position (who is their employer?) and their career. Academic actors, for example, are employed mainly by universities or research units and most of their career takes place within the academic system. Public experts are bureaucrats employed by government to produce knowledge and policy proposals for the government, and they have mainly administrative careers. Private experts are employed by interest groups or non-profit organizations, and their career paths are often more complex: they often circulate to or from the academic world or governmental agencies. Political actors compete for elective mandates and hold different institutional positions (in the legislative or executive branch of government) at different levels (national or local) during their political careers.

Understanding the various kinds of policy actors provides a better understanding of the composition of each policy system. For example, the role of academics inside the advisory system depends on the country, as discussed below. The proportion of public and private experts within the academic system can also widely differ: the number of experts teaching public policy in universities may be high in some countries and very low in others. Similarly, the significance of political actors in the policy formulation process depends on the relationship between the legislative and executive branches. While political actors play an important role in public debate in all countries, the level of participation of experts and academics differs greatly from one country to another.

Adopting an actor-centred perspective also helps us to better understand the *level of compartmentalization* between each system. One may find a high level of compartmentalization; for example, the academic system is mainly composed of academics, policy advisory and formulation systems are essentially composed of experts, and public debates are monopolized by politicians. But one can also find high levels of porosity between policy systems: the academic system includes experts and politicians, academics participate in the policy advisory system and public debates, and politicians play an important role in policy formulation.

In order to grasp the whole policymaking process, it is necessary to include another dimension—*the level of conflict or cooperation in every policy system*. The policy formulation system, for example, is characterized by the intensity of internal conflicts (between departments or between different levels of government) and external conflicts (between departments, local governments, non-profit organizations and interest groups). The level of intra-system conflict is also related to the conflicts between government and parliament. In the policy advisory system, the level of conflict often reflects the diversity of actors (public vs. private) who produce advice. In the academic system, it is generally linked to the significance of a national academic system, the level of competition for jobs and careers, and the dependence on external resources, among other things.

Following a knowledge-centred perspective can help us to better understand *the level of controversies inside each system*. In the policy academic system, a distinction can be made between a context with a dominant paradigm (and thus a low level of controversy) and a context with the co-existence of two or more paradigms (and thus a high level of controversy). In the policy advisory system, the level of controversy depends on the amount of divergent expertise (with different policy analytical styles). In the public debate system, the level of conflict is usually high in every country because of the distinction between political arenas and policy arenas (Edelman, 1988). However, the significance of media criticism, the degree of political pluralism and the level of public contestation of policy proposals can differ.

It is also important to consider the openness of the systems—that is, whether they facilitate (or not) the circulation of policy analysis knowledge. The level of openness is primarily linked to the similarity of policy analytical styles between different systems. In a situation where each system develops a specific style of policy analysis, the capacity of knowledge to circulate between different systems is very weak. At the opposite extreme, the presence of the same type of policy analytical style in different systems facilitates circulation of knowledge and paves the way for knowledge exchange.

The Policymaking Style Matrix

Integrating these different dimensions leads us to propose an analytical matrix that compares the role of policy analysis in the policymaking process. We will use it here to compare the policymaking style in three countries: France, Germany and the United States.

The French policymaking style (Halpern et al., 2017) can be characterized by a high level of compartmentalization and the dominant role of public experts using predictive and causal analytical styles. Academics are restricted to the academic system (using causal and process-oriented analytical styles), and are isolated from the more predictive policy analytical style used in the policy advisory and formulation systems, which are dominated by public experts (senior civil servants)[3] located in ministers' staffs, departments and specific public expertise institutions, mostly related to the prime minister (like the former Commissariat Général au Plan recently transformed into France Stratégie). The separation between the different systems explains the high level of conflict in the public debate system, where actors excluded from the policy formulation system (especially politicians, given the weak role of Parliament, but also academics and private experts) express their criticism of policy proposals and decisions.

The German policymaking style can be characterized by cooperation between different levels of government (cooperative federalism) and between interest groups and government (corporatism) (Blum & Schubert, 2013). The policy analytical styles in France and Germany are similar, but the policy systems in Germany are more porous: academics and private experts are often involved in the policy advisory system, and politicians are highly involved in the policy formulation system through political negotiation in Parliament.

In the United States, we find an even greater circulation of actors between the different policy systems, corresponding to a rather complex and evolving configuration (Radin, 2013). Two other characteristics of the American policymaking style are a high level of conflict in the policy formulation system (especially in Congress but also between levels of government)

Table 4.1 The French policymaking style

Policy System		Academic System	Policy Advisory System	Policy Formulation System	Public Debate System
Actors	Academics	X			
	Public Experts	X	X	X	X
	Private Experts		X		X
	Politicians				X
Level of internal conflict	High/Medium/Low	Medium	Low	Medium	High
Level of compartmentalization	High/Medium/Low	High	Medium	High	Medium
Policy analytical styles	Predictive		X	X	
	Causal	X	X		
	Trial/error				
	Process	X			
	Normative			X	X
Level of internal controversies	High/Medium/Low	Medium	Low	Low	Medium
Level of opening	High/Medium/Low	Medium	Low	High	High

Table 4.2 The German policymaking style

Policy System		Academic System	Policy Advisory System	Policy Formulation System	Public Debate System
Actors	Academics	X	X		X
	Public Experts		X	X	
	Private Experts		X	X	X
	Politicians			X	X
Level of internal conflict	High/Medium/Low	Medium	Low	Medium	Medium
Level of compartmentalization	High/Medium/Low	High	Medium	Low	Medium
Policy analytical styles	Predictive		X	X	
	Causal	X	X	X	X
	Trial/error				
	Process	X			
	Normative				X
Level of internal controversies	High/Medium/Low	Medium	Medium	Medium	Medium
Level of opening	High/Medium/Low	Low	Medium	Low	Medium

Table 4.3 The US policymaking style

Policy Systems		Academic System	Policy Advisory System	Policy Formulation System	Public Debate System
Actors	Academics	X	X		X
	Public Experts	X	X	X	
	Private Experts	X	X	X	X
	Politicians			X	X
Level of internal conflict	High/Medium/Low	Medium	Medium	High	High
Level of compartmentalization	High/Medium/Low	Low	Low	Low	Low
Policy analytical styles	Predictive	X	X	X	X
	Causal	X			
	Trial/error	X	X	X	X
	Process	X			
	Normative			X	X
Level of internal controversies	High/Medium/Low	High	Medium	Medium	High

and a central place taken by predictive and trial-and-error policy analysis, due to the strong role that economics plays in policy studies in the US (in contrast with France and Germany, where political science and sociology play a relatively more important role).

Conclusion

While we consider, like Mayer et al. (2004), that the concept of 'style' can be useful to grasp the different types of policy analysis, we do not seek to go beyond the antagonism between different academic policy paradigms as the aforementioned authors suggest, but rather to categorize different kinds of usable knowledge and to better understand their use, their circulation and their role in the policy process. To this end, we associate their categorization of knowledge with two other paradigms: one based on the different actors who use the paradigms, the other based on the policy systems where actors and knowledge interact. The resulting policymaking matrix allows us to characterize the policymaking process in different countries.

This policymaking style matrix can be used to characterize other countries on the basis of the data collected in the International Library of Policy Analysis series, as well as other policy sectors (either to compare similar policy sectors in different countries or different policy sectors in one country) and local public policies. It is thus a useful framework for the comparative analysis of policymaking that takes into account the type of policy analysis (studied in the literature on policy analytical styles) and the different policy systems by associating an actor-centred approach with a knowledge-centred approach. Its main limitation in understanding the whole policy process is that it does not directly take into account the implementation stage, which is less related to most policy analytical styles; the only exceptions are the trial-and-error style, which is connected to the systematic evaluation of implementation, and the process style, which has been extended to implementation studies (Hill & Hupe, 2002). The next issue is thus to tackle the integration of policy implementation in the analysis of policymaking styles.

Notes

1 'How can you teach (or write a book) on a subject if you can't say what it is?' (p. 2).
2 'Policy studies . . . is conducted mainly by academics and relates to "meta-policy" or the overall nature of the activities of the state. It is generally concerned with understanding the development, logic and implications of overall state policy processes and the models used by investigators to analyse those processes. "Policy analysis", refers to applied social and scientific research—but also involves more implicit forms of practical knowledge—pursued by government officials and non-governmental organizations which usually focus on designing, implementing, and evaluating existing policies, programs and other courses of action adopted or contemplated by states' (p. 1).
3 As the case of healthcare policymaking shows (Genieys & Hassenteufel, 2015).

References

Anderson, James. 1975. *Public Policy-Making*. New York: Praeger.

Bachrach, P.S. and M.S. Baratz. 1963. "Decisions and Non-Decisions: An Analytical Framework" *American Political Science Review* 57: 641–51.

Bardach, Eugene. 2008. *A Practical Guide for Policy Analysis: The Eightfold Path to More Effective Problem Solving*. 3rd revised edition. Thousand Oaks, CA: CQ Press.

Bardach, Eugene and Eric M. Patashnik. 2015. *A Practical Guide for Policy Analysis: The Eightfold Path to More Effective Problem Solving*. 5th revised edition. Thousand Oaks, CA: Sage.

Blum, Sonja and Klaus Schubert. 2013. *Policy Analysis in Germany*. Bristol, UK: Policy Press.

Bourdieu, Pierre and Rosine Christin. 1990. "La Construction Du Marché; Le Champ Administratif et La Production de La 'Politique Du Logement'". *Actes de La Recherche En Sciences Sociales* 81–82: 65–85.

Craft, Jonathan and Michael Howlett. 2012. "Policy Formulation, Governance Shifts and Policy Influence: Location and Content in Policy Advisory Systems". *Journal of Public Policy* 32 (02): 79–98.

Dahl, Robert Alan and Charles Edward Lindblom. 1953. *Politics, Economics, and Welfare: Planning and Politico-Economic Systems Resolved into Basic Social Processes*. New York: Harper.

Dobuzinskis, Laurent, Michael Howlett and David H. Laycock. 2007. *Policy Analysis in Canada: The State of the Art*. University of Toronto Press.

Easton, David. 1965. *A Systems Analysis of Political Life*. New York: Wiley.

Edelman, Murray. 1988. *Constructing the Political Spectacle*. University of Chicago Press.

Feldman, Elliot J., Arnold J. Heidenheimer, Hugh Heclo, Carolyn Teich Adams, T. Alexander Smith, Jack Hayward and Michael Watson. 1978. "Comparative Public Policy: Field or Method?" *Comparative Politics* 10 (2): 287–305.

Genieys, William and Patrick Hassenteufel. 2015. "The Shaping of New State Elites: Healthcare Policymaking in France since 1981". *Comparative Politics* 47 (3): 208–295.

Halpern, Charlotte, Patrick Hassenteufel and Philippe Zittoun. 2017. *Policy Analysis in France*. Bristol, UK: Policy Press.

Hayward, Jack Ernest Shalom and Michael Watson (eds). 1975. *Planning, Politics, and Public Policy: The British, French, and Italian Experience*. London and New York: Cambridge University Press.

Heidenheimer, Arnold J., Hugh Heclo and Carolyn Teich Adams. 1975. *Comparative Public Policy: The Politics of Social Choice in Europe and America*. New York: Macmillan.

Hill, Michael and Hupe, Peter. 2002. *Implementing Public Policy*. London: Sage.

Howlett, Michael and Everts Lindquist. 2007. "Beyond Formal Policy Analysis: Governance Context, Analytical Styles and the Policy Analysis Movement in Canada", in L. Dobuzinskis, M. Howlett and D. Laycock, *Policy Analysis in Canada: The State of the Art*, Toronto: University of Toronto Press.

Jobert, Bruno. 1994. *Le Tournant Néo-Libéral En Europe*. Paris: L'Harmattan.

Jones, Charles O. 1970. *An Introduction to the Study of Public Policy*. Wadsworth Series in Public Policy. Belmont, CA: Wadsworth.

Jordan, G. and J. Richardson. 1982. "The British Policy Style or the Logic of Negotiation?" In J.J. Richardson (ed.), *Policy Styles in Western Europe*. London: Allen & Unwin: 80–110.

Kingdon, John. 1995. *Agendas, Alternatives and Public Policies*. New York: Longman.

Lasswell, Harold D. 1956. *The Decision Process: Seven Categories of Functional Analysis*. Bureau of Governmental Research. Studies in Government. College of Business and Public Administration, University of Maryland,

Lasswell, Harold D. 1971. *The Policy Orientation of Political Science*. Agra, India: Lakshmi Narain Agarwal.

Latour, Bruno. 1988. *La Vie de Laboratoire*. Paris: La découverte.

Lerner, Daniel and Harold D. Lasswell. 1951. *The Policy Sciences: Recent Developments in Scope and Method*. Stanford University Press.

Lindblom, Charles E. 1958a. "Policy Analysis". *The American Economic Review* 48 (3): 298–312.

Lindblom, Charles E. 1958b. "The Science of Muddling Through". *Public Administration Review* 19: 78–88.

Lindblom, Charles E. 1972. *Strategies for Decision Making*. University of Illinois Bulletin. Urbana: Dept. of Political Science.

Lindblom, Charles E. and David K. Cohen. 1979. *Usable Knowledge?: Social Science and Social Problem Solving*. New Haven, CT: Yale University Press.

Lindblom, Charles E. and Edward J. Woodhouse. 1993. *The Policy-Making Process*. 3rd edition. Foundations of Modern Political Science Series. Englewood Cliffs, NJ: Prentice Hall.

Lowi, T.J. 1964. "American Business, Public Policy, Case-Studies, and Political Theory". *World Politics* 16 (4): 677–715.

Lowi, T.J. 1972. "Four Systems of Policy, Politics, and Choice". *Public Administration Review* 32 (4): 298–310.

Majone, G. 1989. *Evidence, Argument, and Persuasion in the Policy Process*. Yale University Press.

Marsh, D. and R.A.W. Rhodes. 1992. *Policy Networks in British Government*. New York: Oxford University Press.

Mayer, Igor S., C. Els van Daalen and Pieter W.G. Bots. 2004. "Perspectives on Policy Analyses: A Framework for Understanding and Design". *International Journal of Technology, Policy and Management* 4 (2): 169–191.

Mishan, E.J., and Euston Quah. 2007. *Cost-Benefit Analysis*. New York: Routledge.

Perelman, Chaïm, and L. Olbrechts-Tyteca. 1950. *La Nouvelle Rhétorique?: Traité de l'Argumentation*. Paris: Presses universitaires de France.

Peters, B. Guy and Jon Pierre. 2006. *Handbook of Public Policy*. Thousand Oaks, CA: Sage.

Peters, B. Guy. 2015. *Advanced Introduction to Public Policy*. Cheltenham, UK: Edward Elgar.

Popper, Karl. 1935. *Logique de La Découverte Scientifique*. Paris: Payot.

Popper, K. R. 1959 [1934]. *The Logic of Scientific Discovery*. London: Routledge.

Popper, Karl R. 1960. *On the Sources of Knowledge and of Ignorance*. London: Routledge.

Pressman, Jeffery L. and Wildavsky, Aaron. 1973. *Implementation*. University of California Press.

Radin, Beryl. 2013. *Beyond Machiavelli: Policy Reaches Mid-Life*, Washington, DC: Georgetown University Press.

Richardson, J., G. Gustafsson and G. Jordan. 1982. "The Concept of Policy Style". In J.J Richardson (ed.), *Policy Styles in Western Europe*. London: Allen & Unwin: 1–16.

Sabatier, Paul A. and Hank C. Jenkins-Smith. 1993. *Policy Change and Learning: An Advocacy Coalition Approach*. Theoretical Lenses on Public Policy. Boulder, CO: Westview Press.

Simon, Herbert A. 1944. *Decision-Making and Administrative Organization*. *Public Administration Review* 4 (1): 16–30.

Smith, T. Alexander. 1975. *The Comparative Policy Process*. Santa Barbara, CA: ABC-Clio.

Wildavsky, Aaron. 1987. *Speaking Truth to Power: The Art and Craft of Policy Analysis*. New Brunswick, NJ: Transaction.

Wilson, Richard. 2006. "Policy Analysis as Policy Advice". In Robert E. Goodin, Michael Moran, and Martin Rein (eds), *The Oxford Handbook of Public Policy*. Oxford University Press: 152–85.

Wittgenstein, Ludwig. 2005. *Recherches philosophiques*. Bibliothèque de philosophie. Paris: Gallimard.

Zittoun, Philippe. 2001. *La Politique Du Logement 1981–1995: Transformations d'une politique publique controversée*. Paris: Editions L'Harmattan.

Zittoun, Philippe. 2014. *The Political Process of Policymaking: A Pragmatic Approach to Public Policy*. Palgrave Macmillan.

5

POLICY ANALYSIS AND BUREAUCRATIC CAPACITY

Jose-Luis Mendez and Mauricio I. Dussauge-Laguna

Introduction

This chapter studies the relationship of policy analysis with bureaucratic capacity. Policy analysis is understood as those analytical activities related to proposing a course of action to solve public problems—that is, defining the nature and causes of such problems, devising and evaluating possible choices, and proposing an alternative to decision makers. Accordingly, we deal here only with a certain type of bureaucratic capacity, namely that related to policy analysis for policy formulation, and a specific type of analyst, the governmental policy analyst.

The chapter is structured as follows. The first section reviews theoretical debates on the concept of policy analysis capacity and related terms. It underlines the relevance that policy analysis has for policymaking, and the variables that may affect its supply and demand. The second section provides an overview of policy analysis in comparative perspective. It synthesizes information drawn from studies about policy analysis in five countries: Australia, Canada, Germany, Brazil and Mexico. Thereafter, it contrasts these cases against the theoretical insights of the first section. The chapter closes with some concluding remarks about policy analysis capacity as a concept and as a basis for conducting comparative research.

The Study of Governmental Policy Analysis: A General Overview

Policy Analytical Capacity and Other State Capacities

As mentioned above, we deal here only with a certain type of bureaucratic capacity, namely that related to policy analysis for policy formulation. Thus, we do not focus on other state capacities, such as those related to agenda setting, policy implementation and policy evaluation. Of course policy analysts may relate to these processes to some extent, but they have been primarily the realm of politicians, managers and non-governmental policy experts, respectively.

Agenda setting is a process that takes place in the broader political arena, mainly involving the intervention of elected politicians, political parties and interest groups. Policy analysts can participate in agenda-setting processes, for instance by advising elected politicians or ministers on the relevance of accepting or not accepting a new issue or considering a state problem as an urgent one. However, the role of analysts here tends to be limited, as such decisions are likely to be taken based on the degree to which an issue is advocated by political actors. Policy implementation, in turn, takes place for the most part within the state. It also tends to involve various types of political games, but here managers play a central role in activities such as organizational leadership, budgeting, human-resource management and monitoring. In this way, Wu, Ramesh and Howlett (2015) speak of 'operational capacity', while Painter and Pierre (2005, p. 2) refer to 'administrative capacity' as 'the ability to manage efficiently the human and physical resources required for delivering the outputs of government'. Finally, policy evaluation is closely related to policy analysis but it is usually performed by policy experts outside the state, at a variety of non-profit organizations such as universities, think tanks and non-government organizations that perform programme evaluations either subcontracted by the government or as part of their own regular activities.

Policy analytical capacity and administrative capacity are components of state capacity. Although state capacity is a somewhat elusive concept (Hendrix, 2010) that has been subject to different views (Mann, 1984; Evans, 1995; Rueschemeyer, Huber Stephens & Stephens, 1992; Norris, 2012), in general it can be conceived as being closely related to policy outcomes and thus to the overall efficacy of the state. Painter and Pierre (2005) depict the relationship between policy analytical capacity, administrative capacity and state capacity as the corners of a triangle, each of them depending on the other to some degree.

As to policy analysis, Gill and Saunders define it as 'a method for structuring information and providing opportunities for the development of alternative choices for the policymaker' (1992, pp. 6–7). For Painter and Pierre, 'policy capacity is the ability to marshal the necessary resources to make intelligent collective choices about and set strategic directions for the allocation of scarce resources to public ends' (2005, p. 2). For Howlett, in turn, 'as part of the policy formulation process, this activity involves policy appraisal, that is, providing information or advice to policy makers concerning the relative advantages and disadvantages of alternative policy choices', while 'the term "policy analytical capacity" thus describes the ability of individuals in a policy-relevant organization to produce valuable policy-relevant research and analysis on topics asked of them or of their own choosing' (2015, p. 173; see also Howlett, Ramesh & Perl, 2009; Sidney, 2007; Wildavsky, 1979).

Riddell (1998) identified several elements of individual policy analytical capacity: environmental scanning, trends analysis and forecasting methods; statistics, applied research and modelling; evaluation of the means necessary to meet goals; consultation and managing relations; and programme design, implementation monitoring and evaluation. These capacities are usually possessed by a certain type of civil servant, the governmental policy analyst, often located at advising bureaus within the executive offices at the local, subnational or national levels. However, it is not necessarily easy to identify their location. As Howlett has stated, 'in many cases it is not clear even if the job classifications and titles typically used by public service commissions to categorize professional policy analysts in government for staffing purposes are accurate or reflect a true sense of what policy analysts actually do on a day-to-day basis' (2015, p. 176).

Governmental policy analysts can be seen as a specific subset of civil servants, as they may or may not belong to the career civil service. Often they are part of the advising bodies within executive offices, but the latter could be also formed by other type of advisors, for instance those offering advice from political or party perspectives. They are also a subset of the more general type of policy analyst, who can work both at governmental and non-profit organizations. Policy analysts usually come from university programmes specializing in certain disciplines, such as economics, public administration, political science and business management, although it is possible that they come also from other fields, such as sociology or engineering. Even when they may not be political activists, they are political actors as they advocate certain choices and may engage in conflicts or 'political games' with elected politicians (Meltsner, 1976; Behn, 1986).

Importance of Policy Analytical Capacity and Policy Analysis

Policy analytical capacity is important for the development of state capacity for several reasons. Policy analysis helps to choose a better alternative by confronting policy problems in a better way and avoiding policy failures resulting from a mismatch between plans and on-the-ground conditions. It is expected that through an empirical and systematic analysis of the causes and consequences of available choices, governments can avoid past mistakes as well as apply new techniques to the resolution of old and new problems (Howlett, 2009). In this way, higher levels of policy analytical capacity are expected to lead organizations to be more successful in solving problems in the short and long term (Aucoin & Bakvis, 2005).

There has been a debate in the policy field about what stage of the policy process is more important. While some authors (Cobb & Elder, 1971) have argued in favour of agenda setting, because it involves decisions that affect later stages, others have highlighted the importance of implementation as a missing link in the policy process (Pressman & Wildavsky, 1973). Authors focusing on policy design (Linder & Peters, 1984; Howlett, 2011) have stressed that it is in the policy formulation stage where decisions leading to the solution of policy problems are taken. Although it could be said that all authors in this debate are right to some extent, the importance of policy formulation and thus governmental policy analysis cannot be denied.

Despite this importance, in the 1990s Peters (1996) pointed to several major trends diminishing the capacity of governments to formulate policy. First, the issues that governments face have become increasingly difficult to manage; second, there has been a general erosion of the public service; third, policy analysis has tended to be replaced by political advice; fourth, the increasing variability of policy issues requires more flexible and creative forms of intervention; finally, policies and the solutions they entail have come to be seen as socially constructed rather than as naturally occurring.

As to the latter point, the assumption that evidence-based policy is a better way to confront policy problems has been questioned from different points of view. In fact, doubts on the capacity of the 'policy sciences' to confront issues have been present since the very start of the policy field, when Laswell (1951) cautioned about some of its limits. Although these doubts were put aside in the 1960s and early 1970s by more optimistic views on the capacity of policies to solve public problems, starting in the late 1970s several authors began to argue that policy analysis was a craft rather than a science (Wildavsky, 1979; Majone, 1989). In the following decades, criticisms of the concept of evidence-based policy became even more prevalent (Stone, 2002; Packwood, 2002; Pawson, 2006). Several works have even questioned the value for policy analysis of the collection and analysis of large amounts of data (Tenbensel, 2004), or have tried to 'demystify' the authority of social statistics (Neylan, 2008).

Among the criticisms of evidence-based policy analysis is that evidence is only one factor involved in policymaking and that systematic data collection and policy analytical techniques may not be superior to the judgment of politicians or citizens, or may impose an elitist, technocratic view on governmental decisions (Jackson, 2007; Majone, 1989). Some of these concerns are justified in many instances, especially in those circumstances when policy analysts trained in highly sophisticated quantitative analysis techniques forget about the limitations of such techniques or of the databases they use, and present quantitative evidence as beyond challenge. However, the criticisms can also be misplaced (Howlett et al., 2009), or may even be the product of an overly rationalistic, 'straw-man' construction of policy analysis. Probably the fairest and most useful way to consider policy analysis is the one indicated by Laswell (1951) and Wildavsky (1979), that is, as a sort of professional trade where, even when it is not 'scientific', some basic rules for the systematic generation and analysis of evidence as well as alternatives apply. With these methods, policy analysts can 'speak truth to power' (Wildavsky, 1979), while decision makers can 'weave' together various strands of information and values advocated by several stakeholder groups to make pragmatic judgments (Head, 2008). In fact, this is what often happens, even in countries with merit civil services and democratic institutions.

Studies and Factors of Governmental Policy Analytical Capacity

Although at the beginning somewhat rare, since the 1970s several works have been produced on the features of policy analysis and the roles of policy analysts. Among the first we can mention are those of Meltsner (1976) and Wildavsky (1979). These initial studies were followed by additional ones in the 1980s (Behn, 1986; Nelson, 1989; Majone, 1989; Aberbach & Rockman, 1989; Wollmann, 1989), and in the 1990s (Bushnell, 1991; Thompson, Yessian & Weiss, 1992; Boston, Martin, Pallot & Walsh, 1996). According to Howlett (2015), most studies have focused on the 'demand' side of the policy advice "market", examining the strengths, weaknesses and other characteristics of the knowledge utilization process in government. However, there are concerns about the accuracy of this work, given that it has tended to employ partial surveys or consist of anecdotal case studies.

Most of the abovementioned studies focus on the United States, but comparative studies have been increasingly produced, such as those of Barker and Peters (1993), Radin (2000), Polidano (2000), and Painter and Pierre (2005). Howlett (2015) identified several comparative studies of the supply of policy advice (Wagner & Wollman, 1986; Malloy, 1989; Hawke, 1993; Halligan, 1995; Thissen & Twaalfhoven, 2001; Mayer, van Daalen & Bots, 2004; Weible, 2008; Gregory & Lonti, 2008), as well as works on 'policy supply' that look at the United Kingdom (Page & Jenkins, 2005), Australia (Weller & Stevens, 1998); New Zealand (Boston et al., 1996), the Netherlands (Hoppe & Jeliazkova, 2006), France (Rochet, 2004), and Germany (Fleischer, 2009). However, Howlett argues that the answers to basic questions, such as how many people are in policy analysis positions or what they do in the various countries, still remain unknown.

Most of the work on policy analysis refers to the national or federal level; very few look at the subnational or local level. There are exceptions, however: Hird (2005) examines nonpartisan policy research organizations operating in U.S. state legislatures through a statistical analysis of those agencies in all 50 states and a survey of 800 state legislators. He details how nonpartisan policy analysis organizations came to be, what they do, and what state legislators want from them, and concludes that policy analysis institutions can play an important role, as long as they remain scrupulously nonpartisan. Howlett (2009) studied the background, training and work of provincial policy analysts in Canada, revealing several substantial differences between analysts working for national governments and their subnational counterparts.

As is evident from the above, there has been a tendency to study policy analysis capacity through a supply-and-demand approach. In this perspective, the level of governmental policy analysis depends on the extent to which policy analysis is demanded by state actors as well as on the degree to which the elements needed to supply it are present. Although such an approach may involve some risks, as we discuss below, it still offers a good way to introduce the issue. Several demand-and-supply factors have been mentioned in the literature (Polidano, 2000; Vining & Boardman, 2007; Howlett, 2015; Weimer, 2015). Demand-side factors include the type of political regime and the level of bureaucratic development—for instance, in democratic regimes where elected politicians and decision makers in general are more accountable to civil society, there is a greater preoccupation with effectively solving public problems and, thus, with evidence and techniques that could be potentially helpful to that effect. A democratic regime could also promote another element conducive to policy analysis, that is, a culture in which openness is encouraged and risk taking is acceptable (Riddell, 1998). Likewise, in those countries with merit civil services, bureaucrats would be more interested in approaching issues in a professional manner, especially if such systems go up to the bureaucratic levels right below ministers and deputy ministers. The opposite would be the case in authoritarian regimes with bureaucratic apparatuses organized under a spoils system, where the goal is simply to distribute benefits to client groups of the 'winning coalition' (De Mesquita, Morrow, Siverson & Smith, 1999). On the supply side, there are two elements that are especially important to facilitating the development of policy analysis: the availability of quality data and information, and the existence of study programmes on public policy, as well as in related disciplines such as economics, public administration and political science.

If we take a demand-supply approach for a first approximation to the understanding of the level of policy analysis and policy analytical capacity, we can develop a demand-supply matrix of governmental policy analysis (see Table 5.1). We would expect a higher level of analysis to be present in those cases where there are high levels of both demand and supply for policy analysis, while lower levels of both demand and supply would be associated with a lower level of policy analysis. In the first category are consolidated bureaucratic democracies, where there is a comparatively higher level of governmental policy analytical capacity, and civil servants— or in some instances, professionalized public/private policy networks—can develop policy analysis, thanks to the availability of quality information on the characteristics of the respective nation, its people and its public problems. Although of course there are important differences, most Western European nations, the United States and Canada, as well as Australia, New Zealand and some East Asian countries could be included in this group.[1] At the other extreme are countries with authoritarian or 'competitive authoritarian' (Levitsky & Way, 2010) regimes and clientelistic bureaucracies, for example a good number of African nations.

In a third, intermediate level, the presence of demand factors is low while the level of supply ones is high, or the other way around. In the first, policy analysis would be at a

Table 5.1 A supply-demand matrix of governmental policy analysis

		Demand	
		Low	*High*
Supply	**High**	*Intermediate* Developing bureaucratic democracies National subcontracting model	*Higher* Consolidated bureaucratic democracies Civil service/professional network model
	Low	*Lower* Clientelistic authoritarian regimes Clientelistic model	*Intermediate* Developing bureaucratic democracies Foreign aid model

Source: Authors' elaboration based on Howlett (2015) and Weimer (2015).

medium level because, even if it is not highly demanded by the state, good levels of quality information and policy analysis capabilities exist in national think tanks or universities, and policy analysis could be facilitated and subcontracted out. In the second case, where the state demands a more systematic and evidence-based policy analysis, but it cannot be supplied internally, governmental agencies turn to international organizations such as the United Nations and the World Bank. Mexico (Mendez, 2017) and several South American nations would be examples of the first case, while most countries in Central America and the Caribbean (as well as in Africa) would be examples of the second.

Despite the potential usefulness of a supply-demand perspective, several authors have criticized it. Nutley, Walter and Davies (2007), for instance, state that looking at policy advice and analysis with this market-like approach has some pitfalls, and that in any case it involves a rather imperfect market, one that has to be mediated or connected by policy networks in order to actually work. Craft and Howlett (2012), in turn, have argued that the market analogy leads to the consideration of three separate locational components: the supply of policy advice, its demand on the part of decision makers, and brokers who match supply and demand. The first component includes the 'knowledge producers' located in academia, statistical agencies and research institutes, providing basic economic and social data upon which analyses are based. The second set is composed of the 'proximate decision makers' who 'consume' policy analysis and advice. In the third group are 'knowledge brokers' who serve as intermediaries between the knowledge producers and the proximate decision makers, translating data and information into usable forms of knowledge. However, such a locational model may no longer be completely applicable as there is increasing evidence that shifts in governance arrangements have blurred both the inside vs. outside and the technical vs. political dimensions of policy formulation environments. Thus, for Craft and Howlett, 'the growing plurality of advisory sources and the polycentrism associated with these governance shifts challenge the utility of [. . .] traditional models of policy advice systems' (2012, p. 79), leading to a revised approach that sees influence more as a product of content than location. However, we consider that the increasing importance of policy analysis brokers and the blurring of inside and outside elements of policy analysis may be phenomena more present in the consolidated bureaucratic democracies, and thus one may still consider the supply-demand approach for the study of policy analysis—and the matrix just proposed—as useful heuristic tools.

Policy Analytical Capacity in Different National Settings

Having discussed the theoretical and conceptual aspects of policy analysis capacity, we will now turn to some country examples to illustrate how different governments have tried to build their own policy analytical capacities, the challenges they have faced, and the variables that seem to either constrain or favor these efforts. The discussion covers both developed and developing countries, drawing mainly on the contributions to the International Library of Policy Analysis,[2] particularly in chapters dedicated to this very subject.

Australia

During the past 30 years, the policy analysis capacity of Australian public organizations has undergone continuous change. According to Head (2015), profound institutional and environmental changes have most likely damaged the analytical capacity of the Australian government in the short term, yet in the longer term may eventually become beneficial in some respects.

The rise of neoliberal values and New Public Management (NPM) ideas since the 1980s, which strongly criticized both 'big government' and the state's monopoly over policy advice, resulted in measures that directly affected the federal government's policy capacity, both analytical and administrative. Outsourcing, privatization and downsizing reforms reduced the size of the public sector, and thus its overall policy expertise, and at the same time private contractors and non-government organizations profited by recruiting former public employees. Changes in the management of the senior civil service increased the risks of politicization and undermined long-standing principles of neutral competence. Marketization reforms reasserted the relevance of efficiency and economy and challenged traditional concerns regarding social equity. On the whole, 'the long-standing role of public agencies as the key providers of trusted and independent expert policy advice became increasingly contested' (Head, 2015, p. 53).

Changes to the government's institutional structure and functions have also been related to other reasons. Just as the federal government's control over revenue collection has grown, so have areas of 'shared funding, policy overlap, and potential conflict' (Head, 2015, p. 56) vis-à-vis subnational governments. Federal involvement in an ever-growing number of policy subjects, many of which are now discussed and followed up within the institutional structure and mechanisms associated to the Council of Australian Governments, have stressed the policy analytical and policy coordination capacities of federal officials. Furthermore, the government's monopoly over policy advice has been disputed by the rise of specialized bodies (some even with statutory independence), including the Productivity Commission and the Australian Competition and Consumer Commission.

Last but not least, Head points at the emergence of other policy actors that are capable of providing alternative sources of policy advice. This is the case of the Australian National Audit Office, which has expanded its menu of assessments; consulting firms, which are frequently hired to produce reports and advice for public organizations; and an increasing number of think tanks, advocacy organizations, and lobbying organizations, all of which currently have easier access than before to information sources and a variety of communication outlets.

As a result of all this, the state of policy analysis capacity in Australia is mixed. On the one hand, the sources of policy advice have multiplied, which may be beneficial for policymakers: they may draw insights and information from a broader market of policy ideas. Moreover, a recent public service capabilities review 'found that the federal agencies were competent' (quoted in Head, 2015, p. 60). On the other hand, the same review stated that agencies 'needed to lift their capacity to respond to the tough challenges of rapid external change and higher community expectations'. Similarly, Head suggests that a context of multiple sources of policy advice and a diversity of stakeholder interests represents a huge challenge for policy analysts, as they may not have the time and skills to process all relevant information, particularly that which may reinforce an evidence-based policymaking process. In addition, policy analytical capacity seems to vary widely across federal departments, as well as between federal and subnational levels.

Canada

The policy analytical capacity in Canada, as depicted by Howlett (2009), seems to vary widely across sectors. On the one hand, several actors that regularly participate in the Canadian policymaking process, such as trade unions, business associations, and even think tanks, actually have rather limited analytical in-house capacity. Therefore, they often rely on work and research conducted by external consultants. On the other hand, government institutions would seem to be the only bodies with the necessary resources (especially personnel and funding) to build in-house policy analytical capacity. Even within the public sector, however, there is 'a very "lumpy" or uneven distribution of policy analytical capacity, varying by level of government and by department or agency involved' (Howlett, 2009, p. 165).

The Canadian federal government's policy analysis capacity has also varied significantly across time and place (see Bakvis, 2000). For example, during the 1980s and early 1990s, budgetary cuts affected the availability of analytical capacity across federal agencies. Once the government was able to sort out the crisis, it set in motion a number of initiatives to recompose its analytical capacity. These included a Task Force on 'Strengthening Our Policy Capacity' and *La Relève* ('renewal of human resources management in the Public Service of Canada'), and collaborations with various think tanks. According to Howlett (2009), the policy analytical capacity has certainly improved and is nowadays higher than it was in the 1980s. Yet variations across agencies still remain, with core executive offices such as the Prime Minister's Office and the Ministry of Finance possessing better analytical capacity than other federal departments.

The Canadian government's policy analysis capacity has also faced significant challenges from the changing political-administrative environment. Howlett (2009) notes that policy processes nowadays mandate consultations from the public. Similarly, recent managerial reforms have underlined a focus on performance management and evidence. As a result, public officials are now required to be able to analyse data coming from polls and focus groups, as well as to manage for results. At the same time, policy analysts are facing new policy challenges, resulting from the 'increased scope, range and complexity' of the government's agenda (Howlett, 2009, p. 167), which includes problems such as climate change.

Moreover, Howlett (2009) suggests that there are important differences in policy analytical capacities between the federal government and the subnational (i.e. provincial, territorial and local) governments. Despite a number of government initiatives that have been advanced in places like British Columbia, Nova Scotia, Manitoba and Alberta to strengthen analytical capacity at the subnational level, capacity remains much weaker in comparison to that existing at the federal level.

Germany

A third interesting case of policy analysis capacity is that of Germany, which shows some similarities but, above all, contrasting features with Australia and Canada. According to Schmid and Buhr (2013), the German administrative system has been subject to many of the same pressures described in the Australian and Canadian cases: significant institutional and policy reforms associated with economic crises, reunification, and more recently the turn to neoliberalism in the management of the economy, and the emergence of scientific advisory boards and commissions of experts, with the latter focused on reform in areas such as labour markets, pensions and health care.

At the same time, Schmid and Buhr stress that the federal government institutions' in-house policy capacities have actually remained strong, and go as far as to argue that 'the basic structures of policy-making [. . .] have remained on track over the post-war era' (Schmid & Buhr, 2013, p. 100). The thousands of civil servants based in the various federal ministries have remained influential because the historical principles of bureaucratic work are still in place. While the Chancellor may set out general policy guidelines, the *Ressortprinzip* implies that ministers are at liberty to organize their ministries as they see fit. The ministries, in turn, are based on units staffed by professional civil servants with significant policy expertise. While the predominance of lawyers is still in place, backed by the legal nature of the German governing tradition, the number of economic experts and social scientists has increased during the past decades.

While the challenges faced by Germany in terms of securing strong policy analysis capacities have not been related to neoliberal principles or NPM reforms, there still are some significant issues that may affect the federal bureaucracy's longer-term capacity. Schmid and Buhr (2015, p. 99) remark on the dangers of 'groupthink', conformity, narrow policy advocacy coalitions and cognitive maps, which come precisely from the tendency to primarily rely on internal staff for producing policy analysis and advice. These are problems that may get even worse once one takes into account the fact that 'a selective and conservative or risk-averse approach prevails' (p. 97), and thus the demand for external sources of policy analytical capacity (in the form of special commissions) may become even more attractive for political actors than before.

Brazil

In contrast to the previous examples, Brazil is a developing country which has faced long periods of authoritarian governments throughout the 20th century, becoming a fully democratic state in 1988. Despite the late advent of democracy, Celina Souza (2013, p. 40) argues that the Brazilian federal bureaucracy has been consistently able to build and adapt its policy capacity so that the key priorities of the various administrations could be implemented.

The development of policy capacity in Brazil has, of course, passed through a number of different stages. The first efforts to build a professional bureaucracy go back to the 1930s, during President Getulio Vargas' administration. Later, a number of decentralized agencies were created, with more flexible hiring practices and set apart from the political dynamics. These agencies (later called 'islands of excellence') were considered to have higher policy capacity than central ministries, and were thus assigned several policy tasks, including key economic ones. In 1989 a new career corps, labelled 'Specialist in Public Policies and Government Management', was established 'to hire professionals with generalist training intended to constitute the upper echelons of the administration' (Souza, 2013, p. 42). During the 1990s, as a response to fiscal crisis and inflation, and backed by the NPM ideology, thousands of employees were laid off from the public sector or took early retirement programmes, and several decentralized agencies were closed. In the early 2000s, however, the federal government again began recruiting aggressively (p. 42), particularly to staff public universities and the social policy sector. More recently, open competition procedures have been strengthened in an effort to end clientelistic practices.

These recurrent efforts to build Brazil's policy capacity have had some limitations. First of all, policy analytical capacities seem to vary across federal institutions. Whereas monetary (Central Bank), technical (Meteorology Institute, Geography and Statistics), and foreign affairs areas are considered to possess high capacity, social policy, infrastructure and cultural institutions have lower capacity (CAF, 2015, pp. 29–31; Souza, 2013, p. 47). Moreover, the recent use of open competitions for entry to government posts has been problematic to some extent: procedures are perceived to be complex, interviews are not used as part of the hiring processes to avoid legal complaints from participants, and the individuals hired do not always possess the expertise that is really required. In the end, according to Souza, '[d]espite the quantitative growth in the bureaucracy and its increased qualifications, bureaucratic capacity-building in the public sector is still incomplete' (2013, p. 47).

Mexico

A fifth and final case is illustrated by the example of Mexico, another developing country that has only recently democratized. However, the development of policy analytical capacities in Mexico's bureaucratic apparatus cannot be traced as far back as in Brazil. In fact, a merit-based system focused in building the capacity of the federal government was established just over a decade ago, in 2003. Thus, as Jesus Hernandez and David Arellano (2017) have argued, 'skills are still being built' within public sector institutions.

The state of policy analytical capacities in the Mexican federal administration has been changing for various reasons. During most of the 20th century, the authoritarian political regime produced a highly politicized administrative system, in which middle and senior officials had to develop analytical skills but also be part of certain political networks. Towards the end of the century, as various economic crises unfolded throughout the 1970s to the 1990s, a new dominant cadre of senior officials emerged. A large number of top positions, from the level of director-general to the presidency, were occupied by highly qualified personnel: almost half of the senior officials possessed graduate degrees, generally obtained from economics-related programmes at universities abroad (Hernandez & Arellano, 2017). While the democratic transition of 2000 brought with it several changes at the highest government positions, the number of public servants with postgraduate degrees has remained high. Hernandez and Arellano report that about 45% of middle- and senior-level officials surveyed possess a master's degree or a PhD. Moreover, during the past two decades, the creation of regulatory agencies and other statutory bodies in fields like telecom-munications, economic competition and education policy, as well as the institutionalization of social policy evaluation practices, have further increased policy analytical skills in Mexico, albeit mainly in organizations outside of the executive branch (autonomous agencies) or even the public sector (e.g. universities and consultancies in charge of evaluating social programmes).

Despite the improvement in policy analytical skills at the middle and senior levels of the federal government and other independent public bodies, significant challenges remain with regard to how much the policy advice provided by these more professional public servants actually influences or turns into good policy decisions. To begin with, policy analysis capacity has historically been stronger in finance and other technical areas than in government sectors like agriculture. Recent administrative changes and capacity-building trends have probably reinforced the capacity divide between economic and regulatory areas vis-à-vis the more politicized social policy fields. Furthermore, there are broader constraints which continue to hinder the work of federal policy analysts. For instance, Hernandez and Arellano report that budget constraints (noted by 30% of respondents) and lack of personnel (also noted by 30% of respondents) are perceived to be the main obstacles hampering policy work. They also found that about 43% of middle- and senior-level officials think that their technically sound policy analyses and recommendations are not taken into account due to political considerations. As a result, Hernandez and Arellano conclude that 'many of the public policies and decisions made at the federal level are not always based on robust technical approaches', and that a logic in which 'decision-makers make decisions before diagnosing the public problem' seems to be prevalent as of this day.

Comparative Overview

While the previous vignettes are hardly conclusive with regards to the state of policy analytical capacity around the world—not least because they draw on works which have been produced on the basis of slightly different conceptualizations and approaches—the descriptions are still useful to present some broader statements on the subject. First, despite the contrasting political and administrative features of these five countries, the task of (re)building policy analytical capacity would seem to be a common and permanent one for all of them. Either because of limited initial capacity, or because of the need to readjust bureaucratic structures after important administrative reforms, all of these countries seem to be regularly engaged in adjusting their central government's policy analytical capacity. Second, despite the similarities, there are some important variations in terms of how the supply of policy analytical capacity has grown outside the main public sector institutions (that is, federal departments). In Australia, NPM-inspired reforms pointed at the need to broaden the market of ideas, thus increasingly relying on consultants and think tanks; in countries like Germany, Brazil and to some extent Mexico, capacity-building outside state institutions has not been as prominent. Third, even within the latter group of nations, policy analytical capacity-building strategies have followed slightly different paths. Whereas Brazil and Mexico have more recently introduced decentralized and other independent public bodies, many of which have reportedly developed stronger analytical capacities than some ministries, in the case of Germany its federal civil service appears to have retained control over the supply of analytical capacity and thus over policy advice. Lastly, policy analytical capacity varies greatly across policy sectors, as well as between the federal and the subnational levels, as shown especially in the Australian and Canadian cases. For instance, financial and technical government areas have apparently been able to build higher policy capacity levels than their social policy counterparts.

In terms of demand for policy analysis, some cases would seem to suggest that governments have tried to draw policy advice from both public institutions and external organizations that are perceived to have greater analytical capacity, at least with regards to some topics. This is clearly the case in Australia, but also in Canada in terms of its recent association with think tanks, and even in Germany and its special commissions for specific topics. On the other hand, in countries like Mexico and Brazil it is not clear how much politicians are really demanding higher analytical capacity levels, and the policy advice that comes with it, as policy decisions are still heavily reliant on (or conditioned by) political considerations. Thus, while the first three countries would tend towards the upper-right cell of Table 5.1, the latter two would fall in the upper-left one.

The supply of policy analysis is quite high in countries with developed systems for the collection of information, as it is the case in all of the examples discussed here (with a slight variation in the Brazilian case). A good indicator to measure the strength of statistical systems in developing nations is the Statistical Capacity Indicator (SCI) of the World Bank. Most of the countries where this supply element for policy analysis is still clearly lacking are in Africa (http://datatopics.worldbank.org/statisticalcapacity/SCIdashboard.aspx), although great efforts have been made recently to change this situation.

On the whole, the experiences of the five national cases here discussed would seem to be quite similar to that of other governments which have been discussed in the broader (albeit limited) literature on policy analytical capacity (Aucoin & Bakvis, 2005; Parrado, 2014). Both analytical capacity limitations within government structures and the search for alternative sources of policy advice have been present in other nations, such as the United Kingdom and New Zealand, where NPM reforms have been implemented during the past decades. Broader issues related to how to build analytical capacity, where to look for analytical capacity regarding specific policy topics, and how to strengthen the links between analytical capacity and evidence-based policymaking (Howlett, 2009; Head, 2015)—or with state effectiveness more broadly—can be found in almost any region of the world (Page & Wright, 2007; Hertie School of Governance, 2014; CAF, 2015).

Conclusions

This chapter focuses on the study of governmental policy analytical capacity. Evidence-based policy analysis has limits and constitutes only one ingredient of overall state capacity. However, there is no doubt that it is an important component of the information needed to solve public problems in more efficient ways. Despite the fact that the literature on governmental policy analysis is still somewhat underdeveloped, a number of studies exist. Many of them use a supply-demand perspective, which involves risks but offers a good first way to approach the study of this subject. Thus, we presented in this chapter a demand-supply matrix as a heuristic tool for the identification of some basic reference points for the comparative study of governmental policy analysis across nations.

In comparative terms, the five country cases provide empirical illustrations of the topic. As they involve only limited evidence, no strong generalizations can be made. Moreover, even while addressing the same topic, authors still have slightly different conceptualizations and different perspectives. In fact, as Howlett has suggested, the policy analytical capacity of governments (and other actors) still is 'an important and largely unanswered empirical question' (2009, p. 163; see also Parrado, 2014). The several texts already produced within the International Library of Policy Analysis (plus other ones) provide a general understanding of the subject across nations. However, more comparative analyses—especially those that start from a common framework—are needed in order to improve such understanding.

Notes

1 If we follow some cross-national comparisons of policy capacity levels (Polidano, 2000), we could also include Chile in this group. The inclusion of specific world zones in these categories is partially based on Norris (2012), who classified countries according to both bureaucratic and democratic development levels.
2 http://press.uchicago.edu/ucp/books/series/POL-ILPA.html

References

Aberbach, J. D. and Rockman, B. A. (1989), On the rise, transformation, and the decline of analysis in the US government, *Governance*, 2 (3).
Aucoin, P. and Bakvis, H. (2005), Public service reform and policy capacity: Recruiting and retaining the best and the brightest, in M. Painter and J. Pierre (eds), *Challenges to state policy capacity, Global trends and comparative perspectives*. London: Palgrave Macmillan.
Bakvis, H. (2000), Rebuilding policy capacity in the era of the fiscal dividend: A report from Canada, *Governance*, 13 (1), 71–103.
Barker, A and B. G. Peters (eds) (1993), *The politics of expert advice: Creating, using and manipulating scientific knowledge for public policy*. University of Pittsburgh Press.
Behn, R. D. (1986), Policy analysis and policy politics, *Policy Analysis*, 7 (2).
Boston, J., Martin, J., Pallot, J. and Walsh, P. (1996), *Public management: The New Zealand model*. Auckland, New Zealand: Oxford University Press.
Bushnell, P. (1991), Policy advice: Planning for performance, *Public sector*, 14 (1).
CAF (2015), *Un Estado más efectivo*. Bogota: Corporación Andina de Fomento.

Cobb, R. W. and Elder, C. D. (1971), The politics of agenda-building: An alternative perspective for modern democratic theory, *The Journal of Politics*, 33(4), 892–915.

Craft, J. and Howlett, M. (2012), Policy formulation, governance shifts and policy influence: Location and content in policy advisory systems, *Journal of Public Policy*, 32 (2).

De Mesquita, B. B., Morrow, J. D., Siverson, R. M. and Smith, A. (1999), Policy failure and political survival: The contribution of political institutions, *Journal of Conflict Resolution*, 43(2), 147–161.

Evans, P. (1995), *Embedded autonomy: States and industrial transformation*. Princeton University Press.

Fleischer, J. (2009), Power resources of parliamentary executives: Policy advice in the UK and Germany, *West European Politics*, 32 (1).

Gill, J. I. and Saunders, L. (1992), Toward a definition of policy analysis, *New Directions for Institutional Research*, 76.

Gregory, R. and Lonti, Z. (2008), Chasing shadows? Performance measurement of policy advice in New Zealand government departments, *Public Administration*, 86 (3).

Halligan, J. (1995), Policy advice and the public sector, in B. Guy Peters and D. T. Savoie (eds), *Governance in a changing environment*. Montreal, Canada: McGill-Queen's University Press.

Hawke, G. R. (1993), *Improving policy advice*. Wellington, New Zealand: Victoria University Institute of Policy Studies.

Head, B. (2008), Three lenses of evidence-based policy, *The Australian Journal of Public Administration*, 67 (1).

Head, B. (2015), Policy Analysis and public sector capacity, in Brian Head and Kate Crowley (eds), *Policy analysis in Australia*. Bristol, UK: Policy Press.

Hendrix, C. S. (2010). Measuring state capacity: Theoretical and empirical implications for the study of civil conflict, *Journal of Peace Research*, 47 (3).

Hernandez-Galicia, J. F. and D. Arellano-Gault, (2017), Policy analysis and bureaucratic capacity in the federal government, in J. L. Mendez and M. I. Dussauge-Laguna (eds), *Policy analysis in Mexico*. Bristol, UK: The Policy Press.

Hertie School of Governance (2014), *The Governance Report 2014*. Oxford University Press.

Hird, J. A. (2005), Policy analysis for what? The effectiveness of nonpartisan policy research organizations, *Policy Studies*, 22 (1).

Hoppe, R. and Jeliazkova, M. (2006), How policy workers define their job: A Netherlands case study, in H. K. Colebatch (ed.), *The work of policy: An international survey*. New York, Rowman & Littlefield.

Howlett, M. (2009), Policy analytical capacity and evidence-based policy-making: Lessons from Canada. *Canadian Public Administration*, 52 (2).

Howlett, M. (2011), *Designing public policies: Principles and instruments*. New York: Routledge.

Howlett, M. (2015), Policy analytical capacity: The supply and demand for policy analysis in government, *Policy and Society*, 34 (3).

Howlett, M. and Ramesh, M. (2015), Achilles' heels of governance: Critical capacity deficits and their role in governance failures, *Regulation & Governance*, 26 May.

Howlett, M., Ramesh, M., and Perl, A. (2009), *Studying public policy: Policy cycles and policy subsystems*. Oxford University Press.

Jackson, P. M. (2007), Making sense of policy advice, *Public Money and Management*, 21 (4).

Laswell, H. D. (1951), The policy orientation, in Lerner, D. and Laswell, H. D. (eds), *The policy sciences*. Stanford University Press.

Levitsky, Steven and Way, Lucan (2010), *Competitive Authoritarianism: Hybrid Regimes after the Cold War*. New York: Cambridge University Press.

Linder, S. and Peters, G. (1984), From social theory to policy design, *Journal of Public Policy*, 4 (3).

Majone, G. (1989), *Evidence, argument, and persuasion in the policy process*. New Haven, CT: Yale University Press.

Malloy, J. (1989), Policy analysts, public policy and regime structure in Latin America, *Governance*, 2 (3), 315–338.

Mann, M. (1984), The autonomous power of the state: Its origins, mechanisms and results, *European Journal of Sociology*, 25 (2), 185–213.

Mayer, B. van Daalen C. E. and Bots, P. W. G. (2004), Perspectives on policy analyses: A framework for understanding and design, *International Journal of Technology Policy and Management*, 4.2 (169).

Meltsner, A. J. (1976), *Policy analysis in the bureaucracy*. Berkeley: University of California Press.

Mendez, J. L. (2017), Evolution of policy analysis as a field of studies in Mexico, in J. L. Mendez and M. I. Dussauge-Laguna (eds), *Policy analysis in Mexico*. Bristol, UK: Policy Press.

Nelson, R. H. (1989), The office of policy analysis in the department of the interior, *Journal of Policy Analysis and Management*, 8 (3).

Neylan, J. (2008), Social policy and the authority of evidence, *Australian Journal of Public Administration*, 67 (1).

Norris, P. (2012), *Making democratic governance work: The impact of regimes on prosperity, welfare, and peace*. Cambridge University Press.

Nutley, S. M., Walter, I. and Davies, H. T. O. (2007), *Using evidence: How research can inform public services*. Bristol, UK: Policy Press.

Packwood, A. (2002), Evidence-based policy: Rhetoric and reality, *Social Policy and Society*, 1 (3).

Page, E. C. and Jenkins, B. (2005), *Policy bureaucracy: Governing with a cast of thousands*. Oxford University Press.

Page, E. C. and Wright, V. (2007), *From the active to the enabling state*, Basingstoke, UK: Palgrave.

Painter, M. and Pierre, J. (eds.) (2005), *Challenges to state policy capacity: Global trends and comparative perspectives*. London: Palgrave Macmillan.

Parrado, S. (2014), Analytical capacity, in M. Lodge and K. Wegrich (eds), *The problem-solving capacity of the modern state*. Oxford University Press.

Pawson, R. (2006), *Evidence-based policy: A realist perspective*. London: Sage.

Peters, B. G. (1996), *The policy capacity of government*. Ottawa: Canadian Centre for Management Development.

Polidano, C. (2000), Measuring public sector capacity, *World Development*, 28 (5).

Pressman, J. L. and Wildavsky, A. B. (1973), *Implementation: How great expectations in Washington are dashed in Oakland*. Berkeley: University of California Press.

Radin, B. A. (2000), *Beyond Machiavelli: Policy analysis comes of age*. Washington, DC: Georgetown University Press.

Riddell, N. (1998), *Policy research capacity in the federal government*. Ottawa, Canada: Policy Research Initiative.

Rochet, C. (2004), Rethinking the management of information in the strategic monitoring of public policies by agencies, *Industrial Management and Data Systems*, 104 (3).

Rueschemeyer, D., Huber Stephens, E. and Stephens, J. D. (1992), *Capitalist development and democracy*. Chicago University Press.

Schmid, J. and D. Buhr (2013), Federal government: In-house capacities—Life within the 'apparatus', in S. Blum and K. Schubert (eds), *Policy Analysis in Germany*. Bristol, UK: Policy Press.

Sidney, M. S. (2007), Policy formulation: Design and tools, in G. J. Fischer and M. S. Sidney (eds), *Handbook of public policy analysis: Theory, politics and methods*. New Brunswick, NJ: Taylor & Francis.

Souza, C. (2013), Modernisation of the state and bureaucratic capacity-building in the Brazilian Federal Government, in J. Vaitsman, J. Mendes and L. Lobato (eds), *Policy analysis in Brazil*. Bristol, UK: Policy Press.

Stone, D. (2002), *Policy paradox: The art of political decision making*. New York, WW Norton.

Tenbensel, T. (2004), Does more evidence lead to better policy? The implications of explicit priority setting in New Zealand's health policy for evidence-based policy, *Policy Studies*, 25 (3).

Thissen, W. A. H. and Twaalfhoven, P. G. J. (2001), Toward a conceptual structure for evaluating policy analytic activities, *European Journal of Operational Research*, 129.

Thompson, P. R. and Yessian, M. R. (1992), Policy analysis in the Office of Inspector General, U.S. Department of Health and Human Services, in C. Weiss (ed.) *Organizations for policy analysis: Helping government think*. London, Sage.

Vining, A. R. and Boardman, A. C. (2007), The choice of formal policy analysis methods in Canada, in L. Dobuzinskis, M. Howlett and D. Laycock (eds), *Policy analysis in Canada: The state of the art*. University of Toronto Press.

Wagner, P. and Wollmann, H. (1986), Social scientists in policy research and consulting: Some cross-national comparisons, *International Social Science Journal*, 38 (4): 99–135.

Weible, C. M. (2008), Expert-based information and policy subsystems: A review and synthesis, *Policy Studies Journal*, 36 (4).

Weller, P. and Stevens, B. (1998), Evaluating policy advice: The Australian experience, *Public Administration*, 76.

Weimer, D. (2015), La evolución del análisis de políticas en Estados Unidos: Cuatro fuentes de demanda, *Foro Internacional*, XV (3).

Wildavsky, A. B. (1979), *Speaking truth to power: The art and craft of policy analysis*. Boston, Little, Brown.

Wollmann, H. (1989), Policy analysis in West Germany's federal government: A case of unfinished governmental and administrative modernization? *Governance*, 2 (3).

Wu, X., Ramesh, M. and Howlett, M. (2015), Policy capacity: A conceptual framework for understanding policy competences and capabilities, *Policy and Society*, 34 (3–4).

6

REFLECTIONS ON A HALF CENTURY OF POLICY ANALYSIS

Beryl A. Radin

The field of policy analysis that exists in the 21st century is quite different from that found in the field's earlier phases (Radin, 2000; Radin, 2013a). The world of the 1960s that gave rise to this field in the US often seems unrelated to the world we experience today. These shifts have occurred as a result of a range of developments—technological changes, changes in the structure and processes of government both internally and globally, new expectations about accountability and transparency, economic and fiscal problems, and increased political and ideological conflict. Increasingly, policy observers have been using the phrase 'wicked problem' to describe problems that are difficult or impossible to solve.[1] At the same time that these developments require shifts in the way that the field operates, however, many of the expectations from the past continue and persist (Radin, 2013b; Radin, 2013a). Indeed, it is not unusual to find reading lists in the field continuing some of the earlier literature such as the technical approach of Stokey and Zeckhauser's book in 1978, Arnold Meltsner's path-breaking study of working policy analysts in 1976, the multiple editions of Weimer and Vining's textbook, first published in 1989, and Harold Lasswell's vision of policy sciences in 1971.

This chapter provides an overview of recent developments in the policy analysis field around the world, drawing on studies in a number of countries.[2] It illustrates both the unique aspect of the field in different countries as well as a number of issues and concerns facing both academics and practitioners within very different cultures, structures and experiences. In addition, it illustrates the impact of globalization on the practice and education of policy analysts in the US. It discusses the shifts that have occurred in the definition of clients as well the ways that clients and analysts interact with one another. It contrasts the development of the field in parliamentary systems with shared power systems (as in the US). It also comments on the relationship between analysis and politics. Policy analysis today exists in a highly volatile environment and the field itself has been defined and evaluated in terms of these pressures.

The comparative dimensions of policy analysis have been acknowledged in the second decade of the 21st century through the publication of a set of books issued as a part of the *International Library of Policy Analysis* published by Policy Press. While published as stand-alone volumes, these works provide the basis for an analysis of several themes. This chapter deals with five of these themes that emerge from three different eras in the development of policy analysis (Radin, 2013a). First, and perhaps most important, is attention to the context in which policy analysis takes place. This involves both the structure and culture of the political system as well as the political shifts that have occurred during the past half century. Second is the acknowledgement that policy analysis is not a function that is easily institutionalized and, as a result, changes over time. Third is the tension between the academic institutions involved in the teaching and training of policy analysis and the practitioner community that actually performs policy analysis. Fourth is the variety of links between policy analysis and existing efforts (such as management reform, fiscal analysis and legal analysis) that take place in the bureaucratic setting. And fifth is the variety of players engaged in something described as policy analysis, such as career public servants, short-term staffers, think tanks, consultants, legislative actors and interest groups.

Policy Analysis Beyond the US

Until *circa* 2000, the literature on policy analysis was focused almost entirely on the experience within the US. The exception to this was found in Great Britain in a 1984 book authored by Brian Hogwood and Lewis Gunn, *Policy Analysis for the Real World*. The preface to that book was prescient and signalled a set of concerns that developed in later years.

> The problem of generating suitable and readily available teaching material for British courses has not yet been overcome. Although our primary interest was in producing policy analysis materials for British students, our experience has made us aware of the limitations of much American literature for *American* students, particularly those who have previously thought of policy analysis as merely American politics rehashed, or as arcane mathematical techniques.
>
> [. . .]
>
> Much of the literature about particular techniques concentrates on technical points and assumes that the 'optimal' decision will automatically be taken and enforced by a single, authoritative decision-maker. This literature fails to discuss the use and limits of policy analysis techniques in real-world political settings.
>
> *Hogwood & Gunn, 1984, pp. v–vi*

By the first decade of the 21st century, the concerns expressed by Hogwood and Gunn were addressed by a range of scholars around the world. The introduction of these issues produced a literature that indicated that the field was rich and varied and, in particular, attentive to the context of the systems in which policy analysis took place. The creation of the *Journal of Comparative Policy Analysis: Research and Practice* was evidence of this interest. It defined its mission as follows:

> The Journal aims to stimulate the further intellectual development of comparative policy studies and the growth of an international community of scholars in the field. It gives priority to comparative studies adhering to the following criteria:
>
> 1. Contribute to comparative theory development;
> 2. Present theory-based empirical research;
> 3. Offer comparative evaluations of research methods;
> 4. Derive the practice implications of theory-based research;
> 5. Use conceptual heuristics to interpret practice;
> 6. Draw lessons based on circumstances in which compared policy related issues have in common certain manipulable policy, program or institutional variables.[3]

Evidence of a global perspective on policy analysis was found in the programmes of a variety of professional meetings (for example, creation of the International Public Policy Association, an offshoot of the International Political Science Association) and in the publication of a number of textbooks and edited volumes from around the world. The following are examples of publications dealing with policy analysis in a number of countries: H. K. Colebatch, *The Work of Policy: An International Survey* (with contributions from the Netherlands, Japan, Croatia, South Korea, New Zealand and Finland); Claudia Scott and Karen Baehler, *Adding Value to Policy Analysis and Advice* (a book written with the support of the ANZSOG, the Australia and New Zealand School of Government); Iris Geva-May, *Thinking Like a Policy Analyst: Policy Analysis as a Clinical Profession*; and Michael Howlett, *Designing Public Policies: Principles and Instruments* (highlighting Canada). Other books could be added to this list.

These and other approaches suggest that there are many ways to sort out developments in the field. One can easily list the range of these developments. They include types of policy issues, the diverse relationships between analysts and clients, the types of analysis required, its time frame, the stage of the policy process where it occurs, where in the system it occurs (e.g. whether it takes place inside government or outside government), the impact of the structure of the government involved, the placement of analysis in central agencies vs. programme agencies, whether analysts and clients are career or political actors, the appropriate skill set found in analysts, and the boundaries between policy analysis and management.

Development of Policy Analysis in a Global Context: Contrasts and Similarities

It is difficult to characterize the patterns that have emerged as a result of the globalization of the policy analysis field. Some countries have actually renamed existing data and planning offices and cast them as policy analysis organizations. In other countries, career staff (usually generalists) who traditionally acted as advisors to the party in power have become the core of the policy analysis enterprise. The demise of the Soviet Union provided the impetus in some nations for an organizational unit that could provide advice on alternatives to previous approaches. In still other settings, policy analysis units have been established within autocratic governments to provide at least a façade of openness and a move toward democracy.

The expansion of the field across both the Atlantic and Pacific oceans provided American policy analysis scholars with a modified view of the field. David Weimer characterized the results of this experience:

> First, the relative importance of different goals, if not the goals themselves, will differ across regimes and societies. Most obviously, different countries are likely to have different constitutional constraints that must be satisfied in routine policy making. Additionally, analysts working in different countries may argue for different tradeoffs among goals because of differences in the societies they are trying to make better. For example, analysts seeking to reflect social values in a materially wealthier society may place greater weight on environmental quality relative to economic growth than their counterparts in poorer societies. These weights must ultimately be related to the values of the people in the society.
>
> Second, the sets of plausible policy alternatives are likely to differ across countries as well. The differences may result from anticipation of goals or tradeoffs among them. It may also be a consequence of certain types of generic policy alternatives not being commonly used in a particular country. Of course, an analyst may wish to present an unusual but potentially desirable alternative that will not be immediately

politically feasible in the hope of making it more feasible in the future. Yet, as it is the policies actually adopted and implemented that will have the most immediate consequences for society, understanding the particular political environment is essential.

Weimer, 2012, p. 4

Variation in policy analysis approaches can be attributed to the structure of government (e.g. whether it is a centralized or federal system) or to the historic demands of ending colonialism, achieving democracy or responding to the end of the Soviet Union.

But if anyone had been pushed to come up with comparisons, they would likely have emphasized the differences in the political structure between a parliamentary system (where the executive branch is viewed as a part of the legislative branch) and the institutional design found in the US (where power is shared between the legislative, executive and judicial systems). It appears that a number of important attributes found in the early stages of policy analysis in the US have parallels to the practice of policy advising.[4]

The classic view of policy advising in a Westminster system is based on working relationships between departmental policy advisors, ministers and members of parliament. These relationships are defined by government guidelines and are viewed as a part of decision-making process involving ministers and cabinet officials. The parliamentary system intertwines the legislative and executive branches to make it clear that this combination produces 'government' policy.

Although the US system involves a more complex decision-making process emerging from the shared powers between the legislative, executive and judicial branches, the early stages of policy analysis in the US focused only on decision making within the executive branch at the federal government level. There was little indication that the original policy analysts were concerned about competing views that would emerge from the Congress or from organizations outside of government.[5] This has changed in more recent years as the development of networks as a decision-making form has further complicated the situation.

The policy advisor in a Westminster system is expected to provide full and accurate information to an elected official who is a part of government. These elected officials are the individuals who are accountable to the electorate through the parliament and the ballot box. Advisors are career public servants who are assumed to provide full and accurate information to the parliament about the factual and technical background of policies and their administration. The concept of 'ministerial responsibility' defines this relationship.

Similarly, the early US policy analysts were also expected to provide full and accurate information to a political appointee involved in the decision-making process. Crucial to the original design of the profession was the relationship between an analyst and a client inside of government. Clients were usually cabinet officials or other high-level political figures (such as those in the White House). This model was later modified with the proliferation of policy analysis units both inside and outside of government.

In a parliamentary system, the relationship between individual policy advisors and their clients is viewed as confidential and the advice that is given during the advising process is not open to public scrutiny. Advisors are expected to remain personally anonymous and particular views should not be ascribed to individual analysts. Given this set of expectations, the presence of competing advice is not acknowledged.

The original policy analysts in the US federal system also emphasized the confidential relationship between themselves and decision makers. Even if they produced policy alternative memos with recommendations, those documents were not accessible to the public.[6] In addition, these analysts were usually the only individuals in the agency or department who were thought to possess analytical capacity and thus there was not competing advice from other parts of the institution.

Because the policy advisor in a parliamentary system usually deals with issues from the perspective of top officials, the advisor's main role is to influence specific actions related to the political, economic and social agenda of the government of the day. Thus the advisor highlights the outcomes of policy change and the strategies and resources required to achieve these outcomes. Details about putting the policy into operation or changing the details of implementing existing policies are not a part of the agenda of the top officials.

Performing Policy Analysis

Early policy analysts in the US also did not focus on the details of policy implementation. Indeed, Yehezkel Dror specifically defined the role as avoiding administrative reforms, implementation management, and other organizational matters. He wrote: 'To move into such items cannot but ruin the essence of policy analysis as focusing on policy-making' (Dror, 1984, p. 107). Rather, policy analysis was limited to the crafting of new policies and programmes. In some cases, the policy analyst provided a way for a cabinet official to conceptualize the department as a whole and provide a sense of how various pieces in the department fit together.

Policy advisors in a parliamentary system are usually experienced officials within the career public service. They are expected to be politically neutral and able to serve any government, regardless of its political complexion, with an equal degree of loyalty and efficiency. For the most part, these advisors are valued for their ability to meet standards of rigour, honesty, relevance and timeliness. In most cases, they are trained as administrative generalists rather than programme or policy specialists.

Here, some differences with the US are evident. The US policy analysts who were found in the federal government in the early years of the profession were expected to come from academia or think tanks and have sophisticated training in analytical skills (often with PhDs in economics or operations research). They were not expected to be career public servants but rather individuals who would stay in government for relatively short periods and then move out—perhaps as a result of changes in the political structure. While the individuals were highly qualified professionals in terms of their analytical abilities, they were generalists in terms of programme or policy. Some of the analysts had links to political officials, but this was rare. This pattern changed in the second generation of developments in the field.

Because policy analysis in parliamentary systems is so clearly integrated into the career public service system, the process involves individual advisors dealing with individual clients. With a few exceptions, the advising process has not featured separate organizational structures that collectively present advice. At the same time, policy advisors seek information from others within and outside government. And when advisors deal with central agencies, they have to develop relationships with others in programme areas.

From the earliest days, policy analysts in the US were organized into organizational units that had significant autonomy in their operations. Often called 'policy shops', these units began as relatively small units ranging between 10 and 30 people. With the exception of the individual who ran the office (and was usually a political appointee), the focus of the activity was on the policy shop itself rather than the individual analysts within it. These policy shops were expected to reach out to others in the policy research infrastructure (such as think tanks, consultants, brain trusts, ad hoc study groups, university institutes and institutions for advanced study), assisting the other offices in data collection and problem analysis but focusing on decisions to be made inside the department.

The parliamentary system advisor is expected to provide policy advice in the context of the specific issue being discussed. Policy advising thus is not formalized as a specialized activity but includes people with a detailed knowledge of technical, legal and administrative aspects of policy issues. At the same time, staff in parliamentary systems typically have a generalist training and background. In addition, advisors are expected to have a clear understanding of the constraints on the effective implementation of policies.

The early policy analysts in the US emphasized the use of formal analytic techniques. These techniques began with the Planning, Programming, and Budgeting System (PPBS), which relied on operations research and some economic analytic approaches, and soon moved to formalized processes related to cost-benefit analysis. Arnold Meltsner described the first generation of analysts as employing both technical and political skills; the analysis approach they selected depended on the preferences of the analyst's client (Meltsner, 1976).

The policy advisor in the parliamentary system is expected to move through several steps in the process of policy analysis. This includes the following:

- Taking a difficult and sometimes poorly understood problem or issue and structuring it so that it can be thought about in a systematic way;
- Gathering the minimum necessary information and applying the appropriate analytical methods;
- Formulating effective options addressing, where necessary, mechanisms for implementation, monitoring and evaluation; and
- Communicating the results of the work to government in a timely and understandable way.[7]

Advisors are not always expected to make a recommendation for the decision maker. However, they are expected to reach a professional judgement about the underlying situation and appropriate possible courses for policy.

By the end of the first decade of policy analysis in the US, the policy analysis process was explicated and formalized. Some of this occurred as a result of the appearance of policy analysis graduate programmes and the growing professionalization of the field. A logic model emerged that defined the analytic process, which tended to follow these steps (Bardach, 2011):

- Define the problem
- Assemble some evidence
- Construct the alternatives
- Select the criteria
- Project the outcomes
- Confront the trade-offs
- Decide
- Tell the story

Dealing with Clients

A parliamentary system allows for coherent policy development across the government. As such, the actors who become the clients for policy advisors include both cabinet-level officials as well as officials found in central agencies (such as prime minister's offices or other government-wide units). Because the executive branch is a part of the legislative branch, decisions that are made by these actors become the formal policy of the system. With a few exceptions (such as times when the upper chamber of the legislature is controlled by different parties than the lower chamber), there is no need to negotiate a policy once it is decided.

The policy analysts operating during the early stages of the profession in the US federal government did not always have clients who had the final authority to determine policy. The policies recommended by the executive branch often had a strong influence over the final determinations worked out between the executive and legislative branches. Unlike in a Westminster system, however, these clients did not have the authority to create new programmes or establish new policies without agreement by the Congress (or, in some cases, by the judiciary).

The US experience not only challenged the assumptions of the parliamentary system but also brought the experience of federalism to the surface. This has turned out to be an issue in other countries that have their own version of federalism. While Australia is characterized as a variation on the Westminster system, it also is a federal structure that provides some level of autonomy and authority to its states (Head & Crowley, 2015, chapter 4). Similarly, policy analysis in Germany takes place in a federal system that provides its decentralized units (the *Länder*) with authority in some important areas (Blum & Schubert, 2013). The Brazilian political structure is also formally a federal system but its development has probably been more affected by its effort to recover from the period between 1964 and 1985 when it was under military control (Vaitsman, Ribeiro & Lobato, 2013, chapter 4).

Efforts at democratization following World War II were a part of the context and environment of the development of policy analysis efforts in Japan and Germany and also experienced by Germany with the reunification of the East and West areas (Adachi, Hosono & Lio, 2015, chapter 1).[8]

Moving Outside of Top Government

In the early days of the policy analysis field, there was significant similarity between the approach taken by the US and by parliamentary systems, since both focused on decisions made inside government. Today, however, policy analysis in the US has moved far beyond government. It is found in all nodes of the policy system: it occurs inside of government as well as in interest groups, non-governmental organizations, and state and local agencies. These groups often approach the policy role with a specific policy agenda in place. In addition, decision making within network systems further complicates the relationship between the analysts and the clients.

Some of these developments have occurred as the policy system itself has emphasized the role of third parties through grants and contracts. Indeed, the growth of these third-party actors has resulted in a situation where the most visible analysts are found not inside government but outside of it. In many parliamentary systems, however, this development has either not occurred or, if outside groups are present, they are not the major actors in the ever-changing policy-advising enterprise. In Australia, for example, career public servants no longer enjoy a monopoly on policy advice as public funds have been allocated to think tanks and government-funded advocacy centres. As a result, some of the similarities between the systems that existed in the early years of policy analysis have diminished.

The shifts that have taken place in the US in the field have changed this category of similarities. Government clients are no longer just top agency officials. As policy analysts and policy analysis offices have proliferated throughout the nooks and crannies of government agencies, the offices found at the top reaches of the departments or agencies no longer have a monopoly on the production of analysis. As a result, analysts attached to these offices now have to negotiate with analysts in other parts of the department. In some cases, ideology—not information—has become the currency of policy debate. In addition, clients have moved from individual officials to collective bodies or even institutional processes within the agency.

Similar developments have occurred in the parliamentary system of Australia, with the introduction of the concept of 'contestability'. Contestability is a belief by governments that policy advice is best when it emerges through a contestable market. In other countries the structure of staff includes a proliferation of policy advisors throughout the system.

Concern about transparency and open access has increased in both settings over the years. In the US, the enactment of the Freedom of Information Act (and its subsequent amendments) shifted at least part of the burden of proof away from the citizen (to establish the right of access to information) to the agency (to show why the information should not be made accessible). The Obama administration has emphasized transparency and made it a formal goal. Agencies are able to restrict access to information if they can show that a document in question is still in draft stage or is part of an ongoing decision-making process. There have been claims that this has led analysts to avoid putting information and options on paper. At the same time, documents and information are easier than ever to access online. While parliamentary systems have increased transparency, they still continue to emphasize the confidential relationship between the policy advisor and the individual official.

During the early stages of the US policy analysis profession, analysts saw their role as primarily focused on the formulation stage of the policy process. During that period they were operating in a context in which new policies and programmes were being developed. The analysts were important actors in an environment characterized by a strong belief in progress, abundance and the possibilities of public-sector change, and high regard for analytical expertise. As the field developed and the mood of the society shifted during the Vietnam era, the analyst's agenda focused less on new programmes and policies and more on changes that might be made in existing efforts. In addition, both policymakers and analysts became more aware of implementation problems with the new programmes and sought to understand the reasons that these problems emerged. Now, in both systems, fiscal realities have led to an emphasis on the budgetary consequences of implementation decisions.

Expanding the Focus

With these developments, analysis can take place at all of the stages of the policy process. Analysis plays a role in bringing policy issues to the policy agenda, in formulating policy details, in ascertaining the details of implementation, and in evaluating policies. In some instances, analysts associated with particular policies or programmes have personally moved from an analytic role to an implementation role and become involved in managing a programme. The increasing focus on implementation has led to a blurring of boundaries between management and policy development, and has also been supported by the contemporary interest in performance management, which sometimes links evaluation activities to performance assessment.

Performance management activities have also been emphasized in some Westminster systems. In addition, the role of central government agencies has provided the setting for what are called 'whole of government' responses, emphasizing coordination across policy, programme and service delivery lines (Management Advisory Committee, 2004). In Australia, for example, policy advisors often have dual responsibilities for policy advice and for programme implementation, which includes the oversight task of dealing with contractors who compete for the rights to deliver services.

By the late 1970s, it became clear that policy analysts in the US system had moved from short-term or 'in-and-outer' career paths to become careerists. With the exception of the top staff, who were political appointees, and some movement between government positions, congressional staff positions, and interest groups or think tanks, most of the analytic staff were permanent career civil servants.

Although there were some attempts in Westminster systems to bring in individuals from the outside to serve as policy advisors, the classic career path continues to predominate in most settings. In Australia, however, large numbers of ministerial advisors have been brought in who are not public servants as such but are public employees employed without pretence to traditional standards of impartiality and merit. As such, they are similar to the political appointees in the US system.

The early US policy analysts were recruited for their expertise in analytical methods, not for their knowledge of specific policy substance. As staff assumed career status they tended to focus on specific policy and programme areas. This new trend solidified, and staff were increasingly recruited for their knowledge of those areas. Career movement usually involved different positions (sometimes outside of the executive branch) involving that policy field. In contrast, most Westminster systems are based on career staff who are viewed as administrative generalists, not as policy specialists—although there are indications that this may be changing in some countries.

The image of the policy analyst as a quasi-academic staffer whose product is a set of written documents no longer describes many practising US policy analysts. However, there are still those who fit the original model of the profession. An increasing number of analysts make their contribution to the process through meetings and other forms of more informal interaction. In some settings, the stylized approach to analysis, leading to formal recommendations, has been replaced by interactions in which the analyst is one of many participants in policy discussions. In addition, there is a sense of urgency about decisions, a blurring of lines between managers and analysts, and a blurring of the differences between analysts and more traditional academic researchers. In the past, information was largely controlled by the analysts; now information is much more available and accessible on the internet.

The proliferation of policy analysis both inside and outside of government has supported an approach to information and data that moves far beyond a positivist orientation. As Carol Weiss has described it, it is difficult to think about information without also acknowledging interests and ideology (Weiss, 1983). Majone's view about information as evidence for policy positions also seems to describe the current situation (Majone, 1989). Policy advisors in a Westminster system rarely wrap themselves in a positivist framework but always frame their approach around their clients. For example, a report by the Australian Auditor-General's office describes information gathering in a way that emphasizes flexibility, quality and transparency (Australian Auditor-General, 2001). In addition, information available on the internet often crosses national boundaries.

Parliamentary systems have also experienced changes that have modified the practice of policy advising. Several patterns are worth emphasizing. First, the coalition governments in some Westminster systems have made it more difficult to establish firm control by one party over government policy (for example, as has occurred in New Zealand). Second, some of the New Public Management approaches have led to changes in the role of central agencies as well as a focus on outcomes and performance assessment, which have resulted in the growth of third-party contracts. Third, there is some movement in the development of analytic groups on the outside of government. Fourth, the basic parliamentary structure allows these systems to work toward a coordinated, 'whole of government' approach that is extremely difficult to achieve within the US system. And fifth, the academic field of policy analysis seems to be further developing in a number of countries.

The policy analysis institutions of the early 1960s shared many of the problems and characteristics of those who practised the ancient art of providing advice to decision makers. Although the functions were similar, something new *had* occurred (Radin, 2013a). What had been a relatively informal set of relationships and behaviours in the past had moved into a formalized, institutionalized world. Although the process began with responsibility for the PPBS process, it became obvious very quickly that the policy analysis task moved beyond a single analytic technique. Other management or budgetary requirements had been imposed in the past, but none seem to have had the breadth of possibility and impact of requirements that stemmed from the initial PPBS activity.[9] Much still depended on personal relationships between the analyst/advisor and the decision maker/ruler, but these organizations took their place in public, open, and legally constituted organizations. As a result, a new field or profession was emerging. Many of the policy analysis activities inside the federal government continued to be closely linked to budget-related decisions.

The new policy analysis field was conceptualized as integral to the formulation stage of the policy process—the stage of the process where analysts would explore alternative approaches to 'solve' a policy problem that had gained the attention of decision makers and had reached the policy agenda. Both decision makers and analysts saw this early stage could be separated from other aspects of policymaking. It did not focus on the imperatives of adopting the preferred alternative (particularly in the legislative branch) or on the details of implementing an enacted policy inside an administrative agency on a day-to-day basis (except as a demonstration experiment). Instead, it focused on the collection of as much information and data as possible to help decision makers address the substantive aspects of the problem at hand.

Development of the Academic Home for Policy Analysis

Less than two years after the diffusion of PPBS throughout the federal government, Yehezkel Dror sounded a clarion call that defined a new profession in what has become a classic article in *Public Administration Review*. Published in September 1967, Dror's 'Policy Analysts: A New Professional Role in Government Service' sought to differentiate policy analysis from systems analysis. He called upon his colleagues to 'develop institutional arrangements, professional training, and job definitions which will provide the desired outputs with good and hopefully very good, but not necessarily outstanding, personnel' (p. 198).

Dror argued for 'a more advanced type of professional knowledge, which can be used with significant benefits for the improvement of public decision making . . . The term *policy analysis* seems to be suitable for the proposed professional discipline, as it combines affinity with systems analysis with the concept of policy in the broad and political sense' (pp. 199–200). He outlined the characteristics of policy analysts as government staff officers—what he described as 'an important new professional role in government service' (p. 201). He called for the establishment of these offices in all government agencies, as close to the senior policy positions as possible.

Dror did not expect policy analysis institutions to focus on the details of policy implementation. Indeed, he believed that policy analysts should not deal with administrative reforms, implementation management, and similar detailed organizational matters: 'To move into such items cannot but ruin the essence of policy analysis as focusing on policy-making' (Dror, 1984, p. 107).

By the early 1970s, the field began to assume both visibility and self-definition. Through support from private foundations, between 1967 and 1970, graduate programmes in public policy were introduced at Harvard, the University of California at Berkeley (Wildavsky, 1997, pp. 275–278), Carnegie-Mellon, the RAND Graduate Institute, the University of Michigan, the University of Pennsylvania, the University of Minnesota, and the University of Texas at Austin (Heineman, Bluhm, Peterson & Kearny, 1990). Almost all of these programmes were at the master's level, focused on training professionals to enter the policy analysis field. As time went on, some policy analysis programmes were established in schools of public administration or in departments of political science.

In the US, perhaps the most dramatic set of changes dealing with globalization of the field has taken place in the classroom. Master of Public Policy programmes in the US increasingly include students from a range of other countries. It has been a challenge for faculty to develop curricula that meet the diversity of interests and needs of this group of students and, at the same time, provide core courses for American students. Some programmes offer separate experiences for international students while others have tried to deal with both sets of students together. There are also American programmes that are structured to simply place international students in the structure and curriculum that had been developed for the US academic market. The combined approach not only provides training in policy analysis for international students but also gives American students some exposure to different political, economic and social settings if the international students are encouraged to contrast their experience with that of their American colleagues. Given the globalization of many policy issues that had traditionally been treated as domestic problems (e.g. environment, health), some advocates of the combined approach believe that this is an effective way to expose American students to global dimensions on various issues.

In many ways, the academic approach to the field has not responded to changes in the world of practice, including the increasing blurring of the boundaries between policy analysis and management and the increased secrecy surrounding policy implementation experiences by state and local governments and private organizations. Perhaps most importantly, these developments have contributed to a significant modification in the skills that are viewed as essential for individuals entering the field.

The gulf between academia and the practitioner world exists in many countries as a result of historical academic styles and preferences embodied in both teaching and research organizations. It has become more and more difficult to assess the impact of policy analysis and policy research activities on decision making, and to defend policy analysis as a function of neutral social science. The original concept of the policy analysis client of the policy was an individual who has authority and is usually located at the top rungs of a public organization. This was modified in the second generation of the profession.

The Situation in the Twenty-First Century

The US experience indicates that policy analysis is not a function that is easily institutionalized. Indeed, in the US and elsewhere, political shifts and fiscal constraints have challenged some of the practices in the profession.[10]

Yet another development has occurred in the 21st century that has had a major impact on the world of the policy analyst and the way they think about clients. Views about decision-making processes have moved to quite a different approach. In the traditional hierarchical decision-making model, the assumed client—usually an individual—would have the authority and power to make a decision. By the end of the 20th century, however, many policy analysts saw decision making as the result of a bargaining process. Thus the proliferation of analysts and analytic organizations fits nicely into the bargaining relationships occurring between multiple players, most of whom were located somewhere within the governmental structure.

By the first decade of the 21st century, another approach was added to the decision-making repertoire: the use of networks. Although networks have captured the interest of scholars in a variety of fields both in the US and abroad, it is not always clear how they operate in the formal decision-making process (Rhodes, 1992). Participants in networks are not always easy to define and networks are often fluid and constantly moving.

Agranoff and McGuire describe a network as a structure that 'includes governmental and non-governmental agencies that are connected through involvement in a public policy-making and/or administrative structure through which information and/or public goods and services may be planned, designed, produced, and delivered' (McGuire & Agranoff, 2011, p. 266). When networks contain a mixture of actors with different resources, it is not always clear how those without formal authority can operate within those relationships. These are issues that are embedded in situations where the client for the work of a policy analyst is the network itself. Since the network is not an entity with clear or simple goals, how does the analyst determine the interests of the body when—by design—it contains players drawn from multiple interests and settings? To complicate things further, many of those interests represent very different perspectives and thus confront substantive policy conflicts. Conflicts can emerge between public-sector and private-sector players, representatives of interest groups, multiple public agencies, and players from the various nodes of the intergovernmental system. In addition, studies of various networks indicate that the interaction of the network itself is crucial; thus it is difficult to focus on substantive policy outcomes when the process of interaction is so important to its success.

Policy analysts have always been concerned about questions related to the cost of proposed action. Reliance on cost-benefit analysis was a common way of thinking about and predicting costs. The early interest in cost-benefit analysis not only pushed analysts to think about the overall cost of an action but also gave them a framework to think about who pays and who benefits from decisions. In that sense, cost-benefit analysis required analysts to think about the consequences of their recommendations for real people and to acknowledge that there might be different costs and benefits to different categories of individuals.

During the early years of the profession, analysts rarely based their decisions only on cost calculations. Recommendations were not expected to be based only on the lowest-cost alternative; analysts tried to trade off multiple values and to determine the ratio between costs and benefits. It certainly helped that the environment of the early 1960s was largely one of growth and possibilities. By the end of the 1960s, analysts were operating in a Vietnam War environment with an understanding that it was hard to have both guns and butter. But it was still possible to ask questions that involved determinations of the abstract idea of 'the public interest'. During the second phase of the profession, beginning in the mid-1970s, the proliferation of policy analysis offices made it obvious that there were multiple interests at play in most policy decisions. Analysts worried about both costs and benefits, but calculated them in terms of their clients. It was the political process that eventually determined the trade-offs between the interests of multiple actors in terms of bargaining and negotiation.

This created a climate in which cost was discussed without thinking about benefits. It pushed analysts to think in short-term rather than long-term frameworks. Debates became increasingly based on budget numbers, not on real assessments of programme effectiveness. The 'green eyeshade' technocrats were much less interested in the details of a programme than in their cost. Advocates of new programmes were pushed to make assessments of future cost even though they knew that they contained significant uncertainties regarding adoption and implementation and thus what their real budget costs would be. The availability of data via the internet reinforced the illusion that budget allocations were complete or even accurate. And fiscal issues combined with increased politicization to push decision makers to further emphasize short-term policy changes.

The specialization in a policy sector that seems to be the norm for recruitment and career development of policy analysts outside of the government seems to be quite different than the pattern inside of government, particularly the federal government. Individuals who become career federal public servants are sometimes likely to have a career structure that involves moving around from policy area to policy area.

Where Are We Today?

This chapter has outlined the modifications that have taken place in the policy analysis field over the past half century. It has emphasized the context in which policy analysis takes place and the impact of the changes in that context that suggest that policy analysis is not a function that is easily institutionalized or predictable. There is a tension between the academic institutions involved in the teaching and training of policy analysis and the practitioner community that actually performs policy analysis. In addition, there are a variety of links between policy analysis and existing efforts (such as management reform, fiscal analysis and legal analysis) that take place in the bureaucratic setting. It is clear that policy analysis involves a variety of players.

The result of these modifications seems to be evidence of a retreat to traditional academic perspectives. First, the differentiation between policy research and policy analysis has become much less clear (Vining & Weimer, 2010). Policy research approaches draw on broad social science research and do not focus on the relationship between the policy analyst and the client he or she is advising. In that sense, the work is less sensitive to the advisory role of policy analysts. Second, faculty members in policy studies programmes are increasingly recruited from traditional academic fields and have been evaluated through the performance criteria of those fields. Third, fewer faculty members than in earlier years either come to the academy with experience as practitioners or are encouraged to spend time in a practitioner role during sabbaticals or other forms of leave. Fourth, the academic work of the faculty tends to assume technocratic postures and avoid policy issues (often those that are termed 'wicked problems') that require attention to framing questions and problems related to defining appropriate strategies. Much of the work that is accomplished may be methodologically important but does not confront the types of policy problems lacking formal data sets that could be used to analyse policy options. Given these patterns, long-term perspectives are much harder to accomplish.

The practice of policy analysis varies across the globe. But at the same time that the field has confronted unique aspects of the field in different countries, it has also found itself sharing experiences and problems. Academics and practitioners in countries with very different cultures, structures and experiences confront similar issues and concerns. This has created a set of contradictions that has made the field both interesting and confusing.

Notes

1 The term was originally described by Rittel and Weber (1973).
2 This chapter draws on the volumes published by the Policy Press for Australia, Japan, Germany, Brazil and the Netherlands.
3 See www.jcpa.ca, accessed 10 January 2012.
4 I have used a draft report of a working group in the Australian government entitled 'Performance Assessment of Policy Work', December 1991, as a classic expression of the world of policy advising in a parliamentary system. While this document provides a picture of activities in just one parliamentary government at one point in time, it is a useful example of the practice of policy advising in a Westminster system. However, since there are important variations in parliamentary system, some of these observations may be less accurate for some systems. See also Uhr and Mackay (1966).
5 While analysts might come from outside of government, competing views from those outside organizations (such as think tanks) were not emphasized.
6 The original Freedom of Information Act was not enacted until 1966. Even with increased coverage, draft memos were not to be accessible to the public.
7 These are spelled out in the Australian 1991 document 'Performance Assessment of Policy Work'.
8 See also Blum and Schubert (2013), chapter 7.
9 For a discussion of the survival of PPBS in the Department of Defense for over 50 years, see West (2011).
10 For example, while political shifts in the Netherlands were not as strong as in some other countries, questions related to political feasibility were dealt within the academic setting. See van Nispen and Scholten (2015), chapter 16.

References

Adachi, Yukio, Sukehiro Hosono and Jun Lio, editors (2015), *Policy Analysis in Japan* (Bristol, UK: Policy Press).
Australian Auditor-General (2001, November), "Developing Policy Advice Better Practice Principles".
Bardach, Eugene (2011), *A Practical Guide for Policy Analysis: The Eightfold Path to More Effective Problem Solving* (Washington, DC: CQ Press).
Blum, Sonja and Klaus Schubert, editors (2013), *Policy Analysis in Germany* (Bristol, UK: Policy Press).
Colebatch, H. K., editor (2006), *The Work of Policy: An International Survey* (New York: Lexington Books).
Dror, Yehezkel (1967), "Policy Analysts: A New Professional Role in Government Service", *Public Administration Review*, Vol. 27, No. 3, pp. 197–203.
Dror, Yehezkel (1984), "Policy Analysis for Advising Rulers", in *Rethinking the Process of Operational Research and Systems Analysis*, edited by Rolfe Tomlinson and Istvan Kiss (Oxford, UK: Pergamon Press).
Geva-May, Iris, editor (2005), *Thinking Like a Policy Analyst: Policy Analysis as a Clinical Profession* (New York: Palgrave Macmillan).
Head, Brian and Kate Crowley, editors (2015), *Policy Analysis in Australia* (Bristol, UK: Policy Press).
Heineman, Robert A., William T. Bluhm, Steven A. Peterson and Edward N. Kearny (1990), *The World of the Policy Analyst: Rationality, Values, and Politics* (Chatham, NJ: Chatham House Publishers).
Hogwood, Brian W. and Lewis A. Gunn (1984), *Policy Analysis for the Real World* (Oxford University Press).
Howlett, Michael (2011), *Designing Public Policies: Principles and Instruments* (Abingdon, UK: Routledge).
Lasswell, Harold (1971), *A Pre-View of Policy Sciences* (New York: American Elsevier).
Majone, Giandomenico (1989), *Evidence, Argument and Persuasion in the Policy Process* (New York: Yale University Press).
Management Advisory Committee (2004, 20 April), "Connecting Government: Whole of Government Responses to Australia's Priority Challenges". Appendix 3 (Canberra, Australia: Public Service Commission).
McGuire, Michael and Robert Agranoff (2011), "The Limitations of Public Management Networks", *Public Administration* Vol. 89, No. 2, pp. 265–284.
Meltsner, Arnold (1976), *Policy Analysis in the Bureaucracy* (Berkeley: University of California Press).

Radin, Beryl A. (2000), *Beyond Machiavelli: Policy Analysis Comes of Age* (Georgetown University Press).

Radin, Beryl A. (2013a), *Beyond Machiavelli: Policy Analysis Reaches Midlife*, 2nd Edition (Georgetown University Press).

Radin, Beryl A. (2013b), "Policy Analysis Reaches Midlife", *Central European Journal of Public Policy*, Vol. 7, No. 1, pp. 8–27.

Rhodes, R. A. W. (1992), "New Directions in the Study of Policy Networks", *European Journal of Political Research*, Vol. 21, No. 1–2, pp. 181–205.

Rittel, Horst and Melvin Weber (1973), "Dilemmas in a General Theory of Planning", *Policy Sciences*, Vol. 4, pp. 155–169.

Scott, Claudia and Baehler, Karen (2010), *Adding Value to Policy Analysis and Advice* (Sydney, Australia: University of New South Wales Press).

Stokey, Edith and Richard Zeckhauser (1978), *A Primer for Policy Analysis* (New York: W.W. Norton).

Uhr, John and Keith Mackay, editors (1966), *Evaluating Policy Advice: Learning from Commonwealth Experience* (Canberra: Federalism Research Centre, Australian National University and Commonwealth Department of Finance).

Vaitsman, Jeni, Jose Mendes Ribeiro and Lenaura Lobato, editors (2013), *Policy Analysis in Brazil* (Bristol, UK: Policy Press).

van Nispen, Frans and Peter Scholten, editors (2015), *Policy Analysis in The Netherlands* (Bristol, UK: Policy Press).

Vining, Aidan R. and David L. Weimer (2010), "Foundations of Public Administration: Policy Analysis", *Public Administration Review: Foundations of Public Administration*, www.aspanet.org/public/aspadocs/par/fpa/fpa-policy-article.pdf (accessed 24 February 2015).

Weimer, David L. (2012), "The Universal and the Particular in Policy Analysis and Training", *Journal of Comparative Policy Analysis*, Vol. 14, No. 1, pp. 1–8.

Weimer David L. and Aidan R. Vining (2011), *Policy Analysis: Concepts and Practice*, 5th Edition (Upper Saddle River, NJ: Prentice Hall).

Weiss, Carol H. (1983), "Ideology, Interests and Information: The Basis of Policy Positions", in *Ethics, the Social Sciences, and Policy Analysis*, D. Callahan and B. Jennings, editors (New York: Plenum Press).

West, William F. (2011), *Program Budgeting and the Performance Movement: The Elusive Quest for Efficiency in Government* (Washington, DC: Georgetown University Press).

Wildavsky, Aaron (1977), "Rescuing Policy Analysis from PPBS", in *Classics of Public Administration*, in Jay M. Shafritz and Albert C. Hyde (Fort Worth, TX: Harcourt Brace College Publishers, 1997), pp. 251–264.

PART II

Policy Analysis by Governments

7

POLICY ANALYSIS IN THE CENTRAL GOVERNMENT

Arnošt Veselý

1. Introduction

The aim of this chapter is to describe and compare policy analysis in central governments in different jurisdictions. This is not an easy task for several reasons. First, there is no common understanding of what counts as 'policy analysis' in various countries. Second, the inclusion of policy analysis in central government can be analysed from different angles: *people* (who produce and use policy analysis); *institutions* (where it is produced); *processes* (how it is produced and used); or *outputs* (in which form and with what effects it is produced). Depending upon the perspective, we can come to quite different conclusions. Third, the nature of policy analysis is influenced by a number of factors, operating at different levels (micro, meso, macro). It is thus very complicated to disentangle the role of these factors, and currently there is no shared theoretical framework that would guide such an undertaking, though much has been done recently (Craft & Howlett, 2012). Last but not least, although our knowledge about policy analysis in different countries has substantially improved during the last decade, we are still not at the stage when rigorous country-level comparison can be realized, because of the lack of reliable and comparable data.

Nevertheless, mainly thanks to the ILPA book series there is now enough information that enables at least some tentative comparisons. We deal with the problems outlined above as follows. First, we provide overview of policy analysis in four central governments: Australia, Canada, Germany and the Netherlands. The aim of this part is to provide the reader with an empirical understanding of the variety of policy analysis in central government. The obvious starting point for the review was a chapter on policy analysis in central government in the ILPA series, supplemented by other sources for each country studied. We focus on the following aspects: (1) context of policy analysis; (2) institutionalization of policy analysis in central government vis-à-vis other institutions; (3) people doing policy analysis; and (4) core issues and problems.

The choice of countries was both pragmatic and intentional. As for the pragmatic reasons, these four countries have been reviewed in the ILPA series. There is also enough further empirical evidence that can be used for comparison (in contrast to other countries already reviewed in the ILPA series). The non-pragmatic reason is that policy analysis in these four countries (1) is comparatively very strong, and has international impact; and (2) has distinctive features that differentiate it from other countries included in the comparison.

In the second part of the chapter we strive to provide a tentative comparison between the four countries. There are many substantial differences among them. However, they share at least two common topics—externalization and politicization. We then focus upon these two trends in more detail showing that even these general trends are present in different forms in particular countries. We conclude with some implications for both theory building and empirical research.

2. Varieties of Policy Analysis in Central Government

2.1. *Australia*

Australia is a federal state, in which the state level is rather strong. At the Commonwealth (federal, central) level Australia has a bicameral legislature. The electoral system is majoritarian and governments are usually dominated by a single party. The dominant style of politics is adversarial (Pollitt & Bouckaert, 2014, p. 232). The Commonwealth of Australia was established in 1901, and for the first few decades of the 20th century the Commonwealth had relatively limited policymaking roles. The new federal government was never conceived as the equivalent of a unitary-style national government. It was given limited resources and had very few exclusive powers (Wanna, 2015, p. 72). From the 1960s, the federal level has been provided with more powers, but the states still possess much autonomy and administrative discretion, meaning that national (federal) goals must be achieved through cooperation with states and territories. This has led to a highly complicated pattern of intergovernmental relations with shared responsibility (p. 72). Cooperation and coordination between federal and state governments, as well as other government and non-government institutions, is crucial, and has been further strengthened by the New Public Management reforms in the 1980s. Consequently, the need for a 'whole-of-government' approach is a common topic in Australian policy discourse.

Policy analysis is a well-established discipline in Australia. However, by contrast with the United States, the term 'policy analysis' is less widely used in Australia, and does not necessarily have a strong association with positivist and quantitative methods (Head & Crowley, 2015, p. 2). In Australia, there has been less orthodoxy about analytical methods and professional skills required for policy work, and policy studies have been anchored more in political science than in economics (p.2).

The original restraint of the Commonwealth in policymaking meant that policy analysis was slow to manifest at that level. From the 1960s, policy analysis was handled through specialist advisory bodies and independent commissions that fed ideas into public debate (Wanna, 2015, p. 76). The federal government also funded think tanks and lobby groups to assist with their research capabilities. This changed in the late 1970s after substantial expansions in Commonwealth programmes and spending, and after university-trained graduates became much more numerous within bureaucracy (p. 76). An influential parliamentary committee report criticized the lack of hard policy analysis and recommended that departments and agencies engage in more-robust and more-transparent methodologies. After that, both scholars and practitioners explored the dimensions of evaluating policy advice and analysing good policy options (Weller & Stevens, 1998). Australia dispensed with its reliance on royal commissions and committees of inquiry in the 1980s, although they are still used occasionally (Craft & Halligan, 2015). It now tends to favour working groups usually with close associations with a servicing department. White papers are now in favour, organized through the Department of the Prime Minister and Cabinet or Treasury, two departments with political oversight because of intergovernmental dimensions.

A notable feature of policy analysis in Australia is the relatively high and increasing role of ministerial advisors. The number of such advisors doubled over the two decades after 1983 (Tiernan, 2007, p. 22). Another trend is an ever-greater role of non-governmental actors. The growth in the use of consultants in the Australian public service has been recorded as concomitant to the development of managerialism (Howard, 1996), and the role of the para-public service has been entrenched. Presumably this leads to increasing contestation of policy advice as well as politicization (Weller, 2015).

In general, it has been argued that 'the Commonwealth has struggled to take seriously the requirements of rigorous policy analysis and evaluation in its own spheres of responsibility, yet has been prepared to impose stringent top-down reporting requirements on the policy implementation of states and territories in the quest for performance results' (Wanna, 2015, p. 71). Commonwealth governments were reluctant to adopt formal or centralized planning, and policymaking has instead been labelled as 'punctuated ad hoc interventionism'. These ad hoc and usually incremental and pragmatic interventions have been shaped by politics rather than policy analysis (p. 71). Without a robust tradition of policy analysis within Commonwealth bureaucracy, policy proposals were not diagnosed before implementation or much evaluated afterwards (with some exceptions, e.g. in social security).

Many Australian scholars have noted declines in the public sector's ability to provide policy advice (Craft & Halligan, 2015; Halligan & Power, 1992; Edwards, 2009; Tiernan, 2011). The Advisory Group on Reform of Australian Government Administration (2009) found that the 'policy capacity of the APS [Australian Public Service] requires strengthening, especially in terms of its ability to provide innovative and creative advice at the strategic level' (2009, p. 21). Discussion of the decline of policy capacity in the federal bureaucracy is indeed widespread in Australian scholarship, but systematic evidence of such a decline is lacking (Tiernan, 2011; O'Flynn, Vardon, Yeatman & Carson, 2011). Thus there is a danger of overestimating the quality of past policy advice, especially because the federal bureaucracy's policy analysis capacity has never been particularly high. As Weller (2015) notes, '[t]he current fad for "evidence-based policy" (usually seen as quantitative measurable policy information) implies that evidence was not used in the past' (Weller, 2015, p. 31).

2.2. Canada

Canada is a federal state with a Westminster system of parliamentary government. There are usually strong majoritarian governments. However, because Canada is a very large country and a multi-ethnic and multi-cultural state, the governing party must try to accommodate a diverse set of interests (Pollitt & Bouckaert, 2011). The impact of the complexity of Canadian federalism and its supporting policy institutions in such a huge, regionally and linguistically diverse country is difficult to overstate (Howlett & Lindquist, 2004, p. 234). Traditionally, the central government has dominated most significant governmental functions, but this has changed in the second half of the 20th century when the balance of power shifted in favour of the provinces and local governments. From the late 1970s, NPM ideas began to influence Canadian public administration, both in the anti-bureaucratic pro-private rhetoric and the measures that were actually implemented. Currently, the portion of public employment in the central government, as opposed to the sub-central government, is one of the lowest in the Organisation for Economic Co-operation and Development (OECD) countries (Bouckaert

& Pollitt, 2014, p. 250). However, despite the reforms, the central agencies have remained strong and some authors even observed movement towards centralization of power (Aucoin & Savoie, 2009).

The public service itself is non-partisan, and nearly all deputy ministers are career civil servants. The capacity of central government personnel has been praised for a long time. Porter, for instance, claimed in the mid-1960s that 'the upper levels [of the federal bureaucracy] constitute what is probably the most highly trained group of people to be found anywhere in Canada' (Porter, 1965, cited in Dobuzinskis, Laycock & Howlett, 2007, p. 32). Generally, non-partisan and professional public service institutions serve governing parties and their executives. The unwillingness of prime ministers to fund competing advice in legislatures meant that, for many years, governments and their public service institutions had analytic capabilities rivalled only by the largest business firms and associations and, to a lesser extent, labour organizations (Howlett & Lindquist, 2007, p. 98). Beginning in the 1960s and carrying on into the 1970s, the federal government took a lead role in the development of policy research and analysis, and this continues even now. Policy research capacity within the Canadian federal government has been described as 'healthy and [comparing] well with the capacity observed in other OECD governments' (Voyer, 2007, p. 235).

In general, Canada is traditionally very strong in policy analysis. A first major impetus for policy analysis training came in the late 1960s when Pierre Trudeau became prime minister and expressed dissatisfaction with the process of policy formulation in Ottawa. He was determined to make policy formation in the federal government more analysis-driven, more scientific and more rational (Geva-May & Maslove, 2007, p. 190). The 1960s and early 1970s were a period of rapid government growth, the result of a generally buoyant economy. This provided fertile conditions for an activist federal government. Canadian governments designed increasingly elaborate planning and budgeting systems predicated on policy analysis and evaluation (Howlett & Lindquist, 2004, p. 235). In the terms expressed by Mayer, van Daalen and Bots (2001), the predominant policy styles of this era could be said to be rationalistic, client-oriented and argumentative (Howlett & Lindquist, 2004, p. 235).

However, Canada's policy *profession* lagged behind its counterpart in the U.S. (Brooks, 2007, p. 34). The earliest cohorts of staff and consultants were primarily drawn from university economics departments. Traditional public administration programmes became more oriented towards policy analysis only in the early 2000s, when new programmes on public policy were established—a time lag of almost 40 years from the U.S. (Geva-May & Maslove, 2007, p. 190). While such institutes have expanded tremendously over the last few years, often serving as home bases for world-renowned specialists in certain fields, they tend to lack the data and specialized expertise required to challenge governments in the policy analytical process (Howlett & Lindquist, 2004, p. 237).

The dominance of governmental policy analysis began to change in the early 1980s when the range of actors and the patterns of power and influence also changed. This created a more complex analytical environment which negated many of the aspirations of purely rational analysis. According to Howlett and Lindquist (2004), the emergence of new state and non-state actors actively shaping public policy and existing programmes led to a shift from the earlier rational, client-oriented advice and argumentative style, to those based on process management, interactivity and participation. Partly because of the emergence of new actors, and partly because of other factors such as public management reforms (and increasing emphasis upon results), the analytical capacity of public administration began to be challenged in the 1990s. In fact, in the literature on the decline of policy capacity in the central government, Canada seems to be the prominent case (Craft & Halligan 2015). The debate started with the deputy minister's Task Force on Strengthening our Policy Capacity that was established in 1995. This task force subsequently issued what is commonly referred to as the *Fellegi Report*, which presented a key examination of the state of policy capacity across the federal government and laid out a roadmap for future investment in capacity. It suggested that most notable weakness centred on the capacity to undertake rigorous, long-term strategic and horizontal analytical work (Voyer, 2007, p. 221).

The argument that departments in the federal government are fairly strong in the provision of short-term advice but much worse in the medium to longer term has been repeated in later documents (Armstrong, Mulder & Robinson, 2002). Similarly, the Public Policy Forum, an Ottawa-based think tank, in its 2007 report identified declining policy capacity as a critical issue facing the Canadian federal civil service. A number of themes were mentioned, including a hollowing out of internal expertise, a tendency to equate analysis with short-term reactions to communications crises and dealing with political sensitivities, and an overemphasis on internal performance reporting (Côté, Baird & Green, 2007).

The most recent analysis, however, provides a more complicated view on policy capacity in Canadian federal government. It has been argued that analytical capacity is 'lumpy' or unevenly distributed across policy domains and public administration units (Craft & Howlett, 2013). Moreover, the assumed decline in policy capacity can also be understood as a *result* of general trends, especially outsourcing and politicization. As for outsourcing, Perl and White (2002) found that in Canada, government expenditures on policy consulting increased from C$239 million in 1981–82 to C$1.55 billion in 2000–01, a 647% increase over 20 years. During the same period, the number of federal public service employees decreased substantially. However, Perl and White also showed that there are significant differences in the extent of outsourcing within the Canadian government: 'it would appear that the central agencies charged with strategic and horizontal policy responsibilities opted for less outsourcing than did line departments and agencies with more technical, specialized, and vertically structured policy responsibilities' (2002, p. 65). New data led to other interesting findings, e.g. that there have been fewer small contracts in recent years, while larger, longer-term contracts have become more common, meaning that expenditures on larger contracts have increased, not declined (Howlett & Migone, 2013).

Another recurrent topic is politicization of the central public administration. Many scholars have argued that in the last decade or so the influence of political appointees and consultants has grown. The number of political advisors in minister's and prime minister's offices in Canada—referred to as 'exempt staff'—is the highest among four Anglophone systems (Australia, Canada, U.K., N.Z.) (Craft & Halligan, 2015). While exempt staff are not considered as public service per se (in terms of political neutrality), they are paid from the public budget. Until 2007, those who were employed as exempt staff for any minister for a total of three years were entitled, if deemed qualified, to be appointed, without competition, to a public service post at an equivalent level of rank. This unique feature of the Canadian system enabled political staff to enter the public service through a 'back door' (Aucoin, 2010, p. 68). According to Aucoin, that rise of political advisors is just one aspect of increased political attention to the staffing of the senior public service.

2.3. Germany

The German administrative system is part of a republican polity whose characteristics are a federal division of powers between national (federal) and 16 *Land* governments, a parliamentary system of government, and the concept of *Rechtsstaat* (Derlien, 2003). State power is divided between the Federation and the *Länder* according to the tasks and functions they perform. The Basic Law assigns everything that has to be regulated and managed in the general interest of the public to the Federation. The *Länder* have been assigned responsibility in all other matters. Consequently, the main force of the legislative lies with the Federation, and the focus of the administrative apparatus with the *Länder.*

Generally speaking, federal government and *Länder* are independent of one another. The federal government, with a few exceptions (foreign service, military, customs, major water ways, labour administration), has no field offices of its own but completely relies on the *Länder* (and local governments) for the execution of federal policies. In practice, there are many links between federal and *Länder* institutions. This forces decision makers and public officials of the Federation and the *Länder* to work together in carrying out tasks. The complicated governance structure calls for a high degree of coordination.

More than 18,000 people are employed at 14 federal ministries, about one half in Berlin and the other half in Bonn. Thus, the ministerial bureaucracy fulfils a very important function within the German political system. However, the German administrative system is largely decentralized, as demonstrated by the division of public sector personnel: only 13% of the entire public sector workforce are federal personnel, while 53% are employed by the *Länder* and 35% by the local government levels (Kuhlmann & Wollmann, 2014, p. 73).

German policymaking and policy analysis takes place in a stable institutional framework that operates in a more structured and standardized way than, for instance, in the U.S. This is because of the need to facilitate communication between various federal and *Länder* institutions. Nevertheless, generally the polity of Germany is characterized by vertical and horizontal fragmentation with many veto players (Schmid & Buhr, 2013). Consequently, the policymaking process is shaped by the pressure to negotiate. Thus the dominant topics of German policy scholars include the problem of consensus and coordination. German policymaking has been labelled as 'fragmented incrementalism' (Wollmann, 1997), because there is rarely an opportunity for a comprehensive reform philosophy.

German federalism may lead to *Verjiechtungsfalle* (joint decision trap), a situation in which interdependent government decisions must be taken at the lowest common denominator because other governments may otherwise veto them. There have been attempts to solve this problem by clearly assigning various competences to particular institutions. This, however, has led to the 'separation decision trap', because many problems are complex in nature and cannot be unambiguously attributed. Moreover, despite the drawbacks of *Verjiechtungsfalle,* the need for cooperation and negotiation also has positive sides; many large-scale reforms, for example, have been consensual and enduring (Schmid & Buhr, 2013).

Another challenge for policymaking stemming from German federalism is a need for *coordination.* By this is meant an attempt to produce coherent government policies. The federal ministers are equipped with strong autonomy and a powerful administrative foundation that is organized in strict hierarchical lines under state secretaries with civil service status. Ministries in Germany are classic bureaucratic organizations, i.e. they are characterized by lifelong tenure, written communication (i.e. communication via various types of formal documents), legal orientation, strict hierarchy and thus a dominance of line organization (ministries are further divided into departments and units) (Veit & Scholz, 2015). This raises the problem of horizontal coordination and departmentalism (Hustedt & Tiessen, 2006).

The nature of policy analysis in the German federal government is incomprehensible without taking into account the background of public officials. Because of legalistic administrative culture in Germany, lawyers are given priority in recruitment to the higher civil service. Similarly, the training for public administration is strongly geared towards a legal curriculum and acquisition of legal expertise (Kuhlmann & Wollmann, 2014, p. 78). This traditional 'lawyers monopoly' was partially weakened in the 1970s, when 'traditional bureaucrats' were supplemented by more 'political' types of officials and the permeability between politics and administration increased. However, since governance still functions largely via the medium of law, the elective affinity to the corresponding discipline continues to exist (Schmid & Buhr, 2013).

The polity, civil service code and policy analysis tradition have their implications for the nature of policy in Germany. Schmid and Buhr (2013, p. 100) argue that policymaking in Germany more often resembles an art than a science. Policy analysis in the federal government is characterized by a high level of communication. Germany has been described as a 'consensus society' (Heinze, 2013, p. 136), which has its impact upon the policy analysis methods employed. For Germany, 'round tables' are typical. They usually combine social and economic interest organizations, scientific experts, political representatives and members of the political administration (p. 136).

Generally, German policy analysis has a clear post-positivist tinge. Heinze (2013) describes the introduction of 'confidential round tables' with politicians and scientific experts to introduce new models of interchange and advice. Advice here relies on dialogue and discourse—it is *advice by dialogue*. This discursive and reflexive form of advice is, of course, very far from traditional textbook accounts of policy analysis. In addition to traditional councils of experts and scientific advisors, new and temporary models of interest intermediation have developed, such as strategic alliances of interest groups and scientific consultancies or think tanks (Heinze, 2013). Although scientists and academics still provide a large portion of political advice in Berlin, important new actors are also involved, such as foundations or commercial organizations. These coexist with institutionalized interest groups and institutes closely linked with these groups (Heinze, 2013).This structural shift in the system of organized interests and the significant changes in the relationship between science and politics has meant that consensus-like round tables, comprised of representatives of organized interests, are increasingly disappearing. In their place have emerged commissions composed of a variety of members, established for a limited period of time (Heinze, 2013).

The forms of policy consulting in Germany are, however, highly varied, and it would be misleading to portray policy analysis in German federal government as 'post-positivist'. Positivist policy analysis, including econometric models, is certainly present in Germany, and 'technocratic models of policy advice' are still used (Heinze, 2013, p. 138). However, the general belief of usefulness of such techniques for policymaking has always been lower than in Canada or the U.S. The fear of the 'scientification of politics' has often been stressed in German policy discussion (p. 138) as scholars have long cautioned that political processes should not be managed and controlled by science. Despite the fact that politicization in the federal ministerial bureaucracy has been convincingly described and challenged (Veit & Scholz, 2015), the 'politics' aspects of policy analysis have been generally acknowledged as natural and legitimate.

2.4. The Netherlands

The Netherlands is a unitary but decentralized state. The political system is consociational, consensual, multi-party and corporatist (Lijphart, 1984). The Dutch political culture is characterized by deliberation, consultation and pursuit of compromise and consensus (Kickert & in 't Veld, 1995). This policymaking style of accommodation and consensus seeking is rooted in a long tradition of 'polder' politics (i.e. consensus decision making) in a highly fragmented, decentralized system, collaboration among the elites of various religious denominations, and neo-corporatist negotiations among the state, employers and unions (van Buuren & Koppenjan, 2014). This consensus policymaking is combined with similarly strong tradition of policymaking based on the knowledge of public scientific institutions (Mayer, 2007).

It is difficult to make generalizations about policy analysis in the Netherlands, because the country includes quite diverse styles (both rational and participatory) that occur under different names. Policy analysis is a multi-faceted phenomenon that has been institutionalized in a diverse set of institutions, including public advisory committees, planning agencies, policy research and consultancy companies, think tanks and universities. Moreover, during its development from World War II, it has undergone a turbulent development and has seen periods with different focuses, beliefs and methods (Mayer, 2007).

Nevertheless, the two aforementioned aspects—consensus-building and a focus on expertise and research—clearly distinguish the Netherlands' case from the other countries described in this chapter. Research and expertise traditionally helped to facilitate consensus in a highly fragmented political system. Consequently, a unique institutionalization of policy analysis, characterized by many independent policy analysis institutions, has been established. Most importantly, there are so-called planning bureaus that are often associated with specific government departments but are allowed to operate relatively independently. It is this relative independence that provides these institutes with the authority needed to forge consensus on a variety of policy topics (Scholten & van Nispen, 2014, p. 4). Consequently, compared to other countries, there is relatively weak politicization of expertise.

The role of policy analysis in national government is relatively low: 'policy analysis in the Netherlands is perhaps not very well *incorporated* inside bureaucracy' (Mayer, 2007, p. 565, original emphasis). The aforementioned advisory bodies are relatively independent from government organizations; very few advisory bodies are embedded within government organizations (Scholten & van Nispen, 2014, p. 140). Nevertheless, some forms of policy analysis have been incorporated into government agencies. The institutionalization of policy analysis in government started in the early 1970s, when the Dutch minister of finance established the Committee for the Development of Policy Analysis (COBA in Dutch) to promote policy analysis within government departments. This committee was composed of top officials of all ministries and its staff was located in the Ministry of Finance. Policy analysis (*Beleidsanalyse* in Dutch) was there understood rather narrowly, as an application of rational techniques such as cost-benefit analysis and objectives analysis. Rigid and bureaucratic implementation of these techniques led to the abolishment of COBA in 1982, and the experiment is generally understood as a failure.

Nevertheless, the institution changed the policy analysis landscape forever and the demise of COBA did not end the pursuit of rational policymaking in bureaucracy (van Nispen & Scholten, 2014, p. 81). On the contrary, rational policymaking ideas have been re-introduced with performance budgeting and new budget format, called From Policy Budget to Accounting for Policy (*Van Beleidsbegroting tot Beleidsverantwoording*, or VBTB). This is clearly indebted to COBA, as the spending departments now have to provide non-financial information about objectives and instruments in an effort to improve efficiency in the public sector (VBTB). The pervasive impact of rational-type techniques is visible also in newly introduced instruments such as policy reviews and spending reviews.

There is a long and well-established tradition of policy analysis as a discipline in the Netherlands. Dutch policy scholars have made many significant global contributions to the field. Few countries have such a high density of institutes specialized in policy analysis, and in few countries have such institutes played and continued to play such a key role in policymaking (van Nispen & Scholten, 2014, p. 1). Almost every sector of government consists of a myriad of consultative and advisory councils, which are deeply intertwined with government and form an 'iron ring' around ministerial departments (Kickert & in 't Veld, 1995). The Netherlands has developed an extensive system of advisory bodies. By the end of the 1970s, the Netherlands had more than 400 advisory councils of some sort. A specific phenomenon in the Dutch setting involves the so-called 'planning bureaus', a specific form of advisory body that not so much actually plans policies, but provides policy-relevant knowledge on developments in society, nature or the economy. However, the system of advisory bodies, as it evolved since the 1970s, came under pressure from the mid-1980s. The number of advisory bodies started to decrease, to about 235 in 1985 and 120 in 1994. Between 1995 and 2015, the number of external advisory bodies further decreased from 119 to 24. This was partly due to the economic crisis of the 1980s and partly because of reform of government bureaucracy in a number of areas (van Nispen & Scholten, 2014, p. 141). However, the remaining advisory bodies have maintained authoritative and influential positions in the policymaking process.

There are many educational programmes in policy sciences in the Netherlands. Most Dutch universities have research groups specialized in policy analysis, sometimes as part of departments of public administration, and sometimes as part of more specialized departments for the technological or agricultural sector (van Nispen & Scholten, 2014, p. 1). Despite the fact that Dutch policy scholars are well known for their contribution to interpretive and participatory policy analysis, policy analysis in bureaucracy was—and still is—strongly influenced by the positivist paradigm, not only from within government but also via the most influential independent advisory bodies such as the Central Planning Bureau (CPB), established in 1947. This is now one of the world's leading institutes in economic modelling (econometrics) to be used for policy support (Mayer, 2007, p. 555). Dutch policy analysis is thus rather divided. On the one hand, the use of positivist rational techniques is widespread and institutionalized. On the other hand, it is criticized by many Dutch scholars as a technocratic and politically naïve approach to policymaking.

To sum it up, in the Netherlands, policy analysis is not usually encompassed in central government organizations, but in advisory bodies and councils, related but independent from central government. When and where policy analysis (*Beleidsanalyse*) is incorporated in bureaucracy, 'it is strongly associated with rationalization of policy formulation and financial control over means and performances—the remnants of COBA. Inside bureaucracy it is strongly influenced by the values and techniques of the Ministry of Finance and institutions such as the CPB, and since about the late 1990s this style of policy analysis might be making a remarkable comeback' (Mayer, 2007, p. 565).

3. Differences, Similarities and Trends

For reasons outlined in the introduction, it is very complicated to compare policy analysis in central government across jurisdictions. With the caution that in the future a more fine-tuned comparison should be made, the tentative comparison of the four countries is summarized in Table 7.1. Although these four countries are the most developed, and have long traditions of policy analysis, there are more differences than similarities.

Let us first examine the institutionalization of policy advice. Australia represents a case of a country which has not traditionally focused upon building strong policy analytical capacities inside federal government. Instead, royal commissions and committees of inquiry had been used, later being replaced by working groups. Similarly, in the Netherlands, policy analysis inside central government has been rather limited in favour of it being conducted in independent advisory councils and planning bureaus. In both countries, policy analysis has been deliberately taken away from internal public administration (but still in close connection to it), and both countries traditionally spent public money to establish policy analysis institutions supporting central government outside the bureaucracy itself. The reasons for this approach, however, differ. In Australia it is the result of the limited power of federal government, while in the Netherlands it was the result of a need to create consensus among many competing parties on the basis of impartial advice.

Canada represents a country with a long and strong emphasis upon policy analytical capacity inside central government. For a long time, the federal government's analytical capacity could not be challenged by other actors. Despite the fact that the policy analysis profession was established with a considerable time lag behind the U.S., the policy analysis style in Canada has been similarly influenced by rational policy analysis techniques, and only recently has moved to more participatory and argumentative styles. Germany also belongs to a cluster of countries with a long-established emphasis upon inside-government capacity. This has, however, never been understood as a mastery of rational policy analysis techniques, but mostly as an ability to communicate, reach consensus and coordinate policy.

Table 7.1 Policy analysis in central government

Country	Institutionalization of policy analysis in central government	Governance context, public administration tradition	Preparation and selection of policy workers	Core issues
Australia	Policy analysis inside federal government traditionally rather limited. Instead working groups usually with close associations with a servicing department.	Federalism. Punctuated ad hoc interventionism.	Public administration. Political science.	Declining policy capacity. Politicization. Whole-of-government.
Canada	Traditional emphasis upon building strong internal policy analytical capacity within federal government.	Federalism.	Economics. Public policy.	Policy capacity. Politicization. Lack of strategic capacity, short-termism. Externalization.
Germany	Traditional emphasis upon internal administrative capacity, but not necessarily analytical capacity.	Federalism. Strong bureaucracies. Stable institutional framework.	Law.	Joint decision trap. Coordination deficit.
The Netherlands	Policy analysis inside central government rather limited. Policy analysis in largely independent advisory councils and planning bureaus.	Consensus-building. Focus on expertise and research.	Economics. Public administration.	Technocratization. Externalization.

There are many factors that can explain the different institutionalization of policy analysis in central government. The most important include governance context (political system, public administration tradition, political culture, etc.) and preparation and selection of policy workers. As for the context, the nature of policy analysis is clearly influenced by a country's level of centralization or decentralization. As we have seen, in all federal states, a need for communication and coordination is unquestionable. In federal countries, any policy design must take into account the multi-level governance structure. Consequently, policy work must be based upon facilitating compromise and reconciling different perspectives, which is at odds with many assumptions of classical textbook policy analysis.

While there is no doubt that federalism *influences* the nature of policy analysis, it does not *determine* it. Australia, Canada and Germany are federal states, yet the form of policy analysis in central government is substantially different. This can be partly explained by the professionalization of policy analysis (i.e. to what extent public policy and policy analysis is taught in higher education), and the preparation and recruitment of central government personnel. In Australia, public policy is a discipline per se, but it does take the same shape as in the U.S.: it is rooted more in political science and public administration than in economics. In Canada, the influence of economics and positivist methodology is clear, although, as recent data demonstrate, this is changing. In Germany, policy analysis is deeply rooted in political science, which leads to more emphasis upon political skills. In practice, however, public administration is dominated by lawyers, which leads to a rather unique policy work style, and a focus on structured policymaking processes.

Differences can also be found in the key problems identified by scholars in each of the countries. In Canada, the core issues concern the assumed decline of policy capacity, short-termism and outsourcing of policy advice. In contrast, in Germany, the most emphasized problems include the coordination deficit, the decision trap and politicization. Despite the differences, there are at least two general issues that are addressed by scholars in all countries: externalization and politicization. These are general trends that are more or less visible in many other countries (Craft & Howlett, 2013).

By externalization I mean the 'relocation of advisory activities previously performed inside government organizations to places outside of government' (Veselý, 2013, p. 200). Externalization has both quantitative and qualitative aspects. The quantitative perspective concerns the proportion of internal and external policy analysis, i.e. the number of policy analysts, the number of policy analyses produced and the expenditures on consulting and advice. The qualitative perspective relates to the quality of internal and external policy analysis institutions and their capacity to provide useful, relevant and high-quality policy advice. This capacity can differ according to the contents of the advice.

While externalization discourse (in terms such as 'contracting out', 'outsourcing' or 'hollowing out') is quite popular in the scholarly literature across jurisdictions (and not limited to the four countries compared here), the empirical evidence is not unequivocal. There is no doubt that 'there has been broadening of sources of advice, with the expanding involvement of actors both within and beyond the governmental system' (Halligan, 1995, p. 138), and that this challenged the primacy of central government in-house policy analysis. Nevertheless, externalization differs across policy domains, departments and jurisdictions and also considerably varies over time. The opposite phenomenon—labelled as 'filling in'—can also occur. Data from countries such as the U.K. show that central government expenditures on external consultants vary substantially over time and between individual departments. It has even been shown that 'outsourcing' and 'filling in' tendencies can coexist in one particular timeframe, i.e., in one governmental agency policy advice is externalized, while in another it is internalized (Veselý, 2013, p. 204).

The qualitative perspective considers whether the production of high-quality advice is actually relocated from central government to places outside government. Again, the discourse on the subject is strong ('policy capacity declines'). One frequent complaint concerns the absorption of policy workers in fire-fighting activities instead of the provision of long-term advice. From the 1990s, various attempts have been made in Canada, the United Kingdom, New Zealand and Australia to review the policy capacity in public administration. Despite these efforts, solid empirical evidence linking reform to improved policy capacity is still rather scarce, and counter-findings also exist. For example, Edwards (2009), focusing upon rail policy and the Department of Transport in Australia, found that after the reforms the government lost considerable analytical capacity to gather and assess information, but at the same time significantly improved its capacity for strategic planning.

The second common trend is that central governments have become more politicized. Politicization of the civil service refers to 'the substitution of political criteria for merit-based criteria in the selection, retention, promotion, rewards, and disciplining of members of the public service' (Peters & Pierre, 2004, p. 2). The increasing politicization of central government is often linked to the fact that the number of political advisors in many countries has risen substantially during the last two decades (OECD, 2011). This view relies on the assumption of a dichotomy between 'political' (partisan-ideological) and 'technical' advice which stresses the importance of technical expertise over political or value-laden issues (Craft & Howlett, 2013, p. 191).

Empirical research has disproved the political versus technical dichotomy and showed that: (1) ministerial advisors play multiple roles beyond mere 'political', and (2) public servants are not—and cannot be—completely inattentive to political wishes. Thus, appointing more ministerial advisors does not necessarily lead to higher politicization (Connaughton, 2015; Maley, 2015), and in fact, may reduce it. Other mechanisms of politicization have also been identified and empirically supported. Hustedt and Salomonsen (2014) have argued that formal politicization (formal rules prescribing that certain civil service positions can be filled by people to the minister's contingent preferences) is accompanied by functional and administrative politicization, while functional politicization refers to a mechanism by which the civil service performs politically responsive bureaucratic behaviour, administrative politicization represents a mechanism by which ministerial advisors politicize the advice provided by the permanent civil service.

4. Conclusion

This tentative comparison of policy analysis in central government reveals striking differences. It has been argued that differences in policy analysis are the result of a combination of contextual elements that 'constrain and create opportunities for different activities and produce discernable policy analytical styles' (Howlett & Lindquist, 2004, p. 226). According to Howlett and Lindquist (p. 232), the concept of policy analytical styles should be reserved for aggregated assessment of policy analysis in a particular jurisdiction. Because there is relative stability in how the government works, the structure of policy networks, the culture of organizations and the nature of policy problems, it is likely that, at the more general level, there is also relative stability in patterns of analytical activities (i.e. how policy analysis is understood and practised). In this sense, the Canadian policy analytical style of the 1960s and 1970s could be considered as 'rational type'—characterized by client orientation and an argumentative style—but the country has gradually shifted to a style based upon process management, interactivity and participation. Similarly, while typical policy analytical style in Germany seems to be coordination (Blum & Schubert, 2013) in the Netherlands it is consensus and cooperation (van Nispen & Scholten, 2014).

However, such generalizations must be taken with caution. As we have seen, analytical styles change over time, and they differ substantially across policy domains and particular institutions. Even more importantly, the assessment of policy analysis styles depends very much on the perspective taken. Different scholars have different—although mostly implicit—beliefs about the *optimal* use of policy analysis in central government that influence their assessment. This can partially explain some contradictory findings. For instance, despite the fact the Canadian federal government is praised as an example of strong in-house policy analysis, it is also the most criticized for the decline of policy analytical capacity. Similarly, while Canadian governments are often accused of not undertaking enough consultation with citizens and various stakeholders, many departments report 'consultation fatigue' (Howlett & Lindquist, 2004, p. 238). Clearly, the assessment depends upon the—often tacit—view of 'how much is too much' and 'how little is too little'.

Comparative research is inevitably a complicated endeavour. It is even more so for such a complex and multi-faceted phenomenon as policy analysis. The travelling problem (Peters, 1996, cited in Kuhlman & Wollmann, 2014, p. 5)—that is, the limited transferability of concepts and terms between different linguistic and cultural contexts—is even more pronounced here than elsewhere. Indeed, even the basic categories of 'policy analysis' and 'policy work' are hard to define in an international context. They inevitably capture not only the actual, real-world differences but also different perspectives on what is *good* or *optimal* policy analysis. The comparison in this chapter, based upon the country reports, necessarily involves not only factually different styles but also reflects different positions and perspectives on policy analysis in various countries. Future research will need to carefully disentangle the discourse or rhetoric about policy analysis, and how it is actually practised.

References

Advisory Group on Reform of Australian Government Administration (2009). *Reform of Australian Government Administration: Building the World's Best Public Service.* Canberra: Commonwealth of Australia, Australian Government Department of the Prime Minister and Cabinet.

Armstrong, J., Mulder, N. & Robinson, R. (2002). *Strengthening Policy Capacity: Report on Interviews with Senior Managers, February–March 2002.* Ottawa, Canada: The Governance Network.

Aucoin, P. (2010). Canada. In C. Eichbaum & R. Shaw (Eds), *Partisan Appointees and Public Servants: An International Analysis of the Role of the Political Adviser* (pp. 64–93). Boston: Edward Elgar.

Aucoin, P. & Savoie, D. (2009). The Politics–Administration Dichotomy: Democracy versus Bureaucracy? In O. Dwivendi, T. Mau & B. Sheldrick (Eds), *The Evolving Physiology of Government: Canadian Public Administration in Transition* (pp. 97–117).

Bakvis, H. (2000). Rebuilding Policy Capacity in the Era of the Fiscal Dividend: A Report from Canada. *Governance, 13*(1), 71–103.

Blum, S. & Schubert, K. (Eds) (2013). *Policy Analysis in Germany.* Bristol, UK: Policy Press.

Brooks, S. (2007). The Policy Analysis Profession in Canada. In L. Dobuzinskis, M. Howlett & D. Laycock (Eds), *Policy Analysis in Canada: The State of the Art.* University of Toronto Press.

Connaughton, B. (2015). Navigating the Borderlines of Politics and Administration: Reflections on the Role of Ministerial Advisers. *International Journal of Public Administration, 38*(1), 37–45.

Côté, A., Baird, K. & Green, I. (2007). *A Vital National Institution: What a Cross-section of Canadians Think about the Prospects for Canada's Public Service in the 21st Century.* Ottawa: Public Policy Forum.

Craft, J. & Halligan, J. (2015, 1–4 July). Looking Back and Thinking Ahead: 30 Years of Policy Advisory System Scholarship. Prepared for T08P06, Comparing policy advisory systems. International Conference on Public Policy, Catholic University of Sacro Cuore, Milan.

Craft, J. & Howlett, M. (2012). Policy Formulation, Governance Shifts and Policy Influence: Location and Content in Policy Advisory Systems. *Journal of Public Policy, 32*(2), 79–98.

Craft, J. & Howlett, M. (2013). The Dual Dynamics of Policy Advisory Systems: The Impact of Externalization and Politicization on Policy Advice. *Policy and Society, 32*(3), 187–197.

Derlien, H.-U. (2003). German Public Administration: Weberian Despite 'Modernization'. In K. K. Tummala (Ed.), *Comparative Bureaucratic Systems* (pp. 97–122). Lanham, MD: Lexington Books.

Dobuzinskis, L., Laycock, D. & Howlett, M. (2007). *Policy Analysis in Canada: The State of the Art.* University of Toronto Press.

Edwards, L. (2009). Testing the Discourse of Declining Policy Capacity: Rail Policy and the Department of Transport. *Australian Journal of Public Administration, 68*(3), 288–302.

Geva-May, I. & Maslove, A. (2007). In Between Trends: Developments of Policy Analysis Instruction in Canada, the United States, and the European Union. In L. Dobuzinskis, M. Howlett & D. Laycock (Eds), *Policy Analysis in Canada: The State of the Art* (pp. 185–217). Toronto University Press.

Halligan, J. (1995). Policy Advice and the Public Service. In B. G. Peters & D. J. Savoie (Eds), *Governance in a Changing Environment* (pp. 138–172). Montreal and Kingston, Canada: McGill-Queens' University Press and Canadian Centre for Management Development.

Halligan, J., & Power, J. (1992). *Political Management in the 1990s.* Melbourne, Australia: Oxford University Press.

Head, B. & Crowley, K. (Eds). (2015). *Policy Analysis in Australia.* Bristol, UK: Policy Press.

Heinze, R. G. (2013). Federal Government in Germany: Temporary, Issue-Related Policy Advice. In S. Blum & K. Schubert (Eds), *Policy Analysis in Germany* (pp. 135–148). Bristol, UK: Policy Press.

Howard, M. (1996). A Growth Industry? Use of Consultants Reported by Commonwealth Departments (1974–1994). *Canberra Bulletin of Public Administration, 80*, 62–74.

Howlett, M. & Lindquist, E. (2004). Policy Analysis and Governance: Analytical and Policy Styles in Canada. *Journal of Comparative Policy Analysis, 6*(3), 225–249.

Howlett, M. & Lindquist, E. (2007). Beyond Formal Policy Analysis: Governance Context, Analytical Styles, and the Policy Analysis Movement in Canada. In L. Dobuzinskis, M. Howlett, & D. Laycock (Eds), *Policy Analysis in Canada: The State of the Art* (pp. 86–115). Toronto University Press.

Howlett, M. & Migone, A. (2013). Searching for Substance: Externalization, Politicization and the Work of Canadian Policy Consultants 2006–2013. *Central European Journal of Public Policy, 7*(1), 112–133.

Hustedt, T. & Tiessen, J. (2006). *Central Government Coordination in Denmark, Germany and Sweden: An Institutional Policy Perspective* (Vol. 2). Universitätsverlag Potsdam.

Hustedt, T. & Salomonsen, H. H. (2014). Ensuring Political Responsiveness: Politization Mechanisms in Ministerial Bureaucracies. *International Review of Administrative Sciences, 80*(4), 746–765.

Kickert, W. & in 't Veld, R. J, (1995). National Government, Governance and Administration. In W. Kickert & F. van Vught (Eds), *Public Policy and Administrative Sciences in the Netherlands*. London: Prentice Hall/ Harvester Wheatsheaf (pp. 45–62).

Kuhlmann, S. & Wollmann, H. (2014). *Introduction to Comparative Public Administration*. Cheltenham, UK: Edward Elgar.

Lijphart, A. (1984). *Democracies: Patterns of Majoritarian and Consensus Government in Twenty-One Countries*. London: Yale University Press.

Maley, M. (2015). The Policy Work of Australian Political Staff. *International Journal of Public Administration, 38*(1), 46–55.

Mayer, I. (2007). The Evolution of Policy Analysis in the Netherlands. In F. Fischer, G. J. Miller & M. S. Sidney (Eds), *Handbook of Public Policy Analysis: Theory, Politics, and Methods* (pp. 553–570). Boca Raton, FL: Taylor & Francis.

Mayer, I. S., van Daalen, C. E. & Bots, P. W. G. (2004). Perspectives on Policy Analyses: A Framework for Understanding and Design. *International Journal of Technology, Policy and Management, 4*(2), 169–191.

OECD (2011). *Ministerial Advisors: Role, Influence and Management*. Paris: OECD.

O'Flynn, J., Vardon, S., Yeatman, A. & Carson, L. (2011). Perspectives on the Capacity of the Australian Public Service and Effective Policy Development and Implementation. *Australian Journal of Public Administration, 70*(3), 309–317.

Perl, A. & White, D. J. (2002). The Changing Role of Consultants in Canadian Policy Analysis. *Policy and Society, 21*(1), 49–73.

Peters, B. G. (1996). Theory and Methodology. In H. A. G. M. Bekke, J. L. Perry & T. A. J. Toonen (Eds), *Civil Service Systems in Comparative Perspective*, Indiana University Press, 1996.

Peters, B. G. & Pierre, J. (2004). *The Politicization of the Civil Service in Comparative Perspective: A Quest for Control*. London: Routledge.

Pollitt, C. & Bouckaert, G. (2011). *Public Management Reform: A Comparative Analysis: New Public Management, Governance, and the Neo-Weberian State* (3rd ed.). Oxford University Press.

Porter, J. (1965). *The Vertical Mosaic*. University of Toronto Press.

Schmid, J. & Buhr, D. (2013). Federal Government in Germany: Permanent In-House Capacities—Life Within the 'Apparatus'. In Sonja Blum & Klaus Schubert (Eds), *Policy Analysis in Germany* (pp. 91–104). Bristol, UK: Policy Press.

Scholten, P. & van Nispen, F. (2014). Advisory Boards and Planning Bureaus. In F. cvan Nispen & P. Scholten (Eds), *Policy Analysis in the Netherlands*. Bristol, UK: Policy Press, pp. 139–154.

Tiernan, A. (2007). *Power Without Responsibility: Ministerial Staffers in Australian Governments from Whitlam to Howard*. Sydney, Australia: University of New South Wales Press.

Tiernan, A. (2011). Advising Australian Federal Governments: Assessing the Evolving Capacity and Role of the Australian Public Service. *Australian Journal of Public Administration, 70*(4), 335–346.

van Buuren, A. & Koppenjan, J. (2014). Policy Analysis in Networks: The Battle of Analysis and the Potentials of Joint Fact-Finding. In F. van Nispen & P. Scholten (Eds), *Policy Analysis in the Netherlands*. Bristol, UK: Policy Press.

van Nispen, F. & Scholten, P. (Eds) (2014). *Policy Analysis in the Netherlands*. Bristol, UK: Policy Press.

Veit, S. & Scholz, S. (2015). Linking Administrative Career Patterns and Politicization: Signalling Effects in the Careers of Top Civil Servants in Germany. *International Review of Administrative Sciences*.

Veselý, A. (2013). Externalization of Policy Advice: Theory, Methodology and Evidence. *Policy and Society, 32*(3), 199–209.

Voyer, J.-P. (2007). Policy Analysis in the Federal Government: Building the Forward-Looking Policy Research Capacity. In L. Dobuzinskis, M. Howlett, & D. Laycock (Eds.), *Policy Analysis in Canada: The State of the Art* (pp. 219–237). University of Toronto Press.

Wanna, J. (2015). Policy Analysis at the Federal Government Level. In B. Head & K. Crowley (Eds), *Policy Analysis in Australia* (pp. 71–86). Bristol, UK: Policy Press.

Weller, P. (2015). Policy Professionals in Context: Advisors and Ministers. In B. Head & K. Crowley (Eds), *Policy Analysis in Australia* (pp. 23–36). Bristol, UK: Policy Press.

Weller, P. & Stevens, B. (1998). Evaluating Policy Advice: The Australian Experience. *Public Administration, 76*(3), 579–589.

Wollmann, H. (1997). Modernization of the Public Sector and Public Administration in the Federal Republic of Germany – (Mostly) A Story of Fragmented Incrementalism. *State and Administration in Japan and Germany. A Comparative Perspective on Continuity and Change*. Berlin, 79–103.

8

POLICY ANALYSIS IN SUB-NATIONAL GOVERNMENTS

Joshua Newman

It seems that a consensus has developed among scholars of public policy that not enough research has been conducted on policy analysis at the sub-national level (Bernier & Howlett, 2012; Howlett & Newman, 2010; Jennings & Hall, 2012; McArthur, 2007; Phillimore & Arklay, 2015; Veselý, Wellstead & Evans, 2014). Paradoxically, this slow development of research into sub-national policy analysis has coincided with a growing interest among scholars and practitioners in policy analysis in general and especially in evidence-based policy (Head, 2013; Legrand, 2012; Newman, Cherney & Head, 2016; Sanderson, 2011; Tseng & Nutley, 2014). It is possible, though unfortunate, that states and provinces and other subordinate units of government might be seen by some as being inferior to, and therefore less interesting than, national governments (McArthur, 2007).

Despite this slow pace of development, international scholarship on policy analysis in state and provincial governments has already accomplished a great deal. Important questions have been posed (even if answers to those questions have not been reached), a research agenda has been framed, methodologies have been piloted, empirical data have been collected and links to the greater dynamics have been drawn. The big question in this area is no longer 'what do we want to know?' but rather, 'where do we go from here?'

Policy Analysis as a Profession

Current conceptions of policy analysis in government see this activity as one of data gathering, knowledge creation, and communication of processed information in the form of advice. In democratic countries, elected representatives are seldom technical experts in their areas of responsibility. Ministers, secretaries and other members of the political executive often find themselves in positions of authority over important policy areas in which they themselves may have little or no experience or expertise (Aberbach, Putnam & Rockan, 1981; Blondel, 1985; Blackham & Williams, 2012; for a dissenting opinion, see Beckman, 2006). Even senior administrators, who may in fact have significant experience and expertise in the policy areas over which they have decision-making capabilities, will not have the capacity to provide recommendations on every policy problem that requires attention. Furthermore, in the complex modern state, no single individual can possibly have full knowledge of all the activity in his or her department. Decisions made by senior levels of authority are necessarily informed by advice from supporting staff.

This advice can take on numerous forms. In modern democracies, the processed information that elected officials and senior administrators receive must be useful for multiple concurrent goals, such as agenda setting, partisan and electoral strategy, and instrumental policy development. Goals can also be in conflict: for example, current trends toward harsher criminal penalties like ever-lengthening prison sentences and the registration of sex offenders can be popular policies among voters in many jurisdictions, and can be used to secure voter support, but they are seldom associated with reduced crime rates and are therefore poor choices from an instrumental perspective (Aos, Miller & Drake, 2007; Freiberg & Carson, 2010). There is a complicated interplay between political and instrumental policy decision making, and therefore the source of the advice that supports those decisions will have an effect on public policy outcomes.

Since the end of the Second World War, there has been a movement in many countries to separate instrumental policy advice from partisan policy advice, mainly by promoting a neutral and permanent workforce of professional policy analysts within the bureaucracy (Dobuzinskis, Howlett & Laycock, 2007; Hollander & Prince, 1993; Jennings & Hall, 2012) and by relocating partisan advisers to dedicated agencies (Gains & Stoker, 2011). This professionalization of the public service has been buttressed by a forced decline in patronage and partisan appointments. The corps of professional policy analysts that has developed over time includes highly specialized experts in particular policy areas, as well as multi-talented generalists who can be assigned to a variety of tasks (Page & Jenkins, 2005), but in either case their purpose is to collect information and process it into advice for senior decision makers (Tiernan, 2011), who can then use it as they see fit in conjunction with the partisan advice they receive from other sources.

More recently, since the turn of the millennium, the concept of neutral instrumental policy advice has taken on a renewed vigour (Bogenschneider & Corbett, 2010; Head, 2008; Nutley & Webb, 2000; Sanderson, 2002). The movement for evidence-based policy, as it has come to be known, insists that the institutionalization of politically neutral policy advice has not yet gone far enough. According to proponents of evidence-based policy, not only should policy advice come from a dedicated and permanent professional corps, but the advice itself should be based on facts that can be verified through rigorous independent processes. Implicit in this argument is the notion that public policy that is based on verifiable research evidence will produce social outcomes that are more equitable, more beneficial to more people, and ultimately more sustainable than policies that are based on traditions, political motives, or unsupported ideologies (e.g., Boaz, Grayson, Levitt & Solesbury, 2008).

In effect, the institutionalization of professional policy analysis within the administrative sphere of government is a move toward evidence-based policy, in that it is an effort to de-politicize the information and advice that is gathered, collated and packaged for senior decision makers' future consumption. It would seem that the concept is popular among decision makers themselves: politicians and bureaucrats around the world have expressed support for increasing evidence-based policy beyond the status quo (e.g., O'Malley, 2014; Organisation for Economic Co-operation and Development, 2013). However, some observers have noted that political uses of evidence continue to take precedence over instrumental uses, including the habit of many political executives to use evidence selectively to justify policy decisions that have already been reached (Newman et al., 2016). Many have argued that evidence-based policy in any strict sense of the term is in fact impossible (Adams, 2004; Freiberg & Carson, 2010; Kay, 2011) because policy choices are ultimately political choices inasmuch as they are decisions about which policies will produce which outcomes. Most moderate voices contend that policies can be informed by evidence but that ultimately political decision making is a legitimate and fundamental part of the process (e.g., Head, 2013).

Some have cautioned that the pendulum may now be swinging too far, and that the movement to de-politicize policymaking is at risk of becoming detrimental to democracy. These critics of evidence-based policy argue that, in a democracy, citizens (through their elected representatives) have the right to pursue whatever policies they desire—no matter what the outcomes of these policies may be (Monaghan, 2010: 1). Pushing evidence-based policy to its logical conclusion, according to this point of view, will eliminate input from the people and replace it with a process-based technocracy in which every problem has a predetermined solution and where human judgement is removed from the equation (Biesta, 2007). These critics also decry what they see as the tyranny of scientific—and especially, statistical—argumentation over human lived experience (Marston & Watts, 2003; Neylan, 2008; Triantafillou, 2015: 174).

These differing conceptions of the use of information in policymaking provide a layout of the terrain over which policy analysis can be positioned. At one extreme, a system akin to the 19th-century (and earlier) practice in many countries of appointing bureaucratic authorities through patronage and cronyism produces policies that are fundamentally political and favour particular groups, corporations or, frequently, individuals over larger populations. At the other end of the spectrum, a brave new technocratic world mechanizes all decision making, obstructing citizens' rights to collective self-determination. These extreme visions are, of course, highly unlikely scenarios. Nevertheless, trends in one direction or another can help to determine the questions that must be asked about what policy analysts should do, how analysis can and should inform decision making, and more general questions about the relationship between administrative and political decision makers in the greater process of formulating and implementing public policy.

Sub-National Governments

The vast majority of inquiry into policy analysis concerns the national level of government, but sub-national government forms an interesting special case of governance that merits much more attention than it has received to date. In addition to the well-known examples of constitutional federations like the United States, Canada, Mexico, Brazil, Germany, Australia and India, a wave of decentralization in numerous countries around the world has produced strong sub-national administrative units and in some cases, fully autonomous regions. Countries like the United Kingdom, Spain, the Philippines and Indonesia all have partially autonomous sub-national government units with rising levels of power, and many developing countries with histories of strong central governments are increasingly devolving responsibility for governance to sub-national units (Bardhan & Mookherjee, 2006).

In many countries, sub-national governments are responsible for delivering public services that affect people's lives in a tangible way and on a daily basis. Policy areas like transportation, health care, education, policing, child care, aged care, sanitation, and urban development are all frequently responsibilities of sub-national governments. By contrast, national government activities are usually either services that are based on transfers of money to individuals, such as unemployment insurance or welfare (McArthur, 2007), or transfers of money to fund programmes at other levels of government, such as occurs with the Goods and Services Tax in Australia. Programmes that are directly run by the national government tend to be in policy areas that either have no physical outcome, like monetary policy or diplomacy, or are not seen or used by individual citizens on a regular basis, like national defence. Of course, there are variations from one country to another—for instance, the provision of health care is almost entirely a sub-national area of responsibility in Canada, but not in the United States—but nonetheless the overall trend is toward sub-national authority for the delivery of many visible public services.

More importantly, sub-national governments allow for variation of public policy *within* a single country. In Australia for example, Queensland, the Northern Territory and Western Australia do not observe daylight savings time, whereas the other states and the Australian Capital Territory do. In the United States, Texas' preference for 'abstinence-only' sex education for adolescents is contrasted by the experience in California, where the state government has repeatedly refused federal funding for abstinence-only education programmes (Raymond et al., 2008). Catalonia, Quebec and Wales all have protective language policies that are not practised in the rest of Spain, Canada and the United Kingdom. Sub-national units of government are designed to allow for regional, ethnic, cultural and religious variations in policy. This variation can sometimes also allow sub-national governments to act as laboratories for policy experimentation, the results of which can be adopted by other governments at sub-national or national levels (Garzarelli, 2006; Oates, 1999).

There is also ample potential for conflict between central and sub-national governments over policy direction. Sub-national governments provide many physical public services, but they do not usually raise sufficient funding to cover the costs of these services and they must often be supported financially by transfers from the central government (Borge & Rattsø, 2002; Dollery, 2002). In effect, because policy areas like health care are becoming more important both in terms of costs and in terms of citizens' expectations (Frenk, 2010), sub-national governments can find themselves in a position of increased policy responsibility without commensurate fiscal transfer. In the developing world, the reverse situation is often a greater problem: sub-national governments can be given sufficient responsibility for funding sources but may not be allowed to share discretionary responsibility for expenditure. In this case, a 'partial decentralization' results in sub-national governments that have the money to pay for services but lack the power to do so and the accountability to make sustainable policy decisions (Devarajan, Khemani & Shah, 2009).

Central and sub-national governments can have highly complex relationships. Because sub-national governments must manage their dependence on grants from their central government, central governments can leverage this power imbalance to circumvent the constitutional limits of their authority. In Canada, this 'federal spending power' has been used by the national government to legislate in areas of provincial jurisdiction, most notably in health care (Telford, 2003). Sub-national governments must also navigate the rough waters of multi-level governance, including negotiating policy in areas of concurrent powers: possession of marijuana, for example, is legal in some US states but is illegal under US federal law (Mikos, 2009). Central governments are responsible for ratifying international treaties, but the implementation of treaty obligations often falls within areas of sub-national jurisdiction, as is the case with conventions on human rights (Spiro, 2008), so sub-national units can find themselves committed to policy decisions to which they may not have been a party. Sub-national governments have little control over immigration, national security, monetary policy or customs and border control, and yet these are things that affect their policy operations daily. In many cases, policy development is further confounded by a misalignment between the party in power in the central government and the parties in power in the states or provinces.

The policy analytical requirements of sub-national jurisdictions are therefore different from, and in some ways more complex than, what is needed to support policy development in a central government. While the activities of policy analysts and their work units in central government bureaucracies may appear to be similar to the activities of policy workers in sub-national administrations, the issues that sub-national policy analysts must deal with as they collect information and craft policy advice for decision makers, and the contexts that shape their understanding of these issues, will necessarily be different from those at the national level.

The Research Agenda

The unique nature of the issues and intergovernmental relationships involved in policy analysis at the sub-national level, as discussed above, has given rise to a set of questions that have begun to take the shape of an early scholarly research agenda. The majority of scholarship on sub-national policy analysis to date falls into one of these categories.

Who Are Policy Analysts? And What Do They Do?

The primary question of academic observers of policy analysis at the sub-national level pertains to who is doing the actual analysis of policy. Despite the long-term institutionalization of policy analysis in the public service, little is known about the people who work in this profession. In some jurisdictions, most of the human-resource information on public servants engaged in policy analysis has been gathered by their unions for purposes of collective bargaining, not by public service commissions, so detailed information may not even be available (Bernier & Howlett, 2012). In many countries very little information exists on how many individuals in the public service do policy analysis at the sub-national level; how many years of experience they bring to their job positions; their ages; what kind of education they have; what kind of on- and off-the-job training they receive; and what kind of work units they are members of, whether they be small or large, hierarchical or autonomous, collaborative or independent, or supportive of evidence-based policy or not.

One inherent problem identified by multiple observers (Howlett & Newman, 2010; Veselý et al., 2014) is that job titles can be misleading. Public servants who do policy work are not always called 'policy analysts' and may not even have the word 'policy' in their job title or position description. In Canada, provincial bureaucracies employ 'policy analysts', 'policy officers' and 'policy advisers' in addition to other employees who do policy work (Howlett & Newman, 2010). In countries where English is not the language of operation, the terms may be even more ambiguous (Veselý et al., 2014), so it can be difficult even to identify people engaged in policy analysis, let alone to learn about their personal and professional characteristics.

But if they could be identified, it would also be useful to know what kind of work these policy professionals do. What kind of analysis are they engaged in, and how do political dynamics affect their work? Do they see themselves as neutral, non-partisan information gatherers and processers or do they see their roles as being more subservient to the whims of the political executive? How much of an individual's time is spent on policy work (as opposed to managerial work, administrative support, or street-level service-delivery-related tasks)? How much time do they spend in their job roles on average, and does this have consequences for the level of continuity of personnel assigned to a particular policy issue?

Do Sub-National Governments Have the Policy Capacity They Need to Govern Effectively?

Accounts of policy analysts' personal characteristics and details related to their professional activities are important, because this can enable a longitudinal examination of public servants' ability to do the job of policy analysis. The capacity of governments to create and enact policy is likely the most studied issue in this area of public administration and this is especially true at the sub-national level. Prominent—though debated—narratives of policy analysis often argue that, since the 1980s, the capacity of governments to do their own policy analysis (and thus, to wield effective control over their own public policy) has waned, due to the forces of globalization, decentralization and the paradigm of New Public Management, which emphasizes smaller, leaner, output-focused bureaucracies (e.g., Baskoy, Evans & Shields, 2011; Conley, 2002; Edwards, 2009).

At play are two separate, but related, concepts. On the one hand, 'capacity' is thought of as the ability of policy workers to conduct the day-to-day business of policy analysis—their training, their education and experience, the size of their workforce, and the material resources they are given to complete their tasks (Rasmussen, 1999; Gleeson, Legge, O'Neill & Pfeffer, 2011; Voyer, 2007). This is sometimes alternatively referred to as 'policy analytical capacity' (Howlett, 2009a; Wellstead, Stedman & Howlett, 2011). On the other hand, 'capacity' can refer to the ability of the state to direct its own policy choices, from formulation through to implementation (Bell, 2004; Knill & Lehmkuhl, 2002; Painter & Pierre, 2005). The former concept is one that focuses on the role of expertise in the policy process; the latter emphasizes autonomy. However, these conceptualizations of policy capacity are similar in that they both intend to evaluate the state's ability to control the process itself, rather than the outcomes that specific policies may produce (Newman & Perl, 2014). In the end, these concepts are complementary, not contradictory, but the use of the single term 'policy capacity' in both contexts can be somewhat confusing.

There are several further issues of interest here. First, the worldwide trend toward decentralization—that is, to increasing responsibility for public service delivery to sub-national units—should drive a stronger demand within sub-national governments for policy analysis in a greater number of policy areas. In theory, further decentralization should be met with greater analytical capacity (i.e. more policy analysts with higher levels of education, better training and stronger resources). It is not known if these needs have been met in many countries or what the general trends might be around the world.

Second, the forces of globalization, including the ease of capital flows in and out of national economies, the transnational nature of corporate activity, the increasing global impact of policy issues like climate change, the proliferation of international treaties and economic agreements and, most recently, the surging wave of migration of millions of refugees to Western countries, have arguably increased the challenge of policy analysis, especially at the sub-national level where governments have little control over the factors that affect their internal situations in these areas. How can local industry be supported when capital investment can easily be relocated to other jurisdictions (or even other countries)? How will sub-national budgets be affected by multi-national corporations operating domestically through online outlets, like the car-sharing company Uber or the short-term home rental agency Airbnb.com, where the evasion of state and provincial sales tax is easy and sanctioned by other levels of government? How can sub-national governments produce local responses to climate change when the causes are global in nature? Will policymakers be able to predict the educational needs of a population affected by the immigration of large numbers of young families coming from countries where base education is likely to be much poorer? With an increasing variety of highly contentious issues, in addition to the many unknown quantities involved in creating policy responses to these issues, the capacity of the state—and especially, sub-national administrations—to engage in effective policy analysis and evidence-based policymaking can be severely curtailed. These challenges can, understandably, affect policy capacity in both its analytical expertise and autonomy of governance conceptions.

Third, the prevailing global trend throughout the 1980s and 1990s and beyond has been one of administrative reform (Christensen & Lægreid, 2002; Pollitt & Bouckaert, 2011). Traditional bureaucracies are now frequently seen as being slow, expensive and wasteful. From the mid-1980s on, many countries attempted to bring in managerial strategies from the private sector, including a focus on outcomes (as opposed to process), improved productivity (implying a downsizing of the workforce), outsourcing of many activities to private firms, and asset sales, privatization, and marketization of public services. These trends may have affected policy analysis, primarily by putting pressure on governments to reduce the size of the policy workforce, but also by embedding market-oriented ideologies throughout the public sector. In addition, these practices may pose greater challenges for sub-national policy analysis, because the growing responsibility of sub-national units for public service delivery increases the pressure to do more with less money.

Where Do Policy Analysts Get Their Information?

The institutionalization of non-partisan policy analysis implies that professional policy analysts are getting their information from independent, reliable and neutral sources. But little is known about the sources that policy workers use for data collection or for explanatory information. Public sector agencies seldom conduct their own field experiments (although they do occasionally use pilot projects—see Sanderson, 2002, for an example), so policy advice cannot always be derived from primary experimental data conducted in-house. More to the point, experimentation in the public sector carries with it a multitude of ethical problems, the most obvious being that if the experiment results in negative outcomes, people's lives will be materially affected (Rittel & Webber, 1973).

Individual policy analysts can rely on internal or external sources of information. In addition to the results of pilot projects conducted by the public sector itself, internal information can include the experience of colleagues within the same department or elsewhere in the public service. More formally, the documented experience of other government agencies or governments in other jurisdictions can provide lessons for how to reform or expand current policies (Rose, 1993). Part of the task of policy analysis is to appraise initiatives from the past or from other jurisdictions and then to decide if the outcomes were favourable or unfavourable and whether the initiative can be adopted domestically. In order to be effective, such appraisals will require information about what outcomes occurred, who was affected and how, and how the local context of the original policy may differ from the context of the location contemplating its adoption (Newman, 2014a).

External sources of information can be valuable as well. Private companies may have research (such as information about pharmaceuticals or information technology) that could be useful to public sector policy analysts, but the reliability of this information may be suspect if it must be paid for. Governments can commission private consultants to conduct research directly, but the short-term contract nature of their work presents questions about the possible loss of institutional memory that this practice can create. Media reports are widely accessible, as are internet search engines, but their reliability and the depth of available information is of course highly questionable.

Academic research is arguably the biggest source of quality information that could be used for policy analysis, and it is available on virtually every topic in every area of public policy. However, it is unclear whether or not, or to what extent, policy analysts use academic research for their policy-related work. The traditional understanding of the relationship between policy workers and academics is one of 'two communities' (Caplan, 1979): policy workers and academics live in separate spaces, speak mutually incoherent languages, respond to conflicting incentives, operate along incompatible timelines, and generally have little or no communication between them. More recently, research has shown that at least in some countries, there is considerably more interaction between the two 'communities' than was previously thought to exist (Newman & Head, 2015). Policy workers may have access to academic research—they just might not be using it as much as they could (Newman, 2014b). It may then be the task of specialized 'bridgers' to close the gap (van der Arend, 2014).

The State of Research to Date

Because governments themselves have not been gathering information on their own policy analysis workforce, interested observers who want to know more about policy analysts and their work must ask them directly. Surveys and interviews are by far the dominant methodology used in studies of policy analysts, including those at the sub-national level.

Unfortunately, there are several limits to survey and interview methods in this context. First and foremost, it is impossible to determine who belongs in the population of study. As discussed above, job titles can be confusing and unhelpful. But, more pertinently, contact information for individual public servants is not always available to the general public. This is, of course, to be expected; one prerequisite for a neutral public sector workforce is that individuals within that workforce must remain anonymous so that ministers and other political appointees can be held responsible for activities within their departments by democratic mechanisms (Pelletier, 1999). Also, the public service is designed to be opaque, so as to preserve its independence from political interference.

From a more technical perspective, because the population is difficult to determine, and also because it is impossible (and unethical) to compel individuals to participate in social research, no study of policy analysts will be able to compile a probability sample. All studies must instead use purposive sampling or snowball methods, or must rely on the statistically weaker practice of asking managers within the public service to distribute surveys or requests for interview to potential participants at their own discretion. Response sets will therefore necessarily be incomplete and will be subject to self-selection bias. Also, results must be interpreted not as a random sample representing a larger group, but more like an incomplete attempt to take a census of the entire population (Veselý, 2013).

Nonetheless, these are the standard practices followed by those who have conducted empirical studies on policy analysts. At present, it appears that these are the best methods for gathering data on a population that is institutionally designed to be resistant to outside investigation. However, some steps can be taken to make the research more robust. Respondents can be targeted by carefully devising survey instruments that can only be completed by people who work in policy development. Managers can be persuaded to assist with distributing surveys with the promise of sharing any human-resource data that comes out of the survey results. Conducting interviews in addition to large-N surveys can help to triangulate data and corroborate results. Lastly, cross-national comparison could be useful for studies of policy analysis; at the moment, very little comparative research has been conducted, especially at the sub-national level (Veselý et al., 2014).

Early empirical studies on policy analysis came out of the United States (Caplan, Morrison & Stambaugh, 1975; Lester, 1993; Weiss, 1980), but in more recent years this area of study has been dominated by research from Canada with much larger response sets (e.g. Landry, Lamari & Amara, 2003; Howlett, 2009a; Wellstead et al., 2011). Studies specifically reporting results from sub-national governments initially came from Canada as well (e.g. Howlett & Newman, 2010) but have more recently been conducted in the Czech Republic (Veselý et al., 2014) and Australia (Head et al., 2014).

Results have been mixed. For instance, in Canada, Howlett (2009b) found that provincial policy analysts were relatively young (70% of respondents were under 50), relatively inexperienced (60% had been with their current organization for fewer than 5 years), and relatively mobile (two-thirds expected not to be in their current position within 5 years), and that these results did not align with data from studies conducted in Canada at the national level. By contrast, in Australia, Head, Ferguson, Cherney & Boreham (2014) found little difference between the length of previous work experience of state-level and national-level respondents. In the Czech Republic, Veselý et al. (2014) found that sub-national policy workers had on average much more prior work experience than Canadian policy workers but about the same as Australians. There does not yet seem to be a pattern emerging.

There are several problems with cross-national comparison at this point, but there is plenty of potential for improvement. For one, there have been so few empirical studies undertaken at the sub-national level that it would be extremely difficult to discern general international trends at this time. Also, the survey instruments used in each study, and for that matter, the general research purposes of the studies themselves, have not been identical, so some of the more material results cannot be compared. For example, Head et al. (2014) were very interested in sources of information and the relationship between academic research and policy development in Australia, and so their survey asked many in-depth questions on this topic. Howlett (2009b) and Veselý et al. (2014) were less interested in this aspect of policy analysis and did not ask for as much detail on similar questions in their surveys. Lastly, most studies to date have been cross-sectional rather than longitudinal, so determining long-term trends (such as whether or not New Public Management has contributed to a decline in policy capacity) would be impossible (but see Baskoy et al., 2011, for a different approach to this problem).

The Path Forward

Where does the research agenda on policy analysis in sub-national governments go from here? The obvious, though superficial, answer is 'more research is required'. Truthfully, more research—preferably from more international sources with some potential for longitudinal analysis—would be extremely beneficial to this area of study, where, despite some fruitful early work and an agenda of clearly defined research questions, so little empirical research has been performed so far.

However, a larger conceptual question looms over the accomplishments that have already been made. In this chapter I have treated policy analysis as something that lies within the purview of a permanent, independent and politically neutral professional policy workforce, performed by dedicated and trained policy analysts. This is, of course, an idealized description. Bureaucrats can make political decisions (Brehm & Gates, 1999) just as politicians can engage in policy analysis (Peters, 2002). Nonetheless, interviews and surveys show that many policy

Policy Analysis at the Sub-National Level

analysts, including highly experienced senior managers, describe their roles as being responsible for non-partisan policy advice that is intended to inform political decision making that is to be carried out by others (Newman et al., 2016; Rasmussen, 1999).

A complex and nuanced network of relationships exists between professional policy analysts, senior bureaucratic managers, political appointees in public service leadership positions, and elected officials, and the structure and internal dynamics of this network are only poorly understood. The classical Weberian paradigm, in which elected officials make policy decisions based on political factors, and then task an independent bureaucratic machine with the implementation of those decisions, is no longer valid—if it ever was (Stoker, 2006). Yet, too many authors conflate policy analysis in the public service and policy development in the political arena (e.g., Herbst, 2002; Hird, 2009). Admittedly, administrative policy analysis and political policy development are two related components of the greater policymaking process, but more precision is necessary in defining the activities of the bureaucratic and political actors involved and their relationships with one another. In sub-national contexts, where the hands-on nature of public service delivery and the difficult challenges of multi-level governance make policy analysis a fundamental component of policy development, future studies will need delve further into the dynamics of sub-national policy analysis if they want to develop a deeper understanding of this aspect of the policymaking process.

References

Aberbach, Joel D., Robert D. Putnam and Bert A. Rockan. 1981. *Bureaucrats and Politicians in Western Democracies*. Cambridge, MA: Harvard University Press.

Adams, David. 2004. Usable Knowledge in Public Policy. *Australian Journal of Public Administration* 63(1): 29–42.

Aos, Steve, Marna Miller and Elizabeth Drake. 2007. Evidence-Based Public Policy Options to Reduce Future Prison Construction, Criminal Justice Costs, and Crime Rates. *Federal Sentencing Reporter* 19(4): 275–290.

Bardhan, Pranab and Dilip Mookherjee. 2006. The Rise of Local Governments: An Overview. In *Decentralization and Local Governance in Developing Countries: A Comparative Perspective*, edited by Pranab K. Bardhan and Dilip Mookherjee, 1–52. Cambridge, MA: MIT Press.

Baskoy, Tuna, Bryan Evans and John Shields. 2011. Assessing Policy Capacity in Canada's Public Services: Perspectives of Deputy and Assistant Deputy Ministers. *Canadian Public Administration* 54(2): 217–234.

Beckman, Ludvig. 2006. The Competent Cabinet? Ministers in Sweden and the Problem of Competence and Democracy. *Scandinavian Political Studies* 29(2): 111–129.

Bell, Stephen. 2004. 'Appropriate' Policy Knowledge, and Institutional and Governance Implications. *Australian Journal of Public Administration* 63(1): 22–28.

Bernier, Luc and Michael Howlett. 2012. The Policy Analytical Capacity of the Government of Quebec: Results from a Survey of Officials. *Canadian Political Science Review* 6(2–3): 281–285.

Biesta, Gert. 2007. Why 'What Works' Won't Work: Evidence-Based Practice and the Democratic Deficit in Educational Research. *Educational Theory* 57(1): 1–22.

Blackham, Alysia and George Williams. 2012. The Appointment of Ministers from Outside of Parliament. *Federal Law Review* 40(2): 253–285.

Blondel, Jean. 1985. *Government Ministers in the Contemporary World*. London: Sage.

Boaz, Annette, Lesley Grayson, Ruth Levitt and William Solesbury. 2008. Does Evidence-Based Policy Work? Learning from the UK Experience. *Evidence & Policy* 4(2): 233–253.

Bogenschneider, Karen and Thomas J. Corbett. 2010. *Evidence-Based Policymaking: Insights from Policy-Minded Researchers and Research-Minded Policymakers*. New York: Routledge.

Borge, Lars-Erik and Jørn Rattsø. 2002. Spending Growth With Vertical Fiscal Imbalance: Decentralized Government Spending in Norway, 1880–1990. *Economics and Politics* 14(3): 351–373.

Brehm, John and Scott Gates. 1999. *Working, Shirking, and Sabotage: Bureaucratic Response to a Democratic Public*. Ann Arbor: University of Michigan Press.

Caplan, Nathan. 1979. The Two-Communities Theory and Knowledge Utilization. *American Behavioral Scientist* 22(3): 459–70.

Caplan, Nathan, Andrea Morrison and Russell J. Stambaugh. 1975. *The Use of Social Science Knowledge in Policy Decisions at the National Level: A Report to Respondents*. Ann Arbor, MI: Institute for Social Research.

Christensen, Tom and Per Lægreid. 2002. *New Public Management: The Transformation of Ideas and Practice*. Burlington, VT and Aldershot, UK: Ashgate.

Conley, Tom. 2002. Globalisation as Constraint and Opportunity: Reconceptualising Policy Capacity in Australia. *Global Society* 16(4): 377–399.

Devarajan, Shantayanan, Stuti Khemani and Shekhar Shah. 2009. The Politics of Partial Decentralization. In *Does Decentralization Enhance Service Delivery and Poverty Reduction?* edited by Ehtisham Ahmad and Giorgio Brosio, 102–121. Cheltenham, UK and Northampton, MA: Edward Elgar.

Dobuzinskis, Laurent, Michael Howlett and David Laycock. 2007. Policy Analysis in Canada: The State of the Art. In *Policy Analysis in Canada: The State of the Art*, edited by Laurent Dobuzinskis, Michael Howlett and David Laycock, 3–17. University of Toronto Press.

Dollery, Brian. 2002. A Century of Vertical Fiscal Imbalance in Australian Federalism. *History of Economics Review* 36 (Summer): 26–43.

Edwards, Lindy. 2009. Testing the Discourse of Declining Policy Capacity: Rail Policy and the Department of Transport. *Australian Journal of Public Administration* 68(3): 288–302.

Freiberg, Arie and W. G. Carson. 2010. The Limits to Evidence-Based Policy: Evidence, Emotion and Criminal Justice. *Australian Journal of Public Administration* 69(2): 152–164.

Frenk, Julio. 2010. The Global Health System: Strengthening National Health Systems as the Next Step for Global Progress. *PLoS Med* 7(1): 1–3.

Gains, Francesca and Gerry Stoker. 2011. Special Advisers and the Transmission of Ideas from the Policy Primeval Soup. *Policy and Politics* 39(4): 485–498.

Garzarelli, Giampaolo. 2006. Cognition, Incentives, and Public Governance: Laboratory Federalism from the Organizational Viewpoint. *Public Finance Review* 34(3): 235–257.

Gleeson, Deborah, David Legge, Deirdre O'Neill and Monica Pfeffer. 2011. Negotiating Tensions in Developing Organizational Policy Capacity: Comparative Lessons to be Drawn. *Journal of Comparative Policy Analysis* 13(3): 237–263.

Head, Brian W. 2008. Three Lenses of Evidence-Based Policy. *Australian Journal of Public Administration* 67(1): 1–11.

Head, Brian W. 2013. Evidence-Based Policymaking – Speaking Truth to Power? *Australian Journal of Public Administration* 72(4): 397–403.

Head, Brian, Michele Ferguson, Adrian Cherney and Paul Boreham. 2014. Are Policy-Makers Interested in Social Research? Exploring the Sources and Uses of Valued Information among Public Servants in Australia. *Policy and Society* 33(2): 89–101.

Herbst, Susan. 2002. How State-Level Policy Managers 'Read' Public Opinion. In *Navigating Public Opinion: Polls, Policy, and the Future of American Democracy*, edited by Jeff Manza, Fay Lomax Cook and Benjamin I. Page, 171–183. Oxford University Press.

Hird, John A. 2009. The Study and Use of Policy Research in State Legislatures. *International Regional Science Review* 32(4): 523–535.

Hollander, Marcus J. and Michael J. Prince. 1993. Analytical Units in Federal and Provincial Governments: Origins, Functions and Suggestions for Effectiveness. *Canadian Public Administration* 36(2): 190–224.

Howlett, Michael. 2009a. Policy Analytical Capacity and Evidence-Based Policy-Making: Lessons from Canada. *Canadian Public Administration* 52(2): 153–175.

Howlett, Michael. 2009b. Policy Advice in Multi-Level Governance Systems: Sub-National Policy Analysts and Analysis. *International Review of Public Administration* 13(3): 1–16.

Howlett, Michael and Joshua Newman. 2010. Policy Analysis and Policy Work in Federal Systems: Policy Advice and its Contribution to Evidence-Based Policy-Making in Multi-Level Governance Systems. *Policy and Society* 29 (1): 123–136.

Jennings, Edward T., Jr. and Jeremy L. Hall. 2012. Evidence-Based Practice and the Use of Information in State Agency Decision Making. *Journal of Public Administration Research and Theory* 22(2): 245–266.

Kay, Adrian. 2011. Evidence-Based Policy-Making: The Elusive Search for Rational Public Administration. *Australian Journal of Public Administration* 70(3): 236–245.

Knill, Christoph and Dirk Lehmkuhl. 2002. Private Actors and the State: Internationalization and Changing Patterns of Governance. *Governance* 15(1): 41–63.

Landry, Réjean, Moktar Lamari and Nabil Amara. 2003. The Extent and Determinants of the Utilization of University Research in Government Agencies. *Public Administration Review* 63(2): 192–205.

Legrand, Timothy. 2012. Overseas and Over Here: Policy Transfer and Evidence-Based Policy-Making. *Policy Studies* 33(4): 329–348.

Lester, James P. 1993. The Utilization of Policy Analysis by State Agency Officials. *Science Communication* 14(3): 267–290.

Marston, Greg and Rob Watts. 2003. Tampering with the Evidence: A Critical Appraisal of Evidence-Based Policy-Making. *The Drawing Board: An Australian Review of Public Affairs* 3(3): 143–163.

McArthur, Doug. 2007. Policy Analysis in Provincial Governments in Canada: From PPBS to Network Management. In *Policy Analysis in Canada: The State of the Art*, edited by Laurent Dobuzinskis, Michael Howlett and David Laycock, 238–264. University of Toronto Press.

Mikos, Robert A. 2009. On the Limits of Supremacy: Medical Marijuana and the States' Overlooked Power to Legalize Federal Crime. *Vanderbilt Law Review* 62(5): 1421–1482.

Monaghan, Mark. 2010. The Complexity of Evidence: Reflections on Research Utilisation in a Heavily Politicised Policy Area. *Social Policy and Society* 9(1): 1–12.

Newman, Joshua. 2014a. Measuring Policy Success: Case Studies from Canada and Australia. *Australian Journal of Public Administration* 73(2): 192–205.

Newman, Joshua. 2014b. Revisiting the 'Two Communities' Metaphor of Research Utilisation. *International Journal of Public Sector Management* 27(7): 614–627.

Newman, Joshua and Brian W. Head. 2015. Beyond the Two Communities: A Reply to Mead's 'Why Government Often Ignores Research'. *Policy Sciences* 48(3): 383–393.

Newman, Joshua and Anthony Perl. 2014. Partners in Clime: Public-Private Partnerships and British Columbia's Capacity to Pursue Climate Policy Objectives. *Canadian Public Administration* 57(2): 217–233.

Newman, Joshua, Adrian Cherney and Brian W. Head. 2016. Do Policy Makers Use Academic Research? Re-examining the 'Two Communities' Theory of Research Utilization. *Public Administration Review* 76(1): 24–32.

Neylan, Julian. 2008. Social Policy and the Authority of Evidence. *Australian Journal of Public Administration* 67(1): 12–19.

Nutley, Sandra and Jeff Webb. 2000. Evidence and the Policy Process. In *What Works? Evidence-Based Policy and Practice in Public Services*, edited by Huw T. O. Davies, Sandra M. Nutley and Peter C. Smith, 13–41. Bristol, UK: Policy Press.

Oates, Wallace E. 1999. An Essay on Fiscal Federalism. *Journal of Economic Literature* 37(3): 1120–1149.

O'Malley, Martin. 2014. Doing What Works: Governing in the Age of Big Data. *Public Administration Review* 74(5): 555–556.

Organisation for Economic Co-operation and Development (OECD). 2013. *Strengthening Evidence-Based Policy Making on Security and Justice in Mexico*. Paris: OECD.

Page, Edward C. and Bill Jenkins. 2005. *Policy Bureaucracy: Government With a Cast of Thousands*. Oxford University Press.

Painter, Martin and Jon Pierre. 2005. Unpacking Policy Capacity: Issues and Themes. In *Challenges to State Policy Capacity: Global Trends and Comparative Perspectives*, edited by Martin Painter and Jon Pierre, 1–18. Basingstoke, UK: Palgrave.

Pelletier, Réjean. 1999. Responsible Government: Victory or Defeat for Parliament? In *Taking Stock of 150 Years of Responsible Government in Canada*, edited by F. Leslie Seidle and Louis Massicotte, 53–72. Ottawa, Canada: The Canadian Study of Parliament Group.

Peters, B. Guy. 2002. *The Politics of Bureaucracy*, 5th Edition. London and New York: Routledge.

Phillimore, John and Tracey Arklay. 2015. Policy and Policy Analysis in Australian States. In *Policy Analysis in Australia*, edited by Brian Head and Kate Crowley, 87–103. Bristol, UK: Policy Press.

Pollitt, Christopher and Geert Bouckaert. 2011. *Public Management Reform: A Comparative Analysis – New Public Management, Governance, and the Neo-Weberian State,* 3rd Edition. Oxford University Press.

Rasmussen, Ken, 1999. Policy Capacity in Saskatchewan: Strengthening the Equilibrium. *Canadian Public Administration* 42(3): 331–348.

Raymond, Marissa, Lylyana Bogdanovich, Dalia Brahmi, Laura Jane Cardinal, Gulielma Leonard Fager, LeighAnn C. Frattarelli, Gabrielle Hecker, Elizabeth Ann Jarpe, Adam Viera, Leslie M. Kantor and John S. Santelli. 2008. State Refusal of Federal Funding for Abstinence-Only Programs. *Sexuality Research & Social Policy* 5(3): 44–55.

Rittel, Horst W. J. and Melvin M. Webber. 1973. Dilemmas in a General Theory of Planning. *Policy Sciences* 4(2): 155–169.

Rose, Richard. 1993. *Lesson-Drawing in Public Policy: A Guide to Learning Across Time and Space.* Chatham, NJ: Chatham House.

Sanderson, Ian. 2002. Evaluation, Policy Learning, and Evidence-Based Policy Making. *Public Administration* (80)1: 1–22.

Sanderson, Ian. 2011. Evidence-Based Policy or Policy-Based Evidence? Reflections on Scottish Experience. *Evidence & Policy* 7(1): 59–76.

Spiro, Peter J. 2008. Resurrecting Missouri v. Holland. *Missouri Law Review* 73(4): 1029–1040.

Stoker, Gerry. 2006. Public Value Management: A New Narrative for Networked Governance? *American Review of Public Administration* 36(1): 41–57.

Telford, Hamish. 2003. The Federal Spending Power in Canada: Nation-Building or Nation-Destroying? *Publius* 33(1): 23–44.

Tiernan, Anne. 2011. Advising Australian Federal Governments: Assessing the Evolving Capacity and Role of the Australian Public Service. *Australian Journal of Public Administration* 70(4): 335–346.

Triantafillou, Peter. 2015. The Political Implications of Performance Management and Evidence-Based Policymaking. *American Review of Public Administration* 45(2): 167–181.

Tseng, Vivian and Sandra Nutley. 2014. Building the Infrastructure to Improve the Use and Usefulness of Research in Education. In *Using Research Evidence in Education: From the Schoolhouse Door to Capitol Hill,* edited by Kara S. Finnigan and Alan J. Daly, 163–175. New York: Springer.

van der Arend, Jenny. 2014. Bridging the Research/Policy Gap: Policy Officials' Perspectives on the Barriers and Facilitators to Effective Links Between Academic and Policy Worlds. *Policy Studies* 35(6): 611–630.

Veselý, Arnošt. 2013. Conducting Large-N Surveys on Policy Work in Bureaucracies: Some Methodological Challenges and Implications from the Czech Republic. *Central European Journal of Public Policy* 7(2): 88–113.

Veselý, Arnošt, Adam Wellstead and Bryan Evans. 2014. Comparing Sub-National Policy Workers in Canada and the Czech Republic: Who are They, What They do, and Why it Matters? *Policy and Society* 33(2): 103–115.

Voyer, Jean-Pierre. 2007. Policy Analysis in the Federal Government: Building the Forward-Looking Policy Research Capacity. In *Policy Analysis in Canada: The State of the Art,* edited by Laurent Dobuzinskis, Michael Howlett and David Laycock, 219–237. University of Toronto Press.

Weiss, Carol H. 1980. Knowledge Creep and Decision Accretion. *Science Communication* 1(3): 381–404.

Wellstead, Adam M., Richard C. Stedman and Michael Howlett. 2011. Policy Analytical Capacity in Changing Governance Contexts: A Structural Equation Model (SEM) Study of Contemporary Canadian Policy Work. *Public Policy and Administration* 26(3): 353–373.

9

POLICY ANALYSIS AT THE LOCAL LEVEL

Martin Lundin and PerOla Öberg

Introduction

Local governments exist in virtually all countries, and decisions made by local governments affect the everyday life of their inhabitants. Local planning, primary education, fire services, parks and recreation, and welfare provision are examples of policy issues often handled within local authorities (e.g., Hague & Harrop, 2007; Norton, 1991). In some countries, such as those in Scandinavia, local government is comparatively strong. In others, such as in France, the United Kingdom and Taiwan, local powers are more limited (e.g., Lijphart, 1999; Sellars & Lidström 2007; Erlingsson & Ödalen, 2013; Fang, 2015). In either case, important policy decisions are made locally, and poor performance by local governments affects trust in local authorities just as trust in national government is responsive to national conditions (Fitzgerald & Wolak, 2014).

It is therefore essential that local policymakers have accurate and sufficient information, so that they can understand the advantages and disadvantages of various policy choices (Lundin & Öberg, 2014; cf. Howlett & Wellstead, 2011). However, administrative capacity for policy analysis varies greatly across countries (Walker, 2014; Liu, Lindquist, Vedlitz & Vincent, 2010). For example, in countries with centralized intergovernmental systems, such as Japan and South Korea, the scope for policy analysis on the local level is restricted and must be understood in relation to decision-making processes on the national level (Kanai, 2015). Moreover, local governments vary enormously in size, even within countries. While smaller municipalities might have limited resources and have to make use of ad hoc solutions in political consensus (Liu et al., 2010), the larger ones often have a more professionalized decision-making structure (Bogumil & Ruddat, 2014).

It is important to understand how information is gathered and analysed when policy alternatives are developed and considered at the local level. However, as will be argued in this chapter, much work remains to be done. The purpose of this chapter is to sort out key topics within the research field of policy analysis at the local level. We also summarize important findings. We do not claim to be exhaustive: the goal is rather to highlight aspects of local policy formulation that we believe are especially important to comprehend. As it stands now, the research on local policy analysis appears scattered and somewhat weak. This is illustrated by the fact that the chapters on local policy analysis within the book series of the *International*

131

Library of Policy Analysis tend to relate to various fields of research and to some extent focus on different things. Thus, studies related to local policy analysis can be found within different literatures, using different terminology and posing somewhat different questions. In many studies, the empirical basis is weak or difficult to use for generalizations beyond the cases investigated. Another general reflection is that comparative evidence is lacking. In fact, some scholars believe that the knowledge of local policy analysis is more or less missing (Liu et al., 2010; Howlett & Walker, 2012). Given this background, the aim here is to develop an agenda for future research.

To What Should Researchers Pay Attention?

The academic study of policymaking commonly distinguishes various stages of the policy process (e.g., Hague & Harrop, 2007; Hill, 1997; Knill & Tosun, 2008; cf. Howlett, 2009). The number of stages and the labels used vary, but at a general level the policy process can be said to include initiation (agenda setting), formulation, decision making (policy adoption), implementation and evaluation. As many scholars have noted before us, this sequential model is a simplification of actual policymaking; in the real world, stages often overlap and the procedures may not be as rational as the ideal type suggests.[1] Nevertheless, it serves well as an analytical tool.

When we discuss policy analysis in this chapter, we focus mainly on the second stage of the policy process: formulation.[2] Policy formulation is the process that takes place when issues are on the agenda of local governments. In the ideal type of the policy process, information is collected, analysed and discussed at this stage. Feasible courses of action are generated and deliberated upon. For example, assume that a local government faces a large increase in the number of children in need of primary education. In order to find out how to formulate public policies to cope with the situation, a lot of information is needed. How large is the new demand? Can existing schools be used, or must new ones be established? What are the advantages and disadvantages of using public or private schools? Is the supply of teachers enough? Where should new schools be located? How should policies be financed? What is a realistic time schedule? Questions like these must be addressed and analysed, and some relevant alternatives on how to take action must be generated and deliberated upon.

Civil servants within local governments are key actors in this process of research (Lundin & Öberg, 2014; Workman, Jones & Jochim, 2009). They often collect information from various sources and write summaries that can provide a basis for decisions by mayors and board and council members. But other actors are also involved: politicians themselves can be active, and 'knowledge generators' and 'knowledge brokers' (cf. Lindquist, 1990) outside local government can supply elected officials and civil servants with relevant information.

As we see it, there are four stages of policy formulation that are especially important to consider in research: (i) information gathering, (ii) analysis, (iii) generation of policy alternatives, and (iv) integration of policy analysis into decision making. In each step, we need to describe what is going on, explain why the processes look the way they do, and identify the consequences for policy. Empirical and theoretical studies on these topics, within various policy areas and various countries, can give us a good map of what role policy analysis has in local policymaking. Hence, in this chapter, we will examine each of these four stages to summarize what current research can tell us about local policy analysis.

Information Gathering

In the first stage, of information gathering, it is important to understand who generates information and to assess the quality of that information.

Who Generates Information?

Actors involved in local policy analysis have the potential to affect how policymaking evolves and how policies are formulated. On the local level, knowledge production is primarily handled within local governments. This has, for example, been recognized by Stewart and Smith's (2007) examination of local policy analysis in Canada (see also Howlett, 2009). However, scholars have noticed that external actors sometimes produce information that local policymakers utilize. For instance, Farah (2013) argues that physicians and engineers, and technical knowledge from universities, played a central role in local decision making on urban development in Brazil. Lundin, Öberg & Thelander (2013) have in a survey asked public sector managers within Swedish municipalities from where they get information when they formulate policy. In line with the argument by Stewart and Smith (2007), managers find that information generated by the local administration itself is most important. But local authorities also employ information produced by other organizations. Reports and documents from national authorities and from the Swedish Association of Local Authorities and Regions are rather significant sources of information, and information produced by other municipalities is also sometimes used. Consultant reports are quite important in certain policy areas, but not in others. Research reports are occasionally employed.

Networks and governance structures are important for local policy formulation, and a number of recent studies have paid attention to local networks. According to Liu et al. (2010), interest groups are influential actors in local policy processes in the US, and findings from research on English and Norwegian local government show that local managers have extensive contacts with the surrounding community (Walker, O'Toole & Meier, 2007; Røseland, 2011). Another study focusing on local policy networks is Dente and Coletti's (2011) analysis of local politics in Italy. They suggest that more-innovative cities have a more complex governance system that includes several local actors. Walker and Andrews (2015) conclude in a recent literature review that there are indications that networking has positive effects on local government performance. But there is still a lack of knowledge on how networking with the surrounding community affects decision making and policy analysis (Walker et al., 2007). More theoretical work is needed to understand these local complexities (Røseland, 2011).

In order to advance our understanding of these complexities, Ansell, Lundin & Öberg (2017) use social network analysis to describe how Swedish municipalities learn from each other before local policy decisions are made. The study demonstrates that geographic proximity is a key contributor to forming networks. Furthermore, the study demonstrates that Swedish municipalities are a 'small world'[3] linked together on a national basis, that county seats often tend to be learning hubs, and that informal personal connections are important for structuring flows of information among municipalities. This demonstrates that additional knowledge of the structure of networks can advance policy analysis on the local level. The structure of learning networks in particular affects if and how information flows between local authorities and consequently how the information generated by these networks can be used by politicians and public administration to improve policy analysis. First, it is important to find out how connected the local authorities are in these learning networks—that is, if they exchange information at all. If a network of local governments is disconnected, or there is a sharp distinction between the centre and periphery of the network, information and experiences from other local governments might not reach many of the governments in the periphery. As a consequence, policy analysis in those peripheral local governments does not include information from other governments. Dissemination of information in strongly connected hierarchical networks may be more efficient and easier to control: it is easier to identify the top actors that all others learn from directly or indirectly, and it is easier to identify how information reaches local governments at the bottom of the hierarchy. A 'small world' network is more difficult to identify (Barthélemy, 2011), but the mutual learning between many equally important hubs and the dense learning networks around each hub is generally considered better for global learning (Cowan & Jonard, 2004) and, hence provides a better context for advanced policy analysis that in the long run may improve quality of decisions. Unfortunately, the literature on learning networks is scarce. The actual structure of information dissemination and learning, as opposed to the theoretical discussion of such networks, is unknown in most countries, and comparative data do not exist.

To this complexity of the information generating process should be added that many countries are now introducing elements of direct democracy in local policy analysis as a strategy to include citizens' opinions and experience in local decision making. These 'democratic innovations' include, for example, citizens' initiatives and advisory committees, referenda, and various arrangements for including civil society in discussion of policy alternatives (Bingham, Nabatchi & O'Leary, 2005; Kim & Schachter, 2013, p. 459). Among others, this trend has been noticed in the UK by Lowndes and Sullivan (2004) and McKenna (2011), in Brazil by Farah (2013), in Germany by Bogumil and Ruddat (2013), in the Netherlands by Michels and De Graaf (2010), and in Sweden by Montin (2002). However, what impact such arrangements have on policy analysis and policy decisions at the local level is still very unclear.

To summarize, we know that much of information generating and gathering is handled by civil servants within local government administrations, although other actors are involved in these processes as well. Networks and elements of direct democracy have received some attention in recent research. However, it seems that not that much is known about who the most influential actors are, how influence varies across countries and policy areas, and what the consequences are for policy analysis and policy decisions (McKenna, 2011).

Quality of Information

The quality of the information on which decisions are based is of course crucial. Information produced by the local organization itself is important and necessary (cf. Lundin et al., 2013; Fang, 2015), but it is seldom built on scientific research. Larger cities and local governments may sometimes have the necessary expertise or staff to produce high-quality information, but this is probably rare. In addition, just like policy analysts on other levels of government, local administrative staff have limited possibilities to keep themselves updated on current research. This means that decisions to a large extent must rely on easily available information from research institutes and government agencies. The internet and other resources have made information much more available than before, possibly presenting situations of information overload for the local administration. Hence, gathering but also sorting out relevant information is a main task for local public administration. While this kind of information to some extent might be found at universities, it is more common to use more popular research surveys and information provided by government agencies (Lundin et al., 2013).

The extent to which expert knowledge is used within local administrations, and thus the quality of information provided to local decision makers, varies depending on the availability of solid information; it is essential to have easy access to accurate information. However, there are many other reasons for variations in information quality. It is well known that the political context is important at the policy formulation stage, perhaps even more so in local politics than on other levels (Lundin & Öberg, 2014; Fang, 2015, p. 73). Lundin and Öberg (2014) have shown that local public administrations tend to include more expert knowledge in their analysis in contexts that involve a higher level of political dispute as well as in contexts with higher levels of public attention. Less politicized decisions, and those that escape the scrutiny of opposition politicians, citizens and media, are based on lower-quality information.

Obviously, it is impossible to evaluate the overall quality of information used in local policy analysis. However, we know that even in contexts where infrastructure and other resources are comparatively well provided, there is dissatisfaction with the information gathered. In Sweden, for example, about 25% of local administration managers are not really satisfied with the information they use in decision making. The level of dissatisfaction is even higher among politicians: 35% of politicians in majority parties, and almost half of the politicians from minority parties, have a critical opinion of the information on which they base their decisions (Lundin et al., 2013). A lack of relevant information has been noted in other countries as well, for instance in Taiwan (Lee, 2015, p. 50).

Overall, it appears that the quality of information available to and used by those involved in policy formulation—both managers and politicians—tends to be somewhat poorer at the local level than at the national level. However, it is difficult to assess how large a problem this is and what the effects are, since there has been very little quantitative research on the subject.

Analysis of Information

There is no systematic data on the kind of techniques that are used within local administration to analyse information. As with the generation of information, the techniques for analysis of this information will most likely vary significantly between urban communities in highly developed countries and small municipalities far from urban centres in less developed countries. However, given that local administrations even in more developed and wealthy countries typically have lower educational levels and less access to resources, it is reasonable to believe that advanced techniques are seldom used on the local level.

There are a few studies that discuss analysis of information at the local level. For instance, according to Walker and Andrews (2015), some local governments use different technical approaches to planning, which are loosely associated with higher levels of performance. Another topic examined in the literature is benchmarking, which is an increasingly common management tool to obtain organizational learning between local government agencies in order to improve performance. There are some weak indications that benchmarking is a useful tool in local policymaking (Askim, Johnsen & Christophersen, 2007; Kuhlmann & Jäkel, 2013; Ammons & Roenigk, 2014). However, there is not much empirical knowledge of how benchmarking works, its effects and the quality of these analyses. Although benchmarking is often described as a neutral technique, its use is dependent on political context and how local governments are positioned in learning networks (Askim et al., 2007), as well as the institutional characteristics of local government systems (Kuhlmann & Jäkel, 2013). Furthermore, different forms of benchmarking produce different results, and there is still no coherent theory of public sector benchmarking that can help us understand these variations (Ammons & Roenigk, 2014).[4]

Because there is a multitude of local governments in many countries, it is possible to test different policies and to learn from the experiences of others (Bogumil & Ruddat, 2013; Farah, 2013; Lundin, Öberg & Josefsson, 2015). Local governments primarily learn from neighbours and other communities that have similar economic and social structures. This might reflect diffusion mechanisms other than learning, but these mechanisms have hardly been disentangled in the literature. Lundin et al. (2015) show that Swedish municipalities try to draw lessons from those municipalities where the inhabitants are satisfied with government services, suggesting that policy analysis, at least to some extent, is based on rational evaluation of best practices. However, less systematic analysis of other local governments' experiences is also common. Policy analysts on the local level often use information from other local governments where they have personal connections or where they can use other coincident channels for information gathering, instead of evaluating relevant examples of successful and unsuccessful policies. The low quality of local analysis appears to be the result of weak traditions of policy analysis in combination with scarce economic resources.

Obviously, the quality of analysis between local administrations will vary significantly, but overall the results are disheartening. It is reported from Canada that 'un- or under-supervised civil servants drive and dominate the policy analysis' (Stewart & Smith, 2007, p. 265). In some countries, the authorities try to increase analytical capacity by offering courses or other collaborations with universities and other institutions (Farah, 2013; Stewart & Smith, 2007; Tsuchyama, 2015).

To sum up, there is very little research indicating how local governments analyse information and how these procedures impinge on local decisions. The general picture from the available studies, however, is that analytical capacity at the local level is often not that good.

Generation of Policy Alternatives

After civil servants have collected and analysed relevant information, they present policy options to politicians, preferably in written documents. This is when it is decided what, and how many, options will be included and evaluated in an open discussion. Local politicians are, of course, sometimes (or even often) involved in the process of discussing alternatives at an earlier stage. However, probably only a small fraction (and the most powerful ones) have the possibility to receive information and take an active part from the beginning of the policy process.

In spite of the importance of the stage when policy alternatives are formulated and presented, little research has examined this stage. Because of the limited resources in local public administration, and scarce assistance available to local politicians, this policy process is likely very different on the local as opposed to the regional or national level. It is sometimes reported that politicians have more policy options to evaluate than they can handle, but empirical research on the local level points in another direction. Based on data on Swedish local governments, Öberg, Lundin and Thelander (2015) found that only on approximately 20% of issues does more than one alternative reach the local board making the decisions.

Most local politicians, in both the majority and opposition factions, think that they lack sufficient information on alternative policy designs. The same study also finds a 'political bias'—that is, alternatives are discarded at an early stage because they are deemed not politically feasible by civil servants. A similar finding is reported from the US, where 'policy compatibility' was mentioned by local policy stakeholders as the attribute that most contributed to an alternative's survival (Liu et al., 2010). Hence, processes based on power relations severely constrain the number of policy alternatives available in local politics. Yet another indication of this is that politicians outside the inner circles, especially those with higher education, would like to see more policy alternatives from which to discuss and choose (Öberg et al., 2015). Since politicians on local levels are much more dependent on the information they receive from local public administration than politicians on the national level, this problem calls for much more research.

Integration of Policy Analysis into Decision Making

The impact of policy analysis on decision making is of course dependent on *how* the information provided in that process is used by politicians. This means that characteristics of politicians and the conditions that embed local decision making are important. In this regard it is necessary to remember that being a local politician is completely different from being a politician on the national level. For one, the context of political conflict is different. For instance, in the US it has been reported that consensus and coalition building is more important on the local level than on the national level (Liu et al., 2010). In addition, the conditions for participation in decision making and the social characteristics of politicians are different. In many countries, local politicians are amateurs who have to combine the difficult assignment of understanding policy analysis with full-time jobs. Individuals with advanced education and well-paid jobs may have restricted possibilities to participate in local government councils if the compensation for loss of income is low or non-existent. Consequently, since local council positions are under-rewarded for the work involved (Stewart & Smith, 2007), it is often difficult to recruit competent politicians and to have them stay for the whole term of office at the local level (Erlingsson & Öhrvall, 2011). In addition, local politicians often lack the kind of personal administrative assistance that parliamentarians have on the national level. Taken together, this makes politicians' power position in relation to public administration weaker than on the national level. This calls for more and perhaps other kinds of studies of knowledge use on the local level.

Although there are very few systematic studies on knowledge use on the local level, it seems like the same kind of processes that can be found elsewhere are important also on the local level—for example, strategic and selective use of information (cf. Boswell, 2009). It has also been shown that the political context affects how politicians approach information. For example, Lundin and Öberg (2014) found that in contexts of political dispute in Sweden, local politicians engage less in critical reflection (deliberation) over the information provided, and are more inclined to ignore the information in such situations (cf. Weible, Pattison & Sabatier, 2010). This implies that even if better information is available in situations of conflict, it may be disregarded by politicians who are unwilling to change their minds or risk losing face. On the other hand, local politicians have been found to reflect more on available information in contexts of high public attention. However, as Lundin and Öberg (2014, p. 44) admit, much more research is needed. Obviously, comparative studies are necessary, but there is also a need to improve the measures of how politicians react to the information produced in local policy analysis.

Conclusion

There are many indications that policy analysis on the local level is more problematic than on the national level: policy analytical capacity is often low within local authorities, and the resources and skills to perform advanced analysis are lacking. Much of the work of collecting information is handled by local civil servants, who depend on easily available information. This makes it essential that information provided by national authorities is sufficient and of good quality. The information produced in local policy analysis is used to varying degrees by local politicians, who often are less competent than national-level politicians and have limited possibilities to perform additional analysis. We know that local governments exchange information with each other, but not always systematically. Theoretically, there are an infinite number of policy options, but the public administration often presents very few options to politicians. Many options are not analysed at all, or are disregarded in the final stage—the integration of policy analysis into decision making—because of political biases. In sum, the current research paints quite a distressing picture of local policy analysis. Yet many things work surprisingly well—for example, in relation to the many decisions taken on the local level every day, citizen protests are marginal.

Before any final conclusions are drawn, it is once again important to emphasize the lack of knowledge about policy analysis on the local level. Although there is extensive research on public policy on the local level and on urban public policy, policy analysis on the local level is seldom one of the explanatory factors emphasized (Deslatte, 2015). Thus, we do not know enough about the effects of different quality, specializations or traditions of policy analysis. It is obvious that our instruments for such analysis have to be improved. As an example, administrative capacity on the local level is often measured very roughly in 'expenditure on central administration per capita' or something equivalent (Andrews, Boyne, O'Toole, Meier & Walker, 2013; Walker, 2014, p. 26).

An obvious problem is the lack of systematic data on how policy analysis is performed on the local level. There is also scarce knowledge of the quality of the information produced by actors involved in policy analysis, as well as how this information is used by local policy decision makers. This chapter is primarily based on research in leading journals and books in English. Apart from the disparate chapters on local policy analysis in the International Library of Policy Analysis (ILPA) book series, a large part of the current empirical evidence is based on information from a few countries, primarily Denmark, Norway, Sweden, the US and the UK. In addition, many of these studies are based on just a few case studies, for example a few cities in the US or a small number of municipalities in Norway. It is difficult to know whether the findings are representative even for other local governments in the same country. Systematic gathered information from a large number of local governments in one country or a strategic selection with reasonable possibilities to generalize are rare. To this we can also add the lack of comparative data: with very few examples, comparisons even between similar countries are missing.

As has been emphasized above, we must acknowledge that it is difficult to perform systematic within-country or cross-country comparisons on local policy analysis. Even within countries, the differences between conditions for policy analysis are huge. In many countries, diverse local contexts produce very different conditions for political leadership and policy analysis, and it has often proved difficult to reform local units into more uniform patterns (Lowndes & Leach, 2004). Moreover, it is difficult to compare local policy in Beijing, New York or Oslo with smaller rural communities in the same country, not to mention rural municipalities in other countries. In addition to size, it is difficult to compare units with different administrative traditions and formal regulations. The degree of independence from the national state, the degree of federalism and regionalism, and differences in public administration traditions and regulations are just a few of the components that make comparisons difficult. Still, this variation in institutional contexts also invites interesting tests of how different political and cultural settings condition local public administration.

Notwithstanding, there are some trends that can be highlighted. One is internally contradictory and for the moment difficult to interpret. There are reports from many countries that administrative reforms with elements of New Public Management (NPM) have been introduced to local government. At the same time, it has been noticed that it has been difficult for national decision makers to implement ideas of NPM at the local level because of resistance from local politicians and civil servants (Bogumil & Ruddat, 2013; Hilterman & Klaassen, 2015). It has also been reported that public administration—comprising actors performing policy analysis on the local level—seems more sceptical of NPM than politicians are (Jacobsen, 2012). This is important since managers' preferences and perceptions have been pivotal for the adoption of NPM ideas (Hansen, 2011). This trend calls for more research attention. How, for example, does implementation of different performance measurements impact learning between municipalities within different contexts?

A second trend, already mentioned, is increasing citizen participation in local policymaking, sometimes called *democratic innovations* (Smith, 2009). These different kinds of citizen consultations are becoming more and more popular around the world. In *deliberative forums*, citizens are invited to discuss specific policy problems in citizen conferences, consensus conferences, planning cells, citizen panels, citizen juries, citizen dialogues and so on (Grönlund, Bächtiger & Setälä, 2014). These forums can have consequences for policy analysis, and are even sometimes considered part of policy analysis. Research in this area is also scarce; in addition, besides the unclear impacts of participation on representative democracy and trust in local government (Fitzgerald & Wolak, 2014; Kim & Lee, 2012), we know very little about the effects on local policy analysis.

Finally, there are indications that we will see an expansion of tasks that must be handled locally. This applies also in some countries where the capabilities for policy analysis on the local level are very weak because of a traditionally strong centralized state (e.g., in Taiwan). Thus, there are good reasons to believe that there are challenges ahead that call for a rebuilding of local government not only financially and democratically, but also managerially (Warner, 2010). For those many nations where we can expect an increase in decision making on the local level, and consequently an augmented need of high-quality policy analysis, knowledge of best practices and pitfalls of local policy analysis would be helpful. Unfortunately, the current state of the field cannot provide much solid empirical evidence. Not yet, anyway.

Notes

1 Other influential perspectives on policymaking exist as well, such as incremental policymaking (Lindblom, 1979) and garbage-can policymaking (Cohen, March & Olsen, 1972). For the purposes of this chapter, it is sufficient to use a more basic idea of the policy process in order to pinpoint key research questions.
2 However, it is hard to separate formulation from initiation and actual decision making, and therefore we will partly reflect on these stages as well.
3 In a 'small world' network, there are tight local clusters of, in this case, municipalities. These different clusters are linked together by key actors; that is, there is a high density of shortcuts between local clusters. Despite highly localizing tendencies, 'small world' networks are well connected on a national basis (Ansell et al., forthcoming).

4 Benchmarking is a component of New Public Management (NPM). In some countries, for example in Germany and Italy, a resistance to NPM has affected benchmarking negatively and it has been "quietly abolished" (Kuhlmann, 2010, p. 1128).

References

Andrews, R., G. Boyne, L. O'Toole, K. Meier, and R. Walker (2013), "Managing Migration? EU Enlargement, Local Government Capacity and Performance in England", *Public Administration* 91(1): 174–194.

Ammons, D. N. and D. J. Roenigk (2014), "Benchmarking and International Learning in Local Government", *Journal of Public Administration Research and Theory* 25: 309–335.

Ansell, C., M. Lundin and PO. Öberg (2017), "Learning Networks among Swedish Municipalities: Is Sweden a Small World?", in J. Glücker, E. Lazega and I. Hammer (eds), *Knowledge and Networks*. Vol 11. Knowledge and Space. Springer, Berlin.

Askim, J., Å. Johnsen and K.-A. Christophersen (2007), "Factors behind Organizational Learning from Benchmarking: Experience from Norwegian Municipal Benchmarking Networks", *Journal of Public Administration Research and Theory*, 18: 297–320.

Barthélemy, M. (2011), "Spatial Networks", *Physics Reports* 499(1):1–101.

Bingham, L. B., T. Nabatchi and R. O'Leary (2005), "The New Governance: Practices and Processes for Stakeholder and Citizen Participation in the Work of Government", *Public Administration Review* 65(5): 547–558.

Bogumil, J. and C. Ruddat (2013), "Local Policy Processes: Economisation, Professionalisation, Democratisation", in S. Blum and K. Schubert (eds), *Policy Analysis in Germany*, Policy Press, Bristol, UK.

Boswell, C. (2009), *The Political Uses of Expert Knowledge: Immigration Policy and Social Research*, Cambridge University Press.

Cohen, M., J. March and J. P. Olsen (1972), "A Garbage Can Model for Organizational Choice", *Administrative Science Quarterly* 17: 1–25.

Cowan, R. and N. Jonard (2004), "Network Structure and the Diffusion of Knowledge", *Journal of Economic Dynamics and Control* 28(8): 1557–1575.

Dente, B. and P. Coletti (2011), "Measuring Governance in Urban Innovation", *Local Government Studies* 37(1): 43–56.

Deslatte, A. (2015), "Reassessing 'City Limits' in Urban Public Policy", *Policy Studies Journal* 43(S1): S56–S77.

Erlingsson, G. and R. Öhrvall (2011), "Why Do Councillors Quit Prematurely? On the Democratic Consequences of Councillors Leaving Their Seats before the End of Their Term", *Lex Localis* 9(2).

Erlingsson, G. and J. Ödalen (2013), "How Should Local Government Be Organized? Reflections from a Swedish Perspective", *Local Government Studies* 39(1): 22–46.

Fang, K.-H. (2015). "Policy Analysis in the Local Councils", in Y.-Y. Kuo (ed.), *Policy Analysis in Taiwan*, Policy Press, Bristol, UK.

Farah, M. F. S. (2013), "Policy Analysis at the Municipal Level of Government", in J. Vaitsman, J. Mendes Ribeiro and L. Lobato (eds), *Policy Analysis in Brazil*, Policy Press, Bristol, UK.

Fitzgerald, J. and J. Wolak (2014), "The Roots of Trust in Local Government in Western Europe" *International Political Science Review*, 5 August.

Grönlund, K., A. Bächtiger and M. Setälä (2014), *Deliberative Mini-Publics: Involving Citizens in the Democratic Process*, ECPR Press, Colchester, UK.

Hague, R. and M. Harrop (2007), *Comparative Government and Politics: An Introduction*, Palgrave Macmillan, Basingstoke, UK.

Hansen, M. B. (2011), "Antecedents of Organisational Innovation: The Diffusion of New Public Management into Danish Local Government", *Public Administration* 89: 285–306.

Hill, M. (1997), *The Policy Process in the Modern State*, Prentice Hall, London.

Hilterman, F. and H. Klaassen (2015), "Policy Analysis at the Local Government Level", F. van Nispen and P. Scholten (eds) *Policy Analysis in the Netherlands*, Policy Press, Bristol, UK.

Howlett, M. (2009), "Policy Analytical Capacity and Evidence-Based Policy-Making: Lessons from Canada", *Canadian Public Administration* 52(2): 153–175.

Howlett, M. and R. M. Walker (2012), "Public Mangers in the Policy Process: More Evidence on the Missing Variable?" *Policy Studies Journal* 40(2): 211–233.

Howlett, M. and A. M. Wellstead (2011), "Policy Analysts in the Bureaucracy Revisited: The Nature of Professional Policy Work in Contemporary Government", *Politics & Policy* 49(4): 613–633.

Jacobsen, D. I. (2012), "Local Authority Bureaucracies: Responsible, Representative, or Divergent?" *Public Administration* 90: 1067–1087.

Kanai, T. (2015), "Local Governments and Policy Analysis in Japan after the Second World War", Y. Adachi, S. Hosono and J. Lio (eds.), *Policy Analysis in Japan*, Policy Press, Bristol, UK.

Kim, S. and J. Lee. (2012), "E-Participation, Transparency, and Trust in Local Government", *Public Administration Review* 72(6): 819–828.

Kim, S., and H. L. Schachter (2013), "Citizen Participation in the Budget Process and Local Government Accountability: Case Studies of Organizational Learning from the United States and South Korea", *Public Performance & Management Review* 36(3): 456–471.

Knill, C. and J. Tosun (2008), "Policy-making", in D. Carmani (ed.), *Comparative Politics*, Oxford University Press.

Kuhlmann, S. (2010), "New Public Management for the 'Classical Continental European Administration': Modernization at the Local Level in Germany, France and Italy", *Public Administration* 88(4): 1116–1130.

Kuhlmann, S. and T. Jäkel (2013), "Competing, Collaborating or Controlling? Comparing Benchmarking in European Local Government", *Public Money & Management*, 33(4): 269–276.

Lee, C.-P. (2015), "Analysis of Innovative Local Government Policies in Taiwan", in Y.-Y. Kuo (ed.) *Policy Analysis in Taiwan*, Policy Press, Bristol, UK.

Lijphart, A. (1999), *Patterns of Democracy: Government Forms and Performance in Thirty-Six Countries*, Yale University Press, New Haven, CT.

Lindblom, C. (1979), "Still Muddling, Not Yet Through", *Public Administration Review* 39: 517–526.

Lindquist, E. (1990), "The Third Community, Policy Inquiry, and Social Scientist", in S. Brooks and A. Gagnon (eds), *Social Scientists, Policy, and the State*, Praeger, New York.

Liu, X., E. Lindquist, A. Vedlitz and K. Vincent (2010), "Understanding Local Policy Making: Policy Elites' Perception of Local Agenda Setting and Alternative Policy Selection", *Policy Studies Journal* 38(1): 69–91.

Lowndes, V. and S. Leach (2004), "Understanding Local Political Leadership: Constitutions, Contexts and Capabilities", *Local Government Studies* 20(4): 557–575.

Lowndes, V. and H. Sullivan (2004), "Like a Horse and Carriage or a Fish on a Bicycle: How Well do Local Partnerships and Public Participation Go Together?" *Local Government Studies* 30(1): 51–73.

Lundin, M. and PO. Öberg (2014), "Expert Knowledge Use and Deliberation in Local Policy Making", *Policy Sciences* 47: 25–49.

Lundin, M., PO. Öberg, and C. Josefsson (2015), "Learning from Success: Are Successful Governments Role Models?" *Public Administration* 93(3): 733–752.

Lundin, M., Öberg, PO. and J. Thelander (2013), "Det välgrundade beslutet: om kommunal beredning i kommunstyrelse-, utbildnings-, arbetsmarknads- och miljöärenden", Report 2013:11, Institute for Evaluation of Labour Market and Education Policy (IFAU), Uppsala, Sweden.

McKenna, D. (2011), "UK Local Government and Public Participation: Using Conjectures to Explain the Relationship", *Public Administration* 89(3): 1182–1200.

Michels, A. and L. De Graaf (2010), "Examining Citizen Participation: Local Participatory Policy Making and Democracy", *Local Government Studies* 36(4):477–491.

Montin, S. (2002), *Moderna kommuner*, Liber, Malmö, Sweden.

Norton, A. (1991), *The International Handbook of Local and Regional Government Status, Structure and Resources in Advanced Democracies*, Edward Elgar, Cheltenham, UK.

Öberg, PO., M. Lundin and J. Thelander (2015), "Political Power and Policy Design: Why Are Policy Alternatives Constrained?" *Policy Studies Journal* 43(1): 93–114.

Røseland, A. (2011), "Understanding Local Governance: Institutional Forms of Collaboration", *Public Administration* 89: 789–892.

Sellars, J. M. and A. Lidström (2007), "Decentralization, Local Government, and the Welfare State", *Governance* 20(4): 609–632.

Smith, G. (2009), *Democratic Innovations: Designing Institutions for Citizen Participation*, Cambridge University Press, UK.

Stewart, K. and P. J. Smith (2007), "Immature Policy Analysis: Building Capacity in Eight Major Canadian Cities", in L. Dobuzinskis, M. Howlett and D. Laycock (eds), *Policy Analysis in Canada: The State of the Art*, University of Toronto Press, Canada.

Tsuchyama, K. (2015), "Policy Research Movements in Local Governments", Y. Adachi, S. Hosono and J. Lio (eds), *Policy Analysis in Japan*, Policy Press, Bristol, UK.

Walker, R. M., L. J. O'Toole, Jr. and K. J. Meier (2007), "It's Where You Are That Matters: The Networking Behaviour of English Local Government Officers", *Public Administration* 85(3): 739–756.

Walker, R. M. (2014), "Internal and External Antecedents of Process Innovation: A Review and Extension", *Public Management Review* 16(1):21–44.

Walker, R. M., and R. Andrews (2015), "Local Government Management and Performance: A Review of Evidence", *Journal of Public Administration Research and Theory* 25(1): 101–133.

Warner, M. E. (2010), "The Future of Local Government: Twenty-First-Century Challenges", *Public Administration Review* 70(1): 145–147.

Weible, C. M., A. Pattison and P. A. Sabatier (2010), "Harnessing Expert-Based Information for Learning and the Sustainable Management of Complex Socio-Ecological Systems", *Environmental Science & Policy* 13: 522–534.

Workman, S., B. D. Jones and A. E. Jochim (2009), "Information Processing and Policy Dynamics", *Policy Studies Journal* 37(1): 75–92.

10

EVIDENCE-BASED BUDGETARY POLICY: SPEAKING TRUTH TO POWER?[1]

Frans K. M. van Nispen and Maarten de Jong

1. Introduction

The relationship between policy analysis and public budgeting has spurred quite some debate since the 1960s when Robert McNamara, Secretary of Defense in the Kennedy administration, launched his Planning, Programming, and Budgeting System (PPBS) in an effort to improve the allocation of resources and efficiency in the public sector. More recently, we have witnessed a revival of performance budgeting due to the New Public Management (NPM) movement, which served as a vehicle to serve old wine in a new bottle. The bouquet is fine as the negotiations about next year's budget are now flavoured by performance information. However, the aftertaste is somewhat backward as the constraints of performance budgeting have become clear. In this chapter we look back at the 50-year history of budgetary reform in the United States and elsewhere to assess the progress that we have made since the first efforts to establish a more evidence-based fiscal policy.

The chapter is structured as follows. We first look at the efforts of budgetary reform from a historical perspective (Section 2). Next, we deal with the revival of performance budgeting as part of the NPM movement that emerged in the late 1980s. We conclude that the efforts to introduce performance budgeting may be characterized best as performance-informed budgeting (Section 3). In addition, some argue that the NPM movement, and consequently performance budgeting, has lost momentum, raising the question of what is on the horizon beyond performance budgeting (Section 4). We feature basically two interrelated developments: the pursuit of an evidence-based budgetary policy (Section 5) and the growing interest in budgetary reviews, notably spending reviews in times of austerity (Section 6). The chapter concludes with further discussion.

2. Budgetary Reform

Performance budgeting has been a key driver of budgetary innovation in the United States for more than 60 years (Schick, 2014, p. 1). Shortly after World War II, the Hoover Committee recommended that "the whole budget should be refashioned by the adoption of a budget based upon functions, activities and projects: this we designate a 'performance budget' " (Hoover, 1950, p. 8; Schild, 1985, p. 21). The advice of the Hoover Committee was followed

Structural Aspects	Analytical Aspects			Informational Aspects
	Planning	*Programming*	*Budgeting*	
Classification of the budget into: Functions Programs Activities Cost elements	Formulation of objectives Identification of alternatives Evaluation of alternatives Selection of the feasible course	Determination of personnel and resources needed for the fulfillment of objectives Determination of costs of such resources Determination of the annual profile of costs	Allocation of resources for selected programs Presentation of the budget in the program structure evolved for the purpose Formulation of operational targets	Progress reports on the implementation of the budget Adjustment in the light of progress Evaluation

Figure 10.1 Schematic presentation of the PPB System

Source: Premchand (1983), p. 328

up in the early 1960s, when Robert McNamara asked the Rand Corporation to design a system that would facilitate communication between the planners and "budgeteers," Since this time, efforts to improve the budgetary process have continued almost non-stop, with new initiatives taken even before previous efforts are implemented (see Annex 1).

The story of PPBS is well known (Figure 10.1). The model worked well at the Department of Defense and so it was declared applicable to all federal departments and agencies. President Lyndon B. Johnson argued that the use of the most modern methods of program analysis would ensure that judgments would be based on more accurate information, highlighting those things that we ought to do more and those we ought to do less (Williams, 1998, p. 61; Radin, 2013, p. 17). Unfortunately, PPBS did not bring what was expected in other policy areas and, not long afterwards, it silently passed away (Schick, 1973; Wildavsky, 1974, p. 206). Various factors may have contributed to its demise—a lack of political leadership, bureaucracy politics, and inbuilt flaws of the system, or a combination of several factors—but whatever the reason, the fact is that policy analysts and their work did not succeed in substantially breaking existing traditions and routines.

> PPB failed because it did not penetrate the vital routines of putting together and justifying a budget. Always separate but never equal, the analysts had little influence over the form or content of the budget.
>
> *Schick, 1973, p. 147*

In an effort to rescue policy analysis—"the heart and soul of PPB" (Rivlin, 1969, p. 915)—from public budgeting, Aaron Wildavsky argued that the "shotgun marriage" between policy analysis and budgeting had to be annulled since it was already hard enough to do a good job of policy analysis without having to meet the arbitrary and fixed deadlines imposed by the budget cycle. He called for more-selective use of policy analysis, for instance the requirement to submit a program memorandum supported by policy analysis for major dollar changes in an agency's budget (Wildavsky, 1969, p. 196). He argued that policy analysis may be considered an "activity that should be distinguished from budgeting, which can and should be carried out alongside it . . . analysis can be accommodated in different ways if it is separated from budgetary structures rather than incorporated in them" (Jenkins, 1978, p. 193). If conventional budgeting is fundamentally anti-analytic, however, it is not clear how receptive budgeting is to policy analysis. Consequently, the efforts to funnel policy analysis through budgetary routines are not very likely to have an effect (Schick, 1977, p. 259).

The rest is more or less history. Many countries experimented with similar devices (Premchand, 1983) and came to basically the same conclusions. In the late 1960s, the French government, inspired by the PPBS, launched a large-scale program, called *Rationalisation des Choix Budgétaires* (RCB), which was abandoned in 1980 for both structural and cyclical reasons (Perret, 2006). In the Netherlands, the *Commissie voor de Ontwikkeling van Beleidsanalyse* (COBA) served very much like McNamara's whiz kids. It adhered to the paradigm of economic rationality and methodological rigidity, and was finally dismantled in 1981 (van Nispen, 2015). The British equivalent, Programme Analysis Review (PAR), had significant impact at first, but gradually faded away because it was "unable to satisfy the technical, organizational and political preconditions for effective analysis" (Gray & Jenkins, 1982, p. 429) and eventually was replaced by the so-called Scrutinies, the critical assessment of draft bills submitted to parliament (House of Lords, 1997–1998).[2]

Later efforts at budgetary reform were similarly unsuccessful, for example the Carter administration's Zero-Base Budgeting (ZBB), of which Aaron Wildavsky has concluded that "some butterflies were caught, no elephants stopped" (Wildavsky, 1975). The pursuit of budgetary reform was reinvigorated in the early 1990s with the emergence of the NPM movement and the associated revival of performance budgeting, i.e., the provision of non-financial information in order to improve the allocation of scarce resources and efficiency by the public sector. Kicking off in New Zealand, performance budgeting soon spread to the Anglo-Saxon world and then to the rest of the world, largely thanks to the annual meeting of the Senior Budget Officers of the Organisation for Economic Co-operation and Development (OECD), which basically serves as an epistemic community.

The latest offspring was the Program Assessment Rating Tool (PART), which was "arguably the most ambitious comprehensive effort to link performance and budgeting of recent times" (de Jong, 2016, p. 18). The coverage of federal programs was almost complete, but the outcome of the exercise in terms of budget allocation was hardly different than traditional budgeting. This leads Gilmour and Lewis to the view that it is significant that the PART scores had any impact at all, given the overwhelming importance of politics in making budgets (2006, p. 750). This applies even more to the utilization of PART scores by the legislative branch, which should have induced interest of Congress in program evaluation for results (Norcross & McKenzie, 2006, p. 4). In reality, largely as a result of Congress's disregard or even distrust of PART, budget authorization by Congress far from followed performance assessments (see Box 10.1). Moreover, PART examinations played only a limited role at best in debates about funding in Congress (Frisco & Stalebrink, 2008, p. 11). As Wildavsky observed with Zero-Based Budgeting, only a few minor programs were terminated as a result of PART.

In the mid-2000s, the Korean government introduced the Self-Assessment of the Budgetary Program (SABP), which was based on PART with some modifications (OECD, 2007). Ineffective programs received automatic spending cuts. In contrast to the US, the Korean parliament's possibilities for amending the budget are more restricted. Not surprisingly, this resulted in a larger impact of the program performance assessment on budget allocation

Box 10.1

Although the relationship between PART scores and funding in the Office of Management and Budget's (OMB) budget proposal has been shown to be slightly positive (Norcross & McKenzie, 2006; Gilmour & Lewis, 2006), there is no evidence that supports a substantial impact on final funding decisions by Congress. In fact, there is some evidence that the impact was limited at best. As an illustration, of the 99 programs that were listed for elimination in the FY 2006 budget proposal, only 15 had been eliminated by 2008. Even the Department of Education—a particular focus of PART, with 48 proposed program eliminations—only saw one of its programs terminated by Congress at the end of the Bush administration. In the 2008 PART-informed budget proposal, 27 programs were rated as ineffective. The breakdown in Figure 10.2 shows that instead of saving more than US$2 billion on ineffective programs, the Bush administration spent an additional US$786 million on these programs. This can hardly be seen as encouraging for a tool that was supposed to improve allocative efficiency by integrating performance and budgets.

Categories	Number	Performance informed savings	
		Proposed by OMB[1]	Enacted by Congress[1,2]
Already eliminated in previous years	2	N/A	N/A
To be eliminated	8	-408 (-100%)	-3 (-0.7%)
To be cut	8	-1,619 (-12.6%)	+789 (+6.0%)
No cuts or increases	9	N/A	N/A
Total		-2,027	+786

Figure 10.2 Breakdown of 27 programs rated ineffective by PART for FY2008

Source: ExpectMore.gov (2007/08)

Notes
1 Millions US$ compared to FY2007 funding
2 These are aggregated figures: some programs were cut while others received increases

(Shin, 2013). With time, however, the gap increased between the self-assessments by ministries and the assessments by the Ministry of Finance and Strategy, as did complaints about the bureaucratic burden. Since this time, Korea has sought to improve the ministries' ownership of assessing performance of budget programs.

3. Performance Budgeting

Although performance budgeting is a container concept that means "different things to different people in different contexts" (Behn, 2003, p. 590), it may be described best

Evidence-Based Budgetary Policy

as the effort "to strengthen the linkage between funding and results (outputs and outcomes), through the systematic use of formal performance information, with the objective of improving the allocative and technical efficiency of public expenditure" (Robinson, 2007, p. xxvi).

First, a distinction can be made between a broad and a strict definition of performance budgeting:

> Broadly defined, a performance budget is any budget that presents information on what agencies have done or expect to do with the money provided to them. Strictly defined, a performance budget is only a budget that explicitly links each increment in resources to an increment in outputs or other results. The broad concept views [performance] budgeting in presentational terms, the strict version views it in terms of allocation.
>
> *Schick, 2003, p. 101*

These two definitions of performance budgeting may be considered as existing at the two poles of a continuum. On one end is "performance as allocation," characterized by the direct and explicit allocation of resources on the basis of units of performance—formula performance budgeting—mainly outputs. In order to obtain "the most effects for the least costs," a budgetary process should create, as Roy Meyers has argued.

> opportunities for comparing ratios of costs and effects: for one program from year to year, for all programs addressing one purpose, and across programs that address different purposes. Such comparisons are viewed as a "conditio sine qua non" by the adepts of formula performance budgeting.
>
> *Meyers, 1996, pp. 178–179*

On the other end is "performance by information," in which inputs are only loosely coupled to outputs or outcomes. Performance information competes with information from other sources (Schick, 2014). A third form of performance budgeting—"presentational budgeting"—refers to the delivery of performance information (either inside or outside the budget) as background information for the purpose of accountability and dialogue with parliament and society (OECD, 2007, p. 21).[3] Arguably, a fourth type might be described as a managerial performance approach that focuses on managerial impacts and changes in organizational behavior, and may de-emphasize a strong budget linkage (von Trapp, 2014, p. 2). In general it should be noted that the line between performance budgeting and performance management is increasingly blurred. In fact, performance budgeting today is seen more and more as a subset of performance management rather than a separate process (Schick, 2014, p. 3).

Taking the traditional line-item budget as a point of reference, Pollitt & Bouckaert (2004, p. 70) distinguish four stages of budgetary reform. It is debatable whether the last step—the switch to accrual-based accounting—is a necessary condition for performance budgeting and, vice versa, if accrual budgeting requires performance budgeting.

1. The provision of performance information;
2. The adaptation of the budget format and addition of other documents;
3. The adaptation of the budget procedures and timetable;
4. The adaptation of the method of charging from cash-based to accrual-based accounting.[4]

147

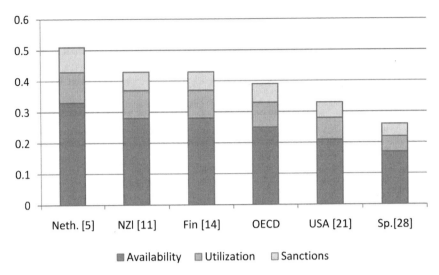

Figure 10.3 Performance budgeting index (PBI) for a selected number of OECD countries
Source: OECD (2013)

In this chapter we primarily focus on the first step—the provision and subsequently the utilization of performance information, both of which are assessed by the OECD on the basis of its 2011 Performance Budgeting Survey. The outcome is reported in *Governance at a Glance 2013*, which, inter alia, contains a *Performance Budgeting Index* (PBI) composed of three components (OECD, 2013, p. 175):

1. Availability of performance information (65%);
2. Utilization of performance information in the budget negotiations (20%);
3. Sanctions in case of not achieving the targets (15%).

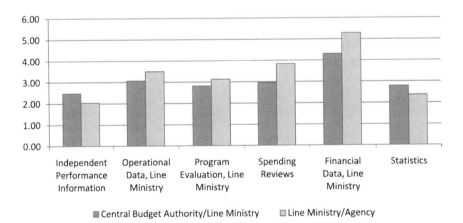

Figure 10.4 The frequency of performance utilization during budget negotiations per category in OECD countries
Source: OECD 2011 (Q7 + Q9)

The outcome may be illustrated in Figure 10.3, which provides the PBI for a selected number of OECD countries with the Netherlands at the high end (0.51) and Spain at the low end (0.26).[5]

The litmus test of performance budgeting is in the utilization of performance information for the allocation of resources or the efficiency of the provision of goods and services.

An assessment is provided by the OECD on the basis of its *2011 Performance Budgeting Survey*.[6] First, the question is raised how often non-financial information is used during the budget negotiations by the Central Budget Authority (CBA) and line ministries, and between line ministries and agencies. Generally, non-financial information is used less frequently at the centralized level, i.e., in the budget talks between CBA and line ministries (mean 3.07) than at the decentralized level, i.e., in the budget talks between line ministries and agencies (mean 3.36). However, the difference is almost negligible (mean 3.07 vs. 3.36). Note that neither financial nor statistical data are specific for performance budgeting, which is geared to the provision of non-financial information.

Non-financial information is used for a variety of reasons, as shown in Figure 10.4, notably the allocation of resources and spending cuts. However, just under 30% of the OECD countries report that they are not using performance information (Figure 10.5) during the budget cycle for any reason.

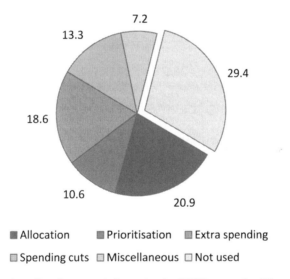

Figure 10.5 The utilization of performance information in OECD countries (%)

Source: OECD 2011 Performance Budgeting Database (Q12)

Notes
The category "allocation" refers to allocation for organizations [9.4%] as well as programs [11.5%]. Similarly "extra spending" stands for increase spending existing programs [8.8%] and the creation of new programs [9.9%]. Spending cuts are composed of the reduction of spending [9.3%] and the elimination of programs [4.0%].

The Sovereign Debt Crisis

Since 2009, the European sovereign debt crisis has arguably increased the priority of performance measurement and reinforced the link between performance measurement and financing (OECD, PBS, Q34). However, with the clear exception of the allocation for line ministries and agencies, line ministries used performance information less during the negotiations about next year's budget as compared with the previous year surveyed (Hawkesworth, 2012, pp. 33–34).[7] In addition, more countries reported that performance information is not used at all: from 10% to about 30% (OECD, 2014, pp. 76–77). In fact we see a massive return to the incremental mode of budgeting on the basis of inputs rather than outputs or outcomes. Even in the case of New Zealand, which is generally considered one of the leading proponents of performance budgeting in the wake of the NPM movement, the budget is input-driven, although authorization takes place on the basis of outputs. However, although the information about outputs is measurable, it is often insufficient to enable the chief executives to purchase the appropriate inputs and to relate inputs to outputs (Posseth, 2010, pp. 138–139). Consequently, the next year's budget is largely shaped by the previous year's budget.

At the same time, a survey of senior executives in ten European countries (n = 4.402) reveals that the relevance of performance information has increased as a result of the fiscal crisis (Hammerschmid, Oprisor & Štimac, 2013).[8] There are two possible reasons for these seemingly contradictory findings. First, the utility of performance information may be still growing in most areas, but the constraints of performance information in the field of public budgeting are widely recognized. Practitioners now acknowledge that only about 20% or 30% of the national budget is applicable to meaningful and budgetary relevant performance indicators. Unfortunately, the survey did not address the relevance and utility of performance information in the field of public budgeting. Second, none of the surveys are conclusive: there is quite a lot of variation at the disaggregated level of the individual countries, both in terms of ambition and intention as well as across sectors.

A detailed analysis of three European countries—Finland, the Netherlands and Spain—indicates that most countries struggle with:

- The formulation of goals and indicators;
- The link between appropriations and outputs and/or outcomes;
- The causal relationship between outputs and outcomes.

van Nispen & Posseth, 2009, p. 20

In addition, the utilization of performance budgeting relies heavily on a country's political setting and administrative capacity. Poland gradually built a sophisticated and detailed system of government-wide performance budgeting, but as political support waned, and with limited and scattered capacity at the Ministry of Finance, the non-financial information that was gathered largely remained unused for budgetary purposes (Kąsek & Webber, 2009; Hardt & de Jong, 2011; OECD, 2013).

Not surprisingly, the added value of non-financial information for the allocation of resources and efficiency in the public sector is low. There is hardly any evidence that non-financial information is used for reallocation of scarce resources during the preparation of the budget in the public sector (Frisco & Stalebrink, 2008, p. 11; de Vries & Bestebreur, 2010, p. 237; OECD, 2007, p. 67; de Jong, van Beek and Posthumus, 2013, pp. 14–15). Insofar as performance information is used to enhance efficiency, it is more likely to occur in the implementation of the budget and by agency managers rather than by politicians (Joyce, 2003, pp. 36–37, Hammerschmid et al., 2013, p. 5; von Trapp, 2014, p. 4). Furthermore, the one-size-fits-all template of performance budgeting does not recognize the uniqueness of programs (Radin, 2006, p. 50; van Nispen & Posseth, 2009, p. 20). The requirement of

Evidence-Based Budgetary Policy

homogeneous goods and services is often not met in the public sector (Van der Kar, 1981, pp. 106–112; Bestebreur & Klaassen, 2003, p. 21); in fact, only a small portion of the budget consists of homogeneous goods and services. Consequently, the provision of non-financial information has become focused on compliance and has failed to deliver insight in effectiveness and efficiency (OECD, 2015, p. 48). These insights would be more likely gained from in-depth program evaluations.

Apart from the characterization of public goods and services as being homogeneous or not, the degree to which public sector officials can be held accountable for program results differs from one program to another. The underlying assumption of NPM seemed to be that financial and results accountability could be integrated for the entire budget, regardless of differences in causality between inputs, outputs and outcomes. In cases of a more problematic causality, government organizations often consider performance accountability as threatening and choose to use performance information opportunistically. A more realistic approach to integrating financial and results accountability in the public sector is provided by a framework that distinguishes between the influence of government and the link between funding and result. As shown in Figure 10.6, there are four broad categories, with the upper left cell representing the best fit for inputs to outputs and outcomes. In the other three cells, the utilization of performance information use is linked only to outputs, or the use of information is disconnected from budget allocation altogether. This framework can be a helpful tool for identifying opportunistic use of performance information, for example dubious claims of effective spending following the attainment of policy goals or legitimizing claims for extra budget using measurable policy outcomes. Such a diversified approach formed the core of the conceptual model of the Accountable Budgeting reform that was introduced in the Netherlands from 2012. This reform addressed some of the persistent shortcomings of the performance budgeting system that had been attempted during the preceding decade.

Many of the disappointing results of performance budgeting with regard to its potential for allocative efficiency may not come as much of a surprise, as we simply lack a criterion to make a choice between extra spending for "guns versus butter." In addition, the utilization of performance information depends on the level of aggregation:

> Performance measurement can help public officials to make budget allocations. At the macro level, however, the apportionment of tax monies is a political decision made by political officials . . . Thus, political priorities—not agency performance— drive macro budgetary choices.
>
> *Behn, 2003, p. 590*

At the micro level of management, performance information may be used to improve efficiency, dividing outcomes by inputs (allocative efficiency) or outputs by inputs (technical efficiency). At the macro level, performance information is simply insufficient for budgeting with an eye on improving cost-effectiveness. What should parliament decide if targets are not met: to allocate more or less money?[9] Additional information is needed about cost-effectiveness to make a decision (Behn, 2003).[10]

While performance budgeting continues to be widely advocated as a public finance management reform, experience shows us that the high expectations regarding the use of performance information in the budget cycle should be tempered. There is no guarantee that non-financial information—whether operational and relevant or not—will be used for the allocation of scarce resources or the improvement of efficiency in delivery of goods and

Potential impact on result / Link funding and result	Strong	Weak
High	PBB/PIB Outputs and Outcomes	PM Disconnected from budget
Low	PBB/PIB Outputs only	PB Presentational use only

Figure 10.6 Diversified approach of performance budgeting depending on policy characteristics

Source: Modified from de Jong in OECD (2015), p. 48

Notes
PBB Performance-based budgeting
PIB Performance-informed budgeting
PB Performance budgeting
PM Performance management

services. Performance information is only one of many variables that are taken into account when making a decision. Despite claims to the contrary, the impact of performance budgeting is still unclear. There is hardly any evidence that the allocation of resources has been improved due to the availability of performance information. The same applies to the improvement of efficiency, linking inputs to outputs, and effectiveness, linking inputs to outcomes.[11] Based on the available evidence, the added value of adopting performance budgeting is more likely to be found in increased government transparency. Other positive effects that have been attributed to performance budgeting are mostly not observable in the budget itself and as such can be attributed more broadly to performance management. These are alignment of goals, supporting a results-oriented culture, policy innovations and better enabling ex post policy evaluation (Posner, 2009, pp. 7–8; Schick, 2014; Speklé & Verbeeten, 2014; van Dooren, 2011, p. 429).

4. What Is on the Horizon Beyond Performance Budgeting?

As the evidence on the added value of performance budgeting becomes clear, one may question what is on the horizon beyond performance budgeting. It could be argued that the NPM movement and consequently the pursuit of performance budgeting is "intellectually dead, an orthodoxy now played out and plagued by evidence of adverse by-product effects" (Dunleavy, Margetts, Bastow & Tinkler, 2006, abstract). The future is in "digital-era governance," focusing on the reintegration of services, holistic and "joined-up" approaches to policymaking, and the extensive digitalization of administrative operations, all of which may incidentally promote efficiency and performance of the public sector.[12] While we do not contest the belief that information and communications technology will play a major role in governance and in public budgeting, we believe that the pursuit of efficiency in the public sector is still alive and kicking. The NPM movement may have sunk below the surface, but is not dead.[13] Performance budgeting is sometimes cynically dubbed a "zombie reform" for this reason: no matter how often it is buried, the call for it keeps haunting us, and it returns time and again. The continued demand for non-financial information is illustrated in a statement of Peter Orszag, the director of the Office of Management and Budget during the first Obama administration:

> I am trying to put more emphasis on evidence-based policy decisions . . . Wherever possible, we should design new initiatives to build rigorous data about what works and then act on evidence that emerges—expanding the approaches that work best, fine-tuning the ones that get mixed results, and shutting down those that are failing.
>
> *Orszag, 2009*

The pursuit of evidence-based budgeting by the Obama administration, dismissed by John Mikesell as a "budgetary wrinkle" (Mikesell, 2014, p. 287), may be considered as an effort to feed the budget talks with evidence from other sources such as policy reviews and, in times of austerity, spending reviews,[14] which may be considered as an "extender" of the continuum from "performance as allocation" and "performance as information."

The impact of the pursuit of evidence-based budgeting may constitute a major leap forward if "the Obama administration actually delivers on the promise by the President and his budget director to fund programs that have strong evidence of success and to end programs that fail to produce impacts" (Haskins, 2009, p. 50). However, proponents of evidence-based decisions should follow one round of the annual congressional appropriations process and critically assess how many decisions are based on any appeal to evidence before getting too excited as has been illustrated earlier by the utilization of the PART scores.

5. The Call for Evidence-Based Budgetary Policy[15]

The call for more evidence-based policy is frequently attributed to the Blair cabinet in the United Kingdom, which launched a large-scale effort to modernize government shortly after it took office. In a statement delivered to parliament, then Prime Minister Tony Blair and the Minister for the Cabinet Office Jack Cunningham argued that the government has to be

> willing constantly to re-evaluate what it is doing so as to produce policies that really deal with problems; that are forward-looking and shaped by the evidence rather than a response to short-term pressures; that tackle causes not symptoms; that are measured by results rather than activity. . . policy making must also be a process of continuous learning and improvement.
>
> *Blair & Cunningham, 1999, p. 15*

Why this "utility turn" in practice as well as research (Solesbury, 2001, p. 4)? After all, evidence-based policy does not constitute a completely novel concept, although its absence and constraints are mainly lamented in practice (Banks, 2009).

A number of qualifications should be made with the focus on "what works." First, what works should not be confused with what is desirable or preferable. The availability of evidence does not imply that the government will act on evidence, or that an evidence-*based* policy will lead to goal attainment. After all, evidence is only one of the many variables that play a role in the design or revision of a policy. At best we can talk about evidence-*informed* policy, although the dividing line between evidence-informed and evidence-based policy is unclear, making the use of knowledge speculative. Second, the relationship between evidence and policy is not linear, and the evidence is highly context-specific (Young & Mendizabal, 2009, p. 1): what works in one setting may not work in another. The external validity is relatively low.

The body of literature on evidence-based policy indicates that what counts as evidence is disputed. Scientific information is frequently challenged by other schools of thought and bodies of expertise. In addition, governments often use a broader definition of evidence than the academic world (Davis, 2004, p. 24). In addition to scientific knowledge—information that has been put to a test—governments often refer to political judgment and practical wisdom, each lens having its distinctive protocol on what counts as "evidence" (Head, 2008, p. 7). It goes without saying that scientific knowledge is often contested by non-scientific information from other "knowledge reservoirs" (Bekkers, 2014). The notion of *evidence-based* policy stands, as such, "in contrast to *opinion-based* policy, which relies heavily on either the selective use of evidence . . . or on the untested views of individuals or groups, often inspired by ideological stand points, prejudices or speculative conjecture" (Davies, 2004, p. 3, emphasis added).

The search for evidence strongly resonates in the current debate about the consequences of the sovereign debt crisis, as articulated by Australian Prime Minister Kevin Rudd's call for a robust, evidence-based policymaking process: "Policy design and policy evaluation should be driven by analysis of all the available options, and not by ideology . . . We're interested in facts, not fads" (Rudd, 2008).

In the summer of 2009, the Australian government organized a large-scale roundtable on strengthening evidence-based policy. The focus was not on budgetary affairs, but the message was clear:

> Undoubtedly, evidence has influenced policy, often for the good. However, practical policy choice is determined by interests, political preferences and power, as well as by evidence. Strident calls for more "evidence-based policy" can reflect a political naiveté; or can hide a claim that politics should be run by "experts"; or can be a cover for the role of interests.
>
> *Pincus, 2009, p. 281*

A more evidence-based policy could, inter alia, prevent a Type I, Type II or Type III error and, as such, may contribute to the reduction of public expenditures (ABS, 2010, p. 2). In order to generate "value for money"—effectiveness and efficiency—interventions should be tested in advance. However, a policy that is proven to have effect in an experimental setting will not necessarily be effective in reality. Therefore, many scholars and practitioners remain skeptical about the merits of evidence-based policymaking (van Twist, Rouw & van der Steen, 2014).

6. Budget Reviews

The pursuit of a more evidence-based budget policy induced a renewed interest in program evaluation as a source of performance information. In an effort to strengthen the ex post evaluation, the Dutch government institutionalized a rotating system of policy reviews that should cover the whole budget in a period of seven years.

Policy Reviews

In the early 1990s, the Dutch government established a "system of involuntary self-assessment" in order to provide better information on relevance, effectiveness, efficiency and cost of government programs to coalition governments at the time of budget formulation (Shaw, 2015, p. 81). A policy review (*beleidsdoorlichting*) is primarily focused on the delivery of policy-relevant information, i.e., the support of current policies. The final report should include a synthesis of the available program evaluations regarding the effects of the policy under scrutiny. Unlike program evaluations, no additional fieldwork is done to balance the positive and negative effects. Program evaluations may lead to conclusions in terms of goal attainment, effectiveness and efficiency, but the consideration of potential alternatives for existing policies is left for what is called Inter-Ministerial Policy Research (Interdepartementale Beleidsonderzoeken, IBO). IBOs usually have a broader scope and generally look at (a specific aspect of) a number of interrelated policies. Finally, a spending review may be considered as an IBO, but geared towards the generation of potential savings.[16] The various modes of policy analysis and evaluation are summarized in Figure 10.7, which highlights the main characteristics of each mode.

In contrast to IBOs and spending reviews, ownership of policy reviews is left in the hands of the line ministries. This is a less centralized, more tailor-made mode of governance than previous efforts to establish performance budgeting, which were applied across the board to all line items, regardless of the characteristics of the output of the government. The role of the Minister of Finance is basically limited to the formulation of the terms of reference and the provision of guidance. In addition, the budget rules contain a rolling plan to ensure that the whole budget is covered in a period of four to seven years. However, only 50% of the policy reviews are actually carried out, due to a lack of priority and capacity. Recently, the number of policy reviews has increased substantially due to closer monitoring by the Minister of Finance, who tables the issue of policy reviews twice a year at the cabinet meeting.

The utilization of the findings of program evaluation (Figure 10.8) during the budget negotiations of the Minister of Finance, also referred to as the Central Budget Authority (CBA), and the line ministries (LM) or spending departments (average 2.81), is slightly lower

Main characteristics	Policy Review[1]	Program Evaluation[1]	Inter-Ministerial Policy Research	Spending Review
Principal	Spending department	Spending department	Joint effort	Cabinet Committee
Role of Ministry of Finance	Programming, Guidelines	None	Selection, Guidelines[2]	Selection, Guidelines[2]
Aim	Arguments/ information	Impact assessment	Policy alternatives	Potential savings
Unit of analysis	Program	Program	Policy	Policy
Focus	Policy relevance	Goal-attainment, effectiveness	Alignment, streamlining	Spending cuts
Decision			Cabinet	Cabinet[3]
Impact budget	Low	Low	Low	Potentially high[4]

Figure 10.7 Modes of policy analysis and evaluation

Source: Minister van Financiën (2004); Schoch & Broeder (2013); van Nispen (2015)

Notes

1 The policy reviews and program evaluations are subject of the *Regulation on Periodic Evaluations.*
2 Representatives of the Ministry of Finance participate in the working groups.
3 The publication of the report is accompanied by a "cabinet view."
4 The utilization of the potential savings is depending on the need for consolidation.

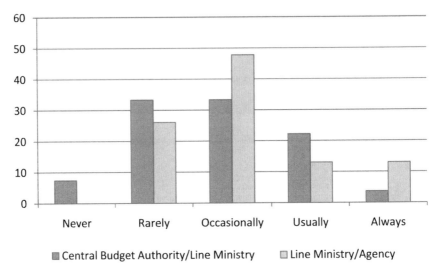

Figure 10.8 The utilization of program evaluation in the budget negotiations in OECD countries (as ratio)
Source: OECD 2011 (Q7 + Q9)

than the utilization of the outcome of program evaluations by the line ministries in the budget negotiations with the agencies (average 3.13). As we will see, program evaluations conducted as part of a CBA-run spending review are used more frequently in budget negotiations than program performance evaluations conducted by the line ministries (OECD, 2015, p. 7).

In times of austerity, across-the-board cuts and one-off measures are not adequate to reduce the budget deficit and public debt. A more evidence-based fiscal policy is needed for fiscal consolidation. However, the path from the utilization of performance information to fiscal consolidation is long. Many other variables are at play.

Spending Reviews[17]

The guidelines for the spending reviews breathe the spirit of integrated policy analysis (Dunn, 2012) or, more precisely, policy evaluation. On the one hand, spending reviews look backward as they are geared to an assessment of timeliness, effectiveness and/or efficiency. On the other hand, spending reviews look forwards as they seek to generate better options for the future and may be characterized as utilization-focused evaluation (Patton, 2008). The main aim of program evaluations is to improve the effectiveness of programs or the efficiency of expenditures. If there is reallocation, it is mostly within programs; if there are savings, they typically are cycled back into the same agencies or programs. This leads Allen Schick to the cynical, but realistic, conclusion that "program evaluation ... comfortably coexists with incremental spending behavior." However, program evaluations may not suffice for countries that face austerity. They may need bolder techniques that promote fiscal consolidation and stabilize public finance (Schick, 2014, pp. 17–18), i.e., spending reviews (Robinson, 2013; van Nispen, 2015).

A recent survey indicated that 16 out of 32 OECD countries experimented with budget reviews as a tool to generate smart or targeted cuts to deal with the consequences of the sovereign debt crisis (OECD, 2012, p. 37). A subtle but crucial distinction should be made between various modes of budget review. Unlike expenditure reviews, which may end up in

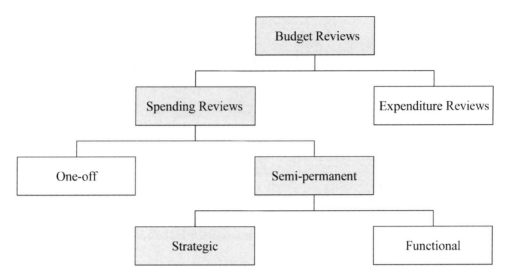

Figure 10.9 A classification of budget reviews
Source: OECD (2012); van Nispen (2015)

proposals for extra funding, spending reviews look for potential savings in relation to the baseline (Robinson, 2013) and, as such, compensate for "the fundamental asymmetry of the regular budget process which is capable of producing good options for new spending, but not of producing good options for new savings" (OECD, 2011, p. 81). Consequently, spending reviews do not take current funding as given, but also examine the consequences of alternative (read: lower) levels of funding (Kraan, 2007, p. 21; OECD, 2012, p. 115).

Budget reviews may be further subdivided into one-off efforts[18] and semi-permanent efforts to generate smart cuts (see Figure 10.9). The latter may be further subdivided into functional reviews, which assess the effectiveness and efficiency of the implementation, and strategic reviews, which also scrutinize the timeliness of the objectives.

The appraisal of proposals for extra funding does *not* belong to spending reviews (Robinson, 2013, pp. 4–5). Consequently, the Australian, British and Irish efforts cannot be considered as spending reviews, but rather as expenditure reviews.[19] In the mid-1970s, the Australian government established the so-called Expenditure Review Committee (ERC), which is at the center of the preparation of the following year's budget.[20] However, its activities are best characterized as strategic reviews that do not require the development of mandatory saving options, rather than spending reviews (OECD, 2012, p. 111). In recent years, however, Australia has carried out a comprehensive *expenditure* review over three budget cycles (2008–10), which has all the characteristics of a comprehensive *spending* review (Robinson, 2013, p. 11).

The institutional setting of spending reviews is more or less similar and characterized by two institutional variables (Kraan, 2010, pp. 14, 41). First, coordination is primarily left in the hands of the Minister of Finance (CBA), rather than the Prime Minister (PM) or the line minister (LM) in charge of the policy under review. In the case of decision making about the potential savings to be generated by the spending reviews, however, the CBA comes second to the Prime Minister (47.4% vs. 31.6%). Line ministries are primarily in charge of the drafting of the report (41.7% vs. 37.5%). See Figure 10.10.

A second characteristic of spending reviews is that the outcome is primarily adopted as part of the budget cycle (as shown in Figure 10.11), although many countries have

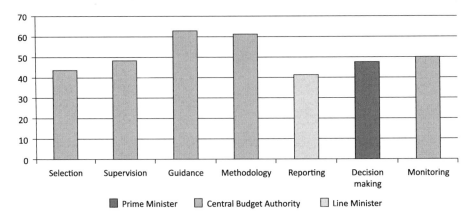

Figure 10.10 Overview of the main actor in charge of spending reviews per category of activity in OECD countries (as ratio)

Source: 2011 OECD Performance Budgeting Survey (Q25)

indicated that the utilization of the potential savings may be attributed to more than one single category. However, even then the budget cycle serves as an important, if not the most important, platform for decision making about the potential savings generated by the spending reviews. After all, the budget comes in the shape of a law and the decision about "who gets what, when, how" belongs to the core of politics (Lasswell, 1936). As Aaron Wildavsky has argued, the allocation of resources is a political rather than an economic process.

Generally, the outcome of spending reviews is used less frequently at the centralized level (CBA/LM) than the decentralized level (LM/agencies), although the mean—2.96 vs. 3.83— is not that far apart.

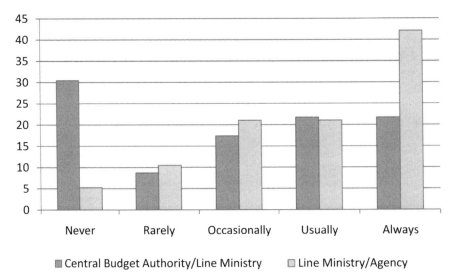

Figure 10.11 The utilization of spending reviews in the budget negotiations in OECD countries (as ratio)

Source: OECD 2011 (Q7 + Q9)

A comparison of two countries with a long-standing tradition of spending reviews—Canada and the Netherlands—indicates that the added value should not be overestimated, even if the savings are measured as a share of "in-scope" spending (van Nispen, 2015; Shaw, 2015). The utilization of the results of expenditure reviews in Anglo-Saxon countries—Canada and the UK—is slightly better due to the close link of the spending reviews with the budget cycle. However, the savings do not exceed 15% of "in-scope" spending (Shaw, 2015, p. 14).

7. Conclusion

This chapter examines the relationship between policy analysis and public budgeting. Taking the PPBS as a point of departure, we addressed the question of whether we have made any progress in transforming the traditional incremental budgeting approach into a more evidence-based fiscal policy. More specifically, have policy analysts succeeded in putting non-financial information on the negotiating table? Is non-financial information taken seriously or merely used as additional background information?

The pursuit of a more evidence-based fiscal policy was supported by the NPM movement, which resulted, inter alia, in a revival of performance budgeting, i.e., the provision of non-financial information for the allocation of scarce resources and efficiency in the public sector. Now that the NPM movement seems to have lost momentum—although not entirely—one may question to what extent the decline of the NPM movement has affected the pursuit of performance budgeting, notably as "governments cannot budget for results unless they manage for results" (Schick, 2014, p. 3).[21]

The current situation is somewhat ambiguous. Most OECD countries that experimented with performance budgeting struggle with the formulation of goals and indicators, the quality of non-financial information, and the links between inputs and outputs and between inputs and outcomes. Not surprisingly, the impact of performance information has been modest so far, even in the case of homogeneous goods and services. Like the results of social research (Weiss, 1979), the utilization of non-financial information is largely eclectic. It is primarily used as additional background information or as political ammunition in budget negotiations, both for extra spending and spending cuts, and is simply ignored if not useful. With few exceptions, there is hardly any evidence that performance information has induced either reallocation of money or increased efficiency in the public sector through the national budgeting process. Agency and program management are probably better places to look for success of this reform.

Second, in many countries we see a retreat of performance budgeting as the constraints of its "one-size-fits-all" approach have become clear. The story of PART is illustrative. The coverage of "the most ambitious comprehensive effort to link performance and budgeting of recent times" was almost complete, but the impact on funding largely negligible. However, that is not to say that the demand for non-financial information has completely disappeared. To the contrary, the global financial crisis has increased the relevance of performance information in general and, more specifically, for budgeting (OECD, 2011; Hammerschmid, Oprisor & Štimac, 2013), although this has not translated into an increase in the utilization of non-financial information. Increasingly, non-financial information is generated, if relevant, by means other than the budget, such as program evaluations and, in times of austerity, spending reviews. However, one may expect that interest in spending reviews (and the results of such reviews) will fade away as the economy recovers and the need for the generation of potential savings disappears.

Finally, what is on the horizon beyond performance budgeting? The call for a more evidence-based fiscal policy clearly deserves the benefit of the doubt, but the initial enthusiasm has been replaced by a growing skepticism, fueled by the relatively low impact of performance budgeting across the world. The outcome is a hybrid mode of public budgeting, a mix of inputs and outputs, which may be characterized at best as performance-informed budgeting. By far the largest part of the budget is still allocated on the basis of inputs rather than outputs or even outcomes. Like its predecessors—PPBS and ZBB—performance budgeting did not manage to break the budgetary routines, i.e., to replace incremental budgeting with a configuration of performance budgeting (Schick, 2014, p. 7). Unfortunately, budgets are still largely decided by power rather than by truth, or by evidence that something works.[22]

Annex 1 *The Stages of Budgetary Reform in the United States*[23]

Date	Reform	Description
1921	Budget and Accounting Act of 1921	Created the executive budget and the Bureau of the Budget (BOB); consistent with the control orientation for budgeting
1937	Brownlow Committee	Created the Executive Office of the President (EOP) with expanded White House staff, including moving BOB from the Department of the Treasury to EOP
1940s–1950s	Hoover Commissions	Focused on "performance budgeting" consisting of establishing closer relationships between resources (inputs) and activities (outputs)
1960	Planning Programming Budgeting System (PPBS)	An effort to more consciously connect resources with results, first in the Department of Defense (successfully) and then with less success in civilian agencies
1970	Management by Objectives (MBO)	Nixon-era strategic planning efforts
1970s	Zero-Based Budgeting (ZBB)	Carter administration's attempt to more systematically review existing programs in the budget process
1990s	Government Performance and Result Act of 1993 (GPRA)	The efforts of the Clinton administration improve service delivery by requiring that federal managers plan for meeting program objectives and providing them with information about program results and service quality
2003–2008	Program Assessment Rating Tool (PART)	The method used by the Bush administration to systematically evaluate federal programs
2010–2016	GPRA Modernization Act of 2010	In an attempt to encourage performance information use, the Obama administration mandated federal agencies to engage in quarterly data-driven reviews of performance information for assessing priority objectives

Source: Joyce (2003), p. 9 (adapted); Moynihan & Lavertu 2011

Evidence-Based Budgetary Policy

Notes

1 An earlier version of this chapter has been published as EUI Working Papers, SPS 2017/1.

2 The British effort to rationalize the budget was part of a three-tier decision-making system that was further composed of the Central Policy Review Staff (CPRS), overseeing PAR, and the Public Expenditures Survey Committee (PESC), which did not embody a detailed analysis of policy options (Premchand, 1983, p. 340).

3 Bouckaert and Halligan (2008) provide a similar trichotomy, putting performance budgeting into context, which distinguishes between performance administration (not consistent, not integrated), management of performance (consistent, not integrated) and performance management (consistent, integrated).

4 The capital budget, setting apart investments, may have the same effect as accrual budgeting. One may question if the relative share of investments in the budgets justifies a completely new accounting system as it is less appropriate for most of the budget, which is geared to consumption.

5 The survey indicates that Korea is doing best (0.66) on the Performance Budgeting Index, while Portugal is lagging behind (0.18).

6 The questionnaire does not match the outcome of the survey as the questions are renumbered. We refer to the numbering of the dataset that is posted on the OECD website.

7 The previous survey took place in 2007. Note that both the wording and the categories have been changed, making the comparison debatable.

8 A European Commission–funded research project, Coordinating for Cohesion in the Public Sector of the Future (COCOPS), comparatively and quantitatively assesses the impact of New Public Management–style reforms in European countries, drawing on a team of European public administration scholars from 11 universities in 10 countries (Hammerschmid et al., 2013).

9 The allocation of scarce resources is often the subject of what in 't Veld has called the "law of policy accumulation," i.e., policymakers tend to respond in the same way regardless of the effectiveness or ineffectiveness of an instrument, namely by calling for "more of the same" (in 't Veld, 1998).

10 This performance information use at the macro level remains largely unobservable by large-scale quantitative research. Therefore the available evidence is largely anecdotal and revealed mostly by qualitative case studies (de Jong, 2015, p. 14).

11 A similar conclusion is drawn by de Lancer Julnes regarding the utilization of performance information not directly related to the budget. Following Weiss, she points at non-instrumental modes of utilization (de Lancer Julnes, 2008). In fact, the utilization of performance information has many faces (Hatry, 2008).

12 The shift away from performance budgeting towards policy evaluation seems to be related to the fact that the NPM movement, of which performance budgeting is an important component, is fading away (Dunleavy, 2005).

13 A similar conclusion is drawn by de Vries, where he states, correctly, that NPM is focused on efficiency, not effectiveness (de Vries, 2010).

14 Agencies are even obliged to employ program evaluation to assess performance, rigorously conducted as part of the budget development process (Mikesell, 2014, pp. 288–289).

15 The section on the pursuit of evidence-based policymaking is taken from van Nispen (2015).

16 The difference between policy reviews and spending reviews is diminishing as policy reviews should also contain a minus 20% alternative from January 1, 2015, onwards.

17 One of the first experiments with spending reviews was the so-called Reconsideration of Public Expenditures (Heroverweging van overheidsuitgaven, HO), a large-scale effort by the Dutch government to cut public spending in order to reduce the sky-high budget deficit in the 1980s. The interest in spending reviews gradually faded away in the early 1990s, when the economy recovered, but spending reviews made a revival in 2010 due to the consequences of the sovereign debt crisis.

18 The one-off spending reviews in both Italy and Spain are mainly due to the rules of the Stability and Growth Pact, rather than the pursuit of a more evidence-based fiscal policy.

19 The Irish spending review—Comprehensive Reviews of Expenditure—is modeled on the British example and constitutes, as such, the preparation of a multi-annual budget which sets three-year ceilings on ministry expenditures (Robinson, 2013, p. 11, fn. 6).

20 The ERC has overseen in earlier times two periods of intense spending review activity focused on delivering fiscal consolidation, the first in the late 1970s and the second in the mid-1980s (Robinson, 2013, p. 10).

21 It should be noted that performance budgeting used the NPM movement as a vehicle, but has dynamics of its own.
22 As Wildavsky's seminal work on the budgetary process noted, it would take a totalitarian regime to fully embrace a normative theory of budgeting, for this would imply the end of politics (Wildavsky, 1992, p. 429).
23 A number of these initiatives refer more to management reform than to budget reform.

References

Australian Bureau of Statistics (ABS) (2010), *A Guide for Using Statistics for Evidence-Based Policy*, Canberra, Australia: ABS.

Australian Expenditure and Strategic Reviews, Presentation at the 7th annual meeting of the OECD Senior Budget Officials Network on Performance and Results, Paris, November 10–11, 2011.

Banks, Gary (2009), *Evidence-Based Policy Making: What Is It? How Do We Get It?* Melbourne: Australian Government Productivity Commission, Commonwealth of Australia.

Bekkers, Victor J. J. M. (2014), Contested Knowledge in Dutch Policy Analysis: Setting the Stage, in: F. K. M. van Nispen and P. W. A. Scholten (eds.) *Policy Analysis and Evaluation in The Netherlands: Institutionalization and Performance* (Bristol, UK: Policy Press).

Blair, Tony and Jack Cunningham (1999), *Modernising Government* (London: The Stationery Office).

Behn, Robert D. (2003), Why Measure Performance? Different Purposes Require Different Measures, *Public Administration Review*, 63 (5).

Bestebreur, Ton and Henk Klaassen (2003), *New Public Budgeting in the Netherlands. Local and National Efforts: A Critical Appraisal.* Paper delivered at 2003 Annual EGPA Conference, Oeiras, Portugal.

Bouckaert, Geert and John Halligan (2008), *Managing Performance: International Comparisons.* London and New York: Routledge.

Davies, Philip (2004), *Is Evidence-Based Government Possible?* Jerry Lee Lecture 2004, delivered at the 4th Annual Campbell Collaboration Colloquium, Washington, February 19, 2004.

de Jong, Maarten (2015), *Managing Spending and Performance in the Netherlands*, Presentation delivered at the Government MI Conference, London.

de Jong, Maarten (2016), *Why Agencies Budget for Results: Exploring Institutional Explanations for Performance Budgeting—The Case of Forestry and Air Traffic Control* (PhD dissertation), Rotterdam: Erasmus University of Rotterdam.

de Jong, Maarten, Iris van Beek and Rense Posthumus (2013), Introducing Accountable Budgeting: Lessons from a Decade of Performance-Based Budgeting in the Netherlands, *OECD Journal on Budgeting* 12 (3).

de Lancer Julnes, Patricia, Performance Measurement Beyond Instrumental Use, in: Wouter van Dooren and Steven van de Walle (eds.) (2008), *Performance Information in the Public Sector: How It Is Used*, Houndmills, UK: Palgrave Macmillan, 58–71.

de Vries, Jouke (2010), Is New Public Management Really Dead? *OECD Journal on Budgeting*, (1): 1–5.

de Vries, Jouke and Ton Bestebreur (2010), Budgetary Reform in The Netherlands: Sadder But Not Wiser Now, in Wanna et al., op cit., 211–239.

Dunleavy, Patrick, Helen Z. Margetts, Simon Bastow and Jane Tinkler (2006), New Public Management Is Dead—Long Live Digital-Era Governance, *Journal of Public Administration Research and Theory* 16 (3): 467–494.

Dunn, William N. (2012), *Public Policy Analysis: An Introduction*, 5th edition. New York: Routledge.

Frisco, Velda and Odd J. Stalebrink (2008), Congressional Use of the Program Assessment Rating Tool, *Public Budgeting & Finance* 28 (2): 1–19.

Gilmour, John B. and David E. Lewis (2006), Does Performance Budgeting Work? An Examination of the Office of Management and Budget's PART Scores, *Public Administration Review*, 66 (5): 742–752.

Gray, Andrew and Bill Jenkins (1982), Policy Analysis in British Central Government: The Experience of PAR, *Public Administration* 60 (4): 429–450.

Hammerschmid, Gerhard, Anca Oprisor and Vid Štimac (2013), *COCOPS Executive Survey on Public Sector Reform in Europe. Research Report* (Work Package 3). Berlin/Rotterdam: Coordination for Cohesion in the Public Sector of the Future.

Hardt, Łukasz and Maarten de Jong (2011), *Improving the Quality of Governance in Poland through Performance Based Budgeting*, "Sprawne pa stwo" Program. Warsaw, Poland: Ernst & Young.

Haskins, Ron (2009), With a Scope so Wide: Using Evidence to Innovate, Improve, Manage, Budget, in: *Productivity Commission, Roundtable on the Strengthening Evidence-Based Policy in the Australian Federation*, Canberra 17–18 August 2009.

Hatry, Harry P. (2008), Epilogue: The Many Faces of Use, in: Wouter van Dooren and Steven van de Walle (eds.), *Performance Information in the Public Sector: How It Is Used*, Basingstoke: Palgrave Macmillan: 227–240.

Hawkesworth, Ian (2012), *Budgeting Levers, Strategic Agility and the Use of Performance Budgeting in 2011/12*, 8th Annual Meeting on Performance and Results, Paris 26–27 November 2012, GOV/PGC/SBO(2012)10.

Head, Brian W. (2008), Three Lenses of Evidence-Based Policy, *Australian Journal of Public Administration* 67(1): 1–11.

Hoover, Herbert (1950), *Budgeting and Accounting: A report to the Congress. Commission on Organization at the Executive Branch of Government*, New York: McGraw-Hill.

House of Lords, *Public Service – Report*, Session 1997–1998, London: www.publications.parliament.uk/pa/ld199798/ldselect/ldpubsrv/055/psrep01.htm (accessed 18 November 2016).

in 't Veld, Roeland J. (1998), The Dynamics of Policy Instruments, in: B. Guy Peters and Frans K. M. van Nispen (eds.), *Public Policy Instruments: Evaluating the Tools of Public Administration*, Cheltenham, UK: Edward Elgar: 153–161.

Jenkins, William I. (1978), *Policy Analysis: A Political and Organizational Perspective*, London: Palgrave Macmillan.

Joyce, Philip G., (2003), *Linking Performance and Budgeting: Opportunities in the Federal Budget Process*. Arlington, VA: IBM Center for the Business of Government.

Kąsek, Leszek and David Webber (2009), *Current Issues in Fiscal Reform in Central Europe & the Baltic States 2008: Performance-Based Budgeting and Medium-Term Expenditure Frameworks in Emerging Europe*, Warsaw, Poland: World Bank.

Kraan, Dirk-Jan (2007), Programme Budgeting In OECD Countries, *OECD Journal on Budgeting* 2007 (4): 1–41.

Kraan, Dirk-Jan (2010), Uitgaven-heroverweging in OESO-landen, *Tijdschrift Voor Openbare Financiën*, 42(2), 117–134.

Lasswell, Harold D. (1936), *Politics: Who Gets What, When, How*. New York: Whittlesey House.

Meyers, Roy T., (1996), Is There a Key to the Normative Budgeting Lock? *Policy Sciences* 29 (3): 171–188.

Minister van Financiën (MvF), (2004), *Eindrapport VBTB-evaluatie*, Tweede Kamer 2004–05, 29 949, no 1.

Mikesell, John L. (2014), *Fiscal Administration: Analysis and Applications for the Public Sector* (9th edition). Boston: Wadworth.

Moynihan, Donald P. and Stéphane Lavertu (2012), Does Involvement in Performance Management Routines Encourage Performance Information Use? Evaluating GPRA and PART, *Public Administration Review* (July/August): 592–602.

Norcross, Eileen C. and Kyle McKenzie (2006), *An Analysis of the Office of Management and Budget's Program Assessment Rating Tool (PART) for Fiscal Year 2007*. Mercatus Center (Working Paper in Government Accountability). Fairfax: George Mason University,

OECD (2007), *Performance Budgeting in OECD Countries*. Paris: Organisation for Economic Co-operation and Development. www.oecd.org/gov/budgeting/performancebudgetinginoecdcountries.htm (accessed 18 November 2016).

OECD (2010), *OECD Value for Money Study Country Assessment of the Netherlands*. Paris: Organisation for Economic Co-operation and Development.

OECD (2011), 2011 OECD Performance Budgeting Survey. Paris: Organisation for Economic Co-operation and Development. http://qdd.oecd.org/subject.aspx?Subject=593d28f2-6f88-4dd1-b59e-f997c3b34c6e (accessed 18 November 2016).

OECD (2012), *Budgeting Levers, Strategic Agility and the Use of Performance Budgeting in 2011/12*, OECD Senior Budget Officials Network on Performance and Results, 8th Annual Meeting, Paris, November 26–27, 2012, GOV/PGC/SBO(2012)10.

OECD (2013), *Government at a Glance 2013*. Paris: Organisation for Economic Co-operation and Development. www.oecd-ilibrary.org/content/book/gov_glance-2013-en (accessed 18 November 2016).

OECD (2014), *Budgeting Practices and Procedures in OECD Countries*. Paris: Organisation for Economic Co-operation and Development. www.oecd-ilibrary.org/content/book/9789264059696-en (accessed 18 November 2016).

OECD (2015), *Performance Budgeting Practices and Procedures: Case Studies*, 11th Annual Meeting of the OECD Senior Budget Officials Performance and Results Network OECD Conference Centre, Paris 26–27 November 2015, GOV/PGC/SBO(2015)12. www.oecd.org/officialdocuments/publicdisplaydocumentpdf/?cote=GOV/PGC/SBO(2015)12&docLanguage=En (accessed 18 November 2016).

Orszag, Peter (2009), Building Rigorous Evidence to Drive Policy, Washington: Office of Management and Budget. www.whitehouse.gov/omb/blog/09/06/08/BuildingRigorousEvidencetoDrivePolicy, retrieved March 22, 2013.

Patton, Michael Q. (2008), *Utilization-Focused Evaluation* (4th edition). Los Angeles, CA: Sage.

Perret, Bernard (2006), De l'échec de la rationalisation des choix budgétaires (RCB) à la loi organique relative aux lois de finances (LOLF), *Revue française d'administration publique* 117 (1): 31–41.

Pincus, Jonathan (2009), Rapporteur's comments, in: *Productivity Commission, Roundtable on the Strengthening Evidence-Based Policy in the Australian Federation*, Canberra on 17–18 August 2009.

Pollitt, Christopher and Geert Bouckaert (2004), *Public Management Reform. A Comparative Analysis*, Oxford: Oxford University Press (2nd edition).

Posner, Paul L. (2009), *Performance Budgeting: Informing Hard Choices Facing the Nation*. Statement prepared for hearing before the Senate Budget Committee, October 29, 2009.

Posseth, Johan J.A. (2010), Does It Pay Off? *On the Experiences of New Zealand and the Netherlands Using the Budget for "managing" Safety*, Delft, Netherlands: Eburon.

Premchand, Arigapudi (1983), *Government Budgeting and Expenditure Controls: Theory and Practice*, Washington: International Monetary Fund.

Radin, Beryl A. (2006), *Challenging the Performance Movement*. Washington: Georgetown University Press.

Radin, Beryl A. (2013), *Beyond Machiavelli, Policy Analysis Comes of Age* (2nd edition). Washington DC: Georgetown University Press.

Rivlin, Alice (1969), The Planning, Programming, and Budgeting System in the Department of Health, Education, and Welfare: Some Lessons from Experience, in: U.S. Congress Joint Economic Committee, *The Analysis and Evaluation of Public Expenditures: The PPB System* Washington: U.S. Government Printing Office, 1969.

Robinson, Marc (ed.) (2007), *Performance Budgeting: Linking Funding and Results*, Houndmills, UK: Palgrave Macmillan.

Robinson, M. (2013), *Spending Review*, Paper delivered at the 34th Annual Meeting of OECD Senior Budget Officials, Paris: OECD, 3–4 June 2013, GOV/PGC/SBO(2013)6.

Rudd, Kevin (2008), *Address to Heads of Agencies and Members of Senior Executive Service*. Great Hall, Parliament House, Canberra, Australia, 30 April.

Schick, Allen (1966), The Road to PPB: The Stages of Budget Reform, *Public Administration Review* 26 (4): 243–258.

Schick, Allen (1973), A Death in the Bureaucracy: The Demise of Federal PPB, *Public Administration Review* 33 (2): 146–156.

Schick, Allen (1977), Beyond Analysis, *Public Administration Review* 37 (3): 258–263.

Schick, Allen (2003), The Performing State: Reflection on an Idea Whose Time Has Come but Whose Implementation Has Not, *OECD Journal on Budgeting*, 3 (2): 71–103.

Schick, Allen (2014), The Metamorphoses of Performance Budgeting, *OECD Journal on Budgeting*, 13 (2).

Schild, Jan A. (1985), De ontwikkeling van de prestatiebegroting, *Beleidsanalyse*, 1–2: 20–27.

Schoch, Mickie and Corina den Broeder (2013), Linking information on Policy Effectiveness and Efficiency to Budget Decisions in the Netherlands, *OECD Journal on Budgeting* 12 (3): 1–22.

Shaw, Trevor (2015), *Performance Budgeting Practices and Procedures: Case Studies*, Paris: OECD, GOV/PGC/SBO(2015)12.

Shin, Sang Hoon (2013), *Dysfunctional Consequences of the Korean Performance Budgeting System and their Policy Implications*. PhD thesis Birmingham University.

Solesbury, William (2001), *Evidence-Based Policy: Whence it Came and Where it's Going*. London: ECRC Centre for Evidence-based Policy and Practice.

Speklé, Roland F. and Roland F. Verbeeten (2014), The Use of Performance Measurement Systems in the Public Sector: Effects on Performance, *Management Accounting Research*, 25 (2): 131–146.

Evidence-Based Budgetary Policy

van der Kar, Hans M., (1981), Beheersen en begroten, in: D. J. Wolfson (ed.), *Naar een beheersbare collectieve sector*. Deventer, Netherlands: Kluwer: 83–124.

van Dooren, Wouter (2011), Better Performance Management: Single and Double Loop Strategies, *Public Performance & Management Review* 34 (3): 421–434.

van Nispen, Frans K. M. (2014), Policy Analysis and Evaluation in National Government, in: Frans K. M. van Nispen and Peter W. A. Scholten (eds.), *Policy Analysis in the Netherlands*, Bristol, UK: Policy Press (International Library of Policy Analysis): 89–105.

van Nispen, Frans K. M. (2015), Policy Analysis in Times of Austerity: A Cross-National Comparison of Spending Reviews, *Journal of Comparative Policy Analysis: Research and Practice*, DOI 10/1080/13876988.2015.1005929.

van Nispen, Frans K. M. and Johan Posseth (2009), *Performance Informed Budgeting in Europe: The Ends Justify the Means, Don't They?* EUI Working Paper RSCAS 2009/39, Robert Schuman Centre for Advanced Studies. Florence, Italy: European University Institute.

van Twist, Mark, Rien Rouw and Martijn van der Steen (2014), Policy Analysis in Practice: Reinterpreting the Quest for Evidence-Based Policy, in: Frans K. M. van Nispen, Peter W. A. Scholten (eds.), *Policy Analysis and Evaluation in The Netherlands: Institutionalization and Performance.* Bristol, UK: The Policy Press.

von Trapp, Lisa (2014). *Note on the Evolving Role of Performance and Results.* Handout at 35th OECD Senior Budget Officials meeting, Berlin, June 12–13, 2014.

Wanna, John, Lotte Jensen and Jouke de Vries (eds.) (2010), *The Reality of Budgetary Reform in OECD Nations. Trajectories and Consequences.* Cheltenham, UK: Edward Elgar.

Weiss, Carol H. (1979), The Many Meanings of Research Utilization, *Public Administration Review* 39(5): 426–431.

Wildavsky, Aaron B. (1969), Rescuing Policy Analysis from PPBS, *Public Administration Review* 29 (2): 189–202.

Wildavsky, Aaron B. (1974), *The Politics of the Budgetary Process.* Boston, MA: Little, Brown and Company.

Wildavsky, Aaron B. (1975), Some Butterflies Were Caught, No Elephants Stopped: The Zero-Base Budget, a Precursor of PPBS, in: A. Wildavsky (ed.), *Budgeting: A Comparative Theory of Budgetary Processes.* Boston: Little, Brown & Company: 278–296.

Wildavsky, Aaron B. (1992), *The New Politics of the Budgetary Process.* New York: HarperCollins.

Williams, Walter (1998), *Honest Numbers and Democracy.* Washington, DC: Georgetown University Press.

Young, John and Enrique Mendizabal (2009), *Helping Researchers Become Policy Entrepreneurs: How to Develop Engagement Strategies for Evidence-Based Policy-Making.* London: Overseas Development Institute (Briefing Paper 53).

PART III

Committees, Public Inquiries, Research Institutes, Consultants and Public Opinion

11

PUBLIC INQUIRIES

Patrik Marier

Introduction

Public inquiries, also frequently referred to as commissions of inquiry or Royal Commissions in the Commonwealth, represent one of the most enduring institutions in Western democracies. In the United Kingdom, their origin dates back to William the Conqueror (Ashforth, 1990) and they have been employed virtually ever since to 'examine everything' (Lauriat, 2010). In Sweden, they originate from the 17th century. In their peak in the first half of the 20th century, an average of 50 inquiries were ongoing yearly, prompting a Prime Minister to enact a 'commission slaughter' in the 1920s that proved futile (Petersson, 2016). Today, public inquiries still address a wide range of social problems such as economic policy (Bradford, 1998), national security (Farson & Phythian, 2011) and nuclear accidents (Dynes, 1983).

Policy analysts and the public in general have a love/hate relationship with public inquiries. On the one hand, they are notoriously infamous for their costs, length and lack of concrete remedial actions. Public inquiries even earned the dubious mention of being 'Canada's biggest industry' (Doern, 1967, p. 417). As stated by Ashforth (1990), 'their labours rarely produce policy results commensurate with the effort and expense of an inquiry' (p. 1). Quebec's latest investigative inquiry, the Charbonneau Commission, illustrates well the doubts and scepticism associated with using public inquiries to tackle societal problems. This commission, created in 2011, scrutinized the attribution process of public contracts to private construction companies following a wave of news reports describing political interference, high cost structures and dubious specifications to rig the process. The hearings of the commission were televised, sustaining strong ratings for speciality news channels with each new allegation of foul play, and they even triggered the resignation of two mayors prior to its conclusion. Four years later, the 1,741-page final report, which concluded that corruption is far more present than first thought, gathered as much attention as the final tally of the resources spent: more than 70,000 pages of transcriptions, 263 days of public hearings, 3,600 documents, and 300 witnesses (Baillargeon, 2015) at a cost of C$44.8 million (Radio Canada, 2015).

On the other hand, public inquiries can have long-lasting influence, and even a transformative effect, despite being lengthy, costly and cumbersome (Inwood & Johns, 2014a), and the public always seems eager to demand an inquiry whenever a major fiasco or disaster hits the newsstands (Sulitzeanu-Kenan, 2006, p. 647). In Sweden, 40% of legislative change from the late 1960s to the early 1980s has been attributed to the work of commissions (Petersson, 2016). They can also play a legitimizing role to signal that governmental authorities are taking appropriate action to address complex societal problems (Hunter & Boswell, 2015). One such example is the Truth and Reconciliation Commission in South Africa that sought to ease the transition into the post-apartheid era and also acted as a tool of transitional justice (Gready, 2011).

Early studies lamented a lack of scholarly interest on public inquiries (Doern, 1967; Ratushny, 2009), but the literature on public inquiries in policy analyses has been expanding. Unfortunately, while there is an impressive number of case studies and within-country comparisons, much less work has been done on cross-country comparative policy analyses involving public inquiries. This chapter focuses on the challenges associated with the study of public inquiries in comparative public policy. Hence, the focus is on the few truly comparative studies that exist, as opposed to engaging the broader literature that consists mostly of individual case studies.

This chapter is divided into four sections. The first section tackles the question of what constitutes a public inquiry and why this definition matters in comparative analysis, and briefly discusses their purpose. The second section summarizes the research contribution of public inquiries into comparative policy analysis by focusing mainly on their characteristics and their impact on policy change. The third section employs examples from recent research to identify the challenges that the study of public inquiries pose for comparative analysis. The conclusion introduces some suggestions on how to stimulate further comparative research in the field.

What is a Public Inquiry?

The term public inquiry is employed to describe multiple kinds of institutions and functions (Sulitzeanu-Kenan, 2006, p. 624). Still, scholars tend to view public inquiries as impartial fact-finding exercises or as tools to develop policy that is public, ad hoc and investigatory (Doern, 1967)—even though the inquiries rarely possess the necessary time or resources to investigate fully the issue at hand (Ashforth, 1990). They are in many ways a 'separate part of government' (Prasser, 2006, p. 9), which distinguishes them from other types of policy advisory bodies and committees (see Chapters 12 and 13 in this volume, respectively). The definitions and meanings attached to public inquiries are most often related to their institutionalization within the broader governmental apparatus. In Westminster parliamentary systems, public inquiries have historically consisted of Royal Commissions (Bulmer, 1993; Jenson, 1994; Prasser, 2006; Lauriat, 2010), although new forms are increasingly common (Rowe and McAllister, 2006), while in Scandinavia they are typically referred to as commissions of inquiry (Premfors, 1983; Petersson, 2016). Complicating matters further, different names are often employed to identify the exact same type of inquiry, most notably in Canada (Makarenko, 2010). For this chapter, I employ the terms commission of inquiry and public inquiry interchangeably, to simplify the discussion.

Defining Public Inquiries in a Comparative Context

To secure comparison across many cases, a broad understanding and a clear definition of public inquiries is essential. Four examples clearly illustrate the definitional barriers when executing comparative analysis with public inquiries and the necessity to focus on specific inquiry attributes to facilitate comparison.

First, Prasser's (2006) thoughtful and in-depth analysis is probably the most engaging discussion of what constitutes a public inquiry. He offers eleven characteristics: (1) they are non-permanent, ad hoc and temporary; (2) they are created and appointed by the executive; (3) they are fully funded by the government; (4) they exist at the discretion of the executive; (5) they are discrete organizational units and not attached to any permanent organization such as a ministry or agency; (6) members usually originate from outside the civil service, government and parliament; (7) they are public and interact with the broader community; (8) they have clear terms of reference that are public; (9) they seek public participation via a host of mechanisms such as public forums, interviews and submissions; (10) they produce a report at the end of the proceedings; (11) they have advisory powers only.

Second, Inwood and Johns (2014b) compare ten public enquiries in Canada and define commissions of inquiry as 'unique, temporary institutional sites meant to supplant regular institutions of policymaking where pre-existing sets of relations in civil society and the state commingle with the new and temporary relations set up within the inquiry itself . . . they are created out of nothing by the Executive, live short lives and then disappear' (p. 9). These two definitions clearly distinguish what is a public inquiry and what is not, but their application remains rooted in Australia and in Canada within a Westminster parliamentary tradition that does not travel well to other countries that have different political institutions.

Third, a special issue of the *American Behavioral Scientist* on commissions as instruments of policy research examines countries with diverse political institutions, such as Sweden, the United Kingdom and the United States. Researchers employ the term 'governmental commissions'. In the introduction to the special issue, Bulmer (1983) describes commissions as being created by the executive to advise on limited issues of public policy and having a specific purpose and limited time to present findings. A commission is expected 'to collect evidence, analyze the problem, report publicly, and make advisory recommendations for governmental actions' (p. 559).

Finally, in his comparative analysis of public inquiries created to tackle pension policies, Marier (2009) defines a commission broadly as 'any working group created and mandated by a government to study a particular policy and/or program'. He emphasizes that it remains subordinate to the government since the government can terminate it at any time and can use the findings as it pleases (p. 1206). While this definition is a rather technocratic view that ignores other aspects of commissions such as their legitimizing functions (Hunter & Boswell, 2015) and notions of impartiality, it makes it possible to compare the eclectic variations offered by France, Sweden and the United Kingdom. This approach even facilitates the comparison of public inquiries within France, which features a lower level of institutionalization, as well as comparison with the United Kingdom and Sweden.

Purpose

Given the broad range of definitions and institutional arrangements related to public inquiries, multiple typologies and classifications have emerged in the literature (Inwood & Johns, 2014b; Prasser, 2006; Petersson, 2016). As a result, it remains quite difficult to engage in comparative analysis, especially when the comparison involves countries that do not have similar political institutions. The most common way to classify and understand public inquiries is to focus on their role or purpose (Ashforth, 1990; Marier, 2009; Rowe & McAllister, 2006). Here it should be noted that a specific inquiry could fulfil more than one purpose; moreover, there can be strong divergence between the official mandate given to an inquiry and the eventual purpose it serves. With these caveats in mind, public inquiries can be grouped as serving three broad aims: to learn, to adjudicate and to fulfil political motives. It is important to note that a single inquiry can fulfil more than one of these objectives.

Learning functions represent a common feature of public inquiries. Governmental authorities usually do not allocate sufficient resources to pause and evaluate broadly the purpose and goals of programs and policies. Such reflection requires a significant commitment both in terms of time and resources (Rose, 1993). The creation of a commission of inquiry allows the government to deploy resources beyond those that are traditionally available within a ministry (Bradford, 1998; Inwood, 2005) and/or the legislative process (Salter, 2003). This is particularly the case for complex issues, such as horizontal policy problems that cut across department lines, where a pooling of expertise is necessary (Bulmer, 1993). Thus, the creation of a public inquiry helps to facilitate learning beyond current practices (March, 1991) or policy paths (Fleckenstein, 2013).

Many authors have claimed that the lessons provided by public inquiries go well beyond problem solving. In the Canadian context, Jenson (1994), Bradford (1998) and Inwood (2005) have argued that the policy ideas promulgated by commissions can have long-lasting influence throughout government, for instance by suggesting new paradigms. Rowe and McAllister (2006) argue that even 'rejected reports' do not simply vanish from the public sphere since the underlying issues that prompted the creation of a public inquiry in the first place remain (p. 110). In fact, the rejection of a report by a government does not necessarily signify the end of policy debates on the matter under scrutiny; it may in fact do the opposite by adding strength to arguments opposed by a government and plant the seeds for the development of an alternative way of thinking about a policy issue. In a web-based experiment featuring contrasting news stories on various scenarios involving public inquiries and ministerial responses, Sulitzeanu-Kenan (2006) concludes that public inquiries are in fact more likely to be trusted if they are critical of the government. Thus, commissions can anchor alternative proposals or actions to those currently favoured or implemented by governmental authorities.

As a learning exercise, an inquiry can help attenuate political conflicts by generating a better understanding of a policy problem and by presenting new kinds of solutions—even challenging and altering problem definitions, thus facilitating the introduction of alternatives that can redefine the common good (Ashforth, 1990; Inwood, 2005). In some countries, like Sweden, public inquiries have long been employed as a means to foster a common understanding of a policy issue (Premfors, 1983; Hermansson, Svensson & Öberg, 1997). The Swedish historical record demonstrates that the Cabinet has frequently employed inquires to 'rationalize' politics and facilitate consensus-building, in an effort to ease the adoption of future legislation (Petersson, 2016).

The second purpose of inquiries, to adjudicate, refers more specifically to the legal traditions of inquiry, which have a long history in Westminster countries (Lauriat, 2010; Howe, 1999). An inquiry is typically put in place to assess what went wrong in the aftermath of a major scandal, a specific controversial event or a disaster. It is an independent judiciary assessment, usually led by a (former) judge or other legal expert (Elliott & McGuinness, 2002). A public inquiry is established because the typical civil and criminal tools are incapable of handling such complex and vast investigations (Howe, 1999). In these circumstances, the public inquiry harnesses the public's image of judges as impartial and unbiased observers to present findings that are considered credible and at arm's-length from government (Drewry, 1975). In the UK, this type of inquiry is far less popular than Royal Commissions; only 24 independent tribunals of inquiry have been set up between 1921 and 2005

(Sulitzeanu-Kenan, 2006). The Charbonneau Commission, discussed in the introduction, serves such a purpose, with the focus clearly more on adjudication than investigation. Still, judiciary-led inquiries are also frequently employed to conduct investigative exercises on policy issues (Inwood & Johns, 2014a).

This type of judicial public inquiry has also been employed to address much broader legal and societal issues. A clear example would be the Truth and Reconciliation Commission in South Africa, which opted to establish a forum to forgive rather than prosecute crimes and violations related to apartheid (Gready, 2011). At the international level, the United Nations has also created adjudicating bodies, which have sometimes paved the way for prosecution in criminal cases (Frulli, 2012).

Finally, public inquiries also serve clear political functions (Hunter & Boswell, 2015; Sulitzeanu-Kenan, 2006), as a result of the fact that they are set up by the executive in the first place. As such, inquiries can be analysed as another tool that government can employ to implement its agenda or to avoid tackling issues that do not fall within this agenda—or those that oppose it. Research on the analytical purposes of inquiries is clearly focused on the motivation for and uses of public inquiries within the political arena—for example, researchers have pointed out that they are regularly established to delay or avoid making a decision on a policy matter (Long, 1994; Bulmer, 1983). This is hardly a recent phenomenon: three of the roles associated with Royal Commissions in a pre-World War II analysis consist of 'passing the buck for solving a problem, forestalling criticism by presenting the appearance of action and kicking a topic into the long grass' (Clokie & Robinson, 1937, p. 123).

Hunter and Boswell (2015) identify three political functions of commissions of inquiry: problem solving, substantiating and legitimizing. While problem-solving commissions of inquiry serve a number of learning purposes, substantiating and legitimizing commissions are less technocratic and presuppose strong political interference. Substantiating commissions are those established by the executive to validate the preferred governmental solution to a particular problem or issue. Commissions can also serve to legitimize a specific agency by demonstrating that it has the capacity and willingness to address problems. In contrast with the Canadian and Swedish cases described above, Hunter and Boswell reject the notion that commissions will likely generate bold policy changes. Instead, they see them as employed to deploy incremental changes aligned with governmental preferences. Thus, the most potent commissions are those that combine problem-solving and substantiating functions.

Public inquiries can also represent another tool of blame avoidance (Sulitzeanu-Kenan, 2010; Fleckenstein, 2013). Sulitzeanu-Kenan (2010) argues that 'inquiries are fundamentally "negative goods" for elected executives' (p. 631). In his analysis of 132 government decisions in the UK, he concludes that the interplay of the politics of blame, issue salience and government popularity explains whether or not governments opt to appoint a public inquiry to manage a crisis. The likelihood that an inquiry will be established is higher when the causes of the policy problems are considered remote and near an election date. Almost half of the calls for an inquiry in British newspapers (49.2%) attribute blame to remote causes (e.g., individual citizens, businesses and other non-governmental organizations) (p. 624). By shifting the discussion on a controversial issue to another venue, governments also hope to confine the terms within which policy learning occurs after a crisis. Sulitzeanu-Kenan's findings challenge the view of public inquiries as facilitating learning under uncertainty; instead, governmental authorities are likely to set them up when they are fairly sure that remote causes are to blame for a crisis and not when public authorities are perceived to be (potentially) at fault.

Public Inquiries and Comparative Policy Analysis

Comparative research on public inquiries has two distinct focus areas: the inner workings of public inquiries and the role of public inquiries in addressing policy problems. The first set of literature aims to elucidate how public inquiries function. As such, it addresses elements such as composition, operating procedures, relationship to other public institutions, and engagement with its mandate (Prasser, 2006; Rowe & McAllister, 2006). These structural elements matter since commissions of inquiry are akin to a 'theatre of power' where the 'truth' of state powers are on display for the general public (Ashforth, 1990).

This research finds particular credence within the adjudicating tradition, where the focus is clearly on the legal foundations within which public inquiries operate. This tradition represents the forum within which judges and politics interact, often in the wake of an incident, a crisis or a tragedy where the government might have been at fault (Howe, 1999). Inwood and Johns (2014b) refer to these as investigative inquiries. As such, these studies often involve discussions on legal aspects, including the various acts that structure commissions and surround the creation and activities of public inquiries (Ratushny, 2009; Drewry, 1975).

Beyond the legal tradition, an increasing number of studies on commissions of inquiry have stressed the changing nature of public inquiries, emphasizing a wide diversity in form and membership. For example, Rowe and McAllister (2006) highlight that Royal Commissions have virtually disappeared from the British political landscape in favour of alternative arrangements consisting of commissions, committees and inquiries. Despite the changes, the ways in which members are selected continue to remain 'opaque' (p. 106). A recent comparative study in the UK employs the broader term 'independent commission' (Hunter & Boswell, 2015), which captures the growing number of different institutional settings. Similar observations have been made in Sweden: in the Working Group on Pensions, for example, politicians played a far more prominent role than they had in previous commissions, and social actors usually involved in public inquiries were excluded (Marier, 2008). As political interventions in commissions of inquiry seem to be on the rise, members are increasingly concerned about their independence, since it is their name that will eventually be attached to the report (Rowe & McAllister, 2006).

Another interesting approach to the inner workings of a public inquiry is to study how it incorporates research. To this effect, Bulmer (1993) identifies seven different ways that research can be used, including serving merely as window dressing, underpinning conclusions, and being the primary motivation behind the creation of a commission (pp. 45–46).

A second set of literature surrounds the role of public inquiries in addressing policy problems. This involves how they facilitate or impede policy change and also the extent to which they legitimize governmental actions to cement the adoption of specific courses of action or to appease controversies. Multiple comparative analyses address the impact of public inquiries on policy change (Bradford, 1998; Marier, 2009; Fleckenstein; 2013) including a special issue (Bulmer, 1983) and edited volumes (Inwood & Johns, 2014a; Farson & Phythian, 2011). These studies all seek to identify the conditions within which public inquiries can be highly influential and alter the policy landscape. One common test is to identify whether a commission triggered a change in policy or was ignored by governmental authorities (Rowe & McAllister, 2006).

Swedish policy analyses feature many references to public inquiries and policy change. According to Lindvall and Rothstein (2006), Swedish policymaking between the 1930s and 1980s operated in the following way: 'Leading politicians at the national level decided the overall aims of policy in collaboration with leaders of major interest organisations, and then government commissions of inquiry engaged experts who compiled the available knowledge about the policy's target area' (p. 49). Supporting these claims, research on the rise of the Swedish welfare state features multiple references to commissions of inquiry (Weir & Skocpol, 1985; Heclo, 1974; Rothstein, 1996) at a time where they became 'semi-permanent institutions' (Petersson, 2016). Despite the ongoing disappearance of the strong state (Lindvall & Rothstein, 2006), featuring a decrease in the participation levels of labour organizations in policymaking activities (Svensson & Öberg, 2002), the influence of commissions of inquiry persists (Marier, 2005; Dahlström, 2009).

Studies on the influence of public inquiries also emphasize different phases of the policy process. For example, Bradford (1998) stresses that Canadian Royal Commissions have had an important role at the agenda-setting stage of economic policymaking. Bradford argues that commissions were responsible for developing the core policy ideas behind the substantial changes in economic policies that accompanied the adoption of the Keynesian welfare state and economic liberalisation, eventually resulting in the North American Free Trade Agreement. Thus, their influence is clearly at the agenda-setting stage where they succeed in defining policy problems, a crucial step well-studied in the policy problems literature (Rochefort & Cobb, 1993). Royal Commissions have assumed this leadership role due to a lack of administrative capacity to tackle large-scale problems and because they succeed in generating policy ideas that are administratively, economically and politically feasible (Bradford, 1998). In a comparative chapter, he argues that similar influential economic ideas have originated from very different actors elsewhere, stressing political parties in the UK, presidents in the US and interest organizations in Sweden.

Marier (2009), in his analysis of pension inquiries, focuses on the sustainability of policy influence of a commission of inquiry *throughout* the policy process. He includes a very diverse set of policy outcomes and identifies five key variables to determine policy influence: membership in the commission, the terms of reference, the level of independence, the institutional environment and, inspired by Bradford (1998), the viability of the output. He concludes that a commission's influence on policy outcomes is highly dependent on governmental responses and ranges from opposition to full endorsement. The two most successful cases of commissions of inquiry, the Swedish Working Group on Pensions and the UK Pensions Commission, involved civil servants early in the deliberative process and paved the way for a broad endorsement of reform across the political spectrum. In the Swedish case, many of the members of the Working Group were eventually integrated within the Implementation Group.

At the opposite end of the spectrum, there is a research agenda devoted to explaining how governmental authorities turn to public inquiries to prevent policy change from occurring. This is rooted in the more cynical literature, cited above, that suggests that public inquiries serve to delay and avoid tackling policy problems.

Finally, other studies do not focus explicitly on policy change, but rather on the signals sent by commissions of inquiries to the broader public. Hunter and Boswell (2015) argue that the symbolic functions of a commission are as important as their problem-solving roles. These symbolic functions can either be substantiating the government's preferred course of action, or legitimizing governmental responses to a policy problem (see also Ashforth, 1990). For Bulmer (1983), these symbolic functions serve to justify, and even encourage, the use of social research by governments.

Governments can, for example, legitimize the adoption of unpopular or controversial policies with their approbation by a commission of inquiry—although this strategy can backfire if the final recommendations point in a different direction. A notable example is the publication in the UK of the final report of the Inquiry into the Value of Pensions (Scott

Inquiry), a commission established to study differences in the pension treatment of public and private sector workers. The report promulgated that private sector workers should receive pension compensation akin to that received by public servants. These findings went firmly against the wishes of Margaret Thatcher who sought to reduce public service pensions to justify retrenchment measures (Nesbitt, 1995, pp. 36–37).

The Difficulties of Engaging in Comparative Policy Analysis on Public Inquiries

Comparative research is usually confined to the same country (Bradford, 1998; Inwood & Johns, 2014a; Prasser, 2006; Hermansson, 1993), closely aligned with a specific policy issue (Farson & Phythian, 2011; Marier, 2009) or a combination of both (Hunter & Boswell, 2015). This section discusses ongoing difficulties associated with a comparative research agenda on public inquiries and provides some illustrations from the literature as to how to resolve them. Three key challenges are addressed: comparison within countries, comparison across a policy field, and measuring influence.

Beyond the traditional difficulties associated with comparative research, comparative studies of public inquiries must also address additional complexities related to elements such as the interpretation of mandates, the diverse forms of inquiries, the eventual policy impact and interpretations of the findings, and the impossibility of knowing the 'true' intentions of the sponsor. In addition, the successful functioning of a commission, and even its influence with policymakers, can be due in large part to the individual leadership role played by a commissioner (Ratushny, 2009). Hunter and Boswell (2015) also stress that commissions can be erratic: they can evolve over time in unanticipated ways and can, for example, shift from performing substantiating tasks for the governments to solving problems. These characteristics are present whether or not researchers opt to compare within and/or across countries, but can quickly become burdensome when comparative work is undertaken.

One of the key hurdles for within-country comparison is the specific nature of the mandates given to public inquiries. Large public inquiries are unlikely to reconvene to tackle a policy issue in the near future. As a result, comparative work involves analyses across various policy fields that may have little in common—for example, a recent Canadian volume covers such diverse issues as the status of women, relationships with Aboriginal people, water quality and pipeline construction (Inwood & Johns, 2014a). Another challenge for comparison is the time period within which they occur. Many historical studies clearly emphasize noticeable variations both with regards to the usage of commissions and the scope of the mandates given to them (Lauriat, 2010; Hermansson, 1993; Ratushny, 2009; Prasser, 2006).

Another type of comparative analyses looks across multiple jurisdictions. Such comparisons are facilitated by the increasing exchanges across countries and the growing similarities in terms of policy activities. Countries do in fact experience very similar policy problems (Rose, 1991)—for example, in designing pension policies suitable for contexts of an ageing population and lower economic growth (OECD, 2009). Commissions are often used even in countries that do not have a long-standing tradition with this policy tool (Marier, 2009). The key difficulty with cross-country comparisons of public inquiries is that various national-level political constellations can significantly impact the ways in which commissions can influence policy change. To facilitate a comparison, it is therefore essential to develop clear parameters (or variables) that can travel across countries.

Another important challenge for all comparative work with public inquiries is how to measure the policy influence achieved by such inquiries. It is already very difficult to come to

Public Inquiries and Policy Analysis

grips with what constitutes a policy change (Green-Pedersen, 2004); assessing the extent to which a public inquiry facilitates this change is even more complicated, as it is difficult to link a change in policy with the influence of a commission. For one, commissions are disbanded once they publish their final report. With the exception of Swedish and Norwegian parliamentarians who are frequently involved in public inquiries, members are usually selected because they are at arm's-length from the administrative and political apparatus of the state. Hence, as a result, they lack the necessary tools to facilitate the adoption of their recommendations. This means that they must gather broad societal endorsement and, more importantly, the support of the governing party if they want their recommendations to see the light of day.

As a result, it is not surprising that researchers conceptualize the role that commissions play in policy change in a variety of ways. Inwood and Johns (2014c) find that commissions of inquiry (COI) can lead to three types of policy change. First, a commission can trigger transformative and direct policy change, which is evidenced by the nature of the changes in ideas, institutions and relations 'that are *directly* attributable to the COI' (p. 292; emphasis added). The entire policy framework is likely affected by the commissions, and this can occur in the medium to long term. A prime example is the Macdonald Commission that was associated with Canada's eventual adoption of the North American Free Trade Agreement with the United States (Inwood, 2005). Second, policy change can be transformative but diffuse, meaning that changes are gradual and some transformation is directly attributable to the COI. Finally, a COI can have marginal and limited impact on policy change, with no change being observable in the short to long term (p. 292).

Marier (2009) argues that a commission can have five kinds of policy influence. First, a public inquiry can be an *alarm raiser* by discovering or bringing up a policy issue that did not originally feature on the policy/political agenda; this is possible especially if the commission has a vague mandate. Second, a report could reinforce the *status quo* and simply gather dust in a parliamentary library. Third, somewhat akin to the marginal policy change described above, a commission can generate *incremental* policy change by suggesting modifications that do not challenge the existing policy structure. Fourth, a commission can be an *idea shaker* whose recommendations simmer for a long time before resulting in an important alteration of the policy framework. Finally, a COI can be akin to a *policy engineer* if it succeeds in having its major recommendations endorsed by the government (Marier, 2009. pp. 1209–1210). In Marier's study, the Swedish Working Group on Pensions and the UK Pension Commission were eventually *policy engineers*.

Conclusion

The review of the literature on public inquiries reveals a wealth of literature concentrated on comparative analyses geared primarily to multiple cases within a single country or across similar policy areas within the same country. As a result, there are two major gaps in the literature.

First, work on the functioning of public inquiries could benefit from analysing cross-country differences. A lot of attention is devoted to defining what is and what is not a public inquiry or a commission; much less attention is given to why different types of public inquiries matter. In an era where various types of forums are being set up, even in countries with such a rich tradition of Royal Commissions like the UK, this generates opportunities for scholars to analyse how these different institutional structures alter the inner working of inquiries. For example, will including politicians or civil servants within an inquiry change significantly the ways in which research is analysed and or even conducted? Are there substantial changes in interactions when the rules of engagement between members of inquiries with the public and societal groups differ?

The diffusion and transfer of policies across regional and national entities have fostered highly interesting comparative analyses that have improved our understanding and knowledge of the policy process. Public inquiries could benefit from similar research attention. There are notable cases of public inquiries being set up in other countries after being successful elsewhere. For example, inspired by the South African Truth and Reconciliation Commission, a similar commission has been set up in Canada to facilitate reconciliation between aboriginal and non-aboriginal peoples. The Norwegian pension reform was not only inspired by the Swedish reform, but also by the ways in which Swedish politicians tackled the inquiries leading to the reforms (Marier, 2016). While circumstances differ, comparative analyses could enhance our knowledge of inquiries and the outcomes they produce.

Second, there is now a truly impressive number of studies comparing policies across regions or countries and a venue, the *Journal of Comparative Analysis*, dedicated to fuelling this enterprise. Unfortunately, few are truly focused on analysing the role of commissions of inquiries within this process. In many cases, inquiries feature in the narrative supporting the comparison, but they do not play a predominant role. This is all the more surprising with the rise of studies involving policy learning and the role of ideas, since inquiries are especially renowned for this specific contribution. The most interesting finding while conducting research for this chapter is the absence of truly comparative, cross-country policy analysis on public inquiries.

References

Ashforth, A. 1990. Reckoning Schemes of Legitimation: On Commissions of Inquiry as Power/Knowledge Forms. *Journal of Historical Sociology*, 3, 1–22.

Baillargeon, Stéphane. 2015. 'À la prochaine . . .' *Le Devoir*, 30 November. Available from www.ledevoir.com/societe/medias/456577/medias-a-la-prochaine. Accessed 5 December 2015.

Bradford, N. 1998. *Commissioning Ideas: Canadian National Policy Innovation in Comparative Perspective*. Toronto: Oxford University Press.

Bulmer, M. 1983. Introduction: Commissions as Instruments for Policy Research. *American Behavioral Scientist*, 26, 559–567.

Bulmer, M. 1993. The Royal Commission and Departmental Committee in the British Policy-making Process. In: Peters, B. G. & Barker, A. (eds), *Advising West European Governments: Inquiries, Expertise and Public Policy*. Edinburgh University Press.

Clokie, H. M. & Robinson, J. W. 1937. *Royal Commissions of Inquiry: The Significance of Investigations in British Politics*. Stanford University Press.

Dahlström, C. 2009. The Bureaucratic Politics of the Welfare State Crisis: Sweden in the 1990s. *Governance*, 22, 217–238.

Doern, G. B. 1967. The Role of Royal Commissions in the General Policy Process and in Federal-Provincial Relations. *Canadian Public Administration*, 10, 417–433.

Drewry, G. 1975. Judges and Political Inquiries: Harnessing a Myth. *Political Studies*, 23, 49–61.

Dynes, R. R. 1983. The Presidential Commission on the Accident at Three Mile Island. *American Behavioral Scientist*, 26, 607–621.

Elliott, D. & McGuinness, M. 2002. Public Inquiry: Panacea or Placebo? *Journal of Contingencies & Crisis Management*, 10.1, 14–25.

Farson, S. & Phythian, M. 2011. *Commissions of Inquiry and National Security: Comparative Approaches*, Santa Barbara, CA: Praeger.

Fleckenstein, T. 2013. Learning to Depart from a Policy Path: Institutional Change and the Reform of German Labour Market Policy. *Government and Opposition*, 48, 55–79.

Frulli, M. 2012. Fact-Finding or Paving the Road to Criminal Justice? Some Reflections on United Nations Commissions of Inquiry. *Journal of International Criminal Justice*, 10, 1323–1338.

Gready, P. 2011. *The Era of Transitional Justice: The Aftermath of the Truth and Reconciliation*. New York: Routledge.

Green-Pedersen, C. 2004. The Dependent Variable Problem within the Study of Welfare State Retrenchment: Defining the Problem and Looking for Solutions. *Journal of Comparative Policy Analysis: Research and Practice*, 6, 3–14.

Heclo, H. 1974. *Modern Social Politics in Britain and Sweden*. New Haven, CT: Yale University Press.

Hermansson, J. 1993. *Politik som Intressekamp*. Stockholm, Sweden: Norstedts Juridik.

Hermansson, J., Svensson, T. & Öberg, P. O. 1997. Vad blev av den svenska korporativismen. *Politica*, 29, 365–384.

Howe, G. 1999. The Management of Public Inquiries. *Political Quarterly*, 70, 294.

Hunter, A. & Boswell, C. 2015. Comparing the Political Functions of Independent Commissions: the Case of UK Migrant Integration Policy. *Journal of Comparative Policy Analysis*, 17, 10–25.

Inwood, G. J. 2005. *Continentalizing Canada: The Politics and Legacy of the Macdonald Royal Commission*. University of Toronto Press.

Inwood, G. J. & Johns, C. M. 2014a. *Commission of Inquiry and Policy Change: A Comparative Analysis*. University of Toronto Press.

Inwood, G. J. & Johns, C. M. 2014b. Why Study Commissions of Inquiry? In: Inwood, G. J. & Johns, C. M. (eds), *Commission of Inquiry and Policy Change: A Comparative Analysis*. University of Toronto Press.

Inwood, G. J. & Johns, C. M. 2014c. Commissions of Inquiry and Policy Change: A Comparative Analysis In: Inwood, G. J. & Johns, C. M. (eds), *Commission of Inquiry and Policy Change: A Comparative Analysis*. University of Toronto Press.

Jenson, J. 1994. Commissioning Ideas: Representation and Royal Commissions. In: Phillips, S. D. (ed.), *How Ottawa Spends 1994–1995: Making Change*. Ottawa: Carleton University Press.

Lauriat, B. 2010. 'The Examination of Everything': Royal Commissions in British Legal History. *Statute Law Review*, 31, 24–46.

Lindvall, J. & Rothstein, B. 2006. Sweden: The Fall of the Strong State. *Scandinavian Political Studies*, 29, 47–63.

Long, M. 1994. The Correct Use of Commissions. *International Review of Administrative Sciences*, 60, 505–511.

Makarenko, J. 2010. *Public Inquiries in Canada*. Available from www.mapleleafweb.com. Accessed 15 November 2015.

March, J. G. 1991. Exploration and Exploitation in Organizational Learning. *Organization Science*, 2, 71–87.

Marier, P. 2005. Where Did the Bureaucrats Go? Role and Influence of the Public Bureaucracy in the Swedish and French Pension Reform Debate. *Governance*, 18, 521–544.

Marier, P. 2008. Empowering Epistemic Communities: Specialised Politicians, Policy Experts and Policy Reform. *West European Politics*, 31, 513–533.

Marier, P. 2009. The Power of Institutionalized Learning: The Uses and Practices of Commissions to Generate Policy Change. *Journal of European Public Policy*, 16, 1204–1223.

Marier, Patrik (forthcoming). The Politics of Policy Adoption: A Scandinavian Tale on the Difficulties of Enacting Policy Diffusion or Transfer Across Industrialized Countries. *Policy Sciences*. Published online: 26 Dec 2016. doi:10.1007/s11077-016-9269-6

Nesbitt, S. 1995. *British Pension Policy Making in the 1980s: The Rise and Fall of a Policy Community*. Aldershot, UK: Avebury.

OECD 2009. *Pensions at a Glance 2009: Retirement-Income Systems in OECD Countries*. Paris: Organisation for Economic Co-operation and Development.

Petersson, O. 2016. Rational Politics: Commissions of Inquiry and the Referral System. In: Pierre, J. (ed.), *Oxford Handbook of Swedish Politics*. Oxford University Press.

Prasser, G. S. 2006. *Royal Commissions and Public Inquiries in Australia*. Chatswood, Australia: LexisNexis Butterworths.

Premfors, R. 1983. Governmental Commissions in Sweden. *American Behavioral Scientist*, 26, 623–642.

Radio Canada. 2015. Commission Charbonneau: 4 ans d'enquête, 44,8 millions de dollars de dépenses totales. Available from http://ici.radio-canada.ca/nouvelles/politique/2015/11/24/001-charbonneau-cout-total-enquete-avocat-politique-commission.shtml. Accessed 5 December 2015.

Ratushny, E. 2009. *The Conduct of Public Inquiries: Law, Policy, and Practice*. Toronto: Irwin Law.

Rochefort, D. A. & Cobb, R. W. 1993. Problem Definition, Agenda Access, and Policy Choice. *Policy Studies Journal*, 21, 56–71.

Rose, R. 1991. What is Lesson-Drawing? *Journal of Public Policy*, 11, 3–30.

Rose, R. 1993. *Lesson-Drawing in Public Policy: A Guide to Learning Across Time and Space,* London: Chatham House.

Rothstein, B. 1996. *The Social Democratic State: The Swedish Model and the Bureaucratic Problem of Social Reforms.* University of Pittsburgh Press.

Rowe, M. & McAllister, L. 2006. The Roles of Commissions of Inquiry in the Policy Process. *Public Policy and Administration*, 21, 99–115.

Salter, L. 2003. The Complex Relationship Between Inquiries and Public Controversy. In: Manson, A. & Mullan, D. (eds), *Commissions of Inquiry: Praise or Reappraise?* Toronto: Irwin Law.

Sulitzeanu-Kenan, R. 2006. If They Get It Right: An Experimental Test of the Effects of the Appointment and Reports of UK Public Inquiries. *Public Administration*, 84, 623–653.

Sulitzeanu-Kenan, R. 2010. Reflection in the Shadow of Blame: When Do Politicians Appoint Commissions of Inquiry? *British Journal of Political Science*, 40, 613–634.

Svensson, T. & Öberg, P. 2002. Labour Market Organisations' Participation in Swedish Public Policy-Making. *Scandinavian Political Studies*, 25, 295–315.

Weir, M. & Skocpol, T. 1985. State Structures and the Possibilities for Keynesian Responses to the Great Depression in Sweden, Britain, and the United States. In: Evans, P. B. (ed.), *Bringing the State Back In*. Cambridge University Press.

12

EXPERT ADVISORY BODIES IN THE POLICY SYSTEM

Kate Crowley and Brian W. Head

This chapter examines transformation, diffusion and variability issues in relation to expert advisory bodies over recent decades. This review of advisory bodies is placed within the broader context of the policy system, which comprises 'interlocking' sets of actors, with 'a unique configuration in each sector and jurisdiction' which provide 'information, knowledge and recommendations for action to policymakers' (Craft & Howlett 2012, p. 80). While the literature on policy advice is decades old, comparative studies of expert advisory bodies and advisory systems have only emerged more recently (Van Damme, Brans & Fobé, 2011; Reinecke, Hermann, Bauer, Pregernig, Karl Hogl & Pistorius, 2013; Schultz, Bressers, van der Steen & van Twist, 2015; Craft & Halligan, 2017); along with the single country studies in the International Library of Policy Analysis (ILPA) (Routledge) series. The chapter proceeds by firstly discussing the place of expert policy advice in policy advisory systems, and the evolving role of the expert advisory council, before reviewing and analysing a range of comparative and single country studies of advisory bodies. The scope of the chapter's review is dependent on the current scope and availability of comparative scholarly analysis on expert advisory bodies and systems, and so ranges widely across the EU countries, Anglophone (English-speaking) countries, and some East Asian countries.

The chapter shows that, while there is still a role for traditional, independent advisory bodies within the government sector, expert advisory bodies today are under great pressure to adapt to changing contexts and expectations. Most importantly, they are not only expected to provide the best available expert advice to government, but increasingly to do so in ways that engage with broader policy contexts and inter-related issue domains. There is growing evidence that some expert bodies are taking on some of the features of 'boundary organizations' specifically by engaging with a range of perspectives across broad policy domains, and by harnessing not only scientific knowledge but also lay knowledge and explicitly value-laden perspectives (Van Damme et al., 2011). Those expert advisory bodies that do engage with sectoral interests and value-based groups are, furthermore, likely to be better placed to leverage support and policy traction on difficult issues. In general, we find that the translation of expert advice into evidence-informed policy action is enhanced where attention is paid to both policy design and engagement processes within specific institutional settings. Nevertheless, the translation and diffusion of expert advice is always difficult and problematic, whatever the socio-political context.

The chapter concludes with a set of key findings on the cross-national variation in advisory bodies and systems (Table 12.5), but also by noting the common themes of the transformation, externalization and politicization of the role of policy advice in recent years.

1. Introduction: The Place of Expert Policy Advice in Policy Advisory Systems

In modern democratic governmental systems, there has long been a tension between the requirements for leaders to be responsive to the views and interests of citizens and stakeholders, and the technocratic requirements of basing decisions on expert technical advice. Debate about policy issues is wide-ranging, and there are many sources of policy ideas and policy advice. Some decades ago, government agencies and statutory bodies constituted the major source of policy analysis and policy advice to ministers. This situation has changed radically in most countries over time as complex advisory systems have emerged. Outside the governmental sector, a vast array of industry associations, think tanks, research centres, consultants, media channels and community organizations typically engage in on-going disputation. Taken together, these non-government or 'external' actors provide a rich variety of contributions to government, ranging from partisan polemics to carefully argued and evidence-informed reports. Within the public sector, administrative departments and ministries play the crucial 'internal' governmental roles of analysing information about the performance of current programmes, and providing evaluations and advice to ministers and their political advisors about options for policy and programme adjustments. In addition, government regulatory bodies monitor compliance with standards and procedural probity. Policy review may also occur in legislatures, not only in everyday debates on legislation but more specifically through legislative committees that investigate particular topics in some depth. Similarly, governments may choose to establish independent public commissions of inquiry into matters of controversy or issues of emerging significance. Finally, it has become common in recent decades for expert advisory bodies to be established within the government sector, but operating with some degree of independence from government agencies. This trend to establish expert advisory bodies can be linked to the growing importance of scientific and technological issues for human well-being, productivity and security, and thus an increased need for reliable and authoritative advice on matters where technical understanding of complex issues is paramount (Prince, 2007; Fischer, 2009).

These diverse, competitive and interacting organizational elements—across the governmental, business and community sectors—constitute the policy advisory system in each country. This chapter focuses on the role and changing functions of advisory bodies that provide independent expert advice to government, and how their work relates to the changing dynamics of the policy advisory system as a whole. In order to situate these specific roles and functions in context, it is useful to outline briefly the types of policy advice that are generated in policy advisory systems. Policy advice goes beyond data analysis by including recommendations about how to understand the issues, and how to respond to them, either in terms of confirming existing settings or arguing for policy change. Policy advice may be pitched at different levels of government (local, regional, national), and may be aimed at different components of the policy system (ranging from strategic long-term policy directions to immediate operational procedures and implementation requirements).

Importantly, some policy issues are seen as relatively routine, with well-established parameters for continued incremental adjustment over time, whereas other issues are seen as controversial matters that call for special handling. Partisan political advisors are likely to be significant background players in handling divisive or sensitive issues and emerging crises. It can be difficult to depoliticize these issues, given the interaction of political staffers with the non-partisan bureaucratic policy system. Public engagement with independent expert bodies and government advisory bodies (for example, statutory authorities that operate independently), could be useful in lowering the 'heat' of sensitive issues. In relation to the content of policy tasks, a useful distinction can be drawn between a focus on short-term tactical issues, medium-term administrative issues, and longer-term strategic policy issues. These different tasks and challenges require different skills, different key actors, and different relationships between expert and lay stakeholder knowledge.

Craft and Howlett (2012) note that advisory systems form part of the total 'knowledge infrastructure' for policy, which comprises diverse flows of information and knowledge in each country. These elements include a vast array of formal bodies including advisory councils, commissions, units, advisors, centres, think tanks, universities, etc. as noted in Table 12.1, which provides an overview of the policy advisory terrain. Expert advisory councils are signalled here as mainly concerned with longer-term issues.

The establishment of expert advisory bodies, as elaborated in later sections, has occurred against the background of wider developments in policy advisory systems. Five significant changes have influenced these developments and gradually made the policy advisory system more complex (Craft & Howlett, 2013; Craft & Halligan, 2017). First, in the decades of the Cold War, the over-riding concerns to promote economic growth and productivity in industrialized countries became closely linked to greater investment in science and technology and a larger role for technical expert advice. Second, from the 1980s the public sector itself became preoccupied with the efficiency and effectiveness of policies and programmes, in the context of revenue pressures and fiscal constraints. Third, the scale and complexity of policy challenges have intensified, as a consequence of the globalization of many policy issues and continued international pressures for productivity and innovation. Fourth, the political

Table 12.1 Policy advisory system actors classified by policy types

	Short-term/reactive	Long-term/anticipatory
Procedural	***'Pure' political and policy process advice*** Political parties, parliaments and legislative committees; regulatory agencies. Internal as well as external political advisors, interest groups, lobbyists, mid-level public service policy analysts and policy managers, pollsters.	***Medium to long-term policy steering advice*** Deputy ministers, agency heads and executives; expert advisory councils, royal commissions, judicial bodies. Agencies, boards and commissions; crown corporations; international organizations (e.g., OECD, ILO, UN).
Substantive	***Short-term crisis and fire-fighting advice*** Political peers (e.g., cabinet); executive office political staff. Expanded ministerial and congressional political staffs; cabinet and cabinet committees; external crisis managers/consultants; political strategists; pollsters; NGOs and community organizations; lobbyists, media.	***Evidence-based policymaking*** Statistical agencies and units; senior departmental policy advisors; strategic policy units; royal commissions; expert advisory councils. Think tanks; scientific and academic advisors; citizen engagement web-enabled initiatives; blue ribbon (eminent persons) panels.

Adapted from Craft & Howlett (2012, p. 91), with expert advisory councils added executive in most countries has moved to assert more control over policy direction, with a notable increase in the politicization of decision-making. And fifth, the traditional role of public servants as the chief advisors to ministers has been undermined in many countries through outsourcing of service delivery, the contestation of policy advice, and a much larger role for external (non-government) players. Particularly in the English-speaking democracies there has been a trend has been towards greater externalization, polycentrism and competition in policy advice and delivery (Halligan, 2010). At the same time, governments are taking responsibility for resolving complex 'wicked' problems that involve disputed values and scientific uncertainty.

Building support for policy positions through participatory processes and enhanced stakeholder communication has become as important for modern governments as building enhanced technical understanding of problems and solutions through best-available science (Van Damme et al., 2011; Head & Alford, 2015). Given that it would be an immense burden for a single jurisdiction to solve policy problems using only its own resources, all countries have moved to take advantage of learning from policy trends and experience elsewhere. While some of this learning is perhaps more about ideological preferences than policy evaluation, it is clear that policies are increasingly being diffused on an international scale (Dolowitz & Marsh, 1996; Evans, 2004; Dobbin et al., 2007; Benson & Jordan, 2011). Domestic politics and international politics are increasingly interdependent. This has implications for the ways in which expertise is incorporated into national advisory systems, and the ways in which expert bodies in specific countries can influence the policy settings adopted in other countries, as policy diffusion occurs alongside convergence through the voluntary uptake of policy ideas.

A related phenomenon is the growth of international policy councils and associated expert advisory bodies attached to international organizations such as the United Nations. A prime example is the Intergovernmental Panel on Climate Change (IPCC), which was established by the United Nations and the World Meteorological Organization in 1988 to provide authoritative assessments of the scientific understanding of climate change (www.ipcc.ch). Researchers in comparative politics have argued for some decades that 'international political processes, actors and institutions increasingly affect national policy decisions' (Busch & Jörgens, 2005, p. 81). In advanced democracies, international treaties and agreements on a range of issues—including those with significant science and technology dimensions—have steered policy and regulatory settings towards harmonization and coordination. Most of the policy learning seems to occur through competition and imitation (Shipan & Volden, 2008) rather than through coercion or the imposition of conditions (for example as conditions of foreign aid). While not the focus of this chapter, comparative analysis would demonstrate that the pattern of policy diffusion is different for each nation-state. Each has a distinctive story of how expert recommendations are considered and filtered within the policy system, and how this experience might vary across policy domains, from technical areas with low levels of political controversy to socially complex areas with significant value-based disputes.

The transition from the production and dissemination of scientific knowledge into policy debate and uptake is uncertain, uneven, and often indirect. There is no royal road from scientific pronouncements to political action via 'evidence-based policymaking' (Head, 2015, 2016), for two main reasons. One is that the strength of technical knowledge consists in its reliability and track record of advising on specific methods, techniques and instruments; but this is very different from understanding and advancing societal goals and priorities. The second is that the prestige of science is more contested now than in previous decades, and other forms of knowledge (held by professionals, stakeholders and citizens) are also important in the policy process. The science sector has therefore switched from a traditional focus on dissemination of authoritative knowledge towards more interactive approaches. Science must still be seen as 'salient, credible and legitimate' (Cash, Clark, Alcock, Dickson, Eckley & Jäger, 2002, p.1) in the eyes of decision-makers and the community, and so, increasingly knowledge brokers are working between researchers and decision makers to ensure this is so. Pielke (2007) argues that adopting an honest-broker role, rather than an advocacy role, will help protect the credibility and legitimacy of science. Other scholars emphasize the need for knowledge brokerage, which provides the human face to the process and idea of knowledge transfer and diffusion (Hargadon, 2002), here seen as an iterative process that takes relationships seriously in a bid to build mutual understanding (Cash et al., 2002; Davies, Nutley & Walter, 2008). Science advisory bodies that are established with the expectation that expert findings will flow directly into policy decision-making will certainly fail this test. Reinecke et al. (2013) argue that bringing together the different worlds of scientific knowledge and policymaking requires a revision of expectations and improved processes. Moreover, the influence of science on policy is just as likely to occur through 'the production of generative ideas and mental models' rather than 'hard scientific data' (p. 3). There are now several methods of knowledge brokerage available for better managing the relationships between science and policy (Reinecke et al., 2013, pp. 4–5), and these methods can be mobilized by expert advisory bodies as well as by individual scientists and their research centres.

2. The Establishment and Development of Expert Advisory Bodies

We define expert advisory bodies as entities established by government to provide on-going advice on matters requiring substantive scientific and/or technical analysis, and whose membership consists largely of experts drawn from non-government organizations and research centres. We distinguish expert advisory bodies from short-term problem-solving groups (such as ad hoc working groups), and from on-going committees of public sector officials (such as government research units, regulatory units, technical monitoring units and legislative committee secretariats). Although expert advisory bodies report to government, they will very often be permitted to release their reports to inform public debate. These bodies were commonly established in an era when science and technology were seen as the key to achieving outcomes, implicitly turning away from the widespread politicization of problem solving. This technocratic approach has been described as the scientization of policymaking (Lentsch & Weingart, 2011).

Expert standing committees established at arm's length from government agencies seem to provide a bulwark against populism and politicization. The most common areas in which these on-going expert advisory bodies have been established are medical and health safety, food and agriculture, education and training, economic development, commerce and trade, environmental standards, and climate change. In recent years, with the growing significance of international frameworks and agreements, there has also been a rapid growth of international expert advisory bodies reporting to the United Nations, the World Trade Organization and the International Labour Organization, on such matters as trade, employment and climate change policies. Haas (2004) draws attention to the contribution of international advisory bodies in resolving major issues around sustainable development and climate change. While the reliability and credibility of the science itself is crucial, legitimacy also depends on communicative networks, which have a key role in shaping high-level strategic thinking and the political will required to initiate policy action. It is well known that climate change response policy has attracted bitter disputes. Given this lack of consensus, the policy advisory structures themselves may be subject to politically driven restructuring following a change in government leadership. Policy councils established by social-democratic governments on sustainable development and climate change have typically been changed or disbanded by incoming conservative governments—for example, Canada's National Round Table on the Environment and Economy was axed by the Harper government for failing to be aligned with government opposition to a carbon tax (Craft & Halligan, 2017), and the Australian Climate Council was de-funded for similar reasons by the conservative Abbott government.

At a detailed level, the forms of analysis and advice may vary enormously. For example, in relation to climate advisory bodies, which study significant biophysical, socio-economic and political aspects of current and future pathways, the advice might range from technical calculations of carbon budgets, to assessments of the effectiveness of policy options. Reinecke et al. (2013, p. 99) explain that 'venues of scientific policy advice range from classical research institutions and governmental agencies, to collaborative research programmes to climate services to information and networking hubs'. Beyond the strictly scientific work, there is also likely to be important background communication to satisfy inquiries from legislators, officials, media commentators and others (Reinecke et al., 2013, p. 95). Indeed, the broad functions and purposes of expert policy advisory councils and committees in contemporary advisory systems have two main aspects:

> On the one hand, they are supposed to contribute to evidence-based policy development and to provide the best available knowledge. On the other hand, they also need to play a role in making the policy-making process transparent, interactive and communicative.
>
> *Van Damme et al., 2011, p. 129*

The capacity of expert advisory bodies to undertake these dual functions will increasingly depend on their capacity and willingness to undertake interactive roles, as Van Damme suggests. Many analysts have argued that governments may seek to use advisory councils to increase policy legitimacy (Cash et al., 2002). Because of the substantive gap between scientific findings and policy action, and the need to combine scientific credibility with outputs and processes that are seen to be legitimate, advisory bodies are increasingly adopting some of the roles of 'boundary organizations', bridging across the domains of science, politics and community. In their study of European education councils, Van Damme et al. (2011, p. 126) suggest that councils are often 'set up by government to increase policy legitimacy' and that councils in turn need to 'gain and sustain access to the policy making process'. Over time, the paradigm has shifted away from that of independent scientific advice and towards one based on interaction and communication with key stakeholders inside and outside government. The contrast between these two frameworks is summarized in Table 12.2.

Issues of transformation, diffusion and variability related to expert advisory councils have been documented by a number of cross-national and single country studies that show varying responses to these pressures to adapt to changing contexts and expectations. Our review below shows that not all advisory bodies have made, or are expected to make, interactive efforts at brokering advice and working across the policy community to ensure better uptake of expert knowledge. Despite pressures for externalization and the argument that knowledge brokerage and bridging roles can enhance evidence-based policymaking, many advisory councils remain in the traditional space (Table 12.2) or are only partially externalized.

Expert Advisory Bodies and Policy Analysis

Table 12.2 The 'externalization' of advisory councils

Councils as traditional, professionalized bodies	Councils as modernized, interactive, responsive bodies
Impetus—Policy needs to move towards greater professionalization (specialized, expert advice).	*Impetus*—Policy needs greater interactiveness (political responsiveness for legitimacy and sustainability).
Policy advice needs to be effective/efficient.	Policy advice needs to be open to challenge.
Councils provide advice efficiently/directly to government.	Councils provide advice accountably/in a transparent fashion.
Councils as government add-on.	Councils as countervailing force.
Short-term instrumental advice.	Long-term strategic advice.
Provide advice on demand.	Provide proactive advice.
Council closely linked to 'mother' department.	Council at a critical distance from government.
High isolation of policy advisory expert bodies.	Expert bodies now 'boundary riders' between interests.
Council stability derives from isolated expert bodies.	Stability derives from being responsive to stakeholders.
Government links constrain network activities.	Interactivity strengthens dialogue between actors.
Advisory and political realms are clearly demarcated.	Advisory-political interaction promotes uptake of advice.

Sources: Craft & Howlett (2013); Van Damme et al. (2011); Reinecke et al. (2013)

3. Advisory Bodies/Systems Comparatively Considered

While there is a rich literature on policy advice, and the manner in which the role of advice has modernized and changed, there are relatively few comparative studies of policy advisory bodies and systems. As Van Damme et al. observe, 'while advisory bodies are now a common feature of the policy-making process in many countries, recent knowledge of their organization and functioning and of their development over time is lacking' (2011, p. 128). In the area of climate change, for example, national and sub-national climate change advisory bodies have not been fully studied, although the International Panel on Climate Change has been well analysed (Reinecke et al., 2013). There has been very little comparative research on advisory systems as a whole in different political and administrative contexts (Schultz et al., 2015). Having identified above the contemporary context of advice giving, we now examine some recent, prominent cross-national comparative studies of advisory bodies (Van Damme et al., 2011; Reinecke et al., 2013) and of advisory systems (Craft & Halligan, 2017; Schultz et al., 2015), looking at the analytic focus of these studies, the countries studied, and the criteria of analysis (see Table 12.3). We then review several single country studies, extending Schultz et al.'s (2015) criteria to consider the issues of externalization, politicization, boundary activity and policy diffusion that are significant in recent literature (Table 12.4). Our interest is not only in the comparative manner by which advisory bodies and systems are studied, but the extent to which there are similarities and/or differences between them, and we conclude this chapter with some observations in that regard (Table 12.5).

Comparing Advisory Councils

We begin with Van Damme et al.'s (2011) comparison of (semi-)permanent education councils in Europe with a view to better understanding 'the functioning of advisory councils' and increasing 'the understanding of the ways in which their functioning can be aligned with modern challenges to policy-making' (p. 128). The authors describe advisory bodies as no longer traditional, apolitical sources of expert advice for governments, but as part of the contemporary complex policy community in which they operate as 'boundary organizations' bringing together multiple players:

> operat[ing] at the crossroads of the different challenges to the policy-making process, pressured by the need to contribute to evidence-based policy development, by the need to assist in building policy support, and by the need to deliver advice that does not infringe too much upon the discretion of political actors to make the final policy decision.
>
> *p. 128*

The traditional boundaries around advisory bodies are breaking down as the political worlds of policymaking and the expert worlds of advisory bodies become 'increasingly interdependent and need to be coordinated so as to increase their functionality and legitimacy' (p. 130). The key dynamic of change is the contemporary need for legitimacy in terms of both 'output legitimacy' to government and 'input legitimacy' from the policy arena. Despite the mix of education council membership types across Europe, there is a clear trend towards seeking greater input legitimacy (p. 140). The authors examine whether councils act as government 'add-ons' or as countervailing forces, and find that those established with reform agendas tend to be more independent. However, in general they find that increased political control is an issue and that councils seek to distance themselves where possible from policymakers. '[M]embership and the relationship of the council with the government serve as a means' of maintaining both relevance and legitimacy, and councils in general try to be relevant, legitimate boundary organizations at the intersection of government, research expertise, and broader policy communities (p. 142).

In reviewing the effectiveness of the advisory function of climate councils across Europe, Reinecke et al. (2013, p. 4) note that where an advisory council observes a clear demarcation of the science–policy boundary, this 'may protect science from politicization and ensure the political acceptability of advice' but it may also act as an obstacle 'to communication, collaboration and concerted action'. They suggest that an advisory council manage the science–policy boundary and facilitate mediation and communication between the two 'worlds' of science and policy, thus creating promising leverage that could more effectively link expert knowledge to policy action (p. 4). These issues of boundary management, boundary work and its relevance for advisory councils is much discussed in the current scientific literature as a means of addressing the science–policy gap. Both experts and policymakers work 'in a brokerage domain in which they negotiate the relevance and cogency of knowledge claims—while still keeping their particular identities and operating conditions as specific societal sub-systems' (p. 4). Traditional advisory councils that are isolated from political and policy communities would therefore have less effective means and mechanisms for pursuing policy uptake and ensuring policy diffusion in practice.

Comparing Advisory Systems

Craft and Halligan (2017) comparatively review trends and developments in the Anglophone family of policy advisory systems—Canada, the UK, Australia and New Zealand. They assess the state of each system by applying spatial, content-based and dynamic concepts to their analysis, the latter capturing the link between advisory systems and their operational context such as the shift to governance, and externalization and politicization issues (Craft & Howlett, 2013). The Anglophone systems have a shared administrative tradition, but the UK, Australia and New Zealand have more closely adhered 'to the precepts of "new public management" than other OECD countries', albeit in differing institutional contexts: unitary (in the UK and New Zealand) and federal (in Australia) (p. 9). Craft and Halligan's (2017) 'trends and developments' analysis is not as criteria-specific as other comparative studies (Table 12.3). The authors note a common decline in policy capacity in countries adopting New Public Management reforms and a concomitant expansion of both political advisors and consultants in response to contraction of the public service. The trend towards centralization of policy advice in Canada and Australia was more marked than elsewhere, and the UK Cabinet Office's policy advisory experimentation is unique to that country.

Schultz et al. (2015) consider how the institutional setup of internal advisory systems in five countries can be understood in relation to the political-administrative regimes in which they are situated. The institutional elements they identify as the basis of comparison include the configuration, administration and composition of the advisory systems (Table 12.3). In terms of *configuration,* there is a trade-off between small, well-functioning and large, more expert councils; temporary bodies serve a specific purpose, while permanent ones run the risk of decline over time. In terms of *administration,* advisory bodies may be regulated or not,

Table 12.3 Comparative approaches to studying advisory bodies/systems

Authors	Analytic focus	Countries	Criteria of analysis
Van Damme, Brans & Fobé (2011)	Semi-permanent advisory bodies in education; councils as boundary organizations	EU focus—Greece, Spain, Belgium, Portugal, the Netherlands, Estonia	Focus on the need for policy legitimacy; i.e., output legitimacy in terms of advice to government; and input legitimacy in terms of broader engagement with the policy community. Council membership and level of autonomy from/relationship with government is comparatively evaluated.
Reinecke, Hermann, Bauer, Pregernig, Karl Hogl & Pistorius (2013)	Climate policy advisory bodies; the integration of climate science and climate policy	EU focus—Germany, the Netherlands, Switzerland and the UK	Focus on the different ways, and the differing institutional/ organizational contexts, in which climate policy brokerage/activity between various actor groups is enacted. The general characteristics of the advisory bodies are a focus, as is their institutionalization, their main activities and their strategies, such as targeted 'boundary management' to ensure knowledge uptake.

(Continued)

Table 12.3 Continued

Authors	Analytic focus	Countries	Criteria of analysis
Craft & Halligan (2017)	*Policy advisory systems analysis*	Anglophone focus—Canada, NZ, Australia, UK	Focus on the state/evolution of the advisory system; utility of spatial, content-based and dynamic approaches (i.e., the shift to governance, and externalization and politicization trends and issues). They conjecture that the influence of a policy advisory system may be linked to an alignment of procedural, substantive, short-/long-term, and reactive/anticipatory conditions.
Schultz, Bressers, van der Steen & van Twist (2015)	*Internal advisory systems in different politico-administrative regimes*	EU focus—France, Germany, Sweden, the Netherlands, UK	Focus on configuration (size of the system, temporal orientation), administration (regulation, financing; obligation for government); and composition (member selection criteria); in differing politico-administrative regimes, i.e., *state structure* (unitary/centralized, unitary/decentralized and federal) and *executive government* (majoritarian, intermediate, consensual).

financed by government or not, and obliged to receive a response from government or not. *Composition* is a significant element of advisory capacity and includes the spread and type of expertise, reputation and representation. Advisory systems must also be understood *in situ*, that is in terms of their fit into a politico-administrative regime. Schultz et al. (2015) look at *state structure* (unitary/centralized; unitary/decentralized; federal), with the more fragmented states likely to have more advisory bodies. They also look at types of *executive government* (majoritarian, intermediate, consensual), with the more consensual states likely to have a relatively larger number of advisory councils.

Single Country Advisory Bodies/Systems Studies

Single country studies of policy advisory bodies and systems are being undertaken for the International Library of Policy Analysis (ILPA) volumes that survey the state of the art of policy analysis in governmental and non-governmental organizations in a range of countries. We review several of the chapters from the series that explicitly consider policy advisory bodies and systems in the Czech Republic, Japan and Taiwan, using Schultz et al.'s

Expert Advisory Bodies and Policy Analysis

(2015) criteria of configuration, administration and composition in differing politico-administrative regimes. These studies provide descriptive overviews of specific advisory councils, committees, boards, and planning bureaus, as depicted in Table 12.4. Prince's (2007) review of 25 years of policy advice in Canada sets the scene for subsequent studies by mapping the externalization of policy advice from 'speaking truth to power' to 'speaking truth with multiple voices'. In the same volume, Dobuzinskis (2007) details the decline of in-house government policy capacity with the abolition of the federal advisory councils for economic and scientific matters in the early 1990s. These developments in externalization and politicization, as well as our interest in boundary activity and policy diffusion, are added to our analysis in Table 12.4.

Yamaya (2015) provides a typology of formal advisory councils at the national level in Japan, noting their regulatory, administrative and political context and the reforms that have followed concerns that councils lack independence. There is concern with their closeness to government, lobbyists and pressure groups, as well as their lack of policy analysis and evaluation expertise and their failure to engage with or engender trust from the general public (Table 12.4). Wang and Chiou's (2015) historical account of advisory committees in Taiwan finds an advisory process that has not democratised in parallel with the political system. Advisory councils largely comprise scholars and experts as well as some representative interests, and are tightly controlled and largely secretive in their proceedings, with low concern about conflict of interest and therefore politicization (Table 12.4). By contrast, the robust, varied internal and external advisory system in the Czech Republic—relatively well advanced for a new democracy—is partly due to the well-established policy advisory system under communism. The Czech Republic has experienced the characteristic shift from state-centred to decentralized governance, and the policy advisory system is now subject to similar types of policy shocks, crises and uncertainties as in other liberal democracies (Merklova & Ptackova, 2016).

4. Findings/Analysis of Cross-National Variations

There are remarkable similarities but also differences between the advisory bodies and systems analysed in these multi-country and single country studies. Some of the relevant details are outlined in Table 12.5. For example, there is very strong evidence that institutional context affects the nature of advisory bodies and systems, and that advisory councils, for example, will vary in relation to different socio-political contexts. In the United States, for instance, the advisory system is openly pluralist: government and advisory bodies maintain a distance from each other, and advice is tendered to government leaders who make the final decisions. The system is more neo-corporatist in parts of Europe, quite elitist or neo-corporatist in Japan with its virtual one-party state, highly controlled but evolving in the post-communist Czech Republic, and relatively closed in the newly democratic state of Taiwan. Van Damme et al. (2011) find that the make-up of education councils across Europe is strongly dependent upon differing political traditions but that councils nevertheless develop similar strategies to maximize their relevance in competitive policy advisory systems. In terms of Anglophone countries, Craft and Halligan (2017) find vastly differing reliance upon political advisors depending on government structure, for example between unitary (UK, NZ) and federal (Canada, Australia) contexts. The literature also suggests that the advisory systems in relatively newly democratized countries (Czech Republic and Taiwan), and in elitist states (Japan), are less externalized and potentially more highly politicized than in longer-established democracies.

Table 12.4 Policy advisory systems—ILPA single country comparisons

Country	Configuration (size, temporal orientation)	Administration (regulation, financing, government response)	Composition (member selection, criteria, etc.)	Policy advice, policy systems, externalization, politicization, boundary activity, policy diffusion
Czech Republic (Merklova & Ptackova, 2016)	Parliamentary democracy since the 1993 transition from communism. There was a well-established advisory system under communist rule. 26 standing, advisory, statutory, permanent and ad hoc committees/councils with many members on more than one body. Political instability affects dynamics of policy advice.	Established by ad hoc *Government Resolution* with activity governed by statutes/rules; and all processes well controlled by government. Significant differences in the resourcing of advisory bodies. Some recommendations/policy proposals adopted in full; in other cases advisory bodies turn to the media and public to exert influence.	No guidelines on balance, partnership, diversity, representation, independence, public good. Selection is ad hoc, not to be expert or representative but committee chairs are from government and appointed by government. Advisory bodies have diverse membership with a mix of independent experts and various representatives.	*Policy advice* typically sought in agenda-setting and formulation stages, not the implementation stage. The *policy system* is robust and diverse within and beyond government, based on advisory tradition. *Externalization*, public deliberation or the accessing of multiple viewpoints is not sought by the system. *Politicization* not explicit but policy advice can be selectively adopted in line with government goals. *Boundary activity*, some bodies coordinate diverse rationales/actors to provide consensual knowledge. *Policy diffusion* failure to impact on policy can be balanced by strong indirect internal/external impact.
Japan (Yamaya, 2015)	Parliamentary democracy; Cabinet system. Powerful, autonomous bureaucracy with in-house expertise. Government councils and committees set up by ministries and agencies. *Shingi-kai*—advisory councils—118 formal councils as of July 2012; many informal councils, including research groups, specialist committees and think tanks.	Regulated by the National Government Organization Act 1948 and the Basic Plan on Reorganization and Rationalization of Councils 1999, and administered by the Shingikai-souran (Council Handbook). There has been periodic concern with the undue policy impact of Councils and their openness to lobbying and where their advice has seen policy change outside of the parliamentary process.	Expert and representative; this can differ according to policy domain; some areas have a closed policy process. Elitist 'Iron Triangle' of policymakers—politicians, bureaucrats, business and only special interest groups. Concern about the prioritization of vested interests, a lack of council neutrality/independence, and about the varying levels of member expertise in policy analysis/evaluation.	Without policy analysis and evaluation skills, the *policy advice* of councils mirrors government data. The *policy advisory system* is elitist/neo-corporatist closely linked to lobbyists/pressure groups. *Externalization*, public deliberation or the accessing of multiple viewpoints do not feature in the system. *Politicization* is a notable feature of the policy advisory system and the work of councils. *Boundary activity* is not a feature of the councils except with government/lobbyists/pressure groups. *Policy diffusion* is sometimes too direct, and too government directed, from councils to policy impact.

| Taiwan (Wang & Chiou, 2015) | Authoritarian dominant-party system now a multi-party democracy. Democratization led to supra-ministerial advisory bodies being created. 43 advisory committees were identified as established within the Executive Yuan and second-level agencies affiliated with the Executive Yuan, as well as several others. | Councils are embedded in a strong administrative tradition. Advisory committees are establish by law, executive orders or government announcement. Minutes, meetings, committee composition and advice are usually kept secret. Given secrecy it is difficult to ascertain whether government acts on council advice. | Membership is usually pre-selected and kept secret. Highly specific, expert professional members advise government. Members (scholars, professionals and interest group members) are unpaid and renewed annually. | Expert *policy advice* from advisory committees is used as a 'management tool' filling knowledge gaps. The *policy advisory system* belongs to a newly democratized but closed bureaucratic practice. *Externalization*, public deliberation or the accessing of multiple viewpoints do not feature in the system. It is difficult to ascertain the degree, if any, of *politicization* given its closed, disengaged nature. *Boundary activity* is not a feature of the councils. *Policy diffusion* is difficult to ascertain because council minutes and advice are kept secret. |

Criteria for Table 12.4 adapted from Schultz et al. (2015)

Table 12.5 Key findings on cross-national variation in advisory bodies/systems

Countries	Authors	Similarities between countries	Differences between countries
EU focus—Greece, Spain, Belgium, Portugal, the Netherlands, Estonia	Van Damme, Brans & Fobé (2011)	Education councils (across Europe) develop similar strategies to maximize their relevance in a competitive policy environment (needing to provide high-quality advice that is highly relevant and from a body that is high 'status'); all councils face challenges to their independence to varying degrees	The make-up of a council is strongly dependent upon that country's dominant political tradition; different levels of neo-corporatist membership exist although the trend is towards greater engagement/legitimacy; councils set up as a reform exercise tend to be more independent
EU focus—Germany, the Netherlands, Switzerland and the UK	Reinecke, Hermann, Bauer, Pregernig, Karl Hogl & Pistorius (2013)	Climate policy knowledge brokers all fund-raise to supplement government funding; Germany/UK share a diverse climate policy advisory landscape that requires networking activities; the landscape is smaller in other countries and more easily organized and accessed; politico-cultural context therefore does make a difference	Climate policy is institutionalized in varied forms, from classic councils to information networks, hubs and service providers; established for differing periods, by different actors, with differing orientations dependent upon their source of funds, funding/staffing levels differ markedly
Internal advisory systems in different politico-bureaucratic regimes	Schultz, Bressers, van der Steen & van Twist (2015)	All internal advisory systems are country specific and internally congruent; the underlying 'struggles' (e.g., attempt to regulate the system) within them are the same for each country; but all advisory systems need to be understood in situ rather than only comparatively	Each country responds differently in terms of the advisory systems configuration, administration and composition; and to tensions between regulation-independence and facts-values; institutional learning and knowledge transfer across advisory systems is therefore difficult
Anglophone advisory systems	Craft & Halligan (2017)	Anglophone countries have an impartial public service but consultants and political advisors are now more common; advisory systems are homogeneous (values, principles, structures, behaviours, cultures, NPM) with a shared administrative tradition, declining public service policy capacity, expanding external supplies of policy advice, a trend to generalist advice and process-heavy policy work, but also 'lumpy' policy capacity across government	Internal advisory systems have different contexts; they are heterogeneous (e.g., varying sizes of public sectors; federal-unitary differences; also differing degrees of politicization, centralization of power and use of partisan advisers); in Canada and Australia there is a strong centralization of power, displacing departmental supplies of advice and influence; less so in UK and not at all in NZ; royal commissions have waned in some countries more than others

Despite their different socio-political and institutional settings, there are nevertheless some aspects of convergence in advisory bodies and systems across various countries. For example, although there are different levels of neo-corporatist arrangements in European education councils, there is a common trend towards seeking greater legitimacy through expanded membership or broader consultation (Van Damme et al., 2011). There are also common tensions in advisory bodies and systems across differing contexts. The issues of policy capacity and policy advising are now more negotiated, complex and contested than ever before (Prince, 2007). Regardless of socio-political context, there are also tensions between regulation and independence, between expert facts/knowledge and non-expert value/opinions, and between expert knowledge transfer and societal relevance. The size of an advisory body can cause tensions. If it is small, it is likely to be flexible, trusted and coherent, but less expert. If it is larger, it will be more expert, but less flexible, more diverse and possibly more fragmented (Schultz et al., 2015). All advisory bodies and systems face the dilemma of deciding on appropriate advisory content.

The trend towards externalization has caused tensions for advisory bodies and systems. If legitimacy in the era of network governance is achieved through social engagement, and operating at some distance from government (Van Damme et al., 2011), this could involve a loss of critical proximity to decision makers. Van Damme et al. (2011, p. 126) observe that councils must 'gain and sustain access to the policy making process' or risk a loss of relevance. In the relatively newly democratized Czech Republic, for example, the success of an advisory body is directly related to its attachment to government, either by including ministers in the membership, or having a strongly positioned chair (Merklova & Ptackova, 2016). Policy leverage must be carefully cultivated by advisory bodies—for example, in climate policy advisory systems, by the knowledge brokers working 'close to the political and societal sphere to ensure their relevance, while at the same time following strict scientific rules and procedures to maintain their independence and credibility' Reinecke et al. (2013, p. 91). Again there are tensions between being too distant from political agendas, and getting too close to political struggles. Distance from government can be readily determined by political decree usually with a mandate about orientation and responsibilities or by resolution, statutes or executive order (Table 12.4). However, neutrality and independence are not easily achieved and maintained. *Lack of neutrality* is sometimes quite obvious. Those advisory bodies with the closest ties to politics may go to the greatest lengths to proclaim their independence (Reinecke et al., 2013, p. 92), and those most lacking in expert evaluation skills may be the most readily swayed by government agendas (Yamaya, 2015).

It is not possible to perform all advisory roles equally well, owing to time, effort, and availability of feedback on performance. As advisory bodies enhance their relevance and political connectedness to decision makers, they strain the associated role of an advisory body as a knowledge broker operating at the intersection of a variety of interests. This is a major theme and concern across the multi-country and single country studies of advisory bodies and systems. If the advisory and political systems are inter-linked to ensure knowledge access, integration and uptake (Merklova & Ptackova, 2016, p. 17), then what becomes of the 'coordinative' functions of advisory bodies in the policy community? In the complex world of policymaking, advisory bodies in many countries are indeed caught between the competing dynamics of seeking output legitimacy to government and input legitimacy though the broader policy arena (Van Damme et al., 2011). Reinecke et al. find that all the climate advisory bodies they studied engage with political *and* societal interests not only through representative involvement in their steering and advisory committees, but also through broad consultation, collaboration and engagement with the community at large. This outward legitimacy is not easy to accomplish, however, given the strong conviction that science should be impartial and disinterested and be an honest broker in providing neutral and objective advice (Pielke, 2007; Reinecke et al., 2013, p. 95).

One interesting suggestion emerging in the studies of advisory bodies is that knowledge uptake by government is determined less by the certainty that the knowledge is 'right' in expert terms, and more by the perception that it is 'accepted' in societal terms. This is consistent with an observation by Wildavsky (1979, p. 405; cited in Prince, 2007) that 'the truth [policy analysts] have to tell is not necessarily in them, nor in their clients, but in . . . their give and take with others whose consent they require . . . over and over again'. This perspective confirms the importance of the boundary-riding and knowledge-brokerage roles by policy experts within a policy system, and their need to balance advice giving to government with knowledge brokerage and diffusion more broadly. This is graphically illustrated in the climate policy space, where a 'super-wicked' problem and a lengthy record of policy failure have spawned a multi-varied climate policy advisory industry attempting to forge and advocate climate solutions. As Prince (2007) and Jasanoff (1990) agree, the production of such knowledge may be systematic and scientific, yet the message and the context in which it is conveyed are inherently highly political. It is not clear, however, from the studies that have been examined here, that boundary spanning, knowledge brokering and policy diffusion are roles for policy advisory bodies that have been mandated by decree, resolution, statutes or executive order. Neither is it clear that governments establish advisory bodies to generate advice that will be equally accepted by decision makers and the public. What is clear, however, is that engagement techniques are likely to promote knowledge uptake, whereas this will not occur through traditional, elitist, academic knowledge production (Reinecke et al., 2013).

5. Conclusions

Expert knowledge can influence the policy process in diverse, but often indirect, ways. The policy advisory system within a country now typically has not only strong internal advisory channels, but also multiple external sources of advice. The global system also has important additional networks and channels of supranational advice and deliberation, including international advisory bodies. Within these systems, the roles and tasks of expert advisory bodies or councils vary broadly: from providing authoritative independent advice on the best available science ('salient, credible and legitimate', in the words of Cash et al., 2002), to reviewing and advising on policy settings, to engaging with stakeholders to influence the agenda for knowledge and action. Expert advisory councils have long been important but low-key actors in the policy advisory system, not only in advanced democracies, but also in at least some relatively centralist, authoritarian and one-party states (Table 12.4). Councils in most settings play useful roles in consolidating technical knowledge and making recommendations in policy areas where reliance on lay knowledge and opinion would not be sufficient to protect and advance the public interest. However, expert technical knowledge no longer suffices to ensure appropriate policy action; it must be legitimated, not only by government, but increasingly by broader publics. As a consequence, policy advisory systems have become, or are being pressured to become, more open to plural voices; science is being challenged as the main source of advice on complex, technical problems; and the role of expert bodies, and expectations of their role, has shifted markedly.

The scholarly literature addresses the transformation dynamics affecting advisory bodies and systems, with a focus on the shift to multiple advisory voices and the concomitant transformation, externalization and politicization of the role of advisory councils. The literature addressing the changing advisory dynamics is now at least three decades old and flourishing. More recent comparative analysis of the impacts of this change is beginning to provide a more detailed picture, for example of the configuration, administration and composition of advisory bodies and systems in specific cross-national contexts. Although the findings of this analysis vary, there are strong common themes emerging, which are being reinforced by single country studies. These confirm that the role of expert advisory bodies, originally intended as enduring contributors to the policy landscape, has shifted. The similarities and differences (Table 12.5) between bodies/systems in differing contexts are becoming clearer as these studies are further extended. Less emphasized, except perhaps in the scientific literature (OECD, 2015) and studies of climate change advisory bodies, is the role of advisory bodies as boundary organizations in ensuring the diffusion of advice and policy action. Here there is much scope for future research.

Acknowledgement

Research assistance by Michele Ferguson is gratefully acknowledged.

References

Benson, D. and Jordan, A. 2011. What have we learned from policy transfer research? *Political Studies Review* 9 (3): 366–378.

Busch, P.O. and Jörgens, H. 2005. International patterns of environmental policy change and convergence. *European Environment* 15 (2): 80–101.

Cash, D.W., Clark, W. C., Alcock, F., Dickson, N., Eckley, N. and Jäger, J. 2002. *Salience, credibility, legitimacy and boundaries: Linking research, assessment and decision making.* Cambridge, MA: Kennedy School of Government, Harvard University.

Craft, J. and Halligan, J. 2017. Assessing 30 years of Westminster policy advisory system experience. Forthcoming in *Policy Sciences.*

Craft, J. and Howlett, M. 2012. Policy formulation, governance shifts and policy influence: Location and content in policy advisory systems. *Journal of Public Policy* 32 (2): 79–98.

Craft, J. and Howlett, M. 2013. The dual dynamics of policy advisory systems: The impact of externalization and politicization on policy advice. *Policy & Society* 32 (3): 187–197.

Davies, H. T., Nutley, S. and Walter, I. 2008. Why 'knowledge transfer' is misconceived for applied social research. *Journal of Health Services Research and Policy* 13(3): 188–190.

Dobbin, F., Simmons, B. and Garrett, G. 2007. The global diffusion of public policies. *Annual Review of Sociology* 33: 449–472.

Dobuzinskis, L. 2007. Back to the future? Is there a case for re-establishing the economic council and/or the science council? (pp 315–350). In L. Dobuzinskis, M. Howlett, D. Laycock (Eds), *Policy analysis in Canada: The state of the art,* University of Toronto Press.

Dolowitz, D. and Marsh, D. 1996. Who learns what from whom: A review of the policy transfer literature. *Political Studies* 44 (2): 343–351.

Evans, M. (Ed.) 2004. *Policy transfer in global perspective.* Aldershot, UK: Ashgate.

Fischer, F. 2009. *Democracy and Expertise.* Oxford University Press.

Haas, P. M. 2004. When does power listen to truth? A constructivist approach to the policy process. *Journal of European Public Policy* 11 (4): 569–592.

Halligan J. 1995. Policy advice and the public sector (pp. 138–172). In B. G. Peters and D. Savoie (Eds), *Governance in a changing environment,* Montreal: McGill-Queen's University Press.

Halligan, J. 2010. The fate of administrative tradition in Anglophone countries during the reform era (pp.129–142). In M. Painter and B. G. Peters (Eds), *Tradition and public administration,* London: Palgrave Macmillan.

Hargadon, A. B. 2002. Brokering knowledge: Linking learning and innovation. *Research in Organisational Behaviour* 24: 41–85.

Head, B. W. 2015. Policy analysis: Evidence-based policy-making (pp. 281–287). In J. D. Wright (editor-in-chief), *International Encyclopedia of the Social & Behavioral Sciences*, 2nd edn, Vol 18, Oxford: Elsevier.

Head, B. W. 2016. Toward more 'evidence-informed' policy-making? *Public Administration Review* 76 (3): 472–484.

Head, B. W. and Alford, J. 2015. Wicked problems: Implications for public policy and management. *Administration and Society* 47 (6): 711–739.

Jasanoff, S. 1990. *The fifth branch: Science advisers as policymakers*. Cambridge, MA: Harvard University Press.

Lentsch, J. and Weingart, P. (Eds) 2011. *The politics of scientific advice: Institutional design for quality assurance*. Cambridge University Press.

Merklova, K. and Ptackova, K. 2016. Policy advisory councils (governmental and departmental advisory bodies) in the Czech Republic (pp 157–176). In *Policy analysis in the Czech Republic*, A. Veselý, M. Nekola and E. M. Hejzlarova (Eds), Bristol, UK: Policy Press.

OECD 2015. *Scientific advice for policy making: The role and responsibility of expert bodies and individual scientists*. OECD Science, Technology and Industry Policy Papers, No 21. Paris: OECD Publishing.

Pielke, R.A. Jr. 2007. *The honest broker: Making sense of science in policy and politics*. Cambridge University Press.

Prince, M. J. 2007. Soft craft, hard choices, altered context: Reflections on 25 years of policy advice in Canada (pp. 95–106). In *Policy analysis in Canada: The state of the art*, Dobuzinskis L., Howlett M. and Laycock D. (Eds), University of Toronto Press.

Reinecke, S., Hermann, A.T., Bauer, A., Pregernig, M., Karl Hogl, K., and Pistorius, T. 2013. *Innovative climate policy advice: Case studies from Germany, the Netherlands, Switzerland and the UK*. Research Report 1–2013, Institute of Forest, Environmental, and Natural Resource Policy, Vienna. www.wiso.boku.ac.at/fileadmin/data/H03000/H73000/H73200/_TEMP_/InFER_RR_13_1_Case_study_report.pdf

Schultz, M., Bressers, D., van der Steen, M. and van Twist, M. 2015. Internal advisory systems in different political-administrative regimes: Exploring the fit of configuration, administration and composition of internal advisory systems in France, Germany, Sweden, the Netherlands and the United Kingdom. Prepared for the International Conference on Public Policy, Milan, 1–4 July.

Shipan, C. R. and Volden, C. 2008. The mechanisms of policy diffusion. *American Journal of Political Science* 52 (4): 840–857.

Van Damme, J., Brans, M. and Fobé, E. 2011. Balancing expertise, societal input and political control in the production of policy advice. A comparative study of education councils in Europe. *Halduskultuur – Administrative Culture* 12 (2): 126–145.

Wang, W.-J. and Chiou, C.-T. 2015. Exploring policy advisory committees in central government (pp. 23–37). In *Policy analysis in Taiwan*, Y-Y. Kuo (Ed.), Bristol, UK: Policy Press.

Wildavsky, A. B. 1979. *Speaking truth to power: The art and craft of policy analysis*. Boston: Little, Brown.

Yamaya, K. 2015. Councils, policy analysis and policy evaluation (pp. 139–148). In *Policy analysis in Japan*, Y. Adachi, S. Hosono and J. Lio (Eds), Bristol, UK: Policy Press.

13

POLICY ANALYSIS IN THE LEGISLATIVE BRANCH

Wouter Wolfs and Lieven De Winter

Introduction

Legislatures, whether they operate in a separation-of-powers system, i.e., 'congresses', or in a fused power system, i.e., 'parliaments' (Kreppel, 2014), play a crucial role in the political decision-making process. The study of legislatures has a very rich and pluralistic research tradition, even pre-dating political science as a discipline. In the last century, legislative studies have evolved from an 'old' institutionalist perspective (dominant between the late 19th century to the end of the Second World War), to a behaviouralist approach in the 1950s and 1960s, to a 'new' institutionalist revival from the middle of the 1980s, associated with more sophisticated research methods and a significant differentiation in subjects and topics (see Martin, Saalfeld & Strom, 2014).

Legislatures fulfil a range of different functions, which can be categorized into three main groups: (1) legitimation and representation; (2) selection and training of political personnel; and (3) decisional functions, including legislating, scrutinizing the budget and controlling the government (Packenham, 1970; Blackburn, Kennon, Wheeler-Booth, Griffith, & Ryle, 2003). The last set of functions is particularly important when considering parliamentary policy analysis. Regarding the legislative function, policy analysis is important because it is the last stage in the decision-making process where a policy initiative can be reshaped before it is implemented. Policy analysis is also required when determining the budget or when scrutinizing the government, as the information and advice from sound policy analysis provides a basis for Members of Parliament to make decisions (Lee, 2015).

One of the principal debates in legislative studies regards the purported decline of parliaments. Many scholars have described a process of deparliamentarization, and identified several reasons for this evolution: a more important role for political parties and 'partitocracy' (Deschouwer, De Winter & Della Porta, 1996; De Winter & Dumont, 2003), a decreased quality of Members of Parliament (Bryce, 1921, although this has been countered by the thesis of professionalization of Members of Parliament (MPs): cf. Borchert, 2003; Gaxie & Godmer, 2007) and an increase of executive tasks following the creation of the welfare state (Martin et al., 2014). An important aspect of the debate on the decline of parliaments is the information asymmetry between the executive and the legislature: parliaments do not possess sufficient information on government policies to properly scrutinize the executive. In recent decades, this information asymmetry has been exacerbated by the process of globalization and—in the EU—the process of Europeanization, developments that have made societies even more complex and have made it more difficult for parliaments to monitor government actions (Raunio, 2011). Nevertheless, others argue that parliaments still matter, because they have concentrated on new tasks, such as communication, or have taken initiatives to 'fight back' to try to influence policymaking (Martin et al., 2014).

Studies focusing on policy analysis in parliaments are scarce and heterogeneous in their focus and approach. Some authors have concentrated on administrative and political support bodies and services, such as the personal assistants of MPs, political group advisors, committee secretariats or parliamentary research services (Marschall, 2013; Lee, 2015; Makita, 2015). Other scholars have focused on political structures, instruments and procedures, such as the committee system, the application of classic parliamentary scrutiny instruments or the use of hearings or parliamentary inquiries (Santos, 2013; Marsh & Halpin, 2015; Siefken & Schüttemeyer, 2013). Furthermore, most work on parliamentary policy analysis consists of case studies, and comparative studies are non-existent to our knowledge.

This wide variety and asymmetry in the literature makes an in-depth comparison of all different aspects of policy analysis in legislatures challenging. The aim of this chapter is to provide a general framework to study policy analysis and support in parliaments, building on the available secondary literature to explore cross-country trends, similarities and differences. Our empirical data is based on a variety of cases: Australia, Belgium, Brazil, the European 'level', Germany, Japan, the Netherlands, Taiwan, the United Kingdom and the United States. In asymmetrical bicameral systems, we will focus on the lower house. The first part of the chapter analyses the internal parliamentary actors that provide policy support to legislators. More specifically, we will assess how the personal assistants to MPs, advisors to political groups, and general parliamentary support services contribute to parliamentary policy analysis. The second part of the chapter examines the political structures and instruments that give legislators the opportunity to incorporate information from the government and expertise from external actors in their work.

Administrative Capacity: Support Services for Members of Parliament

There are three main categories of administrative capacity support for Members of Parliament, corresponding to the different working arenas of the parliamentary system: personal assistants and advisors of individual MPs, who are directly responsible for providing administrative and policy support to the Members; political staff working for party political groups or other groups of MPs; and advisors that provide policy support to committees or the institution as a whole. The staff at all three levels can provide policy analysis and support, but they vary significantly in terms of functions, capacities and operational logic (Marschall, 2005).

Support services in all parliaments have been the subject of reforms and capacity-building in recent decades, albeit to different degrees. Many legislatures have sought to expand research and support capacity in order to reduce the information asymmetry between the parliament and the government. Indeed, the government is in the driver's seat for policy initiation, law passage and implementation, and sometimes even has a privileged position over parliament to obtain information—as is the case in European decision making, where governments also have an advantage regarding available resources. Whereas government ministers can fall back on a large group of personal advisors and civil servants, the staff available to provide policy support to MPs is much more limited. Furthermore, the parliament is also very dependent on information from the government for their scrutiny of that same government. This clearly leads to an imbalance of information between the government under supervision and the parliament as 'controller' (Zaal, 2014, p. 174). Consequently, it is not surprising that many parliaments have taken measures to reduce the information asymmetry by raising their staff levels to increase their policy support capacity.

However, increasing support capacity is not a neutral exercise; the way that the internal services are strengthened entails a certain normative view on the functioning of the parliament. The different levels of the parliamentary administration respond to different demands: personal staff meet the demands of the individual MPs, whereas group staff aim to support partisan interests. Committee staff correspond to the sectoral demands, and the officials working in the parliamentary research service support the collective demands of the institution. Not all categories have been strengthened equally in the different legislatures. A number of contextual factors can explain these differences, including the electoral system (whether it is proportional or majoritarian) and the political system (whether it is a presidential system with strong emphasis on the separation of powers or a parliamentary system characterized by a division between majority and opposition parties).

Personal Assistants to Members of Parliament

The personal staff directly support MPs in their parliamentary work. However, significant variation exists in how this personal assistance is organized in different parliaments, both in terms of the number of assistants and the functions that assistants have.

A first difference relates to the number of assistants each MP has at his or her disposal, and the funding mechanism. In general, there are two systems for providing MPs with personal assistance: staff-based and allowance-based systems. In a staff-based system, the MP receives a maximum number of assistants, directly paid by the parliament, whereas in an allowance-based system, parliament allocates a maximum sum to each MP which he or she can use to hire personnel. Most of the cases studied here use an allowance-based system. One exception is the Belgian Parliament, in which every Member is entitled to one personal assistant who is paid by parliament (Maddens, Smulders, Wolfs & Weekers, 2016; De Winter & Wolfs, 2017).

The difference between the two systems implies a certain trade-off between equality and flexibility. In the staff-based system, every assistant is paid the same, whereas in an allowance-based system the MP has the ability to choose between a smaller group of well-paid policy experts or a larger group of lesser-paid assistants. In the European Parliament (EP), the equality between the Members is also under pressure from the different national backgrounds. Each Member of the European Parliament (MEP) receives a monthly allowance to pay their assistants, who can be hired through European contracts (in the case of parliamentary assistants for work in the EP) or national contracts (in the case of constituency-based assistants). The differences in standard of living between the member states leads to a situation where Members from countries where the wages are lower can hire more (local) assistants than those from countries with a higher standard of living. The average number of assistants ranges from around three for Danish, Swedish and Dutch MEPs to as many as 15 for Lithuanian MEPs.[1] We can assume that these differences have an impact on the support capacity for the legislators.

Although most parliaments use an allowance-based system, the considerable differences in size of the allowance has led to a high variation in the average number of personal assistants that support the MPs in different national parliaments. For example, in the British House of Commons the average number of assistants per MP is four. In Germany and Taiwan, the number is higher, respectively six and eight personal assistants per MP. The best-staffed Members are found in the US Congress: Members of the House of Representatives are supported by an average of 15 personal assistants, and US Senators employ on average 35 assistants. The number can even go as high as 60, depending on the size of the state they represent (Brudnick, 2014).

A second difference relates to the functions of the personal assistants. In general, there are three main types of personal assistants: (1) Administrative assistants, whose tasks include the management of the daily schedule of the MP and other technical-administrative tasks; (2) Policy assistants, who support the MP in legislative tasks, such as drafting bills and amendments, and preparing parliamentary speeches; and (3) Assistants for constituency services, who are responsible for maintaining relations with the local party office and voters of the MP's electoral district (Lee, 2015, p. 56).

In some cases, a part of the allowance for staff is earmarked to hire policy advisors. For US Senators, the Personnel and Office Expense Account of US Senators differentiates between the administrative and clerical assistance allowance and the legislative assistance allowance, with the latter specifically set aside to pay policy support staff (Brudnick, 2014, pp. 6–7). In the Japanese Diet, each MP is entitled to hire one policy and legislative secretary, and two administrative assistants.

Furthermore, in some parliaments, an elaborate hierarchical system determines the functioning of the MPs' personal assistants. The offices of the Members of the US House of Representatives, for example, are characterized by a high degree of specialization, with personal assistants fulfilling up to 15 functions, ranging from Financial Administrator or Executive Assistant to Chief of Staff or Legislative Director.[2] The European Parliament distinguishes between Accredited Assistants, who support the MEP in his or her legislative work, and Local Assistants, who are usually stationed in the electoral district of the MEP to conduct constituency work (Wolfs, 2015, p. 9). However, in most parliaments such a strict distinction is not made and the assistants fulfil a combination of different functions, particularly because the number of staff is rather limited. When MPs have an office of one or two staffers—such as the Belgian Parliament—they will mainly deal with administrative and constituency tasks, and the level of policy analysis and support will be rather limited.

Advisors to Political Groups

This category contains the advisors and assistants who work for the political groups. Similar to the personal staff of the MPs, the assistants of the political groups fulfil myriad functions, ranging from administrative or constituency work to communications and press relations to genuine policy advice and support.

The allocation of group assistants can also follow an allowance-based or a staff-based logic, or a combination of both. In the German Bundestag, political groups receive a group allowance and they can decide themselves what share of the allowance they want to spend on group staff. Political groups in the European Parliament are entitled to a number of policy advisors depending on the group's size. In addition, each political group is equipped with a group allowance—also depending on group size—that can be used to hire additional staff (Maddens et al., 2016, p. 28). In the Belgian House of Representatives, all political groups receive around 1.5 policy advisors per MP.

The policy advisors in the political groups can be organized following logics of centralization, decentralization or secondment. The Brazilian legislature follows a centralized system, with a significant portion of the expert advisors allocated to party leaders (Santos, 2013, pp. 124–125). In the US Congress a similar picture can be observed: additional staff are not allocated to the party groups in general, but are made available to the majority and minority leadership (Speaker, majority and minority leaders, and majority and minority whips). In the European Parliament, most political groups assign political advisors to follow up on the parliamentary committees and support group members in committee work.

In the German Bundestag, the groups follow a logic of decentralization: staff are divided among the different parliamentary committees, and advisors provide support for the individual MPs as well as the so-called 'intergroups'—groups of MPs from all political groups organized around specific themes—and are managed by the group leaders in the committees. Since the resources—and consequently the number of advisors that can be hired—depend on the size of the group, small political groups are at a disadvantage as policy advisors usually need to follow more than one committee, which hampers specialization and reduces overall support capacity. These political group advisors are also expected to keep in close contact with the staff working in the parties' headquarters, and thus function as a liaison between the intra- and extra-parliamentary party expertise (Marschall, 2013, pp. 152–153).

In Belgium, many political groups follow a logic of secondment: the group advisors are posted at the party headquarters to support the party presidency and party research centre. This can be explained by the strong partitocratic nature of the Belgian political system, in which the extra-parliamentary party organization strongly dominates the functioning of the parliamentary group (De Winter & Wolfs, 2017).

General Parliamentary Support Services

In contrast to the previous two categories of advisors, whose work is almost by definition partisan, policy advisors that work in the parliamentary administration cannot be ideologically motivated. Parliamentary officials are expected to take a non-partisan approach and serve the institution as a whole (Marschall, 2013, p. 152). Some authors have described how a more complex global context, and external pressures such as Europeanization, have led to a greater role for administrators, which entails a risk of 'bureaucratization' over 'democratization' (see e.g. Christiansen, Högenauer & Neuhold, 2014). However, the strict neutrality of the administrators is stressed in all legislatures as a precondition for their ability to function. They should refrain from any judgement on political action or any influence on the political discourse if they do not want to become the subject of a political controversy themselves (Zaal, 2014, p. 177).

The main question is to what extent total neutrality and objectivity is possible and desirable. As Lee has stated with regard to policy analysis in the Taiwanese parliament, 'policy analysis cannot be purely objective because this conception determines what data is collected, how the data is analysed, what information is released, and what policy advice is provided' (Lee, 2015, p. 63). At the end of the day, what can be considered as the right or most effective information is a political question (Zaal, 2014, p. 174). Although the provision of policy advice is client-oriented, administrators should uphold scientific standards and try to avoid being loyal to MPs and produce policy analyses that are in line with the legislator's ideology (Lee, 2015, p. 61). In sum, administrators are embedded or even stretched in a complex triangle of principles and interests among the parliamentary administration, legislators and objective research standards, 'which might lead to conflicting internal and external expectations' (von Winter, 2006; Marschall, 2013, p. 152).

In most parliaments, the strengthening of policy support capacity of the parliamentary administration—e.g. by the establishment of a parliamentary research service—was motivated by an aspiration to reduce the information asymmetry with the government, although variation exists depending on the political system. In the US separation-of-powers system, the Congressional Research Service, Congressional Budget Office and Government Accountability Office were created to protect the independence and constitutional authority of the legislature vis-à-vis the US government (Brudnick, 2011, p. 4). In the European Parliament, opposing visions exist on how the institution should develop: either mirroring the US Congress following the separation-of-powers logic or in line with the fusion-power parliamentary systems that exist in most EU member states. The establishment of the European Parliamentary Research Service in 2013 to empower the institution when dealing with the European Commission adopted the separation-of-powers logic by increasing the analytical and support capacity of the Parliament as a whole (Wolfs, 2015).

In parliamentary systems, internal capacity was increased to strengthen the institution, or at least the opposition parties that—in contrast with the majority parties—cannot rely on government expertise. In the Netherlands, the Parliamentary Bureau for Research and Public Expenditure was established following a report that pointed at the parliament's inferior information position and lacking infrastructure compared to the government. However, it is mainly the small opposition parties that rely on policy support from the parliamentary administration to compensate for their lack of resources compared to the larger parties (Zaal, 2014, p. 175). In the German Parliament, the parliamentary research service has an important role to counter the imbalance of information with the government, although it should also be viewed in the context of the 'new dualism' between the opposition and the majority: whereas the majority parties can rely on expertise in governmental ministries, opposition parties have to turn to other sources of information, such as the parliamentary research services (Marschall, 2013, p. 156; Ismayr, 2001, p. 106).

Whether the parliament is actually able to reduce the information imbalance with the executive through policy support by the parliamentary administration depends on a number of factors. The first factor is the overall capacity of the parliamentary administration that differs significantly between countries. Whereas the US Congress employs around 30 administrators per Member, the average staff per MP is less than five, even in most developed democratic countries (not counting personal and group advisors) (Power, 2012, pp. 101–103). Furthermore, in most legislatures only a minority of the administrators are involved in policy analysis; most of the civil servants deal with internal technical-administrative arrangements. The US Congress is an exception: the Congressional Research Service employs more than 600 staff members, 400 of whom are policy analysts working in five research divisions and specialized in a variety of disciplines.[3] In the Dutch Parliament, on the other hand, officials working in the Parliamentary Bureau for Research and Public Expenditure make up only 7% of the total parliamentary staff (Zaal, 2014, p. 175). In Taiwan, the actual staff levels of the parliamentary support bodies are far smaller than stipulated in the law: for example, committees are supported by 8 to 11 administrators, whereas the law foresees 90 to 98. This personnel shortage leads to a work overload for each staff member, so that maintaining a high quality of policy analysis becomes difficult (Lee, 2015, pp. 55–58). In sum, the budget and personnel deployed to do policy analysis is related to the quality of the policy support that is produced. The more administrators that can engage in policy analysis, the more they can specialize, leading to better policy support.

The second factor that has an impact on parliamentary policy analysis is the level of independence and political steering. Two issues are particularly important. First, can the research services conduct policy analysis on their own initiative (in the agenda-setting phase)? In other words, are they proactive or responsive? Second, are they influenced by the political level during the research process (in the preparation phase)? In most parliaments, the research services only respond to questions and assignments from the political level. It is also important who can request support from the research services: are requests limited to the Governing Body of parliament, committees, and political groups, or can individual MPs also make requests?

In the Dutch Parliament, the research service is organizationally separate from the committees so as to emphasize its independence. There is almost no political influence on the conduct of its research: the research service identifies the facts, differences and gaps and leaves the judgement on these to the political level. As far as agenda-setting is concerned, the research service works almost exclusively on the instructions of the parliamentary committees or appointed rapporteurs; the advisors are not able to initiate a research investigation on their own. In the Brazilian Parliament, the research services also work most closely on request and in support of the parliamentary committees, and more specifically the rapporteurs (Santos, 2013, p. 127–128). The in-house research service of the German Bundestag also works almost only on demand from MPs, political groups or committees. Only in very rare cases will the policy advisors draft reports on their own initiative. Most frequently, individual MPs request the research service for support and expertise; generally the advisors do not determine their own research agenda (Marschall, 2013, p. 156).

The European Parliamentary Research Service has a higher degree of independence in conducting its research. A large part of the service is dedicated to responding to research request from Members, but several units have a general goal and significant independence in how to achieve it. For example, the European Added Value Unit has the general mandate to look for policy fields in which efficiency gains can be accomplished by political action at the European level. Which policy fields are examined or how the research is conducted is determined by the research unit itself (Wolfs, 2015, p. 18). In the Taiwanese Parliament, policy advisors in the research service can conduct an investigation on any topic as long as the head of the research service approves (Lee, 2015, p. 57).

The third factor that is important is the actual work done by the parliamentary support services. We can classify their activities into four categories (for an alternative categorization, see for example Makita, 2015, pp. 130–131): (1) Technical-procedural work, such as the preparation of meetings, the collection of amendments, and writing meeting minutes, activities that do not relate to the content of policy work; (2) Data collection, such as the gathering of information on a specific policy topic, an overview of academic literature on a specific topic or a collection of press articles; (3) Data analysis, which also implies the collection of data on a specific topic, but adds the researcher's interpretation by, for example, identifying gaps or discrepancies in the data; and (4) Drafting or writing legislative documents such as bills or amendments on behalf of the MP.

Some scholars have stated that the Europeanization of national parliaments of EU member states has triggered a process of bureaucratization, which implies a more important role for administrators, including in drafting and writing legislative documents (Christiansen et al., 2014). However, in most parliaments, the role of the administration is limited to data collection. For instance, the bulk of the work of the research service of the Japanese Diet received in the last 45 years has consisted of data collection. The share of work dedicated to data analysis has even decreased over time; the requests for drafting have consistently remained very low (Makita, 2015, pp. 130–131). A similar picture can be observed in case of the research services of the German Bundestag. Their main duty is to collect and to a lesser extent analyse and compare research reports that have been produced by other institutions. They do not conduct their own primary research and are not involved in drafting legislative documents (Marschall, 2013, p. 156). In Belgium, most of the support services only provide technical-procedural advice. The support of the library and research services are limited to data collection (De Winter & Wolfs, 2017).

The Dutch Parliamentary Bureau for Research conducts data analysis on a more frequent basis: advisors check government policy documents for internal inconsistencies, assess them in light of the recommendations of the Netherlands Court of Auditors, and check on links with the government's coalition agreement (Zaal, 2014, pp. 176–177). In the European Parliamentary Research Service, a significant number of the advisors are involved in data analysis. It has a unit specifically dedicated to ex ante impact assessments, ex post impact assessments, scientific foresights and policy performance appraisal (Wolfs, 2015, pp. 16–17). The US Congressional Research Service examines complex topics from a variety of perspectives and conducts impact assessments of proposed policy alternatives.[4]

Political Structures and Instruments for Policy Analysis

The second part of this chapter analyses the political structures and instruments of parliamentary policy analysis. We first analyse the instruments that parliaments can use to scrutinize the government as a tool to tackle information asymmetry. Next we examine the role of a parliament's committee system in law-making and scrutiny of the executive. Last, we examine the structures that parliaments have established to incorporate external expertise in their decision-making process.

Oversight and Scrutiny Instruments

Parliaments have a number of instruments to request the government for information and data. Members of Parliament can ask written and oral questions to ministers to gain information on policy issues or to scrutinize government positions or actions. There are many variations of these two instruments. In the Belgian Parliament, a difference exists between regular oral questions—which are mainly aimed at getting information from the government— and 'interpellations'—which are more focused on the scrutiny of a minister's position and can be followed up by a motion of no confidence. Most parliaments regularly organize a 'question time'—often broadcast live on television—when the MPs are given the opportunity to ask questions that the government ministers are obliged to answer.

In most parliaments, the use of these instruments has increased in recent years. The Dutch parliament has seen a rise of the number of written and oral questions in the last 30 years (Zaal, 2014, pp. 172, 184). In the Belgian Parliament, a sharp increase in the number of oral and written questions has occurred in recent decades (De Winter & Wolfs, 2017). Although the trend of a rising number of questions can be recognized in almost all parliaments, uncertainties remain about what purpose they actually serve. Additional research is needed to examine what functions these instruments have and to what extent they can contribute to policy analysis in parliament.

Parliamentary Committees

Committees are a crucial element in parliamentary decision-making and—by extension— the entire political policy process. In most parliaments, committees are the central locus of law making and in shaping public policy. Consequently, authors have dedicated substantial attention to the role of policy analysis in the functioning of committees and have identified a number of factors that have a significant impact on policy analysis in committees.

A first factor that affects the strength of committees and consequently their ability to influence policymaking is the constitutional position of the parliament and information rights. Because of the separation-of-powers system in the United States and the constitutionally strong position of the Congress, its committee system is exceptionally powerful and has a significant impact on agenda-setting, legislation, the budget and even executive appointments (Marsh & Halpin, 2015, p. 138). In many parliamentary systems where a fusion between the parliament and the executive exists, the committees tend to be under the control of the majority and much of the law-making is dominated by the government. These parliaments also often have fewer informational rights and less access to internal government documents, which reduces the parliamentary committees' informational capacity.

A second—though to some extent related—factor is the committee's focus on law-making and its right to initiate and amend legislation, an element that has been the subject of many typologies of parliament. Polsby (1975) has assessed the parliament's level of independence in legislative work and differentiated between 'transformatory legislatures'—with a strong emphasis on committee work to transform proposals into laws—and 'arenas'—which are more focused on debates and confrontations of the significant forces of the political system. A similar typology is Steffani's (1979) classification of 'working parliaments' (or *Arbeitsparlamente*) versus 'debating parliaments' (or *Redeparlamente*), which also distinguishes between parliaments that concentrate on law-making work in committees or on public debates in plenary (see also Marschall, 2015, pp. 150–151). The German Bundestag is considered a good example of a transformative or working parliament that puts significant emphasis on legislative and policy work in the committees. The UK House of Commons, on the other hand, is considered a good example of a parliamentary arena or debating parliament, which is focused on plenary discussions while law-making and policy work is less important (Marschall, 2015, pp. 150–151).

A third factor that influences policy analysis in committees is their internal organization, i.e. the composition and procedures of the committees. In the Australian Parliament, early involvement of the committees through pre-legislative hearings and a focus on agenda-setting seems to have a positive influence on the overall committee impact (Marsh & Halpin, 2015, p. 147). Also in the Australian Parliament, the internal reorganization of committee work following the conclusions of the Selection of Bills Committee in 1990 has raised the capacity of Senate committees to effectively process more bills and based Senate deliberations on much better information (Vander Wyk & Lilley, 2005, cited in Marsh and Halpin, 2015, p. 140). Other important elements are the size of the committee and whether or not there is proportional allocation of committee chair positions and bill rapporteurships to government and opposition groups.

The political culture in a parliamentary committee is a fourth factor. The committees in the German Bundestag are aimed at consensus, which gives them significant policy impact (Steinack, 2012, p. 138). Research on Westminster parliaments has also shown that committees have the most influence when they can reach bipartisan conclusions, particularly on contentious matters (Monk, 2012, cited in Marsh & Halpin, 2015, pp. 141, 144). In the Brazilian parliament, a sharp contrast can be recognized between 'opposition-leaning committees'—where the majority of members take a view that is the opposite of that of the government—and 'pro-government committees'. Opposition-leaning committees have a stronger incentive to consult or produce additional information and policy analyses (Santos, 2013, pp. 122–123).

The final factor is the scope of the committee and their correspondence with ministerial departments. Some committees deal with a very broad range of policy fields, whereas other committees are specifically established for a clearly defined purpose. It is clear that committees with a broad scope on average have a higher workload and have more difficulty in conducting an in-depth analysis of the bills. The Brazilian parliament has no less than 124 standing committees, each of which analyses a specific (sub-)policy field. Furthermore, a large part of the legislative activity takes place in ad hoc committees that are created to examine specific legislative proposals (Santos, 2013, p. 124). In the Australian Parliament, the number of committees was increased from 7 to 24, partly because of a commitment for increased committee legislative activity. Furthermore, some ad hoc committees that were established for a limited time have been able to be very influential. The report of the Long Term Strategies Committee, for example, included comprehensive surveys of public policy issues that had a high strategic value (Marsh & Halpin, 2015, p. 139).

Instruments to Include External Expertise

Parliaments can rely on a number of instruments to incorporate external expertise in the decision-making process. A first instrument is special 'study' or inquiry committees that are established to analyse a specific policy phenomenon. In the Dutch Parliament, legislators can decide to conduct an external investigation, which can take two forms. First, the actual process of policy analysis can be subcontracted to an external research agency. The members of the parliamentary committee determine the exact topic, whereas the actual analysis is conducted by the agency (under the supervision of the committee members). Second, a temporary investigative committee can be established to conduct its own examination through working visits, hearings and the commissioning of studies (Zaal, 2014, p. 178). In Germany, the study commissions consist not only of legislators, but also external experts from academia or organized interests, who are part of the commission on a permanent basis (Siefken & Schüttemeyer, 2013, p. 167). An important factor regarding these types of committees is the threshold for their creation. In the German Bundestag, a quarter of the Members are required to request the establishment of a study committee (Siefken & Schüttemeyer, 2013, p. 166). In other parliaments, for example in Belgium, there is a higher threshold and the majority parties could potentially block the creation of a study commission if it is not in line with the government's policy agenda.

Empirically, significant variation among and within parliaments exists, both in terms of use as well of scope of these committees. In the German Bundestag, study committees were widely used in the 1980s and 1990s and were less popular in the decades before and after. The number of meetings of these committees also varied between 12 and more than 130 (Siefken & Schüttemeyer, 2013, p. 166). The inquiries of the Australian committees also differ significantly in both length and substance (Marsh and Halpin, 2015, p. 142). The establishment of investigation committees has become an increasingly popular practice in the Dutch Parliament: Loeffen (2013) has described an increase of parliamentary investigations in the last 30 years and noted that they were increasingly used as an instrument of parliamentary oversight. Considering the potential policy impact of these study committees, authors have stressed how the committees in the German Parliament follow the parliamentary logic of political conflict. Although most of the committee reports include clear policy suggestions, they are not able to prepare concrete policy decisions (Hampel, 1991, p. 119) or create new knowledge. Instead, they summarize existing research as a starting point for further political discussions (Siefken & Schüttemeyer, 2013, p. 167). In the Australian Parliament, strategic enquiries of committees are most effective when they evaluate the need for policy action before the government has taken a position (Marsh & Halpin, 2015, p. 143).

A second instrument that parliaments can use is hearings: public meetings in which stakeholders or experts are invited to express their opinion and provide expertise on the issue under discussion. One of the first legislatures to establish this practice was the US Congress, and many parliaments have followed its example (Loewenberg, 2006, p. 103). The composition and scope of these meetings can vary extensively between and even within the same parliament. In the Dutch Parliament, a committee can decide to organize a 'technical briefing', with experts or civil servants, a 'hearing', with just a single expert or stakeholder, or a 'roundtable discussion', with several stakeholders simultaneously (Zaal, 2014, pp. 177–178). Most hearings are organized in the framework of new legislation and only rarely as a tool for government scrutiny (with the exception of the US Congress). In the German Bundestag, two thirds of the hearings have a legislative purpose (Siefken & Schüttemeyer, 2013, p. 169). The main aim of hearings is to gather information, even if it is motivated by an intention to strengthen the dominant position of the political groups in parliament (Siefken & Schüttemeyer, 2013, p. 171). Several authors have indeed pointed at a corporatist logic in the organization of hearings: the experts invited represent the positions of certain interest groups (Renn, 1995, p. 152).

Most parliaments have seen a sharp increase in the use of hearings in the last 20 to 30 years. In the German Bundestag, the number of hearings was very low until the middle of the 1980s: the share of laws in which hearings were used rose from less than 10% in the term 1976–1980 to more than 30% in the term 2005–2009 (Siefken & Schüttemeyer, 2013, p. 169). Committees in the Dutch and the Belgian Parliaments have also organized more hearings with better preparation over time (Zaal, 2014, p. 184; De Winter and Wolfs, 2017). Wessels has analysed the differences in the number of hearings held by the parliamentary committees of the German Bundestag and stated that the variation can be explained not only by the number of legislative proposals with which the committee has to deal, but also with the characteristics of the bill: the more conflictual, broad and complex the legislative proposal is, the more likely it is that hearings will be conducted (Wessels, 1987, p. 293).

Parliaments have additional instruments to gain external expertise. Legislators can launch an inquiry for written evidence or written testimony on a certain topic. The Parliament of Australia makes ample use of inquiries to collect information and evidence from citizens, experts and stakeholders (Marsh & Halpin, 2015, pp. 144–145). Additionally, parliaments can contract out studies and reports. The committees of the European Parliament, for example, have a specific budget that they can spend on external studies. Finally, parliaments can conduct study visits in order to gain information. These last instruments have not received much academic attention, however, and the knowledge of their impact on policy-making in parliaments remains limited.

Conclusion

In this chapter, we have given an overview of the different aspects of policy support in legislatures, building on the (scarce) studies of parliamentary policy analysis and the broader tradition of legislative studies. Overall, there is a large variation between legislatures with regard to policy support. Four factors in particular have significant impacts on the level of policy analysis in legislatures.

First, policy analysis is significantly determined by the broader political and institutional context of the parliament. A particularly important element is the information asymmetry between the executive and legislative branch. This asymmetry has triggered the legislatures to increase their internal policy support capacity to improve the institution's informational position, but many parliaments still suffer significant informational disadvantages compared to the executive. This hampers parliamentary policy analysis, particularly in parliaments that are dominated by disciplined majority parties.

Second, size matters. The number of people or structures that are involved in parliamentary policy analysis has an impact on the overall capacity. Overall, the more actors that are engaged—whether it be the total number of parliamentary committees, the personal or group advisors or the administrators working for the parliamentary research service—the lower the individual workload and the greater the specialization that can take place, which could strengthen the overall parliamentary policy analysis capacity. Consider, for example, the US Congressional Research Service, with more than 400 policy advisors subdivided into five research departments, compared with the rather small research institutions in most parliaments. Similarly, compare the 124 specialized standing committees of the Brazilian Parliament in comparison with the seven broad committees the Australian Parliament used to have.

A third difference is the level of discretion and independence, and the intensity of the policy analysis that is conducted, both on the administrative as well as the political level. In some parliaments, the work of the support services or advisors is limited to technical-procedural work and collection of information. In other parliaments, the research services have very specialized units that conduct in-depth impact assessments or other forms of policy analysis that can even shape the parliamentary agenda, although this also entails the risk of 'bureaucratization' of the decision-making process and a lack of political oversight. Not only the discretion of the administrative actors, but also the independence of the political bodies, matters. Parliamentary committees that are not dominated by the majority parties, but are characterized by a non-partisan approach, generally have more influence on the policy outcome.

Fourth, the extent to which parliaments can incorporate external expertise—from the government, civil society, industry, academia or other actors—in their policy work varies significantly and has an impact on the level of policy analysis. Most parliaments have experienced an increase in the number of study committees and hearings with external stakeholders, but nevertheless variations exist in the context and preparation of these tools. The same is true for the parliamentary instruments to scrutinize the executive and to obtain information from the government. In fact, although there is a general rising trend, the application of different types of written and oral questions varies across legislatures.

In general, however, the research on policy analysis in legislatures is still rather limited and many venues for future research remain. First, there is a considerable shortage of comparative studies on parliamentary policy analysis; the field of research is limited to country case studies. Second, many questions remain regarding the use of certain instruments—such as inquiries or studies—and how the parliamentary instruments support the legislators in their policy-making. Third, additional research is required on the work of personal assistants and policy advisors of political groups and their impact on the MPs' policy work. Last, there is a need for a 'policy turn' in the rich field of legislative studies: the gap between political science and public administration with regard to research on legislatures must be bridged to expand our understanding of parliamentary policy analysis.

Notes

1 J. Jancarik (2015): http://jonasjancarik.eu/mep-assistants/
2 For more historical background, see Brudnick, 2014: http://assets.sunlightfoundation.com. s3.amazonaws.com/policy/staff%20salary/2010_house_compensation_study.pdf

3 Congressional Research Service (2016): www.loc.gov/crsinfo/about
4 Congressional Research Service (2016): www.loc.gov/crsinfo/about

References

Blackburn, R., Kennon, A., Wheeler-Booth, M., Griffith, J. & Ryle, M. (2003) *Griffith and Ryle on parliament: Functions, practice and procedures,* London: Sweet & Maxwell.

Borchert, J. (2003), "Professional politicians: Towards a comparative perspective", in J. Borchert & J. Zeiss (eds), *Political class in advanced democracies,* Oxford University Press.

Brudnick, I. (2011) *The Congressional Research Service and the American legislative process,* United States Congressional Research Service.

Brudnick, I. (2014). "Congressional salaries and allowances: In brief", United States Congressional Research Service, www.senate.gov/CRSReports/crs-publish.cfm?pid=%270E%2C★PL%5B%-3D%23P%20%20%0A.

Bryce, J. (1921) *Modern democracies.* 2 Volumes, London: Macmillan.

Christiansen, T., Högenauer A. & Neuhold, C. (2014) "National parliaments in the post-Lisbon European Union: Bureaucratization rather than democratization", in *Comparative European politics,* 12, pp. 121–140.

Deschouwer, K., De Winter, L. & Della Porta, D. (eds) (1996) "Partitocracies between crises and reforms: The cases of Italy and Belgium", special issue of *Res Publica,* 38.2.

De Winter, L. & Dumont, P. (2003) "Belgium: Delegation and accountability under partitocratic rule", in K. Strøm, W. Müller & T. Bergman (eds) *Delegation and accountability in Western Europe,* Oxford University Press, pp. 253–281.

De Winter, L. & Wolfs, W. (2017) "Policy analysis in the Belgian legislatures: The marginal role of a structurally weak parliament in a partitocracy with no scientific and political tradition of policy analysis", in M. Brans & D. Aubin (eds), *Policy analysis in Belgium,* Bristol, UK: Policy Press.

Gaxie, D. & Godmer, L. (2007) "Cultural capital and political selection", in M. Cotta & H. Best (eds), *Democratic representation in Europe,* Oxford University Press, pp. 106–135.

Hampel, F. (1991) "Politikberatung in der Bundesrepublik: Überlegungen am Beispiel von Enquete-Kommissionen", *Zeitschrift für Parlamentsfragen* 1, pp. 111–33.

Ismayr, W. (2001) *Der Deutsche Bundestag im politischen System der Bundesrepublik,* Stuttgart: UTB.

Kreppel, Amie (2014) "Typologies and classifications". In Shane Martin, Thomas Saalfeld, and Kaare Strom (eds), *The Oxford handbook of legislative studies,* Oxford University Press.

Lee, T. (2015) "Policy analysis in the legislative body: The legislative process of the Soil and Groundwater Pollution Remediation Act in Taiwan", in Y. Guo (ed.), *Policy analysis in Taiwan,* Bristol, UK: Policy Press, pp. 53–66.

Loeffen, S. (2013) *Parlementair onderzoek: Een studie van het onderzoeksrecht in Nederland, het Verenigd Koninkrijk en de Verenigde Staten,* The Hague: SDU.

Loewenberg, G. (2006) "The influence of US congressional hearings on committee procedure in the German Bundestag: A case study of institutional diffusion", in T. Power and N. Rae (eds) *Exporting Congress? The influence of the US Congress on world legislatures,* University of Pittsburgh Press, pp. 102–118.

Maddens, B., Smulders, J., Wolfs, W. & Weekers, K. (2016) *Partij- en campagnefinanciering in België en de Europese Unie,* Leuven, Belgium: Acco.

Makita, J. (2015) "A policy analysis of the Japanese Diet from the perspective of 'Legislative Supporting Agencies' ", in Y. Adachi, S. Hosono & J. Lio (eds) *Policy analysis in Japan,* Bristol, UK: Policy Press, pp. 123–138.

Marsh, I. & Halpin, D. (2015) "Parliamentary committees and inquiries", in B. Head & K. Croawley (eds), *Policy analysis in Australia,* Bristol, UK: Policy Press, pp. 137–150.

Marschall, S. (2005) *Parlamentarismus: Eine Einführung,* Baden-Baden, Germany: Nomos.

Marschall, S. (2013) "Parliamentary in-house research services and policy-making in Germany: Sancho Panza or David's sling?" in S. Blum & K. Schubert (eds), *Policy analysis in Germany,* Bristol, UK: Policy Press, pp. 149–160.

Martin, S., Saalfeld, T. & Strom, K. (2014) "Introduction", in S. Martin, T. Saalfeld & K. Strom, *Oxford Handbook of legislative studies,* Oxford University Press.

Monk, D. (2012) "Committee inquiries in the Australian Parliament and their influence on government: Government acceptance of recommendations as a measure of parliamentary performance", *The Journal of Legislative Studies,* 18.2, pp. 137–60.

Ostrogorski, M. (1902) *Democracy and the organization of political parties,* London: Macmillan.

Packenham, R. (1970) "Legislatures and Political Development", in A. Kornberg & L. Musolf (eds), *Legislatures in Developmental Perspective,* Durham, NC: Duke University Press, pp. 521–537.

Polsby, N. (1975) "Legislatures", in F. Greenstein & N. Polsby (eds), *Handbook of political science,* Boston, MA: Addison-Wesley, pp. 257–319.

Power, G. (ed.) (2012) *Global parliamentary report: The changing nature of parliamentary representation,* Geneva and New York: Inter-Parliamentary Union and UNDP.

Raunio, T. (2011) "The gatekeepers of European integration? The functions of national parliaments in the EU political system", *Journal of European Integration,* 33.3, pp. 301–321.

Renn, O. (1995) "Style of using scientific expertise: A comparative framework", *Science and Public Policy,* 22.2: pp. 147–156.

Santos, F. (2013) "The role of the Brazilian legislature in the public policy decision-making process", in J. Vaitsmain, J. Mendes Ribeiro & L. Lobato (eds), *Policy analysis in Brazil,* Bristol, UK: Policy Press, pp. 119–131.

Siefken, S. & Schüttemeyer, S. (2013) "The German Bundestag and external expertise: Policy orientation as counterweight to deparliamentarisation?" in S. Blum & K. Schubert (eds), *Policy analysis in Germany,* Bristol, UK: Policy Press, pp. 161–180.

Steffani, W. (1979) *Parlamentarische un präsidentielle Demokratie: Strukturelle Aspekte westlicher Demokratien,* Opladen, Germany: Westdeutscher verlag.

Steinack, K. (2012) "Government and minority impact in Germany: Policy making in a consensual system", in I. Marsh and J. Wanna (eds), *Contemporary government—fractured or pluralised? Varieties of coalition and minority regimes,* Australia National University Press.

Vander Wyk, J. & Lilley, A. (2005) References of bills to select committees with particular reference to the role of the Selection of Bills Committee, Canberra: the Senate.

von Winter, T. (2006) "Die Wissenschaftlichen Dienste des Deutschen Bundestagen", in S. Falk, D. Rehfeld & M. Thunert (eds), *Handbuch Politikberatung,* Wiesbaden, Germany: VS Verlag, pp. 198–214.

Wessels, B. (1987) "Kommunikationspotentiale zwischen Bundestag und Gesellschaft. Öffentliche Anhörungen, informelle Kontakte und innere Lobby in wirtschafts—und sozialpolitischen Parlamentsausschüssen", *Zeitschrift für Parlametsfragen,* 18.2, pp. 285–311.

Wolfs, W. (2015) "Capacity-building in the European Parliament: Different views on policy support", paper presented at the ECPR General Conference, University of Montréal, 26–29 August.

Zaal, K. (2014) "Policy analysis in the Dutch Parliament", in F. van Nispen & P. Scholten (eds), *Policy analysis in the Netherlands,* Bristol, UK: Policy Press, pp. 171–185.

14

MANAGEMENT CONSULTANCY AND THE VARIETIES OF CAPITALISM

Denis Saint-Martin

Management consultancy is a US$400 billion global business that provides expert advice intended to improve the organizational performance of the world's largest companies and large government bodies, such as the National Health Service in the United Kingdom, and various defence ministries in Europe and North America (IBIS*World*, 2015). Government is a booming sector and accounts for almost a third of the global management consulting market (*The Economist*, 2005). If management consultants from the private sector were once described as being part of a 'shadow government' (Guttman & Willner, 1976), this is no longer the case today. With the rise of New Public Management over the past 30 years, consultants have become increasingly visible actors in the process of government restructuring. Some have written about the 'new cult of the management consultant' in government (Smith, 1994, p. 130), and described consultants as 'intellectual mercenaries' (Leys, 1999) or 'hired guns' that 'politicians use to bypass reluctant civil servants' (Bakvis, 1997, p. 106). Others have coined the term 'consultocracy' (Hood & Jackson, 1991, p. 224) to underline the growing influence of consultants in public policy. In Australia, a study goes as far as suggesting that consultants 'reoriented' the nation's social policy framework (Martin, 1998), while in France, a former minister of industry once claimed that a minister arriving at a cabinet meeting with a report from McKinsey or the Boston Consulting Group is like 'Moses coming down from the mountain with the Tables of the Law' (*Le Monde*, 1999).

Global consulting firms are non-state actors that assume an important political role in today's world. Over time, as they developed more intimate links with governments, large consulting firms mutated into somewhat less 'private' and more 'public' entities by creating arm's-length, not-for-profit, research institutes that produce analyses on key public policy issues (Deloitte, 2009). For instance, the Government of the Future Centre is a think tank established in 2009 by Accenture in partnership with the Lisbon Council and the College of Europe. The Centre is similar to the KPMG Public Governance and Government Institute and the McKinsey Global Institute, the research arm of McKinsey, created in 1990 to 'provide leaders in the commercial, public and social sectors with the facts and insights on which to base management and policy decisions'.

I have described elsewhere the growing inclination of consulting firms to take a more active policy advocacy role as the 'think tank-ization' of management consultancy

(Saint-Martin, 2005). This transformation is an indication of the discursive power that global management consulting corporations increasingly exercise in public debates on the definition of political problems and solutions. This chapter addresses how they have acquired that power and the political legitimacy to become co-pilots in the steering of government organizations. The first section introduces the concept of institutional isomorphism to highlight the role of consultants as experts active in defining norms and disseminating models of appropriate action in the management of large organizations. The second section provides an overview of the origins and evolution of management consultancy cross-nationally. The third section looks at the role of consultants in government since the 1960s and the subsequent growth of the public sector market for management consulting services. The 'varieties of capitalism' approach (Hall & Soskice, 2001) to compare national trajectories reveals that governments and businesses use more consulting services in liberal than in coordinated market economies, and that managerial reforms seeking to make government more 'business-like' have had more impact in liberal market economies (LMEs) than in coordinated market economies (Pollitt & Bouckaert, 2000; Saint-Martin, 2012). This link is not a coincidence. As argued in the conclusion, it is an indication of the institutional complementarities or 'tight coupling' between managerial practices in business and government organizations in modern political economies.

I. Managerial Expertise and Institutional Isomorphism

Expertise and professionalism, as 'new institutionalists' in sociology have argued, play a central role in defining the norms of legitimate behaviour in highly rationalized social contexts (DiMaggio & Powell, 1983; Dobbin, 1994). These contexts, defined as 'organizational fields', are populated by experts and groups of professionals who are densely networked and have considerable resources and incentives to disseminate models of appropriate action (Lodge & Wegrich, 2005; Simmons, Dobbin & Garrett, 2008). Management consultants constitute one such group of experts, acting as agents of institutional isomorphism between large organizations in business and government. The concept of institutional isomorphism focuses on processes of homogenization leading organizations to become more similar to one another. According to DiMaggio and Powell, organizations tend to model themselves after organizations in similar fields that they perceive to be more legitimate or successful (1983, p. 152). Copying organizational structures is a process not driven by efficiency considerations alone; it is also a way of securing legitimacy in political life (Radaelli, 2000, p. 28).

Consultancies disseminate and advocate management 'fashions' and benchmarks that lead to isomorphism (Abrahamson, 1996). They play a knowledge-brokering role between businesses and other large organizations in the public and the not-for-profit sectors (Lapsley, 2001). Consultants have acquired norms-setting power in public management by taking on more active roles in governance processes through contracting-out and public–private partnerships (Saint-Martin, 2000). Consultants are typically brought into government to make it more 'business-like'. As one can read on the website of McKinsey's Public Sector Practice: 'By drawing on our private sector experience, we work to enhance the effectiveness and efficiency of government institutions, enabling them to better fulfill their mission to the public'.[1] Consultants are brought in to government to model public organizations after what is perceived to be the more legitimate or superior management model in the business sector. They provide the language and styles of the corporate world that government organizations imitate to appear more efficient.

Management consultants' claims to expertise are based on their knowledge of business management approaches and practices. Consultants use this knowledge to build and market their reputation as knowledge brokers able to move knowledge among client groups (Semadeni, 2001). A glossy document describing the KPMG Government and Public Sector Services explains that the firm 'is uniquely positioned to deliver highly tailored local solutions, based on key insights gained from our work with similar public and private sector organizations around the world' (KPMG, 2011, p. 1).

Reputation matters crucially for a sector that is unregulated in most countries. Any individual or firm can label their services as 'consulting'. The lack of formal institutional standards and porous industry boundaries create substantial uncertainty when client organizations buy consulting services (Corcoran & McLean, 1998). Reputation, as a result, becomes most important in reducing uncertainty and controlling opportunistic behaviour (Glückler & Armbrüster, 2003, p. 270).

As agents of isomorphism, management consultants facilitate coordination between organizations in the corporate and government sectors. In the words of DiMaggio and Powell, 'similarity can make it easier for organizations to transact with other organizations' (1983, p. 73). Consultants help define what Hall and Soskice describe as the 'set of shared understandings' that lead actors to a specific equilibrium. These 'shared understandings', they argue, 'are important elements of the "common knowledge" that lead participants to coordinate on one outcome, rather than another' (2001, p. 13). According to the 'varieties of capitalism' (VOC) approach, there are two broad types of equilibrium in modern political economies: 'liberal market' and 'coordinated market' institutional arrangements. Each arrangement is characterized by particular institutional structures and power relations that are replicated at multiple levels of the state, market and corporate firm. The institutional framework governing the political economy in LMEs and coordinated market economies (CMEs) are highly path dependent. They consist of interlocking pieces that are, in broad terms, complementary and self-reinforcing over time. As we shall see next, differences between LMEs and CMEs generate systematic differences in the development of the management consulting industry and in the share of public management functions that is assumed by consultants.

II. The Historical Development of Management Consultancy

Management consultancy is an industry largely dominated by US-based firms (McKenna, 2006). In 2015, the size of the global market for consulting services was estimated to be around US$400 billion (IBIS*World*, 2015). The United States represents half of this market, and Europe a third. The European market developed later than in the US. As one study concluded, 'culturally and politically, the United States was a more fertile ground than Europe for embracing consultancy, either as a practical pursuit or as a professional service—or both' (Gross & Poor 2008, p. 70).

Management consulting first emerged in the US in the early 1900s with Frederick Taylor and his 'scientific management' approach to the work process (Rassam & Oates, 1991). Consulting has a background in both engineering and accounting. The industry is diverse and generally divided between the large accountancy-based firms and the so-called elite strategy consultancies such as McKinsey, the Boston Consulting Group, Bain, A.T. Kearney, and Booz & Company. Unlike the accounting firms, which specialize in financial management and information technology, these consultancies focus more on strategic advice, brand management and organizational development, especially business-process re-engineering

(Rassam, 1998, p. 13). It is estimated that large strategy consultancies such as McKinsey spend about US$100 million annually on research.

For large consultancies such as McKinsey, Booz, Gemini and Arthur D. Little, one of the key instruments for disseminating ideas is the publication of articles or books, which has become a favoured marketing tactic in the firms' attempts to increase their market share (Dwyer and Harding, 1996). Consultancies arrange for such books to be serialized in magazines, advertised in newspapers, and endorsed by well-known business figures. For instance, since its publication in 1993, *Re-Engineering the Corporation* by Champy and Hammer has sold nearly two million copies worldwide. The consulting firm that employed the two authors increased its annual revenues from US$70 million the year preceding publication to more than US$160 million the year after (*The Economist*, 1995, p. 57). McKinsey publishes a review (the *McKinsey Quarterly*), and has published 54 books on management since 1980 (*The Economist*, 1995, p. 57). The most famous book produced by two McKinsey consultants is the best-selling *In Search of Excellence* by Peters and Waterman (1982). This book, which has sold more than five million copies, has been described as one of the 'most influential' sources of ideas in the development of the New Public Management (Aucoin, 1990, p. 117).

Strategy consultancies are keen to be seen at the forefront of management thinking. Consultants are often seen as the conduit between business schools and the business world. It is largely management consultants who transfer new ideas from the academic world to the commercial one. This is especially true of the American-owned consultancies (McKinsey, Boston Consulting Group, etc.), which have always had strong links with the leading US business schools (Rassam & Oates, 1991, p. 23). Some firms have formed alliances with business schools by sponsoring research on issues such as the future shape of companies or the changing role of chief executives (Wooldridge, 1997, p. 17). In their search for new ground-breaking ideas, consultancies offer their brightest consultants time to write books, and then throw the full weight of their marketing divisions behind the final products.

The Institutional Link to Accountancy

Although management consulting emerged in the early 20th century, it only started to establish itself as a multi-billion dollar industry in the 1960s when the large international accounting firms moved into consultancy (Stevens, 1991). These firms, then known as the 'Big Eight', included Arthur Andersen, Coopers & Lybrand, Ernst & Whinney, Arthur Young, KPMG Peat Marwick, Deloitte, Haskins & Sells, Touche Ross, and Price Waterhouse. In moving into management consulting, accountants brought with them a reputation for seriousness and professionalism. In addition, because accountants had already developed an organized relationship with their audit clients, they were not seen as 'intruding' or 'snooping' in company operations as industrial engineers sometimes were (Mellett, 1988, p. 5). As auditors for blue chip North American and European businesses and industries, many of the Big Eight firms had earned a reputation for being the world's premiere accountants. The prestige they garnered helped them become the world leaders in management consulting services (Hanlon, 1994). Following a series of mergers, the 'Big Eight' became the 'Big Four'. At the turn of the millennium, their shared global revenues totalled US$25 billion, representing 35% of the world market (*Industry Week*, 2000).

The Big Four trace their origins to London-based accountants who first came to the United States in the 19th century to oversee the interests of British industrialists and entrepreneurs. Deloitte was created in 1845; Price Waterhouse in 1849; KPMG in 1870; and

Ernst & Young in 1849. Together, the Big Four have offices in more than 130 countries and employ a total of about 400,000 professionals worldwide.

These firms have long acted as the reputational agents of large international corporations (Poullaos & Sian, 2010). They emerged in the UK and the US as a result of the separation of ownership and management that came with the corporate form of governance in the 19th century (Stevens, 1991). In LMEs, where firms finance themselves largely through the capital markets, investors stay at arm's length from the companies. They rely heavily on accountants to provide calculable measures on profitability and performance (Vitols, 2001) and investors do not have access to private or inside information about the operation of the company, as their counterparts in CMEs often do (Hall & Soskice, 2001, p. 23). The accounting profession is, accordingly, much older and larger in size in the UK and the US than in more 'coordinated' European markets (Chatfield & Vangermeersch, 1996).

In moving into management consulting, accountants had a head start, since they already knew their audit clients and were party to their business secrets. At the same time, however, they faced potential conflicts of interest between their roles as certified public accountants and management consultants. This is exactly what happened in 2002, when it was found that Arthur Andersen had broken the law by shredding Enron Corp. documents while Enron, a client of Andersen, was under investigation by the US government for hiding debts and concealing its imminent collapse from creditors and investors (Glater, 2002). The fact that over half of the US$52 million Andersen earned from Enron in 2000 came from consulting fees led US observers and legislators to argue that this might have played a role in Andersen's 'decision not to expose Enron's ongoing lies' (Hastings, 2002). Fearing that the US Securities and Exchange Commission might weaken the self-regulatory practices of the accounting profession and intervene to make it illegal for accountants to provide consulting work to their audit clients, the big accounting firms cut their ties with their consulting arms. Arthur Andersen became Accenture and KPMG Consulting became BearingPoint, while Ernst & Young sold its consulting business to Cap Gemini in 2000 and IBM bought PricewaterhouseCoopers' consulting arm in 2002 for US$3.5 billion.

The European Consulting Market

In several European countries (especially those where the Napoleonic code formed the basis of the private law system), government regulation restricts accountants from providing consulting and auditing services to the same client (Ridyard & De Bolle, 1992, p. 67). This is one reason why management consulting has been slower to develop in continental Europe than in the US and the UK. Another is that in Europe, small and medium-sized enterprises (SMEs) are more numerous than in the US and account for a larger share of GDP (European Capital Markets Institute, 2001, p. 2). SMEs have fewer resources than large corporations and cannot as easily afford expensive management consulting services from top elite firms. To address this, European governments have long nurtured the development of the management consulting profession and industry by providing SMEs with resources and incentives to buy management consulting services to improve their efficiency and competitiveness (Saint-Martin, 2001).

In 2010, the European market for management consulting services was estimated at around 90 billion. Germany (32%) and the UK (22%) together constitute more than half of the European market, followed by Spain (11%), France (10%), Italy and the Netherlands (3% each). US consultancies, which benefitted from the growing presence of American multinationals throughout Europe during the postwar period, dominate the European

Table 14.1 European consulting market, 2010 (% of turnover)

	Germany	United Kingdom	Spain	France	Finland	Switzerland	Ireland	Greece
Total turnover (million €)	27 900	19 009	9 903	8 814	1 142	1 056	438	208
Industry	32.4%	6%	6%	14.5%	38.7%	27%	9.8%	11.9%
Banking & Insurance	23.7%	24.4%	25%	30%	5.1%	26%	21.6%	5.6%
Public sector	10.1%	29.9%	16%	15%	11.8%	9%	27.3%	46.6%
Aerospace & Defense	0%	1.7%	8%	3%	0%	n.a.	0.1%	0%
Telecoms & Media	8.2%	3.6%	17%	5%	8.3%	5%	13.3%	12.7%
Wholesale & Retail	4.3%	n.a.	3%	5%	9.4%	5%	3.8%	6%
Energy & Utilities	7.6%	9.7%	11%	11%	7.3%	6%	7%	3%
Transport & Travel	5.3%	3.1%	9%	4%	2.8%	5%	4.7%	1.9%
Healthcare (pharmaceuticals & biotech included)	3.5%	3.3%	2%	3%	7.7%	15%	7.1%	2.8%
Other	4.9%	3%	3%	8.6%	0%	2%	5.3%	9.5%
Total	100%	100%	100%	100%	100%	100%	100%	100%

Source: Modified from FEACO (2011), p. 21

consulting market. The Marshall Plan, in particular, facilitated the expansion of US consulting firms to Europe and the spread of American management ideas and models (Djelic, 1998).

Table 14.1 lists some of the top consulting markets in Europe in 2010 and the percentage of income by client sector. Differences between the UK (liberal market economy) and German (coordinated market economy) varieties of capitalism and corporate governance are most visible when looking at revenues by sector: The category 'industry' represents the most important source of income for the German consulting market, while in the UK the most important source of income is the public sector.

At 46%, Greece—in deep financial and political crisis at the moment of writing—is an exceptional case. In second place is the UK. The public sector in the UK consumes three times more management consulting services than its German counterpart, and twice as much as Spain and France. Ireland closely follows the UK with 27%, suggesting that smaller public sectors consume more management consulting services than in countries where the state plays a larger role in the economy and society. Similar patterns have been in found in Canada and the US (Saint-Martin, 2006). The overall trend reflects the 'laissez-faire' attitude of the state towards the market, as is typical of LMEs and 'liberal' welfare states (Esping-Andersen, 1990).

III. Management Consultants and Public Sector Reform

LMEs have also been leading the way in the dissemination and adoption of New Public Management ideas and practices. The central idea behind the NPM programme is that the efficiency and effectiveness of public services can be improved by lessening or removing differences between the public and private sectors. In their use of market-oriented mechanisms and private sector management techniques, the UK, New Zealand, the US, Canada and Australia have been described as 'first mover countries' (Bach & Bordogna, 2011, p. 2282). As Lynn argued, 'there are really only two groups of great interest in the context of [public sector] reform: the core, Anglo-American NPM marketizers and the continental European modernizers' (2008, p. 1). The first group of NPM enthusiasts is represented by 'the Anglophone countries characterized by majoritarian political systems and an individualist pro-market culture . . . By contrast, the continental European countries embody a strong state tradition reflected in a larger and more active state role' (Bach & Bordogna, 2011, p. 2290). As discussed below, in countries of the first group, politicians have—over time and regardless of party affiliation—made policymaking institutions more open to outside consultants and framed their use in government in three different ways: (1) consultants as rational planners in the 1960s; (2) as 'cost-cutters' and apostles of NPM in the 1980s; and (3) as partners in the new governance in the 21st century.

Rational Planning and Technocratic Politics in the 1960s

In the 1960s, at a time when Keynesianism was still influential and faith in the capacity of the social sciences to help solve public problems was high, government decision makers were looking for new ways to strengthen and rationalize the interventions of the state in society and the economy. This was the era of 'rational management' (Aucoin, 1986), of the Planning, Programming and Budgeting System (PPBS), and the beginning of the so-called 'policy analysis industry' (Pal, 1992, p. 66). The goal was to make management of the modern welfare state more 'scientific' and professional (Fischer, 1990). In Britain, the 1966 Fulton Committee on the Civil Service complained that 'too few civil servants are skilled managers' (Fulton, 1968, p. 12). It argued that the civil service was too closed and sought to open it up: 'there is not enough awareness of how the world outside Whitehall works' (p. 12). Fulton encouraged the 'free flow of men, ideas and knowledge' between the civil service and the world of industry and research (p. 13).

In Canada, the Royal Commission on Government Organization (also known as the Glassco Commission) argued in favour of 'letting the managers manage' (Canada, 1962). The Commission was appointed under J. Grant Glassco, who saw the need for government management to professionalize by learning from the private sector. In becoming more open to the use of consultants from the private sector, both Glassco and Fulton followed a path similar to that taken earlier by the Hoover Commission on the reorganization of the US government in 1947, which had sought to make the presidency more 'managerial' and use business management practices to transform the president into a chief executive officer with centralized authority for decision making (Arnold, 1996). The Commission contracted 15 of its 34 studies to consulting firms. According to McKenna,

> The Hoover Commission represented the first high-profile use of management consulting firms by the Federal Government, and the potential for favorable publicity from the assignment was not lost on the management consulting firms. Each of the firms, in varying degrees, gained prestige and future clients from its work for the Hoover Commission.
>
> *McKenna 1996, p. 104*

In 1968, the UK Treasury, with the support of the British Institute of Management Consultants (IMC), established a register of management consultants that departments were required to consult before using external consulting services (Archer, 1968). In 1970, the Civil Service Department began to develop a secondment programme between Whitehall and large consulting firms. In a speech to the IMC in 1971, Prime Minister Heath noted that 'the practice has grown of seconding management consultants to work alongside civil servants' (Civil Service Department, 1972, p. 5). He added that 'consultants [were] playing a valuable role in improving the quality of central government management'. In Canada, some have argued that 'the practice of using external consultants was given a significant boost by the Royal Commission on Government Organization' (Mellett, 1988, p. 22).

With the emergence of PPBS, the requirement to evaluate policy more systematically opened a lucrative market for management consulting firms (Pattenaude, 1979). PPBS is based on systems theory, which itself became a booming business in the 1960s. As one American critic noted: 'Taught in universities, bought by private business and government agencies, and sold by a cadre of experts, systems analysis is a commodity commanding high prices and ready acceptance at home and abroad' (Hoos, 1972, pp. 1–2). In the early 1970s, it was estimated that the American government was spending 'billions of dollars' in subcontracting to consulting firms work 'concerned with policy formation, organizational models and even the recruitment of Federal executives' (Nader, 1976, p. x). The title of a book published in 1976 by two American lawyers is evocative: *The Shadow Government: The Government's Multi-Billion Dollar Giveaway of its Decision-Making Powers to Private Management Consultants, 'Experts', and Think Tanks.*

New Public Management in the 1980s

In the 1970s, as governments were consolidating their internal policy-making capacities, and as the fiscal crisis led to cutbacks in public expenditures, the use of consultants in the public sector became less prevalent than in previous years (Wilding, 1976, p. 69). However, that changed in the 1980s when, as a result of the influence of public choice theory and the rise of the New Right, governments, seeking to improve efficiency, increased their reliance on outside consultants as a way to transfer business management ideas and practices into the public sector (Saint-Martin, 2000).

When Margaret Thatcher was elected Prime Minister in 1979, the UK government was spending about £6 million a year on consulting services. By the end of her tenure as Prime Minister in 1990, this amount had grown to £246 million. In Canada, when the Conservative Mulroney government was in power, spending on consultancy increased from CAD$56 million in 1984 to almost CAD$190 million in 1993. In Australia, during the Hawke-Keating Labor government, spending on consultancies rose from AUD$91 million in 1987 to AUD$342 million in 1993 (Howard, 1996, p. 70). This increase was so significant that it led to a parliamentary committee inquiry on the engagement of consultants by government departments (Parliament of the Commonwealth of Australia, 1990). In New Zealand, growth in expenditures on consultants also led to an investigation by the Comptroller and Auditor General in 1994 (Audit Office, 1994). That same year, the Efficiency Unit in the UK issued a study on the use of external consultants. It noted: 'Over the past 10 years the Government has substantially increased its use of external consultants' (Efficiency Unit, 1994, p. 19).

The release of that study, which showed that government spending on external consultancy increased 'nearly fourfold' between 1985 and 1990 (Efficiency Unit, 1994, p. 46), created a political backlash as civil service unions, the media and Labour MPs denounced what they saw as a too cozy relationship between consultants and the Tories (Willman, 1994). It has thus been argued that 'the era of Conservative government since 1979 has certainly been the age of management consultancy' (Beale, 1994, p. 13); and that 'the rise of management consultants was one of the distinctive features of the Thatcher years' (Smith & Young, 1996, p. 137). Nevertheless, government spending on management consultants continued to grow even after the election of centre-left governments. Under New Labour, the UK government spent £3 billion on consultants in 2006. In Canada, expenditures on consulting contracts grew from CAD$534 million in 2004 under a Liberal government to almost CAD$1 billion in 2008 under a Conservative government (Donovan, 2008).

The New Governance in the Twenty-first Century

Starting in the mid-1990s, after almost two decades of focusing on reforming the *management* of government, decision makers began to worry more about the *policy* side of the governing process (Peters, 1996). To use Osborne and Gaebler's distinction (1992), the focus of reform shifted from *rowing* to *steering*. After coming to power, the Blair government issued a White Paper on *Modernising Government* (1999). The document argued that whereas earlier management reforms brought improved productivity and better value for money, they paid little attention to the policy process. It underlined in particular the problem of ensuring that policies are devised and delivered in a consistent and effective way across institutional boundaries to address issues that cannot be tackled on a departmental basis—the need for what came to be called 'joined-up' policies. This occurred against a background of increasing separation between policy and delivery, and more diverse and decentralized delivery arrangements (Williams, 1999, p. 452). Similarly, in Canada, once the government had solved its deficit problem, the focus of reform in the mid-1990s shifted to building policy capacity and horizontal management (Bakvis, 2000).

Largely inspired by the new politics of the 'Third Way' developed by Clinton and Blair, these reforms were designed to make government more 'intelligent' and better able to meet the needs of the people (Giddens, 1998). Whereas the political right of the 1980s was anti-statist or anti-bureaucratic, the politics of the Third Way in the late 1990s was more pragmatic and less inclined to denigrate the role of the public sector (Newman, 2001). The new focus was on 'partnerships' with either the private or voluntary sectors. As Neil Williams observed in the case of Britain, modernizing the policy process has meant a 'greater role for outsiders' (1999, p. 456) as a way to ensure that a wider range of viewpoints, knowledge and experience is brought to bear on policy. It is in this context that management consultants re-defined themselves in the late 1990s as 'partners in governance'. As one can read on Accenture's website, 'Citizens now expect government to be more like the 24/7 world of the private sector—more efficient, and always aligned with the people it serves. And government needs a partner who will help improve the way it serves citizens . . . Accenture is that partner.'

Being a partner means that consultancy is no longer simply about providing advice to a client organization that is then solely responsible for subsequently deciding whether to implement the consultants' recommendations. In 1986, the International Labour Office defined a consultant as an expert detached from the employing organization (Kubr, 1986). But now, with the growth of 'outsourcing consultancy', consultants are more involved in service delivery and less detached from their clients than in the past. 'Outsourcing consultancy'—which in the past few years has become the fastest growth sector for consultants—is when an organization assigns whole business or administrative functions to a consulting firm (Tewksbury, 1999). In Britain, a survey of consulting services users found in 2001 that 96% of clients said that they wanted 'some form of relationship with their consultancy firm rather than keeping them at arms length. There is no doubt that consultants are increasingly seen as partners rather than suppliers' (MCA, 2001, p. 4). Quick intervention is less the norm today; the new trend is for large firms to have long-term contracts, such as the six-year contract between PricewaterhouseCoopers and the UK Ministry of Defence, and the ten-year contract with the Home Office covering immigration programs and services

(Huntington, 2001). Consultants are keen to take up large contracts because this is a way of protecting their business from the ups and downs of the economy.

Outsourcing consultancy is especially strong in the field of information technology (IT). Consulting firms have become increasingly active in the development of eGovernment, promoting the use of IT as a tool to transcend organizational boundaries and make government more 'joined up'. Some have described eGovernment as the 'new paradigm' of public sector reform (Accenture) and, according to Patrick Dunleavy and his colleague, it has 'overtaken and superseded' NPM, whose time, they argue, is now 'over' (Dunleavy & Margetts, 2000, p. 1). Whether eGovernment is different from NPM is still an open question. But, like NPM— whose emergence in the 1980s increased public spending on consulting services— eGovernment is also becoming a fast-growing market for management consultancies. In Europe, the eEurope Action Plan adopted by the European Union in 2000 is driving the demand for information technologies in the public sector. Research indicates that eGovernment spending by governments in Western Europe was around US$2.3 billion in 2002 (IDC, 2002).

In the United States, it is estimated that federal, state and local spending on eGovernment was about US$6 billion in 2003 (Labatonjan, 2002). Moreover, in the US, the use of IT in government has taken a new, more security-oriented direction following 9/11 and the creation of the Homeland Security Department. Consulting firms in Washington are now involved in providing the technology that could help, in the words of the Head of the Public Sector Branch of BearingPoint, 'mitigate the risk of exposing valuable information to our enemies' (BearingPoint, 2002). Consultants see the global war against terrorism as a growing market where governments worldwide are expected to spend an estimated US$550 billion on homeland security (Reuters, 2003).

Lobbying Strategies

As the demand for consultancy in government became more pronounced in countries like Britain, Canada and Australia, most consulting firms, as well as the associations that represent their interests, began in the 1980s to develop various institutions and practices designed to build networks of contacts with government officials. In Britain, following the introduction of Mrs Thatcher's 'Efficiency Strategy' in 1980, it was noted that 'the Management Consultancies Association (MCA) moved swiftly to consolidate its position by developing its network of contacts within the civil service' (Smith & Young, 1996, p. 142). In the early 1980s, the MCA created within its organization a 'Public Sector Working Party' (PSWP) in order to develop a more coordinated strategy for promoting management consulting to government. According to the MCA, 'the Group dealing with the public sector has established close links with departments employing management consultancy services with the intention not only of establishing a better understanding within Whitehall of the services that we can offer, but of equal importance, ensuring that our membership is aware of the needs and constraints faced by Ministries' (MCA, 1989, p. 4). The PSWP is made up of various 'sub-groups', one of which is directly linked to the Cabinet Office and whose role is to ensure, in the words of the MCA director, that there is 'a regular dialogue between the MCA and members of Cabinet and with senior officials' (MCA, 1995, p. 3).

Following its creation, the PSWP began to organize a number of events to facilitate the exchange of ideas between Whitehall officials and consultants. Each year, the MCA runs half-day seminars for civil servants on management reform and on the use of consultants in the public sector. In the past, such seminars were sometimes attended by no less than 200 civil

Consultants and Policy Analysis

servants (MCA, 1995, p. 3). The PSWP also holds a series of meetings (four or five a year) attended by member firms and Permanent Secretaries, the purpose of which is to receive an authoritative update on activities within a particular sector of government. As explained in the letters sent by the MCA to the senior officials invited to speak at PSWP meetings, the goal is to see 'how consultants can act as advisers and partners in helping the Civil Service to face future management challenges'. These meetings are supplemented by a series of small monthly business lunches involving the participation of policy-makers and senior staff from member firms. For the MCA, these luncheons 'provided an ideal "off the record" opportunity for wide ranging discussions on subjects of particular interest to both guests and hosts' (MCA, 1996, p. 5). In the past, MCA guests included the head of the Policy Unit, senior Treasury officials, and members of the Efficiency Unit and of the Cabinet Office. Following the example of their business association, MCA member firms began in the 1980s to organize various lobbying activities targeted at Whitehall officials and created 'Government Services Divisions' within their organizational structures. These divisions are often made up of 'former bureaucrats and others with public sector expertise [who] have been hired to develop a rapport with civil servants and to sell the firms' many and varied services' (Bakvis, 1997, p. 109).

As the government became a more important client, management consultants increasingly sought to obtain inside knowledge of Whitehall's current and future plans for management reform. In this search for information, MPs became an important asset in helping to secure valuable Whitehall contacts. In 1988, Tim Smith, a Tory MP and consultant to Price Waterhouse, asked no less than 18 parliamentary questions for detailed information on management consulting. The answers disclosed the nature of the contracts, the successful companies, their assignments and the government expenditures involved (Halloran & Hollingworth, 1994, p. 198).

In Britain, some have also noted the 'revolving door' between government and management consulting firms. For instance, before becoming a minister in Tony Blair's government in 2003, Margaret Hodge worked at PricewaterhouseCoopers. The Secretary of State for Trade, Patricia Hewitt, was research director at Andersen (Simms, 2002, p. 34). Large consultancies also offer some of their staff for free on secondment to various government departments. An investigation by *The Observer* in 2000, which led to the 'staff-for-favours row' (Barnett, 2000), found that firms like PricewaterhouseCoopers and Ernst & Young, which had donated staff free to departments, had subsequently won lucrative government contracts. One consultant to the Treasury quoted in the *Observer* article said: 'I did work on policy issues and got amazing access . . . It is now much easier for me to ring up Treasury officials and get the information I need' (Barnett, 2000).

In the United States, large consulting firms commonly make financial contributions to parties and candidates for Congress. For instance, in the 2000 election cycle, the 'Big Five' donated US\$8 million to the two major political parties: 61% to the Republicans and 38% to the Democrats. Arthur Andersen was the fifth biggest donor to Bush's White House run, contributing nearly US\$146,000 via its employees and political action committee (PAC). Since 1989, Andersen has contributed more than US\$5 million in soft money, PAC and individual contributions to federal candidates and parties, more than two-thirds of this to Republicans. More than half of the current members of the House of Representatives are reported to have received cash from Andersen over the last decade. In the Senate, 94 of the chamber's 100 members reported Andersen contributions since 1989 (Labatonjan, 2002).

Finally, at the European level, management consulting firms' national associations are grouped together in a Brussels-based organization called the FEACO: the European

Federation of Management Consulting Associations. The FEACO presents itself as the 'united voice' of consultants, promoting the 'the interests of management consultants with various international organizations by maintaining close contacts with European institutions, such as the European Commission' (FEACO, 2001, p. 3). The FEACO is organized into various committees such as the European Community Institutions Committee (ECIC). Following publication of the White Paper on Reforming the Commission in 2000, members of the ECIC met to develop their 'action plan'. In that document, one can read that

> [t]he main objective of the ECIC should be to monitor, influence and provide input into the modernization of the European Commission ... The ECIC should maintain close contacts with key persons in the European Commission ... and maintain close contacts with the European Parliament by inviting MEPs to lunches and organize meetings with them, to help them better understand the role of consultants and their contribution to the improvement of the efficient management of all EU activities.
>
> *FEACO, 2000b*

Conclusion

This broad comparative historical overview has focused on the relationships between management consultants and governments and suggested that this link has been closer in some countries than others because of differences in the institutional framework governing the political economy. The management consulting industry has historically been more developed in LMEs than in CMEs, and the available evidence suggests that governments in LMEs have delegated a greater portion of public management functions to outside consultants than governments in CMEs.

One type of reform that consultants helped design and implement in LMEs is 'agencification'—that is, the breaking up of large public sector bodies into semi-autonomous agencies that operate at arm's length and under more business-like conditions than the government bureaucracy (Pollitt, Talbot, Caulfield & Smullen, 2004). This so-called agency model is heavily influenced by corporate governance arrangements characteristic of LMEs. Corporate structures in LMEs concentrate authority in top management. A hands-off approach to regulation prevails, as companies are regarded as a domain of private transaction, regulated by contract rather than by statute. Investors generally stay at arm's length from the companies in which they invest and intervene only in periods of crisis. In government, the application of these practices led to reforms that sought to 'let the managers manage' (James, 2001). Civil servants were turned into managerial executives accountable for performance to legislators and the public, re-defined as 'shareholders' and 'stakeholders', respectively.

As agents of isomorphism, management consultants make organizations more similar to one another. However, making government more 'business-like' in LMEs and CMEs involves different organizational forms and practices. These differences seem to be reinforced rather than weakened by consultants' work in government. The 'agency model' is an illustrative case of isomorphic modelling. It is no coincidence that it was first emulated by governments in LMEs, where there is a greater 'fit' with this form of corporate arrangement than in CMEs, reflecting the institutional complementarities between managerial practices in business and government in modern political economies.

Note

1 www.mckinsey.com/Client_Service/Public_Sector.aspx#Defense_and_Security

References

Abrahamson, E. 1996. "Management Fashion". *Academy of Management Review*, 21, 1: 254–285.

Archer, J. N. 1968. "Management Consultants in Government". *O&M Bulletin*, 23, 1: 23–33.

Arnold, Peri E. 1996. *Making the Managerial Presidency: Comprehensive Reorganization Planning, 1905–1996*. University Press of Kansas.

Aucoin, Peter. 1986. "Organizational Change in the Machinery of Canadian Government: From Rational Management to Brokerage Politics". *Canadian Journal of Political Science*, 19, 2: 3–27.

Aucoin, Peter. 1990. "Administrative Reform in Public Management: Paradigms, Principles, Paradoxes and Pendulums". *Governance*, 3, 2: 115–137.

Audit Office. 1994. "Employment of Consultants by Government Departments". In *Report of the Comptroller and Auditor General: Third Report for 1994*. Wellington, New Zealand.

Bach, Stephan and Lorenzo Bordogna. 2011. "Varieties of New Public Management or Alternative Models?" *The International Journal of Human Resource Management*, 22, 11: 2281–2294.

Bakvis, Herman. 1997. "Advising the Executive: Think Tanks, Consultants, Political Staff and Kitchen Cabinet". In *The Hollow Crown: Countervailing Trends in Core Executives*, edited by Patrick Weller, Herman Bakvis and R. A. W. Rhodes, 84–125. London: Macmillan.

Bakvis, Herman. 2000. "Rebuilding Policy Capacity in the Era of the Fiscal Dividend". *Governance*, 13, 1: 71–104.

Barnett, Anthony. 2000. "Staff for Favours Row Hits Treasury". *The Observer*, June 25. www.guardian.co.uk/Archive/Article/0,4273,4033309,00.html (consulted 12 April 2016).

Beale, Dave. 1994. *Driven by Nissan? A Critical Guide of New Management Techniques*. London: Lawrence & Wishart.

BearingPoint. 2002. Homeland Security Testimonials. Statement of S. Daniel Johnson, Executive Vice-President, Public Services, Committee on House Government Reform.

Canada. 1962. The Royal Commission on Government Organization. *Volume 1: Management of the Public Service*. Ottawa: The Queen's Printer.

Chatfield, Michael and Richard Vangermeersch, eds. 1996. *The History of Accounting: An International Encyclopedia*. New York: Garland.

CIBER. 2003. *Overview of State Government Solutions Provided by CIBER*. http://ciber.com/services_solutions/other_services/egovt/images/CIBER-SGS-Overview.pdf

Civil Service Department. 1972. *CSD News*, 3, 2.

Corcoran, Jan and Fiona McLean. 1998. "The Selection of Management Consultants: How Are Governments Dealing with this Difficult Decision? An Exploratory Study". *International Journal of Public Sector Management*, 11, 1: 37–54.

Deloitte. 2009. *Government Reform's Next Wave: Redesigning Government to Meet the Challenges of the 21st Century*. Washington, DC: Deloitte Research.

DiMaggio, Paul J. and Walter W. Powell. 1983. "The Iron Cage Revisited: Institutional Isomorphism and Collective Rationality in Organizational Fields". *American Sociological Review*, 48, 2: 147–160.

Djelic, Marie-Laure. 1998. *Exporting the American Model: The Postwar Transformation of American Business*. Oxford University Press.

Dobbin, Frank. 1994. *Forging Industrial Policy: United States, Britain and France in the Railway Age*. New York: Cambridge University Press.

Donovan, Kevin. 2008. "Tories Outspent Liberals on Consultants". *The Toronto Star*, 8 December.

Dunleavy, Patrick and Helen Margetts, 2000. "The Advent of Digital Government: Public Bureaucracies and the State in the Internet Age". Paper prepared for delivery at the 2000 Annual Meeting of the American Political Science Association, Washington, 4 September.

Dwyer, A. and F. Harding, 1996. "Using Ideas to Increase the Marketability of Your Firm". *Journal of Management Consulting*, 9, 2: 56–61.

Efficiency Unit, 1994. *The Government's Use of External Consultants: An Efficiency Unit Scrutiny*. London: HMSO.

Esping-Andersen, Gosta. 1990. *The Three Worlds of Welfare Capitalism*. Princeton University Press.

European Capital Markets Institute. 2001. *A Comparison of Small and Medium Sized Enterprises in Europe and in the USA: Manuscript.* www.eurocapitalmarkets.org/system/files/SMEE_book.pdf (consulted 15 April 2016).

FEACO, 2000b. *ECIC Action Plan 2000.*

FEACO, 2011. *Survey of the European Management Consultancy 2010–2011.* Pécs, Hungary: Research Center on Management and Human Resource Management, University of Pécs. www.feaco.org/sites/default/files/Feaco%20Survey%202010-2011.pdf

Fischer, Frank. 1990. *Technocracy and the Politics of Expertise.* Newbury Park, CA: Sage.

Fulton, Lord. 1968. *The Civil Service: Volume 1—Report of the Committee 1966–68.* Cmnd 3638. London: HMSO.

Giddens, Anthony. 1998. *The Third Way: The Renewal of Social Democracy.* Cambridge, UK: Polity Press.

Glater, Jonathan D. 2002. "Longtime Clients Leave Arthur Andersen". *The New York Times,* 16 March, 1.

Glückler, Johannes and Thomas Armbrüster. 2003. "Bridging Uncertainty in Management Consulting: The Mechanism of Trust and Networked Reputation". *Organization Studies,* 24, 2: 269–297.

Gross, Andrew C. and Jozsef Poor. 2008. "The Global Management Consulting Sector". Focus on Industries. *Business Economics,* October, 69–79.

Guttman, Daniel and Barry Willner. 1976. *The Shadow Government: The Government's Multi-Billion Dollar Giveaway of its Decision-Making Powers to Private Management Consultants, 'Experts', and Think Tanks.* New York: Pantheon Books.

Hall, Peter A. and David Soskice, eds. 2001. *Varieties of Capitalism. The Institutional Foundations of Comparative Advantage.* New York: Oxford University Press.

Halloran P. and M. Hollingworth, 1994. *A Bit on the Side: Politicians and Who Pays Them? An Insider's Guide.* London: Simon & Schuster.

Hanlon, G. 1994. *The Commercialization of Accountancy.* London: Macmillan.

Hastings, Alcee. L. 2002. *The Need for Auditor Independence.* U.S. House of Representatives. Congressional Record, V. 148, Part 1, 23 January to 13 February, p. 491.

Hood, Christopher and Michael Jackson. 1991. *Administrative Argument.* Aldershot, UK: Dartmouth.

Hoos, Ida. 1972. *Systems Analysis in Public Policy: A Critique.* Berkeley: University of California Press.

Howard, Michael. 1996. "A Growth Industry? Use of Consultants Reported by Commonwealth Departments, 1974–1994". *Canberra Bulletin of Public Administration,* 80, September, 62–74.

Huntington, Mary. 2001. "Careers: Public Sector – Working in the Public Eye". *Management Consultancy,* 12 March.

IBIS World. 2015. *Global Management Consultants: Market Research Report.* December, Santa Monica, CA. www.ibisworld.com/industry/global/global-management-consultants.html (consulted 21 April 2016).

IDC, 2002. Survey – IT Purchasing Patterns in Western European Public Sector: IDC # PP08J. www.idcresearch.com/getdoc.jhtml?containerId=PP08J (consulted 15 April 2016).

Industry Week, 2000. "Global Manufacturers' Resource Guide". *Top Consulting Firms.* www.industryweek.com/iwinprint/data/chart6-2.html (consulted 15 April 2016).

James, Oliver. 2001. "Business Models and the Transfer of Businesslike Central Government Agencies". *Governance,* 14, 2: 233–252.

KPMG 2011. *Cutting Through Complexity: KPMG Government and Public Sector Services.* KPMG International, 11 pages.

Kubr, Milos. 1986. *Management Consulting: A Guide to the Profession.* Geneva: International Labour Office.

Labatonjan, Stephen 2002. "Enron's Collapse: The Lobbying; Auditing Firms Exercise Power in Washington", *New York Times,* 19 January. www.nytimes.com/2002/01/19/business/enron-s-collapse-the-lobbying-auditing-firms-exercise-power-in-washington.html (consulted 2 December 2016).

Lapsley, Irvine. 2001. "Transforming the Public Sector: Management Consultants as Agents of Change". *European Accounting Review,* 10, 3: 523–543.

Le Monde, 1999. "Les cabinets de conseil, les géo-maîtres du monde". Economic Section, 19 January.

Leys, Colin. 1999. "Intellectual Mercenaries and the Public Interest: Management Consultants and the NHS". *Policy & Politics,* 27, 4: 447–465.

Lodge, Martin and Kai Wegrich. 2005. "Control over Government: Institutional Isomorphism and Governance Dynamics in German Public Administration". *Policy Studies Journal,* 33, 2: 213–233.

Lynn, Laurence E. Jr. 2008. *What Is a Neo-Weberian State? Reflections on a Concept and its Implications.* 24 January.

Martin, John F. 1998. *Reorienting a Nation: Consultants and Australian Public Policy*. Aldershot, UK: Ashgate.

MCA: Management Consultancies Association, 1989. *President's Statement and Annual Report*. London.

MCA: Management Consultancies Association, 1995. *President's Statement and Annual Report*. London.

MCA: Management Consultancies Association, 1996. *President's Statement and Annual Report*. London.

MCA: Management Consultancies Association, 2001. *President's Statement and Annual Report*. London.

McKenna, Christopher D. 1996. "Agents of Adhocracy: Management Consultants and the Reorganization of the Executive Branch, 1947–1949". *Business and Economic History*, 25, 1: 101–111.

McKenna, Christopher D. 2006. *The World's Newest Profession: Management Consulting in the Twentieth Century*. Cambridge University Press.

Mellett, Edward Bruce. 1988. *From Stopwatch to Strategy: A History of the First Twenty-Five Years of the Canadian Association of Management Consultants*. Toronto: CAMC.

Nader, Ralph. 1976. "Introduction". In *The Shadow Government: The Government's Multi-Billion Dollar Giveaway of its Decision-Making Powers to Private Management Consultants, 'Experts', and Think Tanks*, edited by Daniel Guttman and Barry Willner. New York: Pantheon Books.

Newman, Janet. 2001. *Modernising Governance: New Labour, Policy and Society*. London: Sage.

Osborne, David and Gaebler, Ted. 1992. *Reinventing Government: How the Entrepreneurial Spirit is Transforming the Public Sector*. Reading, MA: Addison-Wesley.

Pal, Leslie A. 1992. *Public Policy Analysis: An Introduction*. 2nd edition. Scarborough, ON: Nelson Canada.

Parliament of the Commonwealth of Australia, 1990. *Engagement of External Consultants by Commonwealth Departments*. Report 302, Joint Committee of Public Accounts. Canberra: Australian Government Publishing Service.

Pattenaude, Richard L. 1979. "Consultants in the Public Sector". *Public Administration Review*, May/June: 203–205.

Peters, B. Guy. 1996. *The Policy Capacity of Government*. Research Paper no.18. Ottawa: Canadian Centre for Management Development.

Pollitt, Christopher and Geert Bouckaert. 2000. *Public Management Reform: A Comparative Analysis*. Oxford University Press.

Pollitt, Christopher, Colin Talbot, Janice Caulfield and Amanda Smullen. 2004. *Agencies: How Governments Do Things Through Semi-Autonomous Organizations*. London: Palgrave.

Poullaos, Chris and Suki Sian. 2010. *Accountancy and Empire: The British Legacy of Professional Organization*. London: Routledge.

Radaelli, Claudio. M. 2002. "Policy Transfer in the European Union: Institutional Isomorphism as a Source of Legitimacy". *Governance*, 13, 1: 25–43.

Rassam, Clive. 1998. "The Management Consulting Industry", in *Management Consultancy: A Handbook for Best Practice*, edited by Philip Sadler, 3–29. London: Kogan Page.

Rassam, C. and D. Oates, 1991. *Management Consultancy: The Inside Story*. London: Mercury.

Reuters, 2003. "Governments around the World Will Spend an Estimated $550 Billion on Homeland Security in 2003." Washington, July 7. www.world-am.com/body_03-04-2.html (consulted 15 April 2016).

Ridyard, D. and J. De Bolle, 1992. *Competition in European Accounting: A Study of the EC Audit and Consulting Sectors*. Dublin: Lafferty Publications.

Saint-Martin, Denis. 2000. *Building the New Managerialist State: Consultants and the Politics of Public Sector Reform in Comparative Perspective*. Oxford: Oxford University Press

Saint-Martin, Denis. 2001. "When Industrial Policy Shapes Public Sector Reform: The Case of TQM in Britain and France". *West European Politics*, 24, 4: 105–124.

Saint-Martin, Denis. 2005. "Management Consultancy". In *The Oxford Handbook of Public Management*, edited by Ewan Ferlie, Laurence E. Lynn Jr and Christopher Pollitt, 671–694, New York: Oxford University Press.

Saint-Martin, Denis. 2006. "Le consulting et l'État", *Revue française d'Administration publique*, 120: 743–756.

Saint-Martin, Denis. 2012. "Governments and Management Consultants." In *The Oxford Handbook of Management Consulting*, edited by Matthias Kipping and Timothy Clark, 447–464. New York: Oxford University Press.

Semadeni, Matthew. 2001. "Toward a Theory of Knowledge Arbitrage: Examining Management Consultants as Knowledge Arbiters". In *Current Trends in Management Consulting*, edited by Anthony F. Buono, 43–63. Greenwich, CT: Information Age Publishers.

Simmons, Beth, Frank Dobbin and Geoffrey Garrett, eds. 2008. *The Global Diffusion of Markets and Democracy*. New York: Cambridge University Press.

Simms, Andrew. 2002. *Five Brothers: The Rise and Nemesis of the Big Bean Counters*. London: New Economics Foundation.

Smith, Trevor. 1994. "Post-Modern Politics and the Case for Constitutional Renewal." *Political Quarterly*, 65, 2: 128–138.

Smith, T. and A. Young, 1996. *The Fixers: Crisis Management in British Politics*. Aldershot, UK: Dartmouth.

Stevens, M. 1991. *The Big Six: The Selling Out of America's Top Accounting Firms*. New York: Simon & Schuster.

Tewksbury, 1999. "Survey: Public Sector Go Slow". *Management Consultancy*, 11 February.

The Economist. 1995. "Manufacturing Best-Sellers: A Scam Over a 'Best-Selling' Business Book Shows How Obsessed Management Consultancies Have Become with Producing the Next Big Idea". 5 August, 57.

The Economist. 2005. "From Big Business to Big Government: How Public Sector Work is Re-Shaping Management Consultancy". 8 September, 61.

Vitols, Sigurt. 2001. "Varieties of Corporate Governance: Comparing Germany and the UK". In *Varieties of Capitalism*, edited by Peter A. Hall and David Soskice, 337–360. New York: Oxford University Press.

Wilding, R. W. L. 1976. "The Use of Management Consultants in Government Departments". *Management Services in Government*, 31, 2: 60–70.

Willman, John. 1994. "Con Artists or Cost-Cutters? Do Whitehall's Outside Consultants Provide Value for Money?" *Financial Times Week-End*, 30 April, 7.

Williams, Neil. 1999. "Modernising Government: Policy-Making within Whitehall". *Political Quarterly*, 70, 4, 452–459.

Wooldridge, Adrian. 1997. "Trimming the Fat: A Survey of Management Consultancy." *The Economist*, 22 March, 1–22.

15

PUBLIC OPINION AND POLICY ANALYSIS

Christine Rothmayr Allison

Public opinion research is an essential feature of modern democracies. On a regular basis, and at any stage of the election cycle, we read the results of media polls on various political issues. Governments around the world collect census and other data on their citizens through various tools of public opinion research, and mandate external firms to conduct polls and focus groups on a large variety of issues. Political parties, whether in power or not, use public opinion research to define their electoral strategies. Interest groups also rely on public opinion research to define their public relations strategies, and mobilize the evidence collected in order to advocate for or against policy choices in the policymaking process. Consequently, public opinion research is an important subfield in political science and constitutes an important tool for generating data in various subfields, including policy analysis.

From the perspective of policy analysis, we can think of public opinion and public opinion research through three major lenses. First, there is a longstanding tradition of research about democratic responsiveness—that is, to what extent public policies are responsive to public opinion (e.g. Page, 1994). Various models for understanding the relationship between public opinion and public policy have been developed, all of which roughly conceptualize the causal link between the two in three different ways: public opinion influences public policy; public opinion is shaped by political leadership and policies already in place; the relationship is characterized by mutual dependence and influence. This chapter starts out with a short overview of the debate concerning the relationship between public opinion and public policy on the macro level by addressing one of the key questions about the state of today's democracies: Are public policies responsive to public opinion?

Second, policy studies have integrated public opinion as an explanatory factor in theories of the policy process. The prominence and importance of public opinion for theories of the policy process vary significantly, since other factors such as institutions, actor coalitions or ideational factors can also help explain policy choices and change. In the second part of this chapter, we look therefore at how some of the prominent theoretical frameworks in public policy conceptualize public opinion as an explanatory factor. Theories of the policy process allow us to open up the black box of the relationship between public policies and public opinion within policy subsystems, i.e. on the meso level: how does public opinion as an explanatory factor relate to other factors such as institutions and actor coalitions, which are commonly used within theories of the policy process in order to explain policy choices and change?

229

The third part explores the messy lowlands of public opinion and public policy, and details how policy analysts investigate how political actors actually use public opinion research and data within the policymaking process as a tool and resource at various stages of the policy process. We are particularly interested in governmental public opinion research, namely how various governmental actors utilize public opinion research in the crafting of public policies. This includes, for example, designing various policy instruments or measuring whether policies have reached their target audiences or, alternatively, looking at the impact of specific policy decisions. From a micro-level perspective, this overview therefore addresses the following question: how and to what extent do policymakers actually rely on public opinion research and data in policymaking processes? In terms of empirical research, the actual use of public opinion research in policymaking processes remains the least developed.

The chapter concludes with a brief discussion of how these three different perspectives might mutually inform each other, along with a recommendation for future directions of research on public opinion and policy analysis.

Are Public Policies Really Responsive to Public Opinion?

There is a longstanding tradition of research on the relation between public opinion and public policy, including a very large body of empirical research. Overall, empirical findings point to the fact that public opinion does influence public policies. There are, however, many limits to what can be said about the strength of this influence and the various factors that mitigate it (Burstein, 2010, p. 72; Page, 2002; Shapiro, 2011; Canes-Wrone, 2015). The current debate points to two issues that are of particular interest to policy analysis. The first concerns the theoretical debate about how to conceptualize the relationship between public opinion and public policy, including the issue of what factors mitigate and influence how public opinion impacts public policy. The second pertains to methodological challenges, in particular the availability of public opinion data and the indicators for measuring the relationship between public opinion and public policy.

Despite the longstanding tradition of research on public opinion and public policy, the theoretical debate about the relationship between the two has not been settled. There are roughly three major theoretical approaches for conceptualizing the relationship between public policy and public opinion. The first approach is the democratic responsiveness model, which sees public opinion as influencing public policy (e.g. Page & Shapiro, 1983; Johnston, 1986; Monroe, 1998; Petry, 1999; Petry & Mendelsohn, 2004). In this perspective, electoral pressure leads to responsiveness towards public opinion. In contrast, the democratic control model, along with various other approaches (Lippman, 1925; Margolis & Mauser, 1989), conceives of public opinion as being influenced or manipulated by political elites. In this view, what we perceive as responsiveness is rather the result of conscious communication strategies by elites (e.g. Bourdieu, 1975; Ginsberg, 1986; Chomsky & Herman, 1988). Lastly, other authors conceive of the relationship as being reciprocal: public opinion influences policymakers at the same time as political elites and political decisions shape public opinion (Jacobs, 1992; Geer, 1996; Eisinger & Brown, 1998; Eisinger, 2003; Soroka & Wlezien, 2004). Developing the idea of mutual influence further, public opinion can also be understood as a social construct in which the public, the governing elites, and the media participate simultaneously, structuring the environment in which policy is made (Herbst, 1993; Glasser & Salmon, 1995; Herbst, 1998).

Within the body of research on political representation that is also interested in public opinion as an independent explanatory factor, Canes-Wrone points to a specific school of thought that conceives of the relationship between public opinion and public policy as being a conditional representation. First of all, electoral cycles matter:

> Elected officials increasingly cater to mass opinion as term progresses due to voters' recency bias as well as the lower probability that an initially unpopular policy could produce a popular outcome in time for the election.
>
> *Canes-Wrone, 2015, p. 152*

There is broad evidence that electoral cycles matter for various institutions, including judicial institutions and different types of political systems (e.g. Canes-Wrone & Shotts, 2004). Closer to elections, as electoral pressure mounts, responsiveness towards public opinion increases too. Second, as Burstein, among others, argues, interest group activity may interact with public opinion and mitigate its influence (Burstein, 1998, pp. 115–116). Interest group activity might explain variation in responsiveness across policy domains, as pressure through interest groups renders policy change in accordance with public opinion more likely. The contrary might, however, also be the case: active and powerful interest groups could lobby for solutions that favour their specific interests and reduce government responsiveness towards public opinion.

A third important factor is the salience of an issue, which—according to various studies—increases the responsiveness of policymakers to public opinion (Page & Shapiro, 1983; Monroe, 1998; Burstein, 2003). According to this view, politicians are more likely to engage in public opinion research and use such data for salient issues (Druckman & Jacobs, 2006). For these policy issues, the analysis of media coverage and framing are crucial for understanding the formation of opinions. Advances in studies on framing, priming, and selective exposure highlight the impact of media on opinion formation and on attitudes (Lachapelle, Montpetit & Gauvin, 2014). Media coverage can contribute to increased polarization by exaggerating the disagreement between policy actors (Montpetit, 2016) or by depicting some problems as intractable (Mullinix, 2011, p. 63). Policy scholars are also familiar with the concept of policy feedback, where policies in place have an impact on actors' attitudes, identities (Ingram & Schneider, 2006), and, more generally, on an actor's position within policy networks. In order to better understand policy feedback and also understand policy support (Morgan & Campbell, 2011), it is important to know how people filter information and employ biases.

In addition to the factors already mentioned that mitigate the influence of public opinion on public policy, Gilens' (2012) recent analysis of the impact of wealth on representation points to the fact that together with race (Canes-Wrone, 2015, pp. 152, 156), income and wealth inequalities have to be taken into account in order to better understand whose opinion is actually influencing policymaking. Gilens (2012) shows that depending on the issues at hand, public policy is more responsive to the richest voters than to the median voter, and even more responsive when compared to the opinions of the poorest 10%. In addition to asking under what conditions public opinion influences public policy, research therefore needs to disaggregate public opinion and investigate the variation in the degree of responsiveness for different segments of society.

Mitigating factors help us to better understand variation in responsiveness. Whether we assume interaction between public opinion and other factors, the discussion so far has perceived public opinion as an influencing factor, and therefore not as a result of political and policymaking processes. However, there are other schools of thought that perceive public opinion as the result of political leadership, and therefore propose to conceive of public opinion as a social construct in which various actors, including politicians, the media and interest groups, actively engage. There is general agreement that political elites try to influence public opinion through various communication strategies (Jacobs & Shapiro, 2000; Canes-Wrone, 2015, p. 152) and by using public opinion polls in various ways (Petersen, Hardmeier & Wüest, 2008). In this perspective, the policy–public opinion nexus does not as much mirror responsiveness as it reflects opinion leadership by political elites. The extent to which elites succeed in influencing public opinion has been questioned by various authors, in particular because of competing strategies among various political actors as part of democratic competition (e.g. Chong & Druckman, 2007; Sniderman & Theriault, 2004). An alternative school of thought understands public opinion and how it is mobilized and used in the public sphere through the lens of social construction (Herbst, 1993, 1998). Public opinion in this perspective is neither a dependent nor an independent variable, but is instead the result of how different political actors and the media perceive public opinion and mobilize it in public discourse. The construction of public opinion is thereby based on different types of sources and does not necessarily rely on public opinion polls. Herbst (1998) employs the term 'lay' theories about public opinion to describe the phenomenon of constructing public opinion. Political actors, depending on their function and role, utilize different sources, including the media, their constituency, or lobbyists to gauge and anticipate public reactions. Public opinion does therefore not equate with poll data, and such data might not be of any relevance for forming a judgment about what the public wants. In this sense, Herbst's research supports the results mentioned above, which indicate that public opinion is mitigated by other factors such as interest group activism. These, in turn, likely influence how policymakers conceive and understand 'public opinion', namely as a concept that goes beyond the aggregation of opinions of ordinary citizens.

The second major debate regarding the relationship between public opinion and public policy concerns methodology. As Page and others have argued, the conclusions about the influence of public opinion on public policy are 'based on a biased sample of issues' (Burstein, 2010, p. 64; Page, 2002) since public opinion data is generally available for policy issues that are on the public's radar and of certain importance to the general public and the media. Furthermore, investigating the influence of public opinion on public policy is limited by the fact that citizens do not have necessarily stable and meaningful opinions on many policy issues because of a lack of knowledge as well as interest. In his 2014 book, Burstein addresses the issue of sampling bias through an innovative research design. He starts out with a random sample of public bills from the 101st US Congress (1989–1990) and then analyses to what extent public opinion, interest group activity, and media coverage have an influence on policies. The findings are rather sobering with respect to the influence of public opinion: polling data for specific policy proposals were rarely available and were limited to those issues considered most important (Burstein, 2014). On more general issues, preference data were not available for 24 out of the 60 bills studied. Furthermore, where data were available, only in one out of two cases did the outcome reflect the majority preference. Policy scholars are familiar with the phenomenon that many policy issues don't generate public debate. Whether an issue generates public debate or not impacts the policymaking process, as shown by Culpepper in relation to business regulation: in situations of 'quiet politics', i.e. the absence of public attention, business interests had more influence on shaping regulations than it did in cases where the regulatory issues were highly prominent on the public agenda (Culpepper, 2010). Policy change does not only come from important legislative changes on the macro-political level, but also results from the sum of various smaller steps and adjustments within policy subsystems and networks (Howlett & Cashore, 2007; Howlett & Migone, 2011). Most research on the influence of public opinion on public policy, however, is not interested in day-to-day policymaking processes outside the radar of the media and partisan politics.

The challenge in terms of data and its conceptualizing is not limited to measuring public opinion. There is a longstanding debate in policy analysis on how to conceptualize public policy and generate cumulative research results. Not surprisingly, the lack of standard policy measures is also a challenge for research on the impact of public opinion on public policy. Soroka and Wlezien (2007, 2010) distinguish different ways of conceptualizing and measuring the nexus between policy and public opinion, namely the majoritarian, the consistency, and the co-variation approach. In the majoritarian conceptualization, we look for agreement between the majority opinion and the policy. In the consistency approach, we look at whether preferences for policy change correspond to actual policy change. Finally, in the co-variation approach, we look at whether shifts in opinion go along with policy change over time. A considerable part of policy scholarship is more interested in detailed analysis of policy content (instruments, implementation arrangements, etc.) than it is in changes in expenditure or in the perceived ideological orientation of policy, even though these are meaningful indicators of policy change. Another challenge in investigating the relationship between public policy and public opinion is that it is difficult to determine exactly what constitutes policy change and how to measure what it constitutes.

In short, while there is agreement that public opinion matters for public policy, the extent to which it influences public policies, under what circumstances it does so, and which factors mitigate its impact continue to be the object of extensive research and debate. In addition, different theoretical assumptions about how to conceptualize the link between public opinion and public policy are competing with each other: some researchers assume that public opinion is an independent factor, while others look at public opinion as the result of elite communication and media strategies. Other authors, finally, emphasize a bi-directional relationship. In terms of small N-policy studies and case study research, which continue to occupy an important place in policy analysis, the debate about how various factors interact and mitigate the influence of public opinion on public policy seems particularly promising. As the following section argues in more detail, theories of the policy process emphasize the interaction of public opinion with other factors in order to explain policy outcomes and policy change.

Opening the Black Box: How Theories of the Policy Process Conceptualize the Influence of Public Opinion on Public Policies

Policy process theories perceive of policymaking as a dynamic process where various factors interact in order to explain policy change and policy outcomes. Public opinion is generally just one among other factors taken into account in order to explain policymaking. Policy analysis has a particular interest in the content of public policy—including objectives, instrument choice and implementation arrangements—and is interested not only in fundamental policy change, but also in incremental processes, and changes in implementation practice. Such changes necessarily include issues of limited salience to the public. The focus on policy content goes along with an interest in analysing the subsystems of policymaking instead of focusing on decision making at the macro-political level. Furthermore, public opinion as a concept does not exclusively refer to polling data but includes various sources of information, similar to Herbst's (1993, 1998) concept of lay theories of public opinion mentioned above. In this brief and necessarily incomplete overview, we discuss three approaches that explicitly integrate public opinion into their theoretical framework, namely Kingdon's stream model, the advocacy coalition framework, and the punctuated equilibrium theory. We conclude this section by pointing to a number of other theoretical frameworks and their interest in public opinion as a relevant factor in policymaking.

As discussed above, the rational vision of policymaking suggests that electoral competition induces responsiveness to public opinion. Kingdon's seminal work on agenda-setting (Kingdon, 1984) proposes an alternative model. The basic idea behind Kingdon's model is that in pursuing their interests, policy entrepreneurs seek to couple three independent streams—policy, problems, and politics. Successful coupling can lead to policy change. The public mood, together with election and interest group pressure, is part of the politics stream. Kingdon's understanding of public opinion thereby transcends the use of polling data, as reflected in his use of the term public mood. As Jones and Baumgartner write:

> People in Washington refer to [the concept of the public mood] very often, according to Kingdon, though they do not have in mind particular survey results when they do so. The sense that there is a broad public mood cannot be simply reduced to public opinion alone. Rather it reflects complex interactions among public opinion, elite ideas, and the focus of the media.
>
> *Jones & Baumgartner, 2005, p. 237*

Entrepreneurs succeed in coupling the three streams if a policy window opens in either the problem or the politics stream. A policy window defines the institutional context within which the policymaking takes place (Zahariadis, 2014, p. 74; Jones et al., 2016). Shifts in the public mood can help create such windows, but other factors can do so as well. In order to effect change, a policy entrepreneur must be able to exploit the window. Resources, access to critical decision makers, and communication strategies are important to understanding why entrepreneurs succeed or not. Hence, in this theory of policymaking, the public mood can contribute to creating windows as policy entrepreneurs deploy communication strategies in order to make policy decisions happen. Policies, therefore, are not responsive to the public mood, but the public mood helps explain the behaviour of policy entrepreneurs, although not in the sense of entrepreneurs responding to the public mood. The public mood does not equate with polling data, and political actors might well go ahead with policy reforms even if they don't think the public mood is favourable (Zohlnhöfer, 2016).

Policy studies often analyse policymaking by looking at subsystems, i.e. the network of actors involved in decision making and trying to influence policies around a specific policy issue. The advocacy coalition framework (ACF) integrates public opinion as a factor in the external system, whereby external events can influence the constraints and resources of subsystem actors. Public opinion is one resource among others—such as information or legal resources—that can be mobilized by actor coalitions in order to strengthen their own position. Coalitions strategically mobilize these resources in order to change policy (Sabatier & Weible, 2007, pp. 198–201, 203; Weible, Sabatier & McQueen, 2009). Supportive public opinion is a precious resource because it can lead to greater support by official decision makers (Sabatier & Weible, 2007, p. 203). But external subsystem events are only one of many possible 'paths' leading to policy change (Weible et al., 2009, p. 124). Others include policy-oriented learning, events within the subsystem, and negotiated agreements. External shocks are a necessary, but not sufficient, cause of major policy change, and policy change can also concern secondary aspects of policymaking, a type of change the ACF is equally interested in explaining. In short, as is the case for the streams model, the ACF assumes that policy change is not only driven by exogenous factors, such as a change in public opinion. Furthermore, the level of analysis in terms of policy change is much more fine grained than simply looking at legislative changes, and also concerns various features of public policymaking, such as issues of designing policy instruments or questions related to policy implementation, that less attract the attention of the general public, but instead remain within specialized networks of stakeholders.

Similar to the advocacy coalition framework, the punctuated equilibrium theory is interested in explaining and understanding both major policy shifts and incremental change at the same time. Policymaking largely takes place within subsystems, and as long as a policy issue remains within the subsystem, policies only change in an incremental fashion (through negative feedback). Occasionally, an issue spills over onto the macro-political system, at which level policy punctuations— fundamental changes—can occur (through positive feedback). With positive feedback, modest changes transform in more fundamental policy change over time (Baumgartner & Jones, 2009). The punctuated equilibrium framework adopts a dynamic view of how we perceive problems: issues are constantly defined and redefined through the framing and reframing of policy images. Policy images, which combine factual information with emotional messages, are crucial for understanding agenda-setting processes and the dynamics of policy change. They are key to understanding the process of issue expansion, i.e. why an issue exits the subsystem of specialized interests and experts and appears on the macro-political agenda. As long as a policy image is dominant and broadly accepted within a subsystem, only incremental adjustments are possible. Through 'venue shopping', political actors who mobilize for change will try to challenge the dominant image by offering a new definition. In redefining an issue, they try to expand it and also build new alliances with other actors. Public opinion can be influenced through changing images, as Baumgartner, De Boef and Boydstun show in their analysis of the decline of the death penalty, and public opinion in turn influences public policies and policy decisions (Baumgartner et al., 2008, p. 209). Hence, as discussed above, public opinion is not independent of policy processes, and policy processes are influenced by public opinion on the aggregate level. An additional crucial element of the punctuated equilibrium framework, however, is attention. Policy images are powerful tools for attracting attention and for expanding such attention across various venues in order to break up policy monopolies within subsystems. In this understanding, the interaction between public policy and public opinion is seen as a process over time where institutions provide opportunities for, but also constrain, an actor's strategies. Public opinion is not an independent explanatory variable for policy change, but instead a part of dynamic processes that might cumulate in punctuations, i.e. fundamental shifts in public policies.

The three approaches presented above are by no means the only ones that consider public opinion. For example, the narrative policy framework is interested in how narratives aggregate public opinion and at the same time influence individual opinion (Jones & McBeth, 2010). In the study of policy diffusion, the social contagion model suggests that public opinion is a determining factor for understanding certain processes of diffusion (Pacheco, 2012). All three approaches, however, have similar views on how public opinion is integrated into policy process theories:

(1) Public opinion is a resource and its relevance for policymaking largely depends on actors' strategies and existing networks;

(2) Public opinion can be influenced through framing strategies and images, and policy process theories prefer to understand the relationship between public policy and public opinion as one of mutual influence;

(3) Policy process theories suggest that public opinion is neither a sufficient nor a necessary factor for explaining policy change; as long as policymaking remains within policy

subsystems, factors other than public opinion seem to provide more theoretical leverage for understanding policymaking processes.

In this sense, theories of the policy process point in the same direction as several of the authors mentioned above who assume that responsiveness is conditional, i.e. dependent on various other factors that mitigate the influence of public opinion on public policy.

The Messy Lowlands: How Policymakers Use Public Opinion Research

This last section continues with the discussion of public opinion as a resource and tool within the policymaking process and highlights the utilization of public opinion research by different types of actors throughout the policy cycle.[1] We distinguish between two different sets of research. First, there is research on how politicians and interest groups refer to public opinion in the legislative process. Second, there is literature on how policymakers in a much larger sense use public opinion and public opinion research in designing and implementing public policies.

Opinion polls are mentioned in various institutional arenas at the agenda-setting, formulation, and decision stages. There is very limited comparative research on how politicians evoke public opinion during parliamentary debates. As Petersen et al. (2008) argue in their comparative analysis of four Western democracies, it is generally considered legitimate to evoke public opinion during parliamentary debate. Public opinion can thereby be used in a more partisan fashion, i.e. in order to attack and signal dissent in the case of an opposition politician. Public opinion can also be used to support already developed policy propositions. Furthermore, polling results are often mentioned in a very general way by political elites (Cook, Barabas & Page, 2002). Politicians talk about public opinion without actually making specific claims about how the data relates to their propositions. Most claims involve rather vague assertions in the style of 'Americans I have talked to feel that . . .' (Cook et al., 2002, p. 258). This finding is valid independently of the arena where public opinion is mentioned, whether in hearings, on the congressional floor, or in presidential speeches. Research on interest groups indicates that they also frequently refer to public opinion (see Cook et al., 2002). In fact, the analysis of specific policy issues in the US context implies that organized interest groups commission their own public opinion polls and refer to these results during hearings. Not surprisingly, the formulation of survey questions thereby reflects the framing of the policy issue by the interest group (Gandy, 2003). In sum, and as the policy process theories discussed above have suggested, public opinion is used in a strategic way as a resource in the policymaking process. Political actors refer not only to media polls, but to polling specifically conducted by organized interests to be used in various arenas of representation. In this regard, Petry has argued that the type of sources that political actors, especially politicians, rely on in order to 'measure' public opinion depends on the type of political system (Petry, 2007). He argues that in the Westminster type of parliamentary system found in Canada, where power is concentrated in the hands of the prime minister, public opinion as expressed through electoral results is considered more important than public opinion expressed through organized interests or in opinion polls, in contrast with the US presidential system and its mechanism of checks and balances (Petry, 2007, p. 394).

Empirical research on the use of public opinion research in policymaking processes is relatively sparse and, depending on the theoretical angle taken, arrives at different conclusions. Most research is based on case studies of specific policy issues. Overall, however, there seems to be consensus that political actors do not necessarily equate public opinion with mass

Public Opinion and Policy Analysis

opinion, but rely on various sources and have different views of what are useful indicators of public opinion. In fact, if we adopt a micro perspective on the use of public opinion polls in policymaking, the source of polling results and the question of who conducted these polls become central. As Birch and Petry (2012) argue, policymakers do not see media polls as trustworthy, and prefer to receive public opinion data from other sources, in particular governmental public opinion research. Following their argument, governmental public opinion research can be defined as:

> applied social science and marketing research using surveys and focus groups commissioned by government agencies to map the attitudes and perceptions of citizens in order to produce policy-relevant information that will respond to the knowledge and marketing intelligence needs of policymakers and managers.
>
> *Birch & Petry, 2012, p. 344*

Unlike media polls, governmental public opinion research has more control over the timing and content of the polls, and their methodological soundness (Rothmayr & Hardmeier, 2002, p. 127).

As discussed above, it is generally assumed that the impact of public opinion 'is likely to be greatest on high profile issues' (Page, 2006, p. 8). In this view, governments are responsive to public opinion on high-profile issues because these are crucial in electoral competition and might influence the outcome of future elections. Yet, empirical research reveals that governmental public opinion research is used throughout the policy cycle (Page, 2006, p. 65), not just during election periods. When evoking the reasons for and the usage of public opinion research, in particular public opinion research commissioned by governments, political marketing strategies are mentioned most frequently. Several authors have shown that in the US, presidents use polling for communication purposes and to test ideas, so as to exercise leadership on policy issues. While the evidence on government usage of public opinion research from other political contexts is sparser, Page's examination of the use of public opinion research by the Canadian government also stresses the importance of polling for communication.

Page argues that the impact of polling on governmental policy choices and decision making, however, is overestimated (Page, 2006, p. 55), and emphasizes that public servants are the principal users of public opinion research in policymaking processes (Page, 2006, p. 50).

> Overall, then, public servants play a much larger role than ministers' offices in initiating opinion research, and among public servants, communications staff appear to originate research somewhat more than officials in strategic policy positions.
>
> *Page, 2006, pp. 48–49*

Empirical case studies on the actual use of public opinion research by governments and bureaucracies reveal that public opinion data is one among various sources of information that enters decision making (Page, 2006, p. 184). This body of research also highlights that that polls are not only relevant at the decision stage.

Page's research looks at three different, highly salient policy issues: constitutional renewal, sales and service tax, and gun control. Tracing the timing and usage of public opinion research throughout the policymaking process, he argues that the use and impact of opinion research throughout the policymaking process is quite diverse. The most important use of opinion research is for communication and marketing purposes. Media polls as well as governmental public opinion research can influence the agenda-setting stage as they signal public concerns to the government. Simultaneously, they might also influence priorities within public administration. At the policy formulation stage, public opinion research has a greater impact on the details of policy design, such as instrument choice or design, than it does on the 'direction of a specific policy' (Page, 2006, p. 62). At the implementation stage, opinion research can be used to measure the reception and impact of specific policy instruments (Page, 2006, p. 63). All three case studies reveal that the impact of public opinion on the content and direction of public policy, as well as on the design of the more detailed features of the policy, is very limited. According to Page, the main purpose of public opinion research is to help shape communication strategies in order to achieve previously determined goals. He enumerates the following roles for public opinion research in governmental communication: 'determining target audiences, measuring knowledge and awareness of policies, guiding the language and tone used in communicating policy, gauging the public's responses to different arguments, and influencing the content of communications' (Page, 2006, p. 68). Later in the policy process, 'evaluation of communications' is another role.

No doubt, one important goal of governmental opinion research is improving the persuasiveness of messages (Page, 2006, p. 75). Rothmayr and Hardmeier's (2002) comparison of five health, social, and economic policy issues in Switzerland finds that governmental public opinion research was mainly used as part of public relations and communication strategies. Where it influenced policy-relevant decisions, public opinion research was just one among other types of evidence mobilized, and served to design informational policy instruments such as prevention campaigns, in addition to governmental communication tools like websites and newsletters. Rothmayr and Hardmeier also highlight that changing political contexts create and change opportunities for using public opinion research in order to legitimize and support policies already in place (Rothmayr & Hardmeier, 2002, pp. 133–135). In order to better account for the variation in types of utilization of governmental public opinion research, Birch (2010) suggests mobilizing the literature on research utilization and evidence-based policymaking. This literature, she argues, enables overcoming of the almost exclusive focus on decision making on the macro-political level and to open up the black box of how public opinion research is used throughout the policymaking process. Birch points out that current research is limited to the actual use of findings from public opinion research at specific instances of the policymaking process, as such a case study approach is the most tangible and accessible way to understand governmental public opinion research. As an alternative, she suggests that we should also think of governmental public opinion research as contributing to organizational learning over time, i.e. process use (Birch, 2010, pp. 101–102; Torres & Preskill, 2001). With respect to the use of findings, several types of utilization can be distinguished (Birch, 2010, p. 102). Instrumental use refers to the classic issue of the extent to which public opinion influences policy decisions, either on the macro- or micro-political level. Conceptual use relates to problem definition and policy solution. Strategic use refers to public opinion research being used in order to persuade and successfully pursue governmental policies through political communication. Lastly, managerial use covers utilization for programme monitoring and evaluation.

Public opinion research can improve communication and enable better pursuit of policy goals for all political actors, not just the government. Yet, the utilization of public opinion research is not limited to optimizing political marketing around election periods. Where informational or communication tools are central to the public policy, public opinion research can help to conceptualize, implement, and evaluate these tools in order to improve the policy

Public Opinion and Policy Analysis

design. Conceptual use can also be observed for other types of instruments, and public opinion research is also used to monitor programmes, and as part of evaluation strategies. For example, public opinion research can help public servants and decision makers assess whether target audiences are reached, whether clients are satisfied, or even better understand behavioural impact. In sum, public opinion research is a valuable tool in understanding the effectiveness of public policies. At the same time, polling data is also used for strategic purposes and to legitimize policies where need and opportunity arise through shifting political contexts.

Conclusion

One of the challenges in discussing public opinion and policy analysis is the lack of diversity of political contexts that have been empirically studied. There is no doubt that some of the results discussed above are likely to travel well across different types of political systems. Nevertheless, presidential systems raise a different set of research questions than parliamentary systems, and to what extent theories developed for the US system are also valid for other types of political systems remains a question to be answered empirically. For example, presidents seek to influence the salience of issues in order to increase responsiveness to public opinion in Congress (Canes-Wrone, 2006). In a parliamentary system, where the government generally controls the parliamentary majority, exercising leadership has other strategic aims. More comparative research across different types of political systems and policy issues would help us develop more nuanced theories about how political institutions influence actors' strategies and affect the role that public opinion plays in policymaking. Even within a single political system, however, there is no single answer to how public opinion and policy analysis are interconnected. As discussed above, the concept of public opinion itself does not equate with mass opinion from an actor perspective, and policymakers are critical of media polls and polls conducted by organized interests for good reason. From the perspective of policy analysis, the debate about democratic responsiveness vs. elite leadership through mass opinion polling constitutes an important but incomplete and unsatisfactory theoretical angle. The lack of data on many policy issues and the focus on public and media polls treat the actual utilization of public opinion data within policymaking processes as a black box.

Theories of the policy process suggest that public opinion should be understood as a resource that can be mobilized by political actors and as a factor that interacts with, and is mitigated by, other institutional and actor-specific variables. When looking at policymaking processes in more detail, case study research points to the fact that public opinion is not used only for communication or informational purposes, but is used at various stages of the policymaking process. Case studies also reveal the limited impact of governmental public opinion research on macro-political decision making, i.e. on the direction that policies should take, but indicate that evidence about public opinion is used to conceptualize, implement and evaluate public policies. Polling might serve to legitimize policies, but it might also serve to improve the effectiveness of instruments. In short, although poll results are an important source of evidence and might contribute to policy learning, they are a highly political tool used by different political actors in a highly strategic manner. Future research will need to take into account how new sources of data, such as big data and social media, might change how public opinion is viewed and mass opinion data are used in policymaking—a topic that already attracts attention within policy analysis (Bachner & Hill, 2014).

Note

1 There is abundant literature on political marketing and the use of public opinion polls by political parties, presidents and governments. This literature mainly focuses on the electoral context and is therefore not discussed in this section.

References

Bachner, J. and K. W. Hill (2014). "Advances in Public Opinion and Policy Attitudes Research". *Policy Studies Journal* 42: S51–S70.

Baumgartner, F. R., De Boef, S. L. and A. E. Boydstun. (2008). *The Decline of the Death Penalty and The Discovery of Innocence.* Cambridge University Press.

Baumgartner, F. R. and B. Jones (2009). *Agendas and Instability in American Politics.* University of Chicago Press.

Birch, Lisa M. (2010). L'utilisation de la recherche sur l'opinion publique dans les politiques publiques: Le cas du programme de contrôle du tabagisme. Thèse de (Ph.D.). Département de science politique, Université Laval, Québec, Canada.

Birch, L. M. & Petry, F. (2012). The Use of Public Opinion Research by Governments: Insights from American and Canadian and Research. In J. Less-Marshment (Ed.), *Routledge Handbook of Political Marketing* (pp. 344–355). New York: Routledge.

Bourdieu, P. (1975). Public Opinion Does Not Exist. *Communication and Class Struggle Vol 1: Capitalisme, Imperialisme.* A. Mattelart and S. Siegelbaum. New York, International General: 1240–1259.

Burstein, P. (1998). Interest Organizations, Political Parties, and the Study of Democratic Politics. *Social Movements and American Political Institutions.* A. Costain and A. McFarland. Boulder, CO: Rowman & Littlefield.

Burstein, P. (2003). "The Impact of Public Opinion on Public Policy: A Review and an Agenda". *Political Research Quarterly* 56(1): 29–40.

Burstein, P. (2010). Public Opinion, Public Policy and Democracy. *Handbook of Politics: State and Society in Global Perspective.* K. T. Leicht and J. C. Jenkins, Leiden: Springer: 63–79.

Burstein, P. (2014). *American Public Opinion, Advocacy, and Policy in Congress: What the Public Wants and What It Gets.* New York: Cambridge University Press.

Canes-Wrone, B. (2006). *Who Leads Whom? Presidents, Policy, and the Public.* Chicago University Press.

Canes-Wrone, B. (2015). "From Mass Preferences to Policy". *Annual Review of Political Science* 18(1): 147–165.

Canes-Wrone, B. and K.W. Shotts (2004). "The Conditional Nature of Presidential Responsiveness to Public Opinion." *American Journal of Political Science* 48(4): 690–706.

Chomsky, N. and E. Herman (1988). *Manufacturing Consent: The Political Economy of the Mass Media.* New York, Pantheon Books.

Chong, D. and J. N. Druckman (2007). "Framing Theory". *Annual Review of Political Science* 10: 103–126.

Cohen, M. D., et al. (1972). "A Garbage Can Model of Organizational Choice." *Administrative Science Quarterly* 17(1): 1–25.

Cook, F. L., J. Barabas and B. I. Page. (2002). "Invoking Public Opinion: Policy Elites and Social Security". *Public Opinion Quarterly* 66(2): 235–264.

Culpepper, P. D. (2010). *Quiet Politics and Business Power: Corporate Control in Europe and Japan.* Cambridge University Press.

Druckman, J. N. and L. R. Jacobs (2006). "Lumpers and Splitters: The Public Opinion Information that Politicians Collect and Use". *Public Opinion Quarterly* 70(4): 453–476.

Eisinger, R. M. (2003). *The Evolution of Presidential Polling,* New York: Cambridge University Press.

Eisinger, R. M. and J. Brown (1998). "Polling as a Means Toward Presidential Autonomy: Emil Hurja, Hadley Cantril and The Roosevelt Administration". *International Journal of Public Opinion Research* 10(2): 237–256.

Gandy, O.H. Jr. (2003). "Public Opinion Surveys and the Formation of Privacy Policy". *Journal of Social Issues* 59(2): 283–299.

Geer, J. G. (1996). *From Tea Leaves to Opinion Polls. A Theory of Democratic Leadership.* New York: Columbia University Press.

Gilens, M. (2012). *Affluence and Influence: Economic Inequality and Political Power in America*. Princeton University Press.

Ginsberg, B. (1986). *The Captive Public: How Mass Opinion Promotes State Power*. New York: Basic Books.

Glasser, T. and C. Salmon (1995). *Public Opinion and the Communication of Consent*. New York: Guilford.

Herbst, S. (1993). *Numbered Voices: How Opinion Polling Has Shaped American Politics*. University of Chicago Press.

Herbst, S. (1998). *Reading Public Opinion: How Political Actors View the Democratic Process*. University of Chicago Press.

Howlett, M. and B. Cashore (2007). "Re-Visiting the New Orthodoxy of Policy Dynamics: The Dependent Variable and Re-Aggregation Problems in the Study of Policy Change". *Canadian Political Science Review* 1(2): 50–62.

Howlett, M. and A. Migone (2011). "Charles Lindblom Is Alive and Well and Living in Punctuated Equilibrium Land". *Policy and Society* 30(1): 53–62.

Ingram, H. and A. L. Schneider (2006). Policy Analysis for Democracy. *The Oxford Handbook of Public Policy*. M. Moran, M. Rein and R. E. Goodin. Oxford University Press: 167–189.

Jacobs, L. (1992). "The Recoil Effect: Public Opinion and Policy Making in the United States and Britain". *Comparative Politics* 24 (January): 199–217.

Jacobs, L. R. and R. Y. Shapiro (2000). *Politicians Don't Pander: Political Manipulation and the Loss of Democratic Responsiveness*. University of Chicago Press.

Johnston, R. (1986). *Public Opinion and Public Policy in Canada: Questions of Confidence*. University of Toronto Press.

Jones, B. D. and F. R. Baumgartner (2005). *The Politics of Attention: How Government Prioritizes Problems*. University of Chicago Press.

Jones, M. D. and M. K. McBeth (2010). "A Narrative Policy Framework: Clear Enough to Be Wrong?" *Policy Studies Journal* 38(2): 329–353.

Jones, M. D., H. L. Peterson, J. J. Pierce, N. Herweg, A. Bernal, H. L Raney and N. Zahariadis. (2016). "A River Runs Through It: A Multiple Streams Meta-Review". *Policy Studies Journal* 44(1): 13–36.

Kingdon, J. W. (1984). *Agendas, Alternatives, and Public Policies*. Boston: Little, Brown.

Lachapelle, E., Montpetit, E. and J.-P. Gauvin. (2014). "Public Perceptions of Expert Credibility on Policy Issues: The Role of Expert Framing and Political Worldviews". *Policy Studies Journal* 42(4): 674–697.

Lippman, W. (1925). *The Phantom Public*. New York: Harcourt Brace.

Margolis, M. and G. Mauser (1989). *Manipulating Public Opinion: Essays on Public Opinion as a Dependent Variable*. Pacific Grove, CA: Brooks/Cole.

Monroe, A. D. (1998). "Public Opinion and Public Policy, 1980–1993". *Public Opinion Quarterly* 62(1): 6–28.

Montpetit, É. (2016). *In Defense of Pluralism: Policy Disagreement and Media Coverage*. Cambridge University Press.

Morgan, K. J. and A. L. Campbell (2011). *The Delegated Welfare State: Medicare, Markets and the Governance of Social Policy*. Oxford University Press.

Mullinix, K. J. (2011). "Lingering Debates and Innovative Advances: The State of Public Opinion Research". *Policy Studies Journal* 39: 61–76.

Pacheco, J. (2012). "The Social Contagion Model: Exploring the Role of Public Opinion on the Diffusion of Antismoking Legislation across the American States". *The Journal of Politics* 74(01): 187–202.

Page, B. (1994). "Democratic Responsiveness? Untangling the Links Between Public Opinion and Policy". *Political Science and Politics* 27(25–29).

Page, B. I. (2002). The Semi-Sovereign Public. *Navigating Public Opinion*. J. Manza, F. Cook and R. Y. Shapiro. New York, Oxford University Press: 325–344.

Page, C. (2006). *The Roles of Public Opinion Research in Canadian Government*. University of Toronto Press.

Page, B. I. and R. Y. Shapiro (1983). "Effects of Public Opinion on Policy". *American Political Science Review* 77(1): 175–190.

Petersen, J., Hardmeier, S. and B. Wüest. (2008). "Polls as Public–Politic Linkage: A Comparative Analysis of Poll Use and Roles of MPs in Parliamentary Debate". *The Journal of Legislative Studies* 14(3): 315–338.

Petry, F. (1999). "The Opinion-Policy Relationship in Canada". *The Journal of Politics* 61(2): 540–550.

Petry, F. (2007). How Policymakers View Public Opinion. *Policy Analysis in Canada: The State of the Art.* L. Dobuyinskis, M. Howlett and D. Laycock. University of Toronto Press: 375–398.

Petry, F. and M. Mendelsohn (2004). "Public Opinion and Policy-Making in Canada: 1994–2001". *Canadian Journal of Political Science* 37: 505–529.

Rothmayr, C. and S. Hardmeier (2002). "Government and Polling: Use and Impact of Polls in the Policy-Making Process in Switzerland". *International Journal of Public Opinion Research* 14(2): 123–140.

Sabatier, P. A. and C. M. Weible (2007). The Advocacy Coalition Framework: Innovations and Clarifications. *Theories of the Policy Process*, 2nd edn, Ed. P. A. Sabatier. Boulder. Boulder, CO: Westview: 189–222.

Shapiro, R. Y. (2011). "Public Opinion and American Democracy". *Public Opinion Quarterly* 75(5): 982–1017.

Sniderman, P.M. and S.M. Theriault (2004). The Structure of Political Argument and the Logic of Issue Framing. *Studies in Public Opinion*. W. E. Saris and P. M. Sniderman. Princeton University Press: 133–165

Soroka, S. N. and C. Wlezien (2004). "Opinion Representation and Policy Feedback: Canada in Comparative Perspective". *Canadian Journal of Political Science/Revue canadienne de science politique* 37(03): 531–559.

Soroka, S. N. and C. Wlezien (2007). The Relationship Between Public Opinion and Policy. *Oxford Handbook of Political Behavior*, R. Dalton and H.-D. Klingemann. Oxford University Press: 799–817

Soroka, S. N. and C. Wlezien (2010). *Degrees of Democracy: Politics, Public Opinion and Policy.* Cambridge University Press.

Torres, R. T. and H. Preskill (2001). "Evaluation and Organizational Learning: Past, Present, and Future". *American Journal of Evaluation* 22(3): 387–395.

Weible, C. M., P. A. Sabatier and K. McQueen (2009). "Themes and Variations: Taking Stock of the Advocacy Coalition Framework". *Policy Studies Journal* 37(1): 121–140.

Zahariadis, N. (2014). Ambiguity and Multiple Streams. *Theories of the Policy Process*, P. A. Sabatier and C.M. Weible, 3rd edn. Boulder, CO: Westview Press: 25–58.

Zohlnhöfer, R. (2016). "Putting Together the Pieces of the Puzzle: Explaining German Labor Market Reforms with a Modified Multiple-Streams Approach". *Policy Studies Journal* 44(1): 83–107.

PART IV

Parties and Interest-Group-Based Policy Analysis

16

WHO ARE THE POLITICAL PARTIES' IDEAS FACTORIES? ON POLICY ANALYSIS BY POLITICAL PARTY THINK TANKS

Valérie Pattyn, Gilles Pittoors and Steven Van Hecke

Introduction

Political parties and their role in decision-making processes have been documented extensively in the past few decades. This is not surprising considering the central role that political parties play in the political system of modern democracies (Müller & Strom, 1999). Acting as the main intermediaries between state and society, political parties fulfil a myriad of roles and functions. The literature generally categorizes these functions in three groups: (1) interest aggregation and articulation, i.e., gathering public opinion and the preferences of the electorate, and conveying these in electoral programmes; (2) electoral competition, i.e., mobilizing the electorate in an attempt to compete in elections; and (3) seeking legislative and executive office, i.e., selecting and appointing candidates for political offices both in government and parliament (and other political bodies), and are responsible for drafting government programmes and policies (Müller & Strom, 1999).

The functions of political parties in the political process have been studied intensively and are generally well understood, but the internal processes of these parties have received less attention. While most research has focused on assessing the role of parties in setting the political agenda of governments (Mair, 2008), little evidence is available on how parties generate their own ideas. Considering the importance of political parties in shaping the decision-making process, the lack of understanding of internal idea generation of parties is a significant gap in the literature. This chapter addresses part of this void. To be precise, it focuses on the input side of political parties and addresses questions as: Where do political parties' ideas originate from? Who are the suppliers? What do political parties' 'idea factories' look like?

Research departments, affiliated study centres or party think tanks, as they are often called, are important sources of input for parties. *Political party think tanks*—the term that we will use in this chapter—are hardly covered in the literature, or at least not in a systematic, cross-national, comparative way. When reviewing country case studies (see, for instance, Suzuki, 2015; Cross, 2005; Grunden, 2013; Pattyn, Van Hecke, Brans & Libeer, 2014; Pattyn, Van Hecke, Pirlot, Rihoux & Brans, 2017; Neto, 2013; Timmermans, van Rooyen & Voerman, 2013), one can observe a wide variety of empirical manifestations of political party think tanks. In Western European democracies, for example, most political parties have in-house study groups or affiliated think tanks. By contrast, North American parties get major input from private research centres. The wide diversity of party think tanks makes oversight challenging and means that it is difficult to uncover general trends.

In this chapter, we explore the available literature on party study centres in an effort to develop a heuristic typology that classifies different types of party think tanks worldwide. Although political party think tanks do sometimes take different shapes *within* countries, these differences are usually less outspoken than those differences *across* countries. In this chapter, we particularly focus on these cross-country trends. Our empirical input comes from secondary literature about a wide variety of countries including Australia, Flanders, Wallonia,[1] Brazil, Canada, Germany, Japan, the Netherlands, Taiwan, the United States and the European Union. Without claiming exhaustiveness, the cases under study are sufficiently representative of the variety in political systems of modern democracies that exist worldwide. For instance, the Dutch parliamentary system of consensual politics is quite different from the American presidential system based on majoritarian decision making. We believe that the cases are therefore well representative for the various manifestations of political party think tanks around the world. There also is a sufficiently large geographical spread that prevents a Eurocentric or Western bias.

This chapter is structured in two main parts, which represent the two dimensions around which we expect the most significant cross-country variation. In the first part we address the autonomy of political party think tanks vis-à-vis their mother party. In the second part we zoom into the various functions fulfilled by these organizations. For each of these dimensions, we present a typology based on the empirical reality we discuss. Our approach should be conceived as a mixed inductive-deductive method, with the emphasis on the former aspect. In a concluding section, we combine the two typologies and critically reflect on the meaning of political parties' ideas factories.

1. Autonomy of Political Party Think Tanks

To understand the relationship between political parties and their affiliated think tanks, it is crucial to know how both are related to each other. Screening the various manifestations around the world, heterogeneity prevails. While Canadian political parties, for example, entirely rely on research from external and independent sources, Flemish political parties generally have their own in-house researchers. In between these extremes, various forms of autonomy for political party think tanks exist. Indeed autonomy is conceptually an umbrella term that captures multiple elements. In the framework of the chapter, we refer to organizational, financial and ideological independence.

The most explicit level of autonomy is organizational. Relevant indicators are the (non-) existence of a separate legal personality of the party think tank, and the representation of party executives in the think tank. Financial autonomy is the extent to which the party think tank is dependent on financial support from a political party. The third and final angle is ideological autonomy, i.e., the degree to which political party think tanks approach issues from the same ideological perspective as the political party for which they supply evidence, and the extent to which a party think tank can independently decide on its research agenda.

These aspects of autonomy are strongly correlated. A political party think tank that is situated outside of the political parties' organizational structures is also often financially more independent than a think tank that is structurally embedded in the party. Likewise, a political party think tank that is financially dependent on its mother party is highly unlikely to stray

Policy Analysis by Political Party Think Tanks

Table 16.1 Level of autonomy

Level of Autonomy	Indicators	Cases	Terminology, as featuring in the empirical cases
High	• Separate legal personality • Own financial resources • Ideological freedom	US, Canada, Japan	Research centre, political consulting firm, think tank
Medium	• Separate legal personality • Staffed and/or funded by mother party • Ideologically aligned	Germany, Netherlands, Japan, Wallonia, EU	Political foundation, research institute
Low	• No separate legal personality • Fully financially dependent • Ideologically aligned	Brazil, Japan, Flanders	Study service, study department

too far away from its ideological convictions if it wants to secure future funding. As such, although these three autonomy angles can be distinguished analytically, in reality they are hard to disentangle from each other. In the remainder of the chapter, we therefore consider them together as an aggregate and distinguish between three levels of autonomy: high, medium and low (see Table 16.1).

Highly autonomous party think tanks can be considered to have a high amount of independence from all three angles—that is, they have a separate legal personality, their staff is not appointed by the party, they are financially self-sufficient, and they can set their own ideological line. Conversely, party think tanks with low autonomy are strongly dependent on their mother party in all respects: they are legally incorporated in the party structures, are not viable without party funding and are also ideologically aligned. Party think tanks with a medium level of autonomy are situated in between the two poles of the continuum: they have a separate legal personality, but their staff is usually appointed by the mother party, they are partly financed by party funds, and they are, often as a consequence, not able to follow a separate ideological line. In what follows, we bring the typology to life by referring to empirical examples. Countries can feature more than once, as intra-country differences exist across parties.

a. High Level of Autonomy: US, Canada and Japan

In countries where political parties have little in-house research capacities, they will often rely on outside expertise to back up party ideas and party policies. Outside expertise will be bought in from independent think tanks that might or might not share a political-ideological bond with the party. While relying solely on external research renders political parties as such rather marginal players in the process of policy analysis, it does hold the promise of increased quality of analyses, considering that an independent research centre has no incentive to distort its research to suit political or ideological preferences. On the other hand, if parties lack a reliable supply of policy analysis, they are likely to seek input from outside, organized interests (Cross, 2005).

This situation of relying on external researchers to perform policy analyses is particularly apparent in North America. In the United States, for example, both the Republican and Democratic parties have very weak in-house research capacities, but cooperate intensively with private think tanks. Although these think tanks often have very strong ideological and historical links with the party they cooperate with, they are formally independent both from an organizational and financial point of view. Indeed, Rich (2001) describes the 'dense populated environment' of think tanks and research centres in the US, but these are all private entities and none are directly linked to one particular political party.

Ideologically, the think tanks' independent position can be questioned. The US has seen an explosion of think tanks, political research centres, consulting firms and other bodies concerned with policy analysis since the 1960s. Rich argues that this explosion reflects a simultaneous expansion of 'demand for expertise in policymaking circles and . . . supply of entrepreneurial experts' (Rich, 2001, p. 31). However, despite an apparent abundance of expertise, political interests continually trump expert policy advice, which leads to a general appreciation of advice and expertise as 'little more than the instruments of interests' (Rich, 2001, p. 31; see also Schuck, 1995; Hall, 1989). As such, because policy analysis is ordered by patrons, researchers are often inclined to adapt their work to their patrons' wishes.

Likewise, Canadian parties also rely heavily on external sources of policy advice. Cross argues that 'most Canadian parties essentially have no capacity for on-going policy study' (Cross, 2005, p. 622). It is argued that Canadian political parties conceive their primary role as electoral machines, i.e., they 'exist to choose candidates and leaders and to help them get elected' (Cross, 2005, p. 610). Hence, once elections are over, parties lay off their staff and 'engage in little other than fundraising and housekeeping activities' (Cross, 2005, p. 622). As such, it is not customary for Canadian political parties to sustain an in-house study service, but rather to rely on independent groups to provide policy analysis.

Canadian parties were for a very long time faced with a severe lack of funds in between elections. This is probably one of the main reasons why Canadian parties maintain such a minimalist view on their role during non-election periods. Canadian parties literally do not have the resources to invest in policy analysis, or in gathering in-house contributions such as grassroots and membership input. This situation was slightly altered with the 2003 Campaign Finance Legislation, which provided Canadian parties at the federal level with a significant increase in annual allowances. So far, however, parties have not made use of this legislation to develop capacities for conducting in-house research.

Canadian parties still predominantly appeal to external research centres for policy analysis. Depending on their ideological orientation, parties will resort to centres or institutions such as the Canadian Centre for Policy Alternatives and the Caledon Institute (more left-wing oriented); to the C.D. Howe Institute and the Fraser Institute (more to the right on the ideological spectrum); or to the Institute for Research on Public Policy (located at the centre). These organizations are completely autonomous from political parties, and there has never been a history of formal ties between parties and these research centres. A notable exception is the New Democratic Party (NDP), which is closely affiliated with the Douglas-Coldwell Foundation (DCF). Although the two are not formally connected in terms of organization or finances, the DCF Board of Directors includes high profile figures from the NDP. The DCF played a particularly important role during the 1990s, when the NDP had to reinvent itself following the electoral devastation of 1993 (Jackson & Baldwin, 2005).

A very particular situation of 'external' input also exists in Japan, where political parties only recently started experimenting with establishing their own internal research departments. For a very long time, political parties relied on the government bureaucracy as the 'primary vehicle for policy analysis since the Meiji restoration' (Suzuki, 2015, p. 165). It is the government bureaucracy that provides policy information and ideas, and when drafting bills party executives basically only adapt the proposals provided by the bureaucracy. Until deep in the 1990s, '90% of legislation passed by the Diet was drafted by government bureaucrats ... sponsorship of bills by Diet members made up only 10%' (Tadashi, 2001, p. 73). This renders political parties extremely dependent on analyses performed by the bureaucracy—to such an extent that Japanese politicians find it hard to take the lead on drafting legislation without support from the bureaucracy.

b. Medium Level of Autonomy: Germany, Netherlands, Japan, Wallonia and the EU

A different situation exists where political parties can rely on affiliated bodies for policy analysis and research input. These bodies usually have a separate legal personality, but are often staffed and funded by political parties. The best-known examples of such kind of party think tanks are the German *Stiftungen* or political foundations. Grunden (2013) calls the system of German political parties one of 'organized anarchies', as parties are highly decentralized and get different sorts of input from various and at times contradictory sources— including civil society organizations, internal working groups and temporary advisory commissions.

However, when it comes to research input, German parties rely on their political foundations to deliver. Every political party that is represented in the German parliament has an affiliated political foundation. The *Stiftungen* have a very long history—the Sozialdemokratische Partei Deutschlands' Friedrich Ebert Foundation, for example, was founded in 1925. This does not imply, however, that they are impervious to change. For example, in the 1990s the CDU's Konrad Adenauer Foundation merged several of its smaller groups into one large Department of Political Research, pooling resources, tools and expertise (Thunert, 2001). The system of state funding for political foundations has existed in Germany since the early 1970s, and over the past 40 years foundations have become an inherent part of the German party system.

These foundations are not legally bound to a political party and are funded directly by the state (i.e., not by the party). As Grunden argues, however, although foundations are formally quite autonomous, party executives maintain a tight grip on 'their' political foundations by staffing the foundations' executive positions with party officials, thus preventing the production of any 'unsolicited policy analyses' (Grunden, 2013, p. 184).This ambiguity of autonomy raises some particular problems. On the one hand, political foundations are not allowed to formally provide political consultancy to the affiliated political party because they are officially state-funded and therefore 'independent'. At the same time, however, they are neither entirely free to perform critical or even neutral policy analysis for fear of displeasing party leadership.

The Netherlands is another case where parties rely on affiliated but independent 'scientific institutes' as sources of policy analysis. Similar to the German political foundations, the Dutch institutes are officially autonomous from the parties' organizational structure and 'operate at some distance from the party branches in parliament and government' (Timmermans et al., 2013, p. 187). However, unlike the German foundations, Dutch institutes are directly funded by their affiliated party. Parties get state funds specifically designated to sustain research institutes. It is significant that formal recognition of the institute by the affiliated party is an absolute precondition for financial support (Timmermans et al., 2013).

The latter is a heritage of the Netherlands' strong history of pillarization, where societal cleavages were translated into separate pillars consisting of a political party and ideologically affiliated societal organizations such as unions and health insurers (Lipset & Rokkan, 1990). Similar to the German foundations, the first Dutch institutes date back to the 1920s. The protestant Anti-Revolutionary Party (ARP), for example, established the Abraham Kuyper Foundation in 1921. In 1934 the social democrats (later the labour party PvdA) created the 'Scientific Bureau' with trade union support, which was later renamed the Wiardi Beckman Foundation following the party's reorganization in 1946.

From the very beginning, these foundations were dominated in all but name by their affiliated party. The depillarization of political life that began in the late 1960s (Mair, 2008) forced Dutch political parties to reconsider how they would sustain their foundations. Parties were no longer able to rely on input from other pillarized institutions, such as universities or interest groups, and increasingly counted on the foundations. For that reason state subsidies were introduced in 1972, on the condition—still in the spirit of pillarization—that the foundations be explicitly linked to and recognized by a political party.

This recognition somewhat lessened the problems that German foundations still face. For one, Dutch foundations are not prohibited from formally providing their parties with political consultancy. On the contrary, interactions between party representatives and foundation executives take place regularly in parliament, government and at the lower-level rank and file of the party. Still, the institutes' degree of autonomy varies between parties. While some parties allow their foundations significant degrees of leeway from the party line, other parties require their institutes to obtain approval from party executives for their research agenda (Timmermans et al., 2013).

Since 2008, one can discern a similar system of political foundations emerging at the EU level. In 2007 the European Parliament adopted a regulation that specified the creation of European political foundations to support the political parties affiliated to the groups in the Parliament, and in 2008 the first such foundations were created. Counting 12 in total, the European political foundations have, similar to the Dutch institutes, a legal personality separate from their respective European political party and group, but only receive funding through recognition by that group. Also similar is the proportional system of funding of these foundations: the political group with the most seats in Parliament will receive the bulk of the funds (Gagatek & Van Hecke, 2014). However, considering their relatively recent establishment, it remains to be seen how the relationship between European political foundations and their respective European parties and groups will evolve over time.

Japan can again be mentioned here, with parties that have since the 1990s been experimenting with setting up party think tanks that are independent but firmly linked to the party. For example, Japan's leading Liberal Democratic Party (LDP) established the Institute for Policy Research as an independent think tank, but appointed the chairman of its in-house research department as director of the Institute, while staffing the Institute's board with party officials. Moreover, the actual experts in these foundations often hail from industry or civil society, 'and normally they return to their corporations after two years at the think tank' (Tadashi, 2001, p. 79). This frequent turnover of executives is detrimental for developing a stable relationship between the political party and its think tank and hence reduces the overall capacity to actually deliver policy analyses (Suzuki, 2015).

Belgium also has a particular approach to political party think tanks, although major differences exist between the two main regions. In Wallonia, the country's French-speaking part, parties work with semi-independent political foundations, whereas in Flanders parties work mostly with in-house study services (see below). Although Belgian party think tanks are generally funded through their party, Walloon party think tanks may receive additional funding from the Francophone community by applying for the status of *association reconnue d'éducation permanente*. To be eligible, these think tanks must be able to prove that 'their activities aim at knowledge development addressed to the Belgian francophone society'

(Pattyn et al., 2017). Currently only Etopia (linked to green party Ecolo) and the Institut Emile Vandervelde (linked to the Parti Socialiste) receive such funding, as the others did not apply or were unsuccessful.

c. Low Level of Autonomy: Brazil, Japan and Flanders

Party think tanks with low levels of autonomy do not have a separate legal personality, are instead fully incorporated in the organizational structures of a political party, and hence are also financially dependent. A good example of a system where in-house party think tanks are commonplace is Brazil, where political parties are obliged by law to spend at least 20% of their total budget 'on the establishment and maintenance of party institutes devoted to political research, education, and indoctrination' (de Souza, 2001, p. 140). However, Neto argues that in Brazil 'parties perform less as sources of original ideas than as political processing plants for externally generated proposals' (Neto, 2013, p. 187). Most of these in-house party think tanks predominantly focus on communication with the electorate and supporting MPs rather than on policy analytical research. As a consequence, many parties rely on external (private) think tanks for analytical input (de Souza, 2001). In recent years parties have put effort into cranking up their existing in-house research capacities, but it is not yet clear how this will evolve.

A similar situation can be observed in Japan, where parties were long dependent on the government bureaucracy, as discussed above. Despite their lingering dependence on bureaucratic sources of research input, each of the major Japanese parties has established a large in-house research department. The LDP, Japan's dominant post-Second World War party, has a study service called the Policy Affairs Research Council (PARC), which comprises 'seventeen divisions corresponding to each government agency, forty research committees to deal with broad policy issues, and fifty-nine special committees'—an impressive reach for an overall of thirty staff members (Tadashi, 2001, p. 78). Japan's other major parties have somewhat smaller departments, with the number of staff members ranging from four to twenty-nine across parties (Tadashi, 2001). However, these research departments are not composed of policy experts as such, but rather of political advisors that coordinate the party's position in relation to the bureaucracy and organized interests (see below). For that reason, Japan's political parties have recently been experimenting with creating foundation-type think tanks, discussed in the previous section.

Another example of a system where political parties have well-established in-house study services is Flanders. With the exception of the Christian Democratic party (CD&V)—which relies on an independent think tank CEDER—all Flemish parties have their own study department. These departments are fully integrated in and funded directly by the mother party. This situation makes the study departments very vulnerable and dependent on electoral outcomes. Study departments will often be the first victims in the case of election losses. Moreover, unlike in Brazil, Belgian law does not indicate how much funds a party is obliged to spend on research. As such, a turnover in party leadership can substantially influence the funding of the study service if the new leadership wants to invest more in parliamentary work or propaganda than in research (Pattyn et al., 2014).

d. Categorizing Autonomy

As should be clear from this overview, the autonomy of party think tanks varies significantly between and within countries. While Brazilian parties are obliged by law to establish and maintain in-house think tanks, the non-research nature of these think tanks forces parties to seek additional advice from external research centres. A similar situation exists in Japan, where parties have large and long-standing study departments, but are dependent on external input to such an extent that they are now experimenting with semi-independent think tanks. Contrarily, Canadian and American parties almost exclusively rely on autonomous private think tanks. In the Netherlands and Germany, parties work closely with semi-independent and state-funded political foundations. In Belgium both systems exist, with the Walloon parties working with political foundations and the Flemish parties having a long tradition of internal study departments.

The actual autonomy of party think tanks will clearly be determined by a multitude of institutional (including resources and the historical path that exists within a country) and agency-related factors. As for the latter, it is important to emphasize the core role of party leadership. Party leadership that is not interested in investing in research (and is not obliged by law to do so) might prioritize an investment in, for instance, communication actions. Similarly, leadership may request advice to support pre-existing conceptions or to develop new ideas.

2. Functions Fulfilled by Political Party Think Tanks

Political party think tanks can fulfil a wide spectrum of possible functions. They are the main source of analytical input and policy advice in political parties. Not only do they gather information and expertise one way or another, they also process this information and present the analyses to their political patrons or mother parties. Party think tanks sometimes integrate third-party research in their own reports, but also occasionally produce own research or act as intermediaries between politics and academia. Moreover, beyond issuing reports or writing parliamentary questions, party think tanks also perform a myriad of tasks, ranging from contributing to electoral programmes to writing entire party manifestos (Pattyn et al., 2014).

Clearly, on top of their various levels of autonomy, the nature of the advice that party think tanks deliver also varies significantly. Craft and Howlett (2012) identified two ideal types of such advice: hot vs. cold. On one side of the spectrum is 'hot' policy advice. Party think tanks delivering hot advice usually apply a short-term perspective. The main purpose of hot advice is to support the party's leadership or parliamentarians by supplying them with for instance parliamentary questions and speeches. 'Cold' advice refers to advice produced from a longer-term perspective. Organizations engaged in this type of advice typically perform studies and produce reports that consider a particular policy problem and the appropriate solution from a longer-term perspective, based on thorough analysis and more-or-less complete information. In contrast to cold advice, hot advice is often based on fragmented and incomplete information. As Table 16.2 shows, these classifications are a very useful lens through which to look at the very wide variety of party think tanks worldwide.

Table 16.2 Political party think tank function

	Indicators	*Cases*
Hot advice	• Short-term focus • Interaction with daily party politics • Fragmented information	Japan, Brazil, Flanders, Wallonia
Cold advice	• Long-term focus • Unrelated to daily political frenzy • Rational analysis	US, Canada, Germany, Netherlands, EU

In the following sections, we systematically discuss the different positions that political party think tanks take, following the 'hot' vs. 'cold' typology. We first discuss the party think tanks that predominantly produce hot advice and then those that are mainly engaged in cold advice production.

a. Hot Advice: Japan, Brazil, Flanders and Wallonia

When we consider policy advice production as either political or technical, think tanks that predominantly produce hot advice fall probably somewhere in between the two poles: 'their work is not political, neither technical; . . . the content they create is situated in between: they use scientific statements to build answers in accordance with their ideological narrative, which will be used by politicians' (Pattyn et al., 2017). Party think tanks occupying this function are typically expected to provide immediate facts and figures on certain policy issues should a discussion pop up. They also assist MPs and party leadership in their daily work, preparing parliamentary questions and debates and communicating to the electorate.

This type of function is particularly applicable to the research departments in Japanese political parties. Considering how the actual expertise hails from the government bureaucracy, the parties' think tanks first and foremost spend their time coordinating the party strategy and cooperating with other actors, and developing the overall policy agenda of the party. They have close ties with party leadership, external experts and government administrators. Relying on external expertise, they interpret policy issues to suit the party's interests and communicate such to the different party levels. The LDP's research department PARC, for example, 'coordinates the party's policy positions and works closely with government bureaucrats and interest groups' (Tadashi, 2001, p. 78). Indeed, its main tasks are to organize policy and party meetings and to draft speeches and questions for MPs (Suzuki, 2015).

Even the recent attempts by Japanese political parties to set up their own foundation-type think tanks have done little to alter this key function. The Democratic Party of Japan (DPJ) supported the creation of no less than three think tanks: the Public Policy Platform (Platon), the Citizens Policy Research Council (CPRC), and the Think Net Centre 21 (C21). However, none of these think tanks were created to actually generate cold advice. Rather, they were intended to gather input from different stakeholders and interest groups. Platon and the CPRC aspire specifically to engage citizens in debate, aiming 'to set policy agendas for resolving social issues'. Similarly, the function of C21, 'rather than focussing only on the study of mid-term and long-term policy agendas', was to develop 'networks with other think tanks and specialists' (Tadashi, 2001, p. 79). Hence the fact is that Japanese party think tanks—both the research departments and the external foundations—focus less on providing research input and more on fulfilling their function in political marketing, gathering input from networks and generating public debate (Suzuki, 2015).

As such, the Japanese party think tanks—in all their different forms—can be seen as mainly knowledge brokers and knowledge consumers. They do not produce knowledge themselves, but rather consume the analyses provided by the bureaucracy and act as intermediaries between various stakeholders—e.g., bureaucracy, party leadership, rank and file, experts, industry and civil society. Moreover, they are not sought out by politicians as a source of cold advice, but are conceived as party institutes that gather input and generate hot advice to the party leadership.

Brazilian party think tanks fulfil a similar function. As discussed in the previous section, Brazilian parties are obliged by law to sustain study services, but few are actually involved in research. Most of these institutes busy themselves with 'keeping contact with legislators and the rank and file, and disseminating party materials' (de Souza, 2001, p. 140). They make sure that party members are up to date with the latest news and form a bridge between the parties' upper echelons and the militants. For example, the way the Liberal Front Party's Tancredo Neves Institute (ITN) is involved in research is more akin to a publishing and dissemination outlet for analyses done by other think tanks, rather than actually delivering themselves (de Souza, 2001).

Brazilian party think tanks thus act as both knowledge brokers and knowledge consumers. On the one hand they are very active in gathering expert analyses from external sources, such as private think tanks. On the other hand they act as a platform for all kinds of organizations and researchers to discuss policy issues. They are also intermediaries between the different levels of the party hierarchy. Their focus is clearly short term, as they are mainly active in processing information on salient topics and political events.

The Belgian parties' study departments to a large extent also perform such a function. The Belgian political system—which is characterized by strong electoral motives, rapid time cycles and an abundance of stakeholders—does not allow for rational long-term research to be conducted by study departments. Rather, every new idea is immediately checked for its short-term electoral impact at the different governmental levels, thereby pushing rational long-term research to the fringes of activity. Indeed, these departments 'will help formulate parliamentary questions, will assist their ministers, contribute to the content of electoral programmes, and prepare flash cards for public debates' (Pattyn et al., 2017).

Still, there is a lot of variation among Belgian party think tanks. All of them focus largely on providing their mother party with hot advice, but some claim nonetheless to put this advice in a longer-term ideological perspective. For instance, Etopia, the party think tank of the Francophone green party Ecolo, is very much focused on setting a longer-term agenda away from day-to-day politics. The political department of Ecolo, in turn, is busy responding to the daily party political frenzy. By contrast, the Institut Emile Vandervelde (IEV) of the Francophone Parti Socialiste is a very proactive provider of advice, leaving party officials no discretion and writing very detailed notes to their MPs on what to say—sometimes also being physically present during political negotiations (Pattyn et al., 2017). Overall, Belgian party think tanks are therefore more commonly producers of hot advice than of cold advice. They advise party officials on how to address immediate policy issues, at times from a longer-term perspective, but do not perform long-term analytical research as such.

b. Cold Advice: US, Canada, Germany, Netherlands, EU

Cold advice is typically rational and long term in nature, and depending on the party think tank's autonomy may also be somewhat more neutral and devoid of ideological bias. Unlike those party think tanks that focus on hot advice, these party think tanks will try to avoid getting carried away in the frenzy of day-to-day politics, and instead base their analyses on a broader perspective and more complete information. Cold advice does not respond to political events, but seeks to address a policy problem in all its complexity.

This is the case in North America. As explained above, most American and Canadian political parties rely solely on independent private think tanks to provide policy analysis, investing very little in in-house analytical capacities. Rich (2001) argues that in the US there are generally two kinds of political think tanks. On the one hand, contract-based think tanks 'typically observe standards of neutrality and objectivity in research, maintain a relatively low public profile when promoting research, and are most active in the evaluation of government policies and programmes' (Rich, 2001, p. 53). On the other hand, civil society or industry-sponsored think tanks 'tend to observe a wider range of standards and often promote their research to achieve a higher profile' (Rich, 2001, p. 53). Although these groups generally ensure consistency with the priorities of their sponsors, civil-society-based think tanks have a more direct incentive to influence and therefore tend to produce more research in accordance with the legislative agenda. Contrarily, long-term 'evaluation research is time and resource intensive and produces work that rarely results in products directly suiting the needs or demands of policymakers' (Rich, 2001, p. 59). As such, although experts and researchers of independent American research centres provide important cold advice to policymakers, one can even in this instance observe a difference between freezing cold advice—i.e., evaluations with a largely objective scientific perspective—and somewhat lukewarm advice—i.e., rational research with an agenda.

A similar situation unfolds in Canada, where parties predominantly rely on external input for advice. Cross (2005) refers to a study by the Royal Commission on Electoral Reform and Party Financing, which has quaintly put forward the choices Canadian political parties have made to focus almost exclusively on elections. It follows that they are 'much less interested in discussing and analysing political issues that are not connected directly to winning the next election, or in attempting to articulate the broader values of the party' (Royal Commission vol.1, p. 292, in Cross, 2005, p. 622).

As a result, Canadian parties have fewer ties with political think tanks than their American counterparts. Private think tanks are called upon on an ad hoc basis and only for very specific purposes. Research provided by private think tanks is made to fit the arguments prepared by party officials, leaving little room for deliberation 'removed from a party's immediate political imperatives' (Cross, 2005, p. 626). This results in a public political debate that is highly circular and dominated by parliamentary groups that 'have little capacity to develop new, detailed policy positions' (Cross, 2005, p. 626).

North American party think tanks are in fact private think tanks that sell their analytical services to political parties. The parties and their departments themselves do not as such produce their own knowledge, nor do they act as intermediaries or provide a forum. Rather, they consume the information prepared and seasoned by private think tanks, and adapt these to their own needs and wishes. Although this system of patronage holds that these private think tanks may adapt their analyses to the wishes of their patrons, overall they produce rational and long-term cold advice to political parties that is generally objective in its outlook.

In contrast, the advice produced by Dutch and German party think tanks has a stronger ideological bias. A study conducted by Timmermans, van Rooyen and Voerman shows that the Dutch party think tanks spend most of their time analysing (1) the organization of government and democracy (17.8%), (2) party values and principles (17.6%), and (3) overall international affairs (16.4%). With domestic civil rights coming in as a distant fourth, it becomes clear that these party think tanks 'tend to emphasize themes relating to the organization of the state, the international environment, and to the fundamentals of the party' (Timmermans et al., 2013, p. 191). Concrete policy issues such as the economy or public health receive much less research attention. This is remarkable, to say the least, as these topics feature much more strongly on the electoral agenda.

As such, although government programmes or parliamentary agendas are not usually loaded with fundamental ideological or philosophical references, the Dutch parties' think tanks seem to generally attribute great attention to these issues. Timmermans et al. (2013) explain this according to the parties' government or opposition status. Although overall attention to fundamental issues is high, attention to political-ideological issues is significantly higher when a party is in opposition than when a party is in government. This is likely because being in government forces a party and its think tank to engage in practical policy-technical issues. On the contrary, being in opposition leaves more room to reflect on fundamental issues that question the party values and the overall political system.

Grunden (2013) makes an even broader case for the German *Stiftungen*. He argues that political parties somehow need to define their 'right to exist'—i.e., their societal anchoring, legitimacy, identity and branding. Embedding concrete policy issues into an ideological discourse that strengthens the party's legitimacy is therefore just as crucial for the party's existence as proposing concrete solutions to that issue. Connecting pragmatic solutions to moral legitimations gives the party its identity, which in turn justifies its actions.

The German parties' *Stiftungen* fulfil largely this role of connecting the parties' policy actions with an ideological, legitimizing discourse. The tasks assigned to the foundations are broad, and include 'educational, research-oriented and international activities' (Thunert, 2001, p. 184). Although different foundations have different working agendas, generally 'international networking with like-minded civil society organization is one of their most important functions' (Thunert, 2001, p. 184). In this broad societal role, the foundations hammer out and update the political ideology they represent by adding contemporary political issues to their discourse. As such, the *Stiftungen* also play a major role in their mother party's ideological evolution over time. Throughout the 1990s, for example, the liberal Friedrich Naumann Foundation was active in 'testing the ground for new and generally more radical . . . ideas than the party establishment initially was ready to accept'—but now these radical ideas are part of the liberal party's programme (Thunert, 2001, p. 185).

The Dutch and German party think tanks thus fulfil both tasks of brokering and producing knowledge. Liaising with like-minded institutions, individuals and organizations is one of their core functions, but they also produce their own analyses on political and policy issues. These analyses clearly belong to the cold advice category, as they are not responses to fresh political events, but are conducted in a long-term and rational perspective—albeit from a distinct and unambiguous ideological point of view.

The political foundations that have recently been established at the European level have largely been fashioned after the German model. For one, these European foundations 'emphasise the long-term nature of their activities, which consequently leaves the day-to-day politics to the Europarties and the political groups' (Gagatek & Van Hecke, 2014, p. 95). Moreover, Roland Freudenstein, Head of Research of the Centre for European Studies (since 2014 called the Wilfried Martens Centre for European Studies) of the European People's Party, claimed that the European political foundations 'produce content, provide a forum for people and ideas to meet, emphasize certain issues and throw them into the public, reinforce things that are already there, and thereby promote the goals of our political family' (Gagatek & Van Hecke, 2014, p. 96). Similar to the German *Stiftungen*, the content they produce has a clear long-term perspective, but they do not shy away from presenting this cold advice from a distinct ideological angle. As such, these foundations are mostly active as knowledge brokers that connect various people and organizations and promote public discussion. This also highlights a fundamental difference between the German and European political foundations, as European political foundations are established as umbrella organizations for national party think tanks among which they strive to generate debate and exchange.

c. A Typology of Party Think Tank Functions

The above assessment makes clear that categorizing the various functions of party think tanks is a complicated feat. The discussion has built on Craft and Howlett's (2012) distinction between

Policy Analysis by Political Party Think Tanks

hot and cold advice. However, while the distinction between the delivery of long-term rational analyses and short-term analyses based on incomplete information is important, there is a further distinction related to the context of political parties—namely that between applied and fundamental analysis. The hot/cold distinction relates mainly to the researchers' general approach to their work—i.e., short term based on political events or long term based on analytical facts—while the applied/fundamental distinction relates to the actual topic of these analyses.

Applied analyses focus on the policy-technical side of political parties' activities, and fundamental analyses (in the context of party study centres) focus on the political-ideological side of things. When considering the centres that are engaged in cold advice, the importance of this nuance becomes clear. Compare for instance the Canadian and German party think tanks: while Canadian researchers focus on the more-or-less objective technicalities of applied policy, the German *Stiftungen* have a much stronger ideological predisposition to deal with fundamental questions.

Regardless of how they gather their information—as brokers, consumers or producers—party think tanks deliver advice that can be distinguished according to the hot/cold and applied/fundamental axes. Based on these two axes, one can identify four general types of party think tank functions, as indicated in Figure 16.1.

The first type is that of ideological guardians, i.e., a party think tank that combines long-term analyses with ideologically focused activities. Staff members working for such think tanks will produce studies that strongly reflect the political-ideological line and will elaborate on the party's foundational principles. This is particularly the case in Germany, the EU and the Netherlands, where political foundations and research institutes embed the actions of their mother party in strong ideological rhetoric.

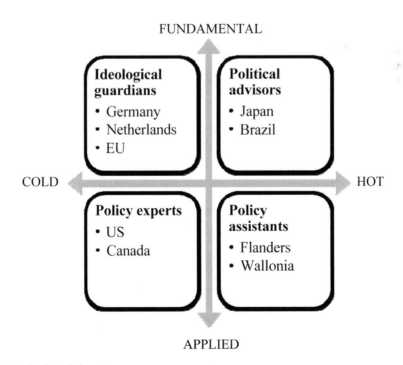

Figure 16.1 Think tank functions

The second type of party think tanks can be labelled as political advisors. They consider fundamental issues, albeit from a short-term view. They are mostly interested in the political-strategic (not the policy-technical) value of a certain policy issue and aim to make the 'right' connection between party and issue—they are known as 'spin doctors'. The Japanese and Brazilian party think tanks are clear cases of this function, as they are important assayers of their mother party's political actions.

A third type of party think tank can be denoted as policy assistants, i.e., those who assist MPs with applied policy-related issues in the short term. Whereas this function is commonly performed by parliamentary assistants, in some instances party think tanks also perform this function. This is particularly the case in most Belgian party think tanks, which often assist their MPs with questions and speeches.

The fourth and final type of party think tanks can be described as policy experts, i.e., they perform research focusing on more technical long-term policy issues. This is the most typical academic-style function of a think tank, and offers parties valuable information about applied policy choices and longer-term outcomes. The American and Canadian private think tanks that work for political patrons clearly belong to this category.

While this typology is helpful in understanding the various functions of political party think tanks according to the type of advice and the topic of analysis, the various possible functions are not mutually exclusive. If the above analysis has showed anything at all, it is that political party think tanks often perform several functions simultaneously, or switch between various roles depending on the particular period of the electoral cycle. In addition, it should be noted that some of these functions could equally be taken up by other entities or actors within or outside the party structure.

Conclusion

The picture of political party think tanks emerging from the above analysis is one of great diversity. This chapter confirms the heterogeneity of party think tanks worldwide, their party-specific nature and the consequential difficulty when trying to compare them. Nonetheless, the chapter has developed on the scarce existing literature in an attempt to create some order in this apparent chaos. It has categorized party think tanks according to two perspectives: autonomy and function. Whereas the former refers to the formal, financial and ideological distance between the mother party and its think tanks, the latter is understood as the nature of the advice party think tanks provide.

As could be expected, the autonomy of party think tanks varies significantly between and within countries. While Brazilian parties are obliged by law to established and maintain in-house think tanks, the non-research nature of these think tanks forces them to seek additional advice from external research centres. A similar situation exists in Japan, where parties have large and long-standing study departments, but are dependent on external input to such an extent that they have recently experimented with establishing semi-independent think tanks. Contrarily, Canadian and American parties almost exclusively rely on independent private think tanks. The Netherlands and Germany are typical cases of yet another tradition, where parties work closely with semi-independent and state-funded political foundations. In Belgium both systems exist, with the Walloon parties working with political foundations and Flemish parties having a long tradition of internal study departments.

Regarding function, the chapter based its approach on Craft and Howlett's (2012) distinction between hot and cold advice. Although this distinction proved a useful analytical perspective, the analysis showed that a further division between applied and fundamental research is necessary in the context of party think tanks. Four possible functions of party think tanks were presented: ideological guardians (cold/fundamental), policy experts (cold/applied), political advisors (hot/fundamental) and policy assistants (hot/applied).

The German, Dutch and European Union political foundations can be viewed mainly as ideological guardians, while the North American research institutes primarily provide policy expertise to political patrons. Among those think tanks that focus on hot advice, the Japanese and Brazilian party think tanks provide short-term strategic advice to their mother party, while the Belgian party think tanks provide more policy-technical support. It is important to highlight that the various functions are not mutually exclusive. Political party think tanks often perform several functions simultaneously, or switch between various roles during an electoral cycle.

Overall, the autonomy and functions of party think tanks are contingently determined by a multitude of institutional and agency-related factors. As for the latter, party leadership plays a crucial role. Leadership that is not interested in investing in research (and is not obliged by law to do so) might prioritize an investment in, for instance, external communication. Conversely, leadership may purposely request advice to support pre-existing conceptions or to develop new ideas. Also the position of the mother party—whether in government or in the opposition—seems to impact the functions carried out by their affiliated think tanks. The Dutch case in particular shows clearly how the parties' research institutes are heavily focused on ideological debate when in opposition, but witness an increase in applied analyses output when their mother party joins the government. Ideally, future research should investigate the external validity of this observation.

On a more institutional level, we assume there to be a linkage between a party think tank's level of autonomy and the nature of the policy advice delivered. In countries where there is very little distance between mother party and think tank, such as Japan or Belgium, party think tanks tend to focus more on providing hot advice. The contrary holds for countries with medium/highly autonomous party think tanks, such as Germany or Canada, which generally provide more cold advice. In addition, one should not underestimate the impact of the prevailing political culture and the historical path of a political party. For example, the different historical experiences of German corporatism and American pluralism have unquestionably affected political parties' perception of policy advice, and the Dutch and Belgian histories of political pillarization have likely influenced how political parties perceive political think tanks.

We would advocate more research to confirm these tentative explanations. Political party think tanks are part of the parties' key machinery. Their input plays a crucial role in the formulation of new and original policy ideas, and hence their influence on policy decisions. Systematic cross-national and cross-party research about think tanks is essential to understand the various roles they play and can provide key insights about the conditions under which they become the parties' ideas factories.

Note

1   The Belgian regions of Flanders and Wallonia are considered as two separate cases, as they have two distinct political party systems. The Brussels capital region of Belgium is not considered separately, as in the capital the Flemish and Walloon systems coexist.

References

Craft, J., & Howlett, M. (2012). Policy Formulation, Governance Shifts and Policy Influence: Location and Content in Policy Advisory Systems. *Journal of Public Policy*, *32*(2), 279–298.

Cross, W. (2005). Policy Study and Development in Canada's Political Parties. In L. Dobuzinskis, M. Howlett & D. Laycock (Eds), *Policy Analysis in Canada: The State of the Art* (pp. 610–635). University of Toronto Press.

de Souza, A. (2001). Brazil. In R. K. Weaver & P. B. Stares (Eds), *Guidance for Governance: Comparing Alternative Sources of Public Policy Advice* (pp. 124–156). Japan Centre for International Exchange.

Gagatek, W. & Van Hecke, S. (2014). The Development of European Political Foundations and Their Role in Strengthening Europarties. *Acta Politica, 49*(1), 86–104.

Grunden, T. (2013). From Hand to Mouth: Parties and Policy-Making in Germany. In S. Blum & K. Schubert (Eds), *Policy Analysis in Germany* (pp. 181–195). Bristol, UK: Policy Press.

Hall, P. (1989). *The Political Power of Economic Ideas: Keynesianism across Nations.* Princeton University Press.

Jackson, A. & Baldwin, B. (2005). Policy Analysis by the Labour Movement in a Hostile Environment. In L. Dobuzinskis, M. Howlett & D. Laylock (Eds), *Policy Analysis in Canada: the State of the Art* (pp. 683–716). Bristol, UK: Policy Press.

Lipset, S. M. & Rokkan, S. (1990). Cleavage Structures, Party Systems, and Voter Alignment. In P. Mair (Ed.), *The West European Party System.* Oxford University Press.

Mair, P. (2008). The Challenge to Party Government. *West European Politics, 31*(1), 211–234.

Müller, W. C. & Strom, K. (Eds) (1999). *Policy, Office or Votes? How Political Parties in Western Europe Make Hard Decisions.* Cambridge University Press.

Neto, P. F. D. (2013). Parties and Public Policy: Programmatic Formulation and Political Processing of Constitutional Amendments. In J. Vaitsman, J. Mendes Ribeiro & L. Lobato (Eds), *Policy Analysis in Brazil* (pp. 177–189). Bristol, UK: Policy Press.

Pattyn, V., Van Hecke, S., Brans, M. & Libeer, T. (2014). Tussen Politieke Partijen en Think Tanks: Een Verkennende Analyse van de Vlaamse Partijstudiediensten. *Res Publica, 3,* 293–316.

Pattyn, V., Van Hecke, S., Pirlot, P, Rihoux, B & Brans M (2017). Ideas as Close as Possible to Power: Belgian Political Parties and their Study Centres. In M. Brans & D. Aubin. *Policy Analysis in Belgium.* Bristol, UK: Policy Press.

Rich, A. (2001). United States. In R. K. Weaver & P. B. Stares (Eds), *Guidance for Governance: Comparing Alternative Sources of Public Policy Advice* (pp. 31–70). Tokyo: Japan Centre for International Exchange.

Schuck, P. (1995). The Politics of Rapid Legal Change: Immigration Policy in the 1980s. In M. K. Landy & M. A. Levin (Eds), *The New Politics of Public Policy.* Baltimore, MD: Johns Hopkins University Press.

Suzuki, T. (2015). Policy Analysis and Policy Making by Japanese Political Parties. In Y. Adachi, H. Sukehiro & I. Jun (Eds), *Policy Analysis in Japan* (pp. 165–184). Bristol, UK: Policy Press.

Tadashi, Y. (2001). Japan. In R. K. Weaver & P. B. Stares (Eds), *Guidance for Governance: Comparing Alternative Sources of Public Policy Advice* (pp. 71–88). Tokyo: Japan Centre for International Exchange.

Thunert, M. W. (2001). Germany. In R. K. Weaver & P. B. Stares (Eds), *Guidance for Governance: Comparing Alternative Sources of Public Policy Advice* (pp. 157–206). Tokyo: Japan Centre for International Exchange.

Timmermans, A., van Rooyen, E. & Voerman, G. (2013). Political Party Think Tanks in the Policy Process. In F. van Nispen & P. Scholten (Eds), *Policy Analysis in the Netherlands* (pp. 187–202). Bristol, UK: Policy Press.

17

BUSINESS ASSOCIATIONS AND THE PUBLIC POLICY PROCESS: WHEN DO THEY DO POLICY ANALYSIS?

Aidan R. Vining and Anthony E. Boardman

Introduction

This chapter examines the role of business associations (BAs) in the policy process and, more specifically, the extent to which they conduct policy analysis, primarily focusing on activity in Canada, the UK, the US and Australia. In these countries and those with similar first-past-the-post institutional structures, most BAs are voluntary organizations whose members consist of individual firms.[1] Reveley and Ville (2010, p. 837) define BAs as a distinctive type of 'meta-organization' (Ahrne & Brunsson, 2008), that is, 'organizations whose constituent members are other organizations'. They further describe each as 'a third party member-based organization with a brokerage role, membership of which is voluntary, and whose members retain their distinctive organization identity' (Reveley & Ville, 2010, p. 839).

Trade associations are an important subset of BAs where members consist of firms *in the same industry*: for example, firms in the dairy farming, construction or pharmaceutical industry. Some BAs are considerably narrower in scope and may only include firms in a particular industry segment or niche. Still others are much broader 'umbrella' organizations whose members are from multiple industries (for example, the U.S. National Association of Manufacturers or the Canadian Manufacturers' Association) (Windmuller & Gladstone, 1984); are of similar size (for example, the Canadian Federation of Independent Business, which represents small businesses), have similar characteristics and interests (such as women's business associations), or come together on a particular distinctive policy issue (such as the Coalition for Secure and Trade-Efficient Borders). Some organizations may encompass both 'upstream' and 'downstream' firms along a supply chain, such as the Canadian Association of Petroleum Producers, which includes exploration and development companies, producers, refiners and retailers as well as some vertically integrated companies.

BAs tend to dominate lobbying interaction with federal officials. Seven out of the eight organizations that lobby federal officials most frequently on an annual basis are BAs (*Maclean's* Magazine, 2012). Table 17.1 lists these high-interaction BAs, as measured by the number of communication reports filed with the federal lobbyist registry. It also summarizes the policy issues that concern them. This chapter concerns policy analyses of these and similar

Table 17.1 Business associations that have the most contact with Canadian federal officials

Number of contacts★	Name of business association	Some recent issues
178	Canadian Association of Petroleum Producers	Pipeline regulation, streamlining of Fisheries Act, tax credits, Clean Air Act related to greenhouse gas regulations
131	Canadian Bankers Association	Do-not-call list, identity theft laws, accounting rules, corporate income tax, mortgage insurance
113	Canadian Cattlemen's Association	Livestock carcass grading regulations, imports of non-NAFTA beef and veal, financial loan guarantees, animal health
105	The Mining Association of Canada	Environmental assessment regulations, skills training, corporate taxation, remediation of abandoned mines
96	Canadian Federation of Independent Business	Credit card code of conduct, budget recommendations, red tape reduction, Canada Pension Plan increases
95	Alliance Manufacturers and Exporters Canada	Various free trade agreements, climate change, foreign workers programme, research funding
92	Chicken Farmers of Canada	Meat inspection regulations, poultry import tariffs, medicated feed mixing regulations, food safety programs

★ The number of communication reports filed with the federal lobbyist registry.

Source: Maclean's Magazine (2012).

policy issues. Obviously, the specific policy issues that interest BAs change over time and particular BAs vary in the intensity of their lobbying from year to year. In spite of this variation, we would expect BAs in aggregate to always be prominent on such lists. BAs are likely to be similarly active at lobbying at the provincial level, although we have no direct empirical evidence of the intensity of their activity. Although BAs engage in extensive lobbying, this chapter focuses on the extent to which they perform policy analysis prior to influencing policy.

Some individual firms engage in policy analysis. However, we do not consider these analyses for three reasons. First, their focus is primarily on competitive strategy (i.e., market strategy) outcomes. Second, and related, some of these policy analyses are necessary in order to comply with regulatory requirements and to stay in business. Thus, for example, we do not consider safety, efficacy or cost-effectiveness studies of new pharmaceutical products that firms undertake in order to gain approval to market drugs or to have them listed on a government formulary. Third, individual firm analysis does not suffer from the 'two (or more) principals-one agent' problems that BAs typically confront (as we explain below).

Although the composition of BAs can vary considerably, as we have described, the primary goal of an individual member firm of any BA is to maximize its profit.[2] In contrast, BAs themselves are almost always incorporated as not-for-profit organizations. Because BAs represent more than one firm, the goal of a BA is not likely to be totally congruent with the individual goals of any particular member(s) over all issues. The multiple principals' nature of a BA has an important theoretical consequence: while the constituent members of BAs are 'profit-maximizing' entities, it is not useful to model BAs as such.

BA member firms maximize profit by engaging in some mix of competitive strategy, which generally concerns how firms compete against other firms in an industry or market segment, and political strategy (also called non-market strategy), where they try to influence public and regulatory policy. Either strategy may be a source of a firm's competitive advantage (Baron, 1995).

The pursuit of political strategy by an individual firm is generally only sensible for large firms or where a particular public policy has a potentially crucial impact on a firm's profitability or survival. More often, it makes more sense for firms with similar political strategy objectives to cooperate and engage in joint action. By doing so, a constituent firm shares the costs of any political strategy action, and thus reduces its share of the total cost. One potentially important purpose of a BA, therefore, is to try to directly influence public policy to the benefit of member firms, whether by supporting or opposing existing or proposed policies (Vining, Shapiro & Borges, 2005).

Unfortunately, there is relatively little academic research concerning the organization and activities of BAs, especially concerning their role in the development and dissemination of public policy analysis. Schmitter and Streeck (1981, p. 9) noted that 'reliable information on, not to speak of analysis of, the resources, organizational characteristics, activities and strategies of formal associations specialized in the promotion and protection of trade or employer interests is rare'. David, Ginalski, Mach & Rebmann (2007, p. 1) claim that 'this statement still has some relevance more than twenty years later' (see also Ahrne and Brunsson, 2008). More recently, Barnett (2012) describes the current management literature on trade associations as 'anemic'.

This chapter aims to shed some light on the ways in which BAs try to influence the policy process and policy outcomes and, more specifically, on the extent to which BAs conduct policy analyses themselves, or use the policy analysis of others, to influence public policy. Although this chapter focuses on BAs in Canada, the UK, the US and Australia, we believe the framework and concepts we propose for thinking about the role of BAs have relevance in countries with similar institutional arrangements.

A limited amount of previous research on BAs has surveyed them about the nature and extent of the public policy analysis that they undertake (Coleman, 1988; Stritch, 2007). However, different observers may have quite different perceptions about what qualifies as public policy analysis. Therefore, it is not surprising that BAs may claim that they engage in public policy analysis, while analysts argue that they do not produce public policy analysis in a meaningful way or that such analysis essentially amounts to firm competitive strategy.

To address these concerns, we first consider the various definitions of public policy analysis and present what we think are its appropriate boundaries. Next, we develop a simple, issue-based model of the public policy process that situates BAs in that process and discusses the key activities that they undertake. The central question for this chapter is: when do BAs engage in public policy analysis? The decision to do so is a complex one that depends on many factors. We then develop some theoretical arguments about the nature and extent of the policy analyses that they undertake. In doing so, we argue that BAs are unlikely to conduct and publicly disseminate a great deal of public policy analysis. Even where BAs do engage in policy analysis, they are likely to prefer to do so through third parties and to obscure (if not hide) their role in the production of the analysis. Finally, we analyse a random sample of 76 (11.8%) of the BAs in Canada. We categorize them into different types based on the characteristics of their members and analyse the extent to which they conduct policy analyses and make them publicly available on their websites. Each policy analysis that we are able to access is examined to determine whether it is, in our estimation, a policy analysis. As far as we know, our research is the first in-depth examination of the policy analyses actually conducted by BAs.

What Counts as Policy Analysis?

Addressing the provincial (and federal) government, Robin Campbell, the president of the Coal Association of Canada (and a former Alberta Minister of Finance and Minister of the Environment), is quoted as saying 'the government should be investing in new technology and research' and 'making sure that we don't lose our competitive advantage when it comes to our other industries in the province that depend on electricity' rather than phasing out coal-powered power plants that will 'throw people out of work, hurt rural communities and undermine industries by boosting electricity costs' (Cotter, 2015). Are these claims summaries of policy analyses or simply examples of political lobbying that contains little or no analysis? To answer this question with any rigour, one needs to be clear about what counts as policy analysis and what does not.

There are a number of different definitions of public sector policy analysis, henceforth 'policy analysis'. At its broadest, policy analysis can be defined as any pronouncement pertaining to public policy. Somewhat more narrowly, it can be defined as any advice or direction to decision makers in the public sector. Although this definition considers the instrumental aspects of policy analysis, it does not distinguish between political lobbying with analytical support and that with no analytical support. More usefully, Weimer and Vining (2011, p. 24) propose a narrower view of policy analysis that stresses 'client-oriented advice relevant to public decisions and informed by social values'. Many other scholars provide similar definitions of policy analysis (Meltsner, 1976; Beckman, 1977).[3]

The 'client' of analysis may be viewed narrowly or broadly. There may be one target client or multiple clients (Richardson, 2000). Policy analysis is most often directed at 'the government' (i.e. politicians)—indeed, this is the ultimate target of all policy analysis. Government might include all (local, provincial or federal) politicians or it might consist of a subset of politicians, such as, the federal Minister of Health or the Prime Minister or the cabinet. Other potential clients include local, provincial or federal government departments or regulatory bodies (such as the Canadian Radio-television and Telecommunications Commission). The client might be a specific bureaucrat, such as a deputy minister or her assistant—or, most broadly, the client might be the public 'writ large' or other policy researchers, with the expectation that there will then be a knock-on process that eventually influences government in the desired direction. Sometimes the client may be a supranational governing body (for example, the EU) or a foreign government.

We argue that there are three ways in which policy analysis can be 'informed by social values' (more, if we include combinations of these three values). One way is to examine science-based facts relevant to a given policy issue. Indeed, in both North America and Europe, many laws require government agencies to base their rulemaking on relevant scientific evidence. For example, in the United States, food safety regulations are based on the science-based transnational system known as Hazard Analysis and Critical Control Point (Wengle, 2016). Second, an argument can be based on some version of aggregate social efficiency—that is, allocative efficiency or economic efficiency. Third, an argument can be made on some notion of equity or fairness, either substantive or procedural. Substantive equity concerns the extent to which the outcomes (i.e., the distribution of benefits or costs) is fair to some specific group (defined in terms of income, race, gender, etc.). Procedural equity concerns the fairness of the process: was each group treated equally, irrespective of the policy outcome? While these normative criteria are conceptually distinct, in practice it is often difficult to disentangle them. Of course, a policy analysis may appeal to more than one (possibly all) of these criteria simultaneously in the form of a multi-goal analysis.

Finally, it is necessary to make a judgment as to whether a social value (for example, efficiency or equity) is a goal in a given analysis. The Coal Association of Canada's argument that Alberta's plan will throw people out of work, hurt rural communities and undermine industries by boosting electricity costs in some larger sense does imply 'social values'. But does it do so in sufficient depth to constitute policy analysis? In our definition, policy analysis requires analysis concerning the impact(s) of the alternative policies on social values. To be convincing, this analysis requires some evidence. At face value, the Coal Association's statement is simply an unsubstantiated claim; one has to look further to determine whether these claims are supported by analysis.

There are a range of definitions of policy analysis that vary in terms of scope or boundaries. One can set a 'low bar', in which a mere assertion that a particular policy is, or will be, bad for the industry, combined with an unsubstantiated fairness or equity argument based on jobs, multipliers or nationality of the firms involved, constitutes a policy analysis. With such a low bar, a larger number of analyses obviously would qualify as policy analyses. In contrast, we argue that to qualify as credible policy analysis, the argument must be directed to a client or clients and contain at least a statement of the issue or problem (rather than a mere statement of symptoms); an analysis of alternative policies based on legitimate social values; and a recommendation (or advice). This represents a higher bar, although not an unrealistically high one.

Business Associations and the Policy Process

There are a number of comprehensive models of the policy process.[4] For the purpose of analysing business associations (BAs), however, we only require a simple framework that explicitly includes BAs in the policy process, while ignoring the complexities of a more comprehensive process model. Our model is summarized in Figure 17.1. It aggregates policy process participants into four major groups: business associations; government actors, including politicians, government administrators, and regulators; aligned coalitions; and opposing coalitions. Our focus is on BAs, which are in row 2. To emphasize this focus, all BA interactions and influences are represented by the thick lines in Figure 17.1. BAs interact considerably with government (row 3), which is the primary target for their analysis, as indicated by the double-headed line between them in the first column. BAs also interact with those firms or BAs from other sectors or interest groups that have goals that are broadly aligned with them on a *specific issue* (row 1), which is also indicated by a thick double-headed line between them in the first column. For example, a citizens' environmental group may help a BA get funding for the development of a new, clean technology, even though this kind of group will be mostly opposed to BAs. Interest groups that oppose BAs on a given issue, such as patient groups opposed to drug price increases, or environmental groups opposed to pipelines or oil tanker traffic, are represented by the bottom row. They also interact primarily with government (row 2), again represented by a double-headed arrow.

Our model is explicitly issue based and has a narrower focus than many other models, such as those based on policy arenas. The particular policy issue may pertain to an existing policy that is under attack, or the issue may be an emerging one, potentially leading to a brand new policy. Government or regulators often signal or communicate new policy issues to BAs. Sometimes, a government may want to make a policy change that it views as beneficial to

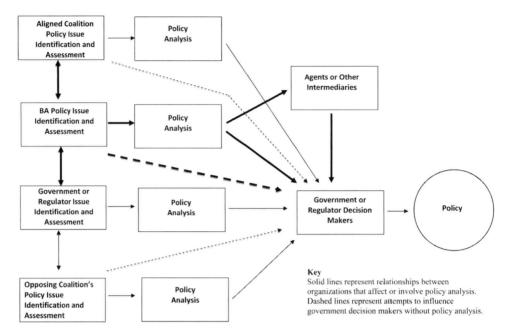

Figure 17.1 The role of business associations in the policy process

society as a whole and may think that a BA may be an ally in effecting change. For example, in 1994 and subsequently, the UK's Department of Trade and Industry (DTI) wanted trade associations to be more influential in contributing to new government initiatives and to help government serve industry better (Bennett, 1997). At other times, government may be considering a policy change that they anticipate businesses will oppose, but believe that it would be advantageous to signal their intentions and learn businesses' views sooner rather than later. In the US, federal agencies are required by law to follow 'notice and comment' procedures, that is, to solicit the views of citizens and take them into account before changing or introducing new agency rules (Yackee & Yackee, 2006). Thus, businesses and BAs, as well as aligned or opposing interest groups, are usually aware of any impending changes that may affect them.

Whatever the origin of a particular policy issue, the first step for all participants in a policy process is to identify and assess the issue to determine their next steps. This stage is shown in the first column of Figure 17.1. More specifically, actors must decide whether they should conduct a policy analysis or not. Except in rare altruistic or strategic circumstances, BAs will only consider conducting policy analysis and subsequently proposing new policy alternatives that are consistent with their interests (Moir & Taffler, 2004). When faced with multiple potential issues, a BA will likely focus on those that have the largest expected net benefit for their members. BAs are much more likely to view the issue as important if it would clearly *reduce* the profitability of the members, such as opening a specific industry to foreign competition.

If the BA decides that some action is appropriate it has two main options. One is to lobby government, which is represented by the (thick) dashed line from 'BA Policy Issue Identification and Assessment' to 'Government or Regulator Decision Makers'. The term 'lobby' is used broadly to include making political contributions, engaging in media campaigns, undertaking advertising aimed at various stakeholders or, more narrowly and directly, meeting with or providing input to members of government responsible in decision making (such as ministers, regulators and deputy ministers). Sometimes, BAs use public relations firms, such as Hill+Knowlton, for this purpose. The second option is to conduct a policy analysis, which is represented by the thicker solid line in Figure 17.1 from the BA Identification and Assessment box to the adjacent Policy Analysis box. The policy analysis may be conducted by the BA or other organizations who are willing to act as an agent for the BA.

If a BA does conduct a policy analysis, then the complete analysis or the conclusions need to be communicated to the appropriate targets. Most importantly, the results need to be distributed to government decision makers directly or through agents, as represented by the thick solid lines in Figure 17.1 from the BA policy analysis box.

Wilson (1980) emphasizes that the purpose of the analysis is to persuade *others*, not the association's own constituency, and therefore the argument or arguments have to be organized to do so: 'Proponents who have a stake in the outcome must make an argument to convince people who do not have a stake, or have a different one' (p. 365). Thus any policy analysis is a strategic document in the technical sense of the word. Policy analyses based on facts or science and conducted by researchers with good credentials generally have high legitimacy and credibility with government and (in most circumstances) with the public. However, policy analyses based purely on efficiency arguments are difficult to get buy-in. Future efficiency gains are often widely distributed and their ultimate resting place is unknown: thus, they have pure public good characteristics and are hard to use to persuade others of the benefits of the policy. BAs that conduct policy analyses themselves have a particular credibility problem because the analysis can be criticized as being merely self-serving profit maximization. Consequently, when efficiency matters, BAs will be tempted to channel the analysis or communication of it through agents, as represented by the thick solid line from the BA policy analysis box to the agents box and then on to government. Both BAs and agents may have incentives to keep the source of the policy analysis itself secret.

It is important to emphasize that BAs or their members do not have to believe that these agents are more credible or legitimate than the BA itself, only that at least one of the other groups view them as such. Given that opposing coalitions (interest groups) and government actors tend to be suspicious of BA goals and motives, whatever the stated goals may be, agents (so-called front groups) will often have more legitimacy and credibility. Unfortunately for the BA, this means that credibility is negatively correlated with (source) transparency.

There are almost always opposing interests in a policy debate as represented in the bottom row in Figure 17.1. Some opposing coalitions have the capability and incentives to conduct their own policy analysis, which they directly communicate to decision makers. Mostly, they lobby decision makers, as indicated by the dashed line. Usually opposing interest groups have fewer incentives to use third-party communication. Indeed, if they are large-number, individual member organizations that represent a significant number of voters, they usually have an incentive to publicize who they are and what their analysis is.

The actual policy outcome in any given issue context will depend on the strength and stability of the different coalitions, consistent with the advocacy coalition framework (Jenkins-Smith & Sabatier, 1993). To some extent, it may also depend on the quality of the policy analyses conducted by the relevant parties (the BA and its coalition partners, the opposing coalition and branches of government) and how they are communicated (Smith, Fooks, Gilmore, Collin & Weishaar, 2015).

The Decision to Engage in Policy Analysis by Business Associations

Oversimplifying somewhat, BAs engage in two kinds of activities: the pursuit of political strategies and the provision of membership services. Political strategies, which are reflected in Figure 17.1, include all types of lobbying, forming coalitions and funding coalition partners, conducting policy analyses, trying to influence policy indirectly by targeting 'influencers', supporting particular politicians or political parties, making political campaign contributions, engaging in media campaigns, advertising aimed at stakeholders, and meeting directly with government bureaucrats or politicians. The targets are external. In contrast, membership services are internal and directed to members (Olson, 1965). This set of activities includes providing networking opportunities for members, which may occur at breakfast or lunch meetings; collecting and disseminating data, often focusing on the sector that members are in, such as industry-wide socio-demographic data on customers; and informing members about current policy issues (e.g., proposed tax and regulatory changes) or other issues that may be relevant to them.

Informal evidence suggests that most BAs spend more time working on member services rather than political strategies. When the UK's DTI introduced policies to work more closely with BAs, Bennett (1997) argues that the chief response of BAs was 'to develop their internal management procedures and relations to their members rather than support Government's emphasis on promoting the competiveness of their members' (p. 5). What affects BAs' decision to engage in political strategies and, more specifically, to conduct policy analysis?

There are a number of different ways to classify the political strategies of firms and BAs. In one influential model, Hillman and Hitt (1999) categorize non-market activities into information strategies, financial incentive strategies and constituency-building strategies. Information strategies target political decision makers by providing information and include 'such tactics as lobbying . . . reporting research and survey results; commissioning research/ think-tank research projects; testifying as expert witnesses and in hearings before other government bodies; and supplying decision makers with position papers or technical reports' (p. 834). Performing policy analysis falls within this category. (Other political strategies fall into Hillman and Hitt's other two categories.) However, such general political strategy theories are too broad for understanding the kind of narrower activities that we are analysing here.

The provision of information that aspires to influence public policy to members of a BA is typically a 'pure' collective (i.e., public) good. The defining characteristics of this kind of good are that it is both 'non-rivalrous in consumption' and 'non-excludable'. Non-rivalrous in consumption means that all BA members can consume the good or service, and one member's consumption does not affect the consumption of others. However, this does not mean that all firms in a BA value the good equally. Non-excludability means that an individual firm cannot be prevented from accessing the information. Not all information is both non-rivalrous and non-excludable. Some information can be kept secret—it is excludable from some parties, or access can be restricted to outsiders (i.e., non-members). However, as discussed in the section on policy analysis, the ultimate target of policy analysis is government, and once a policy analysis has been communicated to government, it becomes a pure collective good.[5]

This characteristic is likely to put a damper on the conduct of policy analysis, and its distribution to government, for two reasons. First, because policy analysis is a pure collective good, no member of a BA has an incentive to contribute any financial or other resources to its production, except in the small numbers situation (Godwin, Ainsworth & Godwin, 2013). They would, of course, like to free ride on policy analysis paid for by others. Second, members

Policy Analysis by Business Associations

of the opposing coalition can free ride as well. They can access the policy analysis and take selective parts of the analysis and use it directly or twist it to suit their purposes.

In addition, the justification for funding can be difficult and requires a balancing act. On one hand, a larger BA membership means there are more analytic resources and a reduction in the per-member (average) cost of any analysis. Furthermore, BAs with broader membership bases represent more firms and are, therefore, more likely to have external validity with government and other stakeholders. The input of broad-based BAs that represent wide sectors of the economy is harder for policymakers to ignore; their breadth of representation gives them greater legitimacy and greater visibility in public arenas. In contrast, Coleman (1988) suggests that, due to the fragmented nature of BAs in Canada, government is not as likely to consult with them. In the UK, the government has explicitly expressed its preference to deal with a few umbrella BAs rather than a bunch of fragmented ones. In 1995, the UK government explicitly encouraged 'the development of well-resourced and effective trade associations . . . the more effective trade associations and professional bodies become, the more influence they will exert on government and the greater the service they will render to their industries' (HM Government, 1995, p. 52).

On the other hand, as the membership increases in size and breadth of sectors, the BA's heterogeneity increases. This presents a problem for the BA executives because, as heterogeneity increases, so does the diversity of individual members' goals. It also becomes less likely that a policy analysis will provide net benefits to an 'average' member. As Hughes, Magat and Ricks (1986) observe, some policies and regulations 'are distributional, with some firms gaining profits and other firms losing'. For example, firms within an industry that import inputs, such as parts, or export finished goods are more likely to favour trade liberalizing policies than other firms in the same industry that do neither. A current member will be tempted to exit the BA when it perceives that its benefits are lower than its cost of membership.

BA executives are often subject to competing pressures from members. At the same time, BAs themselves are generally non-profit organizations and the backgrounds and goals of BA executives may differ from those of the members. In effect, therefore, there are multiple principals and a single agent. This characteristic is likely to have a negative effect on BA organizational behaviour and performance as compared with the more traditional principal-agent situation (Vining & Weimer, 2016). Vining, Boardman and Moore (2014) suggest that mixed enterprises (i.e., companies in which both the private sector and government sector have significant property rights), which also have multiple principals and a single agent, may result in 'the worst of both worlds'. BA executives may be confused about whose needs they should focus on, leading to inaction. They may try to meet the needs of all sub-groups of members, but this can be tricky, it may waste resources and may lead to cognitive dissonance. Sometimes executives act strategically by playing one sub-group off against another and maximizing their own utility at the expense of members.

The situation is further complicated because BA executives have to face government or regulators whose primary goal is often external legitimacy or social value.[6] Often BA executives are either former lobbyists or politicians who have a good understanding of government and how to 'sell' to government. But they may not have a good understanding of business. At the same time, BA members want to maximize profit and may not have a good understanding of government or of the appropriate strategies for influencing government. Obviously, member profit maximization, except in quite limited issue circumstances, does not have external legitimacy and will not be useful in persuading others (Dowling & Pfeffer, 1975). This goal must remain unstated in any policy analysis and any face-to-face meetings with government, or be, at most, highly subservient to other goals. Members of BAs do not naturally consider their responsibilities to society at large and may not understand the importance of social values in affecting policy decisions. Therefore, it is likely to be difficult for BA executives to get their profit-maximizing members to 'buy in' to performing a policy analysis or to agree on how the BA should communicate with government or regulators. These executives may have to 'manage' the relationship between two primary groups that really don't understand each other.

These arguments, combined with the earlier discussion concerning the credibility of BAs, suggest that BAs themselves are often not motivated to conduct a policy analysis and distribute it to government. Of course, it is not surprising that a BA might decide to keep a policy analysis secret if the analysis ends up recommending the 'wrong' answer. Ex ante, however, it is hard to see why a BA would conduct a policy analysis if it does not expect that it is going to be used to try to influence government. BAs are more able to both perform analysis and hide its source when it is channelled through a third party. The third party will have more credibility if it is seen as not as directly concerned with the profit-maximizing goal of BA members. Also, the BA can select an agent that has the necessary specialized skills to conduct the policy analysis. In contrast, most BAs only employ a few administrative staff and do not have the capacity to conduct meaningful policy analysis (Coleman, 1988, p. 45). The third party could also lobby government without releasing the policy analysis, or further subcontract the lobbying task to a different organization. Either way, the BA retains some control of the policy analysis and its uses.

This section argues that BAs are likely to conduct few policy analyses, either by themselves or contracted out. It is difficult to conduct policy analyses (Vining & Weimer, 2017). They are expensive and not many BAs have the skills or resources to conduct them. Even if they did, alternative strategies, including direct lobbying, are often preferable. Members of BAs often have heterogeneous preferences and want government to pursue different goals. Large 'umbrella' BAs may have more credibility with government but have members with more divergent preferences. These preferences often differ from the goals of the BA or the goals of its executives. Thus, it is often difficult for BA executives to justify the expense of conducting policy analysis to profit-maximizing BAs. Policy analysis is more likely to be conducted by BAs with relatively narrow scopes because their members' preferences are more likely to be homogeneous. However, for this very reason, these BAs tend to have fewer members and the average cost is higher. Therefore, the expected net benefits have to be very high.

Analysis of Business Associations in Canada

This section examines the characteristics of BAs in Canada and analyses the extent to which they engage in and publish policy analyses. First, we compiled a list of BAs in Canada and examined some characteristics of these organizations, including size of membership and industry scope. Second, we searched for policy analyses conducted by these organizations that are in the public domain, primarily by going to BA websites. Third, we examined the nature of these policy analyses to determine whether they met our definition of policy analysis and, if not, why not. We find that few BAs conduct 'real' policy analysis and make them publicly available.

Our analysis began with Industry Canada's Directory of Business and Trade Associations in Canada, which lists 760 organizations. However, many of these organizations are not BAs in our view and are not included in the subsequent analysis. On the other hand, the Directory does not include some organizations that we consider to be BAs, or at least are close enough for analytic purposes. We therefore augmented the list of BAs by adding those referred to in

Maclean's Magazine (2012), from newspapers and by searching the internet. Our final population consists of 643 BAs. From this list we randomly sampled 76 BAs (11.8%).

We identified three categories of BAs: industry-based associations, such as The Quebec Hardware and Building Material Association; professional associations, such as The Canadian Gemmological Association; or chambers of commerce, such as St. Albert and District Chamber of Commerce. Using this categorization, 45% of our sample is chambers of commerce, a vast majority of which are local or regional in membership, as shown in the top panel of Table 17.2. The second largest group (32%) consists of industry-based associations, most of which are national in scope. 24% of are professional associations, most of which are provincial in scope. Membership size varies enormously. Some national, industry-based BAs are relatively small and have fewer than 100 members, but others are very large. The Canadian Federation of Independent Business, for example, has more than 109,000 members.

Based on information available on BA websites, only 24 of the 76 BAs in our sample engage in some form of policy analysis and make the findings publicly available. However, most of these analyses provide general information to members about policy issues, and do not appear intended to influence policymakers or to change a particular policy. For example, The Quebec Trucking Association analyses government policy and communicates it to members and the public. The Association's annual reports do mention government advocacy, but no advocacy-related material is published on its website. It is possible that in some cases 'real' policy analyses are available in the 'members only' section of websites. For example, the Automotive Industries Association of Canada claims that it has produced and published policy analyses, but those pages are only available to association members. After carefully reviewing the published policy analyses, we are only able to identify six (8%) BAs that conduct and disseminate real policy analyses. Three of these are industry-based associations, one is a professional association and two are from chambers of commerce, as shown in the bottom panel of Table 17.2.

Table 17.2 Canadian business associations: scope and production of policy analyses

Variable	Business Associations			
	Industry-based	Professional Association	Chamber of Commerce	Total
Geographic Scope of Membership:				
Local/Regional	0	1	29	30
Provincial	7	10	3	20
National	17	7	2	26
Total	24	18	34	76
BAs that Produce Some Policy Analysis:				
Local/Regional	0	0	7	7
Provincial	0	1	2	3
National	8	6	0	14
Total	8	7	9	24
BAs that Produce 'Real' Policy Analysis:				
Local/Regional	0	0	1	1
Provincial	0	0	1	1
National	3	1	0	4
Total	3	1	2	6

Note: Based on a random sample of 11.8% of BAs in Canada.

Although two chambers of commerce conduct 'real' policy analyses, they are very narrowly focused on local interests. Therefore, the following discussion focuses on the other four organizations. In our view, these policy analyses could claim some external validity or are able to make a case that aligns BA members' interests with broader societal interests. For example, the Architectural Institute of British Columbia (AIBC) could plausibly claim that proposed regulatory changes it opposed would create longer delays for consumers (decrease allocative inefficiency) and/or would create inefficiencies in government (also decrease allocative efficiency). Similarly, the Ontario Environmental Industry Association (ONEIA) argues for policies that have environmental or climate change benefits (increases in allocative efficiency). Both BAs also make arguments based on relevant scientific evidence. A notable, although not surprising, characteristic of these policy analyses is that they do not pit members' interests against each other. Implementation of the policy recommendations advocated by both the AIBC and ONEIA would benefit all members individually. This is consistent with our theory that BAs are more likely to provide policy analyses where members have homogeneous interests.

The Canadian Electricity Association (CEA) is one of the few BAs that has produced multiple policy analyses. Most of the corporate utility members are regulated regional utilities that do not compete against one another and share a common interest in a more 'friendly' regulatory environment, investment in new infrastructure and expansion of markets (especially in the US). The CEA's arguments are based on allocative efficiency (greater technical efficiency and lower costs to consumers) as well as on environmental grounds. In contrast, some members of the Canadian Association of Petroleum Producers (CAPP) do compete directly against each other. However, they also share a common interest in a more 'friendly' regulatory environment (and royalty payments) and expansion of markets (especially in the US). These issues are extremely important to many members, especially those operating in Alberta. Both CEA and CAPP specifically target a non-domestic government. While their arguments clearly serve their aggregate profit interests, some have social value related to job creation, the environment or maintenance of government revenues.

Conclusions

This chapter examines the role of BAs in the policy process and, more specifically, in conducting policy analysis. We argue that, for many reasons, BAs are unlikely to undertake much policy analysis. First, producing credible policy analysis is difficult and many BAs do not have the necessary skilled personnel or other resources to do so. Second, BA members—especially in large, umbrella BAs—may have different interests and disagree on the policies they want government to pursue. Third, BA executives may find it impossible to reconcile members' conflicting goals and preferred policies. Indeed, executives have strong incentives to avoid these issues because of potential dissatisfaction and loss of members. Fourth, executives may find it difficult to communicate with government and focus on social value in a way that profit-maximizing members understand. Often, members do not understand that their goal of profit maximization does not have high external legitimacy and BA executives cannot use it manifestly in arguments with government. Fifth, BAs with small membership do not have much political clout either in the eyes of government or other stakeholders. Sixth, the public good nature of policy analyses once they have been communicated to government means that BA members can free ride, benefitting from the production of the analysis without necessarily having to contribute to paying for it. Seventh, alternative strategies, such as direct or indirect lobbying, may be more cost-effective than policy analysis. BAs may reduce some of these problems by having intermediaries conduct the policy analysis and use it to lobby government. In both cases, BAs or front intermediaries may conduct policy analysis to improve the persuasiveness of their position and not release it to government or the public.

There is one caveat to this conclusion. Many governments in Canada have begun to ensure that corporate donations to politicians and political parties are more transparent and to severely limit the amounts (Benzie, 2016). As we noted, political contributions are one of the three types of non-market strategy. To the extent that information strategies and financial incentive strategies are substitutes, which is likely to be the case, the decreasing attractiveness of financial strategies may push businesses to encourage BAs to do more information strategies, including policy analysis.

By their nature, all dialectics are uneasy, but the one represented here regarding policy analysis is particularly uneasy. It is not easy to reconcile the tension between firm/industry profit and 'fairness' to industries on one side versus social efficiency and fairness to non-business interests on the other, so as to develop a coherent policy analysis with wide and transparent appeal. As we have argued earlier, a pleasing synthesis is likely to occur when a BA ignores profit and downplays their equity demands and relies instead on scientific argument and analysis. One consequence is that professional BAs are best suited to engage in this form of argumentation. Within their admittedly narrow areas of (issue) interest and expertise, their scientific knowledge will be largely deferred to: no one messes with lawyers, accountants or doctors on their home turf.

Notes

1   In contrast, BAs in France, Germany, Japan and many other countries play a more formal, institutionalized role in the public policy process. In these countries governments may mandate membership and the payment of dues.
2   Some firms purport to engage in behaviour that benefits society, as Bronn and Vidaver-Cohen (2009) discuss. However, many of these goals are probably highly correlated with long-run profit maximization. The profit maximization goal of members differentiates BAs from other representative organizations that engage in public policy analysis, such as think tanks, trade union associations or other 'peak organizations' (to use Australian terminology).
3   Gormley (2007) provides a useful overview of different definitions. Other scholars place more emphasis on the analytic content and structure of policy analysis and relatively less emphasis on the relationship to specific clients (Williams, 1971; Dunn, 1981).
4   The following policy process frameworks have considerable support: the advocacy coalition framework (Jenkins-Smith & Sabatier, 1993), the multiple-streams framework (Kingdon, 2003; Zahariadis, 1999), policy incrementalism theory (Wildavsky, 1964; Fenno, 1966; Lindblom, 1959), path dependency theory (David, 1985; Hacker, 2002) and punctuated equilibrium theory (Baumgartner & Jones, 1991, 1993).
5   Even if government does not want to allow access to others, it is still difficult to prevent others from acquiring this information because of access to information legislation and for other reasons.
6   Politicians, who are often the intended targets of policy analysis, have political objectives. However, they generally do not want the political popularity of a policy made explicit.

References

Ahrne, Göran and Nils Brunsson. 2008. *Meta-Organizations*. Cheltenham, UK: Edward Elgar.
Barnett, Michael L. 2012. "One Voice, But Whose Voice? Exploring What Drives Trade Association Activity". *Business & Society* 52(2): 213–244.
Baron, David P. 1995. *Business and Its Environment*. 2nd edn, Upper Saddle River, NJ: Prentice Hall.
Baumgartner, Frank R. and Bryan D. Jones. 1991. "Agenda Dynamics and Policy Subsystems". *The Journal of Politics* 53 (4): 1044–1074.

Baumgartner, Frank R., and Bryan D. Jones. 1993. *Agendas and Instability in American Politics*. 2nd ed. Chicago: University of Chicago Press.,

Beckman, Arnold. 1977. "Policy Analysis in Government: Alternatives to 'Muddling Through'". *Public Administration Review* 37(3): 221–22.

Bennett, Robert J. 1997. "The Relations Between Government and Business Associations in Britain: An Evaluation of Recent Developments". *Policy Studies* 18(1): 5–33.

Benzie, Robert. 2016. "Liberals' Legislation Bans Union, Corporate Donations, Reforms Fundraising in Ontario". *The Toronto Star*, 17 May.

Bronn, Peggy Simcic and Deborah Vidaver-Cohen. 2009. "Corporate Motives for Social Initiative: Legitimacy, Sustainability, or the Bottom Line?" *Journal of Business Ethics* 87: 91–109.

Coleman, William. 1988. *Business and Politics: A Study of Collective Action*. Montreal: McGill-Queen's University Press.

Coleman, William. 1990. "State Traditions and Comprehensive Business Associations: A Comparative Structural Analysis". *Political Studies* 38: 231–52.

Cotter, John. 2015, "Coal Association of Canada Warns Alberta Against Power Plant Phase-Out". *Globe and Mail*, November 26: B5,

David, Paul A. 1985. "Clio and the Economics of Qwerty". *The American Economic Review* 75 (2): 332–337.

David, Thomas, Stephanie Ginalski, Andre Mach and Frederic Rebmann. 2007. "Networks of Coordination: Swiss Business Associations as an Intermediary between Business, Politics and Administration During the 20th Century". *Business and Politics* 11(4): Article 4.

Dowling, John and Jeffrey Pfeffer. 1975. "Organizational Legitimacy: Social Values and Organizational Behavior". *Pacific Sociological Review* 18 (1): 122–136.

Dunn, William, N. 1981. *Public Policy Analysis*. Englewood Cliffs, NJ: Prentice Hall.

Fenno, Richard F., Jr. 1966. *The Power of the Purse: Appropriations Politics in Congress*. Boston, MA: Little, Brown.

Godwin, Kenneth, Scott H. Ainsworth and Erik Godwin. 2013. *Lobbying and Policymaking: The Public Pursuit of Private Interests*. Los Angeles, CA: Sage Publications.

Gormley, William T. 2007. "Public Policy Analysis: Ideas and Impacts". *Annual Review of Political Science* 10: 297–313.

Hacker, Jacob S. 2002. *The Divided Welfare State: The Battle over Public and Private Social Benefits in the United States*. New York: Cambridge University Press.

Her Majesty's Government. 1995. *Competitiveness: Forging Ahead*. London: HMSO.

Hillman, Amy and Michael Hitt. 1999. "Corporate Political Strategy Formulation: A Model of Approach, Participation and Strategy Decisions". *Academy of Management Review*, 24: 825–842.

Hughes, J.W. Magat and W. Ricks. 1986. "The Economic Consequences of the OSHA Cotton Dust Standards: An Analysis of Stock Price Behavior". *Journal of Law and Economics*, 29: 29–59.

Industry Canada. 2015. *Directory of Business and Trade Associations in Canada*. Available at www.ic.gc.ca/eic/site/ccc_bt-rec_ec.nsf/eng/h_00001.html, accessed 16 January 2015.

Jenkins-Smith, Hank C. and Paul A. Sabatier. 1993. "The Study of Public Policy Processes". In *Policy Change and Learning: An Advocacy Coalition Approach*, edited by Paul A. Sabatier and Hank C. Jenkins-Smith. Boulder, CO: Westview Press: 1–9

Kingdon, John W. 2003. *Agendas, Alternatives, and Public Policies*. 2nd edn. New York: Longman.

Lindblom, Charles E. 1959. "The Science of 'Muddling Through'". *Public Administration Review* 19(2): 79–88.

Maclean's Magazine. 2012. "The 10 Lobby Groups with the Most Contact with Federal Officials". *Maclean's*, 27 November. Available at www.macleans.ca/news/canada/in-the-lobby, accessed 17 November 2015.

Meltsner, Arnold J. 1976. *Policy Analysts in the Bureaucracy*. Berkeley: University of California Press.

Moir, Lance and Richard J. Taffler. 2004. "Does Corporate Philanthropy Exist? Business Giving to the Arts". *Journal of Business Ethics*. 54: 149–161.

Olson, Mancur. 1965. *The Logic of Collective Action*. Cambridge, MA: Harvard University Press.

Reveley, James and Simon Ville. 2010. "Enhancing Industry Association Theory: A Comparative Business History Contribution". *Journal of Management Studies*, 47(5): 837–858.

Richardson, Jeremy. 2000. "Government, Interest Groups and Policy Change". *Poliktical Studies* 48: 1006–1025.

Schmitter, Phillipe C. and Streeck, Wolfgang. 1981. The Organization of Business Interests: A Research Design to Study the Associative Action of Business in the Advanced Industrial Societies of Western Europe. Discussion Papers IIMV/Arbeitsmarktpolitik, IIM/Labour Market Policy 81 (13).

Smith, Katherine Elizabeth, Gary Fooks, Anna B. Gilmore, Jeff Collin and Heide Weishaar. 2015. "Corporate Coalitions and Policy Making in the European Union: How and Why British American Tobacco Promoted 'Better Regulation' ". *Journal of Health Politics, Policy and Law* 40(2): 325–372.

Stritch, Andrew. 2007. "Business Associations and Policy Analysis in Canada". In Laurent Dobuzinskis, David H. Laycock and Michael Howlett, *Policy Analysis in Canada: The State of the Art*. University of Toronto Press: 443–472.

Vining, Aidan R. and David Weimer. 2016. "The Challenge of Fractionalized Property Rights in Public-Private Hybrid Organizations: The Good, The Bad, and The Ugly". *Regulation & Governance*, 10: 161–178.

Vining, Aidan R. and David Weimer. 2017. "Policy Analysis: A Valuable Skill for Public Administrators". In J.C.N. Raadschelders and R. Stillman (eds), *Foundations of Public Administration*. Irvine, CA: Melvin and Leigh.

Vining, Aidan, Anthony E. Boardman and Mark A. Moore. 2014. "The Theory and Evidence Pertaining to Local Government Mixed Enterprises". *Annals of Public and Cooperative Economics*, 86(1): 53–86.

Vining, Aidan, Daniel Shapiro and Bernhard Borges. 2005. "Building the Firm's Political (Lobbying) Strategy". *Journal of Public Affairs*, 5(2): 1–27.

Walker, Jack. 1983. "The Origins and Maintenance of Interest Groups in America". *American Political Science Review*, 77: 390–406.

Weimer, David and Aidan R. Vining. 2011. *Policy Analysis: Concepts and Practice*. Upper Saddle River, NJ: Prentice Hall.

Wengle, Susanne. 2016. "When Experimentalist Governance Meets Science-Based Regulations; The Case of Food Safety Regulations". *Regulation & Governance*.

Wildavsky, Aaron. 1964. *The Politics of the Budgetary Process*. Boston: Little, Brown.

Williams, Walter. 1971. *Social Policy Research and Analysis*. New York: American Elsevier.

Wilson, James Q. 1980. "The Politics of Regulation". In J. Q. Wilson, *The Politics of Regulation*. New York: Basic Books: 357–394.

Windmuller, John P. and Alan Gladstone. 1984. *Employers Associations and Industrial Associations: A Comparative Study*. Oxford University Press.

Yackee, Jason Webb and Susan Webb Yackee. 2006. "A Bias Towards Business? Assessing Interest Group Influence on the U.S. Bureaucracy". *The Journal of Politics* 68(1): 128–139.

Zahariadis, Nikolaos. 1999. "Ambiguity, Time, and Multiple Streams". In *Theories of the Policy Process*, Paul A. Sabatier (ed.). Boulder, CO: Westview Press: 73–93.

18

POLICY ANALYSIS BY THE LABOUR MOVEMENT: A COMPARATIVE ANALYSIS OF LABOUR MARKET POLICY IN GERMANY, DENMARK AND THE UNITED STATES

Michaela Schulze and Wolfgang Schroeder

1. Introduction

Among the union movement's aims and achievements are high social standards and benefits. As such, unions have always been involved in the policy process and tried to shape labour market policy in the different phases of the policy cycle (e.g., Bonoli & Palier, 2000). Since the 1990s, several policy reforms at the interface of social and labour market policy in various welfare states have been passed. The most important aim is to reconfigure social rights, benefits and obligations. As a result, work (in order to get benefits), obligations and sanctions have been a pivotal part of social policy (Lødemel & Moreira, 2014). *Activation, workfare* or *welfare-to-work* are the terms that have prevailed to describe these policy reforms. As the welfare state has retrenched, the position of labour unions in the political arena has shifted, and unions have had to define their roles and policy goals according to these new challenges. Union research institutions might help to develop political claims in times of welfare state retrenchment.

Denmark, Germany and the United States vary in a number of ways. The countries have different welfare state profiles that are closely connected to the configuration of labour market policy. They represent three different welfare regimes (Esping-Andersen, 1990): Denmark is a social-democratic welfare regime, Germany is a conservative regime and the United States is a liberal regime. Even though the countries vary according to de-commodification and social stratification, all three have implemented labour market reforms that aim at a new balance of rights and duties between the government and citizens. These reforms present challenges to unions, as they run counter to the unions' traditional aims of expanding benefits and worker protections. These developments have major implications for unions' ability to shape and negotiate policy, and thus for labour market policy analysis.

Denmark, Germany and the United States also have different systems of interest groups and interest group representation in the political arena, which has implications for the three union federations. Denmark is known as a model country for a strong role and representation of unions (Jørgensen & Schulze, 2011); its union federation is the Landsorganisationen i Danmark (LO). Germany has a long tradition of union involvement in the political arena, including a strong presence in parliament and committees (Streeck & Trampusch, 2005). The German union federation is the Deutscher Gewerkschaftsbund (DGB). In the US, the role of labour unions in the political arena is weaker and more indirect. Their influence, largely through the American Federation of Labour and Congress of Industrial Organizations (AFL-CIO), can be characterized as direct lobbying, for example via campaign financing (Thunert, 2016, pp. 293ff.).

To compare the unions' analysis of reforms that are located at the interface of social and labour market policy, we focus here on the three relevant organizations that analyse policy for the federations: the Hans Böckler Foundation in Germany, Arbejderbevægelsens Erhvervsråd (the Economic Council of the Labour Movement) in Denmark and The Economic Policy Institute (EPI) in the United States. Besides, federations are the political actors. We are aware of the difficulties and shortage of the results. In addition all three countries have different historical paths of welfare state and labour market policy and the role unions have played.

The main argument of this chapter is that policy counselling and policy analysis can best be described as loosely coupled anarchy. The approach that the three federations take to open up room for policy shaping and counselling is not significantly different. The unions' analyses of labour market policy are closely connected to their role in the political arena. Policy analysis (provided by the policy cycle) enables us to analyse the positions of actors and processes (Howlett & Giest, 2013). In order to compare labour unions' analysis of labour market policy, we focus on the agenda setting and policy change phases of the policy cycle. We exclude the other phases, for example implementation, because the inclusion of the entire policy process would result in a brief country summary without in-depth analysis. In addition, analysis of the agenda setting and policy change phase offers the best way to study the role of unions and institutions in the development of new policies.

Nowadays, unions are facing two important challenges: membership and embeddedness. First, union membership in all countries has been declining since the 1980s, in both absolute and relative terms (OECD, 2016). In the US, as a country with a low union density, union membership has fallen from 22% in 1980 to 11% in 2013 (OECD, 2016). A decline in union density is also obvious in Germany. Whereas in 1980 nearly 35% of employees were organized members of a union, in 2013 only 18% of employees were union members. Denmark, with one of the highest levels of union density, also experienced a decline: from 80% in 1980 to 67 in 2013.

This membership crisis is closely connected to the 'embeddedness' crisis, in which unions are less often involved in parliaments or commissions. Their institutional involvement shrinks because more and more members of parliament are not party or union members (e.g., Allern & Bale, 2012). In addition, the ties between labour unions and parties have weakened in times of welfare state retrenchment. All of this contributes to a changed role of unions in the political system.

The chapter is organized as follows. In section 2, we discuss the most important organizations that analyse policy for and with the unions. These organizations shape the position of the unions in the reform processes. In section 3, we look at labour market policy analyses by the German unions. The Danish model will be analysed in section 4 and the American example will be discussed in section 5. Finally in section 6, we summarize the results from a comparative perspective.

2. Overview of Policy Analyses by Labour Unions in Germany, Denmark and the United States

In order to show how organizations help to analyse labour market policy for the unions we will first discuss the three institutions. In all three countries, there are intensive contacts between labour unions and policy counselling. The organizations conduct their own research in the field of unions' interests. Afterwards they provide results for unions and the public. The organizations seldom conduct research on the direct request of the unions.

Germany: The Hans Böckler Foundation

The Hans Böckler Foundation was established in 1977 as a fusion of the Foundation Co-Determination and the Hans Böckler Society. The organization is the key actor for employee-oriented research in Germany. It deals with co-determination, research linked to the world of work and the support of students on behalf of the DGB. It has a comparatively high budget (approximately 60 million) (Schroeder & Greef, 2013, p. 206). The organization itself finances research on structural change; innovation and employment; changes in co-determination; changes in the field of gainful employment; the future of the welfare state; education for and in the working environment; and history of the labour unions. Representatives often take part in hearings or commissions. Representatives of the Böckler Foundation's two research institutions, the Institute of Economic and Social Research (WSI: Wirtschafts und Sozialwissenschaftliches Institut) and the Macroeconomic Policy Institute (IMK: Institut für Makroökonomie und Konjunkturforschung), are especially active in those areas (WSI, 2016; IMK, 2016) and help shape the policy standpoints of the DGB federation.

For the purposes of this chapter, the WSI's work is more relevant. The organization is engaged in research and consultation related to a fair and humane working and living environment. Economists, social scientists and legal scholars work together on topics that are relevant for unions and employees. Many scholars involved in the WSI have heavily criticized labour market reforms. This is also obvious from the position and influence of the DGB in the reform process, which will be discussed later.

Denmark: Arbejderbevægelsens Erhvervsråd (The Economic Council of the Labour Movement)

The Economic Council of the Labour Movement was founded in 1936 as a forum for unions and social democrats (Arbejderbevægelsens Erhvervsråd, 2016). It describes itself as a place for discussion, consultation and agreement on economic issues. The secretariat is simultaneously a research institute and a think tank. The council's main task is to analyse economic development and policy proposals (Arbejderbevægelsens Erhvervsråd, 2016). It also conducts research on labour market policy, which forms the basis for its representation on behalf of the Landsorganisationen i Danmark (LO) in councils, committees and government-appointed commissions. But the council's influence is not just national: it also holds a seat in the EU Social and Economic Council. Here the representatives advocate the position of the LO and the entire labour movement. Representation on the EU level gives access to information that is useful for new research (Arbejderbevægelsens Erhvervsråd, 2016). The council is mainly funded by the LO and its unions and by the earnings from research, analyses and consultancy projects.

The council's main fields of work are employment; economic growth and wealth; education; inequality; work in general; the financial system; and the tax system. Labour market policy is a major topic of the council's work. This also means that activation has played a pivotal role in the organization's discussion and publications (newsletter, outlooks and newspaper articles). As we have shown, the LO and the council are connected by close thematic and organizational ties. As discussed in section 4, the LO and the council have been integrated in the political process especially of labour market reforms. Our analysis also shows that unions and thus also the council are squeezed out in later reforms. We will argue that the loss of influence will affect both the LO and the Economic Council of the Labour Movement.

United States: The Economic Policy Institute

The Economic Policy Institute (EPI) was founded in 1986 to include the needs of low- and middle-income workers in the policy discussion. The underlying premise of the organization is that every working person deserves a good job with fair pay, affordable health care and retirement security. The Institute supports this premise with its topics of research interest: budget, taxes and public investment; economic growth; education; green economics; health; immigration; inequality and poverty; jobs and unemployment; minimum wage; race and ethnicity; raising America's pay; regulation; retirement; trade and globalization; unions and labour standards; and wages, income and wealth (Economic Policy Institute, 2016). It is obvious that labour market policies are of utmost importance for unions and the EPI, but the relatively recent establishment of the organization indicates that agenda setting (from the mid-1980s until the beginning of the 1990s) and the (re)constitution of the organization have taken place at the same time.

The EPI defines itself as a non-profit, nonpartisan think tank that helps policymakers and opinion leaders to understand public policy. The organization can be characterized as the labour movement's most important voice in the political arena. The EPI conducts research and analyses of politically relevant topics. Its flagship publication is 'The State of Working America', which has been published regularly since 1988 (e.g., Mishel, Bivens, Gould & Shierholz, 2012). The EPI looks at changes in living and working conditions by using data on income, wages, unemployment, wealth and poverty (Economic Policy Institute, 2016). The Institute has also published many other publications that have influenced the labour movement's policy priorities, for example on welfare issues. It also proposes public policies that improve the income situation of workers. One recent example is the EPI's policy recommendations on 'prosperity economics' (2012). According to the EPI, prosperity economics is built on the three key pillars of economic growth, economic security and democracy. Policy recommendations include significant infrastructure investments and increased public investment in research and development for clean energy technologies (Hacker & Loewentheil, 2012).

All three institutions help to develop the political claims of the unions, and their research and analyses influence the unions' political role. Their work is the basis for the self-understanding of labour unions as political actors. In addition, the work of the organizations offers an important landmark and alignment for the unions. Their positions will be found in the different studies and documents that will be discussed in the processes of agenda setting and policy change in the three countries in the following sections.

3. Labour Market Policy Analysis by the German Labour Movement: The Activation Path and the Search for the Deutscher Gewerkschaftsbund's Role

Agenda Setting

The beginning of agenda setting can be traced back to the job placement scandal and the agenda speech of Chancellor Gerhard Schröder (Schroeder, 2006, pp. 263, 264.). The slogan of *Fördern* and *Fordern* (promoting and demanding) has been developed here. Gerhard Schröder and Tony Blair co-authored a position paper on the 'Third Way'/'*Neue Mitte*' concept, which stressed the idea of activation as a new policy principle and the new balance of work (for benefits), obligations and social benefits as described earlier (Schröder & Blair, 1999, pp. 895-896). The most crucial challenge of the German welfare state was seen to be long-term unemployment, due in part to insufficient job incentives, an unqualified work force, and ineffective administration and employment services (Dingeldey, 2006, p. 7). The aim of activation policy was to integrate the unemployed into the labour market and to support recipients to be financially self-reliant. The policy emphasized education, training and job placements.

The agenda-setting phase proved difficult for Böckler Foundation's WSI and its role in analysing labour market policy for two key reasons. First, activation was a controversial topic within the federation. Second, there was relatively little transfer of knowledge from the WSI to the DGB in the field of labour market policy. Most WSI studies show that the researchers held a rather critical attitude towards activation. The publications focus on different country examples, labour market flexibilization or flexicurity (Dingeldey, 1998; Keller & Seifert, 2000; van Oorschot, 2000). It is obvious from the lack of a coherent strategy of the federation DGB that there is relatively little transfer.

The federation was not able to articulate a coherent position of the unions organized under the DGB, nor was it able to bring in the major arguments of the WSI. The DGB vacillated between supporting the ideas of activation to opposing them. The election campaign of 1998 awakened the hope for a governmental change and a stronger role for the federation, and it was for this reason that the unions supported Gerhard Schröder and his election campaign. Schröder approached the unions and raised their hope for a reorganization of labour market policy. The DGB itself hoped for traditional labour market policy instruments and opposed activation. The union's perception of the Schröder-Blair position paper is characteristic for the German labour movement at the turn of the new century. In 1996, the federation argued that the state should not withdraw its responsibility for social policy (DGB Bundesvorstand, 1996, p. 21). During these years the DGB had neither social policy visions nor a clear vision of the federation's role in policy (Schroeder, 2005, p. 74). In 1998, the organization realized a need to reform: it highlighted the overall agreement and acceptance of the activation aims and policy models of Gerhard Schröder (DGB Bundesvorstand, 1998). The traditional welfare state model (of high social benefits) could not be maintained and the traditional aim of full employment had to be reconsidered. The DGB thus postulated a new model that combines social security and activation. Against this background, a further expansion of social policy would neither be financeable nor preferable (DGB Bundesvorstand, 1998, p. 205).

Within the DGB, preferences ranged from (positively) highlighting the need for reform and new social policy ideas to anti-union policy (Schroeder, 2005, pp. 73-74). Some union members labelled the proposals as a blind defamation of the welfare state and a break with the (traditional) political aims of the labour movement (Schulte, 1999). The WSI was not able to contribute to relieve tension or provide a knowledge environment on activation policies.

Policy Change

The major reform step towards activation occurred with the Hartz Commission's proposed reforms, known as Hartz I to Hartz IV (Seeleib-Kaiser & Fleckenstein, 2007). The first and second Hartz reforms (2003) aimed at reforming the job service. Among other things,

Policy Analysis by the Labour Movement

self-employment was fostered and the possibility of sanctioning the unemployed (in case of refusing a job) was further extended. The third reform introduced a new concept of the German job service. Job placement is the primary aim of the policy, and the unemployed are now seen as clients. The Hartz IV (2005) marked the final step towards activation (Lessenich, 2003). Unemployment benefits were reduced to 12 months (18 for older workers) and a new unemployment scheme (unemployment benefit II) was introduced. This replaced the former unemployment assistance and social assistance (for able-bodied persons). Work requirements were part of the new law: Individuals will lose their benefits if they do not take an appropriate job. These reforms are known as Agenda 2010.

The WSI was a critical actor during the policy change phase. Researchers criticized the Hartz reforms from very different perspectives and in different stages. In particular, researchers heavily criticized the role of the unions as counselling experts (Schroeder, 2003, p. 139). Because of their incoherent preferences on activation, they were not able to pursue a coherent union strategy in the Hartz Commission. Other researchers emphasized evaluating self-responsibility and flexibility (in contrast to social rights and benefits). Scientists also looked for experiences in other countries and their experiences in activation policies (Trube & Wohlfahrt, 2001; Klammer & Leiber, 2004; Lessenich, 2003). As during the agenda-setting phase, varying attitudes towards activation policies are obvious. It is not surprising that the different positions within the labour movement in general and within the DGB impeded knowledge transfer or the attempt to find a coherent strategy.

The incoherent strategy of the DGB continued during the process of policy change. All in all, the DGB and the WSI were sceptical of the new activation path of the government. On the one hand they advocated an untouched welfare state and protection against benefit cuts (DGB Bundesvorstand, 1996, pp. 14-15). Consequently, the DGB heavily criticized the Schröder government's Agenda 2010 policy. The different preferences of the unions organized under the DGB and the federation's inability to develop one single strategy for the unions were two of the main problems (Schmoldt & Freese, 2004, pp. 528-529). On the other hand, Chancellor Schröder had promised to develop a new social policy together with the unions. He established the Hartz Commission, comprised of members from unions, labour market experts and employers, to prepare labour market reforms in 2002. This policy of inclusion of labour market parties harks back to the tradition of tripartite alliances as a solution for labour market challenges (Fickinger, 2005, p. 131). However, the Hartz Commission's composition points to a pushback of union influence because union members were selected by the chancellery and seen more as counselling experts without a mandate (Schroeder, 2003, p. 139). The result of the commission's work was published in a report, but it reflects little more than the lowest common denominator (Siegel, 2003, p. 175). Chancellor Schröder announced the full implementation of the suggestions of the Hartz Commission. From this perspective it is not surprising that the federation did not criticize the report (DGB Bundesvorstand, 2002; Tenbrock, 2002, p. 16). Schröder did not stick by his word and later brought in the Hartz IV reform, which imposed more stringent requirements than those suggested by the Hartz Commission (Schulze, 2012, pp. 248-250). As a consequence, the DGB heavily criticized the reform in terms of the level of unemployment benefits, the emphasis on sanctions and the danger of a low-wage labour market (DGB Bundesvorstand, 2004, pp. 7-8, 2003, p. 2; Engelen-Kefer, 2003, p. 700). Most of the criticism refers to major publications and research of the WSI. Within this context, scholars have criticized the labour market policy on a general level (Schäfer & Seifert, 2006), the growing importance of personal responsibility and the enforcement to work (Bothfeld, Gronbach & Seibel, 2004) and the growing gap between rich and poor (Lessenich, 2003).

4. Labour Market Policy Analysis by the Danish Labour Movement: Activation as a Threat to Administrative and Political Corporatism

Agenda Setting

Until the mid-1970s, Danish politicians thought that structural mass unemployment would not affect the Danish economy. As unemployment rose, however, it began to receive attention. Several reports, for example by the Social Commission, came to the conclusion that unemployment was the most urgent challenge and structural problem of the Danish economy. The paradigm of structural unemployment became a reference point for economists, politicians and interest groups (Larsen & Goul Andersen, 2008, pp. 5-7).

As in Germany, the major reasons for unemployment were seen to be an individual's lack of qualifications and insufficient incentives to seek and take a job. In 1992, the Zeuthen Commission was established to elucidate structural problems in the labour market. Commission members suggested that obligatory participation in activation programmes might solve these problems. Job search courses, education and job training were suggested as suitable measures (Larsen & Goul Andersen, 2008).

The Danish case is comparable to the German case in some ways. As in Germany, the Economic Council of the Labour Movement was not able to transfer knowledge on activation during the agenda-setting phase, although for different reasons than in Germany. First, the LO did not see itself as an actor that was in a position to develop political claims. The LO itself did not have its own mission statement until 2003, and the federation did not see its role as developing political claims. They followed the political aims of the social democrats because the LO saw itself as a part of the Social Democratic movement (Gill, Knudsen & Lind, 2003; Galenson, 1998, pp. 62-64). Both actors rejected the paradigm of structural unemployment until the end of the 1980s and opposed the cost-saving reform proposals of the conservative government (Schulze, 2012, p. 123).

Second, researchers often highlight the political character of the LO as a fundamental difference from the German case and an explanation for the minor knowledge transfer in Denmark (Jørgensen, 2003, pp. 156-157). Overall the federation supported a universal welfare state arrangement, full employment, active inclusion and labour market participation. 'Flexicurity', a major principle of Danish society, combines a competitive market economy and high welfare state universalism, including the right of every citizen to basic social protection. As a quid pro quo, the LO accepted comparatively high taxes, which are needed to ensure the Danish welfare state. Another important aspect of the Danish model is the claim for an institutionalized dialogue between social partners to shape labour market policy. The unions' claim for high unemployment benefits seems to be understandable: until the middle of the 1990s, Denmark offered one of the most generous unemployment benefits in Europe. This is also an achievement of the unions; it was not possible for governments to enact reforms without agreement from the unions (Green-Pedersen, 2001, p. 980; Bogedan, 2005, p. 12).

Policy Change

Denmark's activation path extended over a comparatively long period between 1993 and 2011. Here we summarize the most important results. First, unemployment benefits were reduced several times (from a lifelong benefit to maximum two years). During this reform period, individual action plans were introduced to ensure a better placement of the unemployed in the labour market. In addition, the government introduced a requirement that every unemployed individual participate in activation programmes (Goul Andersen & Pedersen, 2007). Since 2002, every unemployed individual or recipient of social assistance is obligated to seek an appropriate job, and accept a job offer, from the first day of unemployment or receipt of social assistance. In addition, all recipients of unemployment or social assistance support are regularly monitored to ensure they are actively seeking employment. From 2009 on, each unemployed individual must submit at least four job applications per week (Jørgensen & Schulze, 2011). During the economic crisis in 2008, Denmark faced higher unemployment and increased inequality, but the country has followed the activation path (as a long-term strategy) and tried to slow the growth in public spending (as a short-term strategy) (Dølvik, Goul Andersen & Vartiainen, 2015; Svarer, 2015). The Economic Council called for further reforms in the field of labour market policy (Svarer, 2015; Danish Government, 2014), but recent discussions show 'welfare chauvinism' (i.e., welfare benefits for certain groups) and a focus on deservingness for migrants (Jørgensen & Thomsen, 2016).

It is not easy to summarize the role of the council. First, the reform period is comparatively long. Second, the reforms were initiated by different governments. Third, reforms also changed the role of the LO dramatically. The Zeuthen Commission laid the foundation for activation, and the LO supported the reforms as a solution to labour market challenges. However, the federation misinterpreted the reform agenda: unionists and the Economic Council of the Labour Movement assumed that it would not have any consequences for their role as a political actor (Scheuer, 2007). The LO did not have its own coherent reform strategy nor any policy to address rising unemployment (Lind, 2000). The LO advocated earlier activation reforms even though it had opposed activation measures until the enactment of the Zeuthen Commission. Because of the strong representation of the LO the first reform was passed without any big quarrel (Madsen, 2005; Martin & Thelen, 2007; Mailand, 2005).

However, in the following years, the LO was overtaken by the changing policy style, and unions were only selectively incorporated in the policymaking process. But the LO gained influence in administrative corporatism, especially in the field of implementation of labour market policies. The years after 2007 mark a path-breaking era for the unions. New and tighter activation reforms have been passed without any clear contribution or protest from the LO. The activation path went hand in hand with the loss of influence and the abolition of regional administrative corporatism (Jørgensen & Schulze, 2011; Lind & Møller, 2006). Since 2009, unions are no longer responsible for activation programmes and have only an advisory role. The right-wing government headed by Lars Løkke Rasmussen abolished tax reductions for trade union membership fees, and unions did not play any role in welfare state policy. It is obvious that the Danish model has to be questioned: within ten years the LO has lost influence in both administrative and political corporatism (Jørgensen & Schulze, 2012).

More generally, however, it can be argued that the Economic Council of the Labour Movement still highlights the Danish model as one of the most successful in the world (e.g., Lykketoft, 2009). In the course of the adoption of the LO's first mission statement, the Economic Council of the Labour Movement's statements and publications on activation reforms have also risen. Before 2003, analysis was mainly published in the yearly labour market reports. It is obvious that the council helped to shape the positions of the LO. Two key aspects are noticeable: First, the council (and as we will show later also the LO) criticizes the malfunction of the new job centres and the labour market policy in times of rising unemployment (Vilhelmsen, 2007, 2010). Second, the Economic Council of the Labour Movement has shared the fear of rising unemployment in times of economic crisis (Bjørsted & Pedersen, 2009; Hansen & Pedersen, 2008).

The policy platform and the mission statement were passed in 2003 and could not impede the dramatic change of the Danish model (LO, 2003, 2007). The LO declared itself to be against further cutbacks in unemployment and social assistance benefits (LO, 2003, 2007). Amazingly enough, the unions' loss of influence is not discussed by the Economic Council of the Labour Movement. Researchers such as Madsen highlight the aim of improving the skills of the unemployed as a positive signal of fostering labour market integration. They also emphasize a need to evaluate the programmes (Madsen, 2014). From a more critical perspective, the council criticizes the character of activation in its function to prevent unemployment (Madsen, 2014). However, it has to be stated that the organization did not contribute to creating a knowledge framework for the LO.

5. Policy Analyses by the American Labour Movement: The American Federation of Labour and Congress of Industrial Organizations's Search for Political Influence

Agenda Setting

As welfare and unemployment rolls had grown dramatically since the 1970s, scientists as well as politicians initiated agenda setting for activation in the United States during the Reagan administration. Three scientists must be highlighted: Charles Murray and Michael Tanner wanted to get rid of the welfare system entirely. Their argument was based on the proposition that work supersedes welfare (Murray, 1984; Tanner, 1994). Lawrence Mead pointed at the growing numbers of illegitimate births and the amount and size of welfare benefits that resulted in dependency on the state (Mead, 1986). Reagan labelled unemployment, poverty and dependency as un–American (Patterson, 1986). In the 1980s, two reforms aimed at removing or cutting rights and expanding work requirements and sanctions. The Family Support Act, passed in 1981, allowed states to introduce workfare programmes, work requirements, time limits on the receipt of benefits, and sanctions (Moffitt, 1986; Zedlewski, Holcomb & Duke, 1998). In 1988, the Family Support Act (FSA) compelled every state to establish welfare–to–work programmes. Basic elements were child support, unemployment and training, support for families and work requirements for recipients of social assistance (O'Connor, 1998).

At the time of the reform, the AFL–CIO did not have much interest in social or labour market policy. In the 1980s and the beginning of the 1990s, under the influence of the (approaching end of) the Cold War, the president of the federation was, not surprisingly, more interested in foreign policy. In addition, the Economic Policy Institute was not founded until 1986, at which point the course for workfare had already been set. Both AFL–CIO and the Institute were critics of the ideas.

The AFL–CIO formulated evaluations on Reagan's reforms (AFL–CIO, 1986) and claimed that all social policy reforms of Reagan should be eliminated. A special focus was on the cutbacks of the welfare system and unemployment insurance (Schulze, 2012, p. 110). The union's major aim was an expansion of social policy programmes and benefits (AFL–CIO, 1986). It criticized the policy for providing too little coverage in unemployment insurance and health care. All in all, the AFL–CIO took a stand for a universal and expanded welfare state, and saw retrenchment policy as a danger for the American welfare state. But the umbrella organization was little more than a toothless tiger. This can be traced back to its informal inclusion in the political process, the historical weakness of federal social policy and the organization's concentration on foreign policy.

The Economic Policy Institute was not able to help sharpen the positions of the AFL-CIO. First of all, the organization was founded in 1986, when agenda setting had already finished. Furthermore, as we have argued, the interest of the federation was more concentrated on foreign policy. Its statements and comments on labour market policy were rare. In time, however, the EPI began to address topics that are more closely connected to labour market issues, such as wage inequality (Mishel, 1995) and problems of making work pay (Bernstein & Mishel, 1995). It is obvious that the organization has grown to become a facilitator of the AFL-CIO.

Policy Change

The long road to the United States' 1996 welfare reform began with the election of President Bill Clinton in 1992. Clinton promised to 'end welfare as we know it' and called for further work requirements and time limits. After a long dispute in Congress, the Act was passed in August 1996 (Weaver, 2000, pp. 242-246). Temporary Assistance for Needy Families (TANF) replaced the former Aid to Families with Dependent Children (AFDC) programme. The law determined mandatory work requirements; required recipients to work as soon as they are job ready or no later than two years after coming on assistance; and established a five-year lifetime limit for receiving TANF benefits. Clinton initiated an extension of public childcare and public transportation for recipients.

Even though the EPI was established as policy change was taking place, the organization's enormous interest in labour market issues is obvious (i.e., evaluating positive and negative issues of the reform) (Boushey, 2002a, 2002b). Nevertheless, it is difficult to ascertain the extent of knowledge transfer from the EPI to the AFL-CIO. The union's lack of interest in labour market developments continued later in times of policymaking. In 1995, John D. Sweeney became the new president of the union federation. He was more in favour of social policy topics and it is not surprising that the union became more visible in these areas. His major topics were insufficient health care and labour market policy in terms of insufficient coverage of unemployment risks (AFL-CIO, 1988, 1989, 1995, 1999, 2000).

The AFL-CIO was engaged in restructuring the union and in organizing campaigns. Sweeney tried to advance claims on labour market policy. At first, the AFL-CIO supported Clinton's campaign, which also advocated workfare programmes. After the reform's enactment, the AFL-CIO heavily criticized it (Hall, 1996; Byrne & Parks, 1996), but the organization was nearly invisible during policymaking (Piven, 1997, pp. 112-113). In the aftermath of the reform Sweeney declared it as 'anti-poor, anti-immigrant, anti-women, anti-children' (Weinstein, 1996). Despite this heavy criticism, the AFL-CIO's statements on labour market issues and reform remained vague (Piven, 1997). Most of the criticism is in accordance with the positions of the EPI and focuses on the labour market situation of workers—for example, the fact that low-wage workers do not fall within the scope of the Fair Labour Standards Act and will have neither the same rights as regularly employed nor equal pay (Simmons, 2002). Overall, the AFL-CIO and the EPI saw the reform as a threat to the American welfare state, as it removes important aspects of the former regulations (e.g., unlimited benefits). In the long run, unions warned that employees would be replaced by low-wage workers; workers' rights would weaken; and workers would lack protection in times of crisis (Simmons, 2002). The AFL-CIO also saw major consequences for the federation. The growing amount of workers who would be shifted to the low-pay sector would make it more difficult for the federation to organize them (Simmons, 2002). It is obvious that the AFL-CIO was reacting ex post facto while it had no visible role during the policymaking process. The AFL-CIO was prevented from having a stronger role in policymaking by both institutional factors and inner union restructuring. This thematic and organizational reconstruction was accompanied by the work of the EPI, which tried to support the AFL–CIO in analysing the consequences of welfare reform. Sawicky and others have contributed to a book on the consequences of federal devolution (Sawicky, 1999). In 1995, Mishel argued that the reform could be a threat to the welfare system in general (Mishel, 1995). Others highlight the potential drop in wages (Eitzen & Zinn, 2000) and the threat to work standards (Simmons, 2002; Boushey, 2002b).

6. Conclusion

In times of welfare state retrenchment, activation policies are central for welfare states. Activation is a rather difficult topic for the labour movement because of the reconfiguration of social rights and obligations. Unions have always fought for a strong role, or even an expansion, of the welfare state. However, newer developments and reforms increasingly challenge these viewpoints. As a consequence, unions have, over time, shifted from a rejection of activation policies towards a cautious approval, though this is not true for all unions organized under the federations we have analysed here.

As we have seen, agenda setting and policy change are the two most important periods in which to understand the reasons for refusal or approval of activation policies. In each of the countries studied here, the three organizations' role in the policy analysis process is different. Denmark and Germany are countries that have strong corporatist traditions and, as such, unions play a pivotal role in labour market polices. In the United States, unions are included more informally. This has major implications for the organization's roles, as analysed here.

Despite the differences, there are certain common results. All three organizations are labour market actors as they provide studies and expertise for the labour movement. All three have published different studies and documents that analyse labour market policy with an emphasis on activation. These studies have not had the character of a Magna Carta nor are they symbolic of an overall policy strategy. Most of them are scientific analyses by critical scientists. A transfer of knowledge or expertise to the union federations remains vague and is difficult to assess empirically. In all three countries, unions are faced with a dilemma, as they find themselves between the conflicting priorities of supporting or opposing activation ideas and reforms. In addition, unions still want to foster high social protection and try to shape social policy. Neither the Hans Böckler Foundation, nor the Economic Policy Institute, nor the Economic Council of the Labour Movement has been able to dissolve these conflicts. Their influence in both agenda setting and policy change remains limited. Nevertheless, they have a broad knowledge on labour market issues. In this sense, special knowledge surrounding is created by the organizations but this knowledge is focused. Besides, unions are not always prepared to incorporate ideas from the organizations.

References

AFL–CIO. 1986. It's Not Working: The Unemployment Insurance in Crisis, in: *The AFL-CIO American Federationist*, 5, April.

AFL–CIO. 1988. America's Needs: Restoring Full Jobless Benefits, *AFL-CIO News* 33(31): 7.

AFL–CIO. 1989. Labor in the 1990s: The New Solidarity, *AFL-CIO News* 34(23): 7–10.

AFL–CIO. 1995. *Executive Council Actions: The Needs of Working America—Welfare Reform*. Available at: www.aflcio.org/aboutus/thisistheaflcio/ecouncil/ec02201995.cfm#WELFARE%20REFORM.

AFL–CIO. 1999. *Executive Council Actions: Medicare Reform*. Available at: www.aflcio.org/aboutus/thisistheaflcio/ecouncil/ec02191999a.cfm.

Policy Analysis by the Labour Movement

AFL-CIO. 2000. *Executive Council Actions: Unemployment Insurance*. Available at: www.aflcio.org/aboutus/thisistheaflcio/ecouncil/ec0217a2000.cfm.

Allern, Elin Haugsgjerd and Tim Bale. 2012. Political Parties and Interest Groups: Disentangling Complex Relationships, *Party Politics* 18(1): 7–25.

Arbejderbevægelsens Erhvervsråd. 2016. *The Economic Council of the Labour Movement*. Available at: www.ae.dk/english.

Bernstein, Jared and Lawrence Mishel. 1995. *Trends in the Low-Wage Labor Market and Welfare Reform*, Washington, DC: Economic Policy Institute.

Bjørsted, Eric and Federik Pedersen. 2009. *Over 80.000 arbejdsløse – risiko for det dobbelte i 2010*, København: Arbejderbevægelsens Erhvervsråd.

Bogedan, Claudia. 2005. *Mit Sicherheit besser? Aktivierung und Flexicurity in Dänemark*, ZeS-Arbeitspapier 6/2005.

Bonoli, Giuliano and Bruno Palier. 2000. How Do Welfare States Change? Institutions and their Impact on the Politics of Welfare State Reform in Western Europe, *European Review* 8(3): 333–352.

Bothfeld, Silke, Sigrid Gronbach and Kai Seibel. 2004. Eigenverantwortung in der Arbeitsmarktpolitik: Zwischen Handlungsautonomie und Zwangsmaßnahmen, *WSI-Mitteilungen*, September: 507–513.

Boushey, Heather. 2002a. The Effects of the Personal Responsibility and Work Opportunity Reconciliation Act on Working Families, *EPI Viewpoints*, 2 March.

Boushey, Heather. 2002b. Staying Employed After Welfare: Work Supports and Job Quality Vital to Employment Tenure and Wage Growth, EPI Briefing Paper, 1 June.

Byrne, Michael and James B. Parks. 1996. Delegates to Raise Workers' Political Voice, *AFL-CIO News* 41(6): 1–2.

Danish Government. 2014. *The National Reform Programme: Denmark 2014*. Available at: http://ec.europa.eu/europe2020/pdf/csr2014/nrp2014_denmark_en.pdf.

DGB Bundesvorstand. 1996. *Die Zukunft gestalten. Grundsatzprogramm des Deutschen Gewerkschaftsbundes*. Berlin: Deutscher Gewerkschaftsbund Bundesvorstand.

DGB Bundesvorstand. 1998. Soziale Gerechtigkeit, Sozialstaat und Innovationen, in Erika Mezger and Klaus W, West (eds), *Aktivierender Sozialstaat und politisches Handeln*. Marburg: Schüren Verlag, 201–211.

DGB Bundesvorstand. 2002. *Stellungnahme des DGB-Bundesvorstandes vom 15. August 2002 zu den Ergebnissen der Kommission "Moderne Dienstleistungen am Arbeitsmarkt" (Hartz-Kommission)*. Available at: http://doku.iab.de/chronik/2x/2002_08_16_20_DGBzuHartz.pdf.

DGB Bundesvorstand. 2003. *Stellungnahme des Deutschen Gewerkschaftsbundes (DGB) zum Entwurf der Bundesregierung sowie der Koalitionsfraktionen eines "Vierten Gesetzes für moderne Dienstleistungen am Arbeitsmarkt"*, 30 September, Berlin.

DGB Bundesvorstand. 2004. Viertes Gesetz für moderne Dienstleistungen am Arbeitsmarkt (Hartz IV), *Informationen zum Arbeits- und Sozialrecht*, April.

Dingeldey, Irene. 1998. Läßt sich die Zahl geringfügiger Beschäftigungsverhältnisse über Steuern und Sozialabgaben beeinflussen? Perspektiven für die deutsche Reformdiskussion durch den europäischen Vergleich, *WSI-Mitteilungen* 51(12): 863–871.

Dingeldey, Irene. 2006. Aktivierender Wohlfahrtsstaat und sozialpolitische Steuerung, *APuZ*. August–September: 3–9.

Dølvik, Jon Erik, Jørgen Goul Andersen and Juhana Vartiainen. 2015. The Nordic Social Models in Turbulent times: Consolidation and Flexible Adaptation, in Jon Erik Dølvik and Andrew Martin (eds) *European Social Models from Crisis to Crisis*. Oxford University Press, 246–286.

Economic Policy Institute. 2016. *About the EPI*. Available at: www.epi.org/about.

Eitzen, D. Stanley and Maxine Baca Zinn. 2000. Elderly Immigrants: Their Composition and Living Arrangements, *Journal of Sociology & Social Welfare* 27(1): 85–114.

Engelen-Kefer, Ursula. 2003. Von einem Paradigmenwechsel in der Sozialpolitik? *Gewerkschaftliche Monatshefte*, December: 696–706.

Esping, Andersen Gøsta., 1990. *The Three Worlds of Welfare Capitalism*. Oxford University Press.

Fickinger, Nico. 2005. *Der verschenkte Konsens: Das Bündnis für Arbeit, Ausbildung und Wettbewerbsfähigkeit 1998–2002*. Wiesbaden: VS Verlag.

Galenson, Walter. 1998. *The World's Strongest Trade Unions: The Scandinavian Labor Movement*. Westport, CT: Quorum Books.

Gill, Colin, Herman Knudsen and Jens Lind. 1997. Are there Cracks in the Danish Model of Industrial Relations? *Industrial Relations Journal* 29(1), 30–41.

Goul Andersen, Jørgen and Jacob J. Pedersen. 2007. *Continuity and Change in Danish Active Labour Market Policy 1990–2007: The Battlefield between Activation and Workfare*, CCWS Working Paper.

Green-Pedersen, Christoffer. 2001. Welfare-State Retrenchment in Denmark, and the Netherlands 1982–1988: The Role of Party Competition and Party Consensus, *Comparative Political Studies* 34(9): 963–985.

Hacker, Jacob S. and Nate Loewentheil 2012. *Prosperity Economics. Building an Economy for All*. Available at: http://isps.yale.edu/sites/default/files/publication/2013/01/2012-prosperity-for-all.pdf.

Hall, Mike. 1996. Information Is Power to Grass Roots, *AFL-CIO News* 41(5): 3.

Hansen, Louise A. and Federik Pedersen. 2008. *Jobfest gavner de udsatte grupper*. København: Arbejderbevægelsens Erhvervsråd.

Howlett, Michael and Sarah Giest. 2013. The Policy-Making Process, in Eduardo Araral, Scott Fritzen, Michael Howlett, M. Ramesh and Xun Wu (eds), *Routledge Handbook of Public Policy*. London: Routledge, 17–28.

IMK 2016. *Das IMK*. Available at: www.boeckler.de/imk_3401.htm.

Jørgensen, Henning. 2003. The Role of the Trade Unions in Social Restructuring in Scandinavia in the 1990s, *Revue Française des Affaires Sociales* 57(4): 151–176.

Jørgensen, Henning and Michaela Schulze. 2011. Leaving the Nordic Path? The Changing Role of Danish Trade Unions in the Welfare Reform Process, *Social Policy and Administration* 45(2): 206–219.

Jørgensen, Henning and Michaela Schulze. 2012. A Double Farewell to a Former Model? Danish Unions and Activation Policy, *Local Economy* 27(5–6): 637–644.

Jørgensen, Martin Bak and Trine Lund Thomsen. 2016. Deservingness in the Danish Context: Welfare Chauvinism in Times of Crises, *Critical Social Policy* 36(3): 1–22.

Keller, Berndt and Hartmut Seifert. 2000. Flexicurity. Das Konzept für mehr soziale Sicherheit flexibler Beschäftigung, *WSI-Mitteilungen* 53(5): 291–300.

Klammer, Ute and Simone Leiber. 2004. Aktivierung und Eigenverantwortung in europäisch-vergleichender Perspektive, *WSI-Mitteilungen* 57(9): 514–521.

Larsen Christian A. and Jørgen Goul Andersen. 2008. *How Ideas Can Have an Independent Causal Effect on Policy Change: The Case of New Economic Ideas that Changed the Danish Welfare State*, Aalborg, Denmark: Centre for Comparative Welfare Studies.

Lessenich, Stephan. 2003. Der Arme in der Aktivgesellschaft. Zum sozialen Sinn des "Förderns und Forderns", *WSI-Mitteilungen*, April: 214–220.

Lind, Jens. 2000. Denmark: Still the Century of Trade Unionism? in Jeremy Waddington and Reiner Hoffmann (eds). *Trade Unions in Europe: Facing Challenges and Searching for Solutions*, Brussels: ETUI, 143–182.

Lind, Jens. 2007. A Nordic Saga? The Ghent System and Trade Unions, *International Journal of Employment Studies* 15(1): 49–68.

Lind, Jens and Iver Hornemann Møller. 2006. Activation for What Purpose? Lessons from Denmark, *International Journal of Sociology and Social Policy* 26(1/2): 5–19.

LO. 2003. LO's værdigrundlag: Vedtaget på LO's ekstraordinære kongres 8. February, in *Værdigrundlag, Fagpolitisk grundlag & Love*, S. 4–7.

LO. 2007. Danish Unemployment Rate Hits All-Time Low: Finding Work for the Remaining Jobless Persons, in *Danish Labour News*, March: 6–7.

Lødemel, Ivar and Amilcar Moreira (eds). 2014. *Activation or Workfare? Governance and the Neo-Liberal Convergence*. Oxford University Press.

Lykketoft, Mogens. 2009. *The Danish Model: A European Success Story*. Copenhagen: AE—Economic Council of the Labour Movement.

Madsen, Per Kongshøj. 2005. The Danish Road to 'Flexicurity': Where Are We? And How Did We Get There? in Thomas Breegard and Flemming Larsen (eds), *Employment Policy from Different Angels*. Copenhagen: DJøF Publishing, 269–289

Madsen, Per Kongshøj. 2014. *Reforming Danish ALMP: An Assessment from a Flexicurity Perspective*, Brussels: OECD.

Mailand, Mikkel. 2005. The Involvement of Social Partners in Active Labour Market Policy: Do the Patterns Fit Exceptions from Regime Theories? in Thomas Breegard and Flemming Larsen (eds), *Employment Policy from Different Angles*. Copenhagen: DJøF Publishing, 135–151.

Martin, Cathie Jo and Kathleen Thelen. 2007. The State and Coordinated Capitalism: Contributions of the Public Sector to Social Solidarity in Postindustrial Societies, *World Politics* 60(1): 1–36.

Mead, Lawrence M. 1986. *Beyond Entitlement: The Social Obligation of Citizenship.* New York: Free Press.

Mishel, Lawrence. 1995. *Recent Wage Trends,* Economic Policy Institute. Available at: www.epi.org/publication/tmp_epwage.

Mishel, Lawrence, Josh Bivens, Elise Gould and Heidi Shierholz. 2012. *The State of Working America.* Ithaca, NY: Cornell University Press.

Moffitt, Robert A. 1986. Work Incentives in the AFDC System: An Analysis of the 1981 Reforms, *The American Economic Review* 76(2): 219–223.

Murray, Charles. 1984. *Losing Ground: American Social Policy 1950-1980.* New York: Basic Books.

O'Connor, John. 1998. US Welfare Policy: The Reagan Record and Legacy, *Journal of Social Policy* 27(1): 37–61.

OECD 2016. *Trade Union Density.* Available at: https://stats.oecd.org/Index.aspx?DataSetCode=UN_DEN#.

Patterson, James T. 1986. *America's Struggle Against Poverty: 1900–1985.* Cambridge (MA): Harvard University Press.

Piven, Frances F. 1997. The New Reserve Army of Labor, in Steven Fraser and Joshua B. Freeman (eds), *Audacious Democracy: Labor, Intellectuals, and the Social Reconstruction of America.* Boston, MA: Mariner Books, 106–118.

Sawicky, Max B. 1999. The New American Devolution: Problems and Prospects, in Max B. Sawicky (ed.), *The End of Welfare? Consequences of Federal Devolution for the Nation.* New York: M.E. Sharpe, 3–24.

Schäfer, Claus and Hartmut Seifert (eds). 2006. *Kein bisschen leise. 60 Jahre WSI,* Hamburg: VSA-Verlag.

Scheuer, Steen. 2007. Dilemmas of Collectivism: Danish Trade Unions in the Twenty-First Century, *Journal of Labor Research* 28(2): 233–254.

Schmoldt, Hubertus and Ulrich Freese. 2004. Für einen sozial gerechten Reformprozess: gegen einen grundsätzlichen Politikwechsel, *Gewerkschaftliche Monatshefte,* September: 528–532.

Schröder, Gerhard and Blair Tony. 1999. Der Weg nach vorne für Europas Sozialdemokraten, *Blätter für deutsche und internationale Politik* 44(7): 888–896.

Schroeder, Wolfgang. 2003. Modell Deutschland und das Bündnis für Arbeit, in Sven Jochem and Nico A. Siegel (eds), *Konzertierung, Verhandlungsdemokratie und Reformpolitik im Wohlfahrtsstaat,* Opladen: Leske + Budrich, 107–147.

Schroeder, Wolfgang. 2005. Sozialdemokratie und gewerkschaftliche Organisation, in Tanja Hitzel-Cassagnes and Thomas Schmidt (eds), *Demokratie in Europa und europäische Demokratien. Festschrift für Heidrun Abromeit.* Wiesbaden: VS Verlag, 56–90.

Schroeder, Wolfgang. 2006. Selbstverwaltungskorporatismus und neuer Sozialstaat, *Zeitschrift für Sozialreform* 52(2): 253–271.

Schroeder, Wolfgang and Samuel Greef. 2013. Policy Analysis by Trade Unions and Business Associations in Germany, in Sonja Blum and Klaus Schubert (eds), *Policy Analysis in Germany.* Bristol, UK: Policy Press, 197–216.

Schulte, Dieter. 1999. Veränderungsdebatte aufnehmen, *Einblick,* December: 7.

Schulze, Michaela. 2012. *Gewerkschaften im Umbau des Sozialstaats. Der Einfluss der Dachverbände im Welfare-to-Work-Reformprozess in Dänemark.* USA and Wiesbaden, Germany: VS Verlag.

Seeleib-Kaiser, Martin and Timo Fleckenstein. 2007. Discourse, Learning and Welfare State Change: The Case of German Labor Market Reforms, *Social Policy & Administration* 41(5): 427–448.

Siegel, Nico A. 2003. Die politische Ökonomie der Konzertierung in Deutschland: Das Beispiel Bündnis für Arbeit, in Sven Jochem and Nico A. Siegel (eds), *Konzertierung, Verhandlungsdemokratie und Reformpolitik im Wohlfahrtsstaat,* Opladen: Leske + Budrich, 148–193.

Simmons, Louise. 2002. Unions and Welfare Reform: Labor's Stake in the Ongoing Struggle over the Welfare State, *Labor Studies Journal* 27(2): 65–83.

Streeck, Wolfgang and Christine Trampusch. 2005. Economic Reform and the Political Economy of the German Welfare State, *German Politics* 14(2): 174–195.

Svarer, Michael. 2015. Labour Market Policies in Denmark: A Story of Structural Reforms and Evidence-Based Policy, in Torben M. Andersen, Michael Bergman and Svend E. Hougaard Jensen (eds), *Reform Capacity and Macroeconomic Performance in the Nordic Countries.* Oxford University Press, 73–98.

Tanner, Michael. 1994. *Ending Welfare As We Know It,* CATO Policy Analysis 212. Washington, DC: CATO.

Tenbrock, Christian. 2002. "Wir sind im Boot", Interview mit Michael Sommer, in: *Die Zeit*, 4 July: 16.

Thunert, Martin. 2016. Hyper-Pluralismus? Die Welt der Interessengruppen, Gewerkschaften, Lobbyisten und Think Tanks, in Christian Lammert, Markus B. Siewert and Boris Vormann (eds), *Handbuch Politik USA*. Wiesbaden, Germany: Springer/VS Verlag, 285–304.

Trube, Achim and Norbert Wohlfahrt. 2001. Der aktivierende Sozialstaat – Sozialpolitik zwischen Individualisierung und einer neuen politischen Ökonomie der Inneren Sicherheit; *WSI-Mitteilungen*, 54(1): 8–16.

van Oorschot, Wim. 2000. *Soziale Sicherheit, Arbeitsmarkt und Flexibilität in den Niederlanden 1980–2000, WSI-Mitteilungen*, 53(5): 330–334.

Vilhelmsen, Jes. 2007. *Styrtdyk i Aktiveringen*. København: Arbejderbevægelsens Erhvervsråd.

Vilhelmsen, Jes. 2010. *Jobcentre bryder loven*. København: Arbejderbevægelsens Erhvervsråd.

Weaver, Kent R. 2000. *Ending Welfare As We Know It*. Washington, DC: Brookings Institution Press.

Weinstein, Kenneth R. 1996. *From Meany to Sweeney: Labor's Leftward Tilt*, Heritage Foundation Background Paper 1094. Available at: www.heritage.org/research/governmentreform/bg1094.cfm.

WSI 2016. *Das WSI*. Available at: www.boeckler.de/wsi_2874.htm.

Zedlewski, Sheila R., Pamela A. Holcomb and Amy-Ellen Duke. 1998. *Cash-Assistance in Transition: The Story of 13 States*, Occasional Paper No. 13. Washington, DC: The Urban Institute.

19

POLICY ANALYSIS AND THE VOLUNTARY SECTOR

Bryan Evans, Juniper Glass and Adam Wellstead

The roles and contributions of voluntary, non-profit organizations in the policy process have been identified as: '(1) identifying issues on the policy agenda; (2) developing policy solutions through research and analysis, i.e. policy-ready research; and (3) promoting particular policy solutions', which includes mobilizing through demonstrating and advocating directly to government (Carter, Plewes & Echenberg, 2005, p. 6). These roles, as with those of other non-governmental policy actors, became a subject of serious interest as a consequence of the ascent of the New Public Governance (NPG) understanding of the policy process. NPG is 'concerned with how policy elites and networks interact to create and govern the public policy process' (Osborne, 2010, p. 6). The long-standing understanding of policy advice construction as a monopoly of government policy workers, labouring within vertical processes, has given way to a more pluralistic, polycentric process of policy co-construction which includes the participation of non-state policy actors (Craft & Howlett, 2012, p. 84). NPG scholars contend that 'we are witnessing a fundamental shift in governing models' marked by a 'pluralization of policy making', where the neoliberal priority allocated to markets and the traditional Weberian hierarchies of public administration have given way to networks. In normative/theoretical terms the 'model rests on interdependence, not power relationships, and centers on negotiation and persuasion, not control' (Phillips & Smith, 2011, pp. 4–5). However, the NPG model is not without its critics; some question whether the policy process is 'actually as open and as participatory as this model of "governance" suggests?' (Phillips, 2007, p. 497). In other words, the multi-actor process of policy co-construction envisaged by NPG may be less prevalent than usually suggested.

While the debate on the participation of non-state actors in the policy process is a meaningful one, the fact is that regardless of the nature of the relationship to the process, non-governmental actors, including non-profit organizations, are serious contributors to the generation and mobilization of policy ideas (Pekkanen & Smith, 2014). The type of policy advocacy activities undertaken by non-profits, the extent of their organizational investment in such work, and the techniques and instruments used will vary from organization to organization depending on their capacities and mission.

After initial remarks on defining the non-profit sector and its constituent organizations, this chapter is composed of three sections. The first examines the theoretical debates regarding non-profits in the policy process. The second part explores how non-profits engage with the policy process, whether through advocacy or co-construction. The third section examines the tools and methods employed by non-profits in the policy process.

The non-profit sector is generally understood to include the 'broad range of social institutions that operate outside the confines of the market and the state' (Salamon et al., 1999, p. 3). The literature reveals an array of terms with which to refer to this collection of non-state, not-for-profit organizations, including 'civil society', 'non-profit', 'voluntary', and 'third sector'. Rather than debate which concept has more merit, this chapter alternates between them, to reflect the wide lexicon used in the referenced literature as well as among non-profit practitioners.

Despite the diversity of non-profit organizations, they share five characteristics: voluntary nature; private and non-governmental structure; absence of profit distribution to shareholders or members; autonomy and self-governance; and service to a public benefit (Salamon, 2000; Phillips & Smith, 2011). Within the sector, there is a considerable amount of fluidity and crossover with interest groups that engage in policy advocacy. This becomes especially clear during attempts to classify such organizations; for example, most business associations are registered non-profits (Baroni, Carroll, Chalmers, Muñoz Marquez and Rasmussen, 2014). This chapter focuses upon non-profit organizations that have a mission to contribute to the public good within fields of activity including health, culture and recreation, social services, development and housing, environment, law and advocacy, volunteerism promotion and international activities, following categories identified in the International Classification of Non-Profit Organizations (United Nations, 2003). Although often constituted as non-profits, certain types of organizations have intentionally been set aside from our analysis, in particular educational institutions, hospitals, business associations and political parties as well as grant-making, labour, religion-focused, and professional trade organizations, many of which are treated elsewhere in this volume.

In most countries, advocacy is a side activity for the majority of non-profit organizations, although some identify policy influence as their central mission. The largest share of non-profit advocacy is undertaken by organizations that combine advocacy with a different primary activity, usually the provision of services (Almog-Bar & Schmid, 2014). In this chapter, the term 'advocacy organization' refers to one in which policy influence is the central part of its mission.

Theorizing Non-Profits in the Policy Process

A central theoretical debate regarding non-profit advocacy examines the nature of non-profit organizations' relationship with the state, including whether or not and how government sources of funding affect organizations' strategies. The state-non-profit relationship may be theorized as one of symbiosis, in which actors from the two sectors work together to improve policies and programs for public benefit, or as one of conflict, in which the government is compelled to maintain its dominant position by ignoring or repressing the voice of non-profits and their constituents (Kimberlin, 2010). Similarly, the receipt of government funding could either provide a privileged position from which a non-profit can influence policies or reduce an organization's willingness to criticize public policies for fear of losing an important revenue source. In North America and Europe, non-profit-government relationships often fit a

> pattern of co-dependency among unequals . . . In addition to depending on segments of the NGO sector to provide services and perform consultative roles, governments

> increasingly rely on NGOs for channeling citizen voice and ultimately for legitimizing state action . . . NGOs, in turn, are rewarded for establishing and preserving positive ties with government . . . in legal, economic, and political currency.
>
> *Lang, 2013, p. 17*

Empirical findings about the influence of revenue sources on non-profit advocacy present contrasting views. A survey of over 700 US non-profits found that the level of dependence on outside donations had no effect on the likelihood that their advocacy followed donor's policy priorities, indicating that 'nonprofits do not speak for their donors' preferences at the expense of their focal groups' (Yoshioka, 2014, p. 1088). A possible explanation for this effect is that organizations have agency in choosing their donors and tend to develop relationships with those whose support will not hinder its policy advocacy goals (Yoshioka, 2014). The scope and intensity of a non-profit's advocacy activities, however, have been found to be inversely related to the proportion of government and private funding in overall revenues, which indicates that excessive dependence on public sector and private donors may restrict advocacy work (Guo & Saxton, 2010). Relatedly, human service non-profits, referring to non-profit organizations whose mission is to provide a range of social services such as child care, immigrant settlement support, and home care for the elderly, tend to have higher levels of government revenue sources and therefore tend to prefer the use of 'insider' advocacy tactics, that is, working directly with policymakers, over influencing public opinion or other external pressure tactics (Mosley, 2011).

A nation's public sector governance approach inevitably influences the nature of its relationship with non-profits. Governments working from a New Public Management (NPM) framework develop relationships with the non-profit sector based on contracts in which the government is the principal and the non-profit is the agent, and extensive accountability mechanisms are in place (Phillips & Smith, 2011). While NPM continues to characterize governance in many developed countries including Canada and Australia, others, such as the United Kingdom, are shifting away from NPM towards greater collaborative engagement with civil society. This change may be motivated in part by acknowledgement that 'both policy problems and service delivery issues are more complex, and governments have recognized that they cannot solve them on their own' (Phillips & Smith, 2011, p. 2).

The nature of government regulation of civil society also has a considerable impact on the ability of non-profits to engage in effective advocacy. A cross-sectional analysis of 28 OECD countries found systematic differences in the regulation and oversight of non-profits between corporatist nations such as Japan, Norway and Switzerland, and pluralist nations such as the US, Australia, the United Kingdom and France. 'In societies where the structures of interest mediation are well established and closed to outside influence', non-profits are more strictly regulated, likely because of the perception that they 'present a potential risk for upsetting the political order and managed social consensus' (Bloodgood, Tremblay-Boire & Prakash, 2014, p. 731). Pluralist countries have enabled non-profits to play a role in the policy process by implementing 'fewer restrictions on NGOs' ability to combine advocacy with service delivery and . . . raise resources from nontraditional channels', seeing non-profits as 'a useful forum for societal voice, a means of organizing and representing social interests, policy information, and welfare provision which are otherwise lacking' (Bloodgood et al., 2014, p. 731). A review of developing countries reveals, in contrast, that autocratic governments tend towards more regulation to limit the activities and influence of the non-profit sector (Rutzen, 2011). In recent years, more than forty nations (many of them developing and transition countries) have created or enacted legislation that limits voluntary associations' contribution to public dialogue and policy processes (Rutzen, 2011). Governments may also support or hinder the influence of non-profits through the provision of resources that support advocacy. For example, many governments around the world have restricted in recent years their funding of public policy research, an important activity through which voluntary associations may contribute to the policy process (McGann, 2014).

The wide range of roles that non-profits are enabled to play in jurisdictions around the world demonstrates that their participation in public policy advocacy is not inherent but contested. Also contested is the notion of what gives non-profits a right to advocate in the first place and to whom they ought to answer. Lang (2013) theorizes that accountability to the public is the primary basis for non-profit legitimacy in the policy process. Applying principal-agent theory to the sector, it has been suggested that when non-profits enter agreements with the public sector, government is their principal, and when they advocate, they are acting as agents for the public (Bryce, 2012). In many cases, organizations are dealing simultaneously with multiple accountability and representational relationships, with a typical non-profit holding responsibilities towards at least six types of stakeholders: donors, government, other non-profits, the public at large, the non-profit's constituents or beneficiaries, and its staff and board (Jordan, 2007). The diverse audiences with whom organizations must communicate and to whose expectations they must live up create a complex accountability environment (Balser & McClusky, 2005; Christensen & Ebrahim, 2006). Because these expectations are rarely formalized, the road to legitimacy and accountability must be navigated by each non-profit. While voluntary associations 'frequently claim to advocate for the general public or underrepresented groups, they usually do not have a legal obligation to those being served. Also, it is within the organizations' discretion to decide how they speak for their focal groups' (Yoshioka, 2014, p. 1064).

Thus, a central question in the study of non-profit advocacy is just whose interests an organization represents (Pekkanen & Smith, 2014). It has been recommended that advocacy analyses conceptually divide non-state policy actors into narrow 'sectional groups', with a circumscribed constituency, and broad 'cause groups' that serve a broad public constituency, since these two groups are posited to act differently based on their key audience (Klüver, 2013). Some scholars distinguish, although few have yet researched the distinctions, between self-interested advocacy to advance the wellbeing of an organization—for example, engaging in government relations in an effort to secure new or additional funding—and advocacy to advance the wellbeing of those whom the organization serves—for example, seeking policy influence to reduce social inequities (Kimberlin, 2010). It should be pointed out that the two types of activities are not necessarily mutually exclusive. For example, benefits gained from government relations, such as increased credibility among decision makers or knowledge of the policy process, could ultimately serve to strengthen the impacts of progressive advocacy. On the other hand, processes of non-profit registration and reporting to regulators have been posited to foster upward accountability to government that hinders accountability to an organization's constituencies (Lang, 2013).

Explicitly at least, non-profits usually declare one of three types of focal groups as the intended beneficiaries of their advocacy work: members (those with an official membership), constituents (the broad group of citizens who share some common interests with the mission of the organization, including both members and non-members), or the general public (Yoshioka, 2014). Organizations that state they represent the entire public tend to formulate public policy priorities and options independently and then attempt to inform or convince the public as well as policymakers, while membership-based organizations are more likely to actively seek their focal groups' perspectives and convey them to policymakers (Yoshioka, 2014). Differences between fields have been noted such that the majority of arts and culture, environmental and animal protection organizations claim to advocate on behalf of the general public, and the majority of those in the education and human service fields claim to speak for their constituents (Yoshioka, 2014). It has also been found that non-profits that make service provision as their primary mission tend to use insider strategies and collaborate with policymakers, and consider them more effective in effecting policy change than attempting to apply outside pressure (Mosley, 2011; Almog-Bar & Schmid, 2014).

Another question that is crucial to deepening understanding about the advocacy role of non-profits is, 'Which interests have organizations to represent them?' (Pekkanen & Smith, 2014, p. 9). To date there has been little research on how policy priorities and positions come about within voluntary associations. One hypothesis is that non-profits will be more active on policy issues that the general public considers important—that is, 'patterns of relative attention to issues among citizens and organised interests should be similar' (Rasmussen et al., 2014, p. 251). Indeed, a study of 142 European Commission consultations found that organized interest groups were more active on issues that fell within policy areas regarded by the public as salient (Rasmussen, Carroll & Lowery, 2014). While this concurrence is of interest, it is likely that there are feedback loops at play that have not been accounted for by research—for example, as organizations raise awareness of an issue, it becomes meaningful for more members of the public. The processes involved in determining and shifting non-profits' advocacy stances are therefore likely complex with many influences.

Non-profit advocacy theorists also debate the effect of growth and bureaucratization on a non-profit's tendency to undertake activities promoting policy change (Kimberlin, 2010). The larger and more professional an organization becomes, the greater its interest may be in maintaining the status quo so as to perpetuate its existence. Non-profits with more resources, credibility and staff may have greater capacity to engage with government and contribute to the policy sphere (Kimberlin, 2010). Size has been found to impact the relationships between an organization and those it claims to represent: 'The more staff members a non-profit employs, the more likely the non-profit is to act on its own initiative based on its own assessment of policy issues', rather than consulting with members or the public (Yoshioka, 2014, p. 1085).

The Policy Work of Non-Profit Voluntary Associations: From Advocacy to Co-Construction

A complex web of iterative relationships links civil society and its organizations to the state; these relations are informed by the state's policies while they in turn seek to shape the policies of the state. A study of government third-sector relations in Quebec identified nine parameters shaping those relations: (1) government openness to the third sector; (2) the inclusion of the sector's activities in government policy; (3) the sharing or lack of objectives; (4) the presence or absence of standards guiding interface; (5) the degree of intensity and formalism of relations; (6) how government finances the third sector; (7) the degree of third-sector autonomy; (8) the extent to which the relationship is institutionalized; and (9) whether the rules and goals of the interface are co-constructed or not (Proulx, Bourque & Savard, 2007, p. 300).

To this point, New Public Governance, which emerged in the late 1990s in part as a theoretical adaptation to the paradox of NPM (Rhodes, 1996), posits that policy advice systems have evolved away from a vertical and essentially monolithic governmental design and towards a 'polycentric' and, from a participant ecology perspective, pluralized structure. NPG established new means of bureaucratic control based on 'centralized decentralization' (Hoggett, 1996). Contemporary governments now possess many alternative sources of policy input. Government decision makers no longer dominate the policy process in a command-and-control manner, but rather occupy a seat at the centre of a 'complex "horizontal" web of policy advisors that includes both "traditional" . . . advisors in government as well as active and well-resourced non-governmental actors in NGOs, think tanks and other similar organisations' (Craft & Howlett, 2012, p. 85). These relationships have been characterized as a 'reciprocal bestowing of legitimacy' in that non-profit organizations, among other non-governmental actors, are relied upon by the state to deliver services and to provide a vehicle to carry citizen's voices to the state, and by doing so legitimating consequent state policy (Lang, 2013, p. 17). For many non-profits, the achievement of their mission—that is, their purpose for existing—is manifested through policy advocacy and engagement with the public policy process (Bryce, 2012, p. xiii).

The study of non-profit advocacy is interdisciplinary in scope, drawing from sociology and political science in particular (Kimberlin, 2010, p. 165). Such studies find non-profit advocacy difficult to analyse for three reasons. First, measuring advocacy presents a methodological challenge. Second, determining causality in cases of successful advocacy outcomes is a tricky endeavour: precise causal attribution of effectiveness given the array of possible factors is not impossible, but requires grounded research. Third, what is meant by advocacy covers a large variety of tactics and strategies which can be easily substituted one for the other depending on objectives, capacities or any number of shifting variables in the environment (Pekkanen & Smith, 2014, p. 2).

Methodological obstacles notwithstanding, the determinants of non-profit advocacy, types of advocacy activities undertaken by non-profits, and the extent and scale of such work are increasingly well understood. For example, key elements endemic to each non-profit organization influence how it will decide to engage with the policy process. These may include the relationship of a specific non-profit to other advocacy actors as well as to government, which issues it has identified as priorities to pursue, and how it mobilizes and relates to the broader public. As the social and political context changes, non-profit organizations engaged in advocacy will often remain loyal to their original mission. This fidelity may either be a source of strength or a detriment to achieving policy goals (Young, 2010). For example, a resolute commitment to a specific policy objective may create sufficient programmatic inflexibility that inevitable compromises cannot be negotiated with either government or other advocacy coalition members. The result is that advocates become relatively marginalized and positioned as 'outsiders' to the process. On the other hand, too much flexibility risks capture by government or may threaten the legitimacy of a non-profit as an advocate.

Venue selection—that is, choosing what level of government to target, identifying who in government to engage with, or which specific part of the government apparatus to engage, and/or including private sector entities—ultimately shapes which specific advocacy strategies are selected by a non-profit organization (Pekkanen & Smith, 2014, p. 10). One study of non-profit organizations working on human rights and immigration issues in the European Union confirmed that venue is a determinant of non-profit advocacy behaviour. In this case, differences in tactics were observed when non-profits' advocacy strategies were guided by the organization's role and proximity to the process. A more external position in government-led consultative mechanisms would require a different array of advocacy strategies and tactics than an internal location. It is acknowledged that some non-governmental policy actors have greater access to the policy process and key government decision makers while others have less so, as explained by the Advocacy Coalition Framework (ACF). A central contention of ACF is that 'policy participants will seek alliances with people who hold similar policy core beliefs among legislators, agency officials, interest group leaders, judges, researchers, and intellectuals' (Sabatier & Weible, 2007, p. 196).

Constructing coalitions also has a pragmatic value. Aligning with other civil society organizations enables organizations to combine limited resources and thus reduces the policy capacity deficit. By working within and through a coalition, and by 'pooling resources', non-governmental organizations 'demonstrate to policymakers that they have resolved their internal differences and achieved a consensus on a position' (Heaney & Lorenz, 2013, p. 252). In addition, the growth in participation through an advocacy coalition is as a practical response to an increasingly crowded field of organizations struggling to gain the attention of government (Heaney & Lorenz, 2013, p. 252). Consequently, non-governmental organizations 'rank coalition participation among their top influence tactics' (Nelson & Yackee, 2012, p. 339).

The choice of venue selection may be informed by the status of a non-profit or other non-governmental actor as a policy insider or outsider. The differences in the 'insider' and 'outsider' status of non-governmental organizations noted in the EU study have been observed in Canada as well. A review of research on non-profit advocacy activities finds that the tactics and strategies employed are 'usually grouped into several clusters that include: legislative advocacy; administrative advocacy; grassroots advocacy; judicial (legal) advocacy; electoral advocacy; media advocacy; research and public education, coalition building; and direct actions' (Almog-Bar & Schmid, 2014, p. 20). The types of activities falling under the rubric of advocacy can be placed on an axis of insider to outsider strategies and indirect to direct activities, as illustrated in Figure 19.1.

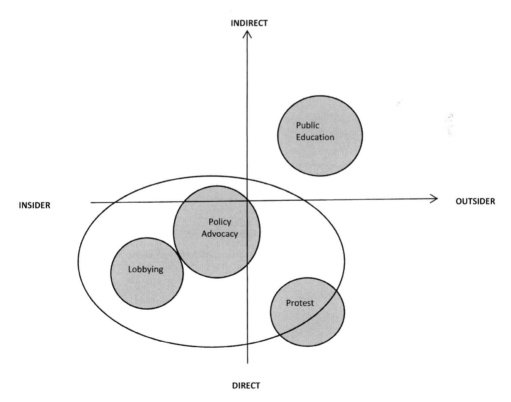

Figure 19.1 Relationship among various types of 'advocacy' activities
Source: Pekkanen and Smith (2014)

An analytical distinction is made between policy advocacy and lobbying (Salamon & Geller, 2008, p. 7). Policy advocacy is a general term referring to activities intended to influence government policy. This includes research, coalition building, and presenting policy alternatives. Lobbying encapsulates a narrower and more focused set of actions and refers to communicating positions to policymakers through direct engagement in deliberative/consultative settings with policymakers, or indirect engagement through mobilizing the public with awareness campaigns or even protests (Pekkanen & Smith, 2014). Insider and outsider tactics are also distinct approaches to policy advocacy. Insider tactics involve working directly with government policy staff and decision makers. Outsider tactics are concerned with working outside the formal advisory system and can involve public education/awareness campaigns, efforts to influence media coverage, and protest events (Onyx et al., 2010; Mosley, 2011).

It must be noted that the process of policy engagement is an iterative dynamic where not only are non-profits transformed in various ways but so too are those state structures charged with engaging with non-governmental policy actors. The process results in the continuous changing and re-constitution of such venues as governmental organizations modify themselves to better adapt and survive in this policy advocacy ecology (Theil & Uçarer, 2014, p. 114).

A variety of exogenous and endogenous factors contribute to constraining or facilitating policy engagement. Advocacy mobilization is often in response to the actions of government, not just the cause of activities of decision makers (Baumgartner, Larsen-Price, Leech & Paul Rutledge, 2011). What governments decide to do (or not do) is obviously a significant exogenous factor informing non-profit advocacy. However, the spectrum of relations between government and non-governmental actors, including non-profit organizations, and the nature of these relationships, are also of significant importance in defining policy advocacy. A significant role of non-profit organizations is concerned with the delivery of services funded by government. Indeed, most non-profit activity combines 'advocacy with the provision of services' where service delivery is the core function (Almog-Bar & Schmid, 2014, p. 12). One crucial question is to what extent this funding relationship constrains the non-profits' latitude in engaging in policy advocacy. Case studies are highly variable with respect to this question. One Belgian study of more than 250 welfare sector non-profits found that receiving government funds as a key source of income 'did not stifle the NPOs' commitment to advocate' (Verschuere & De Corte, 2013). However, other researchers observe a 'skittishness many non-profits have about engaging in, much less admitting to, advocacy' (Pekkanen & Smith, 2014, p. 7). A study of Canadian non-profits providing settlement services for immigrants found that 'advocacy chill' was prevalent, particularly where non-profits operated within a quasi-market of competitive contract funding. Failing to win a government service delivery contract would have dire consequences for the non-profits' viability. In the Canadian case, a serious degree of politicization has come to overshadow the awarding of government contracts at the federal level (Evans & Shields, 2014). The tension can be summed up as one where there is a serious 'desire to engage in effective advocacy, with the government as their primary target, yet they depend heavily on government funding' (Wayland, 2006, p. 3).

Factors endogenous to a non-profit organization also weigh significantly in establishing the extent to which policy advocacy will be included as a task of the organization. Therefore, the capacity of a non-profit organization to engage in policy advocacy derives from the internal characteristics of the organization itself. Resource mobilization theory acknowledges 'that an organization requires personnel, financial, and other resources ... to build the infrastructure and carry out the activities required to sustain advocacy as an agency activity. As a result, larger and more established organizations, which have greater resources and stronger infrastructure, should show more participation in advocacy' (Kimberlin, 2010, p. 172). The resource health of a non-profit organization thus entails significant implications for its policy capacity. Consequently, it has been noted that 'few voluntary sector organizations . . . have the policy capacity to participate effectively' (Phillips, 2007, p. 498). Corroborating this observation is the finding of a 2005 Canadian survey of several thousand non-profit organizations where fewer than 25% indicated they participated directly in the policy process. Non-participation was not a function of disinterest but rather of inadequate capacity (Carter, 2011, pp. 430–31). The rather limited policy capacity inherent to non-profit organizations is highly problematic if the policy process is as open and plurilateral as New Public Governance suggests. If governments increasingly demand evidence-based policy from external sources, non-profit organizations require enhanced policy capacity to effectively participate. The rules of the game have changed, and 'access, influence and overall policy success are no longer determined solely by traditional power politics, where actors leverage their strength through numbers . . . [The new politics] is a politics in which knowledge . . . triumphs' (Laforest & Orsini, 2005, p. 483). Obviously, if knowledge and the capacity to create and mobilize that knowledge is the currency required for full non-profit participation in policy co-construction, then a lack of capacity puts non-profits at a significant disadvantage. This raises the serious question of the uneven distribution of policy capacity— which types of organizations possess sufficient capacity to be effective participants and which do not? Does the NPG framework simply reproduce the hierarchical power relationships existing in the broader society and economy?

Returning to the fundamental supposition of NPG theory that the policy process has become more open to participation from multiple non-state actors, we must examine how policy co-governance is operationalized. First, it is necessary to understand that there are two basic but distinct forms of policy process participation—co-construction and co-production. Co-construction is based upon 'entering into a deliberative process with a variety of other stakeholders . . . working together to construct public policy decisions' (Vaillancourt, 2012, p. 79). It is more than lobbying government decision makers to accept policy proposals tabled by non-governmental actors. Understood in this way, co-construction 'is more promising for fostering greater democratization of public policy and public governance' (Vaillancourt, 2012, p. 79). Co-production, with its emphasis on implementation, is obviously much less concerned with power sharing in the design of public policy with non-governmental actors and is more akin to state-led 'monoconstruction' of policy (Vaillancourt, 2009). While the term has been applied to different contexts, including citizen participation in service provision to 'policy-making and policy implementation' (Pestoff, 2012, p. 17), the literature tends to understand co-production as concerned primarily with 'involvement of third sector actors in the delivery or implementation of public policy' (Vaillancourt, 2012, p. 80). The important difference is that co-construction is concerned with 'public policy when it is being designed and not merely to when it is being implemented' (Vaillancourt, 2012, p. 81). In this sense, co-construction aligns with NPG's frame of a more open and multi-actor-driven policy process.

For co-construction to be successful there must be an institutional framework for civil society participation. A collaborative process can be achieved by building participatory mechanisms into the strategic plans of existing government agencies; creating new agencies with the goal of assuring societal participation in government activities; or enshrining participatory mechanisms in law (Ackerman, 2013, p. 120). A number of conditions contribute to successful, durable co-construction: intermediate locations and institutions where civil and political leaders can meet that are conducive to consensus building; involvement of consensus facilitators; participation of a spectrum of political parties; public, not secret, deliberation; and involvement of not just non-profit organizations but also social movement, labour, and other civil society representatives (Vaillancourt, 2009). The active participation of diverse civil society actors serves to legitimate state action; if 'institutions are properly designed, a virtuous cycle that reinforces both state and society is possible' (Ackerman, 2012, p. 119).

Policy Work in the Voluntary Sector: The Need for an Anthropological Approach

Early in the twenty-first century, Migdal (2001) argued for

> an 'anthropology of the state', namely a means of disaggregating the state through a focus on the different pressures that officials on four different levels (the trenches, the dispersed field offices, the agency's central offices, and the commanding heights) of the state encounter
>
> *Migdal, 2001, p. 99*

Moreover, he argued that 'local interactions cumulatively reshape the state or the other social organizations, or, most commonly, both; these interactions are the foundation of the recursive relationship between the state and other social forces' (pp. 123–124). The original intention of Migdal's work was to steer social scientists away from legalistic approaches to state–society relations. An anthropology perspective of the state is an important contribution to developing an understanding of policy analysis in the voluntary sector. As noted above, the iterative dynamic of the relationship between state and civil society that marks policy deliberation can work to re-shape both state and non-state organizations. Seemingly routine activity such as policy work has significant value when understanding the intersections linking state and society. While routine, policy work is hardly supine and pointless. The contributions of Mayer, Bots and van Daalen (2004) and Colebatch (2006) illustrate the rich diversity of policy work ranging from detached scientific analysis to partisan policy advocacy.

Much of this scholarship is focused on policy work within the state. Surprisingly, very little is known about the policy tools employed by non-state organizations. As earlier noted, Pekkanen and Smith (2014) distinguish between advocacy and lobbying activities, and Vaillancourt (2009) illuminates the process of co-construction. However, neither account provides much insight into what rank-and-file policy staff in non-profit organizations actually do. Hence, Migdal's call for an anthropological focus is germane in understanding what is precisely taking place on the 'shop floor' of policy manufacture.

Several Canadian studies and commentary have examined policy tasks within non-profit organizations. Phillips (2007) was perhaps among the first to acknowledge that 'we know relatively little about how and to what extent such groups conduct policy analysis in the current context, how they use it to exert policy influence, and to what end' (Phillips, 2007, p. 497). To this end, she poses several basic questions requiring further empirical research.

> Have civil society organizations adopted policy styles that are compatible with a supposedly more open, inclusive, and participatory system of governance? Are they effective participants in policy networks and in shaping public policy? Few voluntary sector organizations have the policy capacity to participate effectively in the policy process.
>
> *Phillips, 2007, p. 498*

Carter (2011) reports descriptive results from two national surveys indicating that only a quarter of non-profit organizations participate directly in public policy processes in advocacy functions. This degree of non-participation is not a function of disinterest but rather a lack of capacity to do so (Carter, 2011, pp. 430–31). However, non-profit organizations are often involved in the implementation of public policy regardless of whether they have been active participants in the agenda setting or design phase of the process (Carter, 2011, p. 432).

Similarly, Mulholland (2010) states that, for voluntary organizations to increase their policy capacity, they need to increase their basic understanding of how governments function, and to strive to improve policy analysis skills and advocacy. In the early 2000s, the Canadian federal government funded the Voluntary Sector Initiative (VSI) in an attempt to foster increased policy capacity. One response was the emergence of 'communities of purpose', which Mulholland defines as 'relatively informal collaborations of organizations and individuals, united in support of a shared aspiration or goal, with a strong innovation focus, and highly skilled at building sectoral and cross-sectoral policy consensus and using this to influence policy' (p. 141). Mulholland (2010) reports that the majority of policy-related activities by NGOs occurs around procedural matters and there has been limited input into actual policy development.

Whereas Phillips, Mulholland, and Carter provide anecdotal evidence of the policy shortcomings within the voluntary sector, Evans and Wellstead (2013) conducted a survey of civil society organization employees responsible for policy work in the Canadian provinces of British Columbia, Saskatchewan and Ontario across four sectors (environment, immigration, health and labour). In many cases, their findings supported the earlier conclusions. Evans and Wellstead also conducted a parallel simultaneous survey of government policy workers. Overall, the 603 civil society organization respondents indicated that interaction with government officials, particularly at the senior level, was limited. Moreover, this study found that the nature of NGO policy work differed from government-based policy work in terms of tasks performed, attitudes and demographics. Policy-based civil society organization respondents did not fall under the generic policy role like their government counterparts, but instead undertook a number of different roles (Table 19.1). Thus a significant number of respondents saw themselves as fulfilling multidimensional roles within their organization. This is interpreted here as an expression of the necessity for civil society organization staff to multitask. Furthermore, it can be speculated that the prevalence of multitasking is a reflection of the resource constraints experienced by these organizations. The survey data further explored the work of government and NGO policy analysts, including what manner of work they were involved in, who they consulted with, and where in the policy process they engaged with one another. In most cases, the NGO respondents were much less engaged in common policy tasks (briefing, research, collecting policy information, etc.) than their government counterparts. For example, 48.1% of the government-based respondents collected policy-related data or information, compared to 23.2% of the civil society policy workers. This is not surprising considering that over two thirds (67%) of NGO respondents reported their specific organization had absolutely no dedicated policy staff (Evans & Wellstead, 2013, p. 71). Just over one third of the government respondents (35.2%) indicated that they spent a considerable amount of their time (50% or more) examining issues that required a specialist or technical knowledge, and 40.2% addressed issues where it was difficult to identify a single, clear, simple solution on at least a monthly basis. In contrast, only 23.1% of the civil society organization respondents spent more than half of their time addressing issues which did not lend themselves to a single, clear, simple solution.

Civil society organization respondents provided evidence of 'high expectations', even confidence, with respect to their own policy capacity, but the opportunities to actually

Table 19.1 Role within organization

	Nr	%
Advisor	103	17.1
Analyst	48	7.9
Communication Officer	71	11.7
Coordinator	102	17.0
Director	212	35.1
Liaison Officer	33	5.5
Manager	153	25.4
Planner	63	10.4
Policy Analyst	101	16.8
Researcher	108	17.9
Strategic Analyst	70	11.6
Other	117	20.5

Source: Evans and Wellstead (2014)

engage with government in an advisory capacity were less evident (Evans & Wellstead, 2013). Respondents were asked how often stakeholders were invited to work with the government on both an informal and a formal basis. Nearly a third (29.9%) of government respondents indicated that civil society stakeholders worked with them informally on at least a monthly basis. This perception was different from the perspective of civil society respondents. In the case of civil society organizations, only 9.3% of respondents indicated meeting informally and infrequently with government officials on a monthly basis.

Survey data of Canadian government and non-government policy workers suggest that provincial governments tend to invite specific external policy actors and do so rather frequently, while leaving half or more of the civil society actors either out of the policy process entirely or subject to very infrequent invitations to meet and consult (Evans & Sapeha, 2015, pp. 265–266). The reverse held true for formal encounters between government and civil society officials: a quarter of civil society respondents indicated they met frequently (more than once a month) with government officials, while only 14.8% of the government respondents reported the same sort of formal meetings. More troubling was the finding that a sizeable portion of civil society participation in the policy process occurred either after key decisions had been made or not at all (Table 19.2). Well over a third (38.1%) of civil society respondents interacted frequently (more than monthly) with personnel from other civil society organizations.

A subsequent ordinary least squares (OLS) regression model derived from Evans and Wellstead's data examined what factors shape and drive civil society organization interaction with government. The OLS model revealed that those engaged in coordinating and planning responsibilities were less likely to work with government agencies, whereas those who identified themselves as strategic analysts were more likely to do so. Co-ordination with other NGOs resulted in a greater level of interaction with government officials. Those who implemented policy were less likely to interact with government officials than those who were involved in the policy process at earlier stages. Finally, the frequency of briefing activity was one of the most robust independent variables in the model. The OLS analysis found that sector of employment, location, age and education levels were all important independent variables. Respondents from Saskatchewan and those with advanced university degrees were

Policy Analysis and the Voluntary Sector

Table 19.2 At what stage of the government process is your organization invited to participate?

	Frequency	%
At all stages	121	20.0
At the very early stages before decisions have been made	80	13.3
After the key design/content elements have been determined	169	28.1
At the implementation stage	48	8.0
Not at all	50	8.2
Total	468	77.6

Source: Evans and Wellstead (2014)

more likely to engage with government officials. Those working in the immigration sector and those from two age cohorts (ages 31–40 and 51–60) were less likely to be involved.

Conclusion

Howlett (2009) explicitly noted the importance of the non-profit, voluntary sector in the policy process but found that the precise elements of the contribution required more serious research attention. In this vein, the emergence and increasing prominence of the New Public Governance framework necessitates that policy process researchers seriously interrogate a number of important questions. In what precise ways and means is the policy process open to a broad range of non-governmental policy actors? Are certain non-governmental actors privileged in the process? What factors enable a non-governmental actor to engage or to refrain from engagement on policy matters? Are certain policy domains more amenable to co-construction than others (e.g., social policy vs. those based on natural/physical sciences)? This chapter has briefly canvassed issues relating to voluntary sector capacities and strategies in policy work, advocacy and construction—perhaps not to answer these questions but to profile the potential for additional research, and to emphasize that such research has serious implications for illuminating what the policy process is and what it is not.

References

Ackerman, John M. 2012. "From Co-Production to Co-Governance". In Victor Pestoff, Taco Brandsen and Bram Verschuere (eds), *New Public Governance, the Third Sector, and Co-Production*. New York: Routledge, 101–126.

Almog-Bar, M. & H. Schmid. 2014. "Advocacy Activities of Nonprofit Human Service Organizations: A Critical Review", *Nonprofit and Voluntary Sector Quarterly*, 43(1), 11–35.

Balser, D. & McClusky, J. 2005. "Managing Stakeholder Relationships and Nonprofit Organization Effectiveness". *Nonprofit Management and Leadership*, 15(3), 295–315.

Baroni, Laura, Brendan J. Carroll, Adam William Chalmers, Luz Maria Muñoz Marquez and Anne Rasmussen. 2014. "Defining and Classifying Interest Groups", *Interest groups & Advocacy* 3(2), 141–159.

Baumgartner, Frank R., Heather A. Larsen-Price, Beth L. Leech and Paul Rutledge. 2011. "Congressional and Presidential Effects on the Demand for Lobbying", *Political Research Quarterly* 64, (1), 3–16.

Bloodgood, Elizabeth, Joannie Tremblay-Boire and Aseem Prakash. 2014. "National Styles of NGO Regulation", *Nonprofit and Voluntary Sector Quarterly* 43(4), 716–736.

Bryce, Herrington J. 2012. *Players in the Public Policy Process: Nonprofits as Social Capital and Agents* (2nd edition). New York: Palgrave Macmillan.

Carter, S. 2011. "Public Policy and the Nonprofit Sector", *The Philanthropist*, 23(4), 427–435.

303

Carter, S., Plewes, B. & Echenberg, H. 2005. *Civil Society and Public Choice: A Directory of Non-Profit Organizations Engaged in Public Policy.* Toronto: Maytree Foundation.

Christensen, R. A. & Ebrahim, A. 2006. "How Does Accountability Affect Mission? The Case of a Nonprofit Serving Immigrants and Refugees", *Nonprofit Management and Leadership*, 17(2), 195.

Colebatch, H. K. (ed.) 2006. *The Work of Policy: An International Survey.* Lanham, MD: Rowman & Littlefield.

Craft, Jonathan and Michael Howlett. 2012. "Policy Formulation, Governance Shifts and Policy Influence: Location and Content in Policy Advisory Systems", *Journal of Public Policy* 32, 79–98.

Evans, Bryan and Halina Sapeha. 2015. "Are Non-Government Policy Actors Being Heard? Assessing New Public Governance", *Canadian Public Administration*, 58(2), 249–270.

Evans, Bryan and Adam Wellstead. 2013. "Policy Dialogue and Engagement between Non-Governmental Organizations and Government: A Survey of Processes and Instruments of Canadian Policy Workers", *Central European Journal of Public Policy*, 7(1), 60–87.

Evans, Bryan and John Shields. 2014. "Nonprofit Engagement with Provincial Policy Officials: The Case of NGO Policy Voice in Canadian Immigrant Settlement Services", *Policy and Society* 33, 117–127.

Evans, Bryan and Adam Wellstead. 2014. "Tales of Policy Estrangement: Non-Governmental Policy Work and Capacity in Three Canadian Provinces", *Canadian Journal of Nonprofit and Social Economy Research*, 5(2), 7–28.

Guo, Chao and Gregory D. Saxton. 2010. "Voice-In, Voice-Out: Constituent Participation and Nonprofit Advocacy", *Nonprofit Policy Forum* 1, 1–25.

Heaney, Michael T., and Geoffrey M. Lorenz. 2013. "Coalition Portfolios and Interest Group Influence over the Policy Process", *Interest Groups & Advocacy* 2(3), 251.

Hoggett, Paul. 1996. "New Modes of Control in the Public Service", *Public Administration* 74 (Spring), 9–32.

Howlett, M. 2009. "Policy Analytical Capacity and Evidence-Based Policy-Making: Lessons from Canada", *Canadian Public Administration* 52(2), 153–175.

Joint Accord Table of the Voluntary Sector Initiative. 2002. *Code of Good Practice On Policy Dialogue.* Ottawa, ON: Voluntary Sector Initiative (Canada).

Jordan, Lisa. 2007. "A Rights-Based Approach to Accountability", in A. Ebrahim and E. Weisband (eds), *Global Accountabilities: Participation, Pluralism, and Public Ethics* 151–167. Cambridge University Press.

Kimberlin, Sara E. 2010. "Advocacy by Nonprofits: Roles and Practices of Core Advocacy Organizations and Direct Service Agencies", *Journal of Policy Practice* 9, 164–182.

Klüver, H. 2013. *Lobbying in the European Union: Interest Groups, Lobbying Coalitions, and Policy Change.* Oxford University Press.

Laforest, Rachel and Michael Orsini. 2005. "Evidence-Based Engagement in the Voluntary Sector: Lessons from Canada", *Social Policy and Administration* 39(5), 481–497.

Lang, Sabine. 2013. *NGOs, Civil Society, and the Public Sphere.* New York: Cambridge University Press.

Mayer, I., Bots, P. and van Daalen, E.. 2004. "Perspectives on Policy Analysis: A Framework for Understanding and Design", *International Journal of Technology, Policy and Management*, 4 (1), 169–191.

McGann, James G. 2014. *2014 Global Go To Think Tank Index Report.* Think Tanks and Civil Societies Program. Philadelphia, PA: University of Pennsylvania.

Migdal, J. 2001. *State in Society: Studying How States and Societies Transform and Constitute One Another.* New York: Cambridge University Press.

Mosley, Jennifer. 2011. "Institutionalization, Privatization, and Political Opportunity: What Tactical Choices Reveal about the Policy Advocacy of Human Service Nonprofits", *Nonprofit and Voluntary Sector Quarterly* 40(3), 435–457.

Mulholland, Elizabeth. 2010. "New Ways to Keep Up Our End of the Policy Conversation", *The Philanthropist* 23(2), 140–145.

Nelson, D. & Yackee, S. W. 2012. "Lobbying Coalitions and Government Policy Change: An Analysis of Federal Agency Rulemaking", *Journal of Politics*, 74, 339–353.

Onyx, Jenny, Lisa Armitage, Bronwen Dalton, Rose Melville, John Casey and Robin Banks. 2010. "Advocacy with Gloves On: The 'Manners' of Strategy Used by Some Third Sector Organizations Undertaking Advocacy in NSW and Queensland", *Voluntas: International Journal of Voluntary and Nonprofit Organizations* 21(1), 41–61.

Osborne, Stephen (ed.) 2010. "Introduction: The (New) Public Governance: A Suitable Case for Treatment?" In his *The New Public Governance: Emerging Perspectives on the Theory and Practice of Public Governance*. London: Routledge.

Pekkanen, Robert and Steven Rathgeb Smith. 2014. "Introduction: Nonprofit Advocacy: Definitions and Concepts". In Robert J. Pekkanen, Steven Rathgeb Smith and Yutaka Tsujinaka (eds), *Nonprofits and Advocacy: Engaging Community and Government in an Era of Retrenchment*. Baltimore, MA: Johns Hopkins University Press.

Pestoff, Victor. 2012. "Social Services in Europe: Some Crucial Conceptual Issues". In Victor Pestoff, Taco Brandsen and Bram Verschuere (eds), *New Public Governance, the Third Sector and Co-production*. New York: Routledge.

Phillips, Susan D. 2007. "Policy Analysis and the Voluntary Sector: Evolving Policy Styles". In L. Dobuzinskis, M. Howlett and D. Laycock (eds), *Policy Analysis in Canada: The State of the Art*. University of Toronto Press.

Phillips, S. and S. Smith. 2011. "Between Governance and Regulation". In S. Phillips and S. Smith (eds), *Governance and Regulation in the Third Sector*. New York and London: Routledge.

Proulx, Jean, Denis Bourque and Sebastien Savard. 2007. "The Government–Third Sector Interface in Quebec", *Voluntas* 18(3), 293–307.

Rasmussen, A., B. Carroll and D. Lowery. 2014. "Representatives of the Public? Public Opinion and Interest Group Activity", *European Journal of Political Research* 53(2), 250–268.

Rhodes, R.A.W. 1996. "The New Governance: Governing Without Government", *Political Studies* 44, 652–667.

Rutzen, D. 2011. "Global Perspectives on the Legal Framework for Civil Society and Relational Governance". In S. Phillips and S.R. Smith (eds), *Governance and Regulation in the Third Sector*. London: Routledge, 260–276.

Sabatier, Paul and Christopher Weible. 2007. "The Advocacy Coalition Framework: Innovations and Clarifications". In Paul Sabatier (ed.), *Theories of the Policy Process*, 2nd edition. Boulder, CO: Westview Press.

Salamon, Lester M. and Stephanie Geller. 2008. *Nonprofit America: A Force for Democracy?* Communique # 9. Center for Civil Society Studies, Institute for Policy Studies. Johns Hopkins University.

Salamon, Lester M., Helmut K. Anheier, Regina List, Stefan Toepler, S. Wojciech Sokolowski and Associates. 1999. *Global Civil Society: Dimensions of the Nonprofit Sector*. Baltimore, MD: Johns Hopkins Center for Civil Society Studies.

Salamon, Lester M., Leslie C. Hems and Kathryn Chinnock. 2000. *The Nonprofit Sector: For What and for Whom?* Center for Civil Society Studies. Baltimore, MD: Johns Hopkins University. http://thirdsectorimpact.eu/site/assets/uploads/page/documents-for-researchers/CNP_WP37_2000.pdf

Thiel, Markus and Emek M. Uçarer. 2014. "Access and Agenda-Setting in the European Union: Advocacy NGOs in Comparative Perspective", *Interest Groups & Advocacy* 3 (1), 99–116.

Tsujinaka, Yutaka, Steven Rathgeb Smith, and Robert Pekkanen. 2014. *Nonprofits and Advocacy: Engaging Community and Government in an Era of Retrenchment*, Baltimore, MD: Johns Hopkins University Press.

United Nations. 2003. *Handbook on Non-Profit Institutions in the System of National Accounts*. New York: United Nations. http://unstats.un.org/unsd/publication/seriesf/seriesf_91e.pdf.

Vaillancourt, Yves. 2009. "Social Economy in the Co-construction of Public Policy", *Annals of Public and Co-operative Economics* 80(2), 275–313.

Vaillancourt, Yves. 2012. "Third sector and the Co-Construction of Canadian Public Policy". In Victor Pestoff, Taco Brandsen and Bram Verschuere (eds), *New Public Governance, the Third Sector and Co-production*. New York: Routledge.

Verschuere, Bram and Joris De Corte. 2013. "Nonprofit Advocacy Under a Third-Party Government Regime: Cooperation or Conflict?" *Voluntas* 24(4), 222–241.

Wayland, S.V. (2006). "Collaboration and Conflict: Immigration and Settlement-Related. Advocacy in Canada", *Policy Matters* 26 (June).

Yoshioka, Takayuki. 2014. "Representational Roles of Nonprofit Advocacy Organizations in the United States", *Voluntas* 25, 1062–1090.

Young, McGee. 2010. *Developing Interests: Organizational Change and the Politics of Advocacy*. Lawrence: University Press of Kansas.

PART V

Advocacy-Based and Academic Policy Analysis

20

MEDIA AND POLICY ANALYSIS

Yu-Ying Kuo and Ming Huei Cheng

Introduction

Lasswell (1970) stated that public policy is problem-oriented, and policy analysis applies a variety of methods. The rational model of policy analysis includes problem analysis, solution analysis and communication. The policy analyst gathers information, theory and facts to assess problems and predict consequences of current and alternative policies. Problem analysis is a process of understanding the problem, framing the problem, modelling the problem, choosing and explaining relevant goals and constraints and selecting a solution method. Solution analysis concerns choosing impact categories for goals, concretely specifying policy alternatives, predicting impacts of alternatives, valuing impacts of alternatives, and assessing and recommending alternatives. Communication means to convey useful advice to clients (Weimer & Vining, 2011). Similarly, Bardach (2011) pointed out the eightfold path to policy analysis: (1) define the problem, (2) assemble some evidence, (3) construct the alternatives, (4) select the criteria, (5) project the outcomes, (6) confront the trade-offs, (7) decide, and (8) tell your story. Policy analysis relies on rational, systematic analysis, and the process of communication, an essential element of policy analysis, relies on storytelling.

As communication platforms, traditional media are one-way transmission platforms that lack participation, efficient feedback and communication from and among stakeholders, including city residents and other players in cities (Zhou & Wang, 2014). Social media is ideal for communicating policy analysis and storytelling because of its participative, interactive, and transparent attributes (Kaplan & Haenlein, 2009; Mangold & Faulds, 2009; Mayfield, 2007; Wigmo & Wikstrom, 2010). Participative, interactive and transparent communication of policy analysis emphasizes information sharing through vertical and horizontal transmission systems in governmental departments (Mu, 2013). Social media is now seen as an important tool to identify policy problems, alternatives and solutions, and to tell policy stories in order to engage citizen participation in the policy process.

Following the development of internet information technology, the development of social media policy has transformed communication between local governments and citizens. In recent years, the number of policies and applications dealing with social media and information technologies to improve the quality of government services and enable greater citizen engagement has exploded. Social media offer enormous opportunities for individuals, business and society to enhance efficiency, and are an important tool for internal and external communications in government. Publicly available social media sites, such as Facebook, Twitter, or other microblogging sites like Weibo and WeChat, are providing governments with attractive options for meeting a variety of objectives. The rise of social media also involves the creation of new policies and guidelines to encourage proper use and to mitigate the risks of social media tools. Developing a social media policy can be an important first step for those government agencies considering using social media and can ultimately serve as a key enabler to responsibly and effectively leverage social media tools (Hrdinová, Helbig & Peters, 2010). The rapid adoption of social media in particular has the potential to provide a convenient venue for dialogue between citizens and with the government. As a consequence, governments are faced with creating proper social media policies, so the analyses of media policy practice is worth further investigation.

Fischer and Forester (1993) indicated that public policy, in essence, is the production of argumentation. Argumentation becomes easy with the aid of social media. Fischer and Gottweis (2012) advocated the importance of argumentation and deliberation. Argumentation is a communicative practice in the process of discourse and narrative. Deliberation comes from actors' communication and expression of discourse and narrative. The rise of new media affects the process of problem identification and construction in representative democracy (Coleman, Moss & Parry, 2015). Those who control the agenda or policy debate in virtual space affect policies. Hence, inducing multiple discourses and narratives would promote the quality of argumentation. Public information from the media influences democratic responsiveness and accountability; in particular, it shapes politicians' views of the political costs of benefits (Bertelli & Sinclair, 2015). Grimmelikhuijsen and Meijer (2015) stated that establishing a direct channel with citizens, and using it to communicate successes, helps the police strengthen their legitimacy, but only slightly and for a small group of interested citizens. Social media use can increase perceived police legitimacy by enabling transparency and participation. Public service should thus focus on creating opportunities for citizenship by forging trusting relationships with members of the public. An increasingly important role of the public servant is to serve citizens and communities by helping citizens articulate and meet their shared goals rather than attempting to control or steer society in new directions (Denhardt & Denhardt, 2015).

In the digital era, many people are immersed in daily use of social media. Facebook has 1.44 billion active users per month, Google has 1.17 billion, and Instagram has 0.4 billion (Chen, 2016). A 2015 digital life survey in Taiwan indicated that 87.2% of respondents (n=14,973) use Facebook, and 83.0% use the messaging app Line. Facebook and Line are two primary social media in Taiwan social life (Lo, 2015).

Microblogging, a broadcast medium in the form of blogging, has become an indispensable application of social media in China since 2009. Microblogs differ from traditional blogs in that their content is typically smaller in both actual and aggregate file size. This allows users to exchange small elements of content such as short sentences, individual images, or video links (Zheng, 2013). Because foreign microblogging services such as Twitter are censored in China, Chinese internet users use Weibo (Chinese for 'microblog') or WeChat. The key features of microblogs are large amounts of information, fast transmission speed and high user engagement. Citizens, opinion leaders and traditional media in China are using microblogs actively as a new channel to receive information, distribute messages and express opinions (Zheng & Zheng, 2014). Recent studies have shown that official microblogging has become a sophisticated e-government effort for social governance, especially for local and central governments. It has led to a gradual change in local government's social governance strategy and a functional change from being a service provider to a 'service predictor' (Schlæger & Jiang, 2014).

Media and Policy Analysis

Prior studies have investigated numerous components of media policy and regulation (Braman, 2004; Puppis, 2010; Hrdinová et al., 2010); government's use of social media (Zavattaro & Sementelli, 2014; Zhou & Wang, 2014; Zheng & Zheng, 2014); and the use of social media for citizen engagement (Mossberger, Wu & Crawford, 2013; Bonsón, Royo & Ratkai, 2015). While there are many high-profile examples of local governments engaging social media tools, social media and policy analysis is still fairly new and relatively unexplored. In order to understand the relationship of media context and policy analysis, the study shows experiences of four East Asian capital cities: Taipei, Tokyo, Seoul and Beijing.

Taipei

Taipei Mayor Ko Wen-je insisted that 'change' is the key for Taipei to become a comfortable, prosperous and sustainable city. Breaking with the traditional approach to management, Mayor Ko has endeavoured to streamline procedures and reform administrative behaviour to provide accessible services to citizens. In 2015, in order to realize citizen participation for a better Taipei, the Taipei city government established the platform of i-Voting to encourage citizens to express their opinions and to vote on issues of concern to citizens. i-Voting has five features (i-Voting, 2016):

1. A simple procedure, everyone can participate;
2. Identity verification, on-time check and vote;
3. Information security, privacy is assured;
4. Distance voting, citizens can vote anywhere;
5. Information disclosure, everyone can see the results.

One year into his administration, the Mayor sought to assess the performance of 33 departments. Each department made a poster to manifest the most impressive performance in 2015, and citizens voted for the best five departments. Each citizen was able to vote once per day, after verification of their email address. The voting duration lasted from January 20 at 8am to February 3 at 8pm, and the city forum and news releases promoted the voting. The results are indicated in Table 20.1. The winning departments were the Taipei City Police Department, Taipei Rapid Transit Corporation, Department of Transportation, Department

Table 20.1 i-Voting on performance of Taipei City Government Departments

Department of Taipei City Government	*# of Votes*
Taipei City Police Department	9509
Taipei Rapid Transit Corporation	7559
Department of Transportation	7476
Department of Environmental Protection	6099
Department of Information and Tourism	5083
Department of Urban Development	4513
Department of Education	4211
Department of Civil Affairs	3963
Public Works Department	3896
Taipei City Fire Department	3796
Department of Finance	3654
Department of Rapid Transit Systems	3384
Department of Social Welfare	3341

(*Continued*)

Table 20.1 (Continued)

Department of Taipei City Government	# of Votes
Secretariat	3226
Department of Cultural Affairs	3181
Department of Information Technology	2989
Department of Sports	2908
Department of Labor	2757
Department of Health	2647
Department of Economic Development	2188
Department of Government Ethics	2138
Indigenous Peoples Commission	2081
Department of Personnel	2012
Department of Civil Servant Development	1989
Research, Development and Evaluation Commission	1987
Taipei Water Department	1968
Urban Planning Commission	1949
Department of Budget, Accounting and Statistics	1927
Department of Compulsory Military Service	1886
Taipei Feitsui Reservoir Administration	1873
Department of Legal Affairs	1852
Department of Land	1569
Hakka Affairs Commission	1369

Source: Authors' translation of i-voting, Taipei City Government, https://ivoting.taipei/3-survey-result/1-orderby (accessed on 5 February 2016)

of Environmental Protection, and Department of Information and Tourism. Although some criticized the departments' efforts to manipulate the voting through mass mobilization, most felt that the results generally reveal citizens' satisfaction on the city government's performance.

Tokyo

In a 2013 survey on internet use, Japan's Ministry of Internal Affairs and Communications found that 79% of respondents receive and send emails, 58.8% use the internet for map and traffic information, while 46.1% use social media (Table 20.2). Table 20.3 indicates the

Table 20.2 2013 participants in internet use in Japan (Number of respondents: 3,621; in percent)

Receiving and sending e-mails (excluding e-mail magazine)	79.0
Receiving mail magazines (free)	37.0
Browsing webs and writing blogs	44.9
Use of social media	46.1
Use of sites for video upload and share	51.9
Map or traffic information services (free)	58.8
Use of the weather reports (free)	51.7
Use of news websites	46.9
Transaction of goods or services	51.5

Note: Because response rates varied by prefecture of residence and by age of the heads of households, results were weighted to properly represent the population.

Source: Ministry of Internal Affairs and Communications, Japan

Media and Policy Analysis

Table 20.3 Internet users in Japan, 2012–2016

Year	Internet Users**	Penetration (% of Pop)	Total Population	Non-Users (Internetless)	1Y User Change	1Y User Change	Population Change
2016★	115,111,595	91.1 %	126,323,715	11,212,120	0.1 %	117,385	−0.2 %
2015★	114,994,210	90.9 %	126,573,481	11,579,271	0.1 %	143,694	−0.17 %
2014	114,850,516	90.6 %	126,794,564	11,944,048	0.8 %	932,305	−0.15 %
2013	113,918,211	89.7 %	126,984,964	13,066,753	12.7 %	12,846,631	−0.12 %
2012	101,071,581	79.5 %	127,139,821	26,068,240	0.5 %	472,929	−0.09 %

★ estimate for July 1, 2016
★★ Internet User = individual age 14+ using internet via any device.

Excerpted from Internet Live Stats (www.InternetLiveStats.com)

growth in internet usage in Japan. The Ministry of Internal Affairs and Communications' survey was conducted in 2013, and it is reasonable to assume that the percentage has increased further since then. According to Internet Live Stats, Japan has one of the highest internet penetration rates and ranks number five in total number of internet users worldwide.

The Tokyo metropolitan government seeks citizens' opinions on important issues through surveys, whose process, sample size and results are revealed on the internet so that citizens who are interested in city affairs can access them at any time. Since 2011, some of the important issues that have been surveyed include the following.

2016
- 4 February, Child Abuse

2015
- 21 December, Residency in Tokyo
- 16 December, Satisfaction with Tokyo Government
- 30 October, Tokyo Urban Planning
- 10 August, Agriculture in Tokyo
- 3 August, Assistance to Victims
- 2 February, Healthy Environment for Children

2014
- 22 December, Safe, Reliable and Comfortable Roads
- 26 November, Healthy Food
- 6 November, Interest Rate in Tokyo
- 30 September, Waste and Resource Recycling
- 26 August, Healthy Teeth
- 2 April, Sanitary Sewer
- 8 January, Ocean Park

2013
- 22 November, Prevention of Drug Abuse
- 12 November, Satisfaction with Tokyo Government
- 29 October, Food Safety
- 30 July, Knowledge of Diseases
- 28 January, Road Construction in Tokyo

(Continued)

2012

- 7 December, Tokyo 2020
- 5 November, Travel in Tokyo
- 9 October, Satisfaction with Tokyo Government
- 10 September, Forest and Forestry in Tokyo
- 31 July, Restaurant Eating Habits
- 6 March, Electricity Saving

2011

- 15 December, 2020 Tokyo
- 17 November, Earthquake Policy
- 27 October, Satisfaction with Tokyo Government
- 8 September, Family, School and Social Environment for Children
- 14 July, Prevention of HIV/AIDS

(www.metro.tokyo.jp/POLICY/TOMIN/monitor.htm)

The survey on child abuse in 2016 is an example of how the Tokyo city government obtained citizens' feelings, opinions and suggestions on the prevention of child abuse.

The Tokyo metropolitan government places great emphasis on child counselling and family support. In order to prevent child abuse and to establish a safety network for all stages of child development, a survey was conducted to evaluate the status quo and propose solutions for improvement. Considering gender, age and profession, the survey was sent to 334 sampled targets during 14–28 December 2015; 237 responses were received, a response rate of 71.0%. Table 20.4 describes the characteristics of the respondents.

Table 20.4 Respondents of survey on child abuse

			%
Respondents		*237*	*100*
Gender	Male	119	50.2
	Female	118	49.8
Age	20–29	6	2.5
	30–39	15	6.3
	40–49	44	18.6
	50–59	57	24.1
	60–69	50	21.1
	70 above	65	27.4
Profession	Corporate	51	21.5
	Organization (NPO)	10	4.2
	Self-employed	17	7.2
	Welfare employer	6	2.5
	Welfare employee	33	13.9
	Teacher	4	1.7
	Student	2	0.8
	Housewife	45	19
	Non-employment	35	14.8
	Other	34	14.3

Developed from www.metro.tokyo.jp/POLICY/TOMIN/monitor.htm

For example, when asked in Q1, 'Do you feel the number of cases of child abuse has increased?', 77.2% of respondents believe that it has. Q3 asks: 'If you suspect someone of child abuse, will you report it?' 84.8% of respondents say yes. Q13 asks: 'What are the main causes of child abuse?' 43.5% of respondents indicate the main cause is economic and 39.7% point out the problem comes from family abuse. Q16 asks: 'What are the effective solutions to child abuse?' 41.8% of respondents state that short custody from social institutions can help, 40.5% indicate that family counselling and experience exchange can help, and 38.0% say regular family visits from social workers can help. Q19 asks: 'Where do you receive information about the prevention of child abuse?' 56.5% of respondents indicate that they are informed by 'Tokyo report', issued by the Tokyo city government, or news. The results provide evidence for problem identification and policymaking.

Seoul

In recent years, many governments have worked to increase openness and transparency in their actions. Information and communication technologies are seen by many as a cost-effective and convenient means to promote openness and transparency and to reduce corruption. The number of internet users is growing exponentially in Korea, from 19 million in 2000 to 45 million in 2015, a 2.5 times increase in 15 years. Approximately 92.3% of the population now uses the internet (Internet World Stats). Information systems have been mostly used to enhance the efficiency of administrative procedures as well as help to improve transparency of civil affairs in the Seoul Metropolitan Government. The OPEN (Online Procedures ENhancement for Civil Applications) system is a web-based IT application aimed at ensuring administrative transparency by disclosing administrative procedures. This experience is a good example of how new information technology can be utilized to fight corruption, improve the transparency of urban administration, and bring services closer to citizens.

The OPEN System was initiated by Seoul's former Mayor, Goh Kun, in January 1999, and opened to the public on 15 April of that year (Holzer & Kim, 2002). To open its administration in order to share it with citizens, Seoul announced the Open Administration 2.0 in 2012. Open Administration 2.0 is a citizen-centric administration based on communication, transparency, sharing and collaboration through the establishment of the Seoul Information Communication Center. Citizens are not just recipients of various public services; they are also creators of diverse types of public information for fellow citizens utilizing an entirely new type of participatory administrative platform. In March 2012, the website of the Seoul Government was completely transformed to a state-of-the-art content management system (CMS), enabling employees to post their blog-type writings on the site. Other government websites have been developed into open, participatory web pages so that the information on each site can be scrapbooked to social networks and citizens can make comments directly on each site (Seoul Metropolitan Government, n.d.a).

Furthermore, Seoul has opened the Seoul Open Data Plaza (n.d.) and created its own Instagram account in order to share public information with citizens, create diverse business opportunities for the private sector, and to develop the IT industry. The plaza is an online channel to share and provide citizens with all of Seoul's public data, such as real-time bus operation schedules, subway schedules, non-smoking areas, locations of public Wi-Fi services, shoeshine shops, and facilities for disabled people. Information registered in Seoul Open Data Plaza is provided in the open API (Application Programming Interface) format, and is designed to enable citizens to be able to use it in creating diverse businesses.

The rampant phenomenon of corruption in Korea has been a serious obstacle in the process of its democratic development (Kim, 2003). As a result of Korea's cultural heritage of collectivism and nepotism, citizens generally have low trust in public institutions for the handling process of civil applications. This new policy has sought to increase transparency in the civil administration and prevent unnecessary delays and unjust handling of civil affairs on the part of civil servants. By doing so, the OPEN System contributed to restoring public trust in the Seoul Metropolitan Government. Among the new policies, the system of online disclosure of the civil application process received particularly favourable reviews from Koreans as well as from overseas. For example, citizens, public administration specialists, and government employees voted the OPEN System as the Most Valuable Policy of Seoul in 1999 and 2000. Consequently, the system was recognized as a 'Good Practice' at the 9th International Anti-Corruption Conference in Durban, South Africa, in 1999 and the United Nations' Seoul Anti-Corruption Symposium in 2001. Such international recognition and successful achievements drove local Korean governments to adopt similar IT applications as the OPEN System.

The Audit and Inspection Bureau was put in charge of overall development and implementation of the OPEN System. The Bureau selected target civil applications to be disclosed with a primary focus on those (1) with a history of frequent corruption scandals, (2) whose handling processes are complicated enough to inconvenience citizens, and (3) whose opening to the public is likely to block solicitation of special favours. The Bureau also determined specific items to be entered by front desk officials and monitored system management as a whole. In addition, the Information System Planning Bureau was responsible for technical support, such as task analysis, systems development, and systems introduction. The Bureau also was in charge of personnel training and system maintenance in the implementation stage.

It is notable that the Mayor and the Audit and Inspection Bureau's strong initiative made it possible to overcome civil servants' unwillingness to cooperate, and resistance against computerization. Civil servants were asked to continually input data regarding public services, as the OPEN System is a dynamic system that makes real-time information available on the status of an application and tracks its progress until completion. The Bureau monitors input and process delays, verifies any omitted documents or mistakes in data input, and urges the corresponding departments (or civil officials) in charge to correct the problems detected. According to Park (2005), citizens are allowed to track their applications for permits and approvals by stages, and to access related information (e.g., regulations). They are able to monitor in real time who is handling and reviewing their applications, if there are any problems in the application review process, and when applications are expected to be complete. Applicants can find out why an application is rejected, and raise questions about or objections to administrative decisions. In short, citizens can monitor the entire application handling processes online whenever they want and wherever they are. As a result, the OPEN System improves administrative transparency by allowing citizens to check their applications from submission through the final decision, and to monitor any delays or mistakes in data entry and handling. Citizens save time and money and avoid unnecessary phone calls or in-person visits.

After the system had run for one year, a South Korean research institute conducted a survey in 2000. 55% of respondents thought that government corruption was lower than before the reform. After several years, another follow-up survey showed that the public satisfaction with government officials' integrity increased every year. Now, the system's scope has been extended to 54 areas (see Table 20.5). More than 82,000 officials across 770 municipal government departments are required to input information into the OPEN System.

Media and Policy Analysis

Table 20.5 Areas covered by the OPEN system

area	housing	transportation	construction	culture & tourism	urban planning	others
Number	7	11	6	7	3	20

Sources: http://english.seoul.go.kr; http://english.seoul.go.kr/get-to-know-us/statistics-of-seoul

Seoul's OPEN System policy is a good example of opening up administrative procedures to the public through a real-time online system that allows citizens to monitor the process around the clock. This trend revolutionized administrative practices by enabling Seoul to provide speedy quality services and enhance efficiency. The Seoul Metropolitan Government has also taken full advantage of developments in information technology and reformed its administrative procedures.

Beijing

Internet users in China are facing a different situation than the other countries examined here. As most media are controlled by the state, Chinese citizens have turned to microblogs like Twitter, Weibo and WeChat to openly exchange unfettered news and opinion. Weibo, the Chinese word for 'microblog', refers to mini-blogging services, including social chat sites and platform sharing. Microblogging has been a mainstream internet application and a hub of public opinion in China since 2009. On microblogging sites like Twitter, Weibo and WeChat, individual internet users can set up real-time information sharing communities, and upload and update information in 140-character blocks. By the end of 2015, the total number of Chinese microblogging users had reached 290 million, representing 42% of total internet users in China (National Bureau of Statistics of China, 2016). The Chinese government has recognized the importance of microblogs and has launched its own government microblog accounts to disclose government information and foster interactions between government and citizens (Zheng & Zheng, 2014). Under the concept of 'Microblog for all people', official government microblogs have expanded rapidly, and serve to enhance government communication with the public and release information in a timely manner.

According to the 2015 Annual National Government New Media Report (China Government, 2015), more than 28,000 government microblogging accounts and more than 10,000 chat sites have been launched by government agencies at various levels in China. The majority of government microblogging accounts are run by county-level governments, most by judicial and police departments. The Beijing municipal government was ranked as the number 2 government microblogging site in January 2015 (Table 20.6), and received the highest score in communication and content in China.

The Beijing government's Weibo site, 'Beijing Announcement', launched on 30 November 2011 by the Information Office of the Beijing municipal government, has integrated 39 departments and units to provide a one-stop service covering all aspects of daily life, including food, housing, transportation, education, public security, and health. By the end of February 2016, 7,366,153 users were registered and the total number of Weibos released reached 35,303 (Beijing Release Weibo, 2016).

In 2015, of more than 2,000 official departments and units, the top three blogs—as calculated by using the capability of communication, interaction and service ability—are

Table 20.6 The top 10 provincial microblogs in China

Rank	Unit	Weibo/WeChat	Comprehensive score
1	Shanghai	Shanghai Announcement	102.26
2	Beijing	Beijing Announcement	101.36
3	Sichuan	Sichuan Announcement	101.13
4	Zhejiang	Zhejiang Announcement	101.03
5	Jilin	Jilin Announcement	100.45
6	Guangdong	Guangdong Announcement	100.39
7	Chongqing	Chongqing Micro Release	100.33
8	Jiangsu	Microblog Jiangsu	100.28
9	Anhui	Anhui Announcement	100.20
10	Shandong	Shandong Announcement	100.05

Translated and adapted from http://news.xinhuanet.com/yuqing/2015-02/09/c_127475924.htm (accessed 25 September 2016). See source for individual category scores.

Table 20.7 The top 10 government microblogs in Beijing

Rank	Microblog	Score
1	Safe Beijing	99.71
2	Beijing Subway	97.25
3	Beijing Fabu	88.03
4	Beijing Police	87.24
5	JingKan Subway	82.20
6	Trans Beijing	80.98
7	Weather Beijing	80.39
8	Capital Netpolice	74.33
9	Beijing Bus group	74.31
10	Beijing 12345	74.31

Translated and adapted from http://bj.bendibao.com/news/2015813/198280.shtm (accessed 25 September 2016). See source for individual category scores.

'Safe Beijing', 'Beijing Subway' and 'Beijing Fabu'. Table 20.7 shows the top ten blogs and their total scores.

The operation mechanism of 'Beijing Announcement' is mainly through the 'Beijing Microblog Conference Hall', which is a microblog platform run by the municipal government. It is responsible for collecting all of the resources of government microblog accounts and plays an important role in information transmission, public communication and mobilization. In order to implement point-to-point service between the government and citizens, Beijing Microblog Conference Hall is committed to responding promptly to public queries and complaints. Beijing Microblog Conference Hall has been recognized as a breakthrough innovation of government microblog application.

In an analysis of content from Beijing Announcement in 2012, 40% of messages are related to daily life services, followed by 21.05% related to news information, 14.91% to city promotion information, and 10.53% related to administrative information and citizen participation, respectively. Government microblog accounts post more messages related to service-oriented activities, such as transportation, weather, education, employment and

Media and Policy Analysis

Table 20.8 Message content in Beijing announcements

	category				
	life service	news information	city propaganda	administrative information	interaction
2012	40%	21.05%	14.91%	10.53%	10.53%
2013	38.7%	55.7%		4.6%	

Source: Zheng (2013), Ho (2014).

medical services (see Table 20.8). However, the year after this research was conducted, Ho (2014) found that the category of news information accounts for 55.7% of all Beijing microblogs, followed by daily life services, with 38.7% of all microblogs. The category of news information is focused on the meeting of NPC (National People's Congress) and CPPCC (Chinese People's Political Consultative Conference), policy reports and mayoral affairs. This may indicate a shift towards more major news events and official promotion-oriented use of microblogging by the Beijing government.

In order to assist the government in controlling speech and communication on the internet, the Beijing metropolitan government introduced the real name policy to microblogging in March 2012. The real name policy requires all microblog users to register using the name on their government-issued ID card. The Beijing government also enacted several regulations on microblog development and administration, as shown in the Appendix to this chapter.

Based on the discussion above, Beijing government microblogs have been used widely to disseminate information and deliver public services. Rigorous regulations have been established. As a tool designed for and centred around interaction, microblogs promote two-way conversation, engagement and collaboration between the government and citizens. However, a majority of messages are overly formal and posted for self-promotion by the Beijing government, indicating that the new media policy of the Beijing government tends to avoid interactions with citizens to stay away from potential trouble. As for the dimension of deliberation, Beijing microblogs follow the same news production logic as traditional mass media. To some extent government microblogs are oriented towards public deliberation, but the Beijing government still needs to prove their diversity.

Conclusion

From this examination of the experiences of Taipei, Tokyo, Seoul and Beijing, it is evident that social media have been popular in the process of policy analysis. The use and extent of social media are closely related to a country's institutional environment, and its politics, economy and culture. That's why this paper explores social media and policy analysis, particularly the application of social media for citizen participation, in four capital city governments. The discussion indicates that government agencies increasingly leverage social media to improve the quality of government services and enable greater citizen engagement. Taipei i-Voting has opened a channel for citizens to express their own opinions on government services. The Tokyo city government relies on frequent surveys to obtain information on citizen satisfaction, and opinions and suggestions on policies. In Seoul, the OPEN System policy's transparent data-handling process enables citizens to access public services through the internet and shows the possibility of achieving efficient and democratic administration. The system's success may be attributed to the powerful leadership of the city government, the development of information technologies, and citizens' attitudes. Beijing government microblogging has opened a new stage of 'Microblog Governance'. These online platforms fulfil the purpose of self-promotion and public opinion guidance rather than service delivery. Obviously, social media help enhance accountability, openness, and transparency in the process of policy analysis. Through the practice of social media and policy analysis, lessons can be drawn from one country to another.

References

Bardach, Eugene (2011). *A Practical Guide for Policy Analysis: The Eightfold Path to More Effective Problem Solving* 3rd Ed. Washington, DC: CQ Press.

Beijing Release Weibo. http://gov.weibo.com/2418724427. Accessed 29 February 2016.

Bertelli, Anthony M. and J. Andrew Sinclair (2015). "Mass Administrative Reorganization, Media Attention, and the Paradox of Information", *Public Administration Review*, 75(6), 855–866.

Bonsón, E., Royo, S., and M. Ratkai (2015). "Citizens' Engagement on Local Governments' Facebook Sites: An Empirical Analysis—The Impact of Different Media and Content Types in Western Europe", *Government Information Quarterly*, 32, 52–62.

Braman, S. (2004). "Where Has Media Policy Gone? Defining the Field in the Twenty-first Century", *Communication Law and Policy*, 9(2), 153–182.

Chen, Cheng-Yi (2016). "Why Is Social Media Popular?" *Commonwealth*, 589, 25.

Chen, Liang-Yu (2015). "Book Review: *The Argumentative Turn Revisited: Public Policy as Communicative Practice*", *Taiwan Democracy Quarterly*, 12(2), 161–168.

China Government (2015). Annual National Government New Media Report, http://news.xinhuanet.com/yuqing/128638812_14530. Accessed 15 January 2016

Coleman, S., Moss, G. and Parry, K. (eds.) (2015). *Can the Media Serve Democracy? Essays in Honour of Jay G. Blumler*. Basingstoke, UK: Palgrave Macmillan.

Denhardt, Janet V. and Robert B. Denhardt (2015). "The New Public Service Revisited", *Public Administration Review*, 75(5), 664–672.

Fischer, Frank and John Forester (eds) (1993). *The Argumentative Turn in Policy Analysis and Planning*. Durham, NC: Duke University Press.

Fischer, Frank and Herbert Gottweis (eds). (2012). *The Argumentative Turn Revisited: Public Policy as Communicative Practice*. Durham, NC: Duke University Press.

Grimmelikhuijsen, Stephan G. and Albert J. Meijer. (2015). "Does Twitter Increase Police Legitimacy?" *Public Administration Review*, 75(4), 598–608.

Ho, Jei (2014). "The Comparative Research of Government Microblog Release Contents", *China Newspaper Industry*, April, 33–35.

Holzer, Marc and Byong-Joon Kim (2002). *Building Good Governance: Reforms in Seoul*. The National Center for Public Productivity and Seoul Development Institute.

Hrdinová, J., Helbig, N. and Peters, C. S. (2010). *Designing Social Media Policy for Government: Eight Essential Elements*. Center for Technology in Government, SUNY University at Albany.

Internet Live Stats, www.internetlivestats.com/internet-users/japan. Accessed 17 February 2016.

Internet World Stats, www.internetworldstats.com/top20.htm. Accessed 17 February 2016.

i-voting, Taipei City Government, https://ivoting.taipei/3-survey-result/1-orderby

Kaplan, A. M. and M. Haenlein, (2009). "Users of the World, Unite! The Challenges and Opportunities of Social Media", *Business Horizons*, 53(1), 59–68.

Kim, Young-Jong (2003). "Anti-Corruption System in Korea". *Anti-Corruption Symposium 2001: The Role of On-line Procedures in Promoting Good Governance*. ST/ESA/PAD/SER.E/32. United Nations.

Lasswell, Harold D., (1970). "The Emerging Conception of the Policy Sciences", *Policy Sciences*, 1(1), 3–30.

Lo, J. Y. (2015). "Digital Life". http://topic.cw.com.tw/2015digitallife. Accessed 17 February 2016.

Mangold, W. G. and D. J. Faulds (2009). "Social Media: The New Hybrid Element of the Promotion Mix", *Business Horizons*, 52(1), 357–365.

Mayfield, A. (2007). What is Social Media? iCrossing. www.icrossing.co.uk/fileadmin/uploads/eBooks/What_is_Social_Media_iCrossing_ebook.pdf. Accessed 20 February 2016.

Media and Policy Analysis

Mossberger, K., Wu, Y. and Crawford, J. (2013). "Connecting Citizens and Local Governments? Social Media and Interactivity in Major U.S. Cities", *Government Information Quarterly*, 30, 351–358.

Mu, F. (2013). Old Bell Tower: Microblog Approach for City Marketing. 51 Callcenter website. www.51callcenter.com/newsinfo/206/3542178. Accessed 20 February 2016.

National Bureau of Statistics of China (n.d.), www.stats.gov.cn/english. Accessed 25 February 2016.

Park, Hun Myoung (2005). "A Cost-Benefit Analysis of the Seoul OPEN System: Policy Lessons for Electronic Government Projects". Proceedings of the 38th Hawaii International Conference on System Sciences. https://static.aminer.org/pdf/PDF/000/247/222/a_cost_benefit_analysis_of_the_seoul_open_system_policy.pdf?origin=publication_detail. Accessed 10 January 2016.

Puppis, M. (2010). "Media Governance: A New Concept for the Analysis of Media Policy and Regulation", *Communication, Culture & Critique*, 3, 134–149.

Schlæger, Jesper and Min Jiang (2014). "Official Microblogging and Social Management by Local Governments in China", *China Information*, 28(2), http://cin.sagepub.com/content/28/2/189. abstract. Accessed 12 January 2016.

Seoul Metropolitan Government (n.d.a). http://english.seoul.go.kr/, and http://english.seoul.go.kr/get-to-know-us/statistics-of-seoul. Accessed 20 February 2016.

Seoul Metropolitan Government (n.d.b). "Seoul e-Government." http://citynet-ap.org/wp-content/uploads/2014/06/Seoul-e-Government-English.pdf. Accessed 7 July 2016.

Seoul Open Data Plaza (n.d). data.seoul.go.kr. Accessed 17 February 2016.

Tokyo City Government, www.metro.tokyo.jp/POLICY/TOMIN/monitor.htm. Accessed 17 February 2016.

Weimer, David and Aidan R. Vining, (2011). *Policy Analysis: Concepts and Practice* 5th ed. New York: Longman.

Wigmo, J. and Wikstrom, E. (2010). Social Media Marketing: What Role Can Social Media Play as a Marketing Tool? Bachelor dissertation, Linnaus University.

Zavattaro, S. and A. J. Sementelli (2014). "A Critical Examination of Social Media Adoption in Government: Introducing Omnipresence", *Government Information Quarterly*, 31, 257–264.

Zheng, Lei (2013). "Social Media in Chinese Government: Drivers, Challenges and Capabilities", *Government Information Quarterly*, 30, 369–376.

Zheng, L. and T. Zheng (2014). "Innovation Through Social Media in the Public Sector: Information and Interactions", *Government Information Quarterly*, 31, s106–s117.

Zhou, L. and T. Wang (2014). "Social Media: A New Vehicle for City Marketing in China", *Cities*, 37, 27–32.

Appendix: Beijing Microblog Regulation

(sourced from http://news.xinhuanet.com/newmedia/2011-12/16/c_111249899.htm, and cited from https://en.m.wikipedia.org/wiki/Microblogging_in_China)

1. For standardizing the microblog service and its development and management, maintaining the order of online communication, ensuring information securities, protecting the legitimate interest of the Internet information services sites and the microblog users, satisfying the public's needs to Internet information, and promoting well-ordered development of the Internet, this regulation referred to the actual situation of the city and is enacted according to the 'Telecommunications Regulations of the People's Republic of China', the 'Measures for the Administration of Internet Information Services' and other laws, legislations, and regulations.

2. All website firms developing microblog services within the city's administrative area and all their microblog users ought to comply with this regulation.

3. The microblog development and management adheres to the principles of positive utilization, practical development, rightful administration, and security guarantee. It has positive impact on promoting microblog construction and use, as well as its service to the community.

4. The development of microblog services must comply with the constitution, laws, legislations, and regulations. It should propagate the socialist core value system and the advanced socialist culture, and serve to the establishment of a socialist harmonious society.
5. All rights reserved to the municipal government of Beijing to enact plans for microblog service and development, and to enact regulations on the total amount, structure and layout of the microblog service sites.
6. All microblog service sites within the city's administration area must rightfully ask for permission from the department that is in charge of Internet information content before applying for a telecommunications business license or performing non-operational Internet information services filing procedures.
7. All microblog service sites must comply with relevant laws, legislations, regulations and the following rules:
   (1) Establishing and improving administrative regulations for microblog information security.
   (2) Determining the agency responsible for information security, and equipping with appropriate personnel with professional knowledge and skills according to the number of users and the amount of information on microblogging sites.
   (3) Implementing technical security control measures.
   (4) Establishing and improving the administrative regulations on user information security; protecting the user information security and strictly prohibiting disclosure of user information.
   (5) Establishing and improving the disclosure system of false; publicizing truthful information timely.
   (6) Must not provide information interface to websites without a telecommunications business license or that fails to record performing non–commercial Internet information service to relevant departments.
   (7) Must not create fake microblog user accounts.
   (8) Prohibiting and controlling users who spread harmful information; reporting to the public security bureau if found a violation of public security administration or a suspect of crime.
   (9) Assisting and cooperating with relevant departments to carry out administration and management.
8. All microblog service sites must establish and improve censorship regulations on information content, and regulate the creation, copy, publish and transmit of content on microblogging sites.
9. Any group or person who registers a microblog account and create, duplicate, publish or transmit information must use real identification information; must not use fake or others' residence identification information, business registration information or organization code information to register a microblog account. Microblog service sites must ensure the authenticity of registered users' information.
10. Any organization or person must not unlawfully use microblog to create, duplicate, publish or transmit information containing any content that:
    (1) violates the principles of the constitution;
    (2) endangers national security, leaks state secrets, subverts the national government and regime or undermines national unity;
    (3) harms national honor and national interest;
    (4) incites ethnic hatred, ethnic discrimination or undermines national unity;

Media and Policy Analysis

(5) undermines the state religion policies or propagates cult and feudalistic superstition;

(6) spreads rumors, disturbs social order or undermines social stability;

(7) spreads obscenity, pornography, gambling, violence and terror or abets the commission of crimes;

(8) insults or slanders others, infringes others' lawful rights and interest;

(9) incites unlawful assembly, association, procession, demonstration or gatherings that disturbs social order;

(10) plans activities under the name of illegal civil organizations;

(11) contains other content prohibited by laws and administrative regulations.

11. The news administrative department of the municipal people's government, the municipal public security bureau, the municipal department of telecommunication administration and the municipal department of Internet information content must work on microblog development and administration in accordance with their respective responsibilities.

12. The Association of Online Media, the Internet Industry Association, the Communication Industry Association and other industry organizations must establish and improve the self-regulation in the microblog industry, guide the establishment and improvement of microblog service regulations, and train and educate the websites' employees.

13. Any organization or persons may report acts that violate this regulation to the news administrative department of the municipal people's government, the municipal public security bureau, the municipal department of telecommunication administration and the municipal department of Internet information content. The department that receives the report must handle it in accordance to the law.

14. For microblog users and microblog service sites who violate this regulation, the news administrative department of the municipal people's government, the municipal public security bureau, the municipal department of telecommunication administration and the municipal department of Internet information content must handle it in accordance to the law.

15. Microblog service sites that opened before the publication of this regulation must, within three months from the date of publication of this regulation, apply for relevant formalities at the municipal department that is in charge of Internet information content, and regulates the existing microblog users.

16. This regulation shall come into force as of the date of publication.

21

POLICY ANALYSIS AND THINK TANKS IN COMPARATIVE PERSPECTIVE

Diane Stone and Stella Ladi

1. Introduction

The term *think tank* is one that has been subject to many attempts at definition but there is no settled or agreed meaning. In large part this is due to the significant cross-national differences in the historical development, legal constitution, organizational size and socio-political status of think tanks. The term itself has become problematic as it 'is a verbal container which accommodates a heterogeneous set of meanings' ('tHart & Vromen, 2008, p. 135).

In the broader understanding of the term adopted in this chapter, 'think tanks' engage in research, analysis and communication for policy development within local communities, national governments and international institutions in both public and private domains (Stone, 2013a, p. 64). This broad view contrasts with the dominant Anglo-American notion of think tanks as organizational manifestations of civil society.

Generally, in the Anglo-American tradition, these organizations are constituted as non-governmental organizations (NGOs). However, in Europe and Asia it is not unusual to find think tanks that are either semi-governmental agencies or quasi-autonomous units within government. This is most particularly the case in China (Abb, 2015; Zhu & Xue, 2007). Additionally, some European political parties have created in-house think tanks in the form of party institutes or foundations such as the Konrad-Adenauer-Stiftung associated with the Christian Democratic Party in Germany. In parts of North Asia, think tanks are often affiliated with business corporations such as the Mitsubishi Research Institute, a profit-making institute founded in 1970.

Despite this divergence in legal constitution, the roles and functions of think tanks put them at the intersection of academia, public policy and politics where they aim to make connections between policy analysis and policymaking. However, there is considerable diversity among think tanks in terms of size, ideology, resources, and the quality or quantum of analytic output produced.

Notwithstanding the prosperous, well-known think tanks like RAND, the Brookings Institution, or the Council on Foreign Relations in the United States, the majority of think tanks around the world are relatively small organizations. One of the first extensive analyses of the think tank phenomenon a decade ago noted that most operated with a dozen or so research staff and annual budgets of approximately US$2–$3.5 million (Boucher et al.,

Policy Analysis by Think Tanks

2004). Today, the situation is not much changed. Capacity-building initiatives such as the Think Fund (financed through the Open Society Foundations network) and the Think Tank Initiative (financed through a partnership initially launched by the William and Flora Hewlett Foundation) note that their grantee organizations are in need of both funding assistance towards core operational costs (rather than project funding) as well as mentoring in research standards and for professionalized policy analysis (see Struyk & Haddaway, 2011; Welner, 2010).

Aside from policy analysis, think tanks also perform a range of ancillary activities that help amplify their policy analysis and sometimes propel their policy products into decision-making circles. The diversity of activities and functions has presented dilemmas in defining think tanks (reflected in the broad description above), and this has been compounded by their dramatic proliferation, hybrid forms, and world-wide spread over the past two decades. Think tank modes of policy analysis range, at one end of the spectrum, from highly scholarly, academic, or technocratic in style, to overtly ideological, partisan, and advocacy driven, at the other, with vastly different standards of quality throughout.

Think tank work in applying knowledge to policy problems is complemented by organizational strategies to develop advisory ties to government, industry or the public as brokers of policy analysis. Accordingly, think tank policy analysis is not simply an intellectual exercise that is manifested through expert commentary or policy documents. Instead, policy analysis is also action oriented and reliant on policy entrepreneurship, institution building, and competition in a marketplace of ideas.

This positivist and pluralist conception of think tanks competing nationally and internationally in their advocacy towards governments and international organizations is complicated by understandings of think tank influence that dwell on the longer-term capacity to shape the climate of opinion and develop narratives that structure world views and policy beliefs. Consequently, strategies to directly affect the course of a piece of legislation, or the wording of policy initiatives, must be considered alongside efforts at longer-term, indirect, and subtle influence over discourses of governance.

In this chapter we first discuss the different periods of think tank organizational development and the way these periods relate to different types of policy analysis. We then move to a presentation of the different modes of policy analysis and research methods used by think tanks, followed by a discussion of the way think tanks promote policy analysis to external audiences. The concluding section critically evaluates the utility and influence of think tank policy analysis.

2. Epochs of Think Tank Organizational Development

The periods of think tank development from early in the twentieth century parallel the evolution of policy analysis. Three broad stages can be identified: the first group of think tanks that emerged prior to World War II; the second wave of Cold War, peace research and development studies institutes, alongside those with a domestic social and economic policy focus, found primarily in Organisation for Economic Co-operation and Development (OECD) countries; and the world-wide think tank boom from the 1980s continuing to this day (Stone and Denham, 2004). Signs of a fourth cycle are appearing and point to mature think tank ecologies. Yet there are also issues of policy analysis saturation in some national contexts. There is a dual dynamic of both heightened competition in tandem with increased collaboration with other policy knowledge producers in the internet era.

325

a. Twentieth-Century Think Tank Innovation

The first think tanks emerged in response to societal and economic problems spawned by urbanization, industrialization and economic growth in English-speaking countries, but most prominently in the United States. There are many possible reasons for this heightened degree of development: the US has a strong philanthropic sector, a conducive tax system, political parties that act as electoral coalitions, a pluralist political system, and the division of powers in its federal structure as well as between executive and legislature of the United States (Smith, 1991). The US continues to have a far larger population of think tanks than any other country.

Notwithstanding the numerical supremacy of think tanks in the US, in general, the dynamics behind the first wave of think tank development in North America and the British dominions were symptomatic of, and in response to, the growth of state responsibilities and regulatory reach; industrialization and diversification of economies; the expansion of universities and rising literacy; and the professionalization of public service that facilitated demand for independent policy analysis for the rational improvement of society. Organizations such as the Brookings Institution, the 20th Century Fund, and the Russell Sage Foundation in the United States, and the Fabian Society and National Institute for Economic and Social Research in the UK, are typical. In this early epoch of think tank development, the character of policy analysis had a strong rationalist orientation where 'knowledge spoke to power', reflecting in some degree the limited abilities of government to undertake analysis, or policy perversities that resulted from partisanship, ideological battlefields and corrupt practices.

b. Post World War II

The post-World War II era brought a more extensive role for the state in social and economic affairs, prompting a second epoch of think tank developments in North America and in European liberal and social democracies. The New Deal and the Great Society period in the United States along with the Korean and Vietnam Wars prompted the development of government contract research institutions. RAND and the Hudson Institute were exemplary of the new breed of think tank, which was increasingly reliant on government contracts rather than private philanthropy. A number of other institutes, most notably the Urban Institute, acquired substantial input into social policy and analysed American social problems such as the inner city and urban decline, Medicare, or state work-welfare programmes.

Similar institutes emerged in other developed countries, often aligned with political parties: all of the major German political parties are loosely associated with research foundations that play some role in shaping policy, but in a more disinterested manner than is the case of Anglo systems. These include the Friedrich-Ebert-Stiftung (Social Democratic Party-aligned), the Konrad-Adenauer-Stiftung (Christian Democratic Union-aligned), the Hanns-Seidel-Stiftung (Christian Social Union-aligned), the Heinrich-Böll-Stiftung (aligned with the Greens), Friedrich Naumann Foundation (Free Democratic Party-aligned) and the Rosa Luxemburg Foundation (aligned with Die Linke). Likewise, the major political parties in the Netherlands are linked with policy research bodies. Other countries such as Italy, Spain and Switzerland as well as most Scandinavian countries grew a healthy population of policy research institutes over the decades until the 1980s.

Many of the think tanks in this second epoch pioneered applications of new statistical techniques, economic modelling and cost-benefit analysis. Policy analysis became more sophisticated and professional. Government demand expanded with the growth of

Policy Analysis by Think Tanks

government, but more importantly with the capacity of state officials to absorb and use this kind of analysis. In common with previous epoch, institutes were seen as providing rational knowledge inputs into policy development.

There were also developments in how these policy analysis organizations were organized and structured. In an era defined by the Cold War, superpower rivalries, and Third World issues with regard to international issues, think tanks expanded from general purpose institutes such as the ubiquitous Brookings Institution to reflect a proliferation of foreign policy institutes, centres for the study of security, and development studies institutes. On domestic affairs, depending on the make-up of the host country, other modes of policy analysis specialization emerged, including social policy, race and/or ethnic affairs, and the environment.

With the growing number of policy institutes seeking policy attention as well as funding, observers started talking about a marketplace of ideas. This pluralist perspective was prevalent in the highly competitive US policy ecology (Weidenbaum, 2011). Others, however, depict a 'war of ideas' in which think tanks battle for power and persuasion (Kostić, 2014).

c. The International Diffusion of Think Tanks

From the 1980s, a world-wide boom of think tanks was apparent. In Anglo-American political systems, think tank communities matured. Whether as a cause or a consequence of the rise of environmental considerations, environmental policy institutes burgeoned. Specialization has evolved on other fronts as well, including women's policy institutes, business ethics think tanks, and centres for democracy promotion.

However, the diffusion of the think tank model is not an inevitable dynamic. The extent of think tank spread has been highly variable. And political culture matters: for instance, it has been suggested that the French 'don't do think tanks' (Williams, 2008, p. 53).[1] Nevertheless, the think tank boom has been particularly noticeable in Belgium (Fraussen, Lawarée & Pattyn, 2016).

In the Anglo-American context, many of the new institutes adopted a more strident ideological stance along with a new organizational propensity for advocacy and publicity to enhance their traditional modes of research dissemination. The rise and influence of so-called New Right think tanks such as the Heritage Foundation in Washington, DC, and the Adam Smith Institute in London illustrate how free market and conservative think tanks were key actors in the paradigm shift from Keynesian policymaking towards neoliberal principles of government organization (Denham & Garnett, 2004).

Outside the OECD, the evolution of think tanks occurred later in the twentieth century. In the newly industrialized countries of Asia, rapid economic growth freed resources for policy research while increasing levels of literacy and greater opportunity for university education created new generations of intellectuals. Northeast Asian institutes are relatively numerous but are also more likely to be affiliated with a government ministry or large corporation. There has been a steep increase in the number of Chinese think tanks (Xufeng, 2009), both inside government as well as more independent bodies (Zhu & Xue, 2007; Abb, 2015).

A number of Latin American countries, such as Argentina, Peru, and Chile, also have a healthy population of research institutes; many are affiliated with universities, and have had a new breath of life with democratization in the region. A similar trend of specialization has occurred: alongside those organizations focusing on national social and economic policies (see Garcé & Gerardo, 2010), there are a number of foreign policy think tanks (see Merke & Pauselli, 2015).

Independent, Western-style think tanks in the former Soviet Union appeared after 1989 but the bureaucratic legacy of the old, if impoverished, Soviet-style Academies of Science loomed for a couple of decades. Examples include the Center for Social and Economic Research in Poland and the Centre for Liberal Strategies in Bulgaria. As relatively young organizations, with limited resources, the new policy institutes were often over-stretched in their policy focus on the problems of transition. This difficulty is even more pronounced with think tanks in many African countries, on which there is very little scholarly literature (but see Mbadlanyana, Sibalukhulu & Cilliers, 2011). In weak and failed states, the presence of think tanks tends to be very limited. Nevertheless, the reality is that think tanks are present in ever greater numbers, with rough estimates in the order of 6,500 world-wide (Abelson & Brooks, 2016).

The international extent of think tank development is reflected in the industry that has evolved around the phenomenon. Specialist consultants and academics cater both to think tanks that need management advice and to their donors who require evaluation of the think tank analysis they have funded (Struyk, 2006). Over the past two decades, numerous workshops have been convened by development agencies such as the Department for International Development (DfID) or USAID; NGOs like the Center for International Private Enterprise (CIPE) and Freedom House; and international organizations such as the World Bank, United Nations Development Programme (UNDP) and the European Union (EU), on how to launch a think tank or how a think tank can better target the policy system of a country. A number of foundations, such as the Hewlett Foundation and the Open Society Foundations network, have initiated grant programmes to support think tank development. There are practical guides on how to run a think tank (Struyk, 2006) or how to translate complex ideas for policy and public consumption (Mendizabal, 2014); listserves and blogs for the think tank community;[2] and even a degree programme run by the right-wing Atlas Institute, which in some respects may be thought of as a transnational institute. As expected, the policy analysis focus and the methods used in the era of internationalization vary significantly and depend on the specific national and policy context and needs.

d. The Internet-Era Think Tank

Think tanks are an excellent barometer of the transnationalization of policy analysis. The dual dynamic of globalization and regionalization has transformed the research agendas of these organizations. Institutes have been compelled to look beyond local and national matters to address trans-border policy problems. Many think tanks have been at the forefront of public debate, policy analysis and research on the local ramifications of global governance dilemmas concerning climate change, security, migration, financial crises and human rights.

In conjunction with academics in universities, a notable number of think tank researchers are leading commentators on globalization. Their transnational research agendas have been complemented by global dissemination of policy analysis via the internet.

In the evolving shape of global civil society, think tanks are also prominent players. It is common for think tanks to liaise with like-minded bodies from other countries.

Nevertheless, institutes generally remain committed to the nation-state where they are legally constituted. It is relatively rare to see a genuinely transnational/regional/global think tank. However, the non-partisan Carnegie Endowment for International Affairs (established in 1910) has re-engineered into a federated structure as 'the oldest international affairs think tank in America and a unique global network with policy research centres in Russia, China, Europe, the Middle East, and the United States—and soon in India'.[3] Likewise, the

International Crisis Group has been portrayed as a transnational think tank (Kostić, 2014, p. 635) and, by others, as a media-oriented NGO.

Think tank activity within the EU has been considerable, reflecting the deepening of European integration (Boucher et al., 2004; Missiroli & Ioannides, 2012). Despite differences between think tanks in relation to their specific policy remits, structural and membership profiles, and ideological perspectives on European integration, they have common features such as close relations with the European Commission and a research focus on distinctively European issues (Ladi, 2005). The Centre for European Policy Studies (CEPS) in Brussels is the exemplar of this style. Think tanks have also been key players in European harmonization of national structures through cross-national processes of policy transfer, where they go beyond detached policy analysis to spread certain European standards and benchmarks (Ladi, 2005).

Other regional associations, including the Association of Southeast Asian Nations (ASEAN), the African Union, or the Community of Latin American and Caribbean States (CELAC), have also acted as a magnet for think tank activity. ASEAN in particular has witnessed much informal diplomacy convened by elite and often government-sponsored think tanks that have fed into regional security and economic integration initiatives (Stone, 2013a; Zimmerman, 2015).

However, notwithstanding the pressures for convergence that come with globalization and international best practices, knowledge regimes, of which think tanks are one organizational manifestation, are intimately connected with policymaking and (capitalist) production regimes in nationally specific ways (Campbell & Pederson, 2014). In short, policy analytic capacities and modalities of think tanks will inevitably differ from one country to the next.

e. Reprise

In a maturing world-wide industry, think tanks are in a constant state of reinvention. Consequently, the resultant typologies and categories are 'far from fixed' (Shaw, Russell, Greenhalgh & Korica, 2014, p. 450). The boundaries between think tanks and other policy analysis organizations are becoming increasingly difficult to discern. Advocacy groups, business associations and other NGOs have their own capacity for policy analytic research. Transparency International and Oxfam are well-known examples. Universities around the world have established institutes and policy centres that mirror, up to a point, the concern to bridge research and policy. This is particularly the case in Anglo-American universities, which are increasingly compelled by government and other funders of their research to demonstrate that they have impact upon, and provide 'added value' for, society and economy. Universities in a number of countries now tread on the policy analytic territory of think tanks.

Yet some argue that the impact of American think tanks over the past forty years has been to 'drown out' the voices of academic commentary and has 'autonomously produced social scientific knowledge . . . by fortifying a system of social relations that relegates its producers to the margins of public debate' (Block, 2013, p. 649; Medvetz, 2012). In an increasingly competitive field where organizational identities blend and blur, an epistemological move away from studying organizations to studying the organization of policy analysis is prompted.

Think tank practice is not devoted exclusively to desk-based research and policy analysis: some are 'think-and-do tanks' involved in advocacy, technical assistance, and training. Other institutes are informally incorporated into policy implementation or provide monitoring and evaluation services. In most countries, these organizations strive for media coverage and consequently develop their analysis into digestible formats for public consumptions such as op-eds and 'talking heads' for TV or radio commentary. Consequently, the variety of think tanks in existence quite simply defies simple generalization. At the same time, generalization about standards of research and integrity of policy analysis is similarly impossible. Comparative analysis of think tanks can be further complicated by considerations of regime type where the structures of state monitoring and censorship of (semi-)authoritarian polities restrict the parameters of acceptable inquiry. Quite clearly a government-funded Chinese think tank faces different incentives and pressures than a legally independent and financially autonomous Canadian think tank (see McLevey, 2014) or a financially strapped think tank in the Caucasus (see Buldioski, 2009).

Today there is a wealth of information about, and for, these organizations: league tables and rankings; dedicated prizes and competitions; databases and internet directories, scholarly articles and books; and professional evaluations of the policy analysis proffered by think tanks. Scholarly interest continues to grow and diversify, with new sub-fields of investigation, for instance, including foreign policy institutes (see inter alia, Abb, 2015; Abelson, Brooks & Hua, 2016; Acharya, 2011; Stone, 2013b) and, as discussed in the last section, the development over the past decade of new theoretical considerations on think tank influence.

3. Modes of Policy Analysis and Research Methods Used by Think Tanks

Depending on the think tank, different modes of policy analysis and research methods are preferred. There are at least five questions in think tank policy analysis production, which we now discuss.

a. What is the Character of Research?

A common type are the 'ideological tanks' or 'advocacy tanks'—organizations that have a clearly specified political or, more broadly, ideological philosophy. As 'advocacy organizations', think tanks are driven by normative principles, ideological beliefs, or scholarly and professional standards to broadcast and apply their advice to bring about policy change or reform. In general, the later generations of American, Canadian, British and Australian think tanks have been more advocacy-oriented in order to maintain both media and political attention in the increasingly competitive marketplace of ideas (Misztal, 2012). This may be less apparent in some other OECD contexts but is nevertheless evident.

Other examples include the 'New Right' think tanks in the UK and the think tanks that are affiliated with political parties in Germany. Such think tanks choose their research topics and design and conduct their research in light of their ideological identity, and explicitly state this in their mission statements. Contemporary manifestations include the conservative-funded climate-change-sceptic think tanks (Jacques, Dunlap & Freeman, 2008).

One of the oldest think tanks of this type is the Friedrich-Ebert-Stiftung (Foundation) (FES), which was founded in 1925 and is associated with the German Social Democratic Party. The range of topics that it is interested in is clearly linked to its socialist values and includes educational policy, local government and European policy, but also global policy and development. The research leans towards a case-study methodology: for example, in relation to international energy and climate change policy, FES produces policy papers with specific policy recommendations enriched with German and international case studies (www.fes.de/de).

Policy Analysis by Think Tanks

This approach can be juxtaposed with the non-partisan, neutral or data-driven think tanks like the US National Bureau for Economic Research (NBER), which does economic modelling, and the London-based Institute for Fiscal Studies (IFS), which specializes in micro-economic research. Both of these think tanks can be described as academic think tanks whose target group is not only policymakers but also academics and researchers. They provide innovative research and are proud of the quality of the research that they produce. The NBER website states that 'twenty-five Nobel Prize winners in Economics and thirteen past chairs of the President's Council of Economic Advisers have been researchers at the NBER' (www.nber.org). IFS is host to the Economic and Social Research Council (ESRC) Centre for the Microeconomic Analysis of Public Policy, a prestigious research centre attracting the interest of both academia and policymakers (www.ifs.org.uk). These institutes focus on micro- and macro-economic analysis rather than qualitative methods. Quantitative methods and formal models are often seen as more objective, and this is also the case in the world of think tanks, and to their audiences. Many other institutes around the world prefer this type of methodology—for example, the Malaysian Institute of Economic Research (MIER), the Indian Council for International Economic Research (ICIER), and the many economics-based institutes in sub-Saharan Africa supported by both the regional Africa Capacity Building Foundation and the Global Development Network.

b. What are the Foci of Policy Analysis?

The 'academic' think tanks such as the IFS described in the previous section can also be described as 'specialist' tanks, meaning that their research has a specific thematic focus. Common subjects are foreign policy and specific policy sectors such as the environment. The research that specialist tanks conduct is more in depth since they do not need to cover a variety of diverse topics. This means that they are able to use a mixture of research methods and be innovative in their modes of policy analysis. The Foreign Policy Institute (FPI), a Washington-based think tank affiliated with Johns Hopkins University, is a good example of a specialized think tank. The FPI publishes the *SAIS Review of International Affairs*, where academic articles using all possible research methods can be found. In the same vein of cutting-edge research, the FPI announces the books of its fellows and affiliated researchers. It also publishes policy papers and briefs based on a variety of research methods, with a principal focus on the policy message conveyed (www.fpi.sais-jhu.edu).

Many generalist think tanks still exist, however. Most of the 'advocacy' and 'ideological' tanks, for example the Friedrich-Ebert-Stiftung discussed in the previous section, are preoccupied with a huge variety of social problems and accordingly make use of a variety of research tools. The same applies to think tanks that aim to target the supra-national level, such as the Brussels-based think tanks that are discussed in the next section. Generalist think tanks aim to cover a broader range of issues, but are still likely to gain a reputation for their work on specific issues; this is what happened with Bruegel during the Eurozone crisis when their researchers were invited to almost all relevant discussions and conferences. Bruegel—which stands for Brussels European and Global Economic Laboratory—was launched in 2003, and has become one of the more recognizable and respected sources of analysis in the increasingly crowded think tank community of Brussels.

c. For Which Governance Level is Policy Analysis Produced?

Reflecting on whether the level of governance for which think tanks work affects their policy analysis mode and research methods provides interesting observations. Think tanks could either work at the regional level (for example, the American 'state tanks') or at the supra-national level (for example, the think tanks that are based in Brussels and are aiming at the whole EU).

'State tanks' which operate at the regional level often have a more focused agenda related to the specific problems of their region, but the issues they are working on are not necessarily parochial and may have a global appeal. Next 10, a California-based think tank, aimed to influence the 2015 United Nations Climate Change Conference held in Paris and showcase California's pivotal role in climate change policies in the US and globally with its report titled 'California Green Innovation Index'. State tanks use a mixture of quantitative, qualitative and mixed methods depending on the topic under research.

At the supra-national level, the Centre for European Policy Studies (CEPS) is one of the most well-known think tanks in Brussels and conducts research on a variety of topics that are central for the EU, including the Eurozone crisis, migration, TTIP, and capital markets union. Research draws on the state of the art in European studies and, depending on the exact topic, experts from different backgrounds (e.g. economists, lawyers, etc.) contribute to CEPS' research, bringing their own modes of policy analysis and research methods. An interesting feature is that CEPS is very active in collaborative research since its work focuses on the EU. The European Commission is an important source of funding. In 2015, 23% of its budget derived from European research projects, which by default are collaborative. This influences the type of research that CEPS is involved in. Given CEPS' experience in communicating research to policymakers, quite often its role in the research consortium is the communication of the results.

While the EU context is considered *sui generis* by many, nevertheless, there are a range of other think tank initiatives tackling global policy problems and the new dynamics of transnational administration. For example, Think Tank 20 is a formal network of institutes that have received recognition from the G20, and have some limited input in discussions on global economic governance. The Shangri-La Dialogue is a regular summit of defence ministers and defence professionals initiated by a UK-based think tank—the Institute for Strategic Studies—and into which there is extensive input from the ASEAN-Institute of Strategic and International Studies think tank network as well as that of other expert bodies (Zimmerman, 2015). In 2013, the BRICS (Brazil, Russia, India, China and South Africa) set up a think tank council. These examples are simply illustrative of the considerable ferment of transnational policy analysis undertaken by think tank consortia (Stone, 2013a).[4]

d. How is Think Tank Policy Analysis Operationalized?

The penultimate category is the 'think-and-do tanks'—organizations which, apart from their traditional research activities, are active at a more practical level, such as the funding of charity projects. This type of think tank is closer to NGOs. The research that these organizations conduct is more applied and aims at direct policy results. They often focus on global problems and development issues. The Centre for Global Development (CGD) based in London and Washington is a telling example. In a report on building a think-and-do tank, CGD researchers presented research that produced tangible policy results (MacDonald & Moss, 2014). An example is the work that they produced on impact evaluation, which led to the International Initiative for Impact Evaluation (3ie) and what they call a narrowing of the evaluation gap. Think-and-do tanks may use diverse research methodologies and produce innovative work, but are not very much concerned with academic publishing since their priority is a more direct policy result. The downside is that their work may go unnoticed by the academic public policy community.

e. Who Produces the Research? And is it Any Good?

A think tank's reputation is very important. Human capital is the primary asset in producing policy analysis and sustaining the organization's professional credibility as a repository of policy knowledge. Accordingly, most think tanks seek to ensure that their staff is highly qualified, with most research positions requiring staff to hold a PhD and conform to research protocols of their discipline or profession. Some teach on a part-time basis as adjunct faculty of universities and some think tanks are formally linked with universities. Think tanks also produce human capital in the form of specialized analysts who often move between think tank, university, and government service—with long-term ramifications that indirectly interweave the think tank with government agencies via its former fellows. Nevertheless, due to budgetary constraints, think tanks are often forced to rely on interns who participate in the research process but also in the organization of events. A proliferation in the number of interns may call into question think tanks' capacity to produce a high quality of research.

Some think tank fellows, in a phenomenon known as the 'revolving door', have spent careers working with governments or international organizations before bringing their professional experience to the think tank. Other think tank scholars regularly seek appointment to official committees and advisory boards. Usually, staff can legitimately claim knowledge and detailed awareness of the internal workings of government. Consequently, the mix of staff experiences and formal qualifications is important for the organization to establish credibility with political audiences.

Credibility maintenance thus becomes a delicate balancing act for these 'hybrid' organizations. They are four-footed organizations with 'one foot in academia, one foot in journalism, one foot in the market and one foot in politics' (Block, 2013, p. 648; Medvetz, 2012). Yet in terms of everyday practice, some think tanks may be more bi-podal or tri-podal. A body like the International Crisis Group might work closer to the media world (Kostić, 2014; Misztal, 2012). By contrast, a number of think tanks in Latin America have been founded or based in universities (Chaufen, 2013), while the Centre for International Governance Innovation (CIGI) in Canada is closely connected with the Balsillie School at the University of Waterloo. The key point, however, is that these multiple identities and constituencies present resource dependencies and conflicting organizational logics that result from catering for different groups of funders or patrons (McLevey, 2014).

4. Promoting Think Tank Policy Analysis to External Audiences

One of the most important functions of a think tank is the specialized provision of policy analysis. However, policy analysis comes in a variety of formats and delivery mechanisms. The main targets of think tank analysis are legislatures and executives as well as bureaucrats and politicians at local, national, and international levels of governance, but there are further target communities of other policy actors and opinion-formers in society. To reach these varied audiences, think tanks promote their policy analysis in manifold ways.

a. Think Tanks as Information Interlocutors

As interlocutors between knowledge and power, scholarly work and policy work, think tanks may provide services such as ethics or policy training for civil servants, or organize conferences or seminars. Similarly, they have become useful translators of the abstract modelling and dense theoretical concepts characteristic of contemporary (social) science. For governments concerned with evidence-based policy, think tanks potentially assist a more rational policy process by augmenting in-house research capacities, circumventing time and institutional constraints, and alerting elites to changing policy conditions.

There is a well-known distinction between research 'on' policy and research 'for' policy. Research on policy is more reflective and academic in style whereas research for policy is about evaluating whether a policy is or will be successful or not (Burton, 2006, p. 187). Many think tanks do both types of research, with the exact balance between the two contributing to the diversity of policy analysis styles in think tank ecologies already discussed.

The historical image of think tanks as neutral or dispassionate creators or synthesizers of policy knowledge and advice has been subject to significant criticism, as discussed below. Nevertheless, in an era where too much information is bombarding governments and businesses, one critical role of think tanks is to act as editors and provide validation for various sources of information. Think tanks have created a niche as sifters and synthesizers of policy-relevant knowledge (Stone, 2007; 'tHart & Vromen, 2008). However, this function is very much dependent on the intrinsic quality of their research staff and high standards of intellectual quality. In many parts of the world, the research integrity and ethical standards of inquiry, as well as the wider societal legitimacy of think tanks, remain a concern (inter alia, Buldioski, 2009; Mendizabal, 2014; Struyk, 2006).

b. Think Tank Communication and Marketing

In practice, think tanks no longer communicate their advice and analysis solely through the policy professional domains of seminars, conferences and publications. They publicize their views in public forums such as television, radio, newspaper commentary and Twitter campaigns via 'sound bite' policy analysis. Think tanks, as well as their experts, need to act as policy entrepreneurs—that is, as educators, advocates and networkers. Effective communication to policy audiences is as important to the success of a think tank as the production of high-quality policy analysis.

For the past century, think tanks have been more adept at political communication than universities and NGOs. They located offices close to the centre of power. Indeed, the think tank organizational format was an institutional response to the long-standing dilemma of 'bridging research and policy' or promoting evidence-based policy. Today, however, a consistent theme emerging from donors and directors is that 'communications—and leveraging social media—are critical if think tanks want to maximize their impact' (CIGI, 2011, p. 8).

Advocacy is often the communication strategy of the 'outsider' think tank—one located within civil society or otherwise independent—as it tries to push evidence and analysis into government. However, some think tanks become 'insiders' to policy communities. Here, science and policy are difficult to distinguish and the guidelines for validating knowledge are highly contested. In those cases there can be intense struggles over political and epistemic authority, and evidence-based policy may turn into policy-based evidence (see Strassheim & Kettunen, 2014).

c. Think Tank Policy Networks and Partnerships

Think tanks also contribute to governance and institution building by facilitating exchange between government and private actors such as network entrepreneurs. Networks play an important role for think tanks both in embedding them in a relationship with more powerful actors, and in increasing their constituencies, thereby potentially amplifying their impact. However, too close an affinity with government, a political party, or an NGO can seriously undermine a think tank's authority and legitimacy as an objective (or at least balanced) knowledge provider.

Policy communities and sub-governments are well-understood phenomena of policymaking that represent a policy sector or policy issue mode of governance. Policy communities incorporate actors from inside and outside government to facilitate decision making and joint participation and consensus building around policy implementation. Think tank staff becomes involved in these policy communities through a number of routes—informally, through consultations and personal networking and long-term cultivation of the persons central to the community, and more formally through appointment to advisory bodies. In such circumstances, there is a relationship of trust between a think tank and a government ministry or set of officials; the think tank's expertise is recognized and as relationships are built, some privileged access to policy venues occurs. For instance, there is a close and long-standing relationship between the Overseas Development Institute in London and the UK Department for International Development (Stone, 2013a).

As conveners of conferences, workshops, executive training seminars and research projects, think tanks invite and embed themselves with business executives, government officials, and other experts. Such activities provide convivial environs for off-the-record discussions. Indeed, a number of think tanks around the world that enjoy the trust of governments have played a quiet but effective behind-the-scenes role as agents of 'track two diplomacy' (Acharya, 2011; Zimmerman, 2015).

d. Transnational Think Tanking

Think tank engagements with counterparts in other countries can take multiple forms, including temporary project-related partnerships or longer-term networks and associations. Networks provide an infrastructure for global dialogue and research collaboration, and quite often for capacity building. The Open Society Foundation (OSF) founded PASOS, a regional network of Central and Eastern European institutes that has now expanded geographically and is independent of the OSF. The Global Development Network is an extensive international federal network primarily of economic research institutes (see Plehwe, 2007, for a critique). This is a natural evolution of the cross-border nature of many contemporary policy problems, and of new sources of demand for policy analysis.

International organizations like the World Bank, European Union (EU), World Trade Organization (WTO) and UNDP are important financiers and consumers of research and policy analysis. They have provided capacity building and training programmes throughout the world for local elites to establish new think tanks and policy networks (UNDP, 2003). They also require independent policy analysis and research—not only to support problem definition and outline policy solutions, but also to monitor and evaluate existing policy and provide scholarly legitimation for policy development.

Think tanks have become key actors in a thickening web of global and regional institutions, regulatory activities and policy practices. Global governance structures such as the Global Water Partnership or UNAIDS have emerged in response to the increasing prevalence of global policy problems across national boundaries. These contemporary policy problems provide a structural dynamic for research collaboration, sharing of responsibilities, regularized communication, and expert consultation. Global public policy networks are neo-corporatist arrangements that act alongside international organizations, government officials, business representatives, and stakeholders to a policy area to provide policy analysis. Within these networks, selected think tanks have become useful in building the infrastructure for communication between transnational policy actors—including websites, newsletters, and international meetings—and managing the flow of information coming from numerous sources.

5. The Utility and Influence of Think Tank Policy Analysis

One of the most perplexing questions of think tank analysis, especially in methodological terms, concerns think tank policy influence. As one book asks, *Do Think Tanks Matter?* (Abelson, 2009; see also CIGI, 2011). The rising numbers of these organizations worldwide—no matter how they are defined—would suggest they do matter. But sheer scale does not address the questions of when, how and why they matter, and if they will continue to be of consequence in the longer term.

Notwithstanding their extensive growth, the majority of think tanks do not enjoy automatic political access or regular invitations to contribute to policy processes. Attempting to broker policy analysis to decision makers does not equate with immediate policy impact on forthcoming legislation or executive thinking. Relatively few think tanks make key contributions to decision making in local, national, global or regional forums, or exert paradigmatic influence over policy thinking. Instead, to return to the marketplace or battlefield metaphor, it is more apt to view these organizations as one set of sellers of ideas, or analytic brigades, in the larger policy community ecology.

Furthermore, think tank research and reports do not escape challenges or criticism from other knowledge providers based in universities or NGOs or the media. In addition, they may be ignored or patronized at will by governments, corporations, and international organizations. This is more likely to occur as information technology and social media help unpack policy analysis functions from a specific organizational form.

Think tanks appropriate authority on the basis of their scholarly credentials as quasi-academic organizations focused on the rigorous and professional analysis of policy issues. Many use their presumed 'independent' status as civil society organizations to strengthen their reputation as beholden neither to the interests of the market nor the state. These endowments give think tanks some legitimacy in seeking to intervene with knowledge and advice in policy processes. Think tank league tables and rankings may give an impression of importance, but have been heavily criticized for methodological biases (Abelson & Brooks, 2016).

A 2004 survey of European decision makers, journalists, and academics on the impact of think tanks discovered critical and cautious perceptions of influence: while recognizing the importance of a healthy think tank sector for EU policymaking, many survey respondents criticized think tanks for their lack of impact and relevance; their technocratic and elitist orientation; and their ability to provide added value (Boucher et al., 2004, p. 85). Even think tankers bemoan the limited or lack of influence they exert: for instance at a conference on the theme 'Can think tanks make a difference?' one think tank director said that in an age of 'de-politicicization', 'big ideas are off the table because politicians don't want to take risks' (CIGI, 2011, p. 8).

Nevertheless, these organizations acquire political credibility by performing services for governments and other policy actors. In short, the sources of demand help explain think tank relevance and utility, if not their direct policy influence. Accordingly, the reality may be that governments or certain political groups employ these organizations as tools to pursue their own interests or to provide intellectual legitimation for pre-determined policy approaches—not that think tanks have an impact on government.

Think tank development is also indicative of the wider politicization of policy analysis. In a few countries, think tanks are a means of career advancement or a stepping stone for the politically ambitious. The revolving door of individuals moving between executive appointment and think tanks, law firms, or universities is a well-known phenomenon. Rather than the policy analysis papers—or published output—having influence, it is the policy analytic capacity—or human capital—that has long-term influence and resonance inside government, and increasingly inside international organizations.

The utility and relevance of think tanks can also rest within society more generally. Some think tanks attract more attention from the media than from government. The capacity to gain funds from foundations, governments, and corporations to undertake policy analysis is an indirect recognition of the value of many institutes. Others value the pluralism of debate that think tanks can bring into public deliberation; this is one rationale behind the think tank capacity-building initiatives of development agencies. In neo-pluralist thinking, independent think tanks are portrayed as creating a more open, participatory and educated populace and represent a counter to the influence of powerful techno-bureaucratic, corporate, and media interests on the policy agenda. Moreover, a more informed, knowledge-based policy process could have a long-term, trickle-down effect of 'enlightening' decision making (Weiss, 1992).

Power approaches to the role of think tanks in US policymaking have emphasized how think tanks are key components of the power elite where decision making is concentrated in the hands of a few groups and individuals (Domhoff, 1983; Dye, 1978). Those with neo-Marxist sensibilities argued that establishment think tanks—such as the Brookings Institution and the Council on Foreign Relations—are consensus-building organizations constructing the ideology and long-range plans that convert problems of crisis-prone capitalist economies into manageable and de-politicized objects of public policy. Think tanks help form a coherent sense of long-term class interests and maintain hegemonic control through the constant construction and reconstruction of legitimizing policy discourses (Bohle & Nuenhöffer, 2005; Desai, 1994; Pautz, 2011). However, these studies address high-profile institutes with solid links to political parties or the corporate sector, but neglect the role of smaller, lesser-known institutes which thrive in much larger numbers than the elite think tanks, and which continue to achieve sustainable funding for alternative policy perspectives (McLevey, 2014; Stone, 2013a).

Many contemporary analysts are sceptical of think tanks' ability to exert consistent, direct impact on politics (see the essays in Stone & Denham, 2004). Instead, they develop wider and more nuanced understandings of think tank policy influence and social relevance in their roles as agenda setters who create policy narratives that capture the political and public imagination (see also Fischer, 2003; Wacquant, 2004). Discourse approaches identify how think tanks seek to mould problem definition and the terms of debate (Zimmerman, 2015). The constructivist approach emphasizes inter-subjective knowledge—common understandings and shared identities—as the dynamic for change.

New departures on the study of think tanks focus more upon collectivity than on individual think tanks or particular ideological groupings. For example, work on think tanks as part of an organizational field of resource interdependencies with other policy analysis producers, the media, donors and policymakers draws upon the work of Bourdieu (Medvetz, 2012). A similar approach uses the 'linked ecologies' approach (Stone, 2013a). The idea of 'knowledge regimes' states most systematically that the influence of think tank policy analysis is very much mediated by both nationally specific institutional arrangements and the interplay of powerful political and economic interests that fund, sponsor or otherwise select and patronize (Campbell & Pedersen, 2014, pp. 17–18). Think tank policy analysis and its influence will look different from one political economy to the next. In all these perspectives, it is in the *longue duree* that think tank policy analysis and activity achieves wider social relevance in shaping patterns of governance and either altering or reinforcing policy paradigms.

Notes

1 Others observe that France has developed a sizeable think tank population (see, inter alia, Campbell & Pedersen, 2014).
2 For instance, the Evidence-Based Policy in Development Network listserv, as well as the blog On Think Tanks (http://onthinktanks.org/about).
3 Tom Carver, 'The Global Think Tank', Catalogue; email dated 4 May 2015.
4 www.bricsforum.com/2013/03/15/brics-think-tanks-council-set-up, accessed 15 December 2015.

References

Abb, P. (2015). 'China's Foreign Policy Think Tanks: Institutional Evolution and Changing Roles', *Journal of Contemporary China, 24*(93), 531–553.
Abelson, D. E. (2009). *Do Think Tanks Matter? Assessing the Impact of Public Policy Institutes.* Montreal: McGill-Queen's University Press.
Abelson, D. E. and Brooks, S. (2016). 'Struggling to Be Heard: The Crowded and Complex World of Foreign Policy-Oriented Think Tanks', in Abelson, D. E., Brooks, S. and Hua, X. (eds), *Think Tanks, Foreign Policy and Geopolitics.*
Abelson, D. E., Brooks, S. and Hua, X. (eds) (2016). *Think Tanks, Foreign Policy and Geo-Politics: Pathways to Influence.* Abingdon, UK: Routledge.
Acharya, A. (2011). 'Engagement or Entrapment? Scholarship and Policymaking on Asian Regionalism'. *International Studies Review, 13*(1), 12–17.
Block, F. (2013). 'Think Tanks, Free Market Academics, and the Triumph of the Right', *Theory and Society, 42*(6), 647–651.
Bohle, D. and Nuenhöffer, G. (2005). 'Why Is There No Third Way? The Role of Neoliberal Ideology, Networks and Think Tanks in Combating Market Socialism and Shaping Transformation in Poland', in Plehwe, D., Walpen, B. and Neunhöffer, G. (eds), *Neoliberal Hegemony: A Global Critique.* London: Routledge.
Boucher, S., Hobbs, B., Ebélé, J., Laigle, C., Poletto, M., Cattaneo, D. and Wegrzyn, R. (2004). *Europe and Its Think Tanks; A Promise to be Fulfilled. An Analysis of Think Tanks Specialised in European Policy Issues in the Enlarged European Union*, Studies and Research 35, Paris, Notre Europe.
Braun, M., Chudnovsky, M., Di Nucci, C., Ducote, N. and Weyrauch, V. (n.d. circa 2006). *A Comparative Study of Think Tanks in Latin America, Asia and Africa*, mimeo.
Bruegel, http://bruegel.org (visited 8 December 2015).
Buldioski, G. (2009). 'Think Tanks in Central and Eastern Europe in Urgent Need of a Code of Ethics', *The International Journal of Non-Profit Law, 11* (3), 42–52.
Burton, P. (2006). 'Modernising the Policy Process: Making Policy Research more Significant', *Policy Studies, 27*(3), 173–195.
Campbell, J. L. and Pedersen, O. K. (2014). *Knowledge Regimes and the National Origins of Policy Ideas.* Princeton University Press.
CEPS (Centre for European Policy Studies), www.ceps.eu (visited 30 November 2015).
Chaufen, A. (2013). 'Will Think Tanks Become the Universities of the 21st Century?' *Forbes Opinion*, 22May.www.forbes.com/sites/alejandrochafuen/2013/05/22/will-think-tanks-become-the-universities-of-the-21st-century
CIGI – Centre for International Governance Innovation (2011). *Can Think Tanks Make a Difference?* Conference Report, CIGI.
Denham, Andrew and Garnett, Mark (2004). 'A Hollowed Out Tradition? British Think Tanks in the Twenty First Century', in Diane Stone and Andrew Denham (eds), *Think Tank Traditions: Policy Research and the Politics of Ideas.* Manchester University Press.

Policy Analysis by Think Tanks

Desai, Rhadika (1994). 'Second-hand Dealers in Ideas: Think Tanks and Thatcherite Hegemony', *New Left Review*, 203, 27–64.

Domhoff, William. G. (1983). *Who Rules America Now? A View for the '80s*. Englewood Cliffs, NJ: Prentice Hall.

Dye, Thomas. R. (1978). 'Oligarchic Tendencies in National Policy Making: The Role of Private Planning Organisations', *Journal of Politics*, 40 (May), 309–331.

Fischer, F. (2003). *Reframing Public Policy: Discursive Politics and Deliberative Practices*. Oxford University Press.

Fraussen, B., Lawarée, J. and Pattyn, V. (2016). 'Policy Analysis by Think Tanks'. In M. Brans and D. Aubin (eds), *Policy Analysis in Belgium*. Bristol, UK: Policy Press.

Friedrich-Ebert-Stiftung, www.fes.de/de (visited 26 November 2015).

Garcé, A. and Gerardo, U. (eds) (2010). *Think Tanks and Public Policies in Latin America*. Ottawa: International Development Research Centre.

Jacques, P. J., Dunlap, R. E. and Freeman, M. (2008). 'The Organisation of Denial: Conservative Think Tanks and Environmental Scepticism', *Environmental Politics*, 17(3), 349–385.

Institute for Fiscal Studies (IFS), www.ifs.org.uk (visited 8 December 2015).

Kostić, R. (2014). 'Transnational Think-Tanks: Foot Soldiers in the Battlefield of Ideas? Examining the Role of the ICG in Bosnia and Herzegovina, 2000–01', *Third World Quarterly*, 35(4), 634–651.

Ladi, Stella (2005). *Globalization, Policy Transfer and Think Tanks*. Cheltenham, UK: Edward Elgar.

Lucarelli, Sonia and Radaelli, Claudio (2004). 'Italy: Think Tanks and the Political System', in Diane Stone and Andrew Denham (eds), *Think Tank Traditions: Policy Research and the Politics of Ideas*. Manchester University Press.

MacDonald, L. and Moss, T. (2014), 'Building a Think-and-Do-Tank: A Dozen Lessons from the First Dozen Years of the Centre for Global Development', Centre for Global Development, www.cgdev. org/publication/building-think-and-do-tank-dozen-lessons-first-dozen-years-center-global-development

Mbadlanyana, T., Sibalukhulu, N. and Cilliers, J. (2011). 'Shaping African Futures: Think Tanks and the Need for Endogenous Knowledge Production in Sub-Saharan Africa', *foresight*, 13(3), 64–84.

McLevey, J. (2014) 'Think Tanks, Funding, and the Politics of Policy Knowledge in Canada', *Canadian Review of Sociology/Revue canadienne de sociologie*, 51, 54–75.

Medvetz, T. (2012). *Think Tanks in America*. University of Chicago Press.

Mendizabal, E. Ed. (2014) *Communicating Complex Ideas*, On Think Tanks and Creative Commons. https://onthinktanks.files.wordpress.com/2014/06/communicating-complex-ideas_full-book.pdf

Merke, F. and Pauselli, G. (2015). In the Shadow of the State: Think Tanks and Foreign Policy in Latin America. *International Journal: Canada's Journal of Global Policy Analysis*, 70(4), 613–628.

Missiroli, A. and Ioannides, I. (2012). 'European Think Tanks and the EU', *Berlaymont Paper*, (2).

Misztal, B. A. (2012). 'Public Intellectuals and Think Tanks: A Free Market in Ideas?' *International Journal of Politics, Culture and Society*, 25(4): 127–141.

National Bureau for Economic Research (NBER), www.nber.org (visited 8 December 2015).

Next 10 (2015). *California Green Innovation Index*, http://next10.org.

Pautz, H. (2011). 'Revisiting the Think-Tank Phenomenon', *Public Policy and Administration*, 26(4), 419–435.

Plehwe, D. (2007) 'A Global Knowledge Bank? The World Bank and Bottom-Up Efforts to Reinforce the Neoliberal Developments Perspectives in the Post Washington Consensus Era', *Globalisations*, 4(4), 514–528

Shaw, S. E., Russell, J., Greenhalgh, T. and Korica, M. (2014). 'Thinking About Think Tanks in Health Care: A Call for a New Research Agenda', *Sociology of Health & Illness*, 36 (3): 447–461.

Smith, J. A. (1991). 'The Idea Brokers'. *Think Tanks and the Rise of the New Policy Elite*. New York: Free Press.

Stone, D. (2007). 'Recycling Bins, Garbage Cans or Think Tanks? Three Myths Regarding Policy Analysis Institutes', *Public Administration*, 85(2), 259–278.

Stone, D. (2013a). *Knowledge Actors and Transnational Governance: The Private-Public Policy Nexus in the Global Agora*. Basingstoke, UK: Palgrave Macmillan.

Stone, D. (2013b). '"Shades of Grey": Knowledge Networks, Linked Ecologies and the World Bank', *Global Networks: A Journal of Transnational Affairs*, 13(2), 241–260.

Stone, Diane and Denham, Andrew (eds) (2004). *Think Tank Traditions*. Manchester University Press.

Strassheim, H. and Kettunen, P. (2014). 'When Does Evidence-Based Policy Turn Into Policy-Based Evidence? Configurations, Contexts and Mechanisms', *Evidence & Policy: A Journal of Research, Debate and Practice, 10*(2), 259–277.

Struyk, R. (2006). *Managing Think Tanks*. Budapest: Open Society Institute.

Struyk, R. J. and Haddaway, S. R. (2011). 'What Makes a Successful Policy Research Organization in Transition and Developing Countries?' *Nonprofit Policy Forum, 2*(1).

'tHart, P. T. and Vromen, A. (2008). 'A New Era for Think Tanks in Public Policy? International Trends, Australian Realities', *Australian Journal of Public Administration, 67*(2), 135–148.

The Foreign Policy Institute (FPI), www.fpi.sais-jhu.edu (visited 30 November 2015).

UNDP (2003). *Thinking the Unthinkable: From Thought to Policy*. Bratislava: United Nations Development Program

Wacquant, L. (2004). 'Penal Truth Comes to Europe: Think Tanks and the "Washington Consensus on Crime and Punishment"', in Gilligan, G. and Pratt, J. (eds), *Crime, Truth and Justice: Official Inquiry, Discourse, Knowledge*. Cullompton, UK: Willan Publishing.

Weidenbaum, M. (2011). *The Competition of Ideas: The World of Washington Think Tanks*. New Brunswick, NJ: Transaction Publishers.

Weiss, Carol (1992). *Organizations for Policy Analysis: Helping Government Think*. London: Sage.

Welner, K. G. (ed.) (2010). *Think Tank Research Quality: Lessons for Policymakers, the Media, and the Public*. Charlotte, NC: Information Age Publishing.

Williams, A. (2008). 'Why Don't the French Do Think Tanks? France Faces Up to the Anglo-Saxon Superpowers, 1918–1921', *Review of International Studies, 34*(01), 53–68.

Xufeng, Z. (2009). 'The Influence of Think Tanks in the Chinese Policy Process: Different Ways and Mechanisms', *Asian Survey, 49*(2), 333–357.

Zhu, X. and Xue, L. (2007). 'Think Tanks in Transitional China', *Public Administration and Development, 27*(5), 452–464.

Zimmerman, E. (2015). *Think Tanks and Non-Traditional Security: Governance Entrepreneurs in Asia*. Basingstoke, UK: Palgrave Macmillan.

22

ACADEMIC POLICY ANALYSIS AND RESEARCH UTILIZATION IN POLICYMAKING

Sonja Blum and Marleen Brans

1. Introduction

The product of policy analysis, it has been stated by Weimer and Vining (1992), is advice. Policy analysts, including those from academia, are engaged in numerous activities of policy advice, such as diagnosing policy problems, pre-evaluating different policy options, or studying the effects of reform efforts. And yet, policy analysis has come a long way from the understanding of it as an art and craft that can speak 'truth to power' (Wildavsky, 1979) in a direct or linear way. Caplan (1979, p. 459) described social scientists and policymakers as living in separate worlds, forming two communities—each with 'different and often conflicting values, different reward systems and different languages'. Along with the different languages come cultural dissimilarities and translation difficulties.

The 'two communities' metaphor portrays the relation between social sciences and policymaking as one with clear-cut antipodes. On the one side, there are the social scientists, engaged with conducting 'pure science', gaining knowledge and seeking appreciation for their work. On the other side, there are the policymakers, who are concerned with finding practical solutions for immediate issues on the government agenda and, moreover, practical solutions that stand the test of political power games. Today, the roles and actions of the 'two communities' are mostly no longer understood as so clearly distinct. Rather, both social scientists and policymakers are seen to be engaged in a process of 'making sense together' (Hoppe, 1999), a process that is interactive and complex. Increasingly, research utilization and social scientists as sources of knowledge *themselves* have become objects of policy research, for example in the field of interpretive policy analysis (see Section 2).

Thus, there are high hurdles to research utilization for policymaking, while the need for informed policymaking and reasonable choices remains as high as ever. This chapter deals with academic policy analysis and research utilization in cross-national perspective, starting from the proposition that there are variances, but also similarities, between countries. Cross-country variation concerns the policy advisory systems, that is, the specific configuration of actors providing advice and knowledge to policymakers within a policy sector (Halligan, 1995; Craft & Howlett, 2013). Cross-country variation also concerns the 'art and craft' of policy analysis. How academic policy analysis is understood and exerted will be influenced by a number of factors. One is the disciplinary background: a political scientist will understand

341

something different by 'policy analysis' than an economist or sociologist. Another factor is the understanding of one's own role as academic researcher; that is the individual 'solution' for the 'tension between epistemic and practical concerns' (Mayntz, 2013). A third factor, which also lies on the individual level, is whether the researcher understands public policymaking as 'neat and rational' or as 'chaotic and messy' (see Enserink, Koppenjan & Mayer, 2013, p. 16).

All of these factors that determine the understanding of policy analysis are, we argue, intertwined with respective national traditions and cultures. Thus, it is not only scientific advisory systems that differ between countries, but also the contents, styles and methods of policy analysis. Bringing the two dimensions together, we find significant cross-country variances in the interface of policy analysis and policymaking. In this chapter, we explore these variances, thereby focusing on academic policy analysis—that is, policy analysis conducted by researchers at universities or affiliated research institutes.

To do so, the chapter proceeds as follows: Section 2 deals with different definitions of policy analysis and related terms, such as policy sciences or policy studies. In Section 3 we discuss what can be learned from the research utilization literature on the interface of public policymaking and academic policy analysis. Sections 4 and 5 then turn to the (albeit scanty) empirical evidence on cross-country variation: we distinguish different dimensions of academic policy analysis and research utilization, including how well established the discipline of policy analysis is in a country. We also discuss trends and challenges. Section 6 summarizes the findings and draws some tentative conclusions.

2. What is (Academic) Policy Analysis?

What is policy analysis? Until today, policy analysis is often defined by referring to the demand by two of its founding fathers, Lasswell and Lerner (1951), that it be multi-disciplinary, contextual, problem-oriented, and explicitly normative. It has been stated that the 'product of policy analysis is advice' (Weimer & Vining, 1992, p. 1). Indeed, policy analysis has always been characterized by a 'double claim': to conduct scientifically-sound research on the one hand, and to bring this knowledge to use by providing policy advice on the other (Schubert, 2009). The context is special, however, when we focus our attention on *academic* policy analysis. Policy analysis at universities or affiliated research institutes is often directed at gaining scientific knowledge for which possible applications play a marginal role.

Nevertheless, within the individual academic disciplines, the sub-discipline of public policy analysis, as compared to sub-disciplines such as comparative politics or political theory, is characterized by a high application-orientation. Public policy analysis is connected to a number of core disciplines, namely political science, public administration, and economics. It is also conducted, however, in a vast range of other disciplines such as sociology, education, public health, social work, operations research, or planning (Dye, 1976, p. 5). Depending on the specific academic traditions and processes of institutionalization, there are differences between countries regarding the extent to which academic policy analysis is integrated in each of these different disciplines or not. In one country we may find academic policy analysis primarily housed in political science departments, whereas in another country it may largely be the domain of public administration.

The term 'policy analysis' carries a certain ambiguousness (Enserink et al., 2013), given that it refers both to the analysis *of* public policy and the analysis *for* public policy. To disentangle this ambiguousness, we can take a closer look at four different terms that are widely used in the English-language literature: policy studies, policy research, policy analysis, and the policy sciences.

Policy Analysis by Academics

Looking at the first three of these terms, a distinction is often made between policy research or policy studies as the academic variants of explaining policy change and its consequences (Dobuzinskis, Howlett & Laycock, 2007, pp. 3-4), versus the broader and more applied policy analysis. The latter often denotes applied analyses that are not just conducted at universities or even by researchers, but by a broad range of actors—including in federal government, political parties, or public interest groups. Against that background, van Nispen and Scholten (2014, p. 6) characterize policy studies as theory-driven, nomological, mono-disciplinary, and descriptive/empirical. In comparison, they see policy analysis as utilization-focused, ideographic, multi-disciplinary, and prescriptive. Also, the term policy studies is sometimes associated with 'analysis of policy', while policy analysis is associated with 'analysis for policy' (Dobuzinskis et al., 2007, p. 3).

However, the distinction between policy research/policy studies on the one hand and policy analysis on the other is not always that clear cut. Dye famously associated policy analysis with the questions of 'what governments do, why they do it, and what difference it makes' (1976, title). This definition of policy analysis indicates a wider interest in the outputs, the determinants, and the consequences of government action (or, even more broadly, of political actors), and in that sense with an 'analysis of policy'. Dye (1976, p. 3) writes: 'Policy analysis involves the systematic identification of the causes and consequences of public policy, the use of scientific standards of inference, and the search for reliability and generality of knowledge.' Therefore, the three terms of policy analysis, policy studies and policy research are in practice often used interchangeably.

What is more, the understanding and use of the terms differs decisively between countries. It does not come as a surprise that this can lead to misunderstandings in international collaborations and comparisons in the field of public policy analysis. Often, alternative terms in the national languages also exist, which may be more widespread and carry differing connotations. In Australia, the term 'policy analysis' is used less widely than in the United States and it is not as strongly associated with quantitative methods and positivist approaches (Crowley & Head, 2015, p. 2). In France, in turn, the key expression in the field is not policy analysis but the '(political) sociology of public action' (Hassenteufel & Le Galès, 2017). In Germany, the term *Politikfeldanalyse* (literally: policy-field analysis) is traditionally used to denote the academic analysis of policy. More recently, the terms *Policy-Analyse* (policy analysis) and *Policy-Forschung* (policy research) seem to be on the rise in the German language. However, all three terms are used largely interchangeably, meaning that often no clear distinction is made between policy research and policy analysis. Throughout this chapter, when we talk of 'academic policy analysis' in general, we thereby also include what is often referred to as 'policy research' or 'policy studies'.

An even broader term than the aforementioned seems to be that of the 'policy sciences', which covers the study of public policy in general and is often associated with the book *The Policy Sciences*, published by Lasswell and Lerner (1951). Lasswell (1951) demanded the policy sciences to be multi-disciplinary, following the ambitious aim of ultimately rationalising the policy process. For such an endeavour, political science should be merged with insights from other disciplines, such as sociology, economics, business and law, as well as physics or biology, depending on the nature of the respective problem or issue (see Allison, 2008, p. 63).

[W]here the needs of policy intelligence are uppermost, any item of knowledge, within or without the limits of the social disciplines, may be relevant. We may need to know the harbour installations at Casablanca, or the attitudes of a population of Pacific islanders to the Japanese, or the maximum range of a fixed artillery piece.

Lasswell, 1951, p. 4

Overall, there is agreement that multi-disciplinary approaches are needed to develop solutions for today's challenges, be it population ageing, economic crisis, or climate change. At the same time there are hurdles to multi-disciplinary approaches, especially in the academic sphere. It is here where institutes and departments are usually structured along disciplinary borders, and where young researchers in particular are under pressure to publish in refereed academic journals and show their theoretical or methodological contribution 'for their own discipline' to further their academic career. Furthermore, for many scientific questions, disciplinary approaches can be more useful. Against that background, the practice of multi-disciplinarity is central to applied policy analysis, but not necessarily to academic policy analysis.

With the public policy schools that emerged in the United States from the late 1960s onwards, multi-disciplinarity was anchored in the training and education of policy analysts, for example with a strong focus on quantitative methods such as (micro-)economic modelling (Blätte, 2012, p. 48). As Graham Allison (2008), dean of the Kennedy School at Harvard University between 1977 and 1989, remembers, when a new curriculum was developed in the 1960s, professors were involved from the disciplines of political economy, statistics, public administration, operations research, economics and government. At the beginning, there was not much emphasis on 'courses focussing on the leadership of public organisations' (Allison, 2008, p. 68), but courses in the fields of management and leadership were later offered, including executive courses in addition to the regular degree programmes. Today, there is a specific and dominant US approach for conducting 'policy analysis', regarding both the conception of the policy system and the analytical techniques used and taught for policy analysis—the latter being, in general, 'strongly quantitative, privileging economic cost-benefit analysis and/or the use of randomized controlled trials (RCTs) in evaluation' (Crowley & Head, 2015, p. 2).

Next to these positivist approaches, new research strands were established in the 1990s in the United States, which are often labelled as constructivist. Researchers who have taken this 'argumentative turn' in policy analysis (Fischer & Forester, 1993) are engaged with asking which language policy analysts and planners use, and which arguments they put forward. This literature often employs ideational approaches that look at the role of certain beliefs and paradigms for policymaking. 'Interpretive policy analysis' nowadays is a crucial sub-field of policy analysis in a number of countries, such as the Netherlands and Austria (van Nispen & Scholten, 2014; Bandelow, Sager & Biegelbauer, 2013).

3. Forms and Functions of Research Utilization

Section 1 describes the gaps between researchers and policymakers, as well as the difficulties of 'translating' and utilizing scientific expertise for policymaking. So in what ways *can* scientific expertise be utilized for policy and politics? Research on the science–policy interface and on research utilization accumulated from the late 1970s (e.g. Caplan, 1979; Weiss, 1979). In one of these early works, Knott and Wildavsky (1980) distinguished different stages of a ladder of knowledge utilization (see also Landry, Amara & Lamari, 2001). We take this ladder of research utilization as a starting point (Table 22.1) to trace the shift from a linear model of research utilization towards a more interactive one, which has taken place over the last decades.

This ladder of utilization is useful in conceptualizing research utilization as a process that can culminate in the application of reported research, but can also be terminated before this point. Naturally, as with other stages models, one can discuss to which extent the phases

Policy Analysis by Academics

Table 22.1 Ladder of research utilization

Stage	Description
1 Transmission	Transmission of research results to the practitioners and professionals concerned with an issue
2 Cognition	Practitioners and professionals have read and understood the research reports
3 Reference	Research is cited by practitioners and professionals in their reports, studies, and strategies of action
4 Efforts	Practitioners and professionals have made efforts to adopt the research results
5 Influence	Choices and decisions of practitioners and professionals are influenced by the research results
6 Application	Research results gave rise to applications and extensions by the practitioners and professionals concerned with the issue

Adapted from Landry et al., 2001; Knott & Wildavsky, 1980

are neatly distinguishable, can change their order, or are necessarily passed through at all. However, there are also a number of fundamental things that can be added to this model. First, as described above, research utilization is now usually understood as an interactive process in which both researchers and policymakers are involved. To draw on a picture elaborated by Mayntz:

> Although the televised ritual where the chair of an expert council ceremoniously hands a voluminous report to the chancellor seems to suggest otherwise, the provision of scientific knowledge to decision-makers cannot be organised as a simple process of transportation.
>
> *Mayntz, 2013, p. 280*

Another point is the *form* in which the science–policy interface and exchange take place. The ladder of research utilization very much focuses on written documents such as commissioned research reports: Stage 2 premises that practitioners and professionals have 'read and understood' the research results, Stage 3 then consists in them 'citing' from the respective publications (see Table 22.1). However, publications are not the only way in which policymakers can come to learn about or be influenced by scientific expertise—and arguably not even the most important one. A second form comprises convocation activities (Lindquist, 1990) through which scientific experts disseminate knowledge, such as workshops, conferences, or speeches. A third form consists of informal communications and personal contacts, such as background talks or personal briefings. A main element of scientific policy advice, it has been argued, is to produce 'boundary objects' (Gieryn, 1983) that are at the same time legitimate within the scientific community and politically relevant. Empirically, such boundary objects of scientific policy advice can be statistics, models, simulations and expert reports, but also metaphors or narratives (Rüb & Straßheim, 2012).

The 'utilization ladder' also presents a more or less direct approach towards knowledge acquisition and use in government policies. However, there are also more indirect forms of knowledge utilization. A distinction is often made between instrumental, conceptual and symbolic use of knowledge (Amara, Ouimet & Landry, 2004). These three types are not mutually exclusive, but rather complementary. Instrumental use denotes the direct use of knowledge for policymaking, while conceptual use refers to the cognitive level of ideas and beliefs. Conceptual use is more indirect and difficult to grasp than instrumental use, but it can have a large impact in the longer run:

> On the ground, research is often used in more subtle, indirect and conceptual ways, to bring about changes in knowledge and understanding, or shifts in perceptions, attitudes and beliefs: altering the ways in which policymakers and practitioners think about what they do, how they do it, and why.
>
> *Nutley, Walter & Davies, 2007, p. 301*

Last but not least, research use can also be symbolic. This is often highlighted in public discussions, when policymakers are 'accused' of employing scientific expertise to advance their own interests. Without a doubt, scientific expertise is also an important tool in the course of politics. For instance, it can be employed to convince other political actors, to legitimize predetermined positions, or to delay the policy process and gain time by installing an 'expert commission' after an event. Boswell (2009, p. 7) identifies political knowledge utilization as comprising a *legitimizing* function and a *substantiating* function, the first being directed at increasing the authority of an organization, the latter at helping to substantiate its policy preferences (and undermine those of others). The extent to which academic policy analysts themselves pay attention to or are even engaged with this symbolic, political knowledge utilization will depend on how they understand their role in policy and politics (see Head, 2015; Pielke, 2007).

Four such roles, or groups, are distinguished by Head (2015). The first is the 'mainstream academic', who gives broad interpretations on policy, has limited direct engagement with practitioners, and whose impact will rather be long term and conceptual. A second group 'consists of those who specialize in providing evidence-informed critiques of government policies in a chosen policy sector' (Head, 2015, p. 6). Their influence is more long term and conceptual as well, since the problems they highlight are often dissonant with current government policy preferences. Researchers in the third group provide applied, direct consultancy services to practitioners (e.g. policy evaluations), and those in the (small) fourth group take 'secondments into advisory roles within public agencies or ministerial offices' (Head, 2015, p. 6). The last two groups in particular may serve as what have been called 'knowledge brokers' or, alternatively, a 'third community' (Lindquist, 1990) between policymaking and social science research (for example, through think tanks).

All these forms and functions of scientific expertise for policymaking will differ both between policy sectors and between countries. This is illustrated by the concept of policy advisory systems, which can be defined as systems 'of interlocking actors, with a unique configuration in each sector and jurisdiction, who provide information, knowledge and recommendations for action to policy makers' (Craft & Howlett, 2013, p. 80). Policy advisory systems go beyond the boundaries of internal government expertise and can include a broad range of actors, such as advisory committees, academic experts, think tanks, civil society organizations, or employer and employee associations. Halligan (1995) distinguished advisory systems by the location through which advice is provided to governments, with the assumption that the influence of given advice is mainly a function of proximity to political decision makers. Advice can be given from within the public service, as well as internal or external to government. Furthermore, government control over advisory actors can be high or low (Halligan, 1995). Factors other than location and control have also been highlighted, in particular the content of the advice, and whether advice is 'cold' (long term and anticipatory) or 'hot' (short term and reactive) (Craft & Howlett, 2013).

Others have focused on what could be called scientific advisory systems, and thus the specific context in which academic policy analysis unfolds its role for policy and politics. For example, Straßheim and Kettunen (2014, p. 260) emphasize the importance of the cultural and institutional 'embeddedness' of epistemic and political authority: 'what counts as evidence is defined by institutionally and discursively established conventions that differ between countries and policies'. Building on Jasanoff's work (2005), Straßheim and Kettunen see large variances in what counts as evidence in countries with so-called contentious (e.g. the United States), communitarian (e.g. United Kingdom), or consensus-seeking styles of expertise (e.g. Germany). Both the general advisory systems and the specific styles of expertise differ between countries. For instance, in a neo-corporatist, institution-based system such as Germany one will find more 'expert rationality', often stemming from institutional representatives who are included in advisory bodies, e.g. representatives from the employers' and employees' associations (see Straßheim & Kettunen, 2014; Jasanoff, 2005). In a pluralist, interest-based system such as the United States, evidence is much more directed at 'sound science' provided by experts with strong technical knowledge. The following section will zoom in on these and other cross-country variations in academic policy analysis and research utilization.

4. Comparative Differences and Similarities in Policy Research Utilization

As mentioned above, one way to approach comparative differences on policy research utilization is to look at the configuration of actors in the policy advisory system of a country. In a recent study on policy advice utilization (Bossens, Van Damme & Brans, 2014), we adapted Halligan's (1995) location-based model to include academic actors, who were originally not identified as providers of policy advice, which was strangely at odds with the policy advisory role assigned to academic experts by scholars of knowledge utilization (e.g. Knott & Wildavsky, 1980; Landry, Lamari & Amara, 2003).

We now make a distinction between the internal government arena, external academic arena and external non-academic (lay) arena. We present the different arenas in a Venn diagram instead of a matrix (see Figure 22.1). The advantage of locating actors in this diagram is that it allows us to identify advisory institutions or arrangements comprising or involving actors from different arenas. Presented in this way, we can see that academic policy analysts may safely stay within the confines of their institutional habitat of universities or operate at the intersection of two or even three arenas. We can also see that there is a special category of policy workers in advisory bodies or knowledge centres who 'are specifically tasked with translating or processing scientific evidence and thought into policy advice' (Hoppe, 2014, p. 49). It is policy workers of this special type who are explicitly tasked with boundary work between science and government.

At the intersection of the external academic arena and the internal arena, we find government-financed but independent research institutions such as the Dutch Scientific Council for Government Policy (WRR). This high-level scientific council, composed of scholars on leave, provides strategic and future-oriented science-informed advice on overall and long-term government policy. In Flanders, university consortia are engaged in government-financed policy research centres to produce both short- and long-term policy-relevant research for different Flemish government departments. In Germany, departmental research institutes (*Ressortforschung*) of the national ministries have a special tradition, and operate at an arm's-length distance from the civil service. For policy-relevant research (and also commissioned departmental research) a number of extramural research institutes play

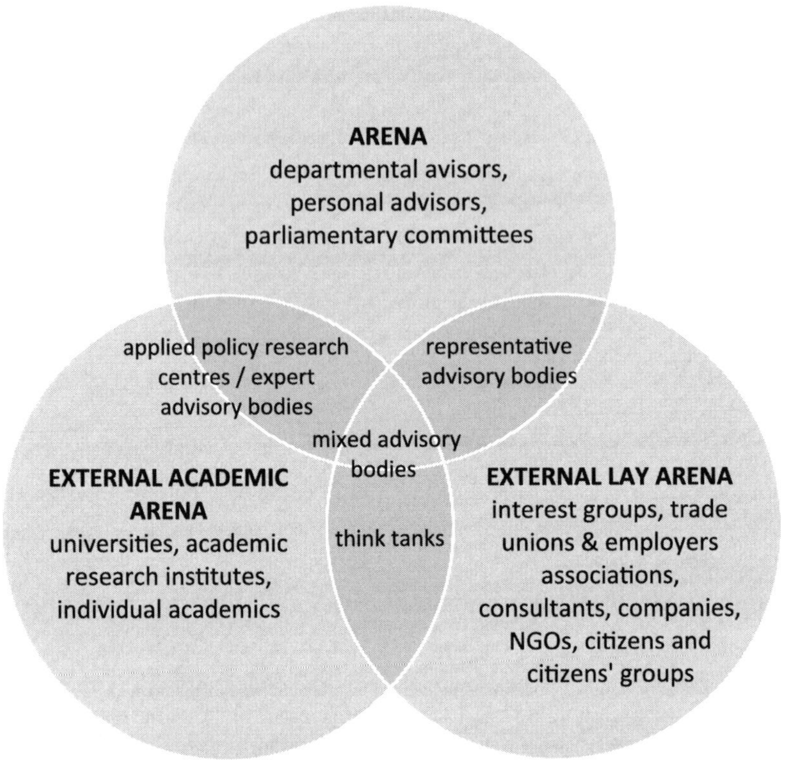

Figure 22.1 Actors and arenas in the policy advisory system
Source: Adapted from Halligan (1995) and Bossens, Van Damme & Brans (2014)

a particular role, such as those of the Leibniz Association and the Fraunhofer institutes (Thunert, 2013).

Academics may also engage at the intersection of the external academic arena and the external non-academic arena, when their expertise is, for instance, sourced by think tanks, or when they team up with private evaluation companies or private consultants for paid consultancy work. The part-time engagement of scholars in think tanks is a longstanding practice in the US and elsewhere where think tanks are well embedded in the policy advisory system, but is relatively new in Europe and other parts of the world where policy think tanks took a longer time to gain ground (see Chapter 21). It is also plausible that some policy-interested academics increasingly turn to private companies, as policy advice externalizes to private players—especially in times when university research financing becomes more scarce. Academics can also, for limited or longer times, trade places with actors in another arena.

The latter phenomenon was described by Head and Walter (2015) in their account of leading academics taking up advisory positions in the Australian bureaucracy. The Netherlands also offers many cases of academics moving to top positions in the bureaucracy. And, in times of political and financial crisis, the technocratic governments of Italy and Greece have been eager to welcome academics as executive ministers, where their expertise is put to use at the apex of decision making. In other countries, such as Germany, this practice is less common.

In a locational model, one can begin to describe comparative differences and similarities in the engagement of academic policy researchers. It helps to locate academic policy researchers in their proper arena and visualize how they engage with actors in other arenas of the policy advisory system. The model can thus serve as a heuristic tool for describing the population density of academic researchers in different arenas and their position vis-à-vis other players. It can show how in some countries policy researchers remain at a distance from other actors and hence engage with both government and the third community in limited ways, while in others the government and third community are more permeable to input from policy researchers. In some cases we find that academic policy researchers tend to stay in the academic arena and only occasionally venture in other arenas; for instance, some have claimed that this is the case for French academics, who view their role as policy critics (Delvaux & Mangez, 2008, p. 113; Nutley, Morton, Jung & Boaz, 2010, p. 135). In the Netherlands, in contrast, all arenas are densely populated with policy-interested academics, who are also found at the intersections. In still other cases, policy-interested academics may shy away from civil society actors and confine their engagements solely to government actors.

The locational model can help to locate policy research and researchers in the world of science, government and society. However, it is too unidimensional to capture the actual functions and roles of academic policy research, which are multifaceted and multi-level. This calls for an investigation at the macro, meso and micro levels. In the remainder of this section, we first zoom in at a number of dimensions at the macro level by pointing at practices, institutions and cultures that bear upon countries' propensity for research utilization in policymaking. Second, we also briefly touch upon meso-level factors that might explain particular sectoral dynamics of research utilization. Third, we discuss how on the micro level individual actors influence the degree to which research is picked up by policymakers.

As we have learned from the literature on knowledge utilization and science and technology studies (STS), the nature and impact of academic policy analysis and research in a particular context will depend on supply and demand as well as on epistemological cultures. Thus, at the macro level, we hypothesize that policy research engagement and utilization is aided by a mature academic policy analysis environment at universities, by strongly institutionalized policy analysis practices in government and governance, and by an epistemological culture of instrumental rationality or technocratic orientations in policymaking. Conversely, policy analytical research utilization is challenged when academic policy analysis is weak, policy analytical practices in government and governance are emergent, and decision making prioritizes considerations of interests and political preferences over scientific and technical evidence.

Mature versus Immature Academic Policy Analysis at Universities

At one end of the continuum we find countries with a mature academic policy analysis at universities, and at the other we find countries with a weak academic policy analysis. Mature academic policy analysis refers to a strong presence of policy analysis in academic curricula and research departments.

The presence and longevity of policy analysis as a subject taught in bachelor and master programmes is comparatively stronger in a number of Anglo-Saxon countries. Without a doubt, the United States—the birthplace of modern policy analysis—also leads in the anchorage of policy analysis in academic curricula and public policy schools. Policy studies are also firmly embedded in academic programmes in Australia. There, 'policy analysis' in its strictest definition has perhaps not caught on as much as in the US (Crowley & Head, 2015), but applied policy analysis is often found under such foci as programme evaluation. In Canada, academic policy analysis emerged comparatively later than in the US, but is now taught at many places, although there is less of a bifurcation between applied policy analysis and policy studies, with policy studies being slightly more dominant (see Dobuzinskis et al., 2007).

The European forerunner in embracing policy analysis in academic curricula is the Netherlands, and the Atlanticism for which the country is reputed may explain the influence of US policy analytical teaching. Policy analysis was institutionalized within Dutch academia in the 1970s, when there was a strong policy orientation and conducive personal ties between academics and policymakers (van Nispen & Scholten, 2014, p. 2).

In many other European countries, policy analysis as an academic subject took longer to find a place in academic curricula; academic policy analysis was generally taught in political science classes, public administration subjects, or under substantive policy analysis such as social policy or socio-economic policy. It is also typical for policy research to have many different homes, with political science departments, public administration departments, and business schools, for instance in the UK, being the university hosts. In Europe, the creation of distinct public policy schools as one finds in the US, and also in Singapore and Korea, are the exception rather than the rule, though some have emerged in the UK and Germany (see Blätte, 2012). In the last two decades, many European countries have caught up with teaching policy analysis at all levels. This is definitely the case for Germany, Belgium, Switzerland and more recently France. In Germany, for instance, two-thirds of all political science BA programmes today contain modules on policy analysis, and 18% of all MA programmes specialize in it; those foci were mostly installed at the respective universities between the mid-1980s and mid-1990s (Reiter & Töller, 2013, p. 275). In Central and Eastern Europe, the policy analysis movement in academia is still modest, with several of the old-style economic planning courses transformed into policy analytical courses.

Hassenteufel and Le Galès' account (2017) of the French trajectory of the institutionalization and automatization of policy analysis shows how policy analysis (although not denoted with that term) was introduced at the margins of the academy, under the cover of 'organization studies' and in particular policy domains such as urban policies, justice and agriculture. In the 1990s and 2000s, policy analysis progressively diffused to French political science, which is now the leading discipline for policy analysis, and emphasizes theory building and policy process studies over more practical policy analysis.

The Netherlands also features a mature approach in policy research: there are many academics doing many different kinds of policy analysis and an astonishing variety of approaches and theoretical perspectives for a comparatively small country. In contrast, in Austria—another small country—there exists only 'a rudimentary disciplinary understanding' (Bandelow et al., 2013, p. 81) of academic policy analysis, mainly due to a small political science community and low resources. Academic policy analysis in Austria specializes in interpretive studies, while the bulk of policy analysis advice is provided by extramural, interdisciplinary research institutes.

Strong versus Weak Institutionalization of Policy Analytical Practices in Government and Governance

Academic policy research requires abstract thinking, the application of methodological standards, and some familiarity with local knowledge of one or more policy domains (Geva-May, 2005). We may assume that professional policy analysts and advisors in government and governance show these competences to a great extent. Hence we hypothesize that professional policy workers, in their endeavour to prepare intelligent solutions to policy problems, will be open to the utilization of research evidence. When policy analytical practices are institutionalized in government and governance, policymaking will be receptive to academic evidence. We find strong institutionalization where policy analysis is recognized as a profession, where policy formulation and evaluation deploy policy analytical procedures, where there are officials at work to gather intelligence and analyse information in a systematic way, where there are reputed planning agencies, and where agencies are custodians of credible databases. These properties relate to the policy analytical capacity of government.

Systematic comparative evidence on the components of policy analytical capacity is lacking, but the available anecdotal and country-specific analyses present mixed accounts and are hence to be approached with caution. Generally speaking, countries with traditions of 'healthy' (Voyer, 2007, p. 235) policy analytical capacity include the US, the UK and Canada, as well as the Netherlands. In these countries, civil service training comprises policy analytical competences, and evaluation is systematically deployed in the policy cycle. In Australia, there is evidence of powerful toolboxes for applied policy analysis in the bureaucracy, but general accounts of policy analytical capacity and its developments are more sceptical. This scepticism is also found in domestic accounts of policy analytical capacity in the Netherlands. Disappointments over the demise of particular government-wide initiatives to reinforce rational policy analysis in the bureaucracy in the 1970s and early 2000s may have blinded critics of the comparatively strong institutionalization of policy analysis in central government, where policy work is indeed well embedded in ministerial departments, where policy analytical procedures and evaluation are frequently practised, and where civil service training comprises a great variety of policy analytical courses, including newer deliberative modes of policy analysis.

Overall, the Netherlands can be regarded as 'one of the strongholds of policy analysis, both in academia and in policymaking' (van Nispen & Scholten, 2014, p. 1). In this it differs from other European countries. In Germany and Austria, for instance, the ministerial civil service is highly professionalized, but the profession of 'policy analyst' therein is not very well recognized. The German governmental departments are largely populated by legal experts and economists. In Austria, public management training curricula for civil servants 'do not usually feature policy analysis units' (Bandelow et al., 2013, p. 81).

It is clear that comparative assessments of governments' policy analytical capacity would benefit from more systematic research on policy workers and their work, and on the structures and procedures in which policy analysis is deployed. It is also important to note that building policy capacity in government may mean different things in different countries. Some countries, like several Central and Eastern European countries in transition, sought to build policy capacity where there was none or little (Lazareviciute & Verheijen, 2000). Others, such as Canada and Australia, aim to re-build their policy capacity, with investments in organizational and human capital within the government apparatus to counter perceived losses. Still others, such as the UK, seem to be re-directing and introducing new dimensions, such as long-term strategic thinking and consultative practices (see Brans & Vancoppenolle, 2005).

Science-Based Rationality in Policymaking versus other Sources of Knowledge

As Straßheim and Kettunen (2014, p. 259) point out, different cultures of evidence take-up help determine what counts as expertise and evidence in the policymaking process. While these epistemological cultures have historical roots in varying traditions of absolutism and enlightenment, they can also be more closely linked to the nature of contemporary policy advisory systems and the power of actors therein. Thus understood, variations in the take-up of academic evidence as opposed to other types of evidence are related to such factors as the nature of governance processes, modes of representation and political rules of conduct.

The conceptualization and comparative understanding of epistemological cultures is still in its infancy (Straßheim & Kettunen, 2014, p. 269). Jasanoff's (2005, 2011) categorization of three types of civic epistemologies—contentious (United States), communitarian (UK), and consensus-seeking (Germany)—point at the impact of pluralist, statist and neo-corporatist governance processes that we also find discussed in Nutley et al.'s (2010) study of evidence take-up in six European countries. These different cultures of evidence take-up can be understood to prioritize different types of knowledge in policy formulation. In Tenbensel's (2008, based on Flyvbjerg, 2001) Aristotelian differentiation of knowledge types these are *episteme* (what is objectively true), *techne* (what works in practice) and *phronesis* (what must be done).

In countries with neo-corporatist traits such as Belgium, Austria and Germany, we would find that the necessary compromises cannot primarily rely on academic evidence with uncompromising claims to the truth. Interests and political knowledge may be prioritized over scientific knowledge, and organizations with strong representational monopolies may crowd out academic expertise in advisory bodies. The Austrian political system, for instance, rests on a unique form of consociationalism based on both political parties and associations, and policy advice in Austria very much reflects this macro-corporatist tradition (Bandelow et al., 2013, p. 80): there are the strong and long-established networks between the social-democratic party and employee organizations on one side, and between the conservative party and employer organizations on the other.

In the Netherlands the neo-corporatist tradition also persists to some degree, but is blended with more pluralist tendencies to incorporate both science and interests, or, in Hoppe's (2014) description, 'knowledge-cum-interests'. This is related to the specific consociational character of Dutch politics: there is the corporatist tradition of the 'Polder model', but research and expertise have a traditionally strong role for consensus building, so the politicization of expertise is low (van Nispen & Scholten, 2014, p. 4). In countries with a statist tradition, like the UK, technical, service-based evidence prevails at the expense of representative organizations' input. Pluralist systems like the US differ from these other systems in some respects: here, different kinds of evidence compete with each other on a more equal footing, and sound science stands a good chance of being picked up.

These cultural differences are a useful point of departure to approach enduring cross-national differences in science-informed policymaking. They can also help us to describe cultural change and challenges to accepted practices, and even the co-existence of different patterns, such as the layering of neo-corporatist advice infrastructure with pluralist modes of advice utilization. We know, for instance, that a number of countries are seeing a trend towards a growing diversification of policy advice sources, which has consequences for the role of academic policy analysis. For Australia, Crowley and Head (2015, p. 1) see a 'growing role of ministerial advisors, consultants, think tanks and media-enabled channels of opinion'. In Germany, since the move of government from Bonn to Berlin after German reunification (completed in 1999), policy advice has grown rapidly as a consulting industry (Heinze, 2013). At the same time, the influence of unions and business associations has decreased significantly, a trend that has not happened in Austria (see above). Government departments in the Netherlands have made increasing use of external consultancies for policy advice since the 1990s (Hoppe, 2014).

To capture the full diversity of the relationship between the supply and demand of policy research, macro-level analysis alone will not suffice, e.g. looking at the practices and cultures of knowledge utilization. The effects of such macro-level features of the relationship between academic policy analysis and policymaking will no doubt be mediated by meso- and micro-level factors. At the meso level, we expect to find variation between policy domains. Some policy domains meet more numerously populated academic communities than others, and the professionalization of policy analysis in government may also be greater in some sectors—for instance education and health. Some policy issue characteristics carry too great an influence over the type of academic policy analysis that is put to use. Domesticated problems might be more instrumentally served with rational policy analysis, while ill-structured problems that are highly controversial and not easily understood with sound science may lend themselves more to deliberative modes of knowledge utilization. Another meso-level factor is political mood swings that may deny academics their previously privileged access to politicians. The decline of the impact of integration and multiculturalist studies in countries such as Australia, the Netherlands and Belgium are cases in point (Scholten, 2008; Head & Walter, 2015, p. 298; Brans et al., 2004).

At the micro level, individuals too may make a difference in the incidence and nature of the utilization of policy research. Some highly reputed and policy-interested academics may individually break through the walls of different arenas or act as policy entrepreneurs (see Head & Walter, 2015), either for brokering research input in certain policies, or to advance the evidence-based movement for better evidence utilization (see e.g. Ron Amann in the UK or Peter Shergold in Australia, in Head & Walter, 2015, p. 293).

5. Dynamics and Trends: Scientification, Societalization and Politicization

Although countries have enduring traditions and characteristics of academic policy analysis, and of the policy engagements of academics, the relationship between academic policy analysis and policymaking is dynamic over time. While this chapter cannot capture historical developments in a systematic way across different nations, we can refer to a number of them. A fine analysis of how at times knowledge production followed policy and at other times policy followed knowledge (van Twist, Rouw & van der Steen, 2014, p. 23) is found in Head and Walter's (2015) historical account of Australian researchers' policy engagements. The interwar optimism about technocratic solutions to social problems, the planning hype following post-war construction, and the Cold War suspicion are historical markers that have given or taken away policy researchers' access to government in other countries too. In Germany, for instance, the discovery and adaptation of policy analysis was 'closely linked to the reform discourses of the 1960s, which soon after were known as "planning euphoria"' (Jann & Jantz, 2013, p. 30). Before that time, 'policy' (for which no German word exists) did not receive much attention and issues of government were seen as adequately addressed within the domain of law, not political science.

Other major developments that since the 1970s have influenced how much weight academic expertise holds in policymaking are the rise of neo-liberalism and deregulation, and wide-scale bureaucratic reforms. In some cases, most notably Thatcher's UK, the neo-liberalist agenda went so far as to cut links with social science research and gave privileged advisory access to think tanks and private consultants. However, the New Public Management (NPM) reforms that followed presented mixed challenges to the demand and supply of policy analysis. They did not weaken the position of policy analysis everywhere (see Brans & Vancoppenolle, 2005, for examples). In New Zealand, for instance, the State Services Commission, which played a central role in the implementation of NPM reforms, carried forward the 'Policy Advice Initiative'. By diffusing classic policy analytical competences among departmental policy managers, this initiative sought to link requirements for professional policy analysis with NPM management principles. In Belgium, the NPM-type structural separation of policy and administration was conducive to building policy analytical capacity in the Flemish departmental administrations and for tightening their links with academic applied research for policy purposes. In Switzerland, the growing public management community gained importance with the introduction of neo-liberal ideas and NPM reforms, and the firm establishment of an evaluation culture strengthened the role of policy analysis for policymaking (Bandelow et al., 2013, p. 84).

More recently, in the last two decades, at least three movements have influenced the interaction between policy research and policymaking: the evidence-based policy movement; the trend towards interactive policymaking (or, to use more fashionable terms, co-production and co-design of policies); and pressures to restore the primacy of politics over evidence in policy choices. In some countries these developments are addressed concurrently, while in others they are addressed consecutively. These developments can also be referred to as scientification, societalization and politicization, for the source of knowledge that they emphasize.

The increasing complexity of the policy environment has been critical for the conduct of advising government on policy, whatever the source of advice. Today, so-called 'wicked problems'—which combine scientific uncertainty with societal dispute—challenge traditional ways of policymaking and of garnering scientific input. Governments are increasingly dependent upon external information, knowledge, expertise and support in order to successfully deliver policies (Peters & Barker, 1993). And, while seeking to underpin policy decisions with evidence is nothing new in the modern world, contemporary democratic governments must contend with these increasingly complex policy topics at the same time as, on every decision taken, they are under increasing scrutiny from media, embedded interest groups, and even individual citizens.

This backdrop has meant that policy research utilization appears to be occurring along two different paths, the first towards scientification and the other towards interactiveness or societalization. Scientification is a movement towards the increased reliance upon academic and scientific policy analysis and evaluation (Weingart, 1999). Thus, this route may increase the government's capacity for problem solving by increasing the scientific knowledge base available to and used for policy decisions. The move to knowledge-intensive policies and public services requires that governments be committed to 'evidence-based policymaking' (Sanderson, 2011, and Nutley et al., 2010, both cited in Straßheim & Kettunen, 2014). Societalization, on the other hand, is based upon the need of democratic governments to garner support for their decisions and to (appear to) be following the wishes of the people or at least acting in their interests. Policy decisions on this path involve direct consultation and interaction with target groups, bringing citizens directly into the policymaking process with the assumption that their support will ensure that the policy solutions are not only in the public's interest but are also sustainable.

This societalization of advice has led to more and more diverse mechanisms of public consultation and participation in the policymaking process, as well as to a broadening of sources of advice, with an expanding involvement of actors from both within and beyond the governmental system. In addition to academic experts and big interests, individual citizens, specific target groups and others are also consulted. Advice has accordingly become more competitive and contested, and the value of academic expertise is itself contested against the value of those with so-called experience-based expertise, or lay expertise, and even the 'wisdom of crowds' (Surrowiecki, 2004, referred to in Bekkers, 2014, p. 239).

As Talbot and Talbot say, some but not all evidence is academic (Talbot & Talbot, 2015). The consequence of greater advice competition is that academic policy analysts are under greater pressure to ensure that their products respond to the government's needs (see Halligan, 1995, and Waller, 1992, for this point on advice in general), as well as to engage with stakeholders outside government. In some cases, the tensions between scientification and societalization have led to symbiotic relationships—for example, when academic experts are called in to set the scientific boundaries for subsequent policy discussions with civil society actors. From the academic side, there is not necessarily a conflict between the trends: The concept of 'deliberative policy analysis' (Hajer & Wagenaar, 2003), for instance, entails a post-positivist view of policy analysis as argumentative practices and of policy issues as necessarily contested. Against that background, the input from academics is seen as contributing to evidence-*informed* policymaking rather than evidence-*based* policymaking, with academic evidence being one source of knowledge among others.

Next to scientification and societalization, a third movement entails different forms of politicization. This is not just the classic observation that research is always used, or possibly misused, for political purposes. There is also sometimes an 'explicit politicization', marked by a discourse that focuses on political primacy, with the underlying fear of interest group 'capture' of a policy domain. One interpretation of this view posits that political decisions should be taken independently by the government, by those officially mandated, and any advice should come from independent experts without even the smallest possible vested interest in particular policy outcomes. This view still favours input from academic policy advice, on the condition that it is independent from societal interests. A more pessimistic view sees the restoration of politics as contributing to the politicization of science, or what is also termed as policy-based evidence-making, where policy-interested academics are pressured to tailor their products to policymakers' needs to the extent that their scientific validity is threatened, or their research subjects become too narrow. In this view, normative selectivity leads to the distortion of scientific facts for political purposes and cognitive selectivity renders policymakers myopic (Straßheim & Kettunen, 2014, pp. 262–3).

This pessimistic view on the politicization of science can help us to discern political manoeuvres towards the political instrumentalization of policy analysis and even 'facts-free policymaking' (Bekkers, 2014, p. 239), where evidence and research is explicitly discredited. However, this scepticism should not blind us from seeing new and interesting experiments and emerging practices where the triple, potentially conflicting pressures are reconciled in procedures and practices that fit with interaction models of research utilization. In non-linear interactions between government, research and stakeholders, 'evidence-based policy is the integration of experience, judgement and expertise with the best available evidence of systematic research' (van Twist et al., 2014, p. 29). There are lessons to be drawn from the way some research funding agencies have begun to sensitize researchers to presenting their scientific output in languages and forms that travel more easily across the boundaries of government and society. The European Union research programmes, for instance, increasingly emphasize that the added value of knowledge for end users be articulated, and projects are called to engage in dialogue and co-production with stakeholders (see Landry, Amara, Pablos-Mendes, Shademani & Gold, 2006, for a discussion on knowledge brokering). Other examples where research is translated for impact to be facilitated include rapid review services, short evidence-based summaries or policy briefs.

Alongside changes to the supply side of knowledge utilization, there are also changes to the demand side. Policy workers and decision makers are challenged to increase external input in policy formulation. In the Netherlands, for example, policy workers engage with academics in knowledge centres, while the UK has established 'what works centres', appointed chief scientific officers in departments, and promoted piloting projects as well as collaborative procedures with evidence producers outside the civil service. The most novel experiments follow opportunities from information and communications technology (ICT) developments and network activities. Talbot and Talbot (2015) mention crowd-sourced wikis, policy hubs, hackathons and policy labs. In Germany, a so-called civil dialogue (*Bürgerdialog*) was carried out by the government in 2015, in which the chancellor and all responsible ministers led dialogues with citizens on quality of life in the country, over the course of the year. The results of these dialogues were then analysed by a consultancy together with researchers from the Free University of Berlin, and monitored by a 'scientific advisory council'.

6. Conclusions

What academics are doing which kind of policy analysis, where, how, with what purpose, and with what effect in the real world of policymaking? In a comparative investigation of policy analysis by academics, these are obvious basic questions, but the answers are not straightforward; systematic research and comparative evidence are rather scarce, and conclusions are tentative at best.

From the available evidence, it can be assumed that the nature of policy analysis by academics is influenced by the institutional habitat of academics and their position in the policy advisory system. In principle, academics should have greater independence than policy analysts in government or in political party organizations and interest groups. As Howlett, Ramesh and Perl (2009, p. 9) point out, academics usually have no direct stake in the outcome of specific policies, except to the extent that they are working with or are committed to a particular ideological stance. They would, therefore, be able to examine policies more abstractly than can other analysts and tend to grapple with the theoretical, conceptual and methodological issues surrounding public policy through the lens of policies studies. While we agree with the above, we also contend that the extent to which academics in a particular country are doing policy studies in such a more abstract and neutral sense, or engaging in more practice-oriented policy analysis, depends on country-specific epistemological traditions and self-understandings of the discipline. Some countries keep their academic policy research at a distance from authorities, and researchers can assume roles of mainstream academics or of policy critics. Another tradition shows a more pragmatic orientation, where policy researchers engage in applied policy analysis offering evaluation and technical advice or advice on policy options. The most common type appears to be mixed, and combines both mainstream and critical policy studies with applied policy analysis, yet with what seems like a dominance of the former. In this context, different kinds of policy researchers are engaged in different kinds of analysis, and portray a variety of roles and engagements vis-à-vis policymaking.

Policy researchers' engagements with policymakers and, ultimately, the weight they can bear upon policy formulation and evaluation are research foci in studies of knowledge utilization. In this chapter, we have hypothesized that policy research engagements and utilization are aided by at least three features: mature academic policy analysis at universities; strongly institutionalized policy analysis practices in government and governance; and an epistemological culture of instrumental rationality or technocratic orientations in policymaking. While we have been able to document some country variations along these dimensions on the basis of literature review and secondary and anecdotal evidence, more systematic research is warranted.

Systematic comparative research could proceed along the following lines. First, a locational model can be used as a comparative heuristic for locating academic policy analysts within and across different arenas in the policy advisory system, as well as describing their engagements

Policy Analysis by Academics

with government and third actors. In such an investigation, it seems worthwhile to explore whether the worlds of policy research utilization correspond to or differ from general advisory systems. Second, comparative research could refine and allocate the roles of academics and the nature of their analysis to certain types. A promising focus for comparison is the understanding of 'policy analysis' in countries, specifically whether there is a self-understanding as an (academic) profession. Research along these lines necessarily requires multi-lingual competences and a thorough understanding of intricate variations of policy analytical terms and concepts in national languages. Third, as policy research utilization depends not only on supply and demand factors but also on the transactions between supply and demand, comparative investigations should include policy analytical capacity and epistemological cultures, both subjects of much current research en route. Finally, the influence of national features of policy research utilization will be mediated by international trends, as well as cross-sectoral characteristics. In this chapter we have referred to a number of overarching trends and developments, some of which are supported by inter- and supranational organizations, such as the scientification and societalization of the research programmes of the European Union. Against the background of these and other trends, more research is needed on the extent to which there is convergence in policy research utilization or whether national heterogeneities prevail.

References

Allison, G. (2008): Emergence of Schools of Public Policy: Reflections by a Founding Dean. In M. Moran, M. Rein & R.-E. Goodin (eds): *The Oxford Handbook of Public Policy*. New York/Oxford: Oxford University Press. 58–79.

Amara, N., Ouimet, M. & Landry, R. (2004): New Evidence on Instrumental, Conceptual, and Symbolic Utilization of University Research in Government Agencies. *Science Communication*, 26 (1). 75–106.

Bandelow, N.C., Sager, F. & Biegelbauer, P. (2013): Policy Analysis in the German-Speaking Countries: Common Traditions, Different Cultures in Germany, Austria and Switzerland. In S. Blum & K. Schubert (eds): *Policy Analysis in Germany*. Bristol, UK: Policy Press. 75–89.

Bekkers, V. (2014): Contested Knowledge in Theory-Driven Policy Analysis: Setting the Dutch Stage. In F. van Nispen & P. Scholten (eds): *Policy Analysis in the Netherlands*. Bristol, UK: Policy Press. 231–247.

Blätte, A. (2012): Der Reformdiskurs in der universitären Vermittlung angewandter Politikforschung: Thesen zur Kontextualisierung und Reorientierung. In M. Glaab & K.-R. Korte (eds): *Angewandte Politikforschung*. Wiesbaden: Springer. 45–60.

Blum, S. (forthcoming): Between Pure Scientist and Policy Entrepreneur: Roles and Functions of Scientific Experts in Policymaking.

Bossens, N, Van Damme, J. & Brans, M. (2014): *Beleidsadvisering in de Vlaamse Overheid: Een analyse van de organisatie van de Vlaamse beleidsadvisering en een verkenning van mogelijkheden voor optimalisering*. Brussels: SBOV.

Boswell, C. (2009): *The Political Uses of Expert Knowledge: Immigration Policy and Social Research*. Cambridge University Press.

Brans, M. & Vancoppenolle, D. (2005): Policy-Making Reforms and Civil Service Systems: An Exploration of Agendas and Consequences. In M. Painter & J. Pierre (eds): *Challenges to State Policy Capacity: Global Trends and Comparative Perspectives*. Basingstoke, UK: Palgrave Macmillan. 164–184.

Brans, M. Jacobs, D., Martiniello, M. Rea, A., Swyngedouw, M., Adam, I. et al. (2004): *Recherche et politiques publiques: le cas de l'immigration en Belgique – Onderzoek en beleid: de gevalstudie van immigratie in België*, Gent: Academia Press.

Caplan, N. (1979): The Two-Communities Theory and Knowledge Utilization. *American Behavioural Scientist*, 22 (3). 459–470.

Craft, J. & Howlett, M. (2013): The Dual Dynamics of Policy Advisory Systems: The Impact of Externalization and Politicization on Policy Advice. *Policy & Society*, 32. 187–197.

Crowley, K. & Head, B. (2015): Policy Analysis in Australia: The State of the Art. In B. Head & K. Crowley (eds): *Policy Analysis in Australia*. Bristol, UK: Policy Press. 1–20.

Delvaux, B. & Mangez, E. (2008): *Towards a Sociology of the Knowledge–Policy Relation*, Literature Review Integrative Report. Available at www.knowandpol.eu

Dobuzinskis, L., Howlett, M. & Laycock, D. (2007): Policy Analysis in Canada: The State of the Art. In L. Dobuzinskis, D. Laycock & M. Howlett (eds): *Policy Analysis in Canada: The State of the Art*. University of Toronto Press. 3–20.

Dye, T.S. (1976): *Policy Analysis: What Governments Do, Why They Do it and What Difference it Makes*. Tuscaloosa: University of Alabama Press.

Enserink, B., Koppenjan, J.F.M. & Mayer, I.S. (2013): A Policy Sciences View on Policy Analysis. In W.A.H. Thissen & W.E. Walker (eds): *Public Policy Analysis, International Series in Operations Research & Management Science*, 179. 11–40.

Fischer, F. & Forester, J. (1993): *The Argumentative Turn in Policy Analysis and Planning*. Durham, NC: Duke University Press.

Flyvbjerg, B. (2001): *Making Social Science Matter: Why Social Inquiry Fails and How it Can Succeed Again*. Cambridge University Press.

Geva-May, I. (2005): *Thinking Like a Policy Analyst: Policy Analysis as a Clinical Profession*. New York: Palgrave Macmillan.

Gieryn, T.F. (1983): Boundary-Work and the Demarcation of Science from Non-Science: Strains and Interests in Professional Ideologies of Scientists. *American Sociological Review*, 48 (6). 781–795.

Halligan (1995): Policy Advice and the Public Sector. In B.G. Peters & D.T. Savoie (eds): *Governance in a Changing Environment*. Montreal: McGill-Queen's University Press. 138–172.

Hajer, M.A. & Wagenaar, H. (2003): *Deliberative Policy Analysis: Understanding Governance in the Network Society*. Cambridge University Press.

Hassenteufel, P. & Le Galès, P. (2017): The Academic World of French Policy Analysis. In: C. Halpern, P. Hassenteufel & E. Zittoun (eds): *Policy Analysis in France*. Bristol, UK: Policy Press.

Head, B. (2015): Relationships between Policy Academics and Public Servants: Learning at a Distance? *Australian Journal of Public Administration*, 74 (1). 5–12.

Head, B. & Walter, J. (2015): Academic Research and Public Policy. In B. Head & K. Crowley (eds): *Policy Analysis in Australia*. Bristol, UK: Policy Press. 285–303.

Heinze, R.G. (2013): Federal Government in Germany: Temporary, Issue-Related Policy Advice. In S. Blum & K. Schubert (eds): *Policy Analysis in Germany*. Bristol, UK: Policy Press. 137–150.

Hoppe, R. (1999): Policy Analysis, Science and Politics: From 'Speaking Truth to Power' to 'Making Sense Together'. *Science and Public Policy*, 26 (3). 201–210.

Hoppe, R. (2014): Patterns of Science–Policy Interaction. In F. van Nispen & P. Scholten (eds): *Policy Analysis in the Netherlands*. Bristol, UK: Policy Press. 49–68.

Howlett, M., Ramesh, M. & Perl, A. (2009): *Studying Public Policy: Policy Cycles and Policy Subsystems*. Oxford University Press.

Jann, W. & Jantz, B. (2013): The Development of Policy Analysis in Germany: Practical Problems and Theoretical Concepts. In S. Blum & K. Schubert (eds): *Policy Analysis in Germany*. Bristol, UK: Policy Press. 29–43.

Jasanoff, S. (2005): *Designs on Nature: Science and Democracy in Europe and the United States*. Princeton University Press.

Jasanoff, S. (2011): The Practices of Objectivity in Regulatory Science. In C. Camid, N. Gross & M. Lamont (eds): *Social Knowledge in the Making*. University of Chicago Press. 307–338

Knott, J. & Wildavsky, A. (1980): If Dissemination is the Solution, What is the Problem? *Knowledge: Creation, Diffusion, Utilization*, 1. 537–578.

Landry, R., Amara, N. & Lamari, M. (2001): Climbing the Ladder of Research Utilization: Evidence from Social Science Research. *Science Communication*, 22 (4). 396–422.

Landry, R., Lamari, M. & Amara, N. (2003): The Extent and Determinants of the Utilization of University Research in Government Agencies. *Public Administration Review*, 63 (2). 192–205.

Landry, R., Amara, N., Pablos-Mendes, A., Shademani, R. & Gold, I. (2006): The Knowledge-Value Chain: A Conceptual Framework for Knowledge Translation in Health. *Bulletin of the World Health Organization*, 84 (8). 597–602.

Lasswell, H.D. (1951): The Policy Orientation. In H.D. Lasswell & D. Lerner (eds): *The Policy Sciences: Recent Developments in Scope and Method*. Palo Alto, CA: Stanford University Press. 3–15.

Lasswell, H.D. & Lerner, D. (1951): *The Policy Sciences: Recent Developments in Scope and Method.* Palo Alto, CA: Stanford University Press.

Lazareviciute, I. & Verheijen, T. (2000): Organizing the Delivery of Policy Advice. In T. Verheijen (ed.): *Politico-Administative Relations: Who Rules?* Bratislava, Slovakia: NISPAcee.

Lindquist, E.A. (1990): The Third Community, Policy Inquiry, and Social Scientists. In S. Brooks & A.-G. Gagnon (eds): *Social Scientists, Policy, and the State.* New York: Praeger. 21–51.

Mayntz, R. (2013): Academics and Policy Analysis: The Tension Between Epistemic and Practical Concerns. In S. Blum & K. Schubert (eds): *Policy Analysis in Germany.* Bristol, UK: Policy Press. 279–85.

Nutley, S., Morton, S., Jung, T. & Boaz, A (2010): Evidence and Policy in Six European Countries: Diverse Approaches and Common Challenges. *Evidence & Policy*, 6 (2). 131–44.

Nutley, S.M., Walter, I. & Davies, H.T.O. (2007): *Using Evidence: How Research Can Inform Public Services.* Bristol, UK: Policy Press.

Peters, B.G. and Barker, A. (1993): *Advising West European Governments: Inquiries, Expertise and Public Policy.* Edinburgh University Press.

Pielke, R.A. (2007): *The Honest Broker: Making Sense of Science in Policy and Politics.* Cambridge University Press.

Reiter, R. & Töller, A.E. (2013): The Role of Policy Analysis in Teaching Political Science at German Universities. In S. Blum & K. Schubert (eds): *Policy Analysis in Germany.* Bristol, UK: Policy Press. 265–277.

Rüb, F. & Straßheim, H. (2012): Politische Evidenz: Rechtfertigung durch Verobjektivierung. In A. Geis, F. Nullmeier & C. Daase (eds): *Der Aufstieg der Legitimitätspolitik.:Rechtfertigung und Kritik politisch-ökonomischer Ordnungen.* Baden-Baden, Germany: Nomos. 377–97.

Sanderson, I. (2011): Evidence-Based Policy or Policy-Based Evidence? Reflections on Scottish Experience. *Evidence & Policy*, 7 (1). 59–76

Scholten, P.W.A. (2008): Constructing Immigrant Policies: Research – Policy Relations and Immigrant Integration in the Netherlands, 1970–2004, dissertation, Twente University.

Schubert, K. (2009): Pragmatismus, Pluralismus und Politikfeldanalyse: Ursprünge und theoretische Verankerung. In K. Schubert & N.C. Bandelow (eds): *Lehrbuch der Politikfeldanalyse 2.0.* München. 39–71.

Straßheim, H. & Kettunen, P. (2014): When does Evidence-Based Policy Turn Into Policy-Based Evidence? Configurations, Contexts and Mechanisms. *Evidence & Policy*, 10 (2). 259–277.

Surrowiecki, J. (2004): *The Wisdom of Crowds.* New York, NY: Double Day.

Talbot, C. & Talbot, C. (2015): Bridging the Academic–Policy-Making Gap: Practice and Policy Issues. *Public Money & Management*, 35 (3). 187–194

Tenbensel, R. (2008): *The Role of Evidence in Policy: How the Mix Matters.* Paper presented at the 12th Annual Conference of the the Research Society for Public Management. Brisbane, Australia.

Thunert, M. (2013): Expert policy advice in Germany. In S. Brooks, D. Stasiak & T. Zyro, (eds): *Policy Expertise in Contemporary Democracies.* Farnham, UK: Ashgate. 123–146.

van Nispen, F. & Scholten, P. (2014): Policy Analysis in the Netherlands: An Introduction. In F. van Nispen & P. Scholten (eds): *Policy Analysis in the Netherlands.* Bristol, UK: Policy Press. 1–14.

van Twist, M., Rouw, R. & van der Steen, M. (2014): Policy Analysis in Practice: Reinterpreting the Quest for Evidence-Based Policy. In F. van Nispen & P. Scholten (eds): *Policy Analysis in the Netherlands.* Bristol, UK: Policy Press. 17–32.

Voyer, J.-P. (2007): Policy Analysis in the Federal Government: Building the Forward-Looking Policy Research Capacity. In: L. Dobuzinskis, D. Laycock & M. Howlett (eds): *Policy Analysis in Canada: The State of the Art.* University of Toronto Press. 317–341.

Waller, M. (1992): Evaluating Policy Advice. *Australian Journal of Public Administration*, 51 (4). 440–446.

Weimer, D.L. & Vining, A.R. (1992): *Policy Analysis. Concepts and Practice.* Englewood Cliffs, NJ: Prentice Hall.

Weingart, P. (1999): Scientific Expertise and Political Accountability: Paradoxes of Science in Politics. *Science and Public Policy*, 26 (3), 151–161.

Weiss, C.H. (1979): The Many Meanings of Research Utilization. *Public Administration Review*, 29. 426–431.

Wildavsky, A. (1979): *Speaking Truth to Power. The Art and Craft of Policy Analysis.* New Brunswick and London: Transaction Publishers.

23

PUBLIC POLICY STUDIES IN NORTH AMERICA AND EUROPE

Johanu Botha, Iris Geva-May and Allan M. Maslove

Introduction

This chapter places academic North American and European public policy programmes in a comparative context and provides an overview of the status of these programmes as pipelines for advancing policy analysis and policy research in light of domestic and global developments.[1]

In this comparative examination, four key themes have been identified for exploration across each region: (1) the historical background of policy analysis and research in light of the nature and scope of U.S. influence; (2) the development of differences and similarities in policy analysis and research, and what might explain them; (3) the roles and impacts of 'experiential learning' tools such as co-ops and internships; and (4) the roles and impacts of accreditation bodies. The conceptual framework applied to public policy programmes across the regions is elaborated before exploring the four themes.

Conceptual Framework and Definitions

Policy analysis is, as Wildavsky coined it, an 'art and craft' (1979) or, rather, a creative and innovative affinity as well as a toolbox of skills. The conceptual difference between these two components can be stretched further to illuminate professional versus academic themes when assessing the teaching and training of public policy in higher education institutions. The professional theme can be conceived as made up of those pedagogical processes and clinical practices that teach and train for the application of skills with specific clients in mind. The 'art' element is here understood as the opportunity to take advantage of and develop innate affinity along with scholarly knowledge. This chapter will characterize such processes and practices under the umbrella of *policy analysis*. The academic theme can be conceived as made up of those pedagogical activities that teach the study of the public policy process writ large for its own sake, as a social sciences and/or liberal arts approach independent of a particular client's needs. Such activities will fall under the umbrella of *policy research*.

Although different in their presentations of policy analytic practices, all methodological policy analysis models across North America and Europe share the common guiding principle that policy analysis is a focal *part of* the policy process, must not be confused with the policy process itself, and is based on a specific professional toolbox of skills in order to reliably

Policy Analysis in North America and Europe

inform public decision making. This consensus is reflected in different definitions of policy analysis that emphasize its unique characteristics. While public policy is defined as 'courses of action or inaction, namely, positions, stances, or political decisions that stress goals, means, values, and practices' (Lasswell, 1950; Lerner & Lasswell, 1951; Cochran & Malone, 1995; Dye, 1995; Pal, 2013), policy *analysis* is a pre-requisite of decision making and 'action', informing each one respectively and providing alternatives for action. Policy analysis is viewed as: 'Creating problems that can be solved' (Wildavsky, 1979), i.e. defining policy problems in such a way that solutions are possible; 'The use of reason and evidence to choose the best policy among a number of alternatives' (MacRae & Wilde, 1985); 'A profession-craft clustering on providing systematic, rational, and science-based help with decision making' (Dror, 1984); 'A problem solving process' (Bardach, 1992); and, especially in line with the conceptual framework of this chapter, '*Client*-oriented advice relevant to *public* decisions' (Weimer & Vining, 2010, emphasis added), implying that solutions suggested are client, time, and loci related.

'Thinking like a policy analyst' requires the acquisition of tacit knowledge common to the members of the professional community (Polanyi, 1966; Gigerenzer, 1999; Reiner & Gilbert, 2000; Sternberg, Forsythe, Hedlund, Wagner & Williams, 2000; Collins, 2001; Geva-May, 2005), which is based on strategies and procedural tools influenced by the real-world context of the problem (March & Simon, 1985) or 'decision frames' leading to *practical* mastery (Tversky & Kahneman, 1981). These 'toolboxes' (Gigerenzer, 1999) distinguish the future-skilled technician or expert from the impostor (Meltsner, 1976). They lead to a higher level of knowledge acquisition that can subsequently be adapted to individual styles and a variety of future contexts (Anis, Armstrong & Zhu, 2004; Geva-May, 2005).[2]

In most North American and European institutions that offer some form of public policy teaching there is, however, an additional component of policy analysis, one that is dedicated to understanding policy processes; that is, they provide 'knowledge about' the policy process, inclusive of some features of policy analysis. This component fits with Weimer and Vining's definition of policy *research* in that it provides tools to critically analyse public policy processes writ large, and to understand them for their own sake as economic, social and political phenomena inherently worthy of study (2010). Howlett and Ramesh note that policy research—they use the term 'policy studies'—is conducted mainly by academics, relates to the 'meta-policy' or the overall nature of the activities of the state, and is generally concerned with understanding the development, logic, and implications of overall state policy processes and the models used by investigators to analyse these processes (Howlett & Ramesh, 2003).

The content of policy research courses and programmes focuses on themes such as the understanding of political institutions in societies, including their 'implications for the formulation and implementation of public policy, the political context of policy making, the policy cycle, federalism, political and administrative responsibilities, the international context of domestic institutions, indigenous rights and institutions, executive leadership in government, Westminster parliamentary [and other] systems, courts and judicial review, public and para-public institutions, institutional designs and paths, etc.' (Clark, Eisen & Pal, 2008).[3] While policy analysis may require knowledge of the above phenomena, courses and programmes that focus on them for their own sake should be viewed as policy research-oriented because they are made up of largely academic activity where specific clients are a secondary concern, or may even harm the quality of the work due to bias (while policy analysis needs to take bias into account either to neutralize it, understand undercurrents, or serve the decision makers/stakeholders and their interests). Policy research by this definition does not train students in *doing* policy analysis.

361

This chapter makes a clear distinction between the two broad and internally complex concepts of policy analysis and policy research because of their comparative nature. Schools and programmes that offer public policy teaching and training across North America and Europe come in a myriad of forms. The official title of a programme or school does not necessarily indicate the type of pedagogical activity it entails, and can obscure differences and similarities across the regions. For example, as will be seen, business schools in the U.K. and schools of public policy in the U.S. both offer comparable courses in policy analysis, yet the former's graduates hold Masters of Business Administration degrees while the latter's graduates holds Masters of Public Policy degrees. A more subtle example—discussed at greater length below—is the case of Masters of Public Administration (MPA) programmes in Canadian political science departments, where some MPAs graduate with a range of skills they can provide to clients *within* the public policy process while other MPAs hold a largely academic knowledge of the public policy process itself. This difference occurs even in Masters of Public Policy/Administration/Service programmes that exist within schools or departments that have 'policy' explicitly in their title and are not housed within political science departments. Europe, in turn, offers policy-related courses and programmes in a wide array of academic homes, from management schools to economics departments. The school and programme titles themselves do not obviously correlate with the type of policy teaching and training that occurs within them.

Furthermore, a constrained definition of policy-related teaching risks excluding important pedagogical activities that are deeply influential in how public policy is understood and practised. For example, using only a definition of policy analysis—as the 'clinical art and craft of providing advice to public decision makers'—excludes not only those programmes that teach the management or implementation of public policies (many MPA programmes),[4] but also those programmes that situate the public policy process in an economic, social, political and historical context (most doctoral programmes). However, if we identify the distinguishing feature of policy analysis as fundamentally client-related in the context of public decision making, and identify the distinguishing feature of policy research as studying the public policy process for its own sake, and include both concepts into our study, we can include both management-heavy MPA and doctoral programmes in public policy in this chapter's analysis. The broadness of the two categories is balanced out by drawing a sharp conceptual line between the two. As will be seen, a lens that distinguishes sharply between policy analysis and policy research as defined above allows for the examination of differences and similarities between and within North America and Europe.

This chapter uses a variety of qualitative and quantitative sources in order to sketch the nature of policy analysis and research across the U.S., Canada and Europe. The online profiles of schools and programmes in each region are assessed to gain an understanding of the way they understand and present their teaching of policy analysis and research, and the skill sets they expect their graduates to acquire. Information provided by accreditation bodies in each region is used to understand the way official organizations responsible for standards define and regulate policy analysis and research. The *Atlas of Public Policy and Management* (http://portal.publicpolicy.utoronto.ca/en/Pages/index.aspx), an innovative project of the Best Practices in Public Management project led by Ian D. Clark and Leslie A. Pal, is used to inform the statistical breakdown of policy analysis versus policy research courses in Masters programmes throughout North America and much of Europe. As fits the definitions established above, policy analysis courses are made up of the project's 'policy and management analysis', 'economic analysis', 'quantitative and analytic methods', and 'leadership and communication skills' courses. 'Management function subjects', such as 'public financial

Policy Analysis in North America and Europe

management', 'evaluation and performance measurement', and 'other management functions', are included under this chapter's policy analysis umbrella when explicitly noted. Policy research courses includes the *Atlas*'s 'democratic institutions and policy process', 'ethics, rights and accountability', and 'socioeconomic, political, and global contexts' courses (Clark & Pal, 2015). The categorization of course types into either policy analysis or policy research illuminates a variety of, at times surprising, differences across the three regions, such as the varying proportions of curricula each region generally allocates to one or the other.

Historical Background

The shared goal of public policy-related programmes in North America and Europe is to provide knowledge, skills and understanding of the craft of policy analysis, the nature of the public policy process itself, and often both. Nevertheless, approaches to policy analysis and research between—and within—the two regions differ. The development of public policy-related programmes in each region is highly dependent on the regional governance context and prevailing analytical culture. In turn, developments in these regions relate to the historical and political events that shaped those contexts – institutional traditions inherited within national governments (Bevir, Rhodes & Weller, 2003; Hajnal, 2003), regulatory bodies (Vogel, 1986), or public agencies (Wilson, 1989; Jordan, 2003). This chapter will address the different contextual triggers that shaped the emergence of public policy studies in North America (the U.S. and Canada) and Europe (Western and Central/Eastern Europe).

The first U.S. programmes that addressed issues of public policy were established in the middle of the twentieth century in political science departments, as well as in distinct public administration schools.[5] While these programmes focused on training students to administer and implement government decisions, rather than on analysing policy problems, developing alternatives and advising decision makers, the beginnings of the discipline were substantially practically driven, with a 'client'—at this early stage, mainly government—explicitly in mind. In contrast, policy research occurring in Canadian political science departments at this time was largely an academic affair, independent of a particular client's needs.

Throughout the 1960s and 1970s U.S. programmes shifted from their management focus to include a greater emphasis on knowledge and skills that could inform policy recommendations.[6] Public affairs programmes spearheaded by economists and political scientists focused on policy problems and 'best alternative' recommendation.[7] At a time of unprecedented investments in warfare and welfare, it was found necessary to become accountable and transparent, as well as to feature systematic rational evidence-based decision making. The U.S. federal government increasingly utilized these services, and the demand for experts in analysis methods increased. The analysts were viewed as 'speaking truth to power' to facilitate rational decision making, enhanced effectiveness and efficiency, as well as political know-how. In time the demand vigorously spread to other levels of government and agencies. The establishment of the first schools of public policy at UC Berkeley and Harvard University marked the first trained policy analysts and developed a new domain of study: 'policy analysis'.

Similarly, the major impetus for policy analysis training in Canada came in the late 1960s, when Pierre Trudeau became prime minister and expressed dissatisfaction with the process of policy formation in Ottawa. Trudeau was determined to make policy formation in the federal government more analysis driven, scientific, and rational. His demands created a market for more analytically trained civil servants to staff the new branches of policy analysis and programme evaluation that were established in virtually every government department and agency, led by the Treasury Board. However, the earliest cohorts of staff and consultants in Canada were drawn primarily from university economics departments. 'Policy analysis'— under that moniker—did not take off as vigorously as it did in the United States, where the market for trained policy analysts quickly expanded and public policy programmes proliferated to deliver the supply.

The distinct impacts of parliamentary government and federalism on Canada's public policy process (Malcolmson & Myers, 2012), along with the highly heterogeneous nature of the country (Howlett & Lindquist, 2007), has served to shape versions of policy analysis and research that, while far from immune to developments elsewhere, are uniquely Canadian. Indeed, despite Canada's geopolitical proximity to the United States, policy analysis and research as *separate* fields within Canadian higher education institutions developed almost 40 years after their U.S. counterparts. While policy research existed under other names (mostly in Canadian political science departments), as is demonstrated by the wealth of twentieth century, largely state-focused, institutional analysis of the Canadian public policy process (Innis, 1930, 1940; Russell, 1965, 1969; Smiley, 1970, 1972; Hodgetts, 1973; Smiley & Watts, 1985; Smith, M, 2005), the shift towards policy analysis in curricula only became visible more recently. Changes of perspective adopted in Carleton University's PhD in Public Policy programme in the early 2000s and in the Simon Fraser University's distinctive Masters in Public Policy programme in 2003, along with even more recent initiatives at the University of Toronto and York University (Toronto), have been instrumental in encouraging a greater emphasis on policy analysis. However, a variety of established and flagship Masters in Public Administration/Policy programmes still allocate up to and at times over half of their curricula to policy research.

The historical development of Western European policy analysis and research programmes was shaped by the unique conditions created by the evolution of a highly conflicted Europe in the mid-twentieth century towards an increasingly united Europe by the end of the century. With unification, the main challenge in Europe in regards to policy analysis and research was to move from largely diverse, culturally driven analytic traditions to a more uniform, common method of policy analytic work. Since the mid-1990s, this new vision has brought significant changes to the way that policy analysis has infiltrated European bureaucracy, such as the increasing demand for common core curricula in policy analysis that form comparable programmes from which to hire expertise.[8] As in the United States context, and unlike in Canada, curricula at the Masters level have developed into promoting policy analysis alongside policy research. Indeed, despite a greater geographical distance from the United States, policy analysis in Europe has been heavily influenced by U.S. developments, to the point where U.S. policy analysis methods are benchmarks for systematic policy analysis in various European countries. The increased adoption of this systematic approach to policy analysis in Europe was driven by a move to accountability, transparency, proof of efficiency, harmonization and corruption deterrence. Hoppe points to the increasing belief in the importance of acquiring maximum rational judgment and of producing viable policy recommendations (Hoppe, 2002, p. 201), both themes that are strongly related to policy analysis, and points to studies showing great pluralism in the way policy issues are understood among European states. He advises that the challenge in Europe in this regard is to 'cope intelligently and creatively with pluralism and diversity' (2002, p. 235).

Central and Eastern Europe offer a particularly interesting intellectual arena for policy analysis because of the challenge presented in the last few decades: to transform perceived obsolete government, public administration and policymaking practices, and to fill a perceived void in systematic, analytical policy development. As in Western Europe, the challenge is intensified by the fact that Central/Eastern Europe includes different regional histories and variations of organizational autonomy. Yet unlike Western Europe, most of the countries have until recently lacked a critical mass of experts in public policy administration and management. This fuelled the need for new orientations, programmes and curricula in teaching and training public policy/administration, and for recruiting. For instance, Budapest University of Economic Sciences (formerly Karl Marx University) initiated a Centre for Public Affairs Studies in 1991, and finally merged with the College of Public Administration. Now called Budapest University of Economic Sciences and Public Administration, it offers public affairs degrees. Ukraine's National Academy of Public Administration is sponsored by the President of Ukraine, and is the first Eastern European institute to be accredited by the European Association for Public Administration Accreditation. Central European University (CEU), also in Budapest, recently initiated and moved programmes into a School of Public Policy. CEU has received significant financial and intellectual support from George Soros' Open Society Institute, which has been instrumental in supporting the diffusion of policy studies in the post-communist countries (Straussman, 2005). Indeed, in the void of administrative tradition after the fall of the communist system, it appears that systematic approaches to policy analysis have been embraced even more aggressively in Central and Eastern European countries than in Western Europe.

Policy Analysis and Research in Each Region

The conceptual framework that applies a distinction between policy analysis and policy research can be usefully applied to the North American and European contexts in order to tease out differences and similarities between and within them. The U.S. system emphasizes policy analysis and deprioritizes policy research at the Masters level, but maintains a comparatively equal balance between the two in doctoral programmes. With policy analysis and research emerging as distinct fields in the United States decades before Canada and Europe, the U.S. system is the most developed in terms of policy-specific scope and variety in its programmes. Canada leans heavily towards policy research, even in Masters programmes that train future policy analysis professionals. The Canadian system is the clear outlier in its strong emphasis on policy research across programme levels and types. The diverse European scene features social science-oriented programmes that are evolving towards a U.S. balance between policy analysis and research. Europe is unique in that its policy-focused programmes are nestled into an array of schools and departments, most of which do not have 'policy' explicitly in their titles.

The balance between policy research and policy analysis is unique in the United States (especially compared to Canada), but the salience of another contrast merits discussing first: the sheer scope of the U.S. context. Even accounting for differences in population size, both the number of policy analysis and research schools and the variety of specialized programmes in the United States is greater compared to Europe, and far greater than in Canada. As is often the case, with a larger scale comes more specialization. In addition to general programmes in public policy, the U.S. schools offer a variety of specialized programmes in areas such as health policy/administration, education, urban government, and the non-profit sector. These programmes, while often carrying their own distinct degree designations, are usually offered by more broadly focused public policy units and share common characteristics of a core programme. The Goldman School of Public Policy at Berkeley, for instance, offers programme specializations in housing and urban policy (among other specializations). The Harris Graduate School of Public Policy Studies at the University of Chicago offers a specialization in environmental science and policy, among others. The Kennedy School at Harvard offers numerous specialization opportunities, including a programme in technology and economic policy. Many schools—certainly the larger ones—offer degree programmes at all three levels (undergraduate, Masters and PhD), as well as a range of specialized certificate and executive programmes. While one can also see evidence of this variety and specialization in Canada (such as the new Master of Philanthropy and Non-Profit Leadership (MPNL) programme and indigenous policy focus options within the regular Master of Arts in Public Administration (MAPA) at Carleton University), the U.S. has a far greater range of offerings.

After the difference in scope, the most obvious contrast between the U.S. and Canadian contexts is the difference in balance between policy research and policy analysis. The U.S. context maintains a more equal balance overall when doctoral programmes are considered, but leans heavily towards policy analysis at the Masters level and below. The greater U.S. emphasis on teaching a craft and skill that provides expert advice to explicitly defined public decision makers (clients) is evident in a variety of ways. U.S. schools of public policy/ administration are more closely linked to governments in terms of the two-way flow of expertise. It is quite common for faculty members to work for a time in government, and for people who have held senior government positions (both appointed and elected) to move to academia. Such cross-fertilization occurs in Canada as well, but to a lesser extent than in the U.S. This may be the consequence of the U.S. political system (where senior bureaucrats come and go with presidents and governors), or the result of a more open and welcoming environment in U.S. universities towards individuals who do not regard academia as their lifetime vocation. Whatever the reason, a client-focused emphasis is commonplace in U.S. schools. The implication of this emphasis is that these tend to put more emphasis on management and analytical techniques themselves, while Canadian programmes tend to contain more theory, where the impact of broad political institutions—i.e. the Westminster parliamentary system—is assessed in the abstract.

Statistical analysis of Masters-level curricula in the United States affirms the observation that their schools prioritize policy analysis. Most programmes allocate more than half of their curricula to the techniques and skills that form policy analysis, with many pushing two-thirds to three-quarters of their entire programme. Very few U.S. schools allocate less than 40% of their courses to policy analysis. The courses allocated to the institutional analysis of the public policy process writ large—policy research—rarely make up more than 20% of courses, with most programmes coming in under 15% and many under 10%.

The training of policy analysts in Canada occurs mostly in graduate and undergraduate university programmes with labels such as 'public policy', 'public administration', and 'policy studies'. The study of policy research occurs in political science departments, doctoral programmes in schools of public policy/administration, as well as in Masters programmes outside political science departments, including schools of public policy/administration. Broadly speaking, there are two types of programmes in Canada. In the first group are those programmes that favour policy research over policy analysis to some degree. Many of these programmes reflect Canada's history of doing policy research within political science departments, such as Manitoba/Winnipeg's MPA, which is located within a political science department and allocates almost 80% of its curricula to policy research, with less than 10% allocated to policy analysis. The management function subjects such as public financial management and performance measurement, part of policy analysis insofar as they relate to a specific client, account for less than 2% of this MPA. While Manitoba/Winnipeg is a disproportionate case compared to U.S. and European programmes, its high percentage of policy research courses is not dramatically far from the mean or median of other Canadian

Policy Analysis in North America and Europe

programmes. Concordia University (Montreal) and Ryerson University (Toronto) both allocate more than half of their MPA curricula to policy research, and University of Ottawa and York University programmes allocate almost half.

Policy research-heavy programmes in Canada are not restricted to political science departments. Masters of public policy/administration/service programmes housed within schools of public policy/administration and other non-political science-specific departments, including programmes offered by Ryerson, the University of Toronto and York University, allocate more than 35% of their curricula to policy research, which is higher than most comparable Masters programmes in the United States and Europe.

The policy research-heavy group is the oldest model in Canada, though there are such programmes in some universities that are relatively recent. Under this model the study of public administration—what governments do, and how they make and carry out their decisions—has inherent academic interest. Those programmes niched in political science departments are heavily influenced by political science, but their policy research as such is not necessarily uni-disciplinary. Many of the policy research-heavy Masters programmes offer policy-area-specific courses (e.g. macroeconomic policy or social policy) that are informed by disciplines ranging from economics to sociology. Often the policy research-heavy programmes allow students to take courses from different departments that can count for credit. Most doctoral programmes lean towards policy research given that the nature of such programmes is to understand phenomena for their own sake and to contribute to formal knowledge (i.e. a specific client interested in the information is secondary), and these programmes are by no means constrained to political science departments. Carleton University's flagship doctoral programme in public policy, within the School of Public Policy and Administration, leans heavily towards policy research.

The second Canadian group is made up of those programmes that favour policy analysis over policy research to some degree. These are many, but not all, of the Masters programmes that have been built in non-political science schools or departments. The Master of Public Policy/Administration/Service programmes offered by the Universities of Victoria, Calgary, Western Ontario, and Waterloo, as well as by Quebec's École nationale d'administration publique (ENAP), all exist in non-political science-specific schools of public policy/ administration/government and all allocate more than 50% of their curricula to policy analysis. Some programmes (Regina, and one of York University's two programmes) are located within schools or faculties of business. Although these programmes tend to lean more towards policy analysis than policy research, they reflect the perspective not common in other programmes that management is generic, and that all organizations—public and private— undertake similar activities. Many other programmes also found in schools of public policy/ administration, such as Carleton University's Master of Arts in Public Administration or Dalhousie University's MPA, allocate around 35% of their curricula to policy analysis. While this figure is average for Canadian programmes in general and higher than the policy research-heavy Canadian programmes, it is far lower than the average percentage that comparable U.S. programmes focus on policy analysis.

The policy analysis-heavy group is the newer model in Canada, lagging almost four decades behind the United States, where policy analysis began its growth in the mid-twentieth century. It is, however, the fastest growing group, as demonstrated by (1) the growing number of schools and programmes that use the practitioner, action-oriented 'policy' in their titles versus disciplinary titles such as political science or economics; and (2) the growing percentage of policy analysis-focused courses in Masters and some undergraduate programmes. Still, Canada heavily emphasizes policy research at the Masters level compared to the United States and Europe. Even generic managerial courses that focus on the implementation of policies for specific clients are less common in Canadian programmes of public administration compared to U.S. ones (Gow & Sutherland, 2004). Policy research is favoured in most programmes based in political science departments and in many schools of public policy/administration, while policy analysis currently resides mainly in Masters programmes and in schools with 'policy' explicitly in their title.

Despite carrying the same designations, Canadian and U.S. graduates of MPA and comparable programmes may have very different knowledge sets, with the former holding a broad academic understanding of the forces that structure the public policy process and the latter holding specific skills that can be applied within the public policy process. This should not be taken to mean that the goals of Canadian and U.S. programmes are different. Like in the United States, Canadian schools and programmes offering public policy/administration at the Masters level, regardless of their balance between policy analysis and research, view themselves primarily as professional programmes, preparing the great majority of their graduates for careers in government or other organizations that participate in some fashion in the public policy process.

The difference between U.S. and Canadian programmes is echoed in the difference between U.S. and European programmes. Most European programmes do not overtly train students in applied policy analysis. In contrast to the common U.S. practice of promoting capstone projects and reflective thinking courses (deLeon & Protopsaltis, 2005; Smith, D., 2005), which often pertain to real-world clients and policy problems as defined by those clients, European programmes commonly require final dissertations based on social science inquiry methods applied to understanding the nature of public administration or public policy writ large. The programmes' curricula themselves often feature welfare economics, public choice, social structure, political/legal philosophy, systematic programming and comparative European policies, all courses that lean more towards policy research than analysis. That said, European Masters programmes in public policy/administration include a greater percentage of policy analysis courses than their Canadian counterparts, with many programmes allocating more than 40% of their courses to policy analysis, and some over 50%. European Masters programmes, especially those few with 'public policy' or 'public administration' explicitly in their titles, appear to be developing more towards the U.S. balance between policy analysis and research than the Canadian one.

A strong similarity among European and U.S. programmes, comparatively absent in the Canadian context, is the wide range of policy-area specializations. The London School of Economics' Department of Social Policy offers more than 15 different specialities (with some specializations possible even at the undergraduate level), ranging from criminal justice policy to gender and social policy, health and international health policy, social policy, social policy and planning in developing countries, youth policy and education policy. Many institutions offer policy studies with an orientation towards science and technology: University of Namur, Belgium; Maastricht University, the Netherlands; University of East London; Louis Pasteur, Strasbourg, France; Universidad del País Vasco/Euskal Herrico Unibersitatea, Bilbao, Spain; University of Madrid; University of Lisbon; University of Oslo; and University of Potsdam (Masters of Public Management, GeoGovernance stream). In France, policy analysis and research are also often offered within faculties of law. An additional orientation in some European institutions is towards urban planning. Examples include the École polytechnique fédérale de Lausanne, Switzerland; Lund University, Sweden; and Erasmus University, Rotterdam, the Netherlands, with its joint programme at the Institute of Housing and Urban Development (HIS) in Rotterdam.

A salient difference between the European and North American contexts is that only a handful of European institutions offer programmes explicitly 'policy' titled, although a current shift towards the establishment of schools of public policy can be observed in the United Kingdom, Germany, and, to a growing degree, in Central and Eastern Europe. Similar to the developments of the field in the U.S. and the prominent models of instruction during the 1970s and 1980s, the main venues for policy analysis and research in European countries fall into four categories: (1) public management departments within business schools; (2) schools of economics; (3) departments of political science; and (4) schools of public administration. This is consistent with Hajnal's (2003), study although his categories and sample countries are somewhat different.

Policy analysis and research curricula are offered (1) in public management departments within business schools in, among others, the U.K. universities of Aston, Sussex and Manchester, and at Bocconi University Center for Applied Social Studies of Management, Italy; (2) in schools of economics, such as at the Erasmus University, Rotterdam, with its School of Economics, and at the University of Minho, Portugal, within the School of Economics; (3) in departments of political science, such as at the London School of Economics, U.K., institutes of political science in France, and political science departments in Switzerland; and (4) in schools of public administration, such as at the École Nationale d'Administration, France, the Department of Public Administration at the University of Leiden, Netherlands, and those universities that participate in the European Master of Public Administration Consortium (EMPA) university exchange programme (where students in a public administration programme or with a public administration focus can spend a semester in another university with a public administration school/department).

Hajnal's (2003) comprehensive statistical comparative study of public administration education programmes identifies three orientation clusters of reference: *legal*—including Greece, Hungary, Italy, Moldova, Poland, Portugal, Romania and Yugoslavia; *public management*—including Belgium, France, Spain and Sweden; and, *corporate*—including Armenia, Bulgaria, Czech Republic, Denmark, Estonia, Ireland, Latvia, Lithuania, the Netherlands, Slovakia and Ukraine.[9]

The E.U. institutions that offer policy analysis and research programmemes do not structure them into a standardized set of core courses, but under a variety of different 'bundles' with a strong penchant towards European governance, organization, management and administration. The aforementioned EMPA includes applying comparative analysis to European policy. A common core Master of European Studies/European Politics and Policies was initiated by Twente University (Nethelands) and the European Group of Public Affairs (EGPA) and involves several E.U. institutions that offer policy-oriented courses dealing with decision making in Europe, comparative federalism, public policy and public management, comparative public administration, and aspects of European integration. The University of Nottingham offers a Public Policy Programme, and the National University of Ireland offers policy analysis alongside a health economics focus. The public policy-specific graduate school in Switzerland, which is known as the IDHEAP and explicitly offers policy analysis courses, joined the University of Lausanne in 2014. The University of Oslo's Masters Programmes' specialization in Health Economics, Policy and Management has an orientation towards policy analysis as well. Several German universities offer clearly stated policy certificates: the Willy Brandt (formerly Erfurt) School of Public Policy—Masters in Public Policy; the University of Potsdam—Masters of Public Management (with Public Policy/Administration and Global Public Policy streams); and the University of Konstanz—Comparative Politics and Policy Analysis (in the Department of Politics and Public Administration). Among the more interesting developments in Germany is the privately funded Hertie School of Governance that began a Masters in Public Policy programme in 2005, and has since established an Executive Masters in Public Management and a doctoral programme in Governance, with 330, 65, and 31 students currently enrolled in each programme, respectively. The Hertie School rapidly established exchange and dual degree agreements with the London School of Economics and Political Sciences, Sciences Po in Paris, and Columbia University in New York, adding to the growing European tradition of exposing public policy/administration students to a variety of pedagogical contexts.

Co-ops, Internships and Think Tanks

'Experiential' components to policy analysis and research programmes can be a marker for an appreciation of policy analytical tools insofar as those components include work experience where techniques and skills taught in the classroom portions of the programme are used to provide advice to actual and specific clients. Policy research can also benefit from experiential learning, but this more often takes the form of interviewing or observing participants in the public policy process and not working towards the goals of a particular organization through a co-op position or internship. Think tanks, in turn, can demonstrate an institution's commitment to understanding the public policy process writ large through policy research that is more explicitly advertised in the public domain, but—in the cases where think tanks are research units that contract services to a specific client—can also provide opportunities for students to exercise policy analysis skills outside the classroom.

While experiential learning is valued in programmes across North America, there are differences within the region. Canada's collection of co-ops and internships is a noteworthy feature of its public policy/administration programmes, but such placements tend to be emphasized even more in the U.S. context. New York University's Wagner School offers an imaginative capstone programme in which teams of students undertake policy analysis projects for client organizations; the same is the case at the Goldman School of Public Policy (Berkeley, California). The public policy programme at the University of Chapel Hill, North Carolina, sends students to Washington, D.C., on a regular basis for internships, as do the large majority of U.S. policy-specific programmes. This greater emphasis on practical experience in the United States compared to Canada fits Radin's (1996) assessment of U.S. programmes as being rooted in a pragmatic tradition that has historically emphasized improving efficiency in resource allocation, the making of actual decisions, and the controlling role of actual top agency officials. *Clients*, not the abstract nature of the state or the public policy process, provide the perspective, values and agenda for U.S. analytical activity, with policy analysis contributing to the improvement of effective, scientifically assessed, and transparent decision making (Dror, 1971; Meltsner, 1976; Wildavsky, 1979).

Many of Canada's Masters-level public policy/administration programmes include a co-op or internship placement component (e.g. Carleton, Dalhousie, Queen's, Simon Fraser, Victoria), which is highly recommended or required of all students, with the exception of those who already have professional experience. Even the policy research-heavy Manitoba/Winnipeg MPA includes a popular and extensive co-op component (perhaps in an effort to balance its otherwise policy research-heavy make-up). Furthermore, many of these programmes have smaller side programmes alongside their regular Masters degrees. In some cases these are executive degree programmes, while in other cases they are specialized certificate or diploma programmes. These programmes are designed to accommodate 'mid-career' public servants or others who view the programmes as vehicles to hone their policy

Policy Analysis in North America and Europe

analysis skills and, relatedly, to enhance their prospects for promotion or other employment opportunities. The executive and certificate programmes, in recognition of the constraints under which students take these programmes, are often offered in various non-standard timetables and formats (e.g. intensive weekends once per month, summer sessions, evening classes, and online teaching or distance education).

The European scene's emphasis on social science-focused programmes has inhibited some of the overtly experiential approaches used in North America. Thesis-driven or more conventionally academic programmes are not especially conducive to the reflective, capstone-style elements found in many North American programmes, especially in the U.S. That said, the aforementioned use of academic exchange programmes in Europe may act as a version of experiential learning insofar as such programmes move students from a specific methodological environment into another that tackles policy problems through different approaches.

All three regions enjoy a wealth of research units that complement and/or are affiliated with specific programmes, schools, departments, or organizations of public policy/administration. These 'think tanks' undertake and publish research on a wide range of public policy issues depending on their respective mandates, and host or participate in seminars, conferences, public consultations and public forums. Such units function mainly as think tanks when they undertake and publish self-initiated research, but function as consulting firms when they undertake research on a contract basis for governments or other clients. Some are quite broad in the range of issues they investigate; others specialize in a particular policy area or sector. The activities of these units constitute another avenue of university participation in the policy analysis and research community, usually in the public domain.

As may be expected given the degree to which U.S. Masters programmes emphasize practical, client-oriented policy analysis, universities in the United States actively engage in *doing* as well as *teaching* policy analysis through research centres attached to their policy analysis schools. Virtually every U.S. programme of policy analysis has a research centre attached to it, and, in most cases, there are several. These centres cover a wide range of specialities, focusing on federal, state and local government levels, and on an array of policy fields (defence and national security, health, education, government/business relations, environment, poverty, and others). At least in some cases, these institutions have a higher public profile than their Canadian counterparts and actively participate in U.S. public policy debates through their publications, conferences, media contributions, and so forth. They are comparable to the university-based centres in Canada in their contribution to policy analysis and in providing policy analysis laboratories for students in training. Nevertheless, U.S. policy analysis research centres are significantly more widespread than in Canada at the federal, state, and non-governmental organization (NGO) level. To enumerate only a few of the many such organizations, which serve also as internship venues, the Urban Institute, Mathematica, the Brookings Institute, the RAND Corporation, and the American Enterprise Institute could be mentioned. Canadian university research units, which include the Education Policy Research Initiative at the University of Ottawa, the Centre for Public Policy Research at Simon Fraser University, and the Local Government Institute at the University of Victoria, also provide a laboratory for the institutions' students of policy analysis, providing them direct participation in policy analysis activities.[10]

A myriad of think tanks and research-oriented centres and institutes exist in Europe as well. The U.K. is home to a particularly large number. Listing them is not the purpose of this chapter, but it is important to observe that they all contribute to the comparative policy database within the E.U., mainly in fields such as economics, migration, welfare and security.

Some of the think tanks are funded and supported by governments fostering inter-nations collaboration within the E.U.[11] Others are funded by political parties or by NGOs.[12]

The slight differences among the 'think tank scenes' of each region generally mirror the themes drawn so far in the chapter. While Canadian research units do provide opportunities for policy analysis, they are by and large attached to universities and generally do research on a part of the public policy process writ large. United States research units span the spectrum in regards to their size and speciality, and emphasize *doing* policy analysis. European programmes fall somewhere in between, and represent the growing importance in European policy analysis and research of finding collaboration among diversity.

Accreditation

Accreditation occurs when a school or programme is certified to have met certain standards that are established by some type of official body. There are benefits that flow from an accreditation process: the appearance to the external world as a 'profession' which, like most professions, establishes a level of quality for training and for admission to the profession. For an individual member institution, the system offers recognition and a seal of approval, which, in the first instance, benefits the graduates of the programme, but ultimately enhances the reputation of the institution and its faculty. Potential disadvantages include (1) diminished institutional autonomy and potential infringement of the right of each university to determine what its faculty collectively decides is an appropriate curriculum and standard of performance; and (2) diminished academic independence and constrained scholarly inquiry. Concerns about diminished autonomy have led some of the leading U.S. public policy schools to not seek accreditation from the Network of Schools of Public Policy, Affairs, and Administration (NASPAA) (e.g. the Harris School at the University of Chicago, and Woodrow Wilson at Princeton University) while concerns about academic independence have kept doctoral programmes largely unregulated. The degree of accreditation across the three regions fits the growing picture that while Europe is moving towards the U.S. model that emphasizes policy analysis at the Masters level and below, Canada still prioritizes policy research at all levels. Accreditation demonstrates especially clearly that differences within regions can be greater than differences between them.

While for the most part resolved in the U.S., the accreditation of public policy/administration schools and programmes has long been and remains a conflictual issue in Canada (Gow & Sutherland, 2004). In the U.S., the NASPAA—established in the mid-1970s—has developed comparatively rigorous, heavily standardized, and widely used accreditation criteria that have built up extensive international reach. In Canada the Canadian Association of Programs in Public Administration (CAPPA) has only recently developed a much looser version with the key criteria a school or programme's good standing with the 'quality assurance body' in each province—regardless of potential discrepancies among provinces—and some connection between school/programme 'goals and outcomes'. In other words, each institution is assessed against the standards it sets for itself. The Canadian model does not currently define a standard core curriculum to which accredited institutions must adhere. The aforementioned Manitoba/Winnipeg MPA, with its near absence of policy analysis elements, is 'eligible for accreditation' under current CAPPA criteria, whereas it would likely not be eligible under NASPAA criteria.

Effective accreditation works when schools and programmes themselves view accreditation important to their own success, and so far this is not the case in Canada. The first paragraph of the CAPPA's 2015 accreditation report puts the matter succinctly:

Policy Analysis in North America and Europe

During the past several years relatively few policy and administration programs have sought accreditation under the existing CAPPA process. Currently only four programs are accredited out of a possible 22 Canadian programs eligible for accreditation. This is not a record of progress that is sustainable or a pace that can bring the benefits from accreditation that have occurred elsewhere.

Atkinson & Rasmussen, 2015, p. 1

While the report does note continued interest in accreditation from schools/departments that teach policy and research at a Masters level, and even launches a new accreditation planning process that includes greater standardization around core 'competencies', Canada's use of an accreditation system stands clearly apart from the other two regions. The desire for professional acceptance and recognition is certainly present in Canada, but a deep tension exists between such a desire and the opposing force of seeking to preserve academic autonomy. This tension has limited the 'template' that schools are willing to utilize in a formal, national accreditation regime.

The initially confounding resistance from Canadian Masters programmes against standardized accreditation is explained once the high percentage of policy research in those programmes is illuminated. Programmes in the U.S. and Europe with high levels of policy research also resist standardized accreditation in order to protect academic freedom, but those programmes tend to exist mainly at the doctoral level. Indeed, PhD programmes in all three regions are less interested in accreditation. The main difference in Canada is that many of its ostensibly professional programmes that train future policy analysts teach more policy research than policy analysis. It is noteworthy that the Masters-level programmes that have gone through CAPPA's accreditation process (Carleton, Ryerson, Western Ontario, and Johnson-Shoyama) all have robust levels of policy analysis in their curricula. Accreditation is seen to advance the goal of being perceived as professional among the 'clients' of programmes—governments, non-academic think tanks, and interest groups. It is little wonder that high levels of academic activity that do not prioritize clients have slowed the development of accreditation in Canada.

In Europe the move to accreditation is following the U.S. example fairly closely, with the European Association for Public Administration Accreditation (EAPAA) pursuing a similar accreditation system to NASPAA, and with the Eastern and Central European countries receiving counsel or sponsorship from U.S. universities. Inspired by NASPAA, EAPAA is, among others, trying to organize Europe-wide accreditation. While some European programmes have been nationally accredited in the past according to national standards (for instance in Germany and the Netherlands), until recently there have not been common European-wide standards for accreditation. Common E.U. accreditation is a rather new, but increasingly adopted, concept. The first EAPAA-accredited programme was the Erasmus Public Administration Programme in the Netherlands (previously already accredited by NASPAA), followed by others. In all cases, European accreditation recognizes that programmes have different missions and approaches, and that they stem from different educational systems. However, a balance is expected between each institution's unique mission and substantial conformance with commonly agreed-upon standards. The willingness to embrace this latter component puts the European scene much closer to the U.S. system than the Canadian one. U.S. schools have definitively opted for the enhanced professionalism associated with programme accreditation, though the regime employed does not prevent a school from designing a diverse set of offerings. Masters programmes, which are widely accepted as 'the professional degree' (a characterization seen as far less problematic than it is in Canada), are accredited against a set of standards that largely focus on defining a standard core. Guidelines even exist for undergraduate programmes.

It is worth noting that a common theme across all three regions is the work that accreditation and related organizations do in an effort to promote public policy/affairs/administration education and research. NASPAA, EAPAA and CAPPA all engage in such promotion to some degree, and each region hosts at least one large organization that focuses primarily on the coordination and promotion of education and research. The most prominent of these organizations include the European Group of Public Affairs, the Institute of Public Administration of Canada (IPAC), and the American Association of Public Policy Analysis and Management (APPAM). Given Eastern Europe's 'later' development in academic policy analysis and research due to the rise and fall of communist bureaucracies, the Network of Institutes and Schools of Public Administration in Central and East Europe (NISPAcee) merits special attention. NISPAcee is an organization of institutes and universities whose main role is to promote education in public affairs through the exchange of ideas, skills and relevant information among institutions. It advocates raising the quality of public administration and developing the civil service in the region. It promotes faculty training, curricula development, development of graduate programmes, conferences and research in order to advance and spread the practices 'of good professional public management, public policy and governance'. NISPAcee also affirms the growing European traditions of promoting discourse across national and pedagogical contexts by providing consultancy services and acting as a nexus between Western European and U.S. consultants and the Central and East European countries.

Conclusion

The central aim of this chapter has been to identify the state of public policy studies across North America and Europe, and to place such studies in a comparative perspective. To achieve this perspective we used a basic conceptual framework that distinguishes between the training of skills meant to inform the actions and decisions of specific clients in the public sector and the study of the public policy process writ large for its own sake. We titled the former category 'policy analysis' and the latter category 'policy research'. The conceptual framework was applied to salient themes across the two regions and allowed coherent differences and similarities to emerge between and within them. We hope that the findings presented may provide a deeper understanding of academic public policy programmes and assist higher education institutional planners in preparing students for their immersion in learning policy analytical skills, understanding the public policy process, or both.

While policy research has existed under other names in non-policy-specific departments such as political science, the development of the field of policy analysis began in the mid-twentieth century in the U.S., and coincided with the emergence of performance-oriented efficient governments, faith in rational decision making, objectivity, systematic policy analysis, and the idea of 'speaking truth to power' (Radin, 1996, 2000). Initially, the notion of policy analysis was that it was 'craft driven', stemming from both positivist social science and normative economic models, with the economic models providing the clearest and most powerful basis for improvement and change orientation (Aaron, 1989; Radin, 1996).

Significant increased demand for policy analysis experts due to developments later in the twentieth century in Canada and Europe has been the driver for public administration, political science and business schools to change their orientation and, increasingly, to include public policy studies and policy analysis in their curriculum offerings. In Canada, the tradition of studying the public policy process writ large has followed programmes, schools and departments as they moved into policy-specific homes, with many Masters of Public Administration/Policy heavily emphasizing policy research. The shift towards adopting policy analytical methods in policy-specific Masters curricula is increasingly visible in recent years, but remains slow.

A key trend across Masters-level policy-focused programmes in Europe is the movement towards a more professional orientation and a determination to be perceived as more professional. Both of these shifts are driven by an expanding standardized accreditation process. This trend has long been embraced and established in the United States. In Canada, Masters-level programmes also understand themselves as professional (and are advertised as such), but—despite the work of the Canadian Association of Programmes in Public Administration—the drive towards accreditation is taking longer. The heavy Canadian Masters-level emphasis on policy research, which eschews standardization and regulation on grounds of academic freedom, helps explain this slower development.

Both Canada and Europe have been influenced by the U.S. scene, mainly due to its scope and early development of policy analysis and research as distinct fields. Reflecting the U.S. pragmatic tradition[13] of systematic policymaking, efficiency and effectiveness, U.S. schools have developed a common core policy analysis methodology, which has led to the U.S. production of a large volume of transferable policy analysis tools that are not necessarily beholden to a particular region's institutions. U.S. methodology and materials therefore influence policy analysis materials utilized internationally. The export of U.S. influence is also due, in part, to the large number of consultants and advisors from the many U.S. institutions of public policy/administration who promote and influence the profession worldwide. Furthermore, a key catalyst in disseminating U.S. influence across the regions is the work of NASPAA, not just as an accreditation body, but also as a producer of a range of other activities one would expect of a professional association, only with international scope. NASPAA offers an annual conference and publishes the *Journal of Public Affairs Education*. It also includes an active international programme that helps to 'export' the U.S. model of policy analysis and research education to other countries. No other region has a comparable programme with an explicit mandate 'to influence'.

Central and Eastern Europe has been especially susceptible to U.S. influence given the void of public policy/administration in this region. A vast demand for policy analysis and research training attracted the most salient, best resourced schools, programmes and organizations, most of them from the United States. Programmes that explicitly teach policy analysis, the aggressive establishment of schools explicitly titled public policy/administration, and public policy/administration associations directly inspired by APPAM and NASPAA are a testament to the U.S. influence in Central and Eastern Europe.

Western Europe and Canada, with more established traditions of their own, have been more particular in adopting elements of the U.S. context. Western Europe has so far retained much of its policy analysis and research in a variety of academic homes that are not universally or explicitly policy focused. For example, unlike the sharp U.S. distinction between Masters of Public Policy/Administration/Affairs and Masters of Business programmes, the United Kingdom continues to provide substantial policy analysis offerings from within many of its business schools.

Specialization in U.S. programmes appears not to have had a serious impact on the make-up of Canadian programmes, whose curricula still lean heavily towards a broad variety of policy areas in its curricula—as makes sense given the policy research focus on the public policy process at large.

The influence of U.S. policy analysis and research is a noteworthy theme across the regions assessed, and there is no obvious sign that such influence is dissipating. But the influence also should not be overstated. U.S. influence, even in the context of a hyper globalized world, does not appear to be enough to render toothless the arguably more powerful influence of each region's unique set of governance institutions and history.

Comparing developments between and within North America and Europe allows us to locate each region on the map of public policy studies. Moreover, a key benefit of this study is that it raises a number of questions pertaining to the future of such studies. Given the developments in the U.S. and Europe, is there a greater need for accreditation and legitimation of policy analysis as a profession in Canada? Given the comparative adaptation stressed in Europe, what should be the content orientation of programmes in North America? What are the appropriate programmatic and institutional arrangements for providing policy analysis versus policy research, or for finding a specific balance between the two? What conceptual frameworks, above and beyond the broad distinction drawn between policy analysis and research in this chapter,[14] can be used to better understand the development of academic public policy studies across different regions? Perhaps most importantly, how does the development of public policy studies in other parts of the world compare to the developments drawn for North America and Europe? Because of their major importance to the field of public policy as a distinct academic discipline and to the nature of actual policymaking itself, these and other related questions should be brought forward on the research agenda.

Notes

1 This study is a restructured and updated version of work that was first published in *Policy Analysis in Canada: The State of the Art* (Dobuzinskis, L., Howlett, M. and Laycock, D. (eds), 2007) by Iris Geva-May and Allan M. Maslove. While public policy studies exists and is growing in other regions, notably Australia, New Zealand, and many parts of Asia, we chose the two regions—North America and Europe—in which public policy studies is especially well established in order to identify development trends. In this context North America refers to the United States and Canada.

2 For detailed discussions on policy analysis, public management and other fields as clinical professions requiring awareness of reasoning processes acquired practice, see I. Geva-May (2005), Chapter 1.

3 2015 refers to the year the quote was retrieved from Clarke et al's online *Atlas of Public Policy and Management*.

4 Note that such 'management/implementation' programmes still involve a specific client, and—as Weimer and Vining make clear—'mere administration' has become more and more involved in the formulation of public policies (2010).

5 Studies by Gow and Sutherland (2004) in Canada, and by Cleary (1990), Henry (1995) and Breaux, Clynch and Morris (2003) in the U.S., present an in-depth account of the development of public policy. DeLeon's 'stages' (1989) and, in the next decade later, Beryl Radin's presidential address (1996) and her *Beyond Machiavelli* (2000) provide a comprehensive account of shifts in the development of the field of policy studies and policy analysis. So does the more finessed account of policy analysis frameworks by Mayer, van Daalen and Bots (2004).

6 This period was marked by post-war policy issues, large-scale social and welfare initiatives, national defence concerns, new economic and budget planning processes, and a reliance on 'scientific management'-style thinking prevalent in the mid-twentieth century.

7 An important stepping stone was the initiation of the Planning Programming Budgeting System (PPBS) in the U.S. and similar developments in Canada and other countries (Heineman, Bluhm, Peterson and Kearny, 1990; Garson, 1986; Lindblom, 1958; Dobuzinskis, 1977; Wildavsky, 1979; Starling, 1979; Radin, 2000; Howlett and Lindquist, 2007; Mintrom, 2003).

8 The European Public Administration Network (EPAN) and the Network of Institutes and Schools of Public Administration in Central and Eastern Europe (NISPAcee) have produced valuable information on the range and type of public policy programmes in Europe. At the 2003 Swiss

Political Science Association annual conference, the working group on public policy chose the topic of comparing the state of the art in public policy analysis across Switzerland, Germany and France. Hajnal (2003) has published an important statistical analysis of programmes in Western and Eastern Europe. Additional data have been collected from the websites of various schools and programmes in Europe. We thank Geert Bouchaert, Bruno Dente, Stephen Osborne, Salvador Parrado Diez, Christine Rothmayr, Monika Steffen, Colin Talbot, Frans van Nispen, Jann Werner, and others for their invaluable comments and explanations.

9 It should be noted that for statistical significance reasons, key countries such as the U.K. and Germany were not included in this study.

10 As do a number of policy research centres such as the C.D. Howe Institute, the Institute for Research on Public Policy, the Fraser Institute, the Canadian Centre for Policy Alternatives, and the Caledon Institute.

11 The following are only some of the many think tanks and research centres in E.U. countries and they were chosen to reflect on intra-E.U. interests and concerns. Country-specific centres can be found in almost every European country and seem to be part of a long-established tradition. Centre for the Study of Public Policy, at the University of Strathclyde, Glasgow, Scotland; Centre for Economic Policy Research based at the University of Essex; The European Policy Centre (EPC) is an example of such an independent not-for-profit think tank. Its *Journal of European Public Affairs* promotes debates on European integration. The Institute for European Studies based in Brussels takes part in many research programmes funded by the European Union, international organizations, and regional Belgian authorities; they publish the journal of *European Integration* and a series, *Etude Europeans*. The Franco-Austrian Centre for Economic Convergence (CFA) is another example of an intergovernmental organization created in 1978 by Jacques Chirac and Chancellor Bruno Kreisky, financed by the European Commission. The Centre for International Studies and Research (CRI) has developed policy partnerships. The European Research Centre of Migration and Ethnic Relation, University of Utrecht; the Geneva Centre for Security Policy (GCSP), an international foundation under the framework of Swiss participation in the Partnership for Peace (1995); the Stockholm International Research Institute, established in 1996, financed by the Swedish government and providing support for studies on arms control, disarmament, conflict management, security building, etc., have also done so.

12 For instance, the U.K.'s Centre of Policy Studies was founded by Conservatives Margaret Thatcher and Keith Joseph in 1974, while the IPPR—Institute for Public Policy Research, London— describes itself as a 'progressive' think tank.

13 This tradition, defined by John Dewey, presented a belief in objectivity and the scientific study of social problems.

14 See, for example, Howlett and Ramesh (2003) for insightful definitions distinguishing between public management, public administration and public policy.

References

Aaron, A. J. 1989. *Politics and the Professors: The Great Society in Perspective.* Washington, DC: The Brookings Institution.

Anis, M., Armstrong, S. and Zhu, Z. 2004. 'The Influence of Learning Styles on Knowledge Acquisition in Public Sector Management'. *Educational Psychology*, 24(4), 549–571.

Atkinson, M. and Rasussen, K. 2005. A discussion paper on CAPPA accreditation. Prepared for a meeting of CAPPA program directors. http://cappa.ca/images/accreditation/New_Accreditation_Process-jan-2015.pdf

Bardach, E. (1992). 'Problem Solving in the Public Sector'. Berkeley: UC Berkeley, GSPP.

Bevir, M., Rhodes, R.A.W. and Weller, P. 2003. 'Traditions of Governance: Interpreting the Changing Role of the Public Sector'. *Public Administration*, 81(1), 1–17.

Breaux, D.A., Clynch, E.J. and Morris, J.C. 2003. 'The Core Curriculum Content of NASPAA-accredited Programs: Alike or Different?' *Journal of Public Affairs Education*, 9(4), 260.

Clark, Ian D. and Pal, Leslie A. (eds) 2015. Curriculum Comparison Tables—North America: How Master's Programs Differ in Distribution of Instruction by Type of Subject and Core Competencies. School of Public Policy and Governance. University of Toronto. http://portal.publicpolicy. utoronto.ca/en/MPPMPAPrograms/CurriculumComparisonTables/Pages/default.aspx

Clark, Ian D., Eisen, Ben and Pal, Leslie A. (eds). 2008. *Atlas of Public Policy and Management*. School of Public Policy and Governance. University of Toronto. http://portal.publicpolicy.utoronto.ca/en/Pages/index.aspx

Cleary, R.E. 1990. 'What do Public Administration Masters Programs Look Like? Do they do What is Needed?' *Public Administration Review*, 50(6), 663–673.

Cochran, C.L. and Malone, E.F. 1999. *Public Policy: Perspectives and Choices* 2nd edn. New York: McGraw-Hill College.

Collins, H. 2001. 'Tacit Knowledge, Trust, and the Q of Sapphire'. *Social Studies of Science*, 31, 71–85.

deLeon, P. 1989. 'The Stages Approach to the Policy Process: What Has It Done? Where Is It Going?' In Coda, S., ed., *The New State*. London: Lynn Rainer Pal, 19–31.

deLeon, P. and Protopsaltis, S. 2005. 'Preparing for the Craft of Policy Analysis: The Capstone Experience'. In I. Geva-May, ed., *Thinking Like a Policy Analyst: Policy Analysis as a Clinical Profession*. New York: Palgrave Macmillan, 171–186.

Dewey, J. 1933. *How We Think: A Restatement of the Relationship of Reflective Thinking to Educative Process*. Boston: Heath.

Dewey, J. 1938. *Logic and the Theory of Inquiry*. New York: Holt, Rinehart & Winston.

Dobuzinskis, L. 1977. 'Rational Government: Policy, Politics and Political Science'. In T.A. Hockin, ed., *Apex of Power: The Prime Minister and Political Leadership in Canada*, 2nd edn, Scarborough, ON: Prentice Hall.

Dror, Y. 1971. *Designs of Policy Sciences*. New York, Elsevier.

Dror, Y. 1984. 'Policy Analysis for Advising Rulers'. In Rolfe Tomlinson and Istavan Kiss (eds), *Rethinking the Profess of Operational Research and Systems Analysis*. Oxford, UK. Pergamon Press.

Dye, T.R. 1995. *Understanding Public Policy*. Englewood Cliffs, NJ: Prentice Hall.

EAPAA Accreditation Eligibility. Accessed 2015. www.eapaa.eu/process

Garson, D. 1986. 'From Policy Science to Policy Analysis: A Quarter Century of Progress'. In William N. Dunn (ed.) *Policy Analysis: Perspectives, Concepts, and Methods*. Greenwich, CT: JAI Press, 3–22.

Geva-May, I. 2002. 'The Missing Variable: Cultural Bias in Policy Analysis'. *Journal of Comparative Policy Analysis, Special Issue: Policy and Culture*, Robert Hoppe ed., 4(3).

Geva-May, I. (ed.) 2005. *Thinking Like a Policy Analyst: Policy Analysis as a Clinical Profession*, New York: Palgrave Macmillan.

Geva-May, I. with Wildavsky, A. 2006 [1997]. *An Operational AppAnalysis: The Craft. Prescriptions for Better Analysis* 2nd edn. Boston: Kluwer Academic Publishers.

Gigerenzer, G. (1999). 'The Adaptive Toolbox'. In *Bounded Rationality: The Adaptive Toolbox*. G. Gigerenzer and R. Selten, eds. Cambridge, MA: The MIT Press.

Gow, J. I. and Sutherland, S.L. 2004. 'Comparison of Canadian Masters Programs in Public Administration, Public Management and Public Policy'. Toronto: Canadian Association of Schools of Public Policy and Administration.

Hajnal, G. 2003. 'Diversity and Convergence: A Quantitative Analysis of European Public Administration Education Programs', *Journal of Public Affairs Education*, 9 (4), 245–258.

Heineman, R.A., Bluhm, W.T., Peterson, S.A. and Kearny, E.N. 1990. *The World of the Policy Analyst: Rationality, Values and Politics*. Chatham, NJ: Chatham House.

Henry, L.L. 1995. 'Early NASPAA History. Washington, DC: NASPAA.' In Breaux et al.

Hodgetts, J.E. 1973. 'Structural Heretics: The Non-Departmental Forms'. *The Canadian Public Service*. University of Toronto Press.

Hood, C. 1998. *The Art of the State*. Oxford University Press.

Hoppe, R. 1999. 'Policy Analysis, Science and Politics: From "Speaking Truth to Power" to Making Sense Together'. *Science and Public Policy*, 26(3), 201–210.

Hoppe, R. 2002. 'Cultural Theory and Its Contribution to Policy Analysis'. *Journal of Comparative Policy Analysis*, Special Issue 4(3), 235–241.

Howlett, M. and Lindquist, E. 2007. 'Beyond Formal Policy Analysis: Governance Context, Analytical Styles, and the Policy Analysis Movement in Canada'. In M. Howlett, L. Dobuzinskis and D. Laycock, eds, *Policy Analysis in Canada: The State of the Art*. Toronto: Toronto University Press.

Howlett, M. and M. Ramesh. 2003. *Studying Public Policy: Policy Cycles and Policy Subsystems*. Oxford University Press.

Innis, Harold Adams. 1930. *The Fur Trade in Canada: An Introduction to Canadian Economic History*. New Haven, CT: Yale University Press.

Policy Analysis in North America and Europe

Innis, Harold Adams. 1940. *The Cod Fisheries: The History of an International Economy.* New Haven, CT: Yale University Press.

Jordan, A. 2003. 'The Europeanization of National Government and Policy: A Departmental Perspective'. *British Journal of Political Science*, 33(1), 261–282.

Lasswell, H.D. 1950. *The World Revolution of Our Time: A Framework for Basic Policy Research.* Stanford University Press.

Lerner, D. and Lasswell, H.D. eds. 1951. *The Policy Sciences.* Palo Alto, CA: Stanford University Press.

Lindblom, C.E. 1958. 'Policy Analysis'. *The American Economic Review*, 48(3), 298–312.

MacRae, D. and Wilde, J.A. 1979. *Policy Analysis for Public Decisions.* North Scituate, MA: Duxbury.

March, J. and Simon, H. 1985. *Organizations.* New York: John Wiley and Sons.

Malcolmson, Patrick N. and Richard M. Myers. 2012. *The Canadian Regime.* University of Toronto Press.

Mayer, I, P., van Daalen, C.E. and Bots, P.W.G. 2004. 'Perspectives on Policy Analysis: A Framework for Understanding and Design'. *International Journal of Technology, Policy and Management*, 4(1), 169–191.

Meltsner, A.J. 1976. *Policy Analysts in the Bureaucracy.* Berkeley: University of California Press.

Mintrom, M. 2003. *People Skills for Policy Analysts.* Washington DC: Georgetown University Press.

Pal, Leslie A. 2013. *Beyond Policy Analysis: Public Issue Management in Turbulent Times.* Toronto, ON: Nelson.

Polanyi, M. 1966. *The Tacit Dimension.* London: Routledge & Kegan Paul.

Radin, B. 1996. The Evolution of Policy Analysis Field: From Conversation to Conversations. Presidential Address, APPAM, Washington DC.

Radin, B. 2000. *Beyond Machiavelli: Policy Analysis Comes of Age.* Washington DC: Georgetown University Press.

Reiner, M. and J. Gilbert. 2000. 'Epistemological Resources for Thought Experimentation in Science Learning'. *International Journal of Science Education*, 22(5), 489–506.

Russell, Peter H. 1965. *Leading Constitutional Decisions: Cases on the British North America Act.* Toronto: McClelland and Stewart.

Russell, Peter H. 1969. *The Supreme Court of Canada as a Bilingual and Bicultural Institution.* Ottawa: Queen's Printer.

Smiley, Donald V. 1970. *Constitutional Adaptation and Canadian Federalism since 1945.* Ottawa: Queen's Printer.

Smiley, Donald V. 1972. *Canada in Question: Federalism in the Seventies.* Toronto, ON: McGraw-Hill Ryerson.

Smiley, Donald V. and Ronald L. Watts. 1985. *Intrastate Federalism in Canada.* University of Toronto Press.

Smith, D. 2005. 'The Wagner Program'. In Geva-May, I. ed., *Thinking Like a Policy Analyst: Policy Analysis as a Clinical Profession,* New York: Palgrave Macmillan.

Smith, Miriam. 2005. 'Institutionalism in the Study of Canadian Politics: The English–Canadian Tradition'. In Andre Lecours, ed., *New Institutionalism: Theory and Analysis.* University of Toronto Press.

Starling, G. 1979. *The Politics and Economics of Public Policy: An Introductory Analysis with Cases.* Homewood, IL: Dorsey.

Sternberg, R., Forsythe, G, Hedlund, J., Wagner, R. and Williams W. 2000. *Practical Intelligence in Everyday Life.* New York: Cambridge University Press.

Straussman, Jeffrey D. (2005). 'Introduction'. *Journal Of Comparative Policy Analysis: Research And Practice.* 7(1).

Tversky, A. and D. Kahneman. 1981. 'Judgment Under Uncertainty: Heuristics and Biases'. *Science.* 185, 1124–1131.

Vogel, D. 1986. National Styles of Regulation: Environmental Policy in Great Britain and the United States. Ithaca, NY: Cornell University Press, 1986.

Weimer, D. L. and Vining, A.R. 2010. *Policy Analysis: Concepts and Practice.* Don Mills, ON: Pearson Canada.

Wildavsky, A. 1979. *Speaking Truth to Power: The Art and Craft of Policy Analysis.* Boston: Little, Brown.

Wilson, J. Q. 1989. *Bureaucracy.* New York: Free Press.

INDEX

Please note: for subjects discussed in the tables, the page number(s) appear in **bold**, and for figures, the page number(s) appear in *italics*. Citations in the endnotes to each chapter are indicated by with an 'n' after the page number. To avoid ambiguity, countries are occasionally placed in parentheses after a particular organisation or institution.

20th Century Fund 326

Aaron, A.J. 374
Abb, P. 324, 327, 330
Abelson, D.E. 328, 330, 336
Aberbach, Joel D. 118, 73
Abraham Kuyper Foundation 250
Abrahamson, E. 214
absolutism 351
academic discipline: definition 57
academic organizations 336
academic policy analysis 341–56: academic system 3, 8, 63–7; academics and advocacy 7, 19–20; comparative differences and similarities in policy research utilization 347–52; context 341–2, 355–6; definition 342–4; dynamics and trends 352–5; forms and functions of research utilization 344–7; ladder of research utilization **345**; politicization 352–5; science-based rationality and sources of knowledge 351–2; scientification 352–5; societalization 352–5; strong and weak institutionalization 350–1; universities 349–50; *see also* media; think tanks
accounting 15, 28, 110, 147, 160, 161n, 215–17, **262**, 365
Acharya, A. 330, 335
Ackerman, John M. 299–300
actor-centred institutionalism 2
actuarial science 28
Adachi, Yukio 7, 27–41, 49, 91
Adam, I. 352
Adam Smith Institute 327

Adams, David 119
Adams, Hugh 56
advisory bodies, *see* expert advisory bodies
Advisory Group on Reform of Australian Government Administration 105
advocacy coalition framework (ACF) 2, 233, 234–5, 267, 273n, 296
advocacy mobilization 18, 19, 292, 298
advocacy organizations 76, 292, 330
Africa Capacity Building Foundation 331
African Union (AU) 329
Agranoff, Robert 96
Ahrne, Göran 261, 263
Aid to Families with Dependent Children (AFDC) 285
Ainsworth, Scott H. 268
Alcock, F. 185–6, 196
Alford, J. 184
Allern, Elin Haugsgjerd 277
Alliance Manufacturers and Exporters Canada 262
Allison, Graham 343–4
Almog-Bar, M. 292, 295, 297–8
Althaus, Catherine 45
Amann, Ron 352
Amara, N. 126, 344–5, 347, 355
American Association for Public Policy Analysis and Management (APPAM) 5, 374, 375
American Enterprise Institute 371
American Federation of Labour and Congress of Industrial Organizations (AFL-CIO) 277, 284–6

Index

Ammons, D.N. 135–6
analytic organizations 96
Anderson, James 61
Andrews, R. 133, 135, 138
Anheier, Helmut K. 292
animal protection organizations 295
Anis, M. 361
announcements: message content **319**
Ansell, C. 133, 139n
anthropology 300–3
Anti-Revolutionary Party (ARP) 250
Aos, Steve 119
API (Application Programming Interface) 315
Archer, J.N. 219
Architectural Institute of British Columbia
    (AIBC) 272
architecture 28
Arellano, David 79
Aristotle 351
Arklay, Tracey 118
Armbrüster, Thomas 215
Armitage, Lisa 298
Armstrong, J. 107
Armstrong, S. 361
Arnold, Peri E. 219
ASEAN-Institute of Strategic and International
    Studies 332; *see also* ASEAN
Ashforth, A. 169–72, 174–5
Askim, J. 135–6
Association of Online Media 323
Association of Southeast Asian Nations (ASEAN)
    329; *see also* ASEAN-Institute of Strategic and
    International Studies
Atkinson, M. 373
Atlanticism 349
Atlas Institute 328
Aucoin, Peter 72, 80, 106–7, 216, 219
Audit and Inspection Bureau (South Korea) 316
Audit Office (NZ) 220
Australian Climate Council 186
Australian Competition and Consumer
    Commission 76
Australian National Audit Office 76
Australian Public Service (APS) 105
Automotive Industries Association of Canada
    271
autonomy: concept 246

Bach, Stephan 218–19
Bachner, J. 239
Bachrach, P.S. 61
Bächtiger, A. 139
Baehler, Karen 46, 51, 52, 87
Baillargeon, Stéphane 169
Baird, K. 107
Bakvis, Herman 72, 77, 80, 213, 221, 223
Baldwin, B. 248

Bale, Tim 277
Balser, D. 294
Bandelow, N.C. 344, 350–1, 353
Banks, Gary 153
Banks, Robin 298
Barabas, J. 236
Baratz, M.S. 61
Bardach, Eugene 2, 3, 40n, 45, 52, 57, 58–9, 90,
    309, 361
Bardhan, Pranab 120
Barker, A. 73, 353
Barnett, Anthony 223
Barnett, Michael L. 263
Baron, David P. 263
Baroni, Laura 292
Barthélemy, M. 134
Basic Plan on Reorganization and Rationalization
    of Councils (1999) (Japan) **192**
Baskoy, Tuna 123, 126
Bastow, Simon 152
Bauer, A. 181, 185–9, 194–6
Baumgartner, F.R. 234–5, 273n, 298
Beale, Dave 220
BearingPoint 222
Beckman, Arnold 264
Beckman, Ludvig 118
Behn, Robert D. 72–3, 146, 151
Bekkers, Victor J.J.M. 154, 354–5
Bell, Stephen 123
benchmarking 11, 135–6, 140n
Bennett, Robert J. 266, 268
Benson, D. 184
Benzie, Robert 273
Bernal, A. 234
Bernier, Luc 118, 122
Bernstein, Jared 285
Bertelli, Anthony M. 310
Bestebreur, Ton 150–2
Bevir, M. 363
Biegelbauer, P. 344, 350–1, 353
Biesta, Gert 120
Bingham, L.B. 134
biology 343
Birch, L.M. 237–8
Bivens, Josh 279
Bjørsted, Eric 283
Blackburn, R. 199
Blackham, Alysia 118
Blair, Tony 153, 223, 280
Blätte, A. 343, 349
Block, F. 329, 333
blogging 19; *see also* micro-blogging
Blondel, Jean 118
Bloodgood, Elizabeth 293
Bluhm, William T. 31, 37, 38, 95, 376n
Blum, Sonja 20, 58, 65, 91, 98n, 115, 341–56
Boardman, Anthony E. 17, 45, 47, 74, 261–73, 269

Index

Boaz, Annette 5, 119, 348, 351, 354
Bogdanovich, Lylyana 121
Bogedan, Claudia 282
Bogenschneider, Karen 119
Bogumil, J. 131, 134, 136, 139
Bohle, D. 337
Bonoli, Giuliano 276
Bonsón, E. 311
Borchert, J. 199
Bordogna, Lorenzo 218–19
Boreham, Paul 126
Borge, Lars-Erik 121
Borges, Bernhard 263
Bossens, N. 347
Boston Consulting Group 213, 215, 216
Boston, J. 73
Boswell, C. 137, 170, 171, 173–6, 346
Botha, Johanu 21, 360–77
Bothfeld, Silke 281
Bots, Pieter 45, 56–7, 67, 73, 106, 300, 376n
Bouchaert, Geert 377n
Boucher, S. 324, 329, 336
Bouckaert, Geert 104–6, 124, 147, 161n, 214
boundary organizations 181, 186, 188–9, 197, 222
Bourdieu, Pierre 62, 230
Bourque, Denis 295
Boushey, Heather 285–6
Bouwen, P. 2
Boydstun, A.E. 235
Boyne, G. 138
Bradford, N. 169, 172, 174–6
Brahmi, Dalia 121
Braman, S. 311
Brans, Marleen 1–22, 181, 184, 186–9, 191, 194–5, 245, 251–4, 341–56
Braybook, D. 37
Brazilian Meteorology Institute 78
Breaux, D.A. 376n
Brehm, John 126
Bressers, D. 181, 187, 189–90, 192–5
Brexit referendum 6
Bridgman, Peter 45
British Institute of Management Consultants (IMC) 219
Broeder, Corina den 155
Bronn, Peggy Simcic 273n
Brookings Institution 324, 326, 327, 337, 371
Brooks, S. 40n, 106, 328, 330, 336
Brown, J. 230
Brownlow Committee (US) 160
Brudnick, I. 202, 204, 211n
Brunsson, Nils 261, 263
Bryce, Herrington J. 294, 296
Bryce, J. 199
Budget and Accounting Act (US) 160
budgetary policy, *see* evidence-based budgetary policy

budgeting, normative theory of 162n
Buhr, D. 77–8, 108–9
Buldioski, G. 330, 334
Bulmer, M. 170, 172–5
Bureau of the Budget (BOB) 160
bureaucratic capacity 9, 70–81: analytical capacity and policy analysis 72–3; Australia 75–6; Brazil 78–9; Canada 76–7; comparative overview 80–1; context 70, 81; cross-national policy analytical capacity 75–81; policy; Germany 77–8; governmental policy analysis 70–5; governmental policy analytical capacity, studies and factors 73–5; Mexico 79; policy analytical capacity 70–2; state capacities 70–2
bureaucratic organizations 108
bureaucratization 203, 205, 210, 295
Burke, E. 37
Burstein, P. 230, 231–2
Burton, P. 334
Busch, P.O. 184
Bush, George W. 223
Bushnell, P. 73
business and law 343
business associations (BAs) 261–73: Canada **262**, 270–2; contact with Canadian federal officials **262**; context 261–4, 272–3; decision to engage in policy analysis 268–70; definition; policy analysis definitions 264–5; policy process and 265–7; role in the policy process *266*; scope and production of policy analyses **271**
Butler, N. 28–9
Byrne, Michael 285

C.D. Howe Institute 248, 377n
Cabinet Office (UK) 153, 189, 222–3
Caledon Institute 248, 377n
Campbell, A.L. 231
Campbell, J.L. 329, 338
Campbell, Robin 264
Canadian Association of Petroleum Producers (CAPP) 261, **262**, 272
Canadian Association of Programs in Public Administration (CAPPA) 372–5
Canadian Bankers Association **262**
Canadian Cattlemen's Association **262**
Canadian Centre for Policy Alternatives 248, 377n
Canadian Electricity Association (CEA) 272
Canadian Federation of Independent Business 261, **262**, 271
Canadian Gemmological Association 271
Canadian Manufacturers' Association 261
Canadian Public Service 77
Canadian Radio-television and Telecommunications Commission 264
Canes-Wrone, B. 230–2, 239
capacity, *see* bureaucratic capacity

Index

capitalism 214, 215; *see also* varieties of capitalism (VOC)
Caplan, Nathan 125–6, 341, 344
Cardinal, Laura Jane 121
Carley, Michael 43
Carroll, Brendan J. 292, 295
Carson, L. 105
Carson, W.G. 119
Carter, S. 291, 299, 301
Carver, Tom 338n
Casey, John 298
Cash, D.W. 185–6, 196
Cashore, B. 232
Cattaneo, D. 324, 329, 336
Caulfield, Janice 224
causal theory 31
Center for Applied Social Studies of Management (Italy) 369
Center for International Private Enterprise (CIPE) 328
Center for Social and Economic Research (Poland) 328
Central and Eastern European institutes 335
central government policy analysis 103–15: Australia 104–5, **112**; Canada 105–7, **112**; context 114–15; differences 111–14; Germany 107–9, **112**; Netherlands 109–11, **112**; policy analysis by country **112**; similarities and trends 111–14; varieties of policy analysis 104–11
Central Planning Bureau (CPB) 111
centralization 14, 106, 113, 189, 194, 202, 295
Centre for Economic Policy Research (UK) 377n
Centre for European Policy Studies (CEPS) 329, 332
Centre for European Studies 256
Centre for Global Development (CGD) 332
Centre for International Governance Innovation (CIGI) 333, 334, 336
Centre for International Studies and Research (CRI) 377n
Centre for Liberal Strategies 328
Centre for Public Affairs Studies (Hungary) 365
Centre for Public Policy Research (Canada) 371
Centre for the Microeconomic Analysis of Public Policy (UK) 331
Centre for the Study of Public Policy (UK) 377n
Centre of Policy Studies (UK) 377n
Chalmers, Adam William 292
chambers of commerce 17, 271–2
Charbonneau Commission 169, 173
Chatfield, Michael 217
Chaufen, A. 333
checks and balances system (US) 236
Chen, Cheng-Yi 310
Cheng, Ming Huei 19, 309–20
Cherny, Adrian 118–19, 126–7

Chicken Farmers of Canada **262**
Chillas, S. 28–9
Chiou, C.-T. 191–3
Chirac, Jacques 377n
Chomsky, N. 230
Chong, D. 232
Christensen, R.A. 294
Christensen, Tom 124, 203, 205
Christian Democratic Party (CDP) 324
Christian Democratic Union (CDU) 249, 326
Christian Social Union (CSU) 326
Christin, Rosine 62
Christophersen, K.-A. 135–6
Cilliers, J. 328
citizen groups 34
Citizens Policy Research Council (CPRC) 253
Civil Service Board (UK) 53
Civil Service Department (UK) 219–20
civil society organizations 5, 21, 249, 256, 297, 300–2, 323, 336
Clark, Ian D. 361–3, 376n
Clark, W.C. 185–6, 196
Clean Air Act (Canada) **262**
Cleary, R.E. 376n
clients: definition 85
climate change 77, 123, 184–7, **189**, 197, **262**, 272, 328, 330, 332, 344
Clinton, Bill 285
Clokie, H.M. 173
Clynch, E.J. 376n
Coal Association of Canada 264, 265
Coalition for Secure and Trade-Efficient Borders 261
Cobb, R.W. 72, 175
Cochran, C.L. 361
Cohen, David K. 59
Cohen, M. 139n
Cold War 183, 284, 325, 353
Colebatch, Hal 45, 87, 300
Coleman, S. 310
Coleman, William 263, 269, 270
Coletti, P. 133
collectivism 316
College of Europe 213
College of Public Administration (Hungary) 365
Collin, Jeff 267
Collins, H. 361
colonialism 88
commercial organizations 109
committees of inquiry (COIs) 4, 6, 10, 15: definition 13, 171, 177
Committee for the Development of Policy Analysis (COBA) (Netherlands) 110–11, 145
Communication Industry Association 323
communism 21, 191, **192**
communities of purpose: definition 301

Index

Community of Latin American and Caribbean
States (CELAC) 329
community organizations 182, **183**
compartmentalization 8, 64–7
computerization 316
Comte, Auguste 30
Congressional Budget Office (US) 51, 204
Congressional Research Service (US) 204, 206,
210
Conley, Tom 123
Connaughton, B. 114
consensus-oriented approaches 4
consociationalism 351
consultants: definition 221; *see also* management
consultancy
consultocracy 213
contestability: concept 92
Cook, F.L. 236
cooperative federalism 65; *see also* federalism
coordinated market economies (CMEs) 15, 215,
217, 224
Coordinating for Cohesion in the Public Sector of
the Future (COCOPS) 161n
Corbett, Thomas J. 119
Corcoran, Jan 215
Corporación Andina de Fomento (CAF) 78
corporatism 17, 65, 109, 209, 259, 283, 286, 293,
351; *see also* neo-corporatism
cost-benefit analysis (CBA) 31, 37, 43–4, 47, 59,
90, 96, 110, 326, 344
Côté, A. 107
Cotter, John. 264
Council of Australian Governments 76
Council of Economic Advisers (US) 331
Council on Foreign Relations (US) 324, 337
Cowan, R. 134
Craft, Jonathan 2, 5, 17, 57, 61, 75, 103–5, 106–7,
113–14, 181, 183, 186–91, 194, 252, 256, 258,
291, 296, 341, 346
Crawford, J. 311
Crick, B. 37
cronyism 120
Cross, W. 245, 247–8, 255
Crowley, Kate 13, 91, 104, 181–97, 343–4, 349,
352
Culpepper, P.D. 232
Cunningham, Jack 153

Dahl, Robert Alan 60
Dahlström, C. 175
Dalton, Bronwen 298
Danish Economic Council of the Labour
Movement 18, 277–9, 282–4, 286
Danish Labour Movement 282–4: administrative
and political corporatism 282–4; agenda setting
282; *Arbejderbevægelsens Erhvervsråd* (Economic
Council of the Labour Movement) 278–9;

policy change 282–4; *see also* Labour Market
Policy
David, Paul A. 273n
David, Thomas 263
Davies, H.T.O. 75, 185, 346
Davies, Philip 154
Davis, Glyn 45
De Boef, S.L. 235
De Bolle, J. 217
De Corte, Joris 298
De Graaf, L. 134
De Jong, Maarten 12, 143–62, 145
De Lancer Julnes, Patricia 161n
De Mesquita, B.B. 74
De Souza, A. 251, 254
De Vries, Jouke 150, 161n
De Winter, Lieven 14, 199–211, 199
debating parliaments 14–15, 207
decentralization 14, 47–8, 113, 120, 121, 123,
202–3, 295; *see also* centralization
DeLeon, P. 2, 32, 40n, 43, 368, 376n
deliberative policy analysis 354
Della Porta, D. 199
Delvaux, B. 348
democracy 78, 87–8, 120, 191: autocracy 87;
bargaining 29–30; Brazil 78; Czech Republic
191; de-politicization and 120; deliberative 40n;
direct 134; multi-party **193**; national examples
78, 87–8, 191; parliamentary **192**; political
process 7, 19, 27, 30; promotion 327; prosperity
economics 279; representative 139, 310; think
tanks 255; *see also* liberal democracy; social
democracy
Democratic Party of Japan (DPJ) 253
democratization 91, 193, 203, 299, 327
Denham, Andrew 325, 327, 337
Denhardt, Janet V. 310
Denhardt, Robert B. 310
Dente, Bruno 133, 377n
dentistry 28
deparliamentarization 199
departmentalism 108
Derlien, H.-U. 107
Desai, Rhadika 337
Deschouwer, K. 199–200
design activity 33
Deslatte, A. 138
Deutscher Gewerkschaftsbund (DGB) 277, 278,
280–1
Devarajan, Shantayanan 121
Dewey, John 377n
Dickson, N. 185–6, 196
Diez, Salvador Parrado 377n
digitalization 152
DiMaggio, Paul J. 214–15
Dingeldey, Irene 280
Djelic, Marie-Laure 218

384

Index

Dobbin, Frank 184, 214
Dobuzinskis, L. 1, 31, 57, 58, 106, 119, 191, 343, 349, 376n, 376n
Doern, G.B. 169–70
Dollery, Brian 121
Dolowitz, D. 184
Dølvik, Jon Erik 283
Domhoff, William G. 337
Donovan, Kevin 221
Douglas-Coldwell Foundation (DCF) 248
Dowling, John 269
Drake, Elizabeth 119
Drewry, G. 172, 174
Dror, Yehezkel 5, 30, 89, 94–5, 361, 370
Druckman, J.N. 231, 232
Dryzeck, John 32
Duke, Amy-Ellen 284
Dumont, P. 199
Dunlap, R.E. 330
Dunleavy, Patrick 2, 152, 161n, 222
Dunn, William N. 2, 156, 273n
Dunrose, Catherine 51
Dussauge-Laguna, Mauricio I. 8–9, 70–81
Dutch institutes 249–50
Dutch Parliamentary Bureau for Research 206
Dutch Scientific Council for Government Policy (WRR) 347
Dwyer, A. 216
Dye, Thomas R. 2, 337 342–3, 361
Dynes, R.R. 169

Easton, David 62
Ebélé, J. 324, 329, 336
Ebrahim, A. 294
Echenberg, H. 291
Eckley, N. 185–6, 196
Ecolo 254
ecology: policy 295, 298, 327, 336
Economic and Social Research Council (ESRC) 331
economic liberalisation 175
Economic Policy Institute (EPI) (US) 18, 277, 279, 285, 286
economics 37, 40n, 43, 53, 61, 66–7, 71, 74, 79, 89, 104, 106, **112**, 113, 213, 216, 278–9, 282, 331–2, 342, 343, 344, 351, 362–4, 367–71
Edelmann, Murray 62, 65
Education Policy Research Initiative (US) 371
Edwards, L. 105, 114, 123
eEurope Action Plan 222
Efficiency Strategy (Thatcher) 222
Efficiency Unit (UK) 220, 223
Eisen, Ben 361, 376n
Eisinger, R.M. 230
Eitzen, D. Stanley 286
Elder, C.D. 72
elitism 5, 14, 72, 191, **192**, 196, 336

Elliott, D. 172
employer organizations 351
endogeneity 18–19
Engelen-Kefer, Ursula 281
engineering: civil 28, 37, 72, 215
Enlightenment era 351
Enserink, B. 342
environmental organizations 295
Erasmus Public Administration Programme 373
Erlingsson, G. 131, 137
Esping-Andersen, Gøsta 218, 276
ethnicity 11, 279
European Added Value Unit 205
European Association for Public Administration Accreditation (EAPAA) 21, 365, 373–4
European Capital Markets Institute 217
European Commission (EC) 161n, 204, 224, 295, 329, 332, 377n
European Community Institutions Committee (ECIC) 224
European Group of Public Affairs (EGPA) 1, 369, 374
European Parliamentary Research Service (EPRS) 204, 205, 206
European People's Party (EPP) 256
European Policy Centre (EPC) 377n
European Public Administration Network (EPAN) 376n
European Research Centre of Migration and Ethnic Relation 377n
European Union (EU) 17, 19, 39, 200, 222, 246, 259, 296, 328, 335, 355, 356, 377n: expert advisory bodies/systems **194**; political party think tank function **252;** think tank functions *257;* think tanks: level of autonomy **247**
Europeanization 200, 203, 205
Evans, Bryan 18, 118, 122–3, 123, 126, 126, 291–303, 301–3
Evans, M. 184
Evans, P. 71
evidence: definition 154, 347
evidence-based budgetary policy 143–62: budget reviews 154–9; budgetary reform 143–6; call for 153–4; classification of budget reviews *157;* context 143, 159–60; modes of policy analysis and evaluation *155;* performance budgeting 146–52; performance budgeting alternatives 152–3; performance information utilization *149;* policy reviews 154–6; program evaluation utilization *156;* sovereign debt crisis 149–52; spending review utilization *158;* spending reviews 156–9; *see also* OECD
Evidence-Based Policy in Development Network 338n
evidence-based policy: concept 72, 119, 153
evidence-based policymaking 5, 20
Executive Office of the President (EOP) (US) 160

Index

Expenditure Review Committee (ERC) (Aus) 157

expert advisory bodies 181–97: advisory bodies/ systems, comparative approaches to **189–90**; advisory councils 187–8; advisory councils, externalization of **187**; advisory systems 188–90; Australia **190**; Belgium **189, 194**; Canada **190**; comparative analysis 187–8; context 196–7; cross-national variations 191–6, **194**; definition 185; establishment and development 185–91; Estonia **189, 194**; evidence-based policy making **183**; fire-fighting advice **183**; France **190**; Germany **189–90, 194**; Greece **189, 194**; ILPA single country comparisons **192–3**; medium to long-term policy steering advice **183**; Netherlands **189–90, 194**; New Zealand **190**; place of expert policy advice in policy advisory systems 182–5; policy advisory system actors by policy type **183**; political and policy process advice **183**; Portugal **189, 194**; short-term crisis **183**; single country studies 190–1; Spain **189, 194**; Sweden **190**; Switzerland **189, 194**; United Kingdom **189–90, 194**

externalization 5, 9, 10, 13, 104, **112**, 113, 182, 184, 186–93, 195, 197

Fabian Society 326
Fager, Gulielma Leonard 121
Fair Labour Standards Act (US) 285
Family Support Act (US) 284, 285
Fang, K.-H. 131, 134–5
Farah, M.F.S. 133, 134, 136
Farson, S. 169, 176
Faulds, D.J. 309
federalism 91, 105, 108, **112**, 113, 139, 361, 364, 369
Federation of Management Consulting Associations (FEACO) **218**, 223–4
Feldman, Elliot J. 56
Fenno, Richard J., Jr. 273n
Ferguson, Michele 126, 197
Fickinger, Nico 281
Fischer, Frank 4, 32, 40n, 182, 219, 310, 337, 344
Fisheries Act (Canada) **262**
Fitzgerald, J. 131, 139
Fleckenstein, Timo 172, 173–4, 280
Fleischer, J. 73
flexicurity 280, 282
Flyvbjerg, B. 351
Fobé, E. 181, 184, 186–9, 191, 194–5
Fooks, Gary 267
Foreign Policy Institute (FPI) 331
Forester, John 4, 32, 310, 344
formal policy analysis methods 43–54: changing policy practices 48–53; concept 43, 53; context 43–4, 53–4; influence on development of policy analysis 44–8 formal/rationalist framework 27, 31–2

Forsythe, G. 361
fragmented incrementalism 108
Franco-Austrian Centre for Economic Convergence (CFA) 377n
Fraser Institute 248, 377n
Frattarelli, LeighAnn C. 121
Fraunhofer institutes (Germany) 348
Fraussen, B. 327
Free Democratic Party (FDP) 326
Freedom House 328
Freedom of Information Act (US) 92, 98n
Freeman, M. 330
Freese, Ulrich 281
Freiberg, Arie 119
Freidson, E. 28, 39n
Frenk, Julio 121
Freudenstein, Roland 256
Friedrich Ebert Foundation 249
Friedrich Naumann Foundation 256, 326
Friedrich-Ebert-Stiftung Foundation (FES) 326, 330
Frisco, Velda 145, 150
Frulli, M. 173
Fulton, Lord 219
Fulton Committee on the Civil Service (UK) 219

Gaebler, Ted 221
Gagatek, W. 250, 256
Gains, Francesca 119
Galenson, Walter 282
Gamper, Catherine 47
Gandy, O.H. Jr. 236
Garcé, A. 327
Garnett, Mark 327
Garrett, Geoffrey 184, 214
Garson, D. 376n
Garzarelli, Giampaolo 121
Gates, Scott 126
Gauvin, J.-P. 231
Gaxie, D. 199
Geer, J.G. 230
Gella, A. 39n
Geller, Stephanie 298
gender analysis framework 50
Geneva Centre for Security Policy (GCSP) 377n
Genieys, William 68n
George Soros' Open Society Institute 365
Gerardo, U. 327
German Labour Movement 279–81: agenda setting 279–80; *Deutscher Gewerkschaftsbund's* Role 279–81; Hans Böckler Foundation 278; job service, concept 281 policy change 280–1; *see also* Labour Market Policy
Geva-May, Iris 1–22, 37–8, 87, 106, 350, 360–77, 376n
Giddens, Anthony 221
Gieryn, T.F. 345

386

Giest, Sarah 277
Gigerenzer, G. 361
Gilbert, J. 361
Gilens, M. 231
Gill, Colin 282
Gill, J.I. 71
Gilmore, Anna B. 267
Gilmour, John B. 145–6
Ginalski, Stephanie 263
Ginsberg, B. 230
Gladstone, Alan 261
Glass, Juniper 18, 291–303
Glassco, J. Grant 219
Glassco Commission *see* Royal Commission on
  Government Organization
Glasser, T. 230
Glater, Jonathan D. 217
Gleeson, Deborah 123
Global Development Network (GDN) 331, 335
global management consultancies 15
globalization 13, 52, 85, 87, 95, 123, 183, 200, 279,
  328, 329
Glückler, Johannes 215
Gluckman, Peter 51
Godmer, L. 199
Godwin, Erik 268
Godwin, Kenneth 268
Gold, I. 355
Goldbach, Stine 47
Gormley, William T. 273n
Gottweis, Herbert 310
Goul Andersen, Jørgen 282–3
Gould, Elise 279
Government Accountability Office (US) 204
Government of the Future Centre 213
Government Performance and Result Act
  (GPRA) (US) 160
government policy analysis 101–62; *see also* central
  government policy analysis; evidence based
  budgetary policy; local level of policy analysis;
  sub-national governments
governmental commissions: concept 171
Gow, J.I. 368, 372, 376n
GPRA Modernization Act (US) 160
Gray, Andrew 145
Grayson, Lesley 119
Gready, P. 170, 173
Great Society 326
Greef, Samuel 278
Green, I. 107
Greenhalgh, T. 329
Green-Pedersen, Christoffer 177, 282
Gregory, R. 73
Griffith, J. 199
Grimmelikhuijsen, Stephan G. 310
Gronbach, Sigrid 281
Grönlund, K. 139

Gross, Andrew C. 215
Grunden, T. 245, 249, 256
Gunn, Lewis 86
Guo, Chao 293
Gustafsson, G. 56
Guttman, Daniel 213

Haas, P.M. 185
Hacker, Jacob S. 273n, 279
Haddaway, S.R. 325
Haenlein, M. 309
Hague, R. 131–2
Hajer, M.A. 354
Hajnal, G. 363, 369, 377n
Hakka Affairs Commission **312**
Hall, Jeremy L. 118–19
Hall, Mike 285
Hall, Peter A. 15, 214–15, 217, 248
Halligan, John 2, 5, 73, 104–7, 106, 113, 161n, 181,
  183–4, 186–91, 194
Halloran, P. 223
Halpern, Charlotte 58, 65
Halpin, D. 200, 207–9
Hammerschmid, Gerhard 150, 159, 161n
Hampel, F. 208
Hanlon, G. 216
Hanns-Seidel-Stiftung Foundation 326
Hans Böckler Foundation 18, 277, 278, 280, 286
Hans Böckler Society 278
Hansen, Louise A. 283
Hansen, M.B. 139
Harding, F. 216
Hardmeier, S. 232, 236, 237–8
Hardt, Łukasz 150
Hargadon, A.B. 185
harmonization 184, 329, 364
Harrop, M. 131–2
Hartz Commission 281
Haskins, Ron 153
Hassenteufel, Patrick 8, 56–68, 343, 349
Hastings, Alcee 217
Hatry, Harry P. 161n
Hawke, G.R. 73
Hawkesworth, Ian 150
Hayek, F.A. 29–30
Hayward, Jack 56
Hazard Analysis and Critical Control Point (US)
  264
Head, Brian 13, 73, 75–6, 81, 91, 104, 118–20,
  125–7, 154, 181–97, 343–4, 346, 348, 349,
  352–3
Heaney, Michael T. 297
Heath, Edward 219
Hecker, Gabrielle 121
Heclo, Carolyn Teich 56
Heclo, H. 175
Hedlund, J. 361

Index

hegemonic class interests 20
Heindenheimer, Arnold J. 56
Heineman, Robert A. 31, 37, 38, 95, 376n
Heinrich-Böll-Stiftung Foundation 326
Heinze, R.G. 109, 352
Helbig, N. 310–11
Hendrix, C.S. 71
Henry, L.L. 376n
Herbst, Susan 127, 232–3
Heritage Foundation 327
Herman, E. 230
Hermann, A.T. 181, 185–9, 194–6
Hermansson, J. 172, 176
Hernandez, Jesus 79
Hersbt, S. 230
Hertie School of Governance 81
Herweg, N. 234
heuristic tools and typology 2, 4, 8, 17, 44–5, 56–7, 62, 75, 81, 86, 246, 348, 356
Hewitt, Patricia 223
Hewlett Foundation 328
Hill, K.W. 239
Hill, Michael 67, 132
Hillman, Amy 268
Hilterman, F. 139
Hird, John A. 73, 127
historical framework 85–98: academic 'home' of policy analysis, development of 94–5; client relationships 90–1; contemporary situation 97; expansive focus 92–4; global development of policy analysis 87–95; moving outside top government 91–2; non-US policy analysis 86–7; performance of policy analysis 89–90; twenty-first century situation 95–7
Hitt, Michael 268
Ho, Jei 319
Hobbs, B. 324, 329, 336
Hodge, Margaret 223
Hodgetts, J.E. 364
Högenauer, A. 203, 205
Hoggett, Paul 295
Hogl, Karl 181, 185–9, 194–6
Hogwood, Brian 86
Holcomb, Pamela A. 284
Hollander, Marcus J. 119
Hollingworth, M. 223
Holzer, Marc 315
Home Office (UK) 221–2
homogenization 214
Hood, Christopher 213
Hoos, Ida 220
Hoover, Herbert 143
Hoover Commission (US) 219
Hoover Committee (US) 143–4
Hoppe, R. 73, 341, 347, 351–2, 364
horizontal coordination 108
Hosono, Sukehiro 49, 91

Howard, Michael 105, 220
Howe, G. 172
Howlett, Michael 1–22, 31, 39, 45, 57, 58, 61, 71–3, 74, 75–7, 81, 87, 103, 105–7, 113–15, 118–19, 122–3, 126–7, 131–3, 181, 183, 189, 232, 252, 256, 258, 277, 291, 296, 303, 341, 343, 346, 349, 355, 361, 364, 376n, 376n, 377n
Hrdinová, J. 310–11
Hua, X. 330
Huber Stephens, E. 71
Hudson Institute 326
Hughes, J. 269
Hunter, A. 170, 171, 173–6
Huntington, Mary 222
Hupe, Peter 67
Hustedt, T. 108, 114

i-Voting 19, 311–12, 319: performance of Taipei City Government departments **311–12**
ideology 10, 78, 92, 93, 154, 203, 256, 324, 337
Iio, Jun 49
in't Veld, Roeland J. 109, 111, 161n
independent commission: term 174
Indian Council for International Economic Research (ICIER) 331
Indigenous Peoples Commission **312**
industrial organizations 34
industrialism 28
industrialization 28, 326
Industry Canada's Directory of Business and Trade Associations 270
industry organizations 323
information and communications technology (ICT) 124, 152, 215, 222, 309, **312**, 315, 317, 336, 355
information interlocutors 20; *see also* think tanks
Information Office (Beijing) 317
Ingram, H. 231
Innis, Harold Adams 364
Institute for European Studies (Belgium) 377n
Institute for Fiscal Studies (IFS) 331
Institute for Policy Research (Japan) 250
Institute for Public Policy Research (IPPR) 377n
Institute for Research on Public Policy (Canada) 248, 377n
Institute for Strategic Studies (UK) 332
Institute of Economic and Social Research (WSI) (Germany) 278, 280–1
Institute of Housing and Urban Development (Netherlands) 368
Institute of Public Administration of Canada (IPAC) 374
institutional framework 215, 224, 299
institutional isomorphism 214
institutionalization of policy analysis 4, 10, 79, 103, 110, 111, **112**, 113, 119, 122, 124, 170, 171, 342, 349–51

388

Index

instrumentalization of policy analysis 355
integrative analytical framework 32
interactive policymaking 20–1
interest groups 11, 16–21, 33, 56, 61, 63–5, 70,
  86, 91, 93, 96, 109, 133, **183, 192–3**, 209, 229,
  231–2, 234, 236, 250, 253, 265–7, 276, 282,
  292, 295, 296, 343, 353–5, 373; *see also* business
  associations (BAs); Labour Market Policy;
  political party think tanks; voluntary sector
interest organizations 175
intergovernmental organizations (IGOs) 377n
International Classification of Non-Profit
  Organizations 292
International Crisis Group (ICG) 329, 333
International Initiative for Impact Evaluation (3ie)
  332
International Labour Office (UK) 221
International Labour Organization (ILO) **183**, 185
International Library of Policy Analysis (ILPA) 3,
  8, 9, 14, 67, 75, 81, 85, 103, 138, 181, 190, **192**
International Monetary Fund (IMF) 39, 189
international organizations (IOs) 9, 75, **183**, 184,
  224, 325, 328, 333, 335–7, 377n
International Political Science Association (IPSA)
  1, 87
International Public Policy Association (IPPA) 1,
  87
internationalization 328
internet: era 19, 325, 328–9; participants in internet
  use **312**; users (2012–2016) **313**
Internet Industry Association 323
Internet Information Services 321n
internships 21, 360, 370–2
Inwood, G.J. 169, 171, 172–3, 174, 176–7
Ioannides, I. 329
Ismayr, W. 204
isomorphism 15, 224

Jackson, A. 248
Jackson, Michael 213
Jackson, P.M. 72
Jacobs, D. 352
Jacobs, L. 230–2
Jacobsen, D.I. 139
Jacques, P.J. 330
Jäger, J. 185–6, 196
Jäkel, T. 135–6
James, Oliver 224
Jann, W. 353
Jantz, B. 353
Jarpe, Elizabeth Ann 121
Jasanoff, S. 196, 347, 351
Jeliazkova, M. 73
Jenkins, Bill 3, 73, 119, 145
Jenkins, William I. 145
Jenkins-Smith, Hank C. 2, 62, 267, 273n
Jennings, Edward T. 118–19

Jenson, J. 170, 172
Jiang, Min 310
Jobert, Bruno 62
Jochim, A.E. 132
Johns, C.M. 169, 171, 173, 174, 176–7
Johnsen, Å. 135–6
Johnson, Lyndon B. 144
Johnston, R. 230
Jonard, N. 134
Jones, Bryan D. 132, 234–5, 273n
Jones, Charles O. 61
Jones, M.D. 235
Jonsen, A.L. 37
Jordan, A. 184, 363
Jordan, G. 56
Jordan, Lisa 294
Jörgens, H 184
Jørgensen, Henning 277, 282–3
Jørgensen, Martin Bak 283
Josefsson, C. 136–7
Joseph, Keith 377n
Journal of Comparative Policy Analysis
  (ICPA/JCPA) 1, 3, 86, 178
Journal of European Integration 377n
Journal of European Public Affairs 377n
Journal of Policy Analysis and Management
  (JPAM) 5
Journal of Public Affairs Education 375
journalism 333
Joyce, Philip G. 150, 160
Jung, T. 5, 348, 351, 354

Kahneman, D. 361
Kanai, T. 131
Kantor, Leslie M. 121
Kaplan, A.M. 309
Karacaoglu, G. 50
Kąsek, Leszek 150
Kay, Adrian 119
Kearny, Edward N. 31, 38, 95, 376n
Keller, Berndt 280
Kennon, A. 199
Kettunen, P. 5, 334, 347, 351, 354
Keynesianism 175, 219
Khemani, Stuti 121
Kickert, W. 109, 111
Kim, Byong-Joon 315
Kim, S. 134, 139
Kim, Young-Jong 316
Kimberlin, Sara E. 292, 294–6, 299
Kingdon, John 59, 234, 273n
Klaassen, H. 139, 151
Klammer, Ute 281
Klüver, H. 294
Knill, Christoph 123, 132
Knott, J. 344–5, 347
Knudsen, Herman 282

Index

Konrad-Adenauer-Stiftung Foundation 249, 324, 326

Koppenjan, J.F.M. 110, 342

Korica, M. 329

Kostic, R. 327, 329, 333

KPMG Government and Public Sector Services 215

KPMG Public Governance and Government Institute 213

Kraan, Dirk-Jan 157

Kreisky, Bruno 377n

Kreppel, Amie 199

Kubr, Milos 221

Kuhlmann, S. 108–9, 115, 135–6, 140n

Kun, Goh 315

Kuo, Yu-Ying 19, 309–20

La Relève 77

Labatonjan, Stephen 222–3

labour market flexibilization 280

Labour Market Policy 276–86: context 276–7, 286; Danish *Arbejderbevægelsens Erhvervsråd* (Economic Council of the Labour Movement) 278–9; German Hans Böckler Foundation 278; Labour Unions 278–9; US Economic Policy Institute 279; *see also* Danish Labour Movement; German Labour Movement; US Labour Movement

labour organizations 34, 106, 175

labour unions 6, 17–18, 276–9

Lachapelle, E. 231

Ladi, Stella 19–20, 324–338

Lægreid, Per 124

Laforest, Rachel 299

Laigle, C. 324, 329, 336

Lamari, Moktar 126, 344–5, 347

Landry, Réjean 126, 344–5, 347, 355

Landsorganisationen I Danmark (LO) 277–9, 282–4

Lang, Sabine 293–4, 296

Lapsley, Irvine 214

Larimer, C.W. 31

Larsen, Christian A. 282

Larsen-Price, Heather A. 298

Lasswell, H. 1–3, 58, 61, 72–3, 85, 158, 309, 342–3, 361

Latour, Bruno 63

Lauriat, B. 169–70, 172, 176

Lavertu, Stéphane 160

Lawarée, J. 327

Laycock, D. 1, 31, 57, 58, 106, 119, 343, 349, 376n

Lazareviciute, I. 351

Le Galès, P. 343, 349

Le Monde 213

Leach, S. 138

Lee, C.-P. 135

Lee, J. 139

Lee, T. 199, 202–5

Leech, Beth L. 298

Legge, David 123

legislative policy analysis 199–211: administrative capacity 200–6; advisors to political groups 202–3; context 199–200, 209–10; general parliamentary support services 203–6; instruments incorporating external expertise 208–9; oversight and scrutiny instruments 206; parliamentary committees 206–8; personal assistance to MPs 201–2; political structures and instruments for 206–9; support services for MPs 200–6

Legrand, Timothy 118

Lehmbruch, G. 2

Lehmkuhl, Dirk 123

Leiber, Simone 281

Leibniz Association 348

Lejano, R.P. 31, 32, 37

Leleur, Steen 47

Lens, Jens 282

Lentsch, J. 185

Lerner, Daniel 58, 342–3, 361

Lessenich, Stephan 281

Lester, James P. 126

Levitsky, Steven 74

Levitt, Ruth 119

Lewis, David E. 145–6

Leys, Colin 213

Libeer, T. 245, 251–2

liberal democracy 191; *see also* democracy

Liberal Democratic Party (LDP) (Japan) 250, 251

liberal market economies (LMEs) 15, 16, 214, 215, 217, 218, 224

librarianship 28

Lidström, A. 131

Lijphart, A. 109, 131

Lilley, A. 207

Lind, Jens 283

Lindblom, Charles E. 30, 37, 57–62, 139n, 273n, 376n

Linder, S. 31–2, 33, 72

Lindquist, E. 31, 39, 45, 61, 105–6, 114–15, 131–3, 137, 345, 346, 364, 376n

Lindvall, J. 174–5

line organization 108

Lio, Jun 91

Lippman, W. 230

Lipset, S.M. 249

Lisbon Council 213

List, Regina 292

Liu, X. 131–3, 137

Living Standards Framework 50

Lo, J.Y. 310

Lobato, Lenaura 91

lobbying: concept 266–7; organizations 76; strategies 222–4; term 266–7; *see also* management consultancy

Local Government Institute (Canada) 371
local level of policy analysis 131–40: context
131–2, 138–9; decision-making integration of
policy analysis 137; information analysis 135–6;
information-gathering 133–7; information
generation 133–4; policy alternatives 136–7;
quality of information 134–5; researchers'
focus 132
Lødemel, Ivar 276
Lodge, Martin 214
Loeffen, S. 208
Loewenberg, G. 209
Loewentheil, Nate 279
logistics 28
Long Term Strategies Committee (Aus) 208
Long, M. 173
Lonti, Z. 73
Lorenz, Geoffrey M. 297
Lowery, D. 295
Lowi, T.J. 56
Lowndes, V. 134, 138
Lundin, Martin 11–12, 131–40, 131–3, 133–4,
135–7, 139n
Lykketoft, Mogens 283
Lynn, Laurence E. Jr. 218

Macdonald Commission
MacDonald, L. 332
Mach, Andre 263
MacIntyre, A. 37
Mackay, Keith 98n
MacNamara, Robert 31
MacRae, D. 5, 31, 40n, 361
Macroeconomic Policy Institute (IMK) 278
Maddens, B. 201–2
Madsen, Per Kongshøj 283, 284
Magat, W. 269
Mailand, Mikkel 283
Mair, P. 245, 250
Majone, G. 57, 72–3, 93
majoritarianism 30
Makarenko, J. 170
Makita, J. 200, 205
Malaysian Institute of Economic Research
(MIER) 331
Malcolmson, Patrick N. 364
Maley, M. 114
Malloy, J. 73
Malone, E.F. 361
Management Advisory Committee (UK) 92
Management Consultancies Association (MCA)
47, 51, 53, 221–3
management consultancy 213–25: accountancy,
institutional link to 216–17; context 213–14,
224; European consulting market 217–**18**;
historical development 215–18; institutional
isomorphism 214–15; lobbying strategies 222–4;

managerial expertise 214–15; New Governance
(21st Century developments) 221–2; New
Public Management (1980s) 220–1; public
sector reform 218–24; rational planning (1960s)
219–20; technocratic politics (1960s) 219–20
managerialism 105
Mangez, E. 348
Mangold, W.G. 309
Mann, M. 71
Maori Potential Framework 50
March, J. 139n, 172, 361
Margetts, Helen Z. 152, 222
Margolis, M. 230
Marier, Patrick 13, 169–71, 174–7
marketization reform 76, 124
Marschall, S. 200, 203–6
Marsh, D. 62, 184
Marsh, I. 200, 207–9
Marshall Plan 15, 218
Marston, Greg 120
Martin, Cathie Jo 283
Martin, J. 73
Martin, John F. 213
Martin, S. 199–200
Martiniello, M. 352
Maslove, Allan M. 21, 106, 360–77, 376n
Mathematica 371
Mauser, G. 230
May, J.P. 2
Mayer, B. 73
Mayer, Igor 45, 56–7, 67, 106, 110–11, 300, 342,
376n
Mayfield, A. 309
Mayntz, R. 342, 345
Mbadlanyana, T. 328
McAllister, L. 170–1, 172, 174
McArthur, Doug 118, 120
McBeth, M.K. 235
McClusky, J. 294
McGann, James G. 294
McGuinness, M. 172
McGuire, Michael 96
McKenna, Christopher D. 215, 219
McKenna, D. 134
McKenzie, Kyle 145–6
McKinsey Consulting Group 213, 215
McKinsey Global Institute 213
McLean, Fiona 215
McLevey, J. 330, 333, 337
McNamara, Robert 143–5
McQueen, K. 234
Mead, Lawrence 284
media 309–23: Beijing 317–19; Beijing microblog
regulation 321–3; child abuse survey **314**;
context 309–11, 319–20; criticism 65; OPEN
system area coverage **317**; Seoul 315–17; Taipei
311–12; Tokyo 312–15; *see also* social media

medicine 27, 28, 29, 34, 37, 60
Medvetz, T. 329, 333, 337
Meier, K.J. 133, 138
Meijer, Albert J. 310
Mellett, Edward Bruce 216, 220
Meltsner, Arnold J. 3, 38, 72–3, 85, 90, 264, 361, 370
Melville, Rose 298
membership-based organizations 294
Mendelsohn, M. 230
Mendez, Jose-Luis 8–9, 70–81
Mendizabal, E. 153, 328, 334
Merke, F. 327
Merklova, K. 191–2, 195
meta-organization 261
Meyers, Roy 147
Michels, A. 134
microblogging 19, 310, 317–23: top ten government microblogs **318**; top ten provincial microblogs **318**; *see also* blogging
Midwest Political Science Association (MPSA) 1
Migdal, J. 300
Migone, A. 107, 232
Mikesell, John 153, 161n
Mikos, Robert A. 121
Miller, Marna 119
Millerson, G. 27–9
Mining Association of Canada **262**
ministerial responsibility: concept 88
Mintrom, M. 38–9, 40n, 376n
Mishan, E.J. 59
Mishel, Lawrence 285–6
Missiroli, A. 329
Misztal, B.A. 330, 333
Mitsubishi Research Institute 324
mobilization of policy ideas 291, 318
modernization 28, 224
Moffitt, Robert A. 284
Moir, Lance 266
Møller, Iver Hornemann 283
Monaghan, Mark 120
Monk, D. 207
Monroe, A.D. 230–1
Montin, S. 134
Montpetit, E. 231
Mookherjee, Dilip 120
Moore, Mark A. 269
Moreira, Amilcar 276
Morgan, K.J. 231
Morris, J.C. 376n
Morrison, Andrea 126
Morrow, J.D. 74
Morton, S. 5, 348, 351, 354
Mosley, Jennifer 293, 295, 298
Moss, G. 310
Moss, T. 332
Mossberger, K. 311

Moynihan, Donald P. 160
Mu, F. 309
Muhr, S.L. 28–9
Mulder, N. 107
Mulholland, Elizabeth 301
Müller, W.C. 245
Mullinix, K.J. 231
multiple-streams framework 273n
Muñoz Marquez, Luz Maria 292
Murrary, Charles 284
Myers, Richard M. 364

Nabatchi, T. 134
Nader, Ralph 220
narrative policy framework 235
National Academy of Public Administration (Ukraine) 365
National Association of Manufacturers (US) 261
National Bureau for Economic Research (NBER) (US) 331
National Bureau of Statistics of China 317
National Government Organization Act (Japan) **192**
National Health Service (NHS) (UK) 213
National Institute for Economic and Social Research (UK) 326
Natural Resources Framework (NZ) 49
Nelson, D. 297
Nelson, R.H. 73
neo-corporatism 2, 5, 14, 110, 191, **192**, **194**, 195, 335, 347, 351–2; *see also* corporatism
neoliberalism 77, 353: principles 78, 327
neo-pluralism 337; *see also* pluralism
nepotism 316
Nesbitt, S. 176
Netherlands Court of Auditors 206
Neto, P.F.D. 245, 251
network entrepreneurs 20; *see also* think tanks
Network of Institutes and Schools of Public Administration in Central and East Europe (NISPAcee) 374, 376n
Network of Schools of Public Policy, Affairs, and Administration (NASPAA) 3, 21, 372–5
Neuhold, C. 203, 205
neutral competence 76
New Deal (US) 326
New Democratic Party (NDP) 248
New Public Governance (NPG) 18–19, 291, 295, 299, 303
New Public Management (NPM) 11–12, 76, 93, 104, 123, 126, 139, 140n, 143, 161n, 189, 213, 216, 218, 220, 293, 353
Newman, Janet 221
Newman, Joshua 10–11, 118–27, 119, 122, 123–5, 126
Neylan, Julian 72, 120
NGOs *see* non-governmental organizations (NGOs)

Index

non-governmental organizations (NGOs) 13, 19, 33, 34, 57, 63, 68n, 71, 76, 91, 173, **183**, 185, 190, 292–3, 296–7, 301–2, 324, 328–9, 332, 334–6, 371–2
nonpartisan policy analysis organizations 73
non-profit advocacy theory 295
non-profit organizations 18, 34, 63, 64, 71, 269, 291, 292, 293, 296, 298–301
non-state organizations 300
not-for-profit organizations 262, 292
Norcross, Eileen C. 145–6
normative policy analysis 4, 8, 61; *see also* style
normative principles 330
Norris, P. 71, 81n
North American Free Trade Agreement (NAFTA) 175, 177, **262**
North American research institutes 259
Northeast Asian institutes 327
Norton, A. 131
NPG theory *see* New Public Governance (NPG)
NPM framework *see* New Public Management (NPM)
Nuenhöffer, G. 337
nursing 28
Nutley, S.M. 5, 75, 118–19, 185, 346, 348, 351, 354

O'Connor, John 284
O'Flynn, J. 105
O'Leary, R. 134
O'Malley, Martin 119
O'Neill, Deirdre 123
Oakeshott, M. 37
Oates, D. 215–16
Oates, Wallace E. 121
Obama, Barack H. 92
Öberg, PerOla 131–40, 131–4, 135–7, 139n, 172, 175
occupational ethics 7
Ödalen, R. 131
OECD (Organisation for Economic Co-operation and Development) 12, 105, 119, 145–50, 151, 156–8, 325: actors in charge of spending reviews *158*; performance budgeting *152*; performance budgeting index (PBI): OECD countries *148*; performance utilization during budget negotiations *149;* utilization of performance information *149;* utilization of program evaluation in budget negotiations *156;* utilization of spending reviews in budget negotiations *158*
Office of Management and Budget (US) 146, 152
Öhrvall, R 137
Olbrechts-Tyteca, L. 62
Olsen, J.P. 139n
Olson, Mancur 268
Ontario Environmental Industry Association (ONEIA) 272

Onyx, Jenny 298
Open Society Foundations network 325, 328, 335
OPEN System 19, 315–17, 319: area coverage **317**
operational definitions 3, 6
operations research 31, 43, 89–90, 342, 344
Oprisor, Anca 150, 159, 161n
optometry 28
organization studies 349
organizational behavior 147
organizational fields: definition 214
Orsini, Michael 299
Orszag, Peter 152–3
Osborne, David 221
Osborne, Stephen 291, 377n
O'Toole, L.J. 133, 138
Ouimet, M. 345
Overseas Development Institute (ODI) 335

Pablos-Mendes, A. 355
Pacheco, J. 235
Packenham, R. 199
Packwood, A. 72
Page, B.I. 229–31, 232, 236
Page, C. 237–8
Page, E.C. 3, 73, 81, 119
Painter, Martin 71, 73, 123
Pal, Leslie A. 219, 361–3, 376n
Palier, Bruno 276
Pallot, J. 73
paradigm concept 56–7
Park, Hun Myoung 316
Parks, James B. 285
Parliamentary Bureau for Research and Public Expenditure (Netherlands) 204
parliamentary policy analysis 4, 14, 199–200, 204, 206, 209–10
Parrado, S. 80–1
Parry, K. 310
Parsons, Wayne 52
participatory approaches 4–5, 7, 10, 45, 48, 56, 110, 184, 299–300
participatory policy analysis (PPA) 40n
parties and interest groups 243–303; *see also* business associations (BAs); Labour Market Policy; political party think tanks; voluntary sector
partitocratic systems 14–15, 203
PASOS Network 335
Patapan, Haig 46
Patashnik, Erik 45, 52, 57
path dependency theory 215, 273n
pathology 34
patronage 119, 120, 255
Pattenaude, Richard L. 220
Patterson, James T. 284
Pattison, A. 137
Patton, C.V. 2

393

Index

Patton, M.Q. 156
Pattyn, Valérie 17, 245–59, 327
Pauselli, G. 327
Pautz, H. 337
Pawson, R. 72
peak organizations 273n
Pedersen, Federik 283
Pedersen, Jacob J. 283
Pedersen, O.K. 329, 338
Pekkanen, Robert 291, 294–6, 297–8, 300
Pelletier, Réjean 125
Pensions Commission (UK) 175, 177
Perelman, Chaïm 62
performance budgeting 12–13, *152*: alternatives
152–3; definition 146–7; evidence-based
budgetary policy 146–52; *see also* evidence-
based budgetary policy; OECD
performance budgeting index (PBI): OECD
countries *148*
performance utilization: OECD countries *149*
Perl, A. 2, 71, 73, 107, 123, 355
Perret, Bernard 145
Pestoff, Victor 299
Peters, B.G. 31–2, 33, 57, 59, 72, 73, 114–15, 126,
221, 353
Peters, C.S. 310–11
Peters, G. 72
Peters, Tom 216
Petersen, J. 232, 236
Peterson, H.L. 234
Peterson, Steven A. 31, 38, 95, 376n
Petersson, O. 169–71, 172, 175
Petry, F. 230, 236–7
Pfeffer, Jeffrey 269
Pfeffer, Monica 123
pharmaceuticals 124, **218**
pharmacology 34
pharmacy 28
Phillimore, John 118
Phillips, Susan D. 291–3, 299–301
physics 343
Phythian, M. 169, 176
Pielke, R.A. 185, 196, 346
Pierce, J.J. 234
Pierre, Jon 57, 71, 73, 114, 123
pillarization 249–50, 259
Pincus, Jonathan 154
Pirlot, P. 245, 251, 253–4
Pistorius, T. 181, 185–9, 194–6
Pittoors, Gilles 17, 245–59
Piven, Frances F. 285
planning-oriented analytical framework 32
Planning-Programming-Budgeting-System
(PPBS) 12, 16, 31, 90, 143, *144*, 160, 219, 376n:
schematic presentation *144*
Plato 30
Plehwe, D. 335

Plewes, B. 291
pluralism 2, 5, 14, 17–18, 65, 191, 199, 259, 291,
293, 325, 326, 327, 337, 347, 351–2, 364
pluralist studies 2; *see also* neo-pluralism
pluralization of policy making 291
Polanyi, M. 361
Polder model 351
Poletto, M. 324, 329, 336
policy academic system 63; *see also* style
policy actors' roles 4
Policy Advice Initiative 353
policy advisors 2
policy advisory system 2–3, 6, 8, 14, 20, 63–7,
181–3, 188–96, 341, 346–8, 351, 355–6: Czech
Republic **192**; definition 346; Japan **192**; Taiwan
193; *see also* style
policy advocacy: concept 298
Policy Affairs Research Council (PARC) 251,
253
policy analysis: academic and advocacy-based
19–22; capacity 9, 70, 71, 123; committees
13–16; conceptual foundations and contribution
1–6, 57, 94, 95, 104, 342; consultants 13–16;
definitions 1–2, 3, 5, 6, 8, 44, 57, 59, 71, 90,
115, 264–5, 270, 273n, 342–3, 349, 361–3;
governments 10–13; modes of policy analysis
and evaluation *155* organizations 87; parties and
interest-group-based 17–19; public 7–10; public
inquiries 13–16; public opinion 13–16; research
institutes 13–16; theory 52–3, 57–8, 70, 75, 86,
104, 132–4, 376n
policy analysis profession 7, 27–41: context 27;
historical overview of academic and practical
foundations 29–32; policy analysis as a
profession 37–9; phases of policy analysis as
policy design 34–6; policy-design approach
to policy analysis 32–4; professionalism 27–9;
systemic thinking capacity 36–7
policy assistants 4, 17, 202, 258, 259
policy capacity: definition 123
policy entrepreneurs 20; *see also* think tanks
policy feedback: concept 231
policy formulation system 8, 63–7; *see also* style
Policy Framework for Pacific People 50
policy incrementalism theory 273n
policy predictive analysis 59–60; *see also* style
policy process models 44
policy process theory 16, 229, 233, 235–6, 239,
273n, 291–2, 350
policy research 21: definition 361–2
policy shops 89–90
policy streams theory 2
policy studies 21: term 343, 361
policy style: concept 56, 114
Policy Unit (UK) 223
policy windows 234
policy work: definition 115

Index

policymaking style: France **66**; Germany **66**; matrix 65–7; United States **67**; *see also* style
policymaking system 4
policy–research utilization 20–1
Polidano, C. 73, 74, 81n
political epistemological cultures 4–5
political parties 3, 6
political party organizations 20, 355
political party think tanks 245–59: autonomy 246–52; autonomy categorization 251–2; Brazil 251, **252**, 253–4; Canada 247–9, **252**, 254–6; cold advice 254–6; context 254–6, 258–9; European Union 249–51, 254–6; Flanders 251, **252**, 253–4; functions **252**–8, *257*; Germany 249–51, **252**, 254–6; high level autonomy 247–9; hot advice 253–4; Japan 247–51, **252**, 253–4; level of autonomy **247**; low-level autonomy 251; medium level autonomy 249–51; Netherlands 249–51, **252**, 254–6; typology of functions 256–8; US 247–9, 254–6; United States **252**, Wallonia 249–51, **252**, 253–4; *see also* think tanks
political pillarization 17
political science 1, 21, 67, 71, 74, 95, 104, **112**, 113, 199, 210, 229, 296, 342–3, 349–50, 353, 362–70, 374
political strategy theory 268
political theory 342
politicization 5–6, 10, 13, 14, 21, 76, 97, 104, 105, 107, 109, 110, 112–14, 182, 184, 185, 187–94, 197, 298, 336–7, 351–5
Pollitt, Christopher 104–6, 124, 147, 214, 224
Polsby, N. 2, 207
polycentrism 75, 184
Poor, Jozsef 215
Popper, K. 37, 57, 60
populism 185
Porter, J. 106
positivist/empiricist framework 27, 32, 40n, 93
Posner, Paul L. 152
Posseth, Johan 150, 150
post-constructionism 31
Posthumus, Rense 150
post-positivist framework 27, 31, 32, 109, 354
Poullaos, Chris 217
Powell, Walter W. 214–15
Power, G. 204
Power, J. 105
Prakash, Aseem 293
Prasser, G.S. 170–1, 174, 176
Pregernig, M. 181, 185–9, 194–6
Premchand, Arigapudi 145, 161n
Premfors, R. 170, 172
Preskill, H. 238
Pressman, Jeffery 61, 72
Prime Minister's Office (Canada) 77
Prince, Michael J. 119, 182, 191, 195–6

principal-agent theory 294
private organizations 95, 215
privatization 76, 124
problem causal analysis 4, 8, 60; *see also* style
Productivity Commission (Aus/NZ) 50, 76
profession: definition 27–9, 38
professional organizations 17, 292
professional: term 28
professionalism 214, 216, 373
professionalization 28, 40, 90, 113, 119, 187, 199, 326, 352: definition 40n
profit maximisation 269, 272, 273n
Program Assessment Rating Tool (PART) 12, 145–6, 153, 159, 160: breakdown of 27 programs *146*
Programme Analysis Review (PAR) 145, 161n
Protopsaltis, S. 368
Proulx, Jean 295
psychology 28
Ptackova, K. 191–2, 195
public administration: definition 377n
public choice theory 2, 220, 368
public debate system 8, 63–7; *see also* style
Public Expenditures Survey Committee (PESC) (UK) 161n
public good 7, 18, 29, 38, **192**, 267–8, 272, 292
public health 255, 342
public inquiries 169–78: comparative context 170–1; comparative policy analysis 174–6; difficulties of engagement 176–7; context 169–70, 177–8; definition 170–3; purpose 171–3
public management: definitions 377n
public mood: concept 234
public opinion 229–40: concept 232, 233, 239; context 229–30, 239; definition 237; influence on public policies 233–6; policy process theories 233–6; research 6, 16; research and use by policymakers 236–9; responsiveness of public policies to 230–3; theories 232, 233
public organizations 9, 13, 75, 76, 214
public policy analysis: definition 263; styles and methods 7–10, 25–98; *see also* bureaucratic capacity; formal policy analysis methods; historical framework; policy analysis profession; style
Public Policy Platform (Platon) 253
public policy studies (Europe and North America) 360–76: accreditation 372–4; co-ops 370–2; conceptual framework and definitions 360–3; context 360, 374–6; historical background 363–5; internships 370–2; regional variation 365–70; think tanks 370–2
public policy theory 52, 229, 230, 233: definitions 377n
Public Sector Working Party (PSWP) 222
public value: definition 35–6
punctuated ad hoc interventionism 105, **112**
punctuated equilibrium theory 233–5, 273n

395

Puppis, M. 311
Putnam, Robert D. 118

Quah, Euston 59
Quebec Hardware and Building Material
    Association 271
Quebec Trucking Association 271

Radaelli, Claudio M. 214
Radin, Beryl 2, 4, 5, 9, 37, 46, 65, 73, 85–98, 144,
    150, 370, 374, 376n
Ramesh, M. 2, 45, 71, 73, 355, 361, 377n
RAND Graduate Institute 95, 324, 326, 371
Raney, H.L. 234
Rasmussen, Anne 292, 295
Rasmussen, Ken 123, 127, 373
Rassam, C. 215–16
rational choice theory 59
Rationalisation des Choix Budgétaires (RCB) 145
rationality: economic 145; evaluative 31; expert
    347; instrumental 20, 349, 356; science-based
    351–2
rationalization of policy formulation 111, **192**
Ratkai, M. 311
Rattsø, Jørn 121
Ratushny, E. 170, 174, 176
Raunio, T. 200
Raymond, Marissa 121
Rea, A. 352
Reagan, Ronald 284
Rebmann, Frederic 263
Rechtsstaat 107–8
regionalism 139
regionalization 328
Reinecke, S. 181, 185–9, 194–6
Reiner, M. 361
Reiter, R. 349
Renn, O. 209
research utilization 341–2, 344–9; see also academic
    policy analysis
Research, Development and Evaluation
    Commission **312**
resource mobilization theory 298–9
resource theory 2
Reuschemeyer, D. 39n
Reveley, James 261
Rhodes, R.A.W. 2, 62, 96, 295, 363
Ribeiro, Jose Mendes 91
Rich, A. 248, 254–5
Richardson, Jeremy 2, 56, 264
Richardson, Liz 51
Ricks, W. 269
Riddell, N. 71, 74
Ridyard, D. 217
Rihoux, B. 245, 251, 253–4
Rittel, Horst 40n, 98n, 124
Rivlin, Alice 144

Robinson, J.W. 173
Robinson, Marc 147, 156–7, 161n
Robinson, R. 107
Rochefort, D.A. 175
Rochet, C. 73
Rockan, Bert A. 118
Rockman, B.A. 73
Roenigk, D.J. 135–6
Rokkan, S. 249
Rosa Luxemburg Foundation 326
Rose, Richard 124, 172, 176
Røseland, A. 133
Rothmayr, Christine 16, 229–40, 377n
Rothstein, B. 174–5
Rouw, Rien 154, 353, 355
Rowe, M. 170–1, 172, 174
Royal Commission on Electoral Reform and Party
    Financing (Canada) 255
Royal Commission on Government Organization
    (Canada) 219–20
Royo, S. 311
Rüb, F. 345
Rudd, Kevin 154
Ruddat, C. 131, 134, 136, 139
Rueschemeyer, D. 71
Russell Sage Foundation 326
Russell, J. 329
Russell, Peter H. 364
Rutledge, Paul 298
Rutzen, D. 293–4
Ryle, M. 199

Saalfeld, T. 199–200
Sabatier, Paul A. 62, 137, 234267, 273n, 296
Sager, F. 344, 350–1, 353
Saint-Martin, Denis 15, 213–25, 214, 217–18, 220
Saint-Simon, Henri de 30
Salamon, Lester M. 292, 298
Salmon, C. 230
Salomonsen, H.H. 114
Salter, L. 172
Sanderson, Ian 5, 118–19, 124, 354
Santelli, John S. 121
Santos, F. 200, 202, 205, 207–8
Sapeha, Halina 302
Saunders, L. 71
Savard, Sebastien 295
Savattaro, S. 311
Savoie, D. 106
Sawicki, D.S. 2
Sawicky, Max B. 286
Saxton, Gregory D. 293
scepticism 45, 160, 169, 350, 355
Schachter, H.L. 134
Schäfer, Claus 281
Scharpf, F.W. 2
Scheuer, Steen 283

Index

Schick, Allen 143–5, 147, 152, 156, 159–60
Schild, Jan A. 143
Schlæger, Jesper 310
Schmid, H. 292, 295, 297–8
Schmid, J. 77–8, 108–9
Schmitter, Phillipe 2, 263
Schmoldt, Hubertus 281
Schneider, A.L. 231
Schoch, Mickie 155
Schoeder, Wolfgang 279–81
Scholten, Peter 48, 98n, 110–11, 115, 343, 344, 349, 350, 352
Scholz, S. 108–9
Schröder, Gerhard 279–81
Schroeder, Wolfgang 18, 276–86, 278
Schubert, Klaus 58, 65, 91, 98n, 115, 342
Schuck, P. 248
Schultz, M. 181, 187, 189–90, 192–5
Schulze, Michaela 18, 276–86, 277, 281–3
Schüttemeyer, S. 200, 208–9
science (discipline) 39n: economic 365; environmental 366; expert advisory bodies 196; natural 60, 303; policy sciences 1, 43, 49, 53, 57–8, 72, 85, 109, 111, 184–8, 264, 267, 334, 342–52, 361; politicization of 354–5; 'pure' 341; rationality 351–2; sociology of 63; Soviet-style academies 328; technology and 13, 14, 183–5, 348, 368; *see also* actuarial science; political science; social science
Scientific Bureau 250
scientific management 15
scientification 21, 352–6
scientization of policymaking 185; *see also* sciences: policy sciences
Scott, Claudia 7, 43–54, 87
Securities and Exchange Commission (SEC) (US) 217
Seeleib-Kaiser, Martin 280
Seibel, Kai 281
Seifert, Hartmut 280, 281
Selection of Bills Committee (Aus) 207
Self-Assessment of Budgetary Programs (SABP) 12, 145
Sellars, J.M. 131
Semadeni, Matthew 215
Sementelli, A.J. 311
Seoul Information Communication Center 315
Seoul Open Data Plaza 315
separation-of-powers system (US) 199, 201, 204, 207
Setälä, M. 139
Shademani, R. 355
Shah, Shekhar 121
Shapiro, Daniel 263
Shapiro, R.Y. 231–2
shareholders: definition 224
Shaw, S.E. 329

Shaw, Trevor 154, 159
Shergold, Peter 352
Shields, John 123, 126, 298
Shierholz, Heidi 279
Shin, Sang Hoon 146
Shipan, C.R. 184
short-termism **112**, 113
Shotts, K.W. 231
Sian, Suki 217
Sibalukhulu, N. 328
Sidney, M.S. 71
Siefken, S. 200, 208–9
Siegel, Nico 281
Simmons, Beth 184, 214
Simmons, Louise 285–6
Simms, Andrew 223
Simon, Herbert 61, 361
Sinclair, J. Andrew 310
Siverson, R.M 74
Skocpol, T. 175
SMEs (small and medium-sized enterprises) 217
Smiley, Donald V. 364
Smith, A. 74
Smith, D. 368
Smith, G. 139
Smith, J.A. 326
Smith, K.B. 31
Smith, K.E. 267
Smith, M. 364
Smith, P.J. 133, 136–7
Smith, Steven Rathgeb 291–3, 294–6, 297–8, 300
Smith, T. Alexander 56
Smith, Tim 223
Smith, Trevor 213, 220, 222
Smulders, J. 201–2
Smullen, Amanda 224
Sniderman, P.M. 232
Social Commission (Denmark) 282
social democracy 19
Social Democratic Party (SDP) (Germany) 249, 326, 330, 351
social media 6, 19, 239, 309–12, 319–20, 334, 336; *see also* blogging; microblogging
social organizations 300
social policy framework 213
social science 31, 40n, 43, 53, 57, 61, 78, 95, 97, 219, 237, 278, 300, 329, 333, 341, 346, 353, 360, 365, 368, 371, 374
social work 28, 315, 342
socialization 21
societal organizations 249
societalization 5, 352–6
sociology 27–8, 63, 67, 72, 214, 296, 342, 343, 367
Sokolowski, S. Wojciech 292
Solesbury, William 119, 153
Soroka, S.N. 230, 233
Soskice, David 15, 214–15, 217

Index

South America 3, 9, 17, 75
South Korean research institutes 316
Souza, Celina 78–9
sovereign debt crisis 149–52; *see also* evidence-based budgetary policy
Soviet Union 19, 87, 88, 328
specialization 14, 97, 138, 202, 203, 210, 327, 365–9, 375
Speklé, Roland F. 152
Spiro, Peter J. 121
stable institutional framework 108, **112**
stakeholders: definition 224
Stalebrink, Odd J. 145, 150
Stambaugh, Russell J. 126
Starling, G. 376n
state capacity: concept 71
State Sector Act (NZ) 47
State Services Commission (NZ) 353
statism/anti-statism 221, 351, 352
Statistical Capacity Indicator (SCI) 80
statistics (discipline) 71, 78, **312**, 317, 344, 345: social 72
Stedman, Richard C. 123, 126
Steffani, W. 207
Steffen, Monika 377n
Steinack, K. 207
Stephens, B. 73
Stephens, J.D. 71
Sternberg, R. 361
Stevens, B. 104
Stevens, M. 216–17
Stewart, K. 133, 136–7
Štimac, Vid 150, 159, 161n
Stockholm International Research Institute 377n
Stoker, Gerry 119, 127
Stokey, Edith 85
Stone, Deborah 30, 72
Stone, Diane 3, 4, 19–20, 324–338
Straßheim, H. 5, 334, 345, 347, 351, 354
Straussman, Jeffrey D. 365
Streeck, Wolfgang 2, 277
Strengthening Our Policy Capacity Task Force 77, 107
Stritch, Andrew 263
Strom, K. 199–200, 245
Struyk, R.J. 325, 328, 334
style: concept 56–8, 67; definition 57
style 56–68: context 67; different policy systems 61–3; policy academic system 63; policy advisory system 63; policy analysis as a field of expertise 57–8; policy analysis as a scientific discipline 57–8; policy formulation system 63; policy predictive analysis 59–60; policy process analysis producing knowledge on the process 61; policymaking style matrix 65–7; normative policy analysis 61; problem causal analysis 60; public debate system 63–4; structure of policy

systems and interaction 64–5; trial/error policy analysis 60–1; typology of policy analytical styles 58–9; *see also* public policy analysis
sub-national government policy analysis 10–11, 118–27: future directions 126–7; policy analysis as a profession 118–20; policy analysts' definition and role 122; policy capacity for effective governance 123–4; research agenda 122–6; research to date 125–6; sources of information for policy analysts 124–5; sub-national governments 120–2
subsystems approach 2, 229, 232–6
Suleiman, E.N. 39n
Sulitzeanu-Kenan, R. 169–70, 172–3
Sullivan, H. 134
supply-and-demand framework 4, 9, 73: matrix **74**
Surrowiecki, J. 5, 354
surveying 28
Sutherland, S.L. 368, 372, 376n
Suzuki, T. 245, 248, 250, 253
Svarer, Michael 283
Svensson, T. 172, 175
Swedish Association of Local Authorities and Regions 133
Swedish Working Group on Pensions 174, 175, 177
Sweeney, John D. 285
Swiss Political Science Association 376–7n
Swyngedouw, M. 352
systems theory 16, 220

Tadashi, Y. 249–51, 253
Taffer, Richard J. 266
Talbot, Colin 224, 354–5, 377n
Tancredo Neves Institute (ITN) 254
Tanner, Michael 284
Taylor, Frederick 15, 215
teaching 7, 19, 21, 28, 64, 86, 95, 97, 349, 360–2, 365, 366, 371
technocratic orientations 20
technocratization **112**
technology 3, 13, 21, 183, 184, 185, 264, 265, 348, 366, 368
Telford, Hamish 121
Temporary Assistance for Needy Families (TANF) 285
Tenbensel, R. 351
Tenbensel, T. 72
Tenbrock, Christian 281
terrorism 222
Tewksbury 221
'tHart, P.T. 324, 334
Thatcher, Margaret 176, 220, 353, 377n
Theil, Markus 298
Thelander, J. 133–4, 135–6
Thelen, Kathleen 283
Theriault, S.M. 232
Think Fund 325

398

Think Net Centre 21 (C21) 253
Think Tank Initiative 325
think tanks 324–38: academic, non-partisan 19–20; advocacy tanks 19; character of research 330–1; communication and marketing 334; context 324–5; definition 19, 324, 325; dissemination of information 20; epochs of organizational development 325–30; foci of policy analysis 331; function 19–20, *257*; generalist 4, 20, 331; governance levels 331–2; ideological tanks 4, 19, 330–1; as information interlocutors 333–4; international diffusion 327–8; internet era 328–9; levels of autonomy **247**; modes of policy analysis 330–3; networks and partnerships 334–5; North American and European studies 370–2; operationalization 332; post-World War II 326–7; promotion to external audiences 333–6; reprise 329–30; research methods 330–3; research production 333; research quality 333; specialist 4, 20, 331; think-and-do-tanks 332; think tank-ization 15, 213–14; transnational think tanking 19, 329, 335–6; twentieth century innovation 326; utility and influence of 336–8; *see also* political party think tanks
Third Way/*Neue Mitte* 280
Thissen, W.A.H. 73
Thompson, P.R. 73
Thomsen, Trine Lund 283
Thunert, Martin 249, 256, 277, 348
Tiernan, A. 105, 119
Tiessen, J. 108
Timmermans, A. 245, 249–50, 255
Tinkler, Jane 152
Toepler, Stefan 292
Töller, A.E. 349
Tong, R. 38
Torres, R.T. 238
Tosun, J. 132
Toulmin, S. 37
Trade Associations 261
Trampusch, Christine 277
transformative parliaments 14–15, 207
transnationalization of policy analysis 328
Treaty of Waitangi 50
Tremblay-Boire, Joannie 293
trial/error policy analysis 4, 8, 60–1, **66–7**; *see also* style
Triantafillou, Peter 120
Trube, Achim 281
Trudeau, Pierre 106, 363
Truth and Reconciliation Commission (South Africa) 13, 170, 173, 178
Tseng, Vivian 118
Tsuchyama, K. 136
Turcanu, Catrinel 47
Tversky, A. 361
Twaalfhoven, P.G.J. 73

typology building 3–4, 56–9, 62, 191, 207, 246–7, 253, 256–8

Uçarer, Emek M. 298
Uhr, John 98n
Ukraine 365
umbrella organizations 261, 284
unemployment 60, 120, 279–85
United Nations (UN) 9, 75, 173, **183**, 184, 185, 292, 316
United Nations Climate Change Conference 332
United Nations Development Programme (UNDP) 328, 335
Urban Institute (US) 326, 371
Urban Planning Commission (Taipei) **312**
urbanization 326
US Labour Movement 284–6: agenda setting 284–5; American Federation of Labour 284–6; Congress of Industrial Organization 284–6; Economic Policy Institute 279; policy change 285–6; *see also* Labour Market Policy

Vaillancourt, Yves 299–300
Vaitsman, Jeni 91
Van Beek, Iris 150
Van Buuren, A. 110
Van Daalen, Els 45, 56–7, 67, 73, 106, 300, 376n
Van Damme, J. 181, 184, 186–9, 191, 194–5, 347
Van der Arend, Jenny 125
Van der Kar, Hans M. 151
Van der Steen, Martijn 154, 181, 187, 189–90, 192–5, 353, 355
Van Dooren, Wouter 152
Van Hecke, Steven 17, 245–59
Van Nispen, Frans 12, 48, 98n, 110–11, 115, 143–62, 343, 344, 349, 350, 352, 377n
Van Rooyen, E. 245, 249–50, 255
Van Twist, Mark 154, 181, 187, 189–90, 192–5, 353, 355
Vancoppenolle, D. 351, 353
Vander Wyk, J. 207
Vangermeersch, Richard 217
Vardon, S. 105
Vargas, Getulio 78
varieties of capitalism (VOC) 215, 218; *see also* capitalism
Vartiainen, Juhana 283
Vedlitz, A. 131–3, 137
Veit, S. 108–9
venue shopping 235
Verbeeten, Roland F. 152
Verheijen, T. 351
Verschuere, Bram 298
Veselý, Arnošt 10, 103–115, 118, 122, 125–6
veterinary medicine 28
Vidaver-Cohen, Deborah 273n
Viera, Adam 121

Index

Vietnam War 96
Vilhelmsen, Jes 283
Ville, Simon 261
Vincent, K. 131–3, 137
Vining, Aidan R. 2, 3, 5, 17, 36, 40n, 45, 47, 50, 52, 74, 85, 97, 261–73, 264, 269–70, 309, 341–2, 361, 376n
Vitols, Sigurt 217
Voerman, G. 245, 249–50, 255
Vogel, D. 363
Vogenbeck, Danielle 43
Volden, C. 184
voluntary organizations 3, 17, 261
voluntary sector 6, 17, 221, 291–303: advocacy and co-construction 295–300; advocacy activities and relationships *297*; anthropological approach to policy work 300–3; civil society participation in the policy process **303**; context 291–2, 303; non-profit voluntary associations 295–300; non-profits in the policy process 292–5; role of civil society organisation respondents **302**
Voluntary Sector Initiative (VSI) 301
voluntary sector organizations 299–301
volunteerism 18, 292
von Oorschot, Wim 280
von Trapp, Lisa 147, 150
von Winter, T. 203
Voyer, J.-P. 106, 107, 123, 350
Vromen, A. 324, 334

Wacquant, L. 337
Wagenaar, H. 354
Wagner, P. 73
Wagner, R. 361
Walker, R.M. 131, 131, 133, 135, 138
Waller, M. 354
Walsh, P. 73
Walter, I. 75, 185, 346
Walter, J. 348, 352–3
Wang, T. 309, 311
Wang, W.-J. 191–3
Wanna, J. 104–5
Warner, M.E. 139
Watanabe, S.P. 39
Waterman, Robert H. 216
Watson, Michael 56
Watts, Rob 120
Watts, Ronald L. 364
Way, Lucan 74
Wayland, S.V. 298
Weaver, Kent R. 285
Webb, Jeff 119
Webber, David 150
Webber, Melvin M. 40n, 124
Weber, Max 28, 40n
Weber, Melvin 98n
Weekers, K. 201–2

Wegrich, Kai 214
Wegrzyn, R. 324, 329, 336
Weible, Christopher 73, 137, 234, 296
Weidenbaum, M. 327
Weimer, David 2, 3, 5, 36, 40n, 50, 52, 74, 85–8, 97, 264, 269–70, 309, 341–2, 361, 376n
Weingart, P. 185, 354
Weinstein, Kenneth R. 285
Weir, M. 175
Weishaar, Heide 267
Weiss, Carol H. 3, 93, 126, 159, 337, 344
welfare chauvinism 283
welfare state 18, 40n, 48, 120, 131, 175, 199, 218, 219, 276–86, 293, 298, 326, 363, 368, 371, 376n: universalism 282
Weller, P. 73, 104–5, 363
Wellstead, Adam M. 18, 118, 122, 126, 131, 291–303,
Welner, K.G. 325
Wengle, Susanne 264
Werner, Jann 377n
Wessels, B. 209
Westminster-style governments 7, 9, 10, 13, 14, 45–6, 48, 53, 88, 91–3, 98n, 105, 170–2, 207, 236, 361, 366
Wheeler-Booth, M. 199
White, D.J. 107
Wiardi Beckman Foundation 250
wicked problems 40n, 97, 184, 353
Wigmo, J. 309
Wikstrom, E. 309
Wildavsky, Aaron B. 2, 3, 5, 31, 32, 57–8, 61–2, 71–3, 144–5, 158, 162n, 196, 273n, 341, 344–5, 347, 360–1, 370, 376n
Wilde, J.A. 5, 31, 40n, 361
Wilding, R.W.L. 220
Wilfried Martens Centre for European Studies 256
Williams, A. 327
Williams, George 118
Williams, Neil 221
Williams, W. 361
Williams, Walter 144, 273n
Willman, John 220
Willner, Barry 213
Wilson, James Q. 267, 363
Wilson, Richard 61
Windmuller, John P. 261
Wittgenstein, Ludwig 59
Wlezien, C. 230, 233
Wohlfahrt, Norbert 281
Wolak, J. 131, 139
Wolfs, Wouter 14, 199–211
Wollman, H. 73, 73, 108–9, 115
Woodhouse, Edward J. 61–2
Wooldridge, Adrian 216
Working Group on Pensions (UK) 174
working parliaments 15, 207

Index

Workman, S. 132
World Bank 9, 39, 75, 80, 328, 335
World Meteorological Organization (WMO) 184
World Trade Organization (WTO) 39, 185, 335
World War II 35, 91, 110, 119, 143, 173, 199, 251, 325–7
Wright, V. 81
Wu, X. 71
Wu, Y. 311
Wüest, B. 232, 236

Xue, L. 324, 327
Xufeng, Z. 327

Yackee, Jason Webb 266
Yackee, Susan Webb 266, 297
Yamaya, K. 191–2, 195
Yeatman, A. 105
Yessian, M.R. 73

Yoskioka, Takayuki 293–5
Young, A. 220, 222
Young, John 153
Young, McGee 296

Zaal, K. 201, 203–4, 206, 208–9
Zahariadis, N. 234, 273n
Zeckhauser, Richard 85
Zedlewski, Sheila R. 284
Zero-Based Budgeting (ZBB) 12, 145, 160
Zeuthen Commission 282, 283
Zheng, Lei 310–11, 317, 319
Zheng, T. 310–11, 317
Zhou, L. 309, 311
Zhu, X. 324, 327
Zhu, Z. 361
Zimmerman, E. 329, 332, 335, 337
Zinn, Maxine Baca 286
Zittoun, Philippe 8, 56–68
Zohlnhöfer, R. 234